Tests Supplement

STAFF

Richard C. Sweetland, Ph.D	Editor
Daniel J. Keyser, Ph.D.	Editor
Terry Faulkner	Managing Editor
Carl T. Edwards	Manuscript Editor
Jane Doyle Guthrie	Production Editor

RESEARCH STAFF: Ann B. Bonner, Kelly Ray

COVER DESIGN: Hal Sandy, Jane Doyle Guthrie

PRODUCTION ASSOCIATE: Lynette Boyer

Richard C. Sweetland, Ph.D.
Daniel J. Keyser, Ph.D.
Editors

Tests

a comprehensive
reference for assessments
in psychology,
education and business

Supplement

Test Corporation of America
Kansas City

The first edition of **TESTS: Supplement** was published in August, 1984

Library of Congress Cataloging in Publication Data

Sweetland, Richard C., 1931-

Tests : a comprehensive reference for assessments in psychology, education, and business. Supplement.

Includes indexes.
1. Psychological tests. 2. Educational tests and measurements.
3. Occupational aptitude tests.
I. Keyser, Daniel J., 1935- . II. Title.
BF176.T43 1983 Suppl. 153.9′028′7 84-8773
ISBN 0-9611286-3-1
ISBN 0-9611286-4-X (lib. bdg.)

Printed in the United States of America

Table of Contents

Preface

We have indeed been gratified by the warm and gracious reception given by the professional community to **TESTS-First Edition**. Within one year of publication, **TESTS** is in its third printing.

Even though great effort was given not to omit any psychological, educational, or business tests published in English world-wide, the near 3,000 original test entries did not in fact cover 100% of the available tests.

With the publication and use of **TESTS**, users of the volume contacted Test Corporation of America with the names of assessment instruments not referenced in the first edition, and an updated "search and find" effort with over 300 publishers has produced **TESTS-Supplement**, with the most current up-to-date information on over 500 new tests. We thank our readers for the numerous suggestions they have offered and, besides the supplementary material, we have also included illustrations from selected tests published since 1980. We hope this will prove to be a continued feature of this desk reference.

We wish to express our special indebtedness to Terry Faulkner, who provided masterful orchestration of this project; Carl Edwards, who wrote the test descriptions; Jane Guthrie, who brought the illustration section to fruition; Kelly Ray, Ann Bonner and Lynette Boyer whose research on new tests continues on a daily basis. Again, we are grateful to the many test publishers and authors who generously and graciously contributed their staff time, information and support for this book.

Throughout the research and production of both **TESTS-First Edition** and **TESTS-Supplement**, Eugene Strauss and Leonard Strauss have given encouragement, suggestions and invaluable advice in all aspects of the business of publishing. Our thanks go to them for their continued association with Test Corporation of America.

Richard C. Sweetland, Ph.D.
Daniel Keyser, Ph.D.
Editors

Introduction

TESTS-Supplement is a continuation of the original work, **TESTS**. It contains over 500 new tests and some older tests that were not included in the primary book. As such, it is an excellent resource of recently published assessments, which allows the user to quickly update information about tests in general or tests in a special field of interest. The user must turn, however, to the original work **TESTS** for a comprehensive overview of all tests related to his reference question.

All tests have been referenced and classified in the familiar **TESTS** format. As before, the main sections Psychology, Education and Business are divided in subgroups within each discipline. Thus, the user will find it easy to move from one volume to the other without shifting his organizational set or disrupting his search.

Each test has been given a primary classification and is described in detail in one of the sections, and may be cross-referenced in a secondary category. For example, the Vineland Adaptive Behavior Scales, described within the Psychology section, is also cross-referenced under the Education section. This system of primary classification and cross-referencing is intended to organize and present the material to the administrator as clearly as possible without further expanding the number of categories and thus reducing the book's accessibility and ease of use.

The format and context of each test entry is designed to give the reader the information that is needed to decide whether or not a particular test is the "right" one for a given assessment needed. The format chosen provides a statement of the test's purpose, a description of the test, relevant cost and availability information, a set of coded visual keys designed to assist in quick screening and the primary owner/publisher.

The PURPOSE statement for each test entry provides a plain-language statement of the test's intended applications. The purpose statement tells what a particular test measures, assesses, diagnoses, evaluates, or identifies, and in most cases indicates application.

The DESCRIPTION provides number of test items, type of test format (paper-pencil, true-false, projective, oral, observational, etc.), factors or variable measured, materials used, the manner in which the test is administered, foreign language availability, and special features according to the test owner's information.

The editors are aware of possibilities for error even though the information is from a primary source. And although each entry has been researched, screened, written, edited and read by professional test administrators, the editors ask that the readers understand that the job of checking and insuring accuracy of a book such as this is a process which will continue throughout the publication of subsequent editions.

The editors had originally designed **TESTS** and **TESTS-Supplement** to include a section presenting data concerning the validity and reliability of each test included in the book. It was soon discovered, however, that this was a project requiring a special publication. Many test publishers do not provide this data in catalogued information regarding their tests and many failed to include such data in the material which they sent to us in response to our requests. Furthermore, research on the validity and reliability of individual tests revealed that more than one set of data is available for many tests and that the conflicting information often proved confusing or misleading. While the purpose of **TESTS** from the outset has been to provide a quick reference of available tests, it soon became clear that an adequate presentation of validity and reliability data is more appropriate to an in-depth, critical review. After much consultation with cooperative publishers and concerned professionals, it was decided not to include a section on test validity and reliability in this edition of **TESTS**. The editors strongly urge all test administrators to contact the test authors or publishers concerning statistical evidence of test validity and reliability.

In terms of style, the editors have chosen to use the commonly acceptable masculine pronoun and to use the word subject for the individual who is being assessed. In doing so, the editors do not intend to show any sexual bias or disregard for those being assessed. British spelling has been retained in proper titles.

How To Use **TESTS**

All tests are listed alphabetically according to test title under their designated subgroups and cross-referenced to other sections where appropriate.

The editors encourage readers to scan sections of the book relevant to their particular assessment needs. By following up on cross-references listed for related fields of testing, the reader will discover tests which will provide a new or more appropriate perspective to a particular assessment situation. For convenience, there are five cumulative indexes (which cover both **TESTS** and **TESTS-Supplement**)—title, author, publisher, scoring service and visually impaired. Preceding the page number in the indexes there will be an S (for **TESTS-Supplement**) and T (for **TESTS-First Edition**) for ready reference purposes.

The PURPOSE statement is set off by bars to direct the reader's attention to the most concise statement of what a test is designed to accomplish.

The KEYS are also designed for quick-scanning reference. They will appear in the following order:

child/teen/adult
grades

☞ ✍ : Symbolizes that an examiner is required.

✍ : Symbolizes that a test is self-administered.

Who May Order Tests

Test publishers adhere to the ethical standards for administering tests as established by appropriate professional organizations for psychology, education and business. The Test Corporation of America fully supports the ethical and professional standards as established by the various national and state professional organizations and encourages each test administrator to contact them. An individual ordering tests of a psychological nature, therefore, should have training and/or the appropriate supervision required by the standards of the American Psychological Association.

While some descriptions in **TESTS-Supplement** state specific restrictions on test accessibility, the inclusion of this information often reflects the wishes of the publisher or author; the fact that a test description does not list restrictions should not be taken to imply that such restrictions do not exist. Test administrators when ordering should ask each publisher for these standards or requirements for purchasing.

How To Order Tests

Order forms, catalogues, and further information regarding tests may be obtained from each publisher. Anyone interested in ordering a specific test should contact the publisher directly, using the Publishers Index which provides mailing addresses and phone numbers.

By necessity, the cost information included is selective and representative. Complete pricing for some tests (covering the various forms, kits, options, etc.) is so lengthy that it makes the inclusion of all cost variables prohibitive. Cost information is as accurate as the editors could establish at the time of publication.

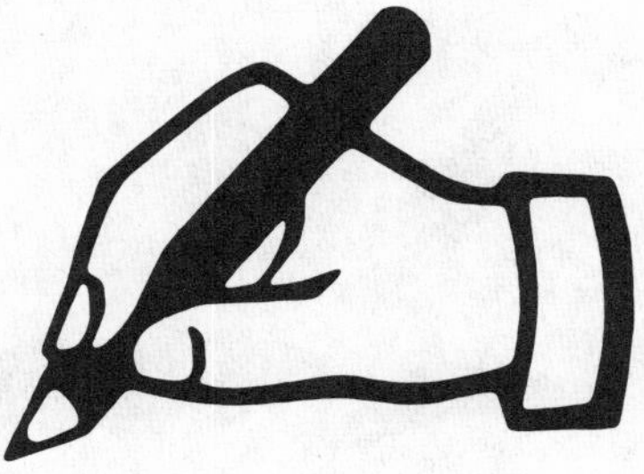

Psychology

The tests presented and described in the Psychology Section have been selected on the basis of their appropriate usage in a clinical or counseling setting. In general, tests found in this section are those which might be used by a mental health professional rather than an educator or human resources specialist.

Tests in this section have been arranged into six subsections on the basis of "typical usage or function." The same guidelines for classification as applied to the tests described in the First Edition of ***TESTS*** *have been used to classify the tests described in this volume.*

The classification of tests on the basis of "typical usage or function" is, of course, an arbitrary one, and the reader is encouraged to review the Education Section and Business Section for additional assessment techniques. Readers are also encouraged to refer to the First Edition of ***TESTS*** *in addition to this supplement for a more complete understanding of the range of tests available within each of the six subsections.*

Psychology Section Index

Child and Child Development

ASSESSMENT IN INFANCY: ORDINAL SCALES OF PSYCHOLOGICAL DEVELOPMENT

Ina C. Uzgiris and J. McV. Hunt

child

Purpose: Assesses the behavioral development of infants in the first two years of life. Used with severely retarded and handicapped infants and to compare different populations of children.

Description: Six paper-pencil observational inventories assessing the following developmental areas: visual pursuit and permanence of objects, means for obtaining desired environmental events, vocal and gestural imitation, operational causality, construction of object relations in space, and schemes for relating to objects. The book *Assessment in Infancy* describes the six scales and provides methodology for testing severely mentally retarded individuals and handicapped infants, analyzing language development, and comparing different populations of children. The Record Forms are designed for use with the book. Each 32 page pamphlet includes forms for each of the six scales (with ample space for recording the infant's actions), a guide for administering the scales, samples of filled-out forms, and a sheet for summarizing results. Supplementary instructional films (16 mm. or video cassette) are available for each of the six scales. The films, depicting infants ranging in age from three weeks to two years, illustrate the behavioral items, eliciting situations, and procedures used in administering the scales. Examiner required. Not suitable for group use.

Untimed: Varies

Range: Ages 3 weeks-2 years

Scoring: Examiner evaluated

Cost: *Assessment in Infancy* (274 pp.) $15.00; Package of five 32 page record forms $10.00.

Publisher: University of Illinois Press

BATTELLE DEVELOPMENTAL INVENTORY

Refer to page 115.

THE BRIGANCE® DIAGNOSTIC INVENTORY OF EARLY DEVELOPMENT

Refer to page 116.

CALLIER-AZUSA SCALE: G-EDITION

Robert Stillman (Editor)

handicapped child

Purpose: Assesses the development of deaf-blind and severely and profoundly handicapped children. Used to plan developmentally appropriate activities and to evaluate a child's developmental progress, particularly at the lower developmental levels.

Description: Multiple item paper-pencil observational inventory measuring 18 developmental subscales in five developmental areas: motor development (postural control, locomotion, fine motor, and visual-motor); perceptual abilities (visual, auditory, and tactile development);

daily living skills (undressing and dressing, personal hygiene, development of feeding skills, and toileting); cognition, communication, and language (cognitive development, receptive communication, expressive communication, and development of speech); and social development (interactions with adults, peers, and the environment). Each subscale is made up of sequential steps describing developmental milestones. Some steps are divided into two or more items describing behaviors which appear at approximately the same time in development. The developmental steps described in the scale take into account the specific sensory, motor, language, and social deficits of deaf-blind and severely and profoundly impaired children (scale items differ from behaviors typically observed among normal children at the same developmental level). Administration of the scale is based on at least two weeks of observation of spontaneously occuring behaviors which typically appear in conjunction with classroom activities. The scale must be administered by someone thoroughly familiar with the child's behavior. No specific testing expertise is required other than good observational skills and a knowledge of the child's repertoire of behaviors. Most accurate results are obtained if several individuals having close contact with the child (teachers, aides, parents, specialists) evaluate the child on a consensus basis. Scale items are rated according to the presence or absence of the specific behaviors listed. Age equivalencies are included only to provide a rough means of comparing functioning levels in different areas of behavior. Interpretation of scale results is based on the sequence in which the behaviors occur, not the age norms for normal children. A profile sheet is provided for summarizing scale results. Self-administered by examiner. Not suitable for group use.

Untimed: Varies

Range: Deaf-blind and severely and profoundly handicapped children

Scoring: Examiner evaluated

Cost: Contact publisher

Publisher: Callier Center for Communication Disorders

DEVELOPMENTAL ACTIVITIES SCREENING INVENTORY-II (DASI-II)

Refer to page 119.

DEVELOPMENTAL HISTORY REPORT

child

Purpose: Assesses information concerning a child's developmental history. Used in preparation for clinical assessment and diagnosis and for educational evaluation and planning.

Description: Multiple item paper-pencil or computer-administered questionnaire assessing a child's development in following areas: pregnancy, birth, development, health, family, education, and behavior. The questionnaire is completed by the individual who knows the most about the child (generally a parent or primary care-giver). A narrative report based on the responses is provided, along with a section identifying two important types of answers: those answers which are clinically significant and those for which the individual indicated a desire to discuss in more detail. Software versions are available for the Apple II + , IIe, III and IBM PC computer systems. Examiner required. Paper-pencil version suitable for group use.

Untimed: 30-45 minutes

Range: Child

Scoring: Computer scored

Cost: Computer program (unlimited usage) $195.00.

Publisher: Psychologistics, Inc.

DEVELOPMENTAL TEST OF VISUAL—MOTOR INTEGRATION (VMI)

Refer to page 16.

THE FIVE P'S: PARENT PROFESSIONAL PRESCHOOL PERFORMANCE PROFILE

Refer to page 122.

FLUHARTY PRESCHOOL SPEECH AND LANGUAGE SCREENING TEST

Refer to page 164.

INITIAL COMMUNICATION PROCESSES

Terris Schery and Ann Glover

child

Purpose: Assesses early behavioral and communication (or pre-communication) processes for at-risk children and handicapped individuals of all ages who are functioning below the developmental level of three years. Used to plan and monitor intervention programs with children and delayed adults who may be autistic, severely or profoundly retarded, multiply-handicapped, or learning disabled.

Description: 92 item observational inventory consisting of 10 subscales assessing the following areas of early behavioral and communication processes: auditory skills, visual skills, manual fine motor skills, oral vocal motor skills, manipulative object play skills, symbolic object play skills, problem-solving skills, affective development, communication skills-comprehension, and communication skills-expression. Interpretive profile distributions allow comparison of an individual with eight groups: autistic, severely/profoundly retarded, multiply handicapped, or trainable mentally retarded, each classified as having a mental age of above two years or below two years. The scales book describes each of the 92 items and provides space for recording the results for one student being observed several times or for six students being observed once. The objectives bank contains a detailed description of each of over 250 objectives with criteria for deciding upon attainment. The progress monitoring log serves as an index to the objectives bank and provides for a sequential record of performance for one student on each of the more than 250 objectives. The manual includes a description of the scales, statistical data, suggestions for interpreting the scores and planning for students. Examiner required. Not suitable for group use.

Untimed: Varies

Range: Developmental age birth-3 years

Scoring: Examiner evaluated

Cost: Starter set (manual objectives bank, scales book, and progress monitoring log) $24.95.

Publisher: CTB/McGraw-Hill

KENT INFANT DEVELOPMENT SCALE (KID SCALE)

Jeanette M. Reuter and Lewis Katoff

child

Purpose: Assesses the developmental age of infants and young handicapped children chronologically or developmentally under one year of age. Used for developmental evaluation and prescriptive programming and as a basis for caregiver/professional conferences.

Description: 252 item paper-pencil inventory in which each item is a sentence stem that describes behaviors characteristic of an infant in its first year of life. Test items cover five behavioral domains: cognitive, motor, language, self-help, and social. The parent or caregiver marks the answer sheet to indicate which behaviors the child has acquired. Computer scored printout lists items in order of developmental age by domain, compares the results for each domain and for the full scale with normative sample of healthy infants, and furnishes developmental ages, a profile of strengths and weaknesses, and a timetable showing which developmental milestones will be acquired next. Examiner required. Suitable for group use. Available in Spanish.

Untimed: 30-40 minutes

Range: Ages 0-1 year

Scoring: Hand key; computer scored

Cost: Contact publisher.

Publisher: Kent Developmental Metrics

LEXINGTON DEVELOPMENTAL SCALES (LDS)

Refer to page 124.

MAXFIELD-BUCHHOLZ SOCIAL MATURITY SCALE FOR BLIND PRE-SCHOOL CHILDREN

Kathryn E. Maxfield and Sandra Buchholz

blind children

Purpose: Measures the social maturity of blind children ages 0-8 years.

Description: Multiple item paper-pencil observational inventory and parent-interview guide assessing the developmental skills and social maturity of blind infants and pre-school children. The examiner's ratings are based on personal observations in the home setting and supplemented by parent interview. This scale is an adaption of Vineland Social Maturity Scale. Examiner required. Not suitable for group use.

Untimed: Varies

Range: Blind children ages 0-8 years

Scoring: Examiner evaluated

Cost: 25 record blanks $2.00; manual $5.00.

Publisher: The American Foundation for the Blind

MEEKER-CROMWELL BEHAVIOR DEVELOPMENTAL ASSESSMENT

Refer to page 168.

MILLER ASSESSMENT FOR PRESCHOOLERS (MAP)

Lucy Jane Miller

preschoolers

Purpose: Identifies children who exhibit moderate preacademic problems which may affect one or more areas of development. Used for screening purposes by psychologists, physicians, occupational and physical therapists, speech pathologists, nurses, teachers, and trained support personnel. Used for comprehensive, clinical assessment by examiners with extensive clinical knowledge and experience.

Description: 27 item oral response and task performance test assessing preschooler's abilities in the following areas: neurological, sensory-motor, cognitive, and combined sensory-motor and cognitive. Provides standardized scores for the child's overall performance and for five performance indices: neurological foundations (abilities comprised of basic motor tasks and the awareness of sensations that are thought to provide the fundamental building blocks for more complex activities), sensory-motor coordination (more complex gross, fine, and oral motor tasks which are not dependent on the interpretation of visual-spatial information), verbal cognitive abilities (memory, sequencing, comprehension, association, and expression in a verbal context), nonverbal cognitive abilities (memory, sequencing, visualization, and the performance of mental manipulations not requiring spoken language), and complex task abilities (the combination of sensory, motor, and cognitive abilities). In addition to the total score and five performance indicies, normative information is provided to establish how a child's individual item performance compares to that of other children the same age.

In addition to the objective test items, a supplemental observations sheet is used to record subjective impressions about the quality of the child's performance, including: movement, touch, vision, language, and draw-a-person (these observations are supplemental and should be administered only by examiners with clinical experience).

Test items are administered and scored with the aid of a scoring notebook. This three-ring binder contains six cue sheets with directions for the examiner and six corresponding score sheets (cue sheets and score sheets are provided for six age groups; the appropriate sheets are inserted into the notebook prior to testing). The front of the score sheet records the child's performance on the objective items, while the back of the sheet records the child's performance on the objective items, while the back of the sheet records the child's behavioral reactions during the testing procedure. The record booklet is suitable for use with all six age groups and includes the following: summary sheet, family information and developmental history questionnaire, supplemental observations sheet, and performance indices. The card notebook includes the figure-ground cards, puzzles, and clown face (stimulus materials required for related test items), as well as the scoring transparency. The materials required for administering the remainder of the test items (over 75 objects, including blocks, toys, crayons, etc.) are contained in a briefcase style portfolio and a carrying case which unfolds to serve as a shield, enabling the examiner to prepare test materials out of view of the child.

The examiner's manual includes: a description of the test; a review of related literature; information concerning the test's development, standardization, reliability, and validity; specific instructions for item administration and scoring; directions for scoring the total test and performance indices; interpretive guidelines; and directions for administration of the supplemental observations sheet. Caution must be used in interpreting the results of the test when it is administered to populations not included in the normative sample, such as children for whom English is not the primary language, or children with known physical, mental, or emotional dysfunction. Examiner required. Not suitable for group use.

Untimed: 20-30 minutes

Range: Preschool children

Scoring: Examiner evaluated

Cost: MAP Kit (manual, scoring materials for 30 children) $249.00

Publisher: The Foundation for Knowledge in Development

PEABODY DEVELOPMENTAL MOTOR SCALES AND ACTIVITY CARDS

Refer to page 125.

PIAGET TASK KIT

Refer to page 125.

PRESCHOOL AND EARLY PRIMARY SKILLS SURVEY (PEPSS)

Refer to page 126.

PRESCHOOL ATTAINMENT RECORD (RESEARCH EDITION)

Refer to page 126.

PRESCHOOL DEVELOPMENT INVENTORY

Harold Ireton

child

Purpose: Preschool Screening: measures the developmental level, symptoms, and behavior problems of children ages 3-5½ years. Identifies children with problems which may interfere with the child's ability to learn.

Description: 84 item paper-pencil questionnaire for obtaining a parent's report (usually mother's) concerning the child's current functioning. The questionnaire (one page, both sides) consists of a 60-item section assessing the child's general developmental status and a 24-item section covering symptoms and behavior problems. The developmental section covers seven areas: language comprehension, expressive language, fine motor, self-help, personal-social, situation-comprehension, and gross motor. The total score on this section identifies possibly low functioning children. The symptoms and behavior problems list includes 14 items pertaining to sensory, motor, language, and somatic problems and 10 items related to immaturity, hyperactivity, behavioral, and emotional problems. Sections are also provided for the parent to describe the child in her own words, report special problems or handicaps of the child, and to raise questions or express concerns she may have about the child. Manual includes instructions for administering, scoring, and interpreting the questionnaire. Self-administered, clerically scored, examiner evaluated. Suitable for group use.

Untimed: Varies

Range: Ages 3-5½ years

Scoring: Examiner evaluated

Cost: Contact publisher.

Publisher: Behavior Science Systems, Inc.

VERBAL LANGUAGE DEVELOPMENT SCALE (VLDS)

Refer to page 175.

VINELAND ADAPTIVE BEHAVIOR SCALES

Sara S. Sparrow, David A. Balla and Dominic V. Cicchetti

child, teen

Purpose: Measures the personal and social sufficiency of individuals from birth to adulthood. Used with mentally retarded and handicapped individuals. This is the 1984 revision of The Vineland Social Maturity Scale.

Description: 244-577 item inventory (depending on which of the three forms is used) assessing adaptive behavior in the following four domains: Communication (receptive, expressive, and written), Daily Living Skills (personal, domestic, and community), Socialization (interpersonal relationships, play and leisure time, and coping skills), and Motor Skills (gross and fine). These four domains are combined to form the Adaptive Behavior Composite. An optional Maladaptive Behavior domain is included in the Survey Form and Expanded Form. The Interview Edition, Survey Form contains 297 items. A trained interviewer administers the inventory to a parent or care-giver in semi-structured interview. The record booklet is used to record item scores and informal observations and contains a score summary page for recording and profiling derived scores.

The Interview Edition, Expanded Form includes 577 items, offers a more comprehensive assessment of adaptive behavior and provides a basis for preparing individual educational, habilitative, or treatment programs. Administration is similar to the Survey Form. Scores are recorded in the item booklet. The score summary and profile booklet includes a page for summarizing derived scores and four program planning profiles, each of which identifies clusters of items which describe activities that should be included in the individual programs.

The Classroom Edition includes 244 items and assesses adaptive behavior in the classroom. This edition is administered in the form of a questionnaire which is independently completed by teachers. A qualified professional is required to determine and interpret derived scores.

All forms include their own manual with guidelines for administration, scoring, and interpreting results. Supplementary materials include: audiocassette presenting sample Survey and Expanded Form interviews; ASSIST microcomputer software programs for score conversion, profiling, and record management; the Technical and Interpretive Manual; and reports to parents explaining an individual's derived scores in relation to strengths and weaknesses. Examiner required. Not suitable for group use. The Survey Form, record booklet and reports to parents for all three versions are available in Spanish.

Untimed: Varies

Range: Survey Form and Expanded Form—birth to 18 years and low-functioning adults; Classroom Edition—ages 3-12 years

Scoring: Examiner evaluated; microcomputer software available

Cost: Survey Form Starter Set (10 record booklets, manual, 1 report to parents) $18.50; Expanded Form Starter Set (10 item booklets, 10 score summary and profile reports, manual, 1 program planning report, 1 report to parents) $30.50; Classroom Edition Starter Set (10 questionnaire booklets, manual, 1 report to parents) $13.50.

Publisher: American Guidance Service

Intelligence and Related

CLIFTON ASSESSMENT PROCEDURES FOR THE ELDERLY (CAPE)

A.H. Pattie and C.J. Gilleard

older adult

Purpose: Assesses level of dependency in the elderly. Used by general practitioners, community nurses, health visitors, occupational therapists, and social workers, as well as hospital personnel.

Description: Two multiple item paper-pencil rating scales assessing cognitive and behavioral competence in the elderly. The Cognitive Assessment Scale is a short psychological test comprised of three sections: information/orientation, mental ability, and a psychomotor test utilizing the Gibson Spiral Maze. The Behavioral Rating Scale consists of 18 items measuring physical disability, apathy, communication difficulties, and social disturbance. Scoring procedure relates level of cognitive and behavioral dependency to likely need for community or hospital care. Examiner required. Not suitable for group use.

Untimed: Varies

Range: Elderly

Scoring: Examiner evaluated

Cost: 20 Cognitive Assessment Scales $5.25; 20 Gibson Spiral Mazes $7.75; 20 Behavioral Rating Scales $5.25; 20 report forms $6.00; manual $8.50.

Publisher: Distributed by The Psychological Corporation

COGNITIVE DIAGNOSTIC BATTERY (CDB)

Refer to page 151.

FOSTER MAZES

adult

Purpose: Measures non-verbal intelligence.

Description: Task performance test assessing spatial orientation and spatial reasoning ability. Blindfolded individual must find his way out of a grooved maze pattern using a stylus or pencil. Mazes are presented in the form of grooves etched into 8½ x 11-inch boards (available in equivalent forms A and B). Manual provides scoring guidelines. Examiner required. Not suitable for group use.

Untimed: Varies

Range: Adult

Scoring: Examiner evaluated

Cost: Maze (form A or B) $92.00.

Publisher: Stoelting Co.

KENDRICK BATTERY FOR THE DETECTION OF DEMENTIA IN THE ELDERLY

Andrew J. Gibson and Don C. Kirkpatrick

older adult

Purpose: Assesses the demented functioning in the elderly. Used by practitioners and nurses under the direction of clinical psychologists.

Description: Two multiple item paper-pencil tests measuring those areas of cognitive functioning most sensitive to the dementing process. The Object Learning Test (available in equivalent forms A and B) measures short-term memory, and the Digit Copying Test measures speed of responding to information. The manual contains information for administration, scoring, and test diagnosis. Examiner required. Not suitable for group use.
BRITISH PUBLISHER.

Untimed: 15 minutes

Range: Age 55 years and up

Scoring: Examiner evaluated

Cost: Manual $5.45; Object Learning Test set $8.65; 25 record forms (includes Digit Copying Test) $4.45.

Publisher: NFER-Nelson Publishing Company Ltd.

LEITER ADULT INTELLIGENCE SCALE (LAIS)

adult

Purpose: Measures general intelligence in adults. Used with individuals from the upper and lower levels of the socio-economic hierarchy and with the psychologically disabled.

Description: Six oral response and task performance tests assessing verbal and non-verbal intelligence. Verbal test includes: similarities-differences, digits forward and backward, and free recall-controlled recall. Non-verbal tests include: pathways (following a prescribed sequence), stencil designs (reproduction of designs), and painted cube test (duplication of designs). Test results identify deficits in cognitive, psychophysical or social areas and provide a measure of functional efficiency for psychologically disabled and superior individuals. Examiner required. Not suitable for group use.

Untimed: 40 minutes

Range: Adult

Scoring: Examiner evaluated

Cost: Test kit (all test materials, manual and 100 record blanks) $132.00.

Publisher: Stoelting Co.

MULTIDIMENSIONAL APTITUDE BATTERY

Douglas N. Jackson

teen, adult ☞ ✍

Purpose: Assesses aptitudes and intelligence for adolescents and adults. Used for clinical and research purposes with normal and deviant populations, including prison inmates, neurotic, psychotic, and neurologically impaired psychiatric patients, persons in business and industry, and high school and college students.

Description: Multiple item paper-pencil multiple choice test consisting of two batteries of five subtests each. The Verbal battery includes the following subtests: Information, Comprehension, Arithmetic, Similarities, and Vocabulary. Performance battery subtests include: Digit Symbol, Picture Completion, Spatial, Picture Arrangement, and Object Assembly. Verbal, Performance, and Full Scale IQ's and standard scores for the ten subtests have been calibrated to those of the WAIS-R and permit appraisal of intellectual functioning at nine different age levels, ranging from 16-74 years. Separate test booklets and answer sheets are provided for the two batteries. One battery of five subtests (seven minutes per test) can be administered in one sitting. An optional tape recording of instructions and timing may be used to administer all subtests. Scoring templates are available for hand scoring. Profiles and scoring sheets may be used for recording raw scores, converting scores to standard form, and recording IQ's. The one-day scoring service provides a five-page computerized report for each individual tested, including a one-page summary for the counselor (tests may be submitted for scoring in any quantity). The manual contains instructions for administering the tests, interpretive and technical information, and norms tables and profiles. Examiner required. Suitable for group use.

Timed/Untimed: 70 minutes (7 minutes per subtest)

Range: High school-adult

Scoring: Hand key; machine-scoring and computer analysis available

Cost: Examination kit (one test booklet and answer sheet for each battery, manual, and one coupon for scoring service) $20.00; 70 test booklets (35 for each battery) $87.50; 70 answer sheets (35 for each battery) $28.00; manual $10.50; 35 record forms $6.00; scoring templates $12.50; computerized scoring (1-24 individuals) $3.25 each; cassette tape of instructions and timing $20.00.

Publisher: Research Psychologists Press, Inc.

NATIONAL ADULT READING TEST

Hazel E. Nelson

adult ☞ ✍

Purpose: Measures the effects of dementia, alcohol, drugs, or illness on the intellectual functioning of adults ages 20-70 years.

Description: 50 item oral response test measuring premorbid intelligence

in the assessment of dementia. Test items comprise a list of 50 words whose pronunciation cannot be guessed by phonemic decoding but must be recognized in order to be read correctly. The individual reads the words aloud. The raw score predicts IQ's which approximate closely to the premorbid IQ level. Examiner required. Not suitable for group use.
BRITISH PUBLISHER

Untimed: Varies

Range: Adult

Scoring: Examiner evaluated

Cost: Word cards £1.05; 25 answer sheets £2.25; manual £2.75.

Publisher: NFER-Nelson Publishing Company Ltd.

NON-LANGUAGE LEARNING TEST

Mary K. Bauman

all ages

Purpose: Measures non-verbal intelligence and learning abilities of blind and visually handicapped individuals.

Description: Multiple item task performance test assessing shape discrimination, flexibility of thinking, and ability to profit from instruction and experience when using concrete materials. The test kit includes: instructions and diagrams for constructing testing materials, instructions for administering the test, and rough norms. Examiner required. Not suitable for group use.

Timed: Varies

Range: Blind and visually handicapped individuals

Scoring: Examiner evaluated

Cost: Test kit $3.00.

Publisher: Associated Services for the Blind

OTIS SELF ADMINISTERING TEST OF MENTAL ABILITY

Arthur S. Otis

teen, adult

Purpose: Measures general mental ability. Used for intelligence screening in educational, clinical, and business settings.

Description: 75 item inventory measuring general intelligence. Test items include: multiple choice, arithmetic problem solving, sequence patterns, and verbal, arithmetic, sequential and abstract reasoning problems. The test consists of a four-page booklet into which the answers are written directly. Scoring chart is used to plot percentile curves showing the distribution of scores in any group of examinees. Raw scores may be converted to IQ's. Available in two forms: Form A Intermediate (ages 9-14 years) and Form A Higher (15-18 years). Also presented on microcomputer diskette by NCS/Professional Assessment Services. Computer report presents a table of item responses, an indication of how much of the test the individual completed before the time limit expired and the IQ. All items answered incorrectly are reproduced on the printout with the individual's answers and the correct answers listed. Diskette may be used on Psychometer only. Examiner required. Suitable for group use (computer administered to individuals).

Timed: 20-30 minutes

Range: Age 12 years-adult

Scoring: Scoring key; microcomputer scoring available

Cost: Contact Psychological Corporation for original inventory; Psychometer diskette (20 administrations) $100.00 from NCS.

Publisher: The Psychological Corporation/Psychometer diskette - NCS/ Professional Assessment Services

SLOSSON PRE-OBSERVATIONAL SCREEN (SPORS)

Steven W. Slosson

all ages

Purpose: Assesses health factors and cognitive, affective and behavioral problem areas which may adversely affect performance on standard intelligence tests. Used to provide contextual clues for a better understanding of an individual's performance on the Slosson Intelligence Test (SIT) and other individually administered intelligence tests.

Description: Three multiple item paper-pencil checklists assessing psychological, medical, and behavioral problems prior to intelligence testing. The Psychological and Medical Profile assesses eight areas of an individual's past medical history: adaptive behavior deficits, developmental ability/disability, medication regimentation, mobility, seizure disorder, expressive language, and receptive language. The Chronic Health Checklist assesses the interplay between physical problems (overall "wellness") and their effect on learning. The Profile of Behavioral Correlations (to optimal independent functioning) measures development in the following behavioral areas: cognitive, receptive language, expressive language, conversational tone, affective, behavioral, attentive listening, and social. The behavioral profile assesses the impact of physical health problems, birth defects, organic and functional disorders, neurochemical and hormonal imbalances, lack of environmental support, peer and adult pressures, and overly critical judgments on testing performance. The checklists are completed by the examiner using past medical records, school files, or the parents' or guardians' knowledge to check appropriate ability or functioning levels. This information should be gathered prior to the testing session so that the examiner can better understand the individual's past performance levels. Examiner required. Not suitable for group use.

Untimed: Varies

Range: Infant-adult

Scoring: Examiner evaluated

Cost: Test kit (individual record forms for SIT and other tests, 50 psychological and medical profiles, 50 chronic health checklists, and 50 profiles of behavioral correlations) $24.00.

Publisher: Slosson Educational Publications, Inc.

SLOSSON POST-OBSERVATIONAL TESTING SCREEN (SPOTS)

Steven W. Slosson and Theodore A. Castillo

---

all ages

Purpose: Assesses an individual's physical appearance, behavior and feelings during the administration of the Slosson Intelligence Test (SIT) and other individually administered intelligence tests. Used to provide contextual clues for a better understanding of an individual's performance on the SIT and other intelligence tests.

Description: Two observational inventories and one structured interview guide assessing physical and behavioral problems as well as the individual's attitudes and feelings at the time of testing. The Visual Scanning For Physical Observations records information regarding physical properties that strike the examiner as being a handicap to the individual's effective functioning (organic deficits, movements and gestures, appearance and dress). The Behavior Profile assesses the individual's observed behaviors during the one-to-one testing situation. Seven factors affecting performance levels are measured: outward behavior, relationship with examiner, recall, affective tone, attitude, work habits, and expression. The Post Test Questionnaire provides a format for an oral question and answer session regarding the individual's anxiety, health levels, ability to concentrate, and time constraints. The examiner records the individual's direct responses in the space provided on the questionnaire. All three forms are used in conjunction with the Slosson Intelligence Test and other individually administered intelligence tests. Examiner required. Not suitable for group use.

Untimed: Varies

Range: Infant-adult

Scoring: Examiner evaluated

Cost: Test kit (forms for SIT and other tests, 50 visual scanning for physical observations forms, 50 behavior profiles, 50 post-test questionnaires) $28.00.

Publisher: Slosson Educational Publications, Inc.

Neuropsychology and Related

ADULT GROWTH EXAMINATION (AGE)

Robert F. Morgan

adult

Purpose: Measures an individual's body age. Identifies individuals in need of further diagnostic screening. Used in employment and medical settings for initial screening purposes.

Description: Three blood pressure tests, a hearing test, and a vision test measuring body age (versus calendar age). Tests are administered in the following order: blood pressure, hearing, blood pressure, vision, and blood pressure. Administration requires the following equipment: portable electronic blood pressure monitor (allowing rapid accurate measurement without a stethoscope), portable audiometric monitor (variable volume dial up to 59 db for two frequencies—1000 cps and 6000 cps), and portable visual near point indicator (visual targets with pica type sentence—near point of clear focus tested). Raw scores for each of the subtests are converted to equivalent age scores. These scores are arranged in rank order with the median score being the tested body age of the individual being examined. Individual stability or reliability is determined by administering the test to the same person several times (a few days apart at varying hours). May be administered by trained paraprofessionals. Identifies individuals in need of professional evaluation. The manual includes: complete instructions for administration and scoring, conversion tables, and discussions of validity, reliability, and uses. Examiner required. Not suitable for group use.

Untimed: 10-15 minutes

Range: Adult

Scoring: Examiner evaluated

Cost: Contact publisher (Or may be purchased as part of R.F. Morgan's *Growing Younger* book, NY: Stein & Day, 1983, $16.95).

Publisher: Robert F. Morgan

AUTISM SCREENING INSTRUMENT FOR EDUCATIONAL PLANNING

Refer to page 52.

BEHAVIOR ASSESSMENT BATTERY

Chris Kiernan and Malcolm Jones

all ages

Purpose: Assesses the ability of handicapped persons to function in their environment.

Description: A battery of tests produced in book form providing a range of assessment procedures. Identifies an individual's developmental strengths and weaknesses as a basis for effective educational planning. Each section consists of a set of items aimed at certain criterion behaviors. Successful completion of the items is an indication of the person's ability to function adequately in his environment. This revision includes a chapter on the use and interpretation of the battery and material on sign language. Examiner required. BRITISH PUBLISHER

Untimed: Varies

Range: Handicapped children and adults

Scoring: Examiner evaluated

Cost: Book £8.45.

Publisher: NFER-Nelson Publishing Company Ltd.

BEXLEY-MAUDSLEY AUTOMATED PSYCHOLOGICAL SCREENING (BMAPS)

William Acker and Clare Acker

adult

Purpose: Assesses psychological defects resulting from organic brain damage. Used to evaluate chronic alcoholics and to screen new patients before referring them for further evaluation.

Description: Six tests assessing psychological functioning presented on floppy disc for computerized administration, scoring, and interpretation. Tests include: visual spatial ability test (little men), symbol digit coding, visual perceptual analysis, verbal recognition memory, visual spatial recognition memory, and the Bexley-Maudsley sorting test (abstract problem solving). Three versions are available for use with Commodore 4040 and 8050 disc drives and Apple II microcomputer. A specially designed patient keyboard clips over the Commodore Pet 4032 and 8032 computer. The keyboard comprises nine response keys. Since some tests use less than nine keys, three masks are provided so that the individual is presented with the exact number of alternatives for each test. Raw and standardized scores are available immediately on completion of the test. Manual provides details of administration, scoring and theoretical background. May be administered by psychologists, psychiatrists, and nurses. Examiner required. Not suitable for group use. BRITISH PUBLISHER

Untimed: Varies

Range: Adult

Scoring: Computer scored

Cost: Complete set (manual, disc, and keyboard adaptor) £195.00.

Publisher: NFER-Nelson Publishing Company Ltd.

BOSTON DIAGNOSTIC APHASIA EXAMINATION

Harold Goodglass and Edith Kaplan

adult

Purpose: Assesses the functioning of aphasic patients. Used for clinical evaluations.

Description: Multiple item oral response, paper-pencil, and task performance test yielding 43 scores that relate to recognized aphasic syndromes: severity rating, fluency (articulation, phrase length, verbal agility), auditory comprehension (word discrimination, body part identification, commands, complex material), naming (responsive, confrontation, animal, body part), oral reading (word reading, oral sentence), repetition (words, high-probability sentences, low-probability sentences), paraphrasia (neologistic distortion, literal, verbal, extended), automatized speech (sentences, reciting), reading comprehension (symbol discrimination, word recognition, oral spelling, word picture matching, sentences, and paragraphs), writing (mechanics, serial writing, spelling to dictation, sentences to dictation, narrative writing), music (singing, rhythm), parietal (drawing to command, stick memory, total fingers, right-left, arithmetic, clock setting, 3-dimensional blocks), plus 7 ratings: melodic line, phrase length, articulatory agility, grammatical form, paraphrasia in running speech, word finding, auditory comprehension. The 80-page text, *The Assessment of Aphasia and Related Disorders,* serves as the test manual and includes: information on the nature of aphasic deficits, common clusters of defects, statistical information, administration and scoring procedures, and illustrations of test profiles that correspond to major aphasic syndromes. Examiner required. Not suitable for group use.

Untimed: Varies

Range: Adult

Scoring: Examiner evaluated

Cost: Complete set (text, 16 stimulus cards, 25 test booklets) $31.00.

Publisher: Distributed by The Psychological Corporation

CALLIER-AZUSA SCALE: G-EDITION

Refer to page 3.

CARD SORTING BOX

Refer to page 255.

DEVELOPMENTAL TEST OF VISUAL-MOTOR INTEGRATION (VMI)

Keith E. Beery and Norman A. Buktenica

child, teen, adult

Purpose: Identifies children with problems in visual perception, hand control, and eye-hand coordination.

Description: 15-24 item paper-pencil test measuring the integration of visual perception and motor behavior. Test items, arranged in order of increasing difficulty, consist of geometric figures which the children are asked to copy. The Short Test Form (15 figures) is used with children ages 2-8 years. The Long Test Form (24 figures) is used with children ages 2-15 years and adults with developmental delays. The manual includes directions for administration, scoring criteria, developmental comments, age norms, suggestions for teaching, percentiles, and standard score equivalents. Supplementary materials include: VMI Monograph and stimulus cards (a 47-page booklet on visual-motor research studies a set of 24 cards for remediation) and assessment worksheets (10 copies each of 40 different worksheets related to tasks on the VMI). Examiner required. Suitable for group use.

Untimed: Varies

Range: Ages 2-15 years, developmentally delayed adults.

Scoring: Examiner evaluated

Cost: Short form (pkg. of 15) $13.25; Long Form (pkg. of 15) $18.79; manual for both forms $11.01; monograph and stimulus cards $12.15; Specimen set $5.48; assessment work sheets $41.54.

Publisher: Modern Curriculum Press, Inc.

DIAGNOSTIC CHECKLIST FOR BEHAVIOR-DISTURBED CHILDREN: FORM E-2

Refer to page 29.

THE DYSINTEGRAL LEARNING CHECKLIST

Mary Meeker and Valerie Maxwell

child

Purpose: Identifies students with potential learning problems. Used by pediatricians, neurologists, special education diagnosticians, and teachers.

Description: Multiple item paper-pencil inventory of symptoms which are predictive of each of the four systems integrated into the cerebellum. Identifies dysintegrated functions for learning. Covers the following areas: vision, speech and auding, motoric, proprioceptor, and behavioral. Test results are coded to training materials for each system involved. Self-administered by examiner and/or parents. Suitable for use with groups of parents.

Untimed: Varies

Range: Children

Scoring: Examiner evaluated

Cost: Checklist (pack of 10) $3.50.

Publisher: SOI Institute

FRENCHAY DYSARTHRIA ASSESSMENT

Refer to page 165.

THE GRADED NAMING TEST

Pat McKenna and Elizabeth K. Warrington

adult

Purpose: Identifies naming deficits. Indicates impaired language functioning in brain damaged patients. Used with psychiatric, neurological, and geriatric patients.

Description: Multiple item oral response test assessing naming deficits with individuals regardless of range of intellectual ability. Test items consist of picture stimuli which the patient is asked to name. Object pictures have been selected so that ambiguous answers are rare. Items of sufficient difficulty are included to adequately assess patients with above average premorbid intelligence. Equivalent scores on Wechsler Adult Intelligence Scale Vocabulary, National Adult Reading Test, and Schonell Graded Word Reading Test can be derived from a conversion table. Examiner required. Not suitable for group use.
BRITISH PUBLISHER

Untimed: Varies

Range: Adult

Scoring: Examiner evaluated

Cost: Manual £4.50; object picture book £9.50; 25 answer/record sheets £3.45.

Publisher: NFER-Nelson Publishing Company Ltd.

HALSTEAD-REITAN NEUROPSYCHOLOGICAL TEST BATTERY FOR ADULTS

Reitan Neuropsychology Laboratory and others

adult

Purpose: Evaluates brain function and dysfunction in adults. Used for clinical evaluation.

Description: A battery of tests assessing adult neuropsychological functioning, including: the Halstead Neuropychological Test Battery, the Wechsler Adult Intelligence Scale, the Trail Making Test, the Reitan-Indiana Aphasia Screening Test, various tests of sensory-perceptual functions, and the Minnesota Multiphasic Personality Inventory. Materials include: category test projection box with electric control mechanism and projector, 208 adults category slides in carousels, tactual performance test (10-hole board, stand, 10 blocks), manual finger tapper, tape cassette for speech-sounds perception test, tactile form recognition test, and manual for administration and scoring. Components may be ordered separately. Examiner required. Not suitable for group use.

Timed/Untimed: Varies

Range: Adult

Scoring: Examiner evaluated

Cost: Adult Battery $1,106.00.

Publisher: Reitan Neuropsychology Laboratory

HALSTEAD-REITAN NEUROPSYCHOLOGICAL TEST BATTERY FOR CHILDREN

Reitan Neuropsychology Laboratory and others

child, teen

Purpose: Evaluates brain function and dysfunction in children ages 9-14 years. Used for clinical evaluations.

Description: A battery of tests assessing the neuropsychological functioning of children, including: the Halstead Neuropsychological Test Battery, the Wechsler Intelligence Scale for Children, the Trail Making Test, the Reitan-Indiana Aphasia Screening Test, various tests of sensory-perceptual functions, and measures of academic achievement. The tests in this battery have been adapted from the Halstead-Reitan Neuropsychological Test Battery for Adults. Much of the equipment used for testing adults can also be used with the children's battery. Adaptations for use with this age group include: new slides (stimulus material) for the category test, a new answer form for the speech-sounds perception test, a 6-hole board instead of a 10-hole board for the tactual performance test, and a shortened form of the Trail Making Test. Materials include: all necessary equipment, test stimuli, slide carousels, recording forms, and manual for administration, scoring, and evaluation of all tests. Components may be purchased separately. Examiner required. Not suitable for group use.

Timed/Untimed: Varies

Range: Ages 9-14 years

Scoring: Examiner evaluated

Cost: Older Children's Battery $1,056.00.

Publisher: Reitan Neuropsychology Laboratory

THE HEARING MEASUREMENT SCALE

Refer to page 158.

LIGHT-SWITCH ALTERNATION APPARATUS

Milton B. Jensen

patients

Purpose: Measures "alternation-type" learning. Used with neuropsychiatric patients to determine degree of mental illness and potential for rehabilitation.

Description: Multiple item task performance instrument consisting of five two-position switches connected to five flashing lights which are used to provide learning tasks at five levels of difficulty: single position, single alternation, double alternation, and a 5-position series. Different and more complex learning tasks can be set up readily by altering the wiring circuit at the control panel (which is screened from the patient's view). Tentative norms are available for each of the five levels of difficulty. Scores of neuropsychiatric patients, when compared with their scores on conventional tests of intelligence, provide an index of severity of mental illness and potential for rehabilitation. Examiner required. Not suitable for group use.

Timed: Varies

Range: Neuropsychiatric patients

Scoring: Examiner evaluated

Cost: Testing apparatus $88.00.

Publisher: Lafayette Instrument Company, Inc.

MULTIDIMENSIONAL APTITUDE BATTERY

Refer to page 11.

NEUROLOGICAL DYSFUNCTIONS OF CHILDRFEN (NDOC)

James W. Kuhns

child

Purpose: Assesses the neurological functioning of children ages 3-10 years. Identifies children in need of further neurological evaluation. Used by school psychologists, education specialists, physicians, nurses, and occupational therapists, and in school psychology training and pediatric residency programs.

Description: 18 item task performance screening instrument measuring a range of neurological functions. For items 1-16, the child is asked to perform a variety of simple tasks, such as walking along a straight line, touching a finger to the nose, and following an object with the eyes. The tasks represent behavior capabilities that are minimally affected by environmental factors. Each task is evaluated on the basis of a "yes-no" decision, depending on whether the child is functioning in a normal, healthy manner or is experiencing mild to moderate impairment in neurological functioning. Item 17 requires measuring the child's head circumference and determining any deviance from the chronological age normal range size as indicated on an included chart. Item 18 is a checklist of discriminating areas of information concerning the child's background. The screening and referral chart relates the child's scores to interpretive clusters and indicates whether referral to an appropriate professional (opthamologist, audiologist, physician, speech specialist, or neurologist) is needed for further evaluation. The manual includes complete information on administering and scoring the tests and interpreting the results, as well as technical data. Examiner required. Not suitable for group use.

Untimed: 50-60 minutes

Range: Ages 3-10 years

Scoring: Examiner evaluated

Cost: Starter set (manual and 20 screening and referral charts) $33.50.

Publisher: CTB/McGraw Hill

NEUROPSYCHOLOGICAL STATUS EXAMINATION (NSE)

Psychological Assessment Resources, Inc.

adult

Purpose: Evaluates, organizes and collates data regarding an individual's neuropsychological functioning. Used for a variety of neuropsychological assessments, ranging from screening procedures to extensive work-ups and preparation for expert-witness testimony.

Description: 10-page multiple item paper-pencil assessment instrument evaluating neuropsychological information such as patient data, observational findings, test administration parameters, neuroanatomical correlates, reports of test findings, clinical impressions, and recommendations for treatment. Consists of 13 sections including: patient and referral data, neuropsychological symptom checklist (93 items), premorbid status, physical, emotional, and cognitive status, results of neuropsychological testing, diagnostic comments, and follow-up and treatment recommendations. All sections designed with consideration of base rate data for common findings in neuropsychological evaluations. The manual includes a discussion of the rationale of the logic underlying the structure of the instrument and provides suggestions for its most efficient use. Examiner required. Not suitable for group use.

Untimed: Varies

Range: Adult

Scoring: Examiner evaluated

Cost: Examination kit (manual and 25 forms) $10.95.

Publisher: Psychological Assessment Resources, Inc.

PAIN AND DISTRESS INVENTORY

Refer to page 60.

PURDUE HAND PRECISION TEST

Refer to page 256.

PYRAMID PUZZLE

Refer to page 256.

RECEPTIVE-EXPRESSIVE OBSERVATION (REO)

Refer to page 145.

REITAN-INDIANA NEUROPSYCHOLOGICAL TEST BATTERY FOR CHILDREN

Ralph M. Reitan and others

child

Purpose: Assesses brain-behavior functioning in children ages 5-8 years. Used for clinical evaluation.

Description: A battery of tests assessing the neurological functioning of young children, including: the Wechsler Intelligence Scale for Children, sensory perceptual tests, modifications of the Reitan-Indiana Aphasia Screening Test and the Halstead Neuropsychological Test Battery, and a number of additional tests (Color Form Test, Target Test, Matching Pictures Test, Progressive Figures Test, Marching Test, and Individual Performance Tests). This battery is related to the Halstead-Reitan Neuropsychological Test Batteries for adults and older children, but a number of adaptations have been made for use with this age group. The Category Test uses a different set of slides for stimuli and colored instead of numbered caps as the guide to lever choice on the answer panel. The Tactual Performance Test uses a 6-hole board in a horizontal instead of a vertical position. The Aphasia Screening Test deletes a number of items from the adult version, adds a number of simple procedures, and uses a different recording form. An electric finger tapping was devised because young children had trouble manipulating the manual apparatus. Materials include: all necessary equipment, test stimuli, slide carousels, recording forms, and manual for administration, scoring, and evaluation of all tests. Components may be purchased separately. Examiner required. Not suitable for group use.

Untimed: Varies

Range: Ages 5-8 years

Scoring: Examiner evaluated

Cost: Young children's battery $1,115.00.

Publisher: Reitan Neuropsychological Laboratory

THE REVERSALS FREQUENCY TEST

Refer to page 149.

STEADINESS TESTER—GROOVE TYPE

Refer to page 257.

STEADINESS TEST—HOLE TYPE

Refer to page 257.

SYSTEM FOR THE ADMINISTRATION AND INTERPRETATION OF NEUROLOGICAL TESTS (SAINT-II)

Dennis Swiercinsky

teen, adult

Purpose: Diagnoses organic brain dysfunction. Differentiates between physiological and psychological contributions to behavior. Used to predict benefits from education, training, or therapy. May also be used for research.

Description: Ten tests of neuropsychological functioning presented on microcomputer diskette. Tests include: number connections, alternating connections, finger tapping, lateral-spatial orientation, rhythm discrimination, abstract sequencing, vocabulary, symbol-number coding, verbal-logical memory, and figural memory. All instructions are presented visually. Eighty-two scores are produced, including: number of correct responses, average response latencies, response latency deviations, response error trends, and psychomotor coordination errors. May be administered only on Psychometer. Examiner required. Not suitable for group use.

Untimed: 60-90 minutes

Range: Age 16 years-adults

Scoring: Microcomputer scored

Cost: Contact publisher.

Publisher: NCS/Professional Assessment Services

TAPPING BOARD

Refer to page 257.

TEST OF ABSTRACT CONCEPT LEARNING (TACL)

teen, adult

Purpose: Evaluates general organic brain dysfunction. Used to screen psychological or medical patients for brain damage when clinical evidence is subtle, contradictory, or confusing.

Description: Multiple item test of abstract reasoning ability presented on microcomputer diskette. Simultaneously assesses several characteristics that indicate cerebral integrity, including mental flexibility, working memory, altertness, deductive reasoning and abstract thinking. In this computer adaptation of the Wisconsin Card Sort, patients sort geometric images into three categories according to color, form and number, utilizing "Right" and "Wrong" feedback to learn the rule for each category. A category is considered learned when 10 consecutive correct sorts are made twice in each category. Results are presented in narrative form and provide information about evidence for general organic impairment, speed of new learning, mental flexibility and influence of anxiety on new learning. May be administered only on Psychometer. Examiner required. Not suitable for group use.

Untimed: 25 minutes

Range: Age 12 years-adult

Scoring: Microcomputer scored

Cost: Psychometer diskette (20 administrations) $90.00.

Publisher: NCS/Professional Assessment Services

TWO ARM COORDINATION TEST

Refer to page 258.

VISUAL FORM DISCRIMINATION

Arthur L. Benton and colleagues

all ages

Purpose: Evaluates the extent to which brain damage has impaired an individual's ability to discriminate visual forms. Used for clinical evaluations of brain damaged patients.

Description: 16 item oral response multiple-choice test measuring the ability to discriminate between complex visual configurations. Test items arranged according to level of difficulty. Comparative data on patients with brain disease provided. Especially useful with patients who have suspected right hemisphere involvement. Normative and validity data are described in *Contributions to Neuropsychological Assessment*, which also includes detailed directions for test administration and scoring, as well as a discussion of the test's application in the clinical assessment of adults and children. Examiner required. Not suitable for group use.

Untimed: Varies

Range: Brain damaged children and adults

Scoring: Examiner evaluated

Cost: Test kit (book of line drawings and 100 record forms) $37.50; *Contributions to Neuropsychological Assessment—A Clinical Manual* $23.00.

Publisher: John Wiley - distributed by Psychological Assessment Resources, Inc.

Marriage and Family

Family

ADULT PERSONAL ADJUSTMENT AND ROLE SKILLS (PARS)

Refer to page 31.

CHILDREN'S VERSION/FAMILY ENVIRONMENT SALE (CV/FES)

C.J. Pino, Nancy Simons and Mary Jane Slawinowsky

child

Purpose: Evaluates the home environment of children ages 5-12 years. Used by guidance counselors, psychologists, clinicians, family therapists, and family educators.

Description: 30 item paper-pencil or oral response test assessing ten areas of family functioning: relationship dimensions (cohesion, expressiveness and conflict), personal growth dimensions (independence, achievement orientation, intellectual-cultural orientation, active-recreational orientation and moral-religious orientation), and system maintenance dimensions (organization and control). Questions are presented to the child in a pictorial non-projective format. The manual describes clinical use, research, and test administration and scoring. Examiner required. Not suitable for group use.

Untimed: Varies

Range: Ages 5-12 years

Scoring: Examiner evaluated

Cost: Test kit (manual, 10 test answer booklets, 50 profiles, 50 examiner's worksheets, and 50 individual student answer sheets) $30.00.

Publisher: Slosson Educational Publications, Inc.

DYADIC PARENT-CHILD INTERACTION CODING SYSTEM (DPICS)

Sheila M. Eyberg and Elizabeth A. Robinson

child, adult

Purpose: Assesses the quality of interaction between parents and young children in the laboratory or clinical setting. Used to aid in evaluation of family functioning, to monitor progress of treatment and to evaluate treatment outcome.

Description: Multiple item paper-pencil coding system comprising a direct observation procedure for monitoring interactions between parents and young children. Data are collected by observing a parent-child dyad in three five-minute semistructured situations which vary in the amount of parental control elicited: child-directed play, parent-direct play, and clean-up. Parents are observed for the following behaviors: descriptive statement, reflective statement, descriptive/reflective question, acknowledgment, physical positive, physical negative, labeled praise, unlabeled praise, critical statement, direct command, and indirect command. Each command is coded as to whether the child complies, noncomplies, or is given no opportunity to comply. Additional child behaviors observed include: whine, cry, yell, smart talk, physical negative, destructive, and changes activity. Whether or not the parent responds to or ignores each deviant behavior is also recorded. In the manual, the behaviors listed above are operationally defined, examples are given, decision rules are delineated, normative data are provided, and research is summarized. Examiner required. Not suitable for group use.

Untimed: 15 minutes

Range: Parents and young children (ages 2-10 years)

Scoring: Examiner evaluated

Cost: Manual $14.50.

Publisher: Psychological Documents, American Psychological Association

HOME OBERVATION FOR MEASUREMENT OF THE ENVIRONMENT

Refer to page 56.

LIFE EVENTS SCALE—CHILDREN

R. Dean Coddington

child

Purpose: Assesses significant events occurring in a child's life. Used for clinical evaluation and counseling of children.

Description: 35 item paper-pencil questionnaire measuring the frequncy of selected important events in a child's family and social life. Scores are provided for three areas: family events over which the child had no control (17 items), desirable extrafamilial events (8 items), and undesirable extrafamilial events (10 items). Total extrafamilial event scores and total scores easily computed. Items are weighted for scoring purposes according to criteria provided by pediatricians, teachers, and mental health workers dealing with children. Materials include the one-page test form and instruction manual. Examiner required. Suitable for group use.

Untimed: Varies

Range: Children

Scoring: Examiner evaluated

Cost: Contact publisher.

Publisher: Distributed by Psychological Assessment Resources, Inc.

MEASURE OF CHILD STIMULUS SCREENING (CONVERSE OF AROUSABILITY)

Albert Mehrabian and Carol Falender

child

Purpose: Measures major components of a child's arousability and stimulus screening. Used for research, counseling and education program selection purposes.

Description: Multiple item paper-pencil observational inventory measuring parent descriptions of their children's arousability (responses of one parent are sufficient). Test results indicate the child's characteristic arousal response to complex, unexpected, or unfamiliar situations. Stimulus screening/arousability has been shown to be a major component of many important personality dimensions such as anxiety, neuroticism, extroversion, or hostility. This test is based on the same conceptual framework used to develop the corresponding adult measure. Examiner required. Suitable for group use.

Untimed: Approximately 20 minutes

Range: Ages 3 months-7 years

Scoring: Examiner evaluated

Cost: Test kit (scale, scoring directions, norms, and descriptive material) $20.00.

Publisher: Albert Mehrabian

MEASURES OF PLEASURE-, AROUSAL-, AND DOMINANCE-INDUCING QUALITIES IN PARENTAL ATTITUDES

Albert Mehrabian

child

Purpose: Evaluates the emotional climate parents create for their children. Used for research and counseling purposes.

Description: Multiple item paper-pencil self-report questionnaire consisting of three orthogonal measures of parental child-rearing attitudes. Measures the levels of pleasure, arousal, and dominance experienced by the child. Provides three scores concerning parental attitudes: pleasure-inducing, arousal-inducing, and dominance-inducing. Examiner required. Suitable for group use.

Untimed: Approximately 20 minutes

Range: Ages 3 months-7 years

Scoring: Examiner evaluated

Cost: Test kit (scales, scoring directions, norms, and descriptive material) $20.00.

Publisher: Albert Mehrabian

MICHIGAN SCREENING PROFILE OF PARENTING (MSPP)

Ray E. Helfer, James K. Hoffmeister and Carol J. Schneider

adult

Purpose: Evaluates an individual's perceptions in areas which are critically important for positive parent-child interactions. Profiles those segments of the individual's early childhood experiences and current relationships which seem to affect that person's ability to interact with others. Used to identify those in need of further assessment.

Description: Multiple item paper-pencil self-report questionnaire for parents and prospective parents consisting of four section (A, B, C, and D). Section A provides information about family characteristics, the respondent's health history, and relationships with employers, social agencies, and spouse. Section B provides information regarding respondent perceptions of childhood experiences and current interactions with family and friends. Section C (answered only by individuals having one or more children) provides information about the respondent's child (or children) and current parent-child interactions. Section D (answered only by individuals who do not have children) provides information with regard to the respondent's expectations for future interactions with prospective children. Section A requires various types of answers depending on the type of biographical information being requested. Sections B, C, and D use seven-point Likert-scales to rate response to individual test items. Computerized scoring generates four scores based on the response to section B: emotional needs met, relationship with parents, expectations of children, and coping. High scores indicate a potential for parent-child interaction problems and may be used to identify individuals in need of further assessment and/or counseling. Scores are not intended to diagnose specific problems, nor do they predict the future behavior of parents. The manual includes: a discussion of the scale's background, development, and content; administration and scoring procedures; item measure characteristics; uses of the scale; and a list of available consulting services. Self-administered. Suitable for group use.

Untimed: Varies

Range: Adult

Scoring: Computer scored

Cost: 25 questionnaires (including scoring service) $50.00.

Publisher: Test Analysis and Development Corporation

PARENT AS A TEACHER INVENTORY: PAAT

Robert D. Strom

adult

Purpose: Assesses the attitudes of parents toward their parent-child relationship.

Description: Multiple item pencil-paper inventory measuring parental attitudes in the following areas: feelings toward the parent-child interactive system, standards for assessing the importance of certain aspects of child behavior, and value preferences as well as frustrations concerning child behavior. Examiner required. Suitable for group use. Available in Spanish.

Untimed: 30-45 minutes

Range: Parents of children 3-9 years of age

Scoring: Examiner evaluated

Cost: Starter set (manual, 20 inventory booklets, 20 identification questionnaires, 20 profiles) $27.50; Specimen set $5.00.

Publisher: Scholastic Testing Service, Inc.

POTENTIAL FOR FOSTER PARENTHOOD SCALE (PFPS)

John Touliatos and Byron W. Lindholm

adult

Purpose: Evaluates candidates for foster parenthood in terms of the quality of foster care that they are capable of providing. Used by social workers in making foster care placement decisions, in training foster family care workers, and in research on foster care.

Description: 54 item paper-pencil rating scale measuring potential for foster parenthood along nine dimensions: health, employment and income, time, opportunities for cultural and intellectual development, opportunities for religious and spiritual development, marriage, ability and motivation for foster parenthood, flexibility, and working with the agency and the child's own parents. Each item presents a statement describing a positive quality of foster parents (such as "has physical ability to care for children" or "has had stable relationships with children"). The social worker rates the husband and wife separately, indicating the degree to which each statement accurately describes the candidates on a four point scale from one (very different) to four (very similar). Ratings can be made at any time during the placement process and are based upon the case worker's past experiences with applicants who have been successful and unsuccessful. Scores are obtained for the total scale and for each of the nine clusters. Cut-off scores are provided for identifying four types of candidates: excellent, good, fair, and poor. The manual includes: directions for administration, scoring, and interpretation; interpretive guidelines; discussions of the four classifications; data concerning the development, reliability and validity of the scales; and a list of references for further research. Use of the scale allows for comparison of different applicants, rating the same applicants at different points in time to assess possible changes, and the identification of a couple's strengths and weaknesses concerning potential for foster care. Self-administered by examiner. Not suitable for group use.

Untimed: Varies

Range: Candidates for foster parenthood

Scoring: Examiner evaluated

Cost: Contact publisher.

Publisher: John Touliatos

PSYCHOSOCIAL ADJUSTMENT TO ILLNESS SCALE (PAIS)

Refer to page 47.

THE SOCIAL BEHAVIOR ASSESSMENT SCHEDULE

Refer to page 50.

THERAPY ATTITUDE INVENTORY (TAI)

Sheila M Eyberg

adult

Purpose: Assesses the amount of satisfaction parents feel in response to parent training programs or individual parent-child interaction training. Used to evaluate therapy programs.

Description: 10 item paper-pencil inventory asking parents to rate their feelings from one (indicating dissatisfaction or deterioration of condition) to five (indicating maximum satisfaction or improvement) regarding the following areas: acquisition of new disciplinary techniques, techniques for teaching their child new skills, their relationship with their child, confidence in ability to discipline, intensity of current behavior problems, level of child's compliance, progress of child, general benefits of treatment program, satisfaction with type of program, and general feeling about the program. Space is provided for personal comments concerning the child and the treatment program. Self administered by parent. Suitable for group use.

Untimed: Varies

Range: Parents

Scoring: Examiner evaluated

Cost: Free.

Publisher: Sheila M. Eyberg

Premarital and Marital Relations

DEROGATIS SEXUAL FUNCTIONING INVENTORY (DSFI)

Leonard R. Derogatis

adult

Purpose: Measures and describes the quality of an individual's sexual functioning.

Description: 10 multiple item paper-pencil subtests assessing the following factors related to an individual's sexual functioning: information, experience, drive, attitude, psychological symptoms, affects, gender role definition, fantasy, body image, and sexual satisfaction. Scaled scores from each subtest are combined to derive an overall sexual functioning score. Norms available separately for men and women. Examiner required. Suitable for group use.

Untimed: 30-40 minutes

Range: Adult

Scoring: Examiner evaluated

Cost: 10 reusable test booklets $30.00; 30 expendable test booklets $33.00; 50 answer sheets $9.00; 50 score/profile forms $10.00; manual $4.00.

Publisher: Clinical Psychometric Research

MINNESOTA-BRIGGS HISTORY RECORD WITH MARRIAGE SECTION

Refer to page 44.

OTTO PRE-MARITAL COUNSELING SCHEDULES

Herbert A. Otto

adult

Purpose: Assesses a couple's compatibility in potential marital problem areas. Used in individual counseling with a pre-marital couple or as a guide in group discussion on marriage planning.

Description: Multiple item paper-pencil rating scale consisting of three separate sections: a general pre-marital survey, a family finance section, and a sexual adjustment section. Intended for use in conjunction with the *Pre-Marital Counseling Manual.* Examiner required. Suitable for group use.

Untimed: Varies

Range: Adult

Scoring: Examiner evaluated

Cost: Counseling kit (manual and 10 copies of each schedule) $12.50; specimen set (manual and one copy of each schedule) $4.50.

Publisher: Consulting Psychologists Press, Inc.

TEMPERAMENT INVENTORY TESTS

Robert J. Cruise and W. Peter Blitchington

adult

Purpose: Assesses an individual's basic temperament traits according to the four temperament theory. Used by professionals and laymen in marital, vocational, social, moral, and spiritual counseling settings.

Description: 80 item paper-pencil test determining an individual's basic temperament traits. Available in two forms: *Understanding Your Temperament* (a forty-two page booklet containing the test and instructions for self-administering, self-scoring, and interpreting the scores from a Christian viewpoint) and the Temperament Inventory (designed for group use and containing only the test itself, to be administered and scored by the examiner/group leader). Temperament templates are necessary for scoring the group form (interpretive material not included). Self-administered. Available in French, German, or Spanish.

Untimed: Varies

Range: Adult

Scoring: Self-scored; examiner evaluated

Cost: *Understanding Your Temperament* $2.95; Temperament Inventory $.60; Temperament Templates (set) $2.95.

Publisher: Andrews University Press

Personality: Normal and Abnormal, Assessment and Treatment

Child

CHILD & ADOLESCENT ADJUSTMENT PROFILE (CAAP)

Robert E. Ellsworth

child, teen

Purpose: Measures the current adjustment of children and adolescents to life and to the community. Used for evaluation of treatment programs.

Description: 20 item paper-pencil rating scale assessing a child's or adolescent's adjustment through five factored dimensions: peer relations, dependency, hostility, productivity, and withdrawal. The child may be rated every three months by a parent, teacher, or probation officer to evaluate the success of the child's mental halth program. The manual explains the rationale and validity of the scales and provides detailed norms for the general and clinical population with respect to adjustment to life and the community. Examiner required. Suitable for group use.

Untimed: 20-30 minutes

Range: Child, adolescent

Scoring: Examiner evaluated

Cost: Manual $5.00; 25 scales and profile sheets $4.50; specimen kit (manual, scale, and profile sheet) $5.50.

Publisher: Consulting Psychologists Press, Inc.

CHILD BEHAVIOR CHECKLIST AND REVISED CHILD BEHAVIOR PROFILE

Thomas H. Achenbach and Craig Edelbrock

child

Purpose: Assesses the behavioral problems and competencies of children ages 4-16 years.

Description: Four multiple item paper-pencil multiple-choice and free response inventories evaluating child behavioral problems from four perspectives: the Child Behavior Checklist assesses behavior from the parents' point of view, the Teacher Report Form assesses the child's classroom behavior, the Direct Observation Form employs an experienced observer to rate the child on the basis of a series of at least six 10-minute observation periods, and the Youth Self-Report (for ages 11-18) gathers information directly from the child. The four-page Child Behavior Checklist contains two pages of questions regarding the child's social history, interests, and school performance. Most items combine free response questions about the child with multiple-choice rating scales for comparing the child with his peers. The last two pages of the checklist present 118 items (item 56 includes a-g) describing a variety of problem behaviors. Parents rate each item from 0 (not true) to 2 (very true) according to their child's behavior over the past six months (time period may vary). Responses are scored according to the Revised Child Behavior Profile, which yields scores for social competence scales and behavior problem scales as well as internalizing, externalizing, and total problem scores. Norms provided in terms of T-scores.

The Teacher's Report Form is presented in a similar four-page format, gathering background information and assessing 118 items related to classroom behavior. Scoring profile includes: standard scores, four general adaptive characteristics, eight behavior problem scales, interalizing and externalizing problems, and total problem scores. The Direct Observation Form rates 96 problem behaviors from 0 (not observed) to 3 (severe intensity) for a 10 minute period. Also provides for scoring on-task behavior at 1-minute intervals. the observer writes a narrative description of the child's behavior during the observation priod and then rates the behavioral items accordingly. Stable scores are obtained by averaging the ratings obtained on six different occasions. Individual item scores, total behavior problem scores, and on-task scores act as direct indices of behavior problems and change over time and provide a basis for group comparison.

The Youth Self-Report form also uses a four-page format to gather first-hand information related to the items on the Child Behavior Checklist. Item scores and total scores act as indices of the child's self-perceived problems and competencies.

The manual for all four instruments (230 pages) discusses: development and construction of the scales; the internalizing-externalizing dichotomy, factor loadings; standardization and norms; reliability and validity; effects of clinical status, socioeconomic status and race; clinical cutoff scores, cluster analyses, profile patterns, and taxonomy; classification of children according to their profile patterns; distribution and correlates of profile types; clinical and research applications; and scoring procedures by hand and computer. Self administered (except for the Direct Observation Form). All self-administered forms suitable for group use.

Untimed: Varies

Range: Children

Scoring: Evaluated by scorer; computer scoring programs available

Cost: Sample packet (Child Behavior Checklist, Revised Child Behavior Profile scoring forms, Teacher Report Form and scoring profile, Direct observation form, and Youth Self-Report form) $5.00.

Publisher: Department of Psychiatry, University of Vermont

DIAGNOSTIC CHECKLIST FOR BEHAVIOR-DISTURBED CHILDREN: FORM E-2

Bernard Rimland

child

Purpose: Diagnoses infantile autism. Differentiates truly autistic from autistic-type children.

Description: 80 item paper-pencil inventory assessing speech and behavior symptoms related to autism in young children. The checklist consists of questions (intended for the child's parents) covering the following topics: social interaction and affect; speech, motor, and manipulative ability; intelligence and reaction to sensory stimuli; family characteristics; illness development; and physiological and other biological data. A total score is derived, as well as separate scores for speech and behavior. Cut-off scores and interpretive guidelines are provided to assist in diagnosing autism and other forms of childhood psychoses. Form E-3 (250) items is also available for obtaining information of etiological, therapeutic, and prognostic importance. Some of the child's symptoms not detailed on Form E-2 are listed on Form E-3, while other questions pertain to medications taken and the effects of drugs and other treatments, the mother's pregnancy, and the child's medical history. Examiner evaluated. Not suitable for group use.

Untimed: Varies

Range: Ages 0-5 years

Scoring: Examiner evaluated

Cost: Contact publisher.

Publisher: Bernard Rimland

PIERS-HARRIS CHILDREN'S SELF-CONCEPT SCALE (PHSCS)

Refer to page 61.

THE REVISED BEHAVIOR PROBLEM CHECKLIST (RBPC)

Refer to page 180.

ROGERS PERSONAL ADJUSTMENT INVENTORY—UK REVISION

Patricia M. Jeffrey, based on original test by Carl Rogers

child

Purpose: Assesses the personal adjustment of problem children. Used for initiation of treatment programs and personality assessment.

Description: Multiple item paper-pencil inventory assessing significant aspects of a child's personality, including: attitude toward environment, adjustment to peers, family, and self, and the manner in which the child approaches problems. Many test items have been completely rewritten, anglicized and updated. Separate test forms have been developed for boys and girls. Suitable for group use.

BRITISH PUBLISHER

Untimed: Varies

Range: Ages 9-13 years

Scoring: Examiner evaluated

Cost: Manual £7.95; booklet for boys (pkg. of 10) £6.95; booklet for girls (pkg. of 10) £6.95; marking keys (set of 3) £3.95.

Publisher: NFER-Nelson Publishing Company Ltd.

Adolescent and Adult

THE ADJUSTMENT INVENTORY: ADULT FORM

Hugh M. Bell

adult

Purpose: Measures the personal and social adjustment of adults.

Description: Multiple item paper-pencil self-report inventory assessing five areas of personal adjustment: home, health, social, emotional, and occupational. Items may be answered on the test booklet or on a separate answer sheet. Examiner must prepare their own scoring stencils for the answer sheets. Self-administered. Suitable for group use.

Untimed: 25 minutes

Range: Adult

Scoring: Examiner evaluated

Cost: Manual and stencil for scoring test booklet $2.00; 25 test booklets $5.00; 50 answer sheets $4.25; specimen set (manual, stencil, test booklet, and answer sheet) $2.00.

Publisher: Consulting Psychologists Press, Inc.

THE ADJUSTMENT INVENTORY: STUDENT FORM

Hugh M. Bell

teen

Purpose: Measures the personal and social adjustment of high school and college students.

Description: Multiple item paper-pencil self-report inventory assessing six scales of adjustment: home adjustment, health adjustment, submissiveness (formerly social adjustment), emotionality (formerly emotional adjustment), hostility, and masculinity-femininity. Norms provided for high school and college students. Self-administered. Suitable for group use.

Untimed: 25 minutes

Range: Junior high-college students

Scoring: Examiner evaluated

Cost: Manual $4.25; 25 reusable test booklets $5.00; 50 answer sheets (includes profile) $8.00; scoring stencils $6.00; specimen set (manual, test booklet, answer/profile sheet) $4.50.

Publisher: Consulting Psychologists Press, Inc.

ADOLESCENT EMOTIONAL FACTORS INVENTORY

Mary K. Bauman

teen

Purpose: Measures emotional and personality factors of visually handicapped adolescents.

Description: 150 item paper-pencil or oral response questionnaire assessing the personal and emotional adjustment of visually handicapped adolescents. Provides scores on the following nine scales: sensitivity, somatic symptoms, social competency, attitudes of distrust, family adjustment, boy-girl adjustment, school adjustment, morale, and attitudes concerning blindnes. A validation score is also provided. Questionnaires are presented in large print format. Instructions for tape recording the questions are included. Supplementary materials provided in the test kit include a discussion of the inventory and a discussion of personality assessment for blind adolescents. This test is an adolescent form of the Emotional Factors Inventory. Examiner required. Paper-pencil version suitable for group use.

Untimed: Varies

Range: Visually handicapped adolescents

Scoring: Examiner evaluated

Cost: Test kit (large print test booklet, set of scoring overlays, 10 IBM answer sheets, supplementary materials, and norms) $15.00.

Publisher: Associated Services for the Blind

ADULT PERSONAL ADJUSTMENT AND ROLE SKILLS (PARS)

Robert E. Ellsworth

adult

Purpose: Measures the adjustment of adult individuals to life and to the community. Used for evaluation of treatment programs.

Description: 31 item paper-pencil observational rating scale assessing eight dimensions of adult personal adjustment and role skills: close relations, alienation-depression, anxiety, confusion, alcohol/drug use, house activity, child relations, and employment. The scale is completed by a spouse, parent, or person close to the individual. The manual explains the rationale and validity of the scale and provides detailed norms for the general and clinical population with respect to adjustment to life and the community. Examiner required. Suitable for group use.

Untimed: 20-30 minutes

Range: Adult

Scoring: Examiner evaluated

Cost: Manual $5.00; 25 scales and profile sheets $4.50; specimen set (manual, scale, and profile sheet) $5.50.

Publisher: Consulting Psychologists Press, Inc.

ADULT PERSONALITY INVENTORY

Samuel Krug

adult

Purpose: Evaluates individual personality characteristics, interpersonal relations, and life style. Used by professionals in industry, public service, health care, and education.

Description: Multiple item paper-pencil inventory assessing personality characteristics in terms of the 16 Personality Factor psychometric profile. While maintaining continuity with the personality model underlying the 16 PF, the questionnaire itself has been redesigned using a systems development approach. Items have been shortened in order to increase the number of items on the inventory (for increased reliability) and the required reading level has been lowered to the fourth-grade level. The computer scoring service provides a nine-page verbal and graphic report examining significant individual characteristics, interpersonal relations, and life style. Examiner required. Suitable for group use.

Untimed: Varies

Range: Adult

Scoring: Computer scored

Cost: 25 test booklets $15.00; 50 answer sheets $6.50; manual $4.00; 1-4 scoring reports $16.00 each; 5-25 scoring reports $5.50 each.

Publisher: Institute for Personality and Ability Testing, Inc.

AFFECTS BALANCE SCALE (ABS)

Leonard R. Derogatis

adult

Purpose: Evaluates psychological adjustment and well-being in terms of mood and affect balance.

Description: 40 item paper-pencil self-report adjective mood scale asssessing four positive affect dimensions (joy, contentment, vigor, and affection) and four negative affect dimensions (anxiety, depression, guilt, and hostility). Scoring and interpretation procedures are structured on the concept that healthy psychological adjustment is based on the presence of active positive emotions and the relative absence of negative emotions. The overall score of the test is expressed as the affect balance index, reflecting the balance between positive and negative affects in terms of standardized scores. Examiner required. Suitable for group use.

Untimed: 3-5 minutes

Range: Adult

Scoring: Examiner evaluated

Cost: 100 test forms $28.00; 100 profile sheets $18.00.

Publisher: Clinical Psychometric Research

BECK DEPRESSION AND HOPELESSNESS SCALE

Aaron T. Beck, M.D.

adult

Purpose: Assesses level of depression and the possibility of suicide. Used for clinical assessment and diagnosis.

Description: Multiple item computer-administered instrument consisting of two scales: the Beck Depression Scale and the Beck Hopelessness Scale. The Beck Depression Scale measures the level of severity of dysphoric mood and assesses the current state of the individual's mood. The Beck Hopelessness scale, when used in conjunction with the depression scale, indicates the level of depression and the possibility of suicide. The Beck Hopelessness Scale was developed on a large sample of patients who had attempted suicide. The program administers and scores the two scales, and provides an interpretive printout of the test. May be used only on Psych Systems-supplied hardware, available in various configurations starting with single-users systems at approximately $25,000. A per-test fee (based on hardware configuration) also applies. Examiner required. Suitable for group use.

Untimed: Varies

Range: Adult

Scoring: Computer scored

Cost: Contact publisher.

Publisher: PSYCH Systems

BECK DEPRESSION INVENTORY

Aaron T. Beck

adult

Purpose: Measures an individual's degree of depression. Used for treatment planning and evaluation in mental health settings.

Description: 22 item multiple choice and true-false invnetory assessing an individual's complaints, symptoms, and attitudes related to his current degree of depression. Scales assessed include: sadness, pessimism, sense of failure, lack of satisfaction, guilty feelings, sense of being punished, self-dislike, self-accusations, suicidal wishes, crying spells, irritability, withdrawal, and indecisiveness. Microcomputer printout indicates severity of depressed mood, lists major symptom-attitude complaints and shows a table of responses. Questions are presented on an eighth-grade reading level. May be administered only on Psychometer. Examiner required. Not suitable for group use.

Untimed: 15-20 minutes

Range: Adult

Scoring: Microcomputer scored

Cost: Psychometer diskette (20 administrations) $90.00.

Publisher: NCS/Professional Assessment Services

BEHAVIORAL OBSERVATION CHECKLIST

Psych Systems, Inc.

adult

Purpose: Assesses an individual's behavior during the testing process. Used for clinical assessment and diagnosis and for personal, marital, and family counseling.

Description: 12 item computer-administered observational checklist consisting of 10 multiple choice items and two free-response inquiries. Checklist items concern the individual's behavior, apparent mood, and responsiveness to the testing process. The computer program administers and scores the checklist, and then provides an interpretive printout of the questionnaire which provides a narrative summary of the individual's current behavioral characteristics. May be used only on Psych Systems-supplied hardware, available in various configurations starting with single-users systems at approximately $25,000. A per-test fee (based on hardware configuration) also applies. Examiner required. Suitable for group use.

Untimed: Varies

Range: Adult

Scoring: Computer scored

Cost: Contact publisher.

Publisher: PSYCH Systems

BERNREUTER PERSONALITY INVENTORY

teen, adult

Purpose: Evaluates the normal adolescent and adult personality.

Description: Multiple item paper-pencil inventory assessing the following six personality traits: neurotic tendency, self sufficiency, introversion-extroversion, dominance-submission, self-confidence, and sociability. The nature of the traits being measured are not readily detectable by the person taking the test. All requred instructions are printed in the test booklet. Norms are provided for high school and college students and adults of both sexes. Self-administered. Suitable for group use.

Untimed: Varies

Range: Adolescent-adult

Scoring: Hand key

Cost: Test kit (50 test booklets, hand scoring stencils and manual) $31.00.

Publisher: Stoelting Co.

THE BIPOLAR PSYCHOLOGICAL INVENTORY (BPI)

adult

Purpose: Measures psychological adjustment. Used for clinical evaluation and diagnosis, personnel screening, and police officer selection.

Description: Multiple item paper-pencil or computer administered self-report inventory assessing affect and behavior along 15 bipolar dimensions: honest/lie, open/defensive, psychic comfort/psychic pain, optimism/depression, self-esteem/self-degradation, self-sufficiency/dependence, achieving/unmotivated, gregariousness/social withdrawal, family harmony/family discord, sexual maturity/sexual immaturity, social conformity/social deviancy, self-control/impulsiveness, kindness/hostility, empathy/insensitivity, and valid/invalid. May be computer scored from keyboard administration or on an optical reader from group administered answer sheets. Hand scored answer sheets may be computer interpreted. Narrative computer printout includes: separate male/female formats, raw scores and percentile scores, personal adjustment profile, prinout of answers to all questions, and printout of significant (problem) items. Computer program sold on disk (with backup disk and instructions) for use with Apple II computer with 48K, one disk drive, and printer (optical reader optional). Normative data available for normal populations. Examiner required. Paper-pencil version suitable for group use.

Untimed: Varies

Range: Adult

Scoring: Examiner evaluated; computer scoring available

Cost: Clinical sample kit (manual, test booklet, 5 answer sheets, set of scoring keys, profiles, scale items booklet and reliability-validity booklet) $20.00; computer program $250.00.

Publisher: Diagnostic Specialists, Inc.

BRIEF SYMPTOM INVENTORY (BSI)

Leonard R. Derogatis

teen, adult

Purpose: Evaluates psychological symptomatic distress. Used with medical and psychiatric patients and adult and adolescent non-patients.

Description: 53 item paper-pencil self-report inventory assessing symptomatic distress in terms of nine symptom dimensions (somatization, obsessive-compulsive, interpersonal sensitivity, depression, anxiety, hostility, phobic anxiety, paranoid ideation, and psychoticism) and three global indices of distress (global severity index, positive symptom index, and positive sympton total). Score/profile forms and published norms are available by sex for four populations: non-patient adult, non-patient adolescent, outpatient psychiatric, and inpatient psychiatric. This inventory is a brief form of the SCL-90-R and may be used in conjunction with the matching observer's scales in the Psychopathology Rating Scales Series (the SCL-90-R Analogue and the Hopkins Psychiatric Rating Scale). Examiner required. Suitable for group use.

Untimed: 10-12 minutes

Range: Adolescent, adult

Scoring: Examiner evaluated

Cost: Manual $15.00; 100 test forms $26.00; 100 score-profile forms $18.00.

Publisher: Clinical Psychometric Research

CLAYBURY ASSESSMENT BATTERY

T.M. Caine, O.B. Wijesinghe, D. Winter and D. Small

adult ✍

Purpose: Directs individuals toward psychological or psychiatric treatment which matches their personal styles. Examines consistency between attitudes and work environment in the selection of therapists. Used also in vocational guidance settings.

Description: Three multiple item paper-pencil questionnaires assessing personal interests, expectancies regarding treatment, and attitudes toward treatment. The Direction of Interest Questionnaire is a 14 item forced choice inventory which distinguishes between two sets of interests: on the one hand ideas, imagination, theory, philosophy, unconventionality and emotional problems; on the other facts, practical problems, biochemistry, common sense, engineering, domestic science, personal ambition, pain and action. This questionnaire is particularly useful in vocational guidance. The Treatment Expectancies Questionnaire is a 15 item factor-analytically devised scale which measures an individual's expectancies regarding psychiatric or psychological treatment. The Attitudes To Treatment Questionnaire is a 19 item factor-analytically devised scale which measures staff attitudes toward psychological and psychiatric treatment and differentiates between psychological and organic approaches to patient care. The manual is based on *Personal Styles in Neurosis* by T.M. Caine, O.B. Wijesinghe and D. Winter (Routledge and Kegan Paul, 1981) and provides a number of applications as well as a full account of the research basis of the questionnaires. Self-administered.
BRITISH PUBLISHER

Untimed: Varies

Range: Adult

Scoring: Examiner evaluated

Cost: Manual £4.65; 50 Direction of Interest Questionnaires £3.75; 50 Attitudes Treatment Questionnaires £3.75; 50 Treatment Expectancies Questionnaires £3.75; set of 3 answer keys £3.50.

Publisher: NFER-Nelson Publishing Company Ltd.

CLIFTON ASSESSMENT PROCEDURES FOR THE ELDERLY (CAPE)

Refer to page 9.

COMPREHENSIVE DRINKER PROFILE (CDP)

G. Alan Marlatt and William R. Miller

adult ☞ ✍

Purpose: Assesses alcoholism in men and women. Used for intake-screening purposes in alcohol abuse treatment programs. Provides a basis for selecting, planning, and implementing individualized treatment programs.

Description: Multiple item paper-pencil structured interview guide assessing an individual's history and current status with regard to the use and abuse of alcohol. Measures items in the following areas: basic demographics, family and employment status, history of problem development, current drinking pattern and problem status, severity of dependence, social aspects of alcohol use, associated behaviors, relevant medical history, motivations for drinking and for seeking treatment, and problem areas other than drinking. Incorporates the Michigan Alcoholism Screening Test as part of the interview, providing a survey of current drinking problems as well as a summary score of problem severity. Also yields scores on other dimensions including: problem duration, family history of alcoholism, alcohol consumption, alcohol dependence, range of drinking situations, quantity/frequency of other drug use, emotional factors related to drinking, and life problems other than drinking. Used by profesionals and paraprofessionals, including physicians, psychologists, psychiatrists, social workers, nurses, and alcohol abuse counselors. Examiner required. Suitable for group use.

Untimed: 1-2 hours

Range: Adult

Scoring: Examiner evaluated

Cost: Interview kit (manual, 25 interview forms, and 8 reusable card sets used in administration of the interview) $25.00.

Publisher: Psychological Assessment Resources, Inc.

CORNELL INDEX (Revised)

Arthur Weider

adult ☞ ✍

Purpose: Evaluates an individual's psychiatric history. Identifies individuals with serious personal and psychosomatic disturbances. Used for clinical evaluations and research purposes.

Description: 101 item paper-pencil questionnaire measuring neuropsychiatric and psychosomatic symptoms. Administered in the form of a structured interview, analysis of responses provides for a standardized evaluation of an individual's psychiatric history and differentiates statistically individuals with serious personal and psychiatric disturbances. Examiner required. Not suitable for group use.

Untimed: 5 minutes

Range: Adult

Cost: 25 questionnaires $7.00; specimen set $2.00.

Publisher: Arthur Weider

DEROGATIS STRESS PROFILE (DSP)

Leonard R. Derogatis

adult ☞ ✍

Purpose: Measures the amount of stress an individual experiences in terms of interactional stress theory.

Description: 77 item paper-pencil test assessing 11 dimensions of stress grouped in the following three domains: environmental stress, personality mediators, and emotional response. In addition to 11 dimension scores and three domain scores, two global stress indices are also derived. Optical scan version available for use with computer scoring and interpetation services. Examiner required. Suitable for group use.

Untimed: 12-15 minutes

Range: Adult

Scoring: Examiner evaluated; computer scoring available

Cost: 100 self-scoring forms $40.00;

100 score/profile forms $16.00; 100 optical scan forms $45.00.
Publisher: Clinical Psychometric Research

DIFFERENTIAL PERSONALITY QUESTIONNAIRE
Auke Tellegen

teen, adult

Purpose: Assesses the normal personality. Used in vocational counseling, personnel selection, career development, and as an adjunct to clinical personality tests in counseling, psychiatric and medical settings.

Description: 300 item paper-pencil self-report inventory measuring factors of the normal personality. Questions are presented in dichotomous forced-choice format at eighth-grade reading level. Measures 20 scales, including: 11 scales measuring primary personality dimensions (well-being, social potency, achievement, social closeness, stress reaction, alienation, aggression, control, traditionalism, absorption, and harm avoidance), three scales measuring higher-order personality traits (positive affectivity, negative affectivity, and constraint); and six scales measuring validity: index of invalid responding, associative slips, unlikely virtues, desireable response inconsistency, true response inconsistency, variable response inconsistency. Norms provided for college students and adults. Examiner required. Suitable for group use.
Untimed: 35-45 minutes
Range: College students-adults
Scoring: Contact publisher
Cost: Contact publisher.
Publisher: NCS/Professional Assessment Services

DISSIMULATION INDEX
Psych Systems, Inc.

adult

Purpose: Assesses a person's ability to undergo on-line testing. Determines the likelihood that the results from such testing will be valid. Used in preparation for clinical use of on-line testing programs.

Description: Multiple item computer-administered test consisting of items from the MMPI validity scales as well as newly constructed items. Predicts for any given individual the validity that can be expected from using on-line test administration techniques. May be used only on Psych Systems-supplied hardware, available in various configurations starting with single-users systems at approximately $25,000. A per-test fee (based on hardware configuration) also applies. Examiner required. Suitable for group use.
Untimed: Varies
Range: Adult
Scoring: Computer scored
Cost: Contact Publisher.
Publisher: PSYCH Systems

EATING DISORDER INVENTORY (EDI)
David M. Garner

teen, adult

Purpose: Assesses psychological and behavioral traits common in eating disorders. Distinguishes individuals with serious psychopathology from "normal" dieters. Used in treatment of individuals with eating disorders.

Description: 64 item paper-pencil self-report inventory consisting of eight subscales measuring specific cognitive and behavioral dimensions related to eating disorders. Identifies individuals with serious eating disorders and differentiates between subgroups of eating disorders. Examiner required. Suitable for group use.
Untimed: Approximately 20 minutes
Range: Adolescent, adult
Scoring: Scoring keys (Also available in computer version)

Cost: EDI Kit (includes manual, scoring key, 25 test booklets and 25 profile forms) $22.00.

Publisher: Psychological Assessment Resources, Inc.

EYBERG CHILD BEHAVIOR INVENTORY (ECBI)

Sheila M. Eyberg

adult

Purpose: Assesses a child's behavioral problems from the parents' point of view. Identifies conduct problem and non-problem children. Used to establish treatment goals, to monitor effects of intervention, to aid in determining need for treatment, and to evaluate treatment outcome.

Description: 36 item paper-pencil inventory comprising a list of the most typical problem behaviors reported by parents, such as: refuses to do chores when asked, whines, dawdles or lingers at mealtime, hits parents, physically fights with brothers and sisters. Parents are asked to rate their child for each behavior on a scale from one (never) to seven (always) and to indicate "yes" or "no" as to whether each behavior listed poses a current problem to the parents. A sum of the frequency rating scores yields an overall problem behavior Intensity Score: a sum of the behaviors listed as current problems yields a Problem Score. Cut-off scores are provided for both scales for discriminating between problem and non-problem children. Ratings on individual behaviors identify specific areas in need of intervention and can be used to monitor treatment effects in respect to specific behaviors. Both the Intensity Score and the Problem Score can be used to monitor the overall effectiveness of treatment programs. Self-administered. Suitable for group use as a screening instrument.

Untimed: Varies

Range: Parents of children ages 2-16

Scoring: Examiner evaluated

Cost: Contact publisher.

Publisher: Distributed by Sheila M. Eyberg

THE FREEMAN ANXIETY NEUROSIS AND PSYCHOSOMATIC TEST

M.J. Freeman

adult

Purpose: Determines the presence of anxiety neuroses disorders and psychosomatic syndromes. Used by physicians concerned with possible functional symptomatology and psychiatrists and clinical psychologists seeking objective evidence of neuroses and functional pathology.

Description: 136 item paper-pencil self-report inventeory using objective and projective methods to determine the existence of anxiety neuroses disorders and to identify distinct psychosomatic syndromes. Part II of the test contains 98 symptoms for checking and measures seven dimensions of neuroses: neurasthenia, psychasthenia, hysteria, hypochondriasis, and structural types of anxiety structures. The projective character of the test prevents the individual taking the test from invalidating the results by consciously manipulating objective answers. Self-administered. Suitable for group use.

Untimed: 30 minutes

Range: Adult

Scoring: Examiner evaluated

Cost: 10 tests and 10 profile sheets $1.75; manual $1.25.

Publisher: Grune & Stratton, Inc.

GERIATRIC SENTENCE COMPLETION FORM (GSCF)

Peter LeBray

older adult

Purpose: Assesses the personal and social adjustment of elderly adults.

Used by clinicians working with the elderly in hospitals, long-term care facilities, out-patient setting, community care programs, and private offices.

Description: 30 item oral response or paper-pencil projective test assessing elderly individuals' adjustment in four domains: physical, psychological, social, and temporal. The individual is asked to complete fragmentary sentence stems via written or verbal responses. The manual includes information on the development, structure, administration, and interpretation of the test, including a number of clinical case illustrations. Examiner required. Not suitable for group use.

Untimed: Varies

Range: Elderly adults

Scoring: Examiner evaluated

Cost: Manual and 50 forms $8.95.

Publisher: Psychological Assessment Resources, Inc.

GIANNETTI ON-LINE PSYCHOSOCIAL HISTORY (GOLPH)

Ronald A. Giannetti

adult

Purpose: Gathers information on an individual's background and current life circumstances. Used to obtain psychosocial history for general or psychiatric patients, to evaluate job applicants' work history, criminal offenders' history of legal difficulties, or training applicants' educational history.

Description: Multiple item, multiple choice and completion item questionnaire presented on microcomputer diskette. Questions and their order of appearance are determined by answers to the preceding items. Examiner selects from the following scales to gather appropriate information: current living situation, family of origin, client development, educational history, marital history/present family, occupational history/current finances, legal history, symptom screening (physical), symptom screening (psychological), and military history. Questions are presented at an eighth-grade reading level. Length of examination depends on the areas chosen for exploration and the extent of the individual's problems. A 3-12 page report presents the individual's responses in narrative fashion. May be administered only on Psychometer. Examiner required. Not suitable for group use.

Untimed: 30 minutes-2 hours

Range: Adult

Scoring: Microcomputer scored

Cost: Psychometer diskette (20 administrations) $130.00.

Publisher: NCS/Professional Assessment Services

THE HILTON QUESTIONNAIRE—A MEASURE OF DRINKING BEHAVIOR

Margaret Hilton

adult

Purpose: Evaluates drinking behavior. Identifies individuals with alcohol abuse problems. Used to support a practitioner's diagnosis, to predict possible danger points, and as a basis for discussion.

Description: 32 item paper-pencil rating scale consisting or simple questions such as "Do you ever feel that once you start drinking you cannot stop?" and "Have you ever felt ashamed of your drinking?" The individual circles a number under one of four answers: never, rarely, occasionally, and frequently. The total score is the sum of the circled numbers. Norms provided for alcoholic unit patients, ex-patients, and other

alcoholics in hospital, and for members of Alcoholics Anonymous. Examiner required. Suitable for group use.
BRITISH PUBLISHER

Untimed: Varies

Range: Adult

Scoring: Examiner evaluated

Cost: Manual £2.75; 25 one-page questionnaires £2.50.

Publisher: NFER-Nelson Publishing Company Ltd.

HOGAN PERSONALITY INVENTORY

Refer to page 227.

HOGAN SELECTION SERIES

Refer to page 227.

HOPKINS PSYCHIATRIC RATING SCALE (HPRS)

Leonard R. Derogatis

teen, adult

Purpose: Evaluates psychological symptomatic distress of medical and psychiatric patients in terms of observer's judgment. Used for psychological screening and in treatment planning and evaluation in mental health setttings.

Description: 17 item paper-pencil observational inventory assessing symptomatic distress in terms of nine primary symptom dimensions (somatization, obsessive-compulsive, interpersonal sensitivity, depression, anxiety, hostility, phobic anxiety, paranoid ideation, and psychoticism) and eight additional dimensions. Each dimension is defined by a brief descriptive paragraph coupled with verbal descriptive anchors at seven discrete scale points. This scale is a part of the Psychopathology Rating Scale Series which includes the SCL-90-R, the SCL-90 Analogue, and the Brief Symptom Inventory (BSI). The nine primary symptoms assessed are common to all four scales. A brief version is available (B-HPRS) which rates only those nine primary symptoms. A microcomputer program (COMPAR-90) is available to calculate and assess differences in terms of standardized scores between HPRS or B-HPRS ratings of patients and self-ratings by the patients on the SCL-90-R or BSI. Examiner required. Not suitable for group use.

Untimed: 2-5 minutes

Range: Adolescent, adult

Scoring: Examiner evaluated

Cost: 100 HPRS forms $32.00; 100 B-HPRS forms $28.00.

Publisher: Clinical Psychometric Research

IMPACT MESSAGE INVENTORY

Donald J. Kiesler, Jack C. Anchin, Michael J. Perkins, Bernie M. Chirico, Edgar M. Kyle and Edward J. Federman

adult

Purpose: Measures the affective, behavioral and cognitive reactions of one individual to another. Used to measure the reactions of individuals to their counselors and other interadants during ongoing transactions in counseling/psychotherapy and other dyads.

Description: 90 item paper-pencil inventory assessing one individual's reactions to the interpersonal or personality style of another person. Test items describe ways in which people are emotionally engaged or affected when interacting with another person. Individuals respond on a four-point scale ranging from "not at all" to "very much so" to indicate the extent to which each item describes the feeling aroused by the other person, behaviors they want to direct toward the other person, or descriptions of the other person which come to mind when in the other person's presence. Each test item describes a reaction characteristically elicited by a person high on one of the following 15 interpersonal dimensions: dominant, competitive, hostile, mistrusting, detached, inhibited, submissive, succorant, abasive, deferent, agreeable, nurturant, affiliative, sociable, and exhibitionistic. Scores are derived for each of the 15 subscales as well as four cluster-scores: dominant, submissive, friendly, and hostile. A revised manual has been completed (Kiesler, D.J. *Research Manual for the Impact Message Inventory*). The manual includes descriptions of the subscales and tables for converting raw scores to T-scores. Examiner required. Suitable for group use.

Untimed: Varies

Range: Adult

Scoring: Examiner evaluated

Cost: Contact publisher.

Publisher: Donald J. Kiesler

INDEX OF SOMATIC PROBLEMS

Psych Systems, Inc.

adult

Purpose: Evaluates somatic problems most frequently found among psychiatric patients. Used for clinical assessment and diagnosis and for personal, marital, and family counseling.

Description: 14-60 item computer-administered true-false inventory assessing the presence and severity of somatic disturbances. Items are presented according to a branching logic (responses to certain questions determine which items will be presented next). The program administers and scores the test, then provides a brief printout of test results which identifies psychosomatic problems an individual is using as a way of coping with emotional difficulties and delineates visible complaints with distinct psychogenic characteristics. May be used only on Psych Systems-supplied hardware, available in various configuations starting with single-users systems at approximately $25,000. A per-test fee (based on hardware configuration) also applies. Examiner required. Suitable for group use.

Untimed: Varies

Range: Adult

Scoring: Computer scored

Cost: Contact publisher.

Publisher: PSYCH Systems

INDIVIDUAL PROBLEM INDEX (IPI)

teen, adult

Purpose: Evaluates the severity of physical, emotional, behavioral and interpersonal problems. Used to plan counseling and treatment programs and to monitor patient progress.

Description: 59 item multiple choice inventory presented on microcomputer diskette. The individual is asked to rate the intensity of his problems in the following areas: feelings, social, thoughts, physical, actions and miscellaneous. Questions are presented at an eighth-grade reading level. Microcomputer printout indicates problems by degree of severity. The problems perceived as most severe are listed first, followed by problems of a lesser degree. May be administered only on Psychometer. Examiner required. Not suitable for group use.

Untimed: 10-15 minutes

Range: Age 14 years-adult

Scoring: Microcomputer scored

Cost: Psychometer diskette (20 administrations) $60.00.

Publisher: NCS/Professional Assessment Services

INDUSTRIAL SENTENCE COMPLETION FORM

Refer to page 228.

INTERACTIVE MEDICAL HISTORY (IMH)

Based on the Harvard Medical History

adult

Purpose: Compiles an individual's medical history. Used for initial screening of adults seeking medical health or a medical checkup.

Description: Multiple item multiple choice and completion question inventory presented on microcomputer diskette. Areas assessed include: reason for appointment, general health list of complaints, present illness, present medications, review of system, lifestyle, family history, comments, and additional information. The questions presented and the order in which they are presented depend on answers to preceding question. A 3-10 page microcomputer report presents the patient's self-reported medical history in narrative style. May be administered only on Psychometer. Examiner required. Not suitable for group use.

Untimed: 30 minutes-2 hours

Range: Adult

Scoring: Microcomputer scored

Cost: Psychometer diskette (20 administrations) $120.00.

Publisher: NCS/Professional Assessment Services

IPS SOCIAL HISTORY (SOCH)

adult

Purpose: Gathers information necessary to assess an individual's social, medical, and psychological history.

Description: Multiple item microcomputer program or paper-pencil test gathering personal information in the following areas: current status, childhood, education, military, criminal, substance abuse, personal relations with friends and family members, and self-descriptive adjectives. As a microcomputer program, a series of questions are presented on the answer screen, and the individual responds by pressing numbers on the keyboard. For paper-pencil administration, item responses are entered directly into the computer by clerical staff. A narrative report is produced describing major problem areas and psychological/medical history. This report can then be used as a guide during subsequent personal interview or to identify topics which need to be further explored. Available for use with OSI and APPLE computers. National scoring service also available. Examiner required. Paper-pencil version suitable for group use.

Untimed: Varies

Range: Adult

Scoring: Microcomputer scored; national computer scoring service available

Cost: Contact publisher for information concerning software requirements and administration costs.

Publisher: Integrated Professional Systems, Inc.

LEITER RECIDIVISM SCALE

adult

Purpose: Measures the potential for recidivism. Used by judges in criminal courts and at each stage of the correctional process to determine in a given case whether society would be best served by probation or incarceration.

Description: Multiple item paper-pencil inventory assessing nine variable related to recidivism: instability, age-time ratio, social immaturity, social control (lack of control), vocational adjustment (lack of adjustment), personality dynamics, abnormal authority reaction, institutional adjustment, and offense level. An individual's recidivism score is the sum of his scores on the nine variables, each of which is a predictor of recidivism in its own right. Self-administered by judge, probation officer, and correctional personnel. Not suitable for group use.

Untimed: Varies

Range: Adult

Scoring: Examiner evaluated

Cost: Test kit (manual, 25 profile sheets and 25 record blanks) $24.00.

Publisher: Stoelting Co.

MEASURE OF ACHIEVING TENDENCY

Albert Mehrabian

adult

Purpose: Assesses an individual's motivation to achieve. Used for research, counseling, and employee selection and placement purposes.

Description: Multiple item verbal questionnaire assessing all major components of achievement. Test items based on extensive factor-analytic investigation of most experimentally identified components of achievement. Examiner required. Suitable for group use.

Untimed: Approximately 15 minutes

Range: Adult

Scoring: Examiner evaluated

Cost: Test kit (scales, scoring directions, norms, and test manual) $28.00.

Publisher: Albert Mehrabian

MEASURE OF AROUSAL SEEKING TENDENCY

Albert Mehrabian

adult

Purpose: Assesses an individual's desire for change, stimulation and arousal. Used for research and counseling purposes.

Description: Multiple item verbal questionnaire measuring an individual's arousal seeking tendencies. Test items are based on extensive factor-analytic and experimental studies of all aspects of change-seeking, sensation-seeking, variety-seeking, and, generally, desire to master high-uncertainty situations. Examiner required. Suitable for group use.

Untimed: Varies

Range: Adult

Scoring: Examiner evaluated

Cost: Test kit (scale, scoring directions, norms, and descriptive material) $20.00.

Publisher: Albert Mehrabian

MEASURE OF DOMINANCE-SUBMISSIVENESS

Albert Mehrabian and Melissa Hines

adult

Purpose: Measures aspects of dominance and submissiveness in an individual's personality. Used for research, counseling and job placement purposes.

Description: Multiple item verbal questionnaire assessing personality characteristics related to dominance and submissiveness. Test items are based on extensive factor-analyltic and experimental studies on aspects of dominance (controlling, taking charge) versus submissiveness characteristics. This measure has been shown to be a basic component of many important personality attributes such as extroversion, dependency, anxiety, or depression. Examiner required. Suitable for group use.

Untimed: Approximately 15 minutes

Range: Adult

Scoring: Examiner evaluated

Cost: Test kit (scale, scoring directions, norms, and descriptive material) $20.00.

Publisher: Albert Mehrabian

MEASURE OF STIMULUS SCREENING (CONVERSE OF AROUSABILITY)

Albert Mehrabian

adult

Purpose: Measures major components of arousability and stimulus screening. Used for research and counseling purposes.

Description: Multiple item verbal questionnaire assessing the extent of an individual's arousal response to complex, unexpected, or unfamiliar situations. Test items are based on extensive factor-analytic and experimental investigations of all major components of arousability and stimulus screening. Stimulus screening/arousability has been shown to be a major component of many important emotional characteristics such as anxiety, neuroticism, extroversion, or hostility. Examiner required. Suitable for group use.

Untimed: Approximately 15 minutes

Range: Adult

Scoring: Examiner evaluated

Cost: Test kit (scales, scoring directions, norms, and descriptive material) $20.00.

Publisher: Albert Mehrabian

MEASURES OF AFFILIATIVE TENDENCY AND SENSITIVITY TO REJECTION

Albert Mehrabian

adult

Purpose: Assesses an individual's interpersonal and social approach-avoidance characteristics. Used for research and counseling purposes.

Description: Multiple item verbal questionnaire consisting of two subscales: affiliative tendency and sensitivity to rejection. Standardized sum of the scores on both subscales also provides a reliable and valid measure of dependency. Examiner required. Suitable for group use.

Untimed: 10 minutes per scale

Range: Adult

Scoring: Examiner evaluated

Cost: Test kit (scales, scoring directions, norms, and descriptive material) $20.00.

Publisher: Albert Mehrabian

THE MINER SENTENCE COMPLETION SCALE: FORM H

Refer to page 230.

THE MINER SENTENCE COMPLETION SCALE: FORM P

Refer to page 230.

MINNESOTA-BRIGGS HISTORY RECORD WITH MARRIAGE SECTION

Peter F. Briggs

adult

Purpose: Gathers information necessary to compile a comprehensive developmental record of the life of an individual under study. Used for counseling and research purposes.

Description: Multiple item paper-pencil inventory consisting of seven scales of personal and developmental history. Optional marriage section available. Standardized scoring system permits the comparison of case histories and is compatible with multi-trait, multi-method analysis. Self-administered. Suitable for group use.

Untimed: Varies

Range: Adult

Scoring: Examiner evaluated

Cost: 10 history records $10.00; 50 history record answer sheets $3.50; 10 marriage sections $5.00; 50 marriage section answer sheets $3.50; user's guide (monograph #36) $4.00.

Publisher: Clinical Psychology Publishing Co., Inc.

MYERS-BRIGGS TYPE INDICATOR: ABBREVIATED VERSION (MBTI:AV)

Katherine C. Briggs and Isabel Briggs Myers

adult

Purpose: Measures personality dispositions and interests based on Jung's theory of types. Used for personal, marital, and vocational counseling, especially in workshops, seminars, or other setting where immediate feedback is needed or time restraints are great.

Description: 50 item paper-pencil inventory assessing personality type along four bipolar scales: introversion-extroversion, sensing-intuition, thinking-feeling, and judging-perceptive. Results for the four scales may be expressed as continuous scores or reduced to a 4-letter code or "type." Presented in self-scoring, self-profiling format, the first page contains the directions for the test taker, followed by the 50 test items and a scoring chart. An individual report form which contains a profile sheet with a brief interpretation of the scores and a chart explanation of each of the 16 MBTI types is also included. Test items on this version represent the first 50 questions from the MBTI form G. Self-administered. Suitable for group use.

Untimed: Varies

Range: Adult

Scoring: Self-scored

Cost: 25 test booklets $16.75; single copy $.75.

Publisher: Consulting Psychologists Press, Inc.

NURSES' OBSERVATION SCALE FOR INPATIENT EVALUATION (NOSIE-30)

Gilbert Honigfeld, Roderic D. Gillis and C. James Klett

adult

Purpose: Assesses the ward behavior of psychiatric inpatients. Used by nonprofessional personnel to evaluated patient status and change.

Description: 30 item paper-pencil observational inventory assessing inpatient psychiatric behavior. Measures six factors: social competence (refuses to do the ordinary things expected of him, has trouble remembering), social interest (shows interest in the activities around him, tries to be friendly to others), personal neatness (keeps his clothes neat, is messy in his eating habits), irritability (gets angry or annoyed easily, is irritable and grouchy), manifest psychosis (hears things that are not there; talks, mutters, or mumbles to himself), and retardation (sits, unless directed into activity, is slow moving and sluggish). A global score, Total Patient Assets, is also calculated as a composite of the six factor scores. Test items consist of statements about the patient's ward behavior rated on a five-point scale from 0 (never) to 4 (always). Factor scores are based on two raters' combined scores in which each item receives unit weight. Profile forms convert raw scores to T-scores or centile ranks for normative comparison. Examiner required. Not suitable for group use.

Untimed: Varies

Range: Adult

Scoring: Examiner evaluated

Cost: Contact publisher.

Publisher: Behavior Arts Center

PERSONAL PROBLEMS CHECKLIST

Psychological Assessment Resources, Inc.

teen, adult

Purpose: Assesses an individual's personal concerns and problems. Used for screening purposes to ensure a thorough review of an individual's concerns and to facilitate the evaluation process.

Description: Multiple item paper-pencil self-report inventory assessing over 200 problems which individuals frequently face in everyday life. Items are grouped into the following 13 areas: social, appearance, vocational, famliy and home, school, finances, religion, emotions, sex, legal, health and habits, attitude, and crises. Items are presented in terms understood by adolescents and adults from most educational and occupational levels. Self-administered. Suitable for group use.

Untimed: 10 minutes

Range: Adolescent, adult

Scoring: Examiner evaluated

Cost: 50 checklists $10.95.

Publisher: Psychological Assessment Resources, Inc.

PROFILE OF ADAPTATION TO LIFE—CLINICAL (PAL-C)

Robert E. Ellsworth

adult

Purpose: Measures the personal and social adaptation of adult individuals. Used as an intake screening instrument in clinical settings.

Description: 41 item paper-pencil self-report inventory providing scores on seven factorial scales: negative emotions, well-being, income management, physical symptoms, alcohol/drugs, close relations, and child relations. May be scored by the counselor or the individual. The manual explains the rationale and validity of the scale and provides detailed norms for the general and clinical populations with respect to adjustment to life and the community. Self-administered. Suitable for group use.

Untimed: 20-30 minutes

Range: Adult

Scoring: Self-scored or examiner evaluated

Cost: Manual $7.50; 25 scales and profile sheets $4.75; specimen set (manual, scale, and profile sheet) $7.75.

Publisher: Consulting Psychologists Press, Inc.

PROFILE OF ADAPTATION TO LIFE—HOLISTIC (PAL-H)

Robert E. Ellsworth

adult

Purpose: Measures an individual's adaptation to life in terms of that person's lifestyle and spiritual awareness. Used by ministers and counselors working with people who are interested in health-related activities and spiritual awareness as part of their remedial program.

Description: Multiple item paper-pencil self-report inventory assessing seven clinical scales (close relations, alienation-depression, anxiety, confusion, alcohol/drugs, house activity, child relations, and employment) and five scales relation to a person's life-style and spiritual awareness (social activity, self-activity, nutrition and exercise, personal growth, and spiritual awareness). The seven clinical scales assessed are the seven scales contained in the Profile of Adaptation to Life—Clinical (PAL-C). The manual explains the rationale and validity of the scale and provides detailed norms for the general and clinical populations in terms of adjustment to life and the community. Self-administered. Suitable for group use.

Untimed: 20-30 minutes

Range: Adult

Scoring: Examiner evaluated

Cost: Manual $7.50; 25 scales and profile sheets $4.75; specimen set (manual, scale, and profile sheet) $7.75.

Publisher: Consulting Psychologists Press, Inc.

PSYCHOEPISTEMOLOGICAL PROFILE (PEP)

Refer to page 191.

PSYCHOSOCIAL ADJUSTMENT TO ILLNESS SCALE (PAIS)

Leonard R. Derogatis

adult

Purpose: Assesses the psychological and social adjustment of medical patients, or their immediate family, to a serious illness.

Description: 46 item paper-pencil self-report instrument or structured interview guide assessing the psychosocial adjustment of medical patients and their immediate families in terms of seven principal domains: health care orientation, vocational environment, domestic environment, sexual relationships, extended family relationships, social environment, and psychological distress. A total score summarizes overall adjustment to illness. The self-report form (PAIS-SR) and the interview guide (PAIS) measure equivalent items. Norms and profile/score sheets are available for lung cancer patients and renal dialysis patients for the self-report form. Examiner required. Self-report form is suitable for group use; the interview guide is individually administered.

Untimed: 20-30 minutes

Range: Adults

Scoring: Examiner evaluated

Cost: Interview booklet $3.00; self-report form $.60; Score/profile sheets for populations listed above $.20.

Publisher: Clinical Psychometric Research

PSYCHOSOCIAL HISTORY REPORT

Giles D. Rainwater and Debra Silver Coe

adult

Purpose: Assesses the basic information necessary for a psychological report. Used for clinical assessment and diagnosis, personnel selection and evaluation, personal and family counseling, vocational guidance and counseling, and educational evaluation and planning.

Description: Multiple item paper-pencil or computer-administered questionnaire assessing an individual's psychological and social history in the following areas: presenting problem, family/-

developmental history, education, financial history and status, employment history, military service, alcohol and drug history, medical history, marital and family life, diet and exercise, and psychological and social stressors. A printed narrative report is provided, in addition to two lists which identify significant responses. One category consists of clinically significant answers. The second category consists of answers which the individual indicated a desire to discuss in more detail. Software versions are provided for the Apple II +, IIe, III, and IBM PC computer systems. Examiner required. Paper-pencil version suitable for group use.

Untimed: Varies

Range: Adult

Scoring: Computer scored

Cost: Computer program (unlimited usage) $295.00.

Publisher: Psychologistics, Inc.

PSYCHOSOCIAL PAIN INVENTORY (PSPI)

Robert K. Heaton, Ralph A.W. Lehman and Carl J. Getto

---

adult

Purpose: Evaluates psychosocial factors related to chronic pain problems. Used in treatment of chronic pain patients.

Description: Eight page multiple item paper-pencil inventory assessing psychosocial factors considered to be important in maintaining and exacerbating chronic pain problems. Evaluates the following factors: several forms of secondary gain, the effects of pain behavior on interpersonal relationships, the existence of stressful life events that may contribute to subjective distress or promote avoidance learning, and components of past history that familiarize the patient with the chronic invalid role and with its personal and social consequences. Ratings also consider the fact that patients differ in the degree to which they are likely to be influenced by potential sources of secondary gain. A total score is obtained, with high scores on the inventory predicting poor response to medical treatment for pain. Examiner required. Not suitable for group use.

Untimed: Varies

Range: Adult

Scoring: Examiner evaluated-Total score is obtained

Cost: Test kit (25 PSPI forms, 1 set of scoring instructions, and 1 copy of the initial research paper on the inventory by Dr. Heaton et al) $13.50.

Publisher: Psychological Assessment Resources, Inc.

ROGERS CRIMINAL RESPONSIBILITY ASSESSMENT SCALES (R-CRAS)

Richard Rogers

---

adult

Purpose: Evaluates the criminal responsibility of individuals who may or may not be held legally accountable for their actions, depending on their sanity or insanity at the time they committed a crime.

Description: Multiple item paper-pencil inventory quantifying essential psychological and situational variables at the time of the crime to be used in criterion-based decision model. This allows the clinician to quantify the impairment at the time of the crime, to conceptualize this impairment with respect to the appropriate legal standards, and to render an expert opinion with respect to that standard. Descriptive criteria are provided on scales measuring the individual's reliability, organicity, psychopathology, cognitive control, and behavioral control at the time of the alleged crime. Part I establishes the degree impairment on psychological variable significant to the determination of insanity. Part II articulates the decision process towards rendering an accurate opinion on criminal responsibility with the ALI standard. Part II also includes experimental criteria and decision models for guilty-but-mentally-ill (GBMI) and M'Naghten standards. Results classify sane and insane individuals across age, sex and race, and all important legal variables. Examiner required. Not suitable for group use.

Untimed: Varies

Range: Adult

Scoring: Examiner evaluated

Cost: Test kit (manual and 15 examination booklets) $22.00.

Publisher: Psychological Assessment Resources, Inc.

SALAMON-CONTE LIFE SATISFACTION IN THE ELDERLY SCALE (LSES)

Michael J. Salamon and Vincent A. Conte

older adult

Purpose: Assesses quality of life in the eldery. Used for screening, counseling, and treatment evaluation purposes with older adults.

Description: 40 item paper-pencil multiple choice sentence-completion inventory asessing older adults' reactions to their ecological, emotional, and social environments. Evaluates the following areas of particular importance to this age group: taking pleasure in daily activites; regarding life as meaningful; relationship between desired and achieved goals; positive mood; positive self-concept; perceived health and financial security; and satisfaction with number and quality of social contacts. Yields a total score and eight subscale scores. Examiner required. Suitable for group use.

Untimed: 20 minutes

Range: Elderly adults

Scoring: Examiner evaluated

Cost: Test kit (manual, 50 test booklets, and 50 scoring sheets) $19.95.

Publisher: Psychological Assessment Resources, Inc.

SCL-90-R

Leonard R. Derogatis

teen, adult

Purpose: Evaluates psychological symptomatic distress of medical and psychiatric patients. Used for psychological screening and in treatment planning and evaluation in mental health setting.

Description: 90 item paper-pencil self-report symptom inventory assessing psychological symptomatic distress in terms of nine symptom dimensions (somatization, obsessive-compulsive, interpersonal sensitivity, depression, anxiety, hostility, phobic anxiety, paranoid ideation, and psychoticism) and three global indices of distress (global severity index, positive symptom index, and positive symptom total). Score/profile forms and published norms are available by sex for four populations: non-patient adult, non-patient adolescent, outpatient psychiatric, and inpatient psychiatric. The SCL-90-R is the pivotal instrument in the Psychopathology Rating Scale Series, which includes the Brief Symptom Inventory, the SCL-90-R Analogue, and the Hopkins Psychiatric Rating Scale. Also available in an optical scan version. A microcomputer scoring program is available for the IBM-PC and Apple computers. Psychometer diskette version available from NCS/Professional Assessment Services.

Examiner required. Suitable for group use.

Untimed: 12-15 minutes

Range: Adolescent, adult

Scoring: Examiner evaluated; machine scoring and microcomputer scoring program available

Cost: Manual $15.00; 100 test forms $28.00; 100 optical scan forms $40.00; 100 score/profile forms $18.00; microcomputer scoring program (SCOR90-1) $150.00.

Publisher: Clinical Psychometric Research

SCL-90-R ANALOGUE

Leonard R. Derogatis

adult

Purpose: Evaluates psychological symptomatic distress of medical and psychiatric patients in terms of observer's ratings. Used for psychological screening and in treatment planning and evaluation in mental health settings.

Description: Ten item paper-pencil observational inventory assessing symptomatic distress in nine primary symptom dimensions (somatization, obsessive-compulsive, interpersonal sensitivity, depression, anxiety, hostility, phobic anxiety, paranoid ideation, and psychoticism) and one global psychopathology scale. Each primary symptom is represented as a continuum along 100 mm lines. The observer marks each continuum line proportionally. This inventory is a part of the Psychopathology Rating Scale Series and is intended to be used in conjunction with either the SCL-90-R or the Brief Symptom Inventory (BSI). The nine primary dimensions are the same as those measured on the other tests in the series. May be used by observers such as physicians, nurses, or technicians without extensive training in psychiatry. Not suitable for group use.

Untimed: 1-2 minutes

Range: Adolescent, adult

Scoring: Examiner evaluated

Cost: 100 inventory forms $28.00.

Publisher: Clinical Psychometric Research

SITUATIONAL PREFERENCE INVENTORY

Carl N. Edwards

adult

Purpose: Assesses an individual's preferred styles of social interaction. Used for counseling and research purposes.

Description: 28 item paper-pencil rating scale assessing preferred styles of social interaction. Each test item consists of a set of three statements, each representing a different style of interaction: cooperational, instrumental, or analytic. Individuals are asked to indicate which of the three statements they agree with most and which they agree with least, leaving the third statement unmarked (neutral). Independent scores are derived for each of the three interactional styles. Norms available by sex for 14 populations. Self-administered. Suitable for group use.

Untimed: Varies

Range: Adult

Scoring: Examiner evaluated

Cost: Contact publisher.

Publisher: Carl N. Edwards

THE SOCIAL BEHAVIOR ASSESSMENT SCHEDULE

Stephen Platt, Steven Hirsch and Anne Weyman

adult

Purpose: Assesses an individual's social functioning, changes in performance arising from psychiatric or physical illness, and the effects of his behavior on other members of the household. Used by health visitors, medical doctors, occupational therapists, social workers, psychologists, and psychiatrists.

Description: Multiple item semi-structured interview guide assessing an individual's behavioral disturbance and altered social performance while also evaluating the related difficulties suffered by the individual's household and close friends. Based on an interview with a relative or close friend (the informant), the schedule describes as fully as possible what the patient actually does, and the extent to which his performance falls short of the main requirements of his role in the household or community. The effect of the individual's behavior on others (objective burden) is assessed in a section of the schedule which takes account of the changes that have occured in the household and the lives of the informant and relatives. Distress caused to the informant (subjective distress) is rated on an item by item basis. Examiner required. Not suitable for group use. BRITISH PUBLISHER

Untimed: Varies

Range: Adult

Scoring: Examiner evaluated

Cost: Complete set (training manual, coding booklet, schedule and presentation wallet) £18.95.

Publisher: NFER-Nelson Publishing Company Ltd.

SOCIAL HISTORY

Psych Systems, Inc.

adult

Purpose: Assesses an individual's social and personal history. Used for clinical intake-screening procedures, as a part of clinical assessment and diagnosis procedures, and for personal/marital/family counseling.

Description: Multiple item computer-administered inventory addressing the following areas of an individual's social history: genetic and childhood history, adolescent adjustment, vocational adjustment, marital adjustment, quality of life, and recent stressful events. A branching strategy is employed by the computer (answers to certain questions dictate which questions will be administered next) to insure that the individual does not encounter items that are inappropriate. The program provides an interpretive report of the questionnaire's results when the administration phase is complete. May be used only on Psych Systems-supplied hardware, available in various configurations starting with single-users systems at approximately $25,000. A per-test fee (based on hardware configuration) also applies. Examiner required. Suitable for group use.

Untimed: Varies

Range: Adult

Scoring: Computer scored

Cost: Contact publisher.

Publisher: PSYCH Systems

STRESS EVALUATION INVENTORY

Refer to page 241.

SYMONDS PICTURE-STORY TEST

Percival M. Symonds

teen

Purpose: Evaluates the personality of adolescents. Used to obtain personal histories related to personality development.

Description: 20 item projective personality test consisting of 20 pictures

for which the adolescent is asked to make up stories. Differs from Murray's TAT in that it is specifically for the study of adolescent fantasy. Quartiles provided for 28 themes. Examiner required. Not suitable for group use.
BRITISH PUBLISHER

Untimed: Varies

Range: Adolescent

Scoring: Examiner evaluated

Cost: Contact publisher.

Publisher: The Test Agency

Multi-Levels

AUTISM SCREENING INSTRUMENT FOR EDUCATIONAL PLANNING

David A. Krug, Joel R. Arick and Patricia J. Almond

all ages

Purpose: Assesses the behavioral, social, and educational development of autistic, mentally retarded, deaf/blind, and emotionally disturbed students. Used to establish IEP's, evaluate program effectiveness, and monitor student progress.

Description: Multiple item paper-pencil observational inventory consisting of five subtests: Autism Behavior Checklist (ABC), Sample of Vocal Behavior, Interaction Assessment, Educational Assessment, and Prognosis of Learning Rate. The Autism Behavior Checklist contains 57 observable behaviors which discriminate autism from other severely handicapped conditions such as deaf/blind, severely emotionally disturbed, and mentally retarded. The Sample of Vocal Behavior assesses spontaneous verbal behavior in low-language developmentally delayed students. The examiner records 50 representative vocalizations in an unstructured setting. The sample is then analyzed for repetitive level, communicative value, vocal complexity, and syntactic complexity. Results yield standardized language age equivalency score. The Interaction Assessment provides a data based assessment of social interaction between an adult and a child, recording observable behaviors such as self-stimulation, crying, laughing, gestures, toy manipulation, conversation, and tantrums. For a 12 minute period, the examiner observes the child for 10 seconds, then in the next 5 seconds codes the interval according to the student's behavior on a matrix coding sheet, which yields a general social interaction profile. The Educational Assessment measures language performance and communicative ability. The student uses either sign language or verbal speech to answer the examiner's questions. Responses are quantitatively interpreted in the following areas: in-seat behavior, receptive language, expressive language, body concept, and speech imitation. The Prognosis of Learning Rate involves teaching each student a standardized task within a specific framework of responses. The student's learning acquisition rate is assessed in terms of responses to learn a black/white sequencing task. The observational methods involved in all five subtests allow all students to be "testable." Examiner required. Not suitable for group use. The Autism Behavior Checklist with instructions and Profile is available in Spanish.

Untimed: Varies

Range: 18 months-adult

Scoring: Examiner evaluated

Cost: ASIEP Test Kit (Administration Manual, 10 record form booklets, all materials needed for administration) $176.00; Spanish Edition of the Autism Behavior Checklist with 20 administration and scoring booklets $24.95.

Publisher: ASIEP Education Company

BALTHAZAR SCALES OF ADAPTIVE BEHAVIOR II: SCALES OF SOCIAL ADAPTATION

Earl E. Balthazar

mentally retarded

Purpose: Evaluates the coping behaviors of profoundly retarded adults and children. Used for program planning and progress evaluation.

Description: Multiple item paper-pencil observational inventory assessing eight categories of social adaptation and coping behaviors: unadaptive self-directed behaviors, unadaptive interpersonal behaviors, adaptive self-directed behaviors, adaptive interpersonal behaviors, verbal communication, play activities, response to instructions, and checklist items. Ratings are based on direct observation of the individual in that person's own environment. Readministration of the scales is sensitive to changes in the individual's behavior. Manual provides instructions for use by technicians, teachers, and other paraprofessionals. Examiner required. Not suitable for group use.

Untimed: Varies

Range: Profoundly retarded children and adults

Scoring: Examiner evaluated

Cost: Complete kit (manual and materials for 25 subjects) $19.50; specimen set (manual and 4 rating sheets) $5.25.

Publisher: Consulting Psychologists Press, Inc.

CULTURE-FREE SELF-ESTEEM INVENTORIES

Refer to page 184.

CULTURE-FREE SELF-ESTEEM INVENTORIES FOR CHILDREN AND ADULTS

James Battle

all ages

Purpose: Measures an individual's perception of self. Identifies individuals in need of psychological assistance. Used as a screening device by psychologists, psychiatrists, counselors, and teachers.

Description: Multiple item paper-pencil self-report form assessing self-esteem for children and adults. Available in three forms. Form A (60 items) and B (30 items) are used with children grades 3-12 and contain the following subscales: general self-esteem, social/peer related self-esteem, parents/home related self-esteem, and lie items (indicating defensiveness). Form A-D is used with adults and contains the following subscales: general self-esteem, social self-esteem, personal self-esteem, and lie items (indicating defensiveness). Results identify individuals who are generally dissatisfied with themselves, as well as individuals experiencing depression. Examiner required. Suitable for group use.

Untimed: Varies

Range: Children and adults

Scoring: Hand key; computer scoring available

Cost: Test kit (manual, Form A, Form B, Form A-D, scoring acetates, computer-scorable answer sheets, and oral administration cassette) $61.50; specimen set $18.75.

Publisher: Stoelting Co.

EMOTIONAL FACTORS INVENTORY

Mary K. Bauman

handicapped

Purpose: Measures emotional and personality factors of visually handicapped individuals.

Description: 170 item paper-pencil or oral response questionnaire assessing the personal and emotional adjustment of visually impaired individuals. Provides scores on the following seven scales: sensitivity, somatic symptoms, social competency, attitudes of distrust, feelings of inadequacy, depression, and attitudes concerning blindness. A validation score is also obtained. Questionnaires are presented in large print format. Instructions for tape recording the questions are included. Supplementary materials provided in the test kit include a discussion of the inventory, instructions for administering and scoring the inventory, and a comparative study of personality factors in blind, other handicapped, and non-handicapped individuals. Examiner required. Paper-pencil version suitable for group use.

Untimed: Varies

Range: Visually handicapped individuals

Scoring: Examiner evaluated

Cost: Test kit (large-print test booklet, set of scoring overlays, 10 IBM answer sheets, supplementary materials, and norms)$15.00.

Publisher: Associated Services for the Blind

MAKE A PICTURE STORY (MAPS)

E.S. Shneidman

all ages

Purpose: Assesses the personality of adults and children six years of age and older. Used for clinical evaluation and therapeutic purposes.

Description: Multiple item projective assessment instrument in which the individual chooses a background, populates it with figures, and tells a story to account for his choices and arrangements, or uses the figures to act out the story dramatically. Twenty-two pictorial backgrounds range from highly structured scenes such as a bedroom or bathroom to ambiguous scenes such as a vague grotto or cave-like opening. Sixty-seven cutout figures include persons (young, old, clothed, nude, wounded, etc.) and animals. Examiner may ask for stories about specific figures and/or backgrounds. An optional miniature theater which also serves as a carrying case makes it possible for the figures to stand erect at varying distances in front of the background; without it the picture is simply laid flat and the figures laid on it. Examiner required. Not suitable for group use.

Untimed: Varies

Range: Ages 6-adult

Scoring: Examiner evaluated

Cost: Complete set (all necessary equipment, manual, 25 figure location sheets, and theater/carrying case) $150.00; without carrying case $75.00.

Publisher: The Psychological Corporation

ROKEACH VALUE SURVEY: FORM G

Milton Rokeach

all ages

Purpose: Measures human values concerning possible end-states of existence and modes of behavior. Used for value therapy, values clarification, and to identify socially undesirable value structures.

Description: 36 item label-ranking test consisting of two sets of 18 values (one set of terminal values and one set of behavioral values) printed on gummed labels which the individual must arrange in order of personal importance. Terminal values include: comfortable life, exciting life, sense of accomplishment, world at peace, world of beauty, equality, family security, freedom, health, inner harmony, mature love, national security, pleasure, salvation, self-respect, social recognition, true friendship, and wisdom. Behavior values include: ambitious, broadminded, capable, clean, courageous, forgiving, helpful, honest, imaginative, independent, intellectual, logical, loving, loyal, obedient, polite, responsible, and self-controlled. Form G is a revision of Form D and includes the values "health" and "loyal" in the place of "happiness" and "cheerful". An extensive list of reference materials is provided. Normative data available for many populations within American society. Self-administered. Suitable for group use.

Untimed: Adults—15-20 minutes; children—20-25 minutes

Range: Child, adult

Scoring: Self-scoring

Cost: Test kit (2 sets of 18 gummed labels with printed array for final rankings) $.75-$1.00 each, depending on quantity.

Publisher: Halgren Tests

SCHEDULE OF RECENT EXPERIENCE (SRE)

Thomas H. Holmes

all ages

Purpose: Measures how often various stress-producing events have occurred in an individual's life during the recent past. Used for counseling and discussion purposes and as an aid to general health maintenance programs.

Description: 42 item paper-pencil inventory assessing the amount of psychological change (adaptive behavior) an individual has undergone in the recent past. Each test item is an event that causes change in a person's life which has been observed in a large number of patients preceding the onset of their medical illness or clinical symptoms. Test items include socially undesirable events as well as socially desirable events (birth of a baby or a promotion at work) which are stress related. The individual is asked to indicate for each item how often it has occurred during a specific time period (ranging from less than one year up to ten years). Inventory may also be used as a framework for a structured interview. Manual includes: instructions for administering the test to individuals of all ages, sample test forms (both one-year and three-year versions), templates for scoring both versions, a report of the studies on which the test is based, and a list of suggested preventive measures for maintenance of health and prevention of illness based on test results. Examiner required. Suitable for group use.

Untimed: Varies

Range: All ages

Scoring: Hand key

Cost: Manual $12.00; 50 one-year test scales with scoring template $10.00; 50 three-year test scales with scoring template $15.00.

Publisher: University of Washington Press

SELF-ESTEEM QUESTIONNAIRE (SEQ-3)

James K. Hoffmeister

all ages

Purpose: Evaluates how individuals feel about various aspects of themselves such as their capabilities, worth, and acceptance by others.

Description: 21 item paper-pencil self-report rating scale consisting of two subscales: Self-Esteem (12 items) and Self-Other Satisfaction (9 items). Self-Esteem is defined to mean the feeling that a person is capable, significant, successful, and worthy. Self-Other Satisfaction is defined to mean the level of satisfaction a person has with respect to those feelings of Self-Esteem. Items on the Self-Esteem subscale consist of statements such as "Most of my friends accept me as much as they accept other people," which the individual rates on five-point scale from one (not at all) to five (yes, very much). Items on the Self-Other Satisfaction subscale immediately follow items on the Self-Esteem subscale and take the form "Does the situation described in [the previous question] upset you?" These items are rated on a similar five-point scale. Scores are provided for both subscales according to the computerized Convergence Analysis process (a score is computed only if the individual has responded in a reasonably consistent fashion to the items used to measure that factor). The manual includes: a description of the test's variables and content, directions for administering and scoring the questionnaire, information concerning development, validity, and reliability, and normative data. Examiner required. Suitable for group use.

Untimed: Varies

Range: Grade 4-adult

Scoring: Computer scored

Cost: 50 questionnaires (includes computer scoring service) $50.00.

Publisher: Test Analysis and Development Corporation

THE STERN ACTIVITIES INDEX (AI)

George Stern and associates

all ages

Purpose: Measures personality in terms of the need-press paradigm of human behavior as conceptualized by Henry Murray. Used for counseling and research purposes.

Description: 300 item (long form) or 91 item (either of two short forms) paper-pencil inventory assessing personality along 30 basic need scales. Test items are descriptions of routine activities and feelings to which the individual indicates a personal "like" or "dislike." The long form provides scores on each of the 30 need scales (10 items per scale), 12 first order scores (self-assertion, audacity-timidity, intellectual interests, motivation, applied interests, orderliness, submissiveness, closeness, sensuousness, friendliness, expressive-constraint, and egoism-diffidence), and four second order scores (achievement orientation, dependency needs, emotional expression, and educability). The two short forms provide scores for the 12 first order dimensions and four second order dimensions. Short forms are used when administration time is a problem, or if scores on the 30 basic need scales are not required. Short form SAI-1158SF is primarily for adults but can be used with individuals as young as 12 years of age who have a minimum seventh grade reading level (the long form also requires a seventh grade reading level). Short form SAI-1173SF is used with younger children who have a minimum fourth grade reading level. Evidence for reliability and validity are presented in the technical manual. Self-administered. Suitable for group use.

Untimed: Long form—40 minutes; short forms—20 minutes

Range: Child, adolescent, adult

Scoring: Examiner evaluated; computer scoring available

Cost: Test booklet $.50; answer sheet $.10; profile form $.10; technical manual $7.50; prices for computer and analysis scoring available on request.

Publisher: Evaluation Research Associates

Research

THE CLASSROOM ENVIRONMENT INDEX (CEI)

Refer to page 183.

CORNELL INDEX

Refer to page 36.

THE D48 TEST (RESEARCH EDITION)

Center for Psychological Applications, Paris

all ages

Purpose: Assesses nonverbal reasoning skills to measure the g-factor in intelligence. May be used with hearing-impaired or nonreading individuals.

Description: 48 item paper-pencil multiple-choice nonverbal analogies test involving pictures of dominoes. Test items cover a wide range of difficulty and can be administered with a minimum need for language. Average scores range from 18 correct answers (in fifth-grade school children) to 31 for college students. The manual provides norms and validity studies on French subjects. Examiner required. Suitable for group use.

Timed: 25 minutes

Range: Child, adult

Scoring: Hand key

Cost: Experimental kit (5 test booklets, 25 answer sheets, manual, and scoring stencil) $12.00; specimen set (manual, test booklet, answer sheet, and scoring key) $8.50.

Publisher: Consulting Psychologists Press, Inc.

THE DEFINING ISSUES TEST OF MORAL JUDGMENT

James R. Rest

teen, adult

Purpose: Measures moral judgment concerning social issues. Used for research purposes only.

Description: 72 item paper-pencil test consisting of six short stories, each followed by 12 related statements. The stories present social problems or moral dilemmas, while the statements provide a range of considerations to be taken into account as one tries to determine what a proper (morally "right") course of action would be in a given situation. Individuals indicate the importance they would place on each consideration by rating each statement on a five-point scale from "none" to "great." Individuals then rank in order of importance the four statements which they consider to be the most important of the 12 statements provided for each story. Provides scores for Stages (of moral development), 2, 3, 4, 4½, 5A, 5B, and 6; the most used index is a combination of Stages 5 and 6, a "principled" morality score ("P" score). An internal consistency check identifies individuals who are randomly checking responses or who do not understand the directions. Inappropriate for use with individuals who are not fluent in English or do not have an eighth-grade reading level. The manual (available from Minnesota Moral Research Projects) contains information on administering and scoring the test, interpretation and sample analyses of test scores, reliability and validity, and norms for various groups. A detailed discussion of the rationale of test development, theoretical issues, and empirical findings is provided in *Development in Judging Moral Issues* (University of Minnesota Press). Examiner required. Suitable for group use.

Untimed: 40 minutes

Range: Age 13 years-adult

Scoring: Examiner evaluated

Cost: Available to professional and student researchers affiliated with recognized institutions free of charge.

Publisher: Minnesota Moral Research Projects

DYADIC PARENT-CHILD INTERACTION CODING SYSTEM (DPICS)

Refer to page 22.

EYBERG CHILD BEHAVIOR INVENTORY (ECBI)

Refer to page 38.

HARDING STRESS-FAIR COMPATIBILITY TEST

Chris Harding

adult

Purpose: Measures an individual's intellectual, social, emotional, and philosophical orientation. Identifies and matches compatible pairs of individuals. Used for research and personal matching services.

Description: 46 item paper-pencil multiple-choice inventory assessing ten factors related to the degree of compatibility between two individuals; intellective (tendency to think things through to a final conclusion), extroversion, sensitivity, idealism, goal setting, awareness (aware beyond immediate concerns), group detachment, advocacy (cooperative maturity), complexity (degree of inner defensiveness), and dominance-agression. Tables printed on the back of the test identify 12 levels of compatibility: optimum compatibility, beginnings of identity fusion, complete mutual reciprocation, equivalent evaluations, "best friend" status, deep friendship possible, reciprocation with reservations in certain areas, awareness of others viewpoint, indifferent relationship, mild antagonism, antagonism, and complete alienation. Scoring sheet contains data on norm distribution, formulae for matching, and explanation. Examiner required. Suitable for group use.

Untimed: Varies

Range: Adult

Scoring: Computer scored

Cost: 1 inventory with computer scoring and matching service $10.00; 1 copy of inventory with scoring sheet available for research purposes free of charge.

Publisher: Harding Tests

THE HIGH SCHOOL CHARACTERISTICS INDEX (HSCI) AND THE ELEMENTARY AND SECONDARY SCHOOL INDEX (ESI)

Refer to page 185.

HOME OBSERVATION FOR MEASUREMENT OF THE ENVIRONMENT (HOME)

Bettye M. Caldwell, Robert H. Bradley and staff

child

Purpose: Measures the quality of the home environment for infants and preschool children. Used for research purposes.

Description: 45 or 55 item (depending on which form is used) paper-pencil inventory assessing the following aspects of a child's home environment: frequency and stability of adult contact, amount of developmental and vocal stimulation, need gratification, emotional climate, avoidance of restriction on motor and exploratory behavior, available play materials, and home characteristics indicative of parental concern with achievement. The examiner completes the inventory on the basis of a one hour visit to the child's home (while the child is awake). The parent is interviewed and parent-child interactions are observed during this period. Roughly two-thirds of the items are based on observed behaviors; one-third are based on parental report. All items are scored plus (+) or minus (–) depending on whether or not the behavior is observed during the visit or the parent reports that the conditions or events are characteristic of the home environment. The form for infants and toddlers (45 items) provides a total score and scores for six subscales; emotional and verbal responsibility of parent, acceptance of child's behavior, organization of physical and temporal environment, provision of appropriate play materials, parent involvement with child, and opportunities for variety in daily stimulation. The form for preschoolers (55 items) provides a total score and scores for eight subscales: learning stimulation, language stimulation, physical environment, warmth and affection, academic stimulation, modeling, variety in experience, and acceptance. Examiner required. Not suitable for group use.

Untimed: 1 hour

Range: Infants-6 years

Scoring: Examiner evaluated

Cost: Contact publisher.

Publisher: University of Arkansas at Little Rock/Center for Child Development

HUMAN INFORMATION PROCESSING SURVEY: HIP SURVEY

Refer to page 219.

IRENOMETER

Panos D. Bardis

all ages

Purpose: Measures attitudes and beliefs concerning peace (Irenology is the study of peace). Used for discussion purposes.

Description: 10 item paper-pencil inventory. Individuals rate 10 statements about peace and its effects on individuals and society on a five-point scale from 0 (strongly disagree) to 4 (strongly agree). All statements express positive attitudes toward peace. Score equals the sum total of the 10 numerical responses. Self-administered. Suitable for group use.

Untimed: Varies

Range: Child-adult

Scoring: Self-scored

Cost: Free.

Publisher: Panos D. Bardis

KRANTZ HEALTH OPINION SURVEY (HOS)

David S. Krantz, Andrew Baum and Margaret V. Wideman

teen, adult

Purpose: Measures preferences for different approaches to health care programs. Assesses the degree to which individuals wish to be involved (i.e., be informed and/or participate) in their own health care and medical treatment programs. Used for research purposes only.

Description: 16 item paper-pencil self-report inventory assessing preferences concerning personal involvement in medical care programs. Consists of two scales: scale B (behavioral involvement) and scale I (information). Scale B contains nine items and measures attitudes toward self-treatment and active behavioral involvement of patients in medical care. Scale I contains seven items and measures the desire to ask questions and be informed about medical decisions. Test items are rated on a binary agree-disagree format. Scores are provided for both scales as well as a total score measuring composite attitudes toward treatment approaches. High scores represent favorable attitudes toward self-directed or informed treatment. Items refer to routine aspects of medical care and do not refer to severe or traumatic illness. The manual (a 14-page excerpt from *The Journal of Personality and Social Psychology*, 1980) includes: the theoretical basis for the scales; information concerning development, reliability, and validity; a list of the scale items; suggested applications; and discussion and results of various research studies using the scale. Self-administered. Suitable for group use.

Untimed: Varies

Range: College student-adult

Scoring: Examiner evaluated

Cost: Contact publisher concerning availability and prices.

Publisher: David S. Krantz

LIGHT-SWITCH ALTERNATION APPARATUS

Refer to page 18.

MEASURE OF ACHIEVING TENDENCY

Refer to page 43.

MEASURE OF AROUSAL SEEKING TENDENCY

Refer to page 43.

MEASURE OF CHILD STIMULUS SCREENING (CONVERSE OF AROUSABILITY)

Refer to page 23.

MEASURE OF DOMINANCE-SUBMISSIVENESS

Refer to page 43.

MEASURE OF STIMULUS SCREENING (CONVERSE OF AROUSABILITY)

Refer to page 44.

MEASURES OF AFFILIATIVE TENDENCY AND SENSITIVITY TO REJECTION

Refer to page 44.

MEASURES OF PLEASURE-, AROUSAL-, AND DOMINANCE-INDUCING QUALITIES IN PARENTAL ATTITUDES

Refer to page 24.

PAIN AND DISTRESS INVENTORY

William W.K. Zung

adult

Purpose: Measures degree of pain and evaluates the characteristics of associated dysfunctions. Used in research and clinical settings to establish pain treatment programs and to monitor the effectiveness of such programs.

Description: 20 item paper-pencil self-report rating scale assessing the presence of somato-sensory pain and associated changes in mood and behavior. Scale items describe the 20 characteristics most commonly described by individuals when pain and associated distress are present. Individuals indicate the degree to which each statement describes their own feelings or behaviors by rating each item on a four-point scale from "none or little of the time" to "most or all of the time." Items include both symptomatically positive and symptomatically negative statements. Standardized analysis provides an index of the pain and distress present. The manual (a six-page excerpt from *The Journal of the Academy of Psychosomatic Medicine*, 1983) includes: directions for administering, scoring, and interpreting the scale; information concerning development, reliability, and validity; normative data; suggested applications; and a list of references for further research. Examiner required. Suitable for group use.

Untimed: Varies

Range: Adult

Scoring: Examiner evaluated

Cost: Contact publisher.

Publisher: William W.K. Zung

PIERS-HARRIS CHILDREN'S SELF-CONCEPT SCALE (PHSCS)

Ellen V. Piers and Dale B. Harris

child, teen

Purpose: Measures self-concept for children grades 4-12. Identifies problem areas in a child's self-confidence. Used for research purposes.

Description: 80 item paper-pencil test assessing six aspects of a child's self-esteem; behavior, intellectual and school status, physical appearance and attributes, anxiety, popularity, and happiness and satisfaction. Test items are written at a third grade reading level and require a simple "yes-no" answer. Percentile and stanine scores are provided for the total score and for each of the six subscales. Scores can be used for research purposes or to identify extreme problem areas. The manual provides all information necessary for administering and interpreting the scale, as well as the information included in Research Monograph #1 concerning use of the scale with minority and special education groups. May be self-administered. Suitable for group use.

Untimed: 15-20 minutes

Range: Grades 4-12

Scoring: Hand key; computer scoring available

Cost: Test kit (25 test booklets, 25 profile forms, 1 scoring key, 2 computer answer sheets, 1 manual) $43.00.

Publisher: Western Psychological Services

PRESCHOOL ATTAINMENT RECORD (RESEARCH EDITION)

Refer to page 126.

PSYCHOSOCIAL PAIN INVENTORY (PSPI)

Refer to page 48.

RESIDENT ASSISTANT STRESS INVENTORY

Gary L. Dickson

college students

Purpose: Identifies the type and level of stress experienced by residence hall personnel. Used by professional housing officers to individualize in-service education in this area.

Description: Multiple item paper-pencil inventory measuring six categories of stress experienced by resident assistants: emotional resiliency, facilitative leadership, counseling skills, environmental adjustment, confrontive skills, and values development. The manual and in-service education guide is divided into two parts: part I for the practitioner and part II for the researcher. Information in these sections includes fifty stress situations, directions for scoring and interpretation, suggestions for in-service training, annotated references, and recommendations for research. Examiner required. Suitable for group use.

Untimed: Varies

Range: College students

Scoring: Examiner evaluated

Cost: Specimen set (inventory, score sheet, profile form, contract form, research form, manual and in-service education guide) $5.00.

Publisher: Andrews University Press

SITUATIONAL PREFERENCE INVENTORY

Refer to page 50.

THE STERN ACTIVITIES INDEX (AI)

Refer to page 56.

SYSTEM FOR THE ADMINISTRATION AND INTERPRETATION OF NEUROLOGICAL TESTS (SAINT-II)

Refer to page 21.

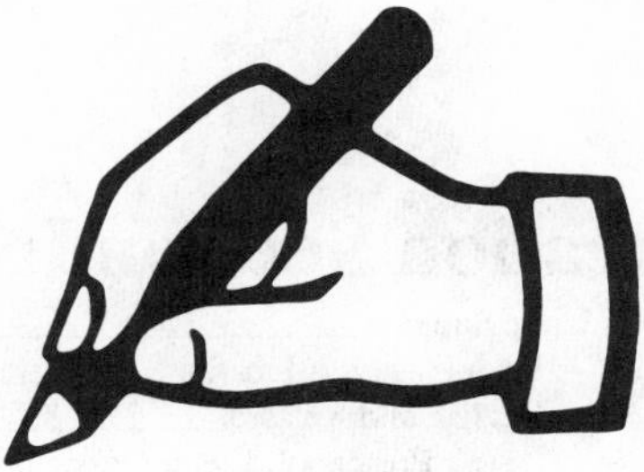

Education

The tests presented and described in the Education Section have been selected on the basis of their appropriate usage in an educational or school setting. In general, tests found in this section are those which might be used by educators or professionals (school psychologists, school counselors, and classroom teachers) concerned with the cognitive and emotional growth and development of persons of all ages.

Tests in this section have been arranged into thirteen subsections on the basis of "typical usage or function." The thirteen subsections listed in the Education Section Index are identical to those listed in the First Edition of ***TESTS****. The same guidelines for classification applied to the tests listed in the First Edition of* ***TESTS*** *have been used to classify the tests listed in this volume.*

Some subsections contain no new test entries in this supplement. In such cases, the title of the subsection will be listed and readers will find the following instructions: "No new tests available. Please refer to the First Edition of ***TESTS*** *for a complete listing and description of tests currently available in this area."*

The classification of tests on the basis of "typical usage or function" is, of course, an arbitrary one, and the reader is encouraged to review the Psychology Section and the Business Section for additional assessment techniques. Readers are also encouraged to refer to the First Edition of ***TESTS*** *in addition to this supplement for a more complete knowledge of the range of tests available within each of the thirteen subsections.*

Education Section Index

Education Section

Academic Subjects

Business Education

*No new tests available. Please refer to the First Edition of **TESTS** for a complete listing and description of tests currently available in this area.*

English and Related

Preschool, Elementary and Junior High School

DENVER HANDWRITING ANALYSIS (DHA)
Peggy L. Anderson

child

Purpose: Assesses the general quality of a student's cursive handwriting and provides detailed information related to handwriting instruction.

Description: Multiple item paper-pencil test consisting of five subtests: near-point copying, writing the alphabet from memory, far-point copying, manuscript-cursive transition, and dictation. Each subtest yields a Mastery Level score that allows for intra-individual comparisons to be made across varying task formats. The DHA Scoring Profile includes a subskill analysis section that classifies errors by type and performance analysis section that yields more general information about spatial organization, speed, slant, and appearance. The manual includes interpretive guidelines, samples of written reports summarizing student performance, and remedial suggestions related to each subtest. Examiner required. Suitable for group use.

Untimed: 20-60 minutes

Range: Grades 3-8. May be extended to younger and older students.

Scoring: Examiner evaluated

Cost: Test Kit (Manual and Wall Chart, 25 Record Forms, 25 Scoring Profiles, in vinyl folder) $21.00; Specimen Set (Manual and Sample Forms) $12.50.

Publisher: Academic Therapy Publications

DIAGNOSIS AND REMEDIATION OF HANDWRITING PROBLEMS (DRHP)
Refer to page 148.

PARALLEL SPELLING TESTS
Dennis Young

child

Purpose: Measures spelling skills at all levels of ability. Used with children ages 6-13 years for program planning and evaluation.

Description: Multiple item paper-pencil test of spelling ability. Test items are selected from banks of sentences presented in the test booklet according to the level of ability of the students being tested. Twelve matched tests without overlap (a

much larger number with partial overlap) can be formed. The abundance of material in the banks and the method of selecting a test render the results less vulnerable to practice effects and coaching. Test booklet also includes: sections on examining and extending the results, an introduction to children's spelling errors and the assessment of spelling in children's writing, fundamental guidance on the teaching of spelling, and a method for systematically charting the progress of children at all levels of ability over a period of six years (ages 6:5-13:0). Examiner required. Suitable for group use.
BRITISH PUBLISHER

Untimed: Varies

Range: Ages 6:5-13:0 years

Scoring: Examiner evaluated

Cost: Test booklet £2.95.

Publisher: Hodder & Stoughton

SPELLMASTER DIAGNOSTIC SPELLING SYSTEM

Claire R. Cohen and Rhoda M. Abrams

---

child

Purpose: Measures spelling abilities and diagnoses individual spelling difficulties. Used to plan instructional and remedial spelling programs. Used by classroom teachers, reading specialists, L.D. specialists, E.S.L. teachers, special education teachers, and adult education teachers.

Description: Multiple item paper-pencil tests measuring eight levels of spelling abilities corresponding to grade levels 1-8. Diagnostic tests, irregular words tests, and homonym tests are provided for all levels. Diagnostic tests measure 160 phonic and structural elements in regular words. Each test contains a scoring key which identifies and analyzes errors. On the basis of the diagnostic tests, students are placed for individual or group instruction, and other levels of diagnostic tests, irregular word tests, or homonym tests are administered according to individual need. Students can correct their own errors and find out why they made them. The testing and evaluating manual describes how to administer and score all tests. The teaching and learning manual provides specific teaching suggestions, learning activities, and approximately 5000 supplementary words for individual study. Correlation charts show how to use other published spelling materials. Examiner required. Suitable for group use.

Untimed: Varies

Range: Grade levels 1-8

Scoring: Examiner evaluated; self-scored

Cost: Sampler package (one each of the tests, manuals, charts, and forms that make up the program) $16.95.

Publisher: Learnco, Inc.

High School and College

COLLEGE ENGLISH PLACEMENT TEST

Oscar Haugh and James Brown

---

college freshmen

Purpose: Measures English composition skills of incoming college freshmen. Used to place college freshmen in English composition classes.

Description: Multiple item paper-pencil test consisting of two parts. Part 1 is a 45-minute objective test of English composition skills. Part 2 (optional) consists of two 25-minute essays. Test items reflect the results of a survey of college English professors concerning the relative importance of

elements of composition in the assignment of freshmen to composition classes. The four areas found to be vital in English composition and placement (and their weight on the test) are as follows: organization and paragraph structure (36%), syntax and grammar (17%), and conventions, usage, and capitalization (22%). Sections of the test are arranged to follow the actual steps in writing a composition. Examiner required. Suitable for group use.
CANADIAN PUBLISHER

Timed: 45 or 95 minutes

Range: College freshmen

Scoring: Examiner evaluated

Cost: 50 test booklets $40.10; 50 answer sheets $33.40; manual $4.00; examination kit $5.25.

Publisher: Nelson Canada

ESSENTIALS OF ENGLISH TESTS

Constance McCullough, Dora V. Smith, and Carolyn Greene

teen grades 7 and up

Purpose: Evaluates proper use of the mechanics of English . Used by secondary English teachers and for placing college freshmen.

Description: Multiple item paper-pencil test measuring five areas of English mechanics: spelling, grammatical usage, word usage, sentence structure, punctuation and capitalization. Selected national percentiles for each subtest and the total raw score are provided for grades 7-12. The Diagnostic Key to Errors and a scoring tabulation form ascertains specific student needs and helps teachers group students with common needs. Raw scores and percentile ranks (along with comments) are recorded on the class record form. Available in two forms, A and B, for pre- and post-testing. Examiner required. Suitable for group use.

Untimed: 45 minutes

Range: Grades 7-12 and college freshmen

Scoring: Hand key; examiner evaluated

Cost: Test kit (manual, 25 test booklets form A or B, scoring key, score tabulation and class record form, and Diagnostic Key to Errors) $7.25; Specimen set $3.25.

Publisher: American Guidance Service

PURDUE HIGH SCHOOL ENGLISH TEST

R. Franklin, J. McKee, H. Remmers, and G. Wykoff

teen grades 9-13

Purpose: Measures English language skills of high school students and college freshmen.

Description: Multiple item paper-pencil test measuring knowledge and ability in five areas of English: grammar, punctuation, effective expression, vocabulary, and spelling. Fall and spring norms provided for high school students in terms of percentiles and standard scores by grade and sex. Norms for college freshmen and other interpretive data are also included. Examiner required. Suitable for group use.

Timed: 36 minutes

Range: Grades 9-13

Scoring: Hand key; computer scoring available

Cost: (1983-84) 35 test booklets $18.99; 100 self-marking answer sheets $39.60; 100 IBM 1230 answer sheets $23.73; IBM 1230 scoring mask $4.95; manual $3.81; 35 class record sheets $5.28.

Publisher: The Riverside Publishing Company

Multi-Level

DIAGNOSTIC SPELLING POTENTIAL TEST (DSPT)

John Arena

all ages

Purpose: Assesses the spelling skills of students age 7 through adult.

Description: Multiple item paper-pencil test consisting of four subtests: Spelling, Word Recognition, Visual Recognition, and Auditory-Visual Recognition. Tables are provided for converting raw scores to standard scores, percentile ranks, and grade ratings. Standard scores and percentiles may be plotted on a profile chart that compares spelling efficiency with requisite skills such as decoding, utilization of phonetic generalizations, visual recall, and matching auditory with visual representations. Two parallel forms available for pre- and post-testing. The manual includes provisions for group administration of three of the subtests and presents a wide range of remedial activities. Examiner required. Suitable for group use.

Untimed: 25-40 minutes

Range: Age 7-adult

Scoring: Examiner evaluated

Cost: Test Kit (Manual, Form A-1: 25 Spelling/Word Recognition Record Forms, Form A-2: 25 Visual/Auditory-Visual Recognition Record Forms, Pad of 25 Profile Sheets, in vinyl folder) $32.50; Specimen Set (Manual and Sample Forms) $17.50.

Publisher: Academic Therapy Publications

LAURITA-TREMBLEY DIAGNOSTIC WORD PROCESSING TEST

Raymond E. Laurita and Phillip W. Trembley

child, teen gr. 1 and up

Purpose: Identifies the level of categorical word processing that a student is able to utilize in spelling. Used for program planning, to establish IEP's, for monitoring progress, and for evaluating instructional programs in spelling.

Description: 64 item paper-pencil test using a dictation spelling format to assess the ability to discriminate among fifteen vowel forms at five sequentially organized levels of difficulty. Criterion-referenced test items are based on an orthographic model that holds that spelling relies on a given set of word processing generalizations. Results are profiled on the Individual Progress Chart, which details the student's level of word processing ability, identifies categories of words that the student is ready to learn, and provides an estimate of the number of words in the student's spelling vocabulary. Suitable for group use.

Untimed: 20-30 minutes

Range: Grade 1-college

Scoring: Examiner evaluated

Cost: Test Kit (manual, 10 Individual Progress Charts, and 20 record forms for pre- and posttesting) 25.00.

Publisher: L & T Educational Materials

WRITTEN LANGUAGE SYNTAX TEST

Sharon R. Berry

hearing impaired K-12

Purpose: Measures hearing impaired students' command of the English language. Used for academic placement and evaluation of hearing impaired students.

Description: Multiple item paper-pencil test assesing hearing impaired students' command of the written syntax. The test includes three levels of assessment as well as a preliminary exercise to determine which levels of the test are appropriate for a given student. The task that students perform entails viewing a picture, scanning a short list of randomly ordered English words, and making a sentence with those words based on the picture. Manual includes information for administering and scoring the tests and interpreting the results. Picture stimuli is included on the test forms. Examiner required. Suitable for group use.

Untimed: Varies

Range: Hearing impaired students primary-grade 12

Scoring: Examiner evaluated

Cost: Test kit (manual, one each of four levels of tests, one folder) $10.00; screening test (10 copies) $4.00; Level 1 test (10 copies) $4.00; Level 2 test (10 copies) $4.00; Level 3 test (10 copies) $4.00; 10 folders $4.00.

Publisher: Gallaudet College Press

Fine Arts

MUSICAL APTITUDE PROFILE

Edwin Gordon

child, teen **grades 4-12**

Purpose: Assesses basic musical needs, abilities, and aptitudes for elementary and high school students.

Description: 250 item paper-pencil test consisting of seven subtests arranged in three musical categories: tonal imagery (melody, harmony), rhythm imagery (tempo, meter) and musical sensitivity (phrasing, balance, style). Test items consist of short musical selections (played by professional artists) administered via audio tape. Scores are provided for each of the seven subtests. The Complete Musical Aptitude Profile contains materials for testing 100 students, including: three full-track 7½ ips tapes on seven-inch open-recorder reels, one manual (includes information on scoring and using test results, and technical data), 100 MRC answer sheets, scoring masks, 100 record file folders for cumulative musical records, 100 musical talent profiles for students and parents, and two class record sheets. Examiner required. Suitable for group use.

Untimed: 110 minutes

Range: Grades 4-12

Scoring: Examiner evaluated

Cost: Complete Musical Aptitude Profile $134.79.

Publisher: The Riverside Publishing Company

Foreign Language and English As A Second Language

AATG NATIONAL STANDARDIZED GERMAN TESTS

teen **grades 9-12**

Purpose: Measures academic achievement in German language study of high school students who are in their second, third, and fourth year of study. Used to place transfer students, assess the progress of students and entire classes, and to compare the results of various teaching methods.

Description: Multiple item paper-pencil test assessing German language competency of high school students. Test sections include: listening comprehension (via tape cassette), grammar, situational questions (testing reading as well as conversational skills), and comprehension of connected passages of approximately 200 words each. Questions in each section are of graded difficulty. The tests are administered once a year in January and may be administered in-school or at an AATG chapter test center. In-school testing is accomplished under the direct supervision of the school's testing or guidance personnel. In the interest of security all parts of the test must be returned (answer sheets are sent to American College Testing and the test booklets and tapes are returned to the AATG Administrative Offices). Teachers who are unable or who prefer not to have their students tested in-school may have their students tested at a chapter test center. ACT will send Regional Chairpersons (list available) a copy of all test orders submitted from their chapter area. Regional chairpersons will establish chapter test centers and inform teachers who have requested this service when and where testing is to occur. Students are eligible to take the test designed for the level on which they are studying at the time of the test administration. Students who take a test below their current level of work, or take more than one test, will be excluded from any awards program. ACT returns scores to test administrators and regional chairpersons in February. Scores are provided for the several sections of the test as well as a total score, enabling teachers to determine in which areas individuals or groups demonstrate high achievement and in which areas remedial assistance might be desirable. Two sets of percentiles are given, one set based on a norming population consisting only of students who took the test with their whole class and a second set based on the entire population taking the tests exclusive of those students whose knowledge of German was acquired in part by other experience than that gained in American secondary schools. ACT report also includes tables showing what percentage of the two groups answered each question correctly as well as a delta (difficulty) index for each item. Students scoring in the 90th to 100th percentile are eligible to apply for the AATG-PAD Study Trip Award to Germany. Practice tests available. Examiner required. Suitable for group use.

Timed: One hour

Range: High school students

Scoring: All tests scored by American College Testing (ACT) Program

Cost: $3.00 per student.

Publisher: AATG (American Association of Teachers of German)

BASIC INVENTORY OF NATURAL LANGUAGE (BINL)

Refer to page 160.

BILINGUAL ORAL LANGUAGE TEST: BOLT-ENGLISH AND BOLT-SPANISH

Sam Cohen, Roberto Cruz, and Raul Bravo

teen grades 7-12

Purpose: Measures oral language skills in English or Spanish. Determines a student's level of bilingualism. Used for academic placement and planning and for reporting accurate results on enrollment and language dominance to federal and state agencies.

Description: Two multiple item oral response tests assessing oral language skills in English (BOLT-English) or Spanish (BOLT-Spanish). The two tests are independent components of the same instrument and based on the same organization. They assess oral language skills from simple sentence patterns to more complex syntactical forms of the language. Students are classified into one of four language categories: non-English/Spanish speaking, very limited English/Spanish speaking, limited English/Spanish speaking, English/Spanish speaking. Results of both tests are combined to determine a student's level of bilingualism. The summary page is used to record the level of bilingualism and to organize data for enrollment and language dominance reports. May be used on a pre/post test basis to determine gain of proficiency in English and/or Spanish. Information concerning the results of field testing are presented in the technical reports. Examiner required. Not suitable for group use.

Untimed: 6 minutes

Range: Intermediate and secondary school students

Scoring: Examiner evaluated

Cost: Classroom packets—English or Spanish (manual, picture booklet, 30 answer sheets and class record chart) $25.00; bilingual test summary page $.50; technical reports, $1.75.

Publisher: Bilingual Media Productions, Inc.

BILINGUAL TWO LANGUAGE BATTERY OF TESTS

Adolph Caso

all ages

Purpose: Measures language proficiency in English and five native languages: Spanish, Italian, Portugese, Vietnamese, and French. Assesses language dominance and determines point of bilinguality. Used for academic placement and evaluation and to determine LAU categories.

Description: A battery of paper-pencil and oral response tests comparing proficiency in English with proficiency in any of five native languages. Tests for all languages consist of four parts (although the content in English is not necessarily the same as that in the native languages): phonetics (letter recognition and spelling), comprehension situations (opposites, similarities, comparisons, reading and listening), writing sentences related to pictures, and an optional supplement measuring oral language proficiency (questions related to Limited English Proficiency Students). Students listen to directions presented on a pre-recorded tape (English on one side and the native language on the other) and write their answers in the student booklet of the appropriate language. The native language test is given first (21 minutes), and the one in English (also 21 minutes) must follow within two weeks. The battery may be administered at any time during the year, but optimal administration is in two sessions per school year (spring-fall) for three consecutive years. Results for both language tests are recorded on the student score profiles card, which includes the following charts: composite scores, proficiency levels, language dominance, point of bilinguality, and LAU category. Cassette player required. Examiner required. Suitable for group use.

Timed: English test—21 minutes; native language test—21 minutes

Range: Students and adults at any level of language proficiency

Scoring: Examiner evaluated

Cost: Contact publisher.

Publisher: Branden Press

LANGUAGE ASSESSMENT BATTERY

Staff of the New York City Board of Education

child, teen K-12

Purpose: Assesses students' verbal abilities in English and/or Spanish. Identifies Spanish-speaking students who cannot participate effectively in English-speaking classrooms and provides a comparable measure of their communication skills in Spanish. Used for academic evaluation and placement of Spanish-speaking students.

Description: Multiple item paper-pencil and oral response subtests measuring students' achievement of basic skills (in English and/or Spanish) in the following areas: reading, writing, listening, comprehension, and speaking. Test item difficulties are low in order to differentiate among students in the lower quartile. All items in both editions (English and Spanish) were carefully reviewed for vocabulary load, grammatical construction, appropriateness of Spanish usage, racial and gender bias, and correctness of item content. Both editions are presented in three levels: level I (grades K-2), level II (grades 3-6), and level III (grades 7-12). All level I subtests are individually administered. The speaking subtests for levels II and III are also individually administered so that regional differences in vocabulary usage or dialect can be accommodated by the teacher. The use of criterion-referenced interpretation and locally developed cut-off scores is recommended. Test development and related research are described in the technical manual. The examination kit includes: one Spanish and one English test booklet for each level, examiner's directions for each level, picture stimulus booklet or card for each level, and one technical manual. Examiner required. Level II and III (except speaking subtests) suitable for group use.

Untimed: 41 minutes per edition

Range: Grades K-12

Scoring: Hand key

Cost: 35 level I test booklets (English or Spanish Edition: includes examiner's directions and picture stimulus booklet) $11.28; 35 level II or level III test booklets (either edition: includes examiner's directions and picture stimulus card) $19.95; 35 Digitek answer sheets for level I or levels II and III (for use with both editions) $9.24; Digitek scoring masks (Spanish levels II and III, English level II, or English level III) $1.95; 250 NCS answer sheets $65.91; technical manual $5.67; examination kit $11.61.

Publisher: The Riverside Publishing Company

ORAL LANGUAGE EVALUATION (OLE)

Nicholas J. Silvaroli, Jann T. Skinner, and J.O. "Rocky" Maynes

child

Purpose: Assesses the language development in English and Spanish of bilingual children. Used for academic planning and placement. Used by teachers with limited language evaluation experience and/or structural linguistic training.

Description: Multiple item oral response test assessing oral language skills in English and Spanish. Classifies the children's development in English and/or Spanish along a six-point continuum of language development: labeling, basic sentences, language expansion, connecting-relating-modifying, storytelling-concrete, and storytelling-abstract. Part I (assessment) establishes a beginning oral language level in either English or Spanish. Part II (diagnosis) identifies pre-post test data and specific language responses that pinpoint specific oral language needs. Part II (prescription) provides the teacher with general and specific instructional activities and/or suggestions for helping students develop their oral language. Examiner required. Not suitable for group use.

Untimed: Varies

Range: Children

Scoring: Examiner evaluated

Cost: Test manual $8.95.

Publisher: EMC Publishing

TEST OF ENGLISH FOR INTERNATIONAL COMMUNICATION (TOEIC)

Refer to page 216.

Mathematics

Basic Math Skills

ASSESSMENT IN MATHEMATICS

R. W. Strong and Somerset Local Education Authority

child, teen

Purpose: Assesses the mathematics competencies of primary and lower secondary students. Determines readiness to progress to new work.

Description: 86 multiple item paper-pencil graded test sheets assessing student abilities in five areas of work common to most mathematics instructional programs: number measure, probability and statistics, shape, and relations. Test sheets are printed as reproducible photocopy masters, providing a flexible assortment of graded tests for use in conjunction with existing instructional programs. The teacher's book provides the background to the tests, objectives and information for each test, and scoring procedures (including reduced reproductions of the pupils' sheets with correct answers indicated). Record cards are available for systematically recording each child's achievement and progress. Examiner required. Suitable for group use. BRITISH PUBLISHER

Untimed: Varies

Range: Primary and lower secondary school students

Scoring: Examiner evaluated

Cost: Teacher's book and 86 pupils' sheets £12.95; 25 record cards £4.25.

Publisher: Macmillan Education

BASIC VISUAL-MOTOR ASSOCIATION TEST

Refer to page 143.

DIAGNOSTIC TEST OF ARITHMETIC STRATEGIES (DTAS)

Herbert P. Ginsburg and Steven C. Mathews

child

Purpose: Evaluates the strategies grade school children use to solve basic arithmetic problems. Used to plan instructional programs.

Description: Multiple item paper-pencil test measuring the procedures children use to perform arithmetic calculation in addition, subtraction, multiplication, and division. Results provide a profile of each student's faulty calculational strategies and potential strengths. The examiner's manual includes an extensive section dealing with interpretation of test results as well as suggested remedial approaches. Examiner required. Suitable for group use.

Untimed: Varies

Range: Elementary school children

Scoring: Examiner evaluated

Cost: Complete kit (examiner's manual, 25 addition, subtraction, multiplication, and division answer sheets and student worksheets) $48.00.

Publisher: Pro-Ed

EARLY MATHEMATICAL LANGUAGE

Margaret K.R. Williams and Heather J. Somerwill

child

Purpose: Assesses children's capacity to understand and use mathematical language. Used for preventive testing in the first years of schooling, and for diagnostic testing with older children who are known to have difficulties in mathematics.

Description: Six multiple item paper-pencil pupil test booklets

assessing student knowledge and use of mathematical language in the following areas: position in space, weight and shape, number, volume and capacity, length, and time. The books are completely non-verbal, containing picture story sequences about the adventures of a family of bears. Test items are designed to stimulate and assess the use of relevant mathematical language. The teacher's book provides guidelines on using the pupil books and making the assessments, as well as suggestions for follow-up remedial work. Key pages from the pupils' books (printed as spirit duplicator masters) are available as worksheets for use as part of the assessments, or for follow-up work as suggested in the teacher's book. Examiner required. Suitable for group use.
BRITISH PUBLISHER

Untimed: Varies

Range: Children

Scoring: Examiner evaluated

Cost: Teacher's book and 6 pupil books £5.50; 16 worksheets £5.50; 25 record sheets £1.75.

Publisher: Macmillan Education

THE ENRIGHT™ DIAGNOSTIC INVENTORY OF BASIC ARITHMETIC SKILLS

Brian E. Enright

child grades 1-6

Purpose: Measures abilities in basic arithmetic computation skills. Used for academic placement, to plan remedial instruction programs, and to establish IEP's for students with special arithmetic needs (typically the lowest 20%).

Description: Four multiple item paper-pencil components assessing 144 arithmetic skills arranged in 13 computation skill sections (addition, subtraction, multiplication, and division of whole numbers, fractions, and decimals, and conversion of fractions). Components include: the wide-range placement test (26 items; available in equivalent forms A and B), skill placement tests (one test for each of the 13 skill sections, all available in forms A and B), basic facts tests (four tests of 50 items each measuring basic facts in addition, subtraction, multiplication, and division), and the skill tests (five items for each of the 144 skills assessed). The examiner administers only the skill placement tests indicated by the wide-range placement test or the student's current classroom problems, and then administers only the skill tests indicated by the student's performance on the skill placement tests. An instructional objective is listed for each of the 144 skills, and the error patterns associated with that skill. Error analysis leads directly to planning and development of remedial instruction. The arithmetic record book is used to track the progress of an individual student in each of the 13 sections of the inventory. The class record sheet is used to track the progress of each class member in each of the 13 sections. The student tests and arithmetic books combine consumable copies of all tests included in the inventory as well as a record-keeping system for teacher use. Three optional individual progress report sheets (one each for whole numbers, fractions, and decimals) are available for use as a tool in discussing with parents the student's growth in arithmetic and in developing IEP's. Video tape for inservice of examiners available. Examiner required. Suitable for group use.

Untimed: Varies

Range: Grades 1-6

Scoring: Examiner evaluated

Cost: Student tests and arithmetic record books (10-pack) $29.50; individual progress record sheets (30-pack) $14.95.

Publisher: Curriculum Associates, Inc.

KRANER PRESCHOOL MATH INVENTORY

Robert E. Kraner

child

Purpose: Assesses the math skills of preschool children. Used for planning early math programs.

Description: Multiple item oral response test measuring attainment of criterion-referenced mathematics skills and concepts by preschool children. Areas measured include 7 categories and 77 quantitative concepts. A receptive age and mastery age are identified in the development of each skill/concept. Examiner required. Not suitable for group use.

Untimed: Varies

Range: Ages 3-6.5 years

Scoring: Examiner evaluated

Cost: Complete program (test manual, 25 scoring forms, classroom record sheet, 5 instructional record forms, 25 math/screen test booklets) $53.00.

Publisher: DLM Teaching Resources

INDIVIDUALIZED CRITERION REFERENCED TESTING (ICRT)

Refer to page 87.

MATHEMATICS 8-12

National Foundation for Educational Research with Alan Brighouse, David Godber and Peter Patilla

child

Purpose: Assesses progress in the acquisition of mathematical skills and concepts taught in primary and first year secondary school programs. Administered at the end of the school year to measure individual and class achievement in mathematics.

Description: 50 item paper-pencil test measuring academic achievement in mathematics. Test items, many of which incorporate drawings or diagrams, are presented in a 12-page test booklet. Measures four skill areas: understanding, computation, application and factual recall. Available for five levels: Mathematics 8 (first year junior), Mathematics 9 (second year junior), Mathematics 10 (third year junior), Mathematics 11 (fourth year junior), and Mathematics 12 (first year secondary). Test titles indicate the age range for which they were designed; for example Mathematics 9 should be used towards the end of the academic year during which the pupils attain their ninth birthday. An overall standardized score compares each pupil's ability with the national average for the same age, and with classmates of differing ages. Consistent use of the series enables progress to be monitored from year to year. Subscores for each of the four skill areas indicate individual strengths and weaknesses in understanding, computation, application and factual recall. Manual includes: discussion of background, content and use of tests, administration and scoring instructions, scoring keys, interpretation guidelines, conversion tables, and technical information. Mathematics 9-12 are currently available. Mathematics 8 will be available in 1985. Examiner required. Suitable for group use.
BRITISH PUBLISHER

Untimed: Varies

Range: Ages 8-12

Scoring: Examiner evaluated

Cost: Manual (9-12 only) £3.45; 25 test booklets (9, 10, 11, or 12) £5.95; specimen set (manual and one of each test booklet 9-12) £3.95.

Publisher: NFER-Nelson Publishing Company Ltd.

MATHEMATICS TOPIC TESTS
Frances Cook Morrison

child, teen

Purpose: Measures skill and understanding of mathematical concepts. Identifies individual student's weaknesses in mathematics. Measures individual and group achievement in mathematics.

Description: Five multiple item paper-pencil subtests covering the following areas of mathematics: number and numeration, addition and subtraction with whole numbers, multiplication and division with whole numbers, operations with fractions, and multiplication and division with fractions. Manual includes directions for administration and scoring. Percentiles are derived for each group or class tested. Examiner required. Suitable for group use. BRITISH PUBLISHER

Untimed: Varies

Range: Ages 10-15 years

Scoring: Hand key

Cost: Specimen set (1 copy of each subtest and manual) £6.10.

Publisher: The Test Agency

MICHIGAN PRESCRIPTIVE PROGRAM IN MATH
William E. Lockhart

teen, adult

Purpose: Measures student abilities in mathematics skills. Identifies skill deficits. Used to help students obtain a 10th grade equivalency and pass the GED test in mathematics.

Description: Multiple item paper-pencil test assessing the following high school level mathematics skills: addition, subtraction, multiplication, division, fractions, averaging, decimals, changing decimals to percents, simple and compound interest, denominate numbers, reading line, bar and circle graphs, finding perimeter, area, and volume, square roots, proportions, set theory, laws of operation, Roman numerals, exponents, signs, simple equations, inequalities, sum of angles, coordinate geometry, theorems, graphical solutions, and slope. The test booklet, answer key, and math study materials are reusable; the student response sheet and individual prescription sheet are consumed. Math study materials have allowed students 1.5 to 3.5 math grade gain in 24 clock hours of study. Examiner required. Suitable for group use.

Untimed: Varies

Range: Middle school-adult

Scoring: Examiner evaluated

Cost: Test book $1.50; 7 response and prescription sheets $2.00; answer key $1.00; math study materials $9.00.

Publisher: Ann Arbor Publishers, Inc.

MORETON MATHEMATICS TESTS: LEVEL II
Andrews, Cochrane and Elkins

child grades 3-5

Purpose: Measures the mathematical abilities of primary school children.

Description: Multiple item paper-pencil test consisting of two subtests (Forms N and P). Form N measures numerical abilities. Form P measures mathematical operations. Metric measurement is used. Australian norms provided in terms of arithmetic ages, 15 point scale scores, and percentiles for grades 3, 4, and 5. Examiner required. Suitable for group use. AUSTRALIAN PUBLISHER

Untimed: Varies

Range: Grades 3-5

Scoring: Examiner required

Cost: Classroom kit (manual 40 form N and 40 form P tests) $14.00.

Publisher: Teaching and Testing Resources

MORETON MATHEMATICS TESTS: LEVEL III

Elkins, Andrews and Cochrane

child grades 5-7

Purpose: Measures the mathematics abilities of primary school children.

Description: Multiple item paper-pencil test measuring mathematical abilities involving numerical operations. Metric measurement is employed. Australian norms provided in terms of arithmetic ages, 15 point scale scores, and percentiles for grades 5, 6, and 7. Examiner required. Suitable for group use.
AUSTRALIAN PUBLISHER

Untimed: Varies

Range: Grades 5-7

Scoring: Examiner evaluated

Cost: Standard kit (manual and 100 tests) $14.00.

Publisher: Teaching and Testing Resources

PROGRESS TESTS IN MATHS

Roy Hollands

child

Purpose: Assesses mathematics achievement throughout the primary and middle school years. Measures both individual and group performance. Used for program planning and assessment.

Description: Six multiple item paper-pencil tests measuring the yearly progress in mathematics of children ages 7-12 years. Test items measure achievement of particular skills and sub-skills in the following mathematical areas: number, measure, shape, and pictorial representations. Each of the six tests corresponds to one year's work in mathematics and is intended for use with a particular age group, ranging from age seven (math 1) to age 12 (math 6). The tests are also suitable for diagnostic use with older students in remedial classes. Tests for the first three years can be read aloud by the teacher to minimize problems caused by the children's limited reading abilities. Test objectives are based on reference to existing math schemes, government and LEA guidelines, and the recommendations of a panel of teachers and advisers. Tests are scored on an A-E grading system. The teacher's manual provides information on the background of the series, objectives, administering the tests, modifying them to suit individual needs, and recording and interpreting the results. Suggestions are also provided for remedial and follow-up work where necessary. A secondary teacher's manual is available for use with tests 5 and 6 only. Examiner required. Suitable for group use.
BRITISH PUBLISHER

Untimed: Varies

Range: Ages 7-12 years

Scoring: Examiner evaluated

Cost: Evaluation pack (teacher's manual for levels 1-6 and one copy of each test) £4.50; secondary teacher's manual with one copy each of test 5 and 6 £2.50.

Publisher: Macmillan Education

TEST OF EARLY MATHEMATICS ABILITY (TEMA)

Herbert Ginsburg and Arthur J. Baroody

child

Purpose: Measures the mathematics performance of children ages 4-8 years. Diagnoses individual strengths and weaknesses. Used to plan instructional programs in mathematics.

Description: 26 item oral response or paper-pencil test assessing mathematical abilities in two domains: informal mathematics (concepts of relative magnitude, counting, and calculation) and formal mathematics (knowledge of convention number facts, calculation, and base ten concepts). A picture card is used to present each test item. Raw scores may be converted to standard scores, percentiles, and age equivalences. Criterion referenced interpretation leads directly to instructional objectives. Examiner required. Suitable for group use.

Untimed: Varies

Range: Ages 4-8 years

Scoring: Examiner evaluated

Cost: Complete kit (manual, 50 record forms, and 26 picture cards) $37.00.

Publisher: Pro-Ed

TEST OF MATHEMATICAL ABILITIES (TOMA)

Virginia L. Brown and Elizabeth McEntire

child, teen grades 3-10

Purpose: Assesses the mathematical attitudes and aptitudes of students grades 3-10. Used to plan and assess instructional programs in mathematics.

Description: Five paper-pencil subtests assessing knowledge, mastery, and attitudes in two major skill areas: story problems and computation. In addition to measuring the student's abilities, the following broad diagnostic areas are assessed: expressed attitudes toward mathematics, understanding of vocabulary as applied to mathematics, the functional use of mathematics as applied to our general culture, and the relationship between a student's attitudes and abilities and those of his peers. Normative information related to age and IQ is given for students ages 8-17 years, as well as graded mastery expectations for the "400" basic number facts. Scores differentiate diagnostically between students who have problems in mathematics and those who do not. Examiner required. Suitable for group use.

Untimed: Varies

Range: Grades 3-10

Scoring: Examiner evaluated

Cost: Complete kit (examiner's manual, 25 profile sheets, 25 student worksheets, 25 story problems) $39.00.

Publisher: Pro-Ed

Upper Math Skills

AMERICAN INVITATIONAL MATHEMATICS EXAMINATION (AIME)

teen grades 9-12

Purpose: Measures mathematical achievement of high school students with exceptional mathematical ability. Used to select students with the specific talents necessary for doing well on examinations such as the U.S.A. Mathematical Olympiad (USAMO).

Description: 15 item paper-pencil free-response test measuring mathematics abilities of selected high school students. No multiple-choice questions are included. Students submit their answers which are graded right or wrong. All problems can be solved using precalculus methods. Only students scoring above a cut off score announced each fall on the American High School Mathematics Examination (ASHME) are invited to participate in the examination, which in turn serves as the qualifying examination for the USAMO. Participating schools must register each fall with the Regional Examination Coordinators. Examiner required. Suitable for group use.

Timed: 3 hours

Range: High school students

Scoring: Scored by MAA Committee on High School Contests

Cost: Contact Dr. Walter E. Mientka at M.A.A. address.

Publisher: M.A.A. Committee on High School Examinations

ARITHMETIC AND MATH SPLIT FORM (FORM M)

Mary Meeker and Robert Meeker

teen grades 7 and up

Purpose: Assesses arithmetic and mathematics skills of intermediate, high school, and college students.

Description: Multiple item paper-pencil test assessing potential in arithmetic and mathematics. Discipline-focused test items are selected from the SOI-LA Basic Test. Administration requires Basic Test manual. Materials available to train any abilities not developed. Examiner required. Suitable for group use.

Timed: 1 hour

Range: Intermediate, high school, and college students

Scoring: Hand key; computer scoring and analysis available

Cost: Examiner's manual $22.00; test forms $1.95 each.

Publisher: SOI Institute

Religious Education

*No new tests available. Please refer to the First Edition of **TESTS** for a complete listing and description of tests currently available in this area.*

Science

General Science

GENERAL CHEMISTRY TEST: FORM 1983-S

college student

Purpose: Measures achievement upon completion of a year's course in freshman college chemistry.

Description: 80 item paper-pencil test measuring the following chemistry subject areas: states of matter, stoichiometry, carbon chemistry, solutions, acid-base chemistry, equilibria, electrochemistry and redox, thermodynamics and kinetics, descriptive chemistry, special topics, and laboratory skills. This form is a scrambled version of Form 1983. For use only by authorized chemistry teachers and administrators. Normative data available. Examiner required. Suitable for group use.

Timed: 110 minutes

Range: College

Scoring: Hand key

Cost: 25 tests $18.00; 25 answer sheets $3.00; scoring stencils $1.00; specimen set $5.00.

Publisher: Examinations Committee—American Chemical Society

HIGH SCHOOL ADVANCED CHEMISTRY: FORM 1984-ADV

teen grades 12 and up

Purpose: Measures achievement in advanced honors courses, typically at end of two years of high school chemistry. May be used for advanced placement and/or college credit at the freshman college level.

Description: Paper-pencil multiple-choice test measuring individual student achievement upon completion of two years of high school chemistry. Test contains general and quantitative questions in 10 areas: atomic structure (includes nuclear); chemical bonding, molecular geometry and carbon chemistry; thermodynamics; kinetics; solids, liquids, gases and solutions; acid-base chemistry; electrochemistry; chemical periodicity; and laboratory procedures and techniques. For use only by authorized chemistry teachers and administrators. Normative data available. Examiner required. Suitable for group use.

Timed: 110 minutes

Range: High school students and college freshmen

Scoring: Hand key

Cost: 25 tests $15.00; 25 answer sheets $3.00; scoring stencils $1.00; specimen set $5.00.

Publisher: Examinations Committee—American Chemical Society

HIGH SCHOOL CHEMISTRY: FORM 1983-S

teen grades 12 and up

Purpose: Measures achievement in high school chemistry upon completion of one year course. Used as end of course test. May also be used for placement in first-year college chemistry course.

Description: Paper-pencil multiple-choice test measures individual student achievement in a one year high school chemistry course. Form 1983-S is a scrambled version of the High School Chemistry Form 1983 examination. The test consists of two parts containing four sections each—Introductory Concepts; Physical Concepts; Atomic and Molecular Concepts; and Solutions Concepts. For use only by authorized chemistry teachers and administrators. Normative data available. Examiner required. Suitable for group use.

Timed: Form 1984 ADV—110 minutes; form 1983-S—80 minutes

Range: High school students and college freshmen

Scoring: Hand key

Cost: 25 tests (either form) $15.00; 25 answer sheets (either form) $3.00; scoring stencils (either form) $1.00; specimen set $5.00.

Publisher: Examinations Committee—American Chemical Society

ORGANIC CHEMISTRY: FORM 1984-B

college student

Purpose: Measures achievement in college brief organic chemistry courses, typically of one semester or one quarter duration.

Description: 70 item paper-pencil multiple-choice test measuring knowledge of organic chemistry. This test is designed for a brief course in organic chemistry, typically one semester or one quarter, for programs requiring only an introduction to organic chemistry, and not for majors in chemistry. (For the latter, see Organic Chemistry 1978 and/or 1982.) For use only by authorized chemistry teachers and administrators. Normative data available. Examiner required. Suitable for group use.

Timed: 90 minutes

Range: College

Scoring: Hand key

Cost: 25 tests $18.00; 25 answer sheets $3.00; scoring stencils $1.00; specimen set $5.00.

Publisher: Examinations Committee—American Chemical Society

Health Science

*No new tests available. Please refer to the First Edition of **TESTS** for a complete listing and description of tests currently available in this area.*

Social Studies

*No new tests available. Please refer to the First Edition of **TESTS** for a complete listing and description of tests currently available in this area.*

Achievement and Aptitude

Academic

AMERICAN SCHOOL ACHIEVEMENT TESTS

Willis E. Pratt, George A. W. Stouffer, Jr. and Jean R. Yanuzzi

child grades 1-9 ☞ ✍

Purpose: Measures the basic skills and subject matter content incorporated in elementary and junior high school programs. Identifies students with learning disabilities.

Description: Multiple item paper-pencil tests measuring achievement in reading, mathematics, language, science, and social studies. Available in equivalent forms X and Y for four levels: primary 1 (grade 1), primary 2 (grades 2-3), intermediate (grades 4-6) and advanced (grades 7-9). In addition to measuring progress in a subject area, each test yields results for analysis of skills and disabilities. All test kits include necessary accessories and 35 test booklets. Examiner required. Intended for group use.

Untimed: Varies

Range: Grades 1-9

Scoring: Self-scored

Cost: Primary 1 (X or Y) $19.00; Primary 2 (Y only) $24.00; Intermediate (X or Y) $29.00; Advanced (X or Y) $29.00.

Publisher: Pro-Ed

BASIC ACHIEVEMENT SKILLS INDIVIDUAL SCREENER (BASIS)

The Psychological Corporation, Measurement Division staff

child, teen grades 1-12 ☞ ✍

Purpose: Measures achievement in reading, mathematics, and spelling for students grades 1-12 (with an optional writing test for grades 3-8). Assesses individual students' academic strengths and weaknesses with both norm-referenced and criterion-referenced information. Used in program planning and evaluation, academic placement, and establishing IEP's.

Description: Three subtests assessing academic achievement in reading, mathematics, and spelling. Test items are grouped in grade-referenced clusters, which constitute the basic unit of administration. Testing begins at a grade cluster with which the student is expected to have little difficulty, and continues until the student fails to reach the criteria for a particular cluster. The clusters range from Readiness through Grade 8 for reading and mathematics, and from Grades 1-8 for spelling. The reading test assesses comprehension of graded passages. The student is required to read the passages aloud and supply the missing words (cloze technique). Comprehension at the lower levels is assessed by word reading and sentence reading, and readiness is measured by letter identification and visual discrimination. The mathematics test consists of a Readiness subtest and assesses computation and problem solving above that level. The student works on the computation items directly in the record form. Word problems are dictated by the teacher and require no reading on the part of the student. The spelling test consists of clusters of words, Grades 1-8, which are dictated in sentence contexts. The student writes the words on the record form. An optional writing exercise (average samples provided for grades 3-8) requires the student to write descriptively for ten minutes. Samples are scored by comparison with criterion samples for each grade. Criterion-referenced scores for the subtests describe performance in basic skills and suggest grade and textbook placement. Raw scores can be converted to standard scores, age- and grade-based percentile ranks, stanines, grade equivalents, and age equivalents. Manual includes information for administering, scoring, and interpreting the tests. Examiner required. Not suitable for group use.

Untimed: 1 hour (including Writing Test)

Range: Grades 1-12

Scoring: Examiner evaluated

Cost: Examiner's kit (manual, content booklet, 2 record forms) $30.00.

Publisher: The Psychological Corporation

THE BRIGANCE® DIAGNOSTIC ASSESSMENT OF BASIC SKILLS—SPANISH EDITION

Albert H. Brigance

---

child, teen   pre K-9

Purpose: Measures the academic skills of Spanish-speaking students. Distinguishes language barriers from learning disabilities. Used by bilingual, ESL, migrant, and bilingual special educators to identify, develop, implement, and evaluate appropriate academic programs for Spanish-speaking students.

Description: 102 multiple item paper-pencil, oral response and direct observation diagnostic tests and eight multiple item paper-pencil or oral response screening forms assess Spanish-speaking students' abilities in the following areas: readiness, speech, functional word recognition, oral reading, reading comprehension, word analysis, listening, writing and alphabetizing, numbers and computation, and measurement. The 102 diagnostic assessments are presented in a loose-leaf binder. Many of the tests include both a student and examiner page, oriented so that the student faces the examiner during oral assessments. Directions to the examiner are written in English; directions to the student are written in Spanish. For assessments involved in dominant language screening, directions to the student are written in English as well as Spanish. For individual or group written assessments, the student page can be removed from the binder and used as a black-line master. Some assessments, such as those evaluating gross-motor and listening skills, include only the examiner page.

The diagnostic tests identify which skills the student has and has not mastered, indicate which students might have learning disabilities, and determine individual instructional objectives. The screening forms include the dominant language screening form and seven screening forms assessing skills that indicate grade-level competency from kindergarten to grade 6. The dominant language form provides a means of comparing a student's performance in English and Spanish on all of the oral language and literacy diagnostic assessments. Results of this screening are used to place students in appropriate ESL and bilingual programs. Results of the grade level screening forms can be used to place students at the appropriate instructional level and to identify students in need of further evaluation. Individual student record books graphically record at each testing the level of competency that the student has achieved.

An optional class record book tracks the progress of 35 students. The diagnostic tests and screening forms together facilitate compliance with: the Lau Remedies, Bilingual Education Act, Chapter I Basic and Chapter I Migrant Education programs, and P.L. 94-142 as well as nondiscriminatory testing requirements for Spanish-speaking students. An extensive bibliography includes research and textbooks used to validate the scope, sequence, and grade levels of the skills assessed. Video tape program for inservice training of examiners available. Examiner required. Many sections suitable for group use.

Untimed: Varies

Range: Preschool-junior high school students

Scoring: Examiner evaluated

Cost: Assessment book and 10 student record books $89.00; class record book $6.95; additional record books available in packages of 10 ($15.95) and 100 ($144.00).

Publisher: Curriculum Associates, Inc.

THE BRIGANCE® DIAGNOSTIC COMPREHENSIVE INVENTORY OF BASIC SKILLS (CIBS)

Albert H. Brigance

child, teen pre K-9

Purpose: Measures attainment of basic academic skills from pre-kindergarten to junior high school. Used to screen kindergarten and first-grade students, to meet minimal competency requirements, to develop IEP's, and for academic placement.

Description: 203 multiple item variable format tests assessing skill sequences in the following 22 sections: readiness, speech, word recognition grade placement, oral reading, reading comprehension, listening, functional word recognition, word analysis, reference skills, graphs and maps, spelling, writing, math grade placement, numbers, number facts, computation of whole numbers, decimals, per cents, word problems, metrics, and math vocabulary. Different assessment methods may be used to accommodate different situations: parent interview, teacher observation, group or individual administration, and informal appraisal of student performance in daily work. Assessment is initiated at the skill level at which the student will clearly be successful and continues until the student's level of achievement for that skill is attained. More than half of the assessments can be used for group as well as individual administration. Alternate forms A and B are available for 51 skill sequences for pre- and post-testing. All skill sequences are referenced to specific instructional objectives and grade level expectations. The comprehensive record book indicates graphically at each testing what level of competency the student has achieved. An optional class record book tracks the progress of 30 students. IEP objective forms are available for readiness, reading, mathematics, and individual use (blank forms). An extensive bibliography lists research and textbooks used to validate the scope, sequence, and grade levels of the skills assessed. Video tape for inservice training of examiners available. Examiner required. Many sections suitable for group use.

Untimed: Varies

Range: Pre-kindergarten to junior high school students

Scoring: Examiner evaluated

Cost: Test book and 10 comprehensive record books $99.00; class record book $6.95; 30 IEP objective forms $15.95; CIBS excerpts available at no charge; 10 additional record books $15.00; 100 additional record books $145.00.

Publisher: Curriculum Associates, Inc.

THE BRIGANCE® DIAGNOSTIC INVENTORY OF BASIC SKILLS

Albert H. Brigance

---

child grades K-6

Purpose: Measures student mastery of basic academic skills from kindergarten to grade 6. Used for academic placement, mainstreaming students, competency evaluations, and IEP development and evaluation.

Description: 143 paper-pencil or oral response tests assessing student mastery in the subskill areas of readiness, reading, language arts, and math. Test items are arranged in developmental and sequential order. Major skill sections include: readiness, word recognition, reading (fluency and level), word analysis, vocabulary, handwriting, grammar mechanics, spelling, reference skills, math placement, numbers, operations, measurement, and geometry. IEP objectives are included for each of the 143 academic skills assessed. The individual student record book shows graphically at each testing to what point of competency the student has progressed and identifies the student's current instructional goals. An optional class record book monitors the progress of 35 students and forms a comprehensive matrix of individual student's levels. IEP objective forms available for reading, readiness, mathematics, and individual use (blank form). Video tape program for inservice training of examiners also available. Examiner required. Some sections suitable for group use.

Untimed: Varies

Range: Grades K-6

Scoring: Examiner evaluated

Cost: Assessment book and 10 individual record books $69.95; class record book $5.95; test excerpts available free of charge; 10 record books $10.95; 100 record books $95.00.

Publisher: Curriculum Associates, Inc.

THE BRIGANCE® DIAGNOSTIC INVENTORY OF ESSENTIAL SKILLS

Albert H. Brigance

---

child, teen grades 4-12

Purpose: Measures a student's mastery of skills essential to success as a citizen, consumer, worker, and family member. Used in secondary programs serving students with special needs—typically the lowest 20%. Used to develop IEP's.

Description: 186 paper-pencil or oral response skill assessments in grade levels 4-12 measuring minimal academic and vocational competencies. Assesses basic skills in the areas of reading, language arts and math, and includes rating scales to measure applied skills that cannot be assessed objectively, including: health and attitude, responsibility and self-discipline, job interview preparation, auto safety, and communication. Other practical assessments include: food and clothing, money and finance, travel and transportation, and communication and telephone skills. Test results identify basic skills which have and have not been mastered, areas of strengths and weaknesses in academic and practical skills, and instructional objectives for a specified skill level. Individual record books indicate graphically at each testing what level of competency the student has achieved and indicate the student's current instructional goals. An optional class record book monitors the progress of 30 students and forms a matrix of specific student competencies. IEP objective forms are available for reading, writing and spelling, mathematics, and individual use (blank form). Tests may be administered by teachers, aides or parent volunteers. Video tape program for inservice training of examiners also available. Examiner required. Some sections suitable for group use.

Untimed: Varies

Range: Grades 4-12

Scoring: Examiner evaluated

Cost: Assessment book and 10 individual record books $99.95; class record book $7.50; test excerpt available free of charge; additional record books available in packages of 10 ($16.95) and 100 ($149.00).

Publisher: Curriculum Associates, Inc.

CHECK UP TESTS

Betty Kerr, Ronald Deadman, Melvyn Nolan, Redvers Brandling and Peter Pile

child

Purpose: Measures student progress in core subjects during the last four years of primary school. Used for classroom planning and program assessment.

Description: Six books, each containing 22 multiple item paper-pencil tests, assessing student abilities in the following subjects: English composition, English language, mathematics, workskills, general knowledge, and science. The English composition, English language, mathematics, and workskills tests are available for three levels: first check ups (ages 8-9 years), intermediate check ups (ages 9-10 years), and check ups (ages 10-11 years). The general knowledge and science tests are available for check ups (10-11 years) only. Each book includes: practice and revision material to build up student confidence, a resource bank of ideas and methods for teaching and testing, and feedback for teachers, showing where teaching is most effective and where extra attention might need to be directed. Each book is also available in a teacher's edition with a complete set of answers. Examiner required. Suitable for group use.
BRITISH PUBLISHER

Untimed: One class period

Range: Ages 8-11 years

Scoring: Examiner evaluated

Cost: Pupils' books each 95p; teacher's books (except science test) £2.25; teacher's book for science test £2.50.

Publisher: Macmillan Education

THE CHILD CENTER OPERATIONAL ASSESSMENT TOOL (OAT)

CHILD Center multidisciplinary team

child

Purpose: Diagnoses the learning needs of elementary school children. Identifies students in need of further evaluation. Monitors educational progress during the course of the year. Used by both regular and special classroom teachers.

Description: Six subtests assess skills in the following areas: reading, spelling, math concepts, math operations, language, and behavior. Criterion-referenced tests in reading, spelling, math concepts and math operations present test items in logical sequence from pre-academic to most complex. The language test assesses underlying learning abilities and identifies modality preferences. The behavior questionnaire identifies the child's profile in the following behavioral areas: learning, coordination, self-esteem, concentration, emotional lability, motor expression, involuntary behavior, and school attitude. Results yield precise instructional skill levels for each child in reading, spelling, and math and identify specific teaching objectives. Parents and aides may administer the test. Additional materials available include: *How to Use OAT Reading/Spelling Tests* and *The OAT Reading/Spelling Program.* Examiner required. Not suitable for group use.

Untimed: Varies

Range: Grades K-6; Spec Ed Grades K-12

Scoring: Examiner evaluated

Cost: OAT specimen set (includes one each: reading test, spelling test, examiner's manual-spelling tests, and *How To Use the OAT Reading/Spelling Tests* $7.00.

Publisher: The CHILD Center

CLYMER-BARRETT READINESS TEST

Refer to page 118.

DIAGNOSTIC ACHIEVEMENT BATTERY (DAB)

Phyllis L. Newcomer and Delores Curtis

child, teen

Purpose: Assesses a child's ability to listen, speak, read, write, and do simple mathematics. Diagnoses learning disabilities.

Description: 10 paper-pencil and oral response subtests assess the following five components of a child's verbal and mathematical skills: listening (listening comprehension test and characteristics test), speaking (synonyms test and grammar completion test), reading (alphabet/word knowledge test and reading comprehension test), writing (written conventions test and creative writing test), and math (math reasoning test and math calculation test). Results, converted to standard scores, provide a profile of the child's strengths and weaknesses on each of the five components as well as the ten subtests. The components of the test may be administered independently, depending on the needs of the child being tested. Examiner required. The creative writing, writing conventions, and math computation subtests may be administered to small groups; the other subtests must be individually administered.

Untimed: Varies

Range: Ages 5-14 years

Scoring: Examiner evaluated

Cost: Complete kit (manual, 25 student work sheets, 25 profile/answer sheets, and picture book, all in a storage box) $51.00.

Publisher: Pro-Ed

HARRISON-STROUD READING READINESS PROFILE

M. Lucille Harrison and James B. Stroud

child K-1

Purpose: Measures specific abilities and skills that children use in learning to read. Identifies areas in which children may need help before or during initial reading instruction.

Description: Five multiple item paper-pencil tests assessing the following pre-reading skills: using symbols, making visual discriminations, using context, making auditory discriminations, and using context and auditory clues. These tests may be administered to groups of 12-15 students at a time. An optional individual test identifies in approximately three minutes how well a student knows the names of the diffferent capital and lower case letters. Raw scores for the tests are plotted on a chart which determines the percentile rank of each score and identifies the strengths and weaknesses of each student. Examiner required. Suitable for group use.

Untimed: 80 minutes

Range: Grades K-1

Scoring: Examiner evaluated

Cost: Test kit (35 consumable test booklets each for parts 1, 2, and 3; manual class record sheet, letter card, and scoring mask) $26.07; examination kit $4.74.

Publisher: The Riverside Publishing Company

INDIVIDUALIZED CRITERION REFERENCED TESTING (ICRT)

child

Purpose: Measures student progress and achievement against a specific set of objectives in reading and mathematics. Measures student mastery of specific skills. Used for program planning, instructional management, and program assessment.

Description: 718 item paper-pencil test assessing student skills in math and reading. The reading test (334 items) measures skills in the following areas: phonetic analysis, structural analysis, word function skills, and comprehension. Items are arranged in 38 color-coded test booklets divided into eight levels. The mathematics test (384 items) measures knowledge of whole number operations, fractions, measurement, geometry, decimals/per cent, and special topics. Items are arranged in 51 test booklets divided into six levels. Tests measure the students' mastery or lack of mastery for each skill or concept tested. Placement tests and procedures are provided for both reading and math to insure that students are tested at a level compatible with their abilities. These placement tests indicate which five reading tests and which five mathematics tests should be administered for the actual testing. Three computer reports are provided. The student report identifies for each student which skills have been mastered, which skills need review, and which skills should be attempted next. The teacher report provides a list of students who attempted each objective, a list of students who passed each objective, a list of students in need of review for each objective, and groupings of students by their approximate working level in the subject tests. The administrative report provides a narrative and statistical summary of objectives tested (a summary that is compiled by class, building, and district), as well as a statistical summary of the number of students who either mastered, partially mastered, or failed to master each objective.

Individual student records are kept in separate student profile folders for reading (four-page folder) and mathematics (six-page folder). The profile folders list each objective sequentially by objective number, booklet number, and level, with spaces for recording initial mastery or subsequent mastery of each objective. Benchmark tests are also provided for interim assessment of student progress. These tests are in the form of color-coded cards which contain two test items for one objective per side of card. Objective-by-objective correlations are also provided for more than 150 reading materials and more than 50 mathematics materials. Examiner required. Suitable for group use.

Untimed: Varies

Range: Elementary school students

Scoring: Placement tests—examiner evaluated; ICRT tests—computer scored

Cost: Reading tests (level 1-8) each level $20.00; math tests (level 1-5) each level $20.00; math tests level 6 up $97.00, sample sets (reading or math) $26.00.

Publisher: Educational Development Corporation

LIFE SKILLS: FORMS 1 AND 2

Kenneth Majer and Dena Wadell

teen grades 9-12

Purpose: Assesses student and group competency in basic reading and mathematics skills that students and adults must use daily.

Description: Two multiple item paper-pencil subtests measuring functional competencies in reading and mathematics. The reading test includes four objectives which measure the ability to follow directions (labels, signs); three objectives which measure locating and understanding references (phone books, catalogs); five objectives which measure interpretation and use of information (want ads, lease agreements); and two objectives which measure the understanding of forms (taxes, installment purchases). The mathematics test objectives are computing basic consumer problems; applying principles of per cent, interest, and fractions; identifying, estimating, and converting time, currency, and measurements; and interpreting graphs, charts, and statistics. The manual includes test administration procedures, scoring, and basic technical data. The technical supplement provides comprehensive information. Two forms of the test are available for pretest-posttest experimental studies. Examiner required. Suitable for group use.

Timed: Reading test—40 minutes; mathematics test—40 minutes

Range: Grades 9-12

Scoring: Examiner evaluated; computer scoring available

Cost: (1983-84) 35 test booklets (form 1 or 2) $36.09; 35 self-mark answer sheets $20.61; 35 MRC answer sheets $15.45; manual $2.70; technical supplement $11.01; examination kit (both test booklets and manual) $2.88.

Publisher: The Riverside Publishing Company

MARTINEZ ASSESSMENT OF THE BASIC SKILLS

David Martinez

LD students

Purpose: Diagnoses deficiencies in basic academic skills. Used with learning disabled, mildly to moderately retarded, and other academically troubled students.

Description: Multiple item paper-pencil test consisting of six subtests, each testing proficiency in a different basic skill area. The Diagnostic Counting and Numerals Test covers fourteen beginning mathematical skills. The Diagnostic Arithmetic Test identifies computational performance in seven skill areas. The Diagnostic Reading Test assesses prereading skills, symbol-sound correspondences, phonically irregular sight words, sound patterns, silent letters, and related word study skills. The Diagnostic Spelling Test assesses spelling skills in writing letters, words, and sentences. the Diagnostic Primary Language Concepts Test assesses twenty-four language concept skills relating to such classroom activities as circling, underlining, and crossing out. The Diagnostic Time Telling Test assesses fourteen skill areas with optional assessment of digital clock time available. Individual student performance profiles provide for pre-post test comparison. Suitable for group use.

Untimed: Varies

Range: Learning disabled, mildly to moderately retarded, and academically troubled students

Scoring: Examiner evaluated

Cost: Complete Test Kit (1 administration manual, 5 student profile charts, 5 student response and record booklets for each diagnostic test: Spelling, Arithmetic, Counting and Numerals, Time Telling, Primary Language Concepts, and Reading) $69.95.

Publisher: ASIEP Education Company

THE MARYLAND-BALTIMORE COUNTY DESIGN FOR BASIC EDUCATION (BCD TEST)

Adult educators under a federal 310 grant

adult

Purpose: Measures the skills adults must master to achieve literacy. Used for program planning and placement in adult literacy courses.

Description: 21 oral response subtests assessing strengths, weaknesses, and deficits in pre-reading skills. Subtests may be given in any order. The manual includes instructions for administering and scoring the test, as well as criterion-referenced guidelines for interpreting the results. Correlation charts identify appropriate remediation programs for specific pre-reading skill deficits. May be administered by non-specialists. Examiner required. Not suitable for group use.

Untimed: 10 minutes per subtest

Range: Non-reading adults

Scoring: Examiner evaluated

Cost: Test $2.50; manual $9.95.

Publisher: Cambridge

NLN ACHIEVEMENT TESTS FOR PRACTICAL NURSING (ALL PRACTICAL NURSING PROGRAMS)

nursing student

Purpose: Appraises achievement in practical/vocational nursing programs. Measures individual student achievement in the nursing program and enables faculty to evaluate specific course or program objectives in terms of nationally accepted objectives in nursing, and to compare the scores of students in a nursing program with those of students throughout the country.

Description: 8 paper-pencil multiple-choice tests, each consisting of 80-170 questions and requiring 1½-3 hours to complete, are given in the following areas: comprehensive nursing achievement test for practical nursing students, medical-surgical nursing for practical nursing students, maternity nursing for practical nursing students, mental health concepts for practical nursing students, nursing of children for practical nursing students, pharmacology for practical nursing students, psychiatric nursing concepts for practical nursing students, and three units of content (TUC) for practical nursing students. Test items have been developed in cooperation with faculty members throughout the United States, reflecting the objectives and subject-matter content of practical/vocational nursing programs from all geographic areas.

All test papers must be returned to NLN Test Service for scoring. Reports on test results are returned to the program within ten working days after the receipt of the answer sheets. Reports include: raw scores and percentiles, item descriptors, a list of omitted or incorrectly answered items for each student, and an additional group analysis when more than ten students are tested as a group. NLN encourages faculty members to review the tests before ordering them to insure that appropriate subject-matter content areas have been covered. NLN achievement tests may be used in the United States, its territories, and Canada by state- or province-approved programs preparing students for nurse practice; by hospitals and colleges which are approved to provide instruction to students from such programs; and by nurse licensing authorities in the United States and Canada or their agents. Requests for use by any other program are evaluated individually. Tests are available in English only. Examiner required. Suitable for group use.

Untimed: 1½-3 hours per test

Range: Students in practical/vocational nursing programs

Scoring: Computer scored

Cost: Test service (test booklets, answer sheets, directions for administration, and scoring service) $3.00-$7.00 per student per test.

Publisher: National League for Nursing

NLN ACHIEVEMENT TESTS FOR PRACTICAL NURSING: COMPREHENSIVE NURSING ACHIEVEMENT TEST FOR PRACTICAL NURSING STUDENTS (FORM 3513)

nursing student

Purpose: Measures general achievement of graduating students in practical/vocational nursing programs. Measures individual student achievement and evaluates program objectives in terms of nationally recognized objectives in nursing.

Description: 170 item paper-pencil multiple-choice test measuring the full range of knowledge presented in programs that prepare students for practical nursing. Questions pertain to case situations that are representative of conditions commonly encountered by the beginning practitioner in health care settings. The situations presented include: medical-surgical nursing, nursing during childbearing, and nursing of children. The questions call for the application of knowledge in the assessment of client status; planning; intervention in basic nursing situations; evaluating; recording, and reporting. Questions related to growth and development, mental health concepts, basic communication techniques, medication administration and effects, as well as nutrition, are integrated throughout. A total score along with subscores in broad clinical areas are reported in the form of individual diagnostic profiles (two copies are provided—one for distribution to students and one for faculty analysis). Norms provided for practical nursing students. Intended for administration at the end of the students' program to assess readiness for the nurse licensure examination and for practice. Sample test available for faculty review. Examiner required. Suitable for group use.

Untimed: 3 hours

Range: Graduate students in practical/vocational nursing programs

Scoring: Computer scored

Cost: Test service (test booklets, answer sheets, directions for administration, and scoring service) $7.00 per student tested.

Publisher: National League for Nursing

NLN ACHIEVEMENT TESTS FOR PRACTICAL NURSING: MATERNITY NURSING FOR PRACTICAL NURSING STUDENTS (FORM 1182)

nursing student

Purpose: Measures achievement of practical/vocational nursing students in maternity nursing. Measures individual student achievement and program objectives in terms of nationally accepted objectives in nursing.

Description: 110 item paper-pencil multiple-choice test measuring student knowledge of the objectives of maternity nursing related to nursing measures, including medications, nutrition, and communication. A total score and three subscores (antepartum; intrapartum and postpartum; and neonate) are provided based on a correction-for-guessing formula. Norms are reported for practical nursing students. Intended for administration after the students' completion of the course in maternity nursing. Sample test available for faculty review. Examiner required. Suitable for group use.

Untimed: 2 hours

Range: Students in practical/vocational nursing programs

Scoring: Computer scored

Cost: Test service (test booklets, answer sheets, directions for administration, and scoring service) $3.00 per student tested.

Publisher: National League for Nursing

NLN ACHIEVEMENT TESTS FOR PRACTICAL NURSING: MEDICAL SURGICAL NURSING FOR PRACTICAL NURSING STUDENTS (FORM 1982)

nursing student

Purpose: Measures achievement of practical/vocational nursing students in medical-surgical nursing. Measures individual achievement and evaluates program objectives in terms of nationally accepted objectives in nursing.

Description: 120 item paper-pencil multiple-choice test measuring knowledge and application of the facts and principles related to the care of medical and surgical patients. Questions refer to patient situations and represent a variety of ages and common conditions. Items relating to the practical nurse's role in drug and diet therapy are integrated throughout the test. A total score and two subscores (medical nursing and surgical nursing) are reported based on a correction-for-guessing formula. Norms are reported for practical nursing students. Intended for administration late in the students' program. Sample test available for faculty review. Examiner required. Suitable for group use.

Untimed: 2 hours

Range: Students in practical/vocational nursing program

Scoring: Computer scored

Cost: Test service (test booklets, answer sheets, directions for administration, and scoring service) $3.00 per student tested.

Publisher: National League for Nursing

NLN ACHIEVEMENT TESTS FOR PRACTICAL NURSING: MENTAL HEALTH CONCEPTS FOR PRACTICAL NURSING STUDENTS (FORM 0481)

nursing student

Purpose: Measures achievement of practical/vocational nursing students in mental health concepts. Measures individual student achievement and evaluates program objectives in terms of nationally accepted objectives in nursing.

Description: 100 item paper-pencil multiple-choice test measuring knowledge and application of mental health concepts to the general practice of practical nursing. About half of the questions are presented in case situations, testing mental health concepts relating to common conditions in general hospital practice. The balance of the test consists of individual questions, two-thirds of which relate to the care of adults and one-third of which relate to the care of children. A total score is reported based on a correction-for-guessing formula. Norms provided for practical nursing students. Sample test available for faculty review to determine the appropriate time for administration. Examiner required. Suitable for group use.

Untimed: 1½ hours

Range: Students in practical/vocational nursing programs

Scoring: Computer scored

Cost: Test service (test booklets, answer sheets, directions for administration, and scoring service) $3.00 per student tested.

Publisher: National League for Nursing

NLN ACHIEVEMENT TESTS FOR PRACTICAL NURSING: NURSING OF CHILDREN FOR PRACTICAL NURSING STUDENTS (FORM 4113)

nursing student ☞ ✍

Purpose: Measures achievement of practical/vocational nursing students in nursing care of children. Measures individual student achievement and evaluates program objectives in terms of nationally accepted objectives in nursing.

Description: 120 item paper-pencil multiple-choice test measuring achievement in nine objectives which are arranged in the following three subscores related to nursing of children. The questions in subscore A (normal growth and development) measure knowledge of growth and development in children, and nursing measures based on age-related needs including preventive measures. Items in subscore B (pathophysiologies and treatments) measure knowledge and recognition of various pathophysiological processes and treatments including nutrition and expected outcomes. Questions in subscore C (nursing measures) test knowledge of nursing measures commonly used in the care of children who are ill, including drug administration and communication skills. Questions about teaching and giving emotional support to family members are also included. A total score is provided in addition to the three subscores. All scores are based on the number of questions answered correctly. Norms are reported for practical nursing students. Intended for administration to students who have completed their major learning experience in the content area of the test. Sample test available for faculty review. Examiner required. Suitable for group use.

Untimed: 2 hours

Range: Students in practical/vocational nursing programs

Scoring: Computer scored

Cost: Test service (test booklets, answer sheets, directions for administration, and scoring service) $3.00 per student tested.

Publisher: National League for Nursing

NLN ACHIEVEMENT TESTS FOR PRACTICAL NURSING: PHARMACOLOGY FOR PRACTICAL NURSES (FORM 1782)

nursing student ☞ ✍

Purpose: Measures achievement of practical/vocational nursing students in pharmacology. Measures individual student achievement and evaluates program objectives in terms of nationally accepted objectives in nursing.

Description: 100 item paper-pencil multiple-choice test measuring general knowledge of pharmacology chiefly through the interpretation of orders, the observations necessary to detect the effects of common drugs, and the basic principles of drug administration. In addition to a total score, the following two subscores are provided: (A) principles of drug administration, calculations, and other implications for nursing; and (B) effects, therapeutic and other. All scores are based on a correction-for-guess formula. Norms are reported for practical nursing students. Intended for administration at the completion of the students' program. Sample test available for faculty review. Examiner required. Suitable for group use.

Untimed: 1½ hours

Range: Students in practical/vocational nursing programs

Scoring: Computer scored

Cost: Test service (test booklets, answer sheets, directions for administration, and scoring service) $3.00 per student tested.

Publisher: National League for Nursing

NLN ACHIEVEMENT TESTS FOR PRACTICAL NURSING: PSYCHIATRIC NURSING CONCEPTS FOR PRACTICAL NURSING STUDENTS (FORM 4313)

nursing student

Purpose: Measures achievement of practical/vocational nursing students in psychiatric nursing. Measures individual student achievement and evaluates program objectives in terms of nationally accepted objectives in nursing.

Description: 80 item paper-pencil multiple-choice test measuring knowledge and application of facts and principles related to the care of persons with mental disorders. A total score and two subscores (facts and principles of psychiatric nursing; and application of facts and principles of psychiatric nursing) are provided based on the number of questions answered correctly. Norms are reported for practical nursing students. Intended for administration after students have completed a course in psychiatric nursing. Sample test available for faculty review. Examiner required. Suitable for group use.

Untimed: 1½ hours

Range: Students in practical/vocational nursing programs

Scoring: Computer scored

Cost: Test service (test booklets, answer sheets, directions for administration, and scoring service) $3.00 per student tested.

Publisher: National League for Nursing

NLN ACHIEVEMENT TESTS FOR PRACTICAL NURSING: THREE UNITS OF CONTENT (TUC) (FORM 1482)

nursing student

Purpose: Measures achievement of practical/vocational nursing students in body structure and function, nursing procedures, and normal nutrition. Measures individual student achievement and evaluates program objectives in terms of nationally accepted objectives in nursing.

Description: 110 item paper-pencil multiple-choice test measuring achievement in three basic fields of instruction: body structure and function, nursing procedures, and normal nutrition. A total score and scores for each of the three areas covered are provided based on a correction-for-guessing formula. Norms are reported for practical nursing students. Suitable for administration early in the students' program after completion of the basic leanring experiences that are covered in the test. Sample tests available for faculty review. Examiner required. Suitable for group use.

Untimed: 2 hours

Range: Students in practical/vocational nursing programs

Scoring: Computer scored

Cost: Test service (test booklets, answer sheets, directions for administration, and scoring service) $3.50 per student tested.

Publisher: National League for Nursing

NLN ACHIEVEMENT TESTS FOR REGISTERED NURSING (ALL REGISTERED NURSING PROGRAMS)

nursing student

Purpose: Appraises achievement in all RN programs associate degree, baccalaureate, and diploma. Measures individual achievement in the nursing program and enables faculty to evaluate specific course or program objectives in terms of nationally accepted objectives in nursing, and to compare the scores of students in a nursing program with those of students throughout the country.

Description: Paper-pencil multiple-choice tests, each consisting of 80-210 questions and requiring 1½-3½ hours to complete, are given in the following areas: anatomy and physiology, basics in nursing (three tests: I, II, and III), chemistry, comprehensive nursing achievement, diet therapy and applied nutrition, fundamentals of drug therapy, maternity and child nursing, microbiology, natural sciences in nursing, normal nutrition, nursing care of adults with pathophysiological disturbances (two tests: I and II), nursing of children, nursing the childbearing family, pharmacology in clinical nursing, and psychiatric nursing. Test items have been developed in cooperation with faculty members throughout the United States, reflecting the objectives and subject-matter emphases of teachers from all geographic areas. Some achievement tests are designed to be given at the end of a course, some after the completion of major learning experiences that may include more than one course, or toward the end of the program. The timing of administration is dependent upon the individual school's curriculum organization.

All test papers must be returned to NLN Test Service for scoring. Reports on test results are returned to the program within ten working days after the receipt of the answer sheets. Reports include: raw scores and percentiles, item descriptors, a list of omitted or incorrectly answered items for each student, and an additional group analysis when more than ten students are tested as a group. NLN encourages faculty members to review the tests before ordering them to insure that appropriate subject-matter content areas have been covered.

NLN achievement tests may be used in the United States, its territories, and Canada by state- or province-approved programs preparing students for nurse practice; by hospitals and colleges which are approved to provide instruction to students from such programs; and by nurse licensing authorities in the United States and Canada or their agents. Requests for use by any other program are evaluated individually. Tests are available in English only. Examiner required. Suitable for group use.

Timed/Untimed: 1½-3½ hours per test

Range: Nursing students in RN programs

Scoring: Computer scored

Cost: Test service (test booklets, answer sheets, directions for administration, scoring of answer sheets, and reporting of test results) $3.00-$8.00 per student per test.

Publisher: National League for Nursing

NLN ACHIEVEMENT TESTS FOR REGISTERED NURSING: ANATOMY AND PHYSIOLOGY (FORM 1213)

nursing student

Purpose: Measures achievement of students in RN programs in anatomy and physiology. Used to evaluate individual student achievement and program objectives in terms of nationally accepted objectives in nursing.

Description: 115 item paper-pencil multiple-choice test measuring knowledge of anatomy and physiology in the following subject-matter areas: cellular metabolism and integumentary system, musculoskeletal system, circulatory system (including lymphatics and fetal circulation), respiratory system, gastrointestinal system, endocrine system, reproductive system, nervous system, special senses, urinary system, and water, electrolyte, and acid-base regulation. A total score and two subscores (anatomy and physiology) are provided based on the number of questions answered correctly. Separate norms are reported for students in associate degree, baccalaureate, and diploma programs. Sample test available for faculty review. Examiner required. Suitable for group use.

Untimed: 2 hours

Range: Students in registered nursing programs

Scoring: Computer scored

Cost: Test kit (test booklets, answer sheets, directions for administration, and scoring service) $3.00 per student tested.

Publisher: National League for Nursing

NLN ACHIEVEMENT TESTS FOR REGISTERED NURSING: BASICS IN NURSING I (FORM 0413)

nursing student

Purpose: Measures achievement of students in RN programs in the basics of nursing care. Used to evaluate individual student achievement and program objectives in terms of nationally accepted objectives in nursing.

Description: 80 item paper-pencil multiple-choice test measuring knowledge of nursing care basics related to fluid balance, medication administration, nursing procedures, and infection control. A total score and two subscores (fluid balance and medication administration; and nursing procedures and infection control) are provided based on a correction-for-guessing formula. Separate norms are reported for students in associate degree, baccalaureate, and diploma programs. Sample test available for faculty review. Examiner required. Suitable for group use.

Untimed: 1½ hours

Range: Students in registered nursing programs

Scoring: Computer scored

Cost: Test service (test booklets, answer sheetes, directions for administration, and scoring service) $3.00 per student tested.

Publisher: National League for Nursing

NLN ACHIEVEMENT TESTS FOR REGISTERED NURSING: BASICS IN NURSING II (FORM 0423)

nursing student

Purpose: Measures achievement of students in RN programs in the basics of nursing care. Used to evaluate individual student achievement and program objectives in terms of nationally accepted objectives in nursing.

Description: 80 item paper-pencil multiple-choice test measuring knowledge of nursing care basics related to technical skills, scientific concepts, and assessment. A total score and two subscores (technical skills; and assessment and scientific concepts) are provided based on a correction-for-guessing formula. Separate norms reported for students in associate degree, baccalaureate, and diploma programs. Sample test available for faculty review. Examiner required. Suitable for group use.

Untimed: 1½ hours

Range: Students in registered nursing programs

Scoring: Computer scored

Cost: Test service (test booklets, answer sheets, directions for administration, and scoring service) $3.00 per student tested.

Publisher: National League for Nursing

NLN ACHIEVEMENT TESTS FOR REGISTERED NURSING: BASICS IN NURSING III (FORM 0433)

nursing student

Purpose: Measures achievement of students in RN programs in the basics of nursing care. Used to evaluate individual student achievement and program objectives in terms of nationally accepted objectives in nursing.

Description: 70 item paper-pencil multiple-choice test measuring knowledge of nursing care basics related to the psychosocial aspects of nursing, ethical/legal situations, nutrition, and other items generally within the confines of basics in nursing. A total score and two subscores (psychosocial and legal/ethical; and nutrition and other fundamentals) are provided based on correction-for-guessing formula. Separate norms are reported for students in associate degree, baccalaureate, and diploma programs. Sample test available for faculty review. Examiner required. Suitable for group use.

Untimed: 1½ hours

Range: Students in registered nursing programs

Scoring: Computer scored

Cost: Test service (test booklets, answer sheets, directions for administration, and scoring service) $3.00 per student tested.

Publisher: National League for Nursing

NLN ACHIEVEMENT TESTS FOR REGISTERED NURSING: CHEMISTRY (FORM 1013)

nursing student

Purpose: Measures achievement in the principles and concepts of chemistry for students in RN programs. Used to evaluate individual student achievement and program objectives in terms of nationally accepted objectives in nursing.

Description: 120 item paper-pencil multiple-choice test measuring recognition of the concepts and principles of general chemistry that pertain to the health sciences; organic compounds and structures that form the basis for understanding phsyiological reactions; and concepts and principles of biochemistry as they relate to human functioning. A total score and three subscores (general chemistry, organic chemistry, and biochemistry) are provided based on the number of questions answered correctly. Separate norms are reported for students in associate degree, baccalaureate, and diploma programs. Sample test available for faculty review. Examiner required. Suitable for group use.

Untimed: 2 hours

Range: Students in registered nursing programs

Scoring: Computer scored

Cost: Test service (test booklets, answer sheets, directions for administration, and scoring service) $3.25 per student tested.

Publisher: National League for Nursing

NLN ACHIEVEMENT TESTS FOR REGISTERED NURSING: COMPREHENSIVE NURSING ACHIEVEMENT TEST 1984 EDITION (FORM 3014)

nursing student

Purpose: Measures achievement of graduating students in RN programs in the range of knowledge needed by the beginning practitioner. Assesses readiness for the nurse licensure examination. Used to evaluate individual student achievement and program objectives in terms of nationally accepted objectives in nursing.

Description: 210 item paper-pencil multiple-choice test measuring the range of knowledge needed by the beginning practitioner in the areas of human functioning, nursing process, and clinical content. Questions are presented in case situations and written within the framework of the nursing process. Case examples are drawn from the various clinical areas. A total standard score and a variety of subscores in the areas above are reported for each student. Scores are reported in the form of individual diagnostic profiles. Two copies are provided: one for distribution to students and one for faculty analysis. Norms are reported for registered nursing students. Sample test available for faculty review. Examiner required. Suitable for group use.

Untimed: 3½ hours

Range: Students finishing registered nursing programs

Scoring: Computer scored

Cost: Test service (test booklets, answer sheets, directions for administration, and scoring service) $8.00 per student tested.

Publisher: National League for Nursing

NLN ACHIEVEMENT TESTS FOR REGISTERED NURSING: DIET THERAPY AND NUTRITION (FORM 3313)

nursing student

Purpose: Measures achievement of students in RN programs in diet therapy and applied nutrition. Used to evaluate individual student achievement and program objectives in terms of nationally accepted objectives in nursing.

Description: 120 item paper-pencil test measuring knowledge of the facts and principles of nutrition and the ability to apply that knowledge to situations involving patients who have specific nutritional problems. A total score and two subscores (facts and principles; and application of knowledge) are provided based on the number of questions answered correctly. Separate norms are reported for students in associate degree, baccalaureate, and diploma programs. It is intended for administration at the end of the students' program and is not a substitute for the NLN achievement test in normal nutrition. Sample test available for faculty review. Examiner required. Suitable for group use.

Untimed: 2 hours

Range: Students in registered nursing programs

Scoring: Computer scored

Cost: Test service (test booklets, answer sheets, directions for administration, and scoring service) $3.00 per student tested.

Publisher: National League for Nursing

NLN ACHIEVEMENT TESTS FOR REGISTERED NURSING: FUNDAMENTALS OF DRUG THERAPY (FORM 1414)

nursing student

Purpose: Measures achievement of students in RN programs in drug therapy. Used to measure individual student achievement and program objectives in terms of nationally recognized objectives in nursing.

Description: 110 item paper-pencil multiple-choice test measuring knowledge of the general principles of drug administration, calculations, and drug effects. A total score and three subscores are reported based on the number of questions answered correctly. The subscores are: calculations, principles of drug adminstration, and drug effects. Separate norms are reported for associate degree, baccalaureate, and diploma programs. This test is intended for use relatively early in the students' program (knowledge of clinical nursing is not required) and is not a substitute for the NLN achievement test in pharmacology in clinical nursing. Sample test available for faculty review. Examiner required. Suitable for group use.

Untimed: 2 hours

Range: Students in registered nursing programs

Scoring: Computer scored

Cost: Test service (test booklets, answer sheets, directions for administration, and scoring service) $3.00 per student tested.

Publisher: National League for Nursing

NLN ACHIEVEMENT TESTS FOR REGISTERED NURSING: MATERNITY AND CHILD NURSING (FORM 0513)

nursing student

Purpose: Measures achievement of students in RN programs in maternal and child nursing. Used to evaluate individual student achievement and program objectives in terms of nationally recognized objectives in nursing.

Description: 125 item paper-pencil multiple-choice test measuring understanding of the facts and principles of maternal and child nursing and the ability to apply these principles. Test items include both case situations and individual questions. Some cases are structured to follow a family over a period of time and require the student to apply principles from both maternal and child nursing to that particular situation. A total score and two subscores (nursing care during the pregnancy cycle and nursing care of children) are provided based on a correction-for-guessing formula. Separate norms are reported for students in associate degree, baccalaureate, and diploma programs. This test is intended for administration late in the students' program after completion of all major learning experiences that contribute to understanding of maternity and child nursing. It is not a replacement for NLN's separate achievement tests in nursing the childbearing family and nursing of children, which are designed to be used relatively early in the program. Sample test available for faculty review. Examiner required. Suitable for group use.

Untimed: 2 hours

Range: Students in registered nursing programs

Scoring: Computer scored

Cost: Test service (test booklets, answer sheets, directions for administration, and scoring service) $3.00 per student tested.

Publisher: National League for Nursing

NLN ACHIEVEMENT TESTS FOR REGISTERED NURSING: MICROBIOLOGY (FORM 1113)

nursing student

Purpose: Measures achievement of students in RN programs in microbiology as it applies to nursing. Used to evaluate individual student achievement and program objectives in terms of nationally accepted objectives in nursing.

Description: 115 item paper-pencil multiple-choice test measuring the nursing student's understanding of facts and principles related to the causative microorganisms of infectious diseases. In addition to a total score, subscores are provided for the following three areas: (1) the basic processes occurring during the cellular activity of microorganisms, the structural and functional differences of the microorganisms, techniques and measures for studying and culturing microorganisms that cause infectious disease; (2) substances developed for immunization, the body's immunological response to foreign substances, and the antimicrobials used in controlling diseases; and (3) the transmission of organisms, the incidence, manifestation, and progression of communicable diseases, as well as methods used to destroy microorganisms. Each score is based on the number of questions answered correctly. Separate norms are provided for students in associate degree, baccalaureate, and diploma programs. Sample test available for faculty review. Examiner required. Suitable for group use.

Untimed: 2 hours

Range: Students in registered nursing programs

Scoring: Computer scored

Cost: Test service (test booklets, answer booklets, directions for administration, and scoring service)$3.00 per student tested.

Publisher: National League for Nursing

NLN ACHIEVEMENT TESTS FOR REGISTERED NURSING: NATURAL SCIENCES IN NURSING (FORM 3213)

nursing student

Purpose: Measures achievement of students in RN programs in the natural sciences. Used to evaluate individual student achievement and program objectives in terms of nationally accepted objectives in nursing.

Description: 110 item paper-pencil multiple-choice test measuring understanding of facts and principles from the natural sciences as they relate to patient care. Questions cover the areas of physiology, chemistry, physics, microbiology, and anatomy. A total score and two subscores (facts and principles; and application of knowledge) are provided based on the number of questions answered correctly. Separate norms are reported for students in associate degree, baccalaureate, and diploma programs. This test is intended for administration after the students have completed the science courses pertaining to the fields listed above. Sample test available for faculty review. Examiner required. Suitable for group use.

Untimed: 2 hours

Range: Students in registered nursing programs

Scoring: Computer scored

Cost: Test service (test booklets, answer sheets, directions for administration, and scoring service) $3.25 per student tested.

Publisher: National League for Nursing

NLN ACHIEVEMENT TESTS FOR REGISTERED NURSING: NORMAL NUTRITION (FORM 1313)

nursing student

Purpose: Measures achievement of students in RN programs in normal nutrition. Used to evaluate individual student achievement and program objectives in terms of nationally accepted objectives in nursing.

Description: 110 item paper-pencil multiple-choice test measuring knowledge of the facts and principles of normal nutrition and the ability to apply those principles. Test items cover the following areas: nutrients, the bodily processes involved in the utilization of nutrients in food, and the role of nutrition in health. A total score and two subscores (knowledge and interpretation of information basic to normal nutrition; and application of knowledge of normal nutrition) are provided based on a correction-for-guessing formula. Separate norms are reported for students in associate degree, baccalaureate, and diploma programs. This test is intended for administration after the completion of the student's initial major learning experience in normal nutrition (knowledge of clinical nursing is not required). Sample test available for faculty review. Examiner required. Suitable for group use.

Untimed: 2 hours

Range: Students in registered nursing programs

Scoring: Computer scored

Cost: Test service (test booklets, answer sheets, directions for administration, and scoring service) $3.00 per student tested.

Publisher: National League for Nursing

NLN ACHIEVEMENT TESTS FOR REGISTERED NURSING: NURSING CARE OF ADULTS WITH PATHOPHYSIOLOGICAL DISTRUBANCES-PARTS I AND II (FORMS 0213 and 0223)

nursing student

Purpose: Measures achievement of students in RN programs in nursing care of adults with pathophysiological disturbances. Used to measure individual student achievement and evaluate program objectives in terms of nationally accepted objectives in nursing.

Description: Two 130 item paper-pencil multiple-choice tests measuring knowledge about the nursing care of adults with the following pathophysiological disturbances: Part I, Form 0213, (problems related to deficiencies in providing oxygen or nutrients to cells, difficulty in elimination, and failures in regulation of metabolism) and Part II, Form 0223, (alterations in renal function and reproductive organs, defects in musculoskeletal or neurological functions, sensory defects, and integumentary problems). Most of the question are presented in case situations and relate to patients who are hospitalized. The health problems selected reflect those occurring most frequently in the adult population of the United States. Questions emphasize the nursing care required by the patient's condition and are written to reflect the nursing process. Questions to measure knowledge of pharmacology and nutrition are integrated throughout both tests.

For each test, a total score and two sets of subscores are reported based on a correction-for-guessing formula. One set of subscores reflects the objectives of the test: pathophysiology, nursing measures, and therapeutic management (including drugs and diet). The second set of subscores reflects the nursing process: (1) assessing, analyzing, and evaluating—steps that required the ability to gather and interpret information about a patient; and (2) planning and implementing—steps that require the ability to select appropriate measures to provide care to a patient. Separate norms are reported for students in associate degree, baccalaureate, and diploma programs. This test is intended for administration as an end-of-course test after the students have completed the major learning experiences in the content described. Sample test available for faculty review. Examiner required. Suitable for group use.

Untimed: Part I - 2 hours; Part II - 2 hours

Range: Students in registered nursing programs

Scoring: Computer scored

Cost: Test service for either Part I or Part II (test booklets, answer sheets, directions for administration, and scoring service) $4.00 per student tested.

Publisher: National League for Nursing

NLN ACHIEVEMENT TESTS FOR REGISTERED NURSING: NURSING OF CHILDREN (FORM 0113)

nursing student

Purpose: Measures achievement of students in RN programs in nursing care for children. Used to measure individual student achievement and program objectives in terms of nationally accepted objectives in nursing.

Description: 120 item paper-pencil multiple-choice test measuring understanding of facts and principles relating to the nursing care of children and the ability to apply these principles. Questions relating to growth and development, teaching, interpersonal relations, nutrition, pharmacology, and the basic sciences are integrated throughout the test. A total score and three subscores (care of infants, care of toddlers and preschoolers, and care of school age children) are provided based on the number of questions answered correctly. Separate norms are reported for students in associate degree, baccalaureate, and diploma programs. Sample test available for faculty review. Examiner required. Suitable for group use.

Untimed: 2 hours

Range: Students in registered nursing programs

Scoring: Computer scored

Cost: Test service (test booklets, answer sheets, directions for administration, and scoring service) $3.00 per student tested.

Publisher: National League for Nursing

NLN ACHIEVEMENT TESTS FOR REGISTERED NURSING: NURSING THE CHILDBEARING FAMILY (FORM 0581)

nursing student

Purpose: Measures achievement of students in RN programs in nursing the childbearing family. Used to measure individual student achievement and program objectives in terms of nationally recognized objectives in nursing.

Description: 120 item paper-pencil multiple-choice test measuring understanding of facts and principles relating to nursing the childbearing family and the ability to apply these principles. Questions related to nutrition, pharmacology, the basic sciences, and interpersonal relations are interspersed throughout the test. While the emphasis is on the normal, questions dealing with common abnormalities of the mother and newborn are included. A total score and three subscores (antepartal care, partal and postpartal care, and fetal and newborn development) are provided based on a correction-for-guessing formula. Separate norms are reported for students in associate degree, baccalaureate, and diploma programs. This test is intended for administration after the students have completed their major learning experience in maternity nursing. Sample test available for faculty review. Examiner required. Suitable for group use.

Untimed: 2 hours

Range: Students in registered nursing programs

Scoring: Computer scored

Cost: Test service (test booklets, answer sheets, directions for administration, and scoring service) $3.00 per student tested.

Publisher: National League for Nursing

NLN ACHIEVEMENT TESTS FOR REGISTERED NURSING: PHARMACOLOGY IN CLINICAL NURSING (FORM 0982)

nursing student

Purpose: Measures achievement of students in RN programs in applied pharmacology. Used to measure individual student achievement and program objectives in terms of nationally accepted objectives in nursing.

Description: 110 item paper-pencil multiple-choice test measuring understanding of facts and principles related to drugs and drug administration. Questions relate to the actions of pharmacologic agents, untoward effects of drugs and their control, drug administration, and the calculation of dosages. Case situations for the questions are drawn from medical-surgical nursing, the nursing of children, obstetric and gynecologic nursing, and psychiatric nursing. A total score is reported based on a correction-for-guessing formula. Separate norms are reported for students in associate degree, baccalaureate, and diploma programs. This test is intended for administration late in the nursing program after considerable clinical experience. Sample test available for faculty review. Examiner required. Suitable for group use.

Untimed: 2 hours

Range: Students in registered nursing programs

Scoring: Computer scored

Cost: Test service (test booklets, answer sheets, directions for administration, and scoring service) $3.00 per student tested.

Publisher: National League for Nursing

NLN ACHIEVEMENT TESTS FOR REGISTERED NURSING: PSYCHIATRIC NURSING (FORM 0314)

nursing student

Purpose: Measures achievement of students in RN programs in psychiatric nursing. Used to measure individual student achievement and program objectives in terms of nationally accepted objectives in nursing.

Description: 110 item paper-pencil multiple-choice test measuring knowledge of theory and practice in psychiatric nursing. Questions relate to patient situations, and the emphasis throughout is on the therapeutic role of the nurse in the care of patients with mental disorders. A total score and two subscores (concept/process and intervention) are reported based on the number of questions answered correctly. Separate norms are reported for students in associate degree, baccalaureate, and diploma programs. Intended for administration after the students have completed their major learning experiences in psychiatric nursing. This form is a revision of Form 0781. Sample test available for faculty review. Examiner required. Suitable for group use.

Untimed: 2 hours

Range: Students in registered nursing programs

Scoring: Computer scored

Cost: Test service (test booklets, answer sheets, directions for administration, and scoring service) $3.00 per student tested.

Publisher: National League for Nursing

NLN BACCALAUREATE-LEVEL ACHIEVEMENT TESTS FOR REGISTERED NURSING

nursing student

Purpose: Appraises achievement of students in baccalaureate level registered nursing programs. Measures individual student achievement and enables faculty to evaluate program objectives in terms of nationally accepted objectives in nursing.

Description: 7 multiple item paper-pencil multiple-choice tests, each consisting of 80-210 questions and requiring 1½-4 hours to complete, are given in the following areas: applied natural sciences, community health nursing, comprehensive nursing achievement test for baccalaureate students, leadership in nursing, medical-surgical nursing, parent-child care, and psychiatric nursing (nursing care in mental health and mental illness). Test items have been developed in cooperation with faculty members throughout the United States, reflecting the objectives and subject-matter content of baccalaureate programs from all georgraphic areas. All test papers must be returned to NLN Test

Service for scoring. Reports on test results are returned to the program within ten working days after the receipt of the answer sheets. Reports include: raw scores and percentiles, item descriptors, a list of omitted and incorrectly answered items for each student, and an additional group analysis when more than ten students are tested as a group. NLN encourages faculty members to review the tests before ordering them to insure that appropriate subject-matter content areas have been covered. Examiner required. Suitable for group use.

Untimed: 1½-4 hours per test

Range: Students in baccalaureate level RN programs

Scoring: Computer scored

Cost: Test service (test booklets, answer sheets, directions for administration, and scoring service) $3.00-$6.00 per student per test.

Publisher: National League for Nursing

NLN BACCALAUREATE-LEVEL ACHIEVEMENT TESTS FOR REGISTERED NURSING: APPLIED NATURAL SCIENCES (FORM 0981)

nursing student

Purpose: Measures achievement in the applied natural sciences for students in baccalaureate-level RN programs. Measures individual student achievement and evaluates program objectives in terms of nationally accepted objectives in nursing.

Description: 110 item paper-pencil multiple-choice test measuring students' ability to use their knowledge of the natural sciences in providing patient care. Questions cover the areas of physiology, pathophysiology, chemistry, physics, microbiology, and anatomy. The test is arranged in two sections (A and B). Section A consists of four-option questions similar to those in other NLN achievement tests. Section B consists of six-option questions which measure the students' comprehension of cause-and-effect relationships. Four subscores are provided, but no overall score. Two subscores, A and B, reflect performance on sections A and B respectively in terms of the number of questions answered correctly. The knowledge subscore measures the number of section B questions in which the student demonstrated knowledge of only the facts in the paired statements. The application subscore measures the number of section B questions in which the student also knew the correct relationship between the two statements. Norms are provided for students in baccalaureate programs only. Intended for administration toward the end of the students' program. A sample test and a fuller description of the six-option questions in section B are available for faculty review on request. Examiner required. Suitable for group use.

Untimed: 2 hours

Range: Students in baccalaureate-level RN programs.

Scoring: Computer scored

Cost: Test service (test booklets, answer sheets, directions for administration, and scoring service) $3.00 per student tested.

Publisher: National League for Nursing

NLN BACCALAUREATE-LEVEL ACHIEVEMENT TESTS FOR REGISTERED NURSING: COMMUNITY HEALTH NURSING (FORM 2314)

nursing student

Purpose: Measures student achievement in community health nursing in baccalaureate-level RN programs. Measures individual student achievement and evaluates program objectives in terms of nationally recognized objectives in nursing.

Description: 100 item paper-pencil multiple-choice test measuring students' ability to apply principles of community health planning and organization of health care services in contemporary society. This test measures knowledge of the nursing process as it is applied to the community and to family groups and individuals in community settings. The test is based on an approach to community health nursing that stresses promotion of maximum health with respect for cultural differences and individual values and with recognition of the ethical-legal constraints within which the community health nurse functions. Knowledge basic to nursing practice in any setting—such as communication, nutrition, and pharmacology—is tested within the context of the community settings where nurses practice. A total score and three subscores (human ecology, individual in systems, community health planning/health care system) are provided based on the number of questions answered correctly. Norms are reported for baccalaureate-level students only. This test is intended for administration to students in baccalaureate programs who have completed a major learning experience in community health nursing. Sample test available for faculty review. Examiner required. Suitable for group use.

Untimed: 1½ hours

Range: Students in baccalaureate-level registered nursing programs

Scoring: Computer scored

Cost: Test service (test booklets, answer sheets, directions for administration, and scoring service) $3.00 per student tested.

Publisher: National League for Nursing

NLN BACCALAUREATE-LEVEL ACHIEVEMENT TESTS FOR REGISTERED NURSING: COMPREHENSIVE NURSING ACHIEVEMENT TEST FOR BACCALAUREATE NURSING STUDENTS (FORM 3113)

nursing student

Purpose: Measures achievement of students about to graduate from baccalaureate-level registered nursing programs. Measures individual student achievement and enables faculty to evaluate program objectives in terms of nationally accepted objectives in nursing.

Description: 210 item paper-pencil multiple-choice test measuring students' ability to apply knowledge derived from nursing science, as well as from the natural, behavioral, and social sciences. The focus of the test is on the cumulative results of the educational program rather than on the content of individual clinical components. To accommodate the heterogeneity of baccalaureate nursing curricula, an attempt has been made to construct a test that reflects a number of representative conceptual frameworks. Subscores are reported for each of the following content areas: clients being assessed for health status including risk factors; clients experiencing a knowledge deficit; clients experiencing maturational or situational crisis; clients experiencing alteration of physiological functioning; clients with dysfunctional patterns of behavior; leadership and research process. The six subscores reflect the percentage of questions within the diagnostic cluster answered correctly. The total score based on the number of questions answered correctly, is a standard score. Score report includes information about individual student performance as well as group performance. Norms are reported for baccalaureate students. Intended for administration to students who are about to graduate from a baccalaureate program in registered nursing. Sample test available for faculty review. Examiner required. Suitable for group use.

Untimed: 4 hours

Range: Students in baccalaureate registered nursing programs

Scoring: Computer scored

Cost: Test service (test booklets, answer sheets, directions for administration, and scoring services) $6.00 per student tested.

Publisher: National League for Nursing

NLN BACCALAUREATE-LEVEL ACHIEVEMENT TESTS FOR REGISTERED NURSING: LEADERSHIP IN NURSING (FORM 0381)

nursing student

Purpose: Measures knowledge of leadership skills of students in baccalaureate-level RN programs. Measures individual student achievement and evaluates program objectives in terms of nationally accepted objectives in nursing.

Description: 80 item paper-pencil multiple-choice test measuring knowledge of general principles and their utilization in the techniques and skills of nursing leadership. The questions present a variety of clinical situations requiring the judgment and intervention of the nurse as first-line manager. A total score is reported based on a correction-for-guessing formula. Norms are provided for baccalaureate students. Intended for administration to students in baccalaureate programs who have completed a sequence of learning activities that introduce the concepts of leadership and management. Sample test available for faculty review. Examiner required. Suitable for group use.

Untimed: 1½ hours

Range: Students in baccalaureate-level RN programs

Scoring: Computer scored

Cost: Test service (test booklets, answer sheets, directions for administration, and scoring service) $3.00 per student tested.

Publisher: National League for Nursing

NLN BACCALAUREATE-LEVEL ACHIEVEMENT TESTS FOR REGISTERED NURSING: MEDICAL-SURGICAL NURSING (FORM 0182)

nursing student

Purpose: Measures student achievement in medical-surgical nursing for students in baccalaureate-level RN programs. Measures individual student achievement and evaluates achievement of program objectives in terms of nationally accepted objectives in nursing.

Description: 120 item paper-pencil test measuring students' knowledge of fact and principles of medical-surgical nursing and the ability to apply these principles to patient care situations. The questions relate to adult patients in a variety of age groups and to situations that focus on the healthy individual, the individual presenting early changes in health status, the individual with acute health problems, and the individual with rehabilitation needs. The situations presented emphasize the nursing care of acutely ill hospitalized patients. A total score and two subscores are provided: care of healthy patients and those with early changes in health status; and care of acutely ill patients and those in need of rehabilitation. All scores are based on a correction-for-guessing formula. Norms are reported for baccalaureate students. Intended for administration to students in baccalaureate programs after they complete their major learning experience in medical-surgical nursing. Sample test available for faculty review. Examiner required. Suitable for group use.

Untimed: 2 hours

Range: Students in baccalaureate-level RN programs

Scoring: Computer scored

Cost: Test service (test booklets, answer sheets, directions for administration, and scoring service) $3.00 per student tested.

Publisher: National League for Nursing

NLN BACCALAUREATE-LEVEL ACHIEVEMENT TESTS FOR REGISTERED NURSING: NURSING CARE IN MENTAL HEALTH AND MENTAL ILLNESS (FORM 2214)

nursing student

Purpose: Measures student achievement in psychiatric nursing in baccalaureate-level RN programs. Measures individual student achievement and evaluates program objectives in terms of nationally accepted objectives in nursing.

Description: 120 item paper-pencil multiple-choice test measuring knowledge of the concepts and principles essential in the care of clients with a variety of mental disorders. The case situations are placed in a number of different settings, and there are questions included on primary and tertiary prevention. Although the chief focus of the test is on knowledge needed in the care of clients with mental disorders, an effort was also made to test concepts of a broader nature. These are integrated throughout the test. The test also includes questions on the newer approaches to treatment. A total score and three subscores (knowledge/concepts; assessing/analyzing/evaluating; planning/implementing) are reported based on the number of questions answered correctly. Norms reported for baccalaureate students. Intended for administration to students who have completed their major learning experience in psychiatric nursing. Sample test available for faculty review. Examiner required. Suitable for group use.

Untimed: 2 hours

Range: Students in baccalaureate-level RN programs

Scoring: Computer scored

Cost: Test service (test booklets, answer sheets, directions for administration, and scoring service) $3.00 per student tested.

Publisher: National League for Nursing

NLN BACCALAUREATE-LEVEL ACHIEVEMENT TESTS FOR REGISTERED NURSING: PARENT-CHILD CARE (FORM 0882)

nursing student

Purpose: Measures student achievement in parent-child nursing care in baccalaureate-level RN programs. Measures individual student achievement and evaluates program objectives in terms of nationally accepted objectives in nursing.

Description: 110 item paper-pencil multiple-choice test measuring knowledge of nursing interventions for individuals during infancy, childhood, adolescence, and families during childbearing and childrearing years. In addition to measuring the achievement of learning objectives pertinent to all areas of nursing practice, such as principles of communication, the test measures learning objectives specific to nursing of parents and children (including psychosocial and physical development of children and parents, and normal and unexpected physical changes related to childhood and childbearing). The test presents nursing situations in a variety of inpatient and outpatient settings where parents and children requiring health care are encountered. A total score and two subscores (childbearing including fetal development and the neonate to one month of age; and care of the child from one month to young adulthood including family health concepts) are provided based on a correction-for-guessing formula. Norms are reported for baccalaureate students. The test requires that students use their knowledge of all steps of the nursing process, and is intended for administration to students in baccalaureate programs who have completed all of the major learning experiences in the content area. Sample test available for faculty review. Examiner required. Suitable for group use.

Untimed: 2 hours

Range: Students in baccalaureate-level RN programs

Scoring: Computer scored

Cost: Test service (test booklets, answer sheets, directions for administration, and scoring service) $3.00 per student tested.

Publisher: National League for Nursing

NLN NURSING MOBILITY PROFILE I

nursing student

Purpose: Evaluates previous learning and experience in order to establish credit and placement in programs preparing for registered nursing practice. Administered to licensed practical nurses seeking placement.

Description: 400 item paper-pencil multiple-choice test assessing three content areas: Book One measures foundations of nursing (200 items) and Book Two measures nursing care during childbearing (100 items) and nursing care of the child (100 items). The two test books may be administered separately or together as determined by individual needs. Book One (foundations of nursing) includes content related to nursing care to meet basic physiological and psychosocial needs. The first section of Book Two (nursing care during childbearing) includes content related to nursing care during antepartal, intrapartal, and neonatal periods. Part two of Book Two (nursing care of the child) includes content related to nursing care of the infant, toddler, preschooler, school age child, and adolescent. Questions are based on the nursing care of clients in health care settings and are presented in case situations that are a representative sample of those commonly encountered in nursing practice. Test items are written within the framework of the four steps of the nursing process (assessment, planning, implementation, and evaluation).

The tests may be administered by faculty at individual schools of nursing on uniform test dates selected by NLN Test Service to safeguard the security of the examination. (Contact NLN Test Service to arrange alternate dates.) It is suggested that the tests be administered in a one-day session to be scheduled by faculty at participating schools of nursing during the restricted periods.

A total score (decision score) is reported for each of the three content areas. Diagnostic scores are also provided as a supplement to faculty evaluations of students and students' self-assessments of strengths and weaknesses. An information bulletin is available upon request providing more detailed information about the content, scoring, and administration of the examination. Suggested methods for institutional standard setting are available upon request. Examiner required. Suitable for group use.

Timed: Book one—3½ hours; Book two—3½ hours

Range: Licensed practical nurses

Scoring: Computer scored

Cost: Book One or Book Two (with scoring service) each $25.00 per student tested.

Publisher: National League for Nursing

NLN NURSING MOBILITY PROFILE II

nursing student

Purpose: Evaluates previous learning and experience in order to establish credit and placement in nursing education programs. Administered to registered nurses seeking placement in a baccalaureate nursing program.

Description: 560 item paper-pencil multiple-choice test assessing four content areas arranged in three test books: Book One measures care of the adult client (220 items), Book Two measures care of the client during childbearing (110 items) and care of the child (110 items), and Book Three measures care of the client with mental disorder (120 items). Test books may be administered in any order or combination as determined by individual needs. Book One (care of the adult client) includes content related to nursing care of individual clients who have deficiency in the delivery of oxygen to the cells; clients with problems in digestion, metabolism and providing nutrients to the cells; clients with impairment in sensorimotor function; and clients with dysfunction of the genitourinary or reproductive system. The first section of Book Two (care of the client during childbearing) includes content related to nursing care during the antepartal, intrapartal, postpartal, and neonatal periods. The second section of Book Two (care of the child) includes content related to nursing care of the infant, the toddler and preschooler, and the school age child and adolescent. Book Three (care of the client with mental disorder) includes content related to nursing care of children and adults who have mental disorders from causes that are psychological, adjustmental, and organic. Most of the questions on the profile are presented in case situations representative of health problems and conditions commonly encountered in nursing practice. Questions relate to the promotion, maintenance, and restoration of health. Items emphasize normal findings, as well as deviations from normal, treatment modalities including drugs and nutrition, and nursing interventions.

The tests may be administered by faculty at individual schools of nursing on uniform test dates selected by NLN Test Service to safeguard the security of the examination. (Contact NLN Test Service to arrange alternate dates.) It is suggested that the tests be administered in a one and one-half day session to be scheduled by faculty at participating schools of nursing during the restricted periods. Standardized scores for each of the four main content areas are reported for faculty use in making decisions about placement or awarding/denying specific course credits. Subscores for content and nursing process are also reported to provide additional advisory information. Two copies of the performance report are provided: one for student use and a second for faculty use. An information bulletin is available providing more detailed information about the scoring, content, and administration of the examination. Examiner required. Suitable for group use.

Timed: Book One—four hours; Book Two—four hours; Book Three—2 hours

Range: Registered nurses

Scoring: Computer scored

Cost: Book One, Two, or Three (with scoring service) each $25.00 per student tested.

Publisher: National League for Nursing

NLN NURSING SERVICE TEST: PROFICIENCY IN PHARMACOLOGY FOR NURSING PRACTICE

nursing student

Purpose: Measures basic knowledge of pharmacology required for safe practice. Used with registered and practical nurses to establish educational objectives for in-service training programs with new or currently employed nursing staff.

Description: 92 item paper-pencil multiple-choice test measuring knowledge of the principles of drug administration and the effects of commonly used drugs, as well as the ability to carry out simple dosage calculations. Test items emphasize essential knowledge required for safe practice, making the test suitable for use with both registered and practical nurses. Raw scores are provided for the total test and three subsections: drug administration, dosage calculations, and drug effects. Examiner required. Suitable for group use.

Untimed: 1½ hours

Range: Registered and practical nurses

Scoring: Computer scored

Cost: Test service (test booklet, answer sheet, directions for administration, and score reporting) $3.75 per test scored.

Publisher: National League for Nursing

NLN PRE-ADMISSION EXAMINATION-PN (PAX-PN)

nursing student

Purpose: Measures ability and scholastic achievement in specific content areas which predict academic success in practical nursing programs. Assists in admissions and placement decisions by schools preparing students for practical nursing.

Description: 3 paper-pencil multiple-choice tests measuring aptitudes in the following areas: verbal ability, science achievement, and mathematics achievement. The verbal ability test consists of word knowledge and reading comprehension sections. The word knowledge section measures the ability to recognize the meaning of a word as it is used in a sentence by choosing the answer that best completes a statement. The reading section is composed of passages of scientific or general nature and associated questions suitable for measuring the reading comprehension skills of applicants to schools of practical nursing. The mathematics test measures the ability to solve computational or word problems involving proportions, ratios, decimals, fractions, percentages, and elementary algebraic concepts. The science test measures knowledge of general principles of chemistry, physics, biology, and health. Most of the questions concern information from secondary school general science and health classes that have useful applications to practical nursing. Experimental questions are included for test development purposes only and are not scored. The tests, administered as a single battery, are administered at scheduled sessions throughout the country at test sites established by NLN Test Service. (Contact NLN if alternate dates are required.) Test performance of each applicant is reported in terms of raw scores and percentiles. Percentile norms are based on performance of applicants to practical/vocational nursing programs. A composite score based on a weighted combination of the subscores is also reported. Interpretive material is provided with each report. Examiner required. Suitable for group use.

Timed: 3½ hours

Range: Applicants to practical nursing programs

Scoring: Computer scored

Cost: One administration of examination with two score reports (one for applicant and one for desginated school of practical nursing) $15.00; additional reports $4.00.

Publisher: National League for Nursing

NLN PRE-ADMISSION EXAMINATION-RN (PAX-RN)

nursing student

Purpose: Measures ability and academic achievement in specific content areas which predict academic success in programs preparing students for beginning registered nursing practice. Assists schools in making admissions and placement decisions.

Description: A battery of three multiple item paper-pencil multiple-choice tests measuring aptitudes in the following areas: verbal ability, mathematics, and science. The verbal ability test consists of word knowledge and reading comprehension sections. The word knowledge section asks individuals to recognize the meaning of a word as it is used in a sentence by choosing the answer that best completes a statement. The reading section is composed of passages of a scientific or general nature with associated questions suitable for measuring the reading comprehension skills of applicants to registered nursing programs. The mathematics test measures skills in basic arithmetic calculations as well as elementary algebraic and geometric concepts. Straight computational as well as reading problems are included. The science test evaluates knowledge of high school-level general science, chemistry, physics, and biology, with particular emphasis on those areas most applicable to the nursing curriculum. Experimental questions are included for test development purposes only and are not included in scoring.

The test is administered at scheduled sessions throughout the country at test sites established by NLN Test Service. (Contact NLN if alternate dates are required.) Test performance of each applicant is reported in terms of raw scores and percentiles. Separate percentile norms are provided for applicants to associate degree programs, diploma programs, and all RN programs. A standardized composite score based on a weighted combination of subscores is also reported. Interpretive material is provided with each report. Examiner required. Suitable for group use.

Timed: 3½ hours

Range: Applicants to registered nursing programs

Scoring: Computer scored

Cost: One administration of the examination with two score reports (one for the applicant and one for a designated school of nursing) $15.00; additional reports $4.00 each.

Publisher: National League for Nursing

NURSING TESTS

Thelma Hunt

teen grades 12 and up

Purpose: Measures aptitude for nursing. Used in selection of applicants for nursing or practical nursing schools, or for assistance in guidance and counseling of pre-nursing students.

Description: Four multiple item paper-pencil tests assessing aptitude for nursing: the Nursing Aptitude Test (specialized general ability test), the Arithmetic Test for Prospective Nurses, the General Science Test for Prospective Nurses, and the Interest-Preference Test for Prospective Nurses. The tests may be administered separately or as a complete battery. Norms available for high school seniors. Examiner required. Suitable for group use.

Timed: Varies

Range: High school seniors and above

Scoring: Examiner evaluated

Cost: 25 aptitude tests $6.00; 25 arithmetic tests $3.00; 25 general science tests $4.00; 25 interest-preference tests $5.00; specimen set for all four tests $5.00.

Publisher: The Center for Psychological Service

OFFICIAL GED PRACTICE TEST

GED Testing Service of the American Council on Education

teen, adult

Purpose: Determines readiness to take the full-length GED. Alleviates anxiety associated with taking the GED Test.

Description: Multiple item paper-pencil test parallelling the content, format, and range of difficulty of the full-length GED Tests. Five subtests cover the following academic areas: writing skills, social studies, science, reading skills, and mathematics. The answer sheet accommodates responses for all five subtests on both sides of a single sheet and contains a summary profile chart that identifies general strengths and weaknesses in various subject areas. Scoring templates and a detailed teacher's manual are provided in the administrator's set. Available in forms A and B in both English and Spanish. All forms are statistically equated to a full-length secure GED Test. Audiotapes available for forms A and B in English. Examiner required. Suitable for group use.

Untimed: Varies

Range: High school students and adults

Scoring: Examiner evaluated

Cost: English form A or B (10 test booklets, 10 answer sheets, 10 info. bulletins) $14.50; administrator's set $10.00.

Publisher: American Council on Education, distributed by Cambridge

SCALES OF INDEPENDENT BEHAVIOR

Refer to page 128.

SECONDARY SCHOOL ADMISSION TEST (SSAT)

child, teen grades 5-10

Purpose: Measures the abilities of students applying for admission to grades 6-11 of independent schools. Used for student selection purposes by independent schools.

Description: Multiple item paper-pencil multiple-choice test measuring verbal and quantitative abilities and reading comprehension. Consists of four sections: one section measuring verbal ability, two sections measuring mathematical ability, and one measuring reading comprehension. An upper level form is administered to students who are in grades 8-10 at the time of testing; a lower form is administered to students in grades 5-7. Scores are normed on the student's grade level at the time of testing. Norms for each grade level are developed annually on the basis of the most recent three-year sample of candidates tested.

The test is administered on specific dates (six Saturdays during the school year and bi-weekly during the summer) at designated test centers. Educational Testing Service (ETS) publishes a *Bulletin of Information for Candidates* containing a list of test centers and test dates as well as information concerning registration and a registration form. The *Bulletin* is mailed to participating schools in August for distribution to candidates, who then complete the form and return it with the test fee to ETS. A booklet entitled *Preparing for the SSAT* is available for candidates who want to familiarize themselves with the test. This booklet contains a description of the test, examples and explanations of test questions, a sample test, and instructions for scoring the test and interpreting scores.

Reading comprehension, verbal, quantitative, and total verbal and quantitative scaled scores as well as program percentiles are mailed to participating schools approximately 15 working days after each administration. Each participating school receives: a roster of scores for candidates who designated it as a score recipient, two gummed label reports for each of those candidates, current program norms, and an interpretive booklet which explains how this information can be used. Students may have their scores reported up to six participating schools (designated by the student at the time of testing). A report of the candidate's scaled scores and percentiles is sent to parents about four days after the reports are sent to the schools, along with a booklet to help them interpret scores.

A program for the handicapped permits physically or visually handicapped students to take the SSAT with up to double the amount of testing time per section. Examiner required. Suitable for group use.

Timed: Varies

Range: Grades 5-10

Scoring: Computer scored; hand scoring available

Cost: Domestic test fee (administration, parents' score report, and up to six designated school reports) $25.00; foreign test fee (including Canada, Puerto Rico, and U.S. territories) $45.00.

Publisher: Educational Testing Service

TEST OF AUDITORY COMPREHENSION (TAC)

Refer to page 159.

THE 3-R's® TEST

Nancy S. Cole, E. Roger Trent, Dena C. Wadell, Robert L. Thorndike and Elizabeth P. Hagen

child, teen K-12

Purpose: Measures achievement in reading, language skills, and mathematics for elementary and high school students. Assesses verbal and quantitative abilities as well. Satisfies all Title I requirements.

Description: Three multiple item paper-pencil batteries assessing academic achievement and ability from kindergarten to grade 12: the Achievement Edition, the Achievement and Abilities Edition, and the Class-Period Edition. The Achievement Edition measures reading and mathematics abilities for grades K-2 and reading, mathematics, and language skills for grades 3-12. A Grade Developmental score (GDS) is provided for each subject, as well as a composite GDS indicating overall academic functioning. Subscores are provided for the following areas: reading (reading comprehension, vocabulary, and study skills), language (grammar, spelling, capitalization, and punctuation), and mathematics (mathematics computation and mathematics problem solving). In addition to these achievement tests, the Achievement and Abilities Edition includes tests measuring verbal and quantitative abilities. Both tests yield scores in terms of national age percentile, national grade percentile ranks and stanines, and standard age scores. Score reports for this edition also contrast actual achievement with the level of achievement expected on the basis of the ability scores.

The Class-Period Edition is a short version of the Achievement Edition for use with grades K-12. Composite achievement is reported in terms of GDSs and percentile ranks. Subscores are provided for the following subjects: reading, language, and mathematics. Machine-scored narrative and graphical reports are available for all three editions (all which may also be scored by hand).

All editions test 11 different levels to match curriculum in each grade. The Achievement Edition provides two forms for purposes of pre- and post-testing. Available options include: multiple scores for special school uses, special norms (Catholic norms, large-city norms) for comparative purposes, achievement scores linked to verbal/quantitative ability scores for considering achievement in the light of student achievement, and criterion-referenced achievement scores in reading which provide diagnostic information on students' strengths and weaknesses.

La Prueba is the Spanish edition of *The 3-R's Test,* Form A, Levels 6-14. It is designed to determine the degree to which students are literate in Spanish, and to assess the achievement of students whose primary language is Spanish. Each level is designed for administration in one or two grades. In addition to *The 3-R's Test* content coverage, it includes science and social studies. Examiner required. Suitable for group use.

Timed: Varies (50-190 minutes depending on edition and grade level)

Range: Grades K-12

Scoring: Hand scored; machine scoring available

Cost: Contact publisher concerning price and availability.

Publisher: The Riverside Publishing Company

Vocational

BALL APTITUDE BATTERY

Refer to page 211.

THE BRIGANCE® DIAGNOSTIC INVENTORY OF ESSENTIAL SKILLS

Refer to page 84.

DAILEY VOCATIONAL TESTS

John T. Dailey

teen, adult gr. 9 and up

Purpose: Assesses knowledge and potential in electrical, mechanical, and scholastic ability and business English skills. Used in career counseling and vocational guidance settings.

Description: 150 item paper-pencil Technical and Scholastic test (TST) and 111 item paper-pencil Business English Test (BET) measuring vocational aptitude for trade, technical, and business careers. The TST yields scores for seven subtests: electricity, electronics, mechanical information, physical sciences, arithmetic reasoning, algebra, and vocabulary. The BET yields a single score, but subscores in spelling, punctuation, capitalization, and grammar can be obtained for local interpretation using the BET scoring mask. The Spatial Visualization Test (SVT) is no longer published. However, for those who already have the SVT booklets, combined BET/SVT answer sheets are available. The examiner's manual includes information for administering, scoring, and interpreting all three tests. The individual profile sheet and the group report form are also designed for use with all the tests. Examiner required. Suitable for group use.

Timed: TST—65 minutes; BET—30 minutes

Range: Grades 9-12, college, adult

Scoring: Hand key

Cost: (1983-84) 35 TST test booklets $23.64; 35 BET test booklets $12.81; 100 answer sheets (TST or BET) $15.66; set of 4 TST scoring masks $7.60; BET scoring mask $2.01; 35 individual profile sheets $5.76; 35 group report forms $5.76; examination kit $9.66.

Publisher: The Riverside Publishing Company

Educational Development and School Readiness

ANALYSIS OF READINESS SKILLS

Mary C. Rodriques, William H. Vogler and James F. Wilson

child K-1

Purpose: Measures a child's readiness for introductory reading and mathematics programs.

Description: 30 item oral response test consisting of the following three subtests (10 items each): visual perception of letters, letter identification, and mathematics (identification of numerals and counting numerals). The teacher's manual provides directions for administering the tests in English or Spanish and includes norms for both English-speaking and Spanish-speaking children. Examiner required. Individually administered; suitable for screening groups of children.

Untimed: 35 minutes

Range: Grades K-1

Scoring: Examiner evaluated

Cost: Test kit (25 test booklets, teacher's manual, scoring key, class record sheet, and sample item chart) $13.56; examination kit $4.38.

Publisher: The Riverside Publishing Company

BATTELLE DEVELOPMENTAL INVENTORY

DLM Teaching Resources staff

child

Purpose: Evaluates the development of children from infant to primary levels. Screens and diagnoses developmental strengths and weaknesses. Used to establish IEP's and to aid in placement and eligibility decisions.

Description: Multiple item test assessing key developmental skills in five domains: personal-social, adaptive, motor, communications, and cognition. Information is obtained through structured interactions with the child in a controlled setting, observation of the child, and interviews with the child's parents, caregivers, and teachers. Test items contain content and sequence directly compatible with infant and preschool curricula for use in generating IEP's. Obtained scores include standard scores, percentile ranks, and age equivalent scores. Administered by teacher or trained paraprofessional; may be administered to handicapped children using various modifications devised for this purpose. Examiner required. Not suitable for group use.

Untimed: Screening examination 10-30 minutes; diagnostic evaluation 1-2 hours

Range: Ages 0-8 years

Scoring: Examiner evaluated

Cost: Test kit (15 scoring booklets, 15 screening test booklets, test items, manual) $95.00.

Publisher: DLM Teaching Resources

BRIEF INDEX OF ADAPTIVE BEHAVIOR (BIAB)

R. Steve McCallum, Maurice S. Herrin, Jimmy P. Wheeler and Jeanette R. Edwards

child, teen

Purpose: Evaluates the development of adaptive behavior in children ages 5-17 years. Used for counseling purposes.

Description: 39 item paper-pencil observational inventory assessing three domains of adaptive behavior: independent functioning, socialization, and communication. Completed and scored by either parent or teacher. Manual includes a discussion of the test and procedures for administration and scoring. Self-administered. Not suitable for group use.

Untimed: Varies

Range: Ages 5-17 years

Scoring: Examiner evaluated

Cost: Starter set (manual, 20 response sheets) $8.00; specimen set $4.00.

Publisher: Scholastic Testing Service, Inc.

THE BRIGANCE® DIAGNOSTIC INVENTORY OF EARLY DEVELOPMENT

Albert H. Brigance

child

Purpose: Measures the development of children functioning below the developmental age of seven years. Diagnoses developmental delays and monitors progress over a period of time. Used to develop IEP's.

Description: 200 item paper-pencil, oral response, and direct observation inventory assessing psychomotor, self-help, communication, general knowledge and comprehension, and academic skill levels. Test items are arranged in developmental sequential order in the following sections: pre-ambulatory skills, gross motor skills, fine motor skills, pre-speech, speech and language skills, general knowledge and comprehension, readiness, basic reading skills, manuscript writing, and basic math skills. An introductory section outlines how to administer the tests, assess skill levels, record the results, identify specific instructional objectives, and develop IEP's. Results, expressed in terms of developmental ages, are entered into the individual record book, which shows graphically at each testing to what point an individual has progressed. An optional group record book monitors the progress of 15 individuals. Examiner required. Not suitable for group use.

Untimed: Varies

Range: Developmental ages 0-7 years

Scoring: Examiner evaluated

Cost: Assessment book and 10 individual developmental record books $67.95; group record book $7.95; test excerpts available free of charge; 10 record books $12.95; 100 record books $105.00.

Publisher: Curriculum Associates, Inc.

THE BRIGANCE® K & 1 SCREEN

Albert H. Brigance

child K-1

Purpose: Assesses the basic skills necessary for success in kindergarten and grade 1. Identifies students in need of special service referral, determines appropriate pupil placement and assists in planning instructional programs and developing IEP's.

Description: 12 (for kindergarten) or 13 (for grade 1) multiple item paper-pencil, oral response and direct observation assessments measuring the following basic skills: personal data response, color recognition, picture vocabulary, visual discrimination, visual-motor skills, standing gross motor skills, draw a person (body image), rote counting, identification of body parts, recites alphabet, follows verbal directions, numeral comprehension, recognition of lower case letters (upper case alternate), auditory discrimination, prints personal data, syntax and fluency, and numerals in sequence. Point values assigned to each skill add up to 100 for "perfect" score. This criterion-referenced score is used to rank or group students according to a composite score. Five optional advanced assessments are included for students scoring 95 or above on the basic first grade assessment: response to picture, articulation of sounds, basic preprimer vocabulary, preprimer/primer oral reading, and basic number skills. Also includes optional forms for teacher rating, parent rating, and examiner observations.

Personal information, assessment results, scoring, testing observations, comparative summary of the screening, and recommendations are all recorded on the pupil data sheet, printed on 3-part carbonless sets to facilitate distribution of the completed data to teachers, administrators, and parents. An optional class summary record folder collects and summarizes data for 30 pupils. Separate pupil data sheets and class summary record folders are required for the kindergarten and grade 1 assessments. Criterion-referenced results are translated directly into curriculum or program objectives to meet the needs of individual pupils. Test items are cross-referenced to the Brigance Inventory of Basic Skills and the Inventory of Early Development to facilitate further evaluation of skill deficiencies. Examiner required. Not suitable for group use.

Untimed: 12 minutes

Range: Grades K-1

Scoring: Examiner evaluated

Cost: Assessment manual $29.95; 30 pupil data sheets and 1 class summary record folder for grade K $11.95; 30 pupil data sheets and 1 class summary record folder for grade 1 $12.00.

Publisher: Curriculum Associates, Inc.

CALLIER-AZUSA SCALE: G-EDITION

Refer to page 3.

CENTRAL INSTITUTE FOR THE DEAF PRESCHOOL PERFORMANCE SCALE (CID PRESCHOOL PERFORMANCE SCALE)

Refer to page 154.

CLYMER-BARRETT READINESS TEST

Theodore Clymer and Thomas C. Barrett

child K-1

Purpose: Measures the important skills and background necessary for success in beginning instruction—especially reading. Identifies students with serious skill deficits. Used at the end of kindergarten to assess the results of a readiness program and at the beginning of grade 1 to group students and determine instructional goals.

Description: 116 item paper-pencil multiple-choice test and 24 item observational inventory (completed by the child's classroom teacher) assessing readiness for first grade instruction. Six tests measure three types of skills: recognizing letters (35 items) and matching words (20 items) visual discrimination, beginning sounds (20 items) and ending sounds (20 items) auditory discrimination, and completing shapes (20 items) and copy-a-sentence (1 item) measuring visual-motor coordination. The tests are given in three separate administration periods, one for each skill area. The readiness survey collects teacher observations concerning oral language facility, concept development, listening and thinking skills, social and emotional development, and work habits. The first test of visual discrimination (recognizing letters) and the first test of auditory discrimination (beginning sounds) may be administered as a short form of the test for quick screening purposes. All six tests, the readiness survey, and a student summary page are all contained in one 16-page booklet, available in equivalent forms A and B for pre- and posttesting. The class record sheet compiles data on up to 40 students. The manual includes: information on administering and scoring the tests and analyzing the results, normative data, cutoff scores, and technical data. This instrument is a revised version of the Clymer-Barrett Prereading Battery. Examiner required. Suitable for group use.

Untimed: Varies

Range: Grades K-1

Scoring: Examiner evaluated

Cost: Contact publisher.

Publisher: Chapman, Brook & Kent

THE COMMUNICATION SCREEN: A PRESCHOOL SPEECH-LANGUAGE SCREENING TOOL

Refer to page 162.

DABERON SCREENING FOR SCHOOL READINESS

Virginia A. Danzer, Mary Frances Gerber and Theresa M. Lyons

handicapped child

Purpose: Assesses the school readiness of 4-6 year old children and other handicapped and difficult to manage children. Used to develop IEP's for young children.

Description: Multiple item oral response and task performance test assessing language skills, knowledge of body parts, color and number concepts, functional use of prepositions, plurals, ability to follow directions, general knowledge, visual perception, gross motor development, and the ability to categorize. A high percentage of accurate responses indicates school readiness. Innaccurate responses indicate future problem areas, the need for further diagnostic and prognostic study, and information that needs to be taught. Results yield a Learning Readiness Equivalency age score to identify children with learning difficulties. A *Report On Readiness* is provided for parents and teachers to discuss. The manual includes information regarding administration and assessment procedures and instructional objectives for writing IEP's. Examiner required. Not suitable for group use.

Untimed: 20-40 minutes

Range: Ages 4-6; handicapped and difficult to handle children

Scoring: Examiner evaluated

Cost: Complete Test Kit (manual, materials needed for administration, 25 screening forms, 25 *Report On Readiness,* and 5 classroom summary forms) $59.95.

Publisher: ASIEP Education Company

DEVELOPMENTAL ACTIVITIES SCREENING INVENTORY-II (DASI-II)

Rebecca R. Fewell and Mary Beth Langley

child

Purpose: Detects early developmental disabilities in children functioning between the ages of birth and 60 months.

Description: 67 item oral response and task performance test assessing 15 developmental skills categories ranging from sensory intactness, means-end relationships, and causality to memory, seriation, and reasoning. Test items may be administered in different sequences in one or two settings. Instructions are given either verbally or visually. Each test item includes adaptations for use with visually impaired children. The following stimulus items are included in the test kit: 37 picture cards, 5 set-configuration cards, two pairs of numeral cards, three pairs of word cards, and 4 shape cards. The manual includes: a matrix for identifying the concepts tapped by each test item, simple instructional programs for teaching the specific skills assessed by the test items, and an example of the type of program that might be used for a child assessed with this instrument. May be administered by classroom teachers with a minimum of testing experience. Examiner required. Not suitable for group use.

Untimed: Varies

Range: Ages birth-60 months (lowest scorable age is one month)

Scoring: Examiner evaluated

Cost: Complete kit (manual, 50 record forms, and stimulus items in storage box) $39.00.

Publisher: Pro-Ed

DEVELOPMENTAL HISTORY REPORT

Refer to page 4.

DEVELOPMENTAL INDICATORS FOR THE ASSESSMENT OF LEARNING-REVISED (DIAL-R)

Carol D. Mardell-Czudnowski and Dorothea S. Goldenberg

child

Purpose: Assesses a child's developmental level. Identifies potential problem, average, and gifted young children who may have special educational needs.

Description: 24 item oral response and task performance test assessing developmental abilities in three skill areas: motor (catching, jumping, hopping and skipping, building, touching fingers, cutting, matching, copying and writing name), concepts (naming colors, identifying body parts, rote counting, meaningful counting, positioning, identifying concepts, naming letters, sorting chips), and language (articulating, giving personal data, remembering, naming nouns, naming verbs, classifying foods, problem solving, sentence length). The movable plastic dial which is used to present test items reduces distractions by presenting only one stimulus at a time. Social and emotional considerations are noted through behavioral observations, and a parent questionnaire is available to collect parent information. The test kit includes: plastic dials and stands, blocks, scissors, beanbag, cutting cards, scoresheets, pencil, colored marking pens and tape. A small mirror or the child's photograph is used to assist in self-identification. Empirical scoring system based upon national norms. Administered by a team of paraprofessionals and/or professionals at three stations. Training procedures available separately. Examiner required. Not suitable for group use.

Untimed: 20-30 minutes

Range: Ages 2-6 years

Scoring: Examiner evaluated

Cost: DIAL-R assessment kit $149.95.

Publisher: Childcraft Education Corp.

DEVELOPMENTAL TEST OF VISUAL-MOTOR INTEGRATION (VMI)

Refer to page 16.

EARLY IDENTIFICATION SCREENING PROGRAM

Office of Continuum Services, Baltimore City Public Schools

child K-1

Purpose: Identifies children in grades K-1 who lack basic school readiness skills. Used by classroom teachers for program planning and referral purposes.

Description: Multiple item paper-pencil and oral response test assessing a child's ability to perform tasks generally required for academic success. Three subtests screen for proficiency levels in auditory, visual and articulation skills: Hear-Write Tasks (auditory discrimination, short-term memory, beginning penmanship, fine muscle control), See-Write Tasks (visual discrimination, eye-hand coordination, beginning penmanship, fine muscle control), and See-Say Tasks (general information, verbal skills, reading readiness, eye-hand coordination, articulation skills). Scoring is based on frequency measure, counting the number of correct responses per minute, the period allowed for each subtest. The tests are administered over a three day period, one subtest per day. The children being tested within a class or school are ranked according to their performance, identifying those needing further attention. Not suitable for group administration. Available in Spanish.

Timed: 20 minutes per child

Range: Grades K-1

Scoring: Examiner evaluated

Cost: Kindergarten screening booklet (pkg. of 15) $9.99; First-Grade screening booklet (pkg. of 15) $9.99; administration and scoring manual $6.96.

Publisher: Modern Curriculum Press, Inc.

EARLY LEARNING ASSESSMENT AND DEVELOPMENT

Audrey Curtis and Mary Wignall

child

Purpose: Assesses developmental skills and capacities of children in the first years of school. Identifies appropriate remedial activities for children who need to practice and develop certain skills.

Description: Multiple item task-performance and teacher-observation

instrument assessing five developmental areas: motor skills (fine motor and gross motor), perceptual skills (visual, auditory, and tactile perception), communication skills, learning and memory, and emotional and social development. Eleven cards (for sequencing and auditory perception activities) and nine spirit duplicator masters (for individual child profile and visual perception activities) are provided for eliciting activities which allow teachers to observe and pinpoint children's individual developmental abilities. Using guidelines presented in the handbook, teachers can identify and remedy areas of weakness in the first year of infant school before the child becomes used to failure. The materials are also useful for older children who have specific learning difficulties. Specific remedial suggestions are provided in the handbook. Record sheets are provided to monitor class progress. Examiner required. Not suitable for group use.
BRITISH PUBLISHER

Untimed: Varies

Range: Infant school students

Scoring: Examiner evaluated

Cost: Test kit (handbook, 11 cards, 9 spirit duplicating masters, and 5 record sheets, all packed in ring-binding folder) £14.95.

Publisher: Macmillan Education

EARLY SCREENING INVENTORY (ESI)

Samuel J. Meisels and Martha Stone Wiske

child

Purpose: Assesses the ability of a 4-6 year old child to acquire new skills. Identifies children who may need further evaluation and special educational services.

Description: Multiple item task performance and oral response screening instrument assessing the development of kindergarten-aged children. The test is divided into four sections. The initial screening items section assesses the child's ability to respond to an unstructured drawing task and fine motor control. The visual-motor/ adaptive section examines fine motor control, eye-hand coordination, the ability to remember visual sequences, the ability to draw visual forms, and the ability to reproduce three-dimensional structures. The language and cognition section assesses language comprehension and verbal expression, the ability to reason and count, and the ability to remember auditory sequences. The gross motor/ body awareness section assesses balance, large motor coordination, and the ability to imitate body positions from visual cues. Non-consumable stimuli for all tests are provided. The manual includes: directions for administration, scoring, and interpreting the tests and statistical information. The parent questionnaire provides relevant information about the child's family, medical, and developmental history. Examiner required. Individually administered; suitable for screening groups of children.

Untimed: Varies

Range: Ages 4-6 years

Scoring: Examiner evaluated

Cost: Test kit (manual, screening materials, 30 score sheets, 30 parent questionnaires) $39.95.

Publisher: Teachers College Press

EDINBURGH PICTURE TEST

Godfrey Thomson Unit for Educational Research, University of Edinburgh

child

Purpose: Assesses the non-verbal reasoning abilities of children ages 6-8 years. Identifies children in need of further evaluation. Used to measure achievement in the infant school and to aid in selection procedures.

Description: Multiple item paper-pencil test consisting of five subscales: doesn't belong, classification, reversed similarities, analogies, and sequences. Each subscale is separately timed with its own instructions and examples. Test items use pictures and shapes to present tasks of a similar type to those used in verbal reasoning tests. Items are based on ideas used in the former Moray House Picture Tests, but have been completely redrawn and retested. The manual contains information for administering and scoring the test, and details of the test's construction and standardization. Examiner required. Suitable for group use. BRITISH PUBLISHER

Timed: 30-40 minutes

Range: Ages 6:6-8:0 years

Scoring: Examiner evaluated

Cost: Test booklet £4.75 per set (20 copies); manual £2.00; specimen set £2.75.

Publisher: Hodder & Stoughton

THE FIVE P's: PARENT PROFESSIONAL PRESCHOOL PERFORMANCE PROFILE

Judith Simon Bloch

child

Purpose: Assesses the development of preschoolers (and older children functioning at this level) with behavioral, emotional, or developmental disorders. Used to plan IEP's for emotionally disturbed, schizophrenic, autistic, and language impaired students.

Description: 505 item paper-pencil observational assessment tool consisting of 15 scales grouped in five developmental areas: routines and self-help skills (classroom adjustment-school component, classroom adjustment-home component, toileting/hygiene, mealtime behaviors, dressing), motor development (gross motor/balance/coordination skills, perceptual/fine motor skills), language (communicative competence, receptive language, expressive language), social development (emerging self, relationship to adults, relationship to children), and cognitive development (attitude toward learning, cognitive skills). Items in each of the 15 scales (27-58 items each) describe developmental milestones and interfering behaviors. Items are rated "Yes," "No," or "Sometimes," according to which behaviors are demonstrated by the child. Parent (or primary caregiver) and teacher simultaneously and independently complete the scales in the fall and spring of each school year, providing a means of ongoing assessment. Test kit also includes IEP Forms, graphic profile sheet, and a Learning Style and Effective Teaching Methods Page, identifying the child's particular style of learning and corresponding methods of intervention. Instructional and technical manuals provided. Not suitable for group administration.

Untimed: Varies

Range: Ages 0-5 years

Scoring: Examiner evaluated

Cost: Contact publisher.

Publisher: Variety Pre-Schooler's Workshop

FLUHARTY PRESCHOOL AND LANGUAGE SCREENING TEST

Refer to page 164.

HOWELL PREKINDERGARTEN SCREENING TEST

Joseph P. Ryan, Ronald Mead and Howell Township Schools, Howell, N.J.

child

Purpose: Measures the school readiness of children entering kindergarten. Identifies children with learning disabilities, special talents and English language deficiencies. Used for academic placement at the kindergarten level.

Description: A battery of oral response and task performance subtests assessing 21 critical skills related to school readiness. Skills assessed include: shape and letter identification, listening comprehension, visual, motor and fine coordination, auditory memory and prereading and math skills. Scoring provides a profile of each child's strengths and weaknesses and identifies children in need of special placement: learning disabled, gifted and talented, and E.S.L. programs. Consumable student test booklets are scored according to guidelines provided in the manual. Individual record sheets are included in each test booklet for teacher reference. May be administered by teachers, paraprofessionals or volunteers. Examiner required. Individually administered; suitable for screening large groups of children.

Timed: 90 minutes, 2 sittings

Range: Ages 4-5 years

Scoring: Examiner evaluated

Cost: Student test booklets (set of 10) $14.95; user's guide and technical manual $11.95; specimen set (student test booklet and user's guide) $12.95.

Publisher: Book-Lab

INFANT SCREENING

Humberside Local Education Authority

child

Purpose: Identifies children who are "at risk" in terms of educational, social or emotional failure in their early school years. Diagnoses exact areas where problems exist. Suggests appropriate teaching programs to deal with the problems. Used for inservice training of teachers of young children.

Description: Two two-page multiple item paper-pencil observational checklists and one eight-page multiple item paper-pencil test assessing developmental areas of ability ranging from visual and auditory discrimination to managing behavior. Checklist 1 is completed for children ages 5 years and older; checklist 2 is completed for children ages 6 years and older. The test booklet is administered to children ages 6 years and older and is used in conjunction with the second checklist. Individual pupil profiles record children's progress and problems, forming a basis from which decisions about remedial work can be made. The teacher's book explains use of the materials for initial screening and provides ideas for follow-up diagnosis and remediation throughout the infant and lower junior years. Examiner required. Suitable for group use.
BRITISH PUBLISHER

Untimed: Varies

Range: Ages 5-6 years and up

Scoring: Examiner evaluated

Cost: Checklist 1 or 2 (pack of 20) £1.75; test booklet (pack of 10) £1.95; pupil profiles (pack of 25) £1.75; teacher's book and 8 diagnostic test cards £6.50.

Publisher: Macmillan Education

INITIAL COMMUNICATION PROCESSES

Refer to page 5.

AN INVENTORY OF PRIMARY SKILLS

Robert E. Valett

child K-1

Purpose: Measures primary skills necessary for success in kindergarten and first grade. Used by parents to identify areas in which their child is in need of developmental assistance.

Description: 20 item oral response, task performance, and paper-pencil inventory assessing development in the following areas: self information, body identification, body spatial relations, copying designs, alphabet printing, writing numbers, symbol matching, sentence copying, counting, basic arithmetic, copying house, draw-a-man, sight vocabulary, paragraph reading, alphabet knowledge, number knowledge, class concepts, position in space concepts, and descriptive concepts. Provides a total score as well as subscores for each of the areas listed. Administered by parent. Examiner required. Not suitable for group use.

Untimed: Varies

Range: Grades K-1

Scoring: Examiner evaluated

Cost: Package of 10 inventories $6.95.

Publisher: Pitman Learning, Inc.

KENT INFANT DEVELOPMENT SCALE (KID Scale)

Refer to page 5.

KRANER PRESCHOOL MATH INVENTORY

Refer to page 75.

LEXINGTON DEVELOPMENTAL SCALES (LDS)

Child Development Centers of the Bluegrass, Inc. staff

child

Purpose: Assesses the development of handicapped and nonhandicapped preschool children. Identifies a child's needs and abilities. Used for program planning and to evaluate the effectiveness of classroom and child instruction.

Description: Multiple item observational inventory assessing development in the following areas: gross and fine motor, language, personal and social, and cognitive. Test items are organized according to developmental area and are listed by age. Results are plotted on an interpretive chart and age norms are arranged in sequence denoting four continuous stages of development. The LDS Long Form provides an in-depth assessment and requires approximately two hours to administer. The LDS Short Form is a screening tool which takes 30-45 minutes to administer. Examiner required. Not suitable for group use.

Untimed: 30 minutes-2 hours

Range: Ages 2-6 years

Scoring: Examiner evaluated

Cost: LDS Long Form manual $6.00; LDS Long Form chart $1.25; LDS Short Form manual $4.00; LDS Short Form chart $1.00.

Publisher: Child Development Centers of the Bluegrass, Inc.

THE LOLLIPOP TEST: A DIAGNOSTIC SCREENING TEST OF SCHOOL READINESS

Alex L. Chew

child pre K-1

Purpose: Evaluates the school readiness of preschool, kindergarten, and first grade students. Used to plan individualized programs in grades K-1.

Description: Multiple item oral response and task assessment test measuring a preschool child's attainment of the developmental skills necessary for success in grades K-1. Test items are culture-free. Results identify both deficiencies and strengths for each child tested. May be administered before and after preschool programs to assess progress in readiness skills. Examiner required. Individually administered; suitable for screening groups of children.

Untimed: 15-20 minutes

Range: Preschoolers, grades K-1

Scoring: Examiner evaluated

Cost: Test kit (manual, 7 cards, 5 booklets) $37.00.

Publisher: Stoelting Co.

MAXFIELD-BUCHHOLZ SOCIAL MATURITY SCALE FOR BLIND PRE-SCHOOL CHILDREN

Refer to page 6.

MEEKER-CROMWELL BEHAVIOR DEVELOPMENTAL ASSESSMENT

Refer to page 168.

MILLER ASSESSMENT FOR PRESCHOOLERS (MAP)

Refer to page 6.

MOTOR SKILLS INVENTORY (MSI)

Refer to page 144.

PEABODY DEVELOPMENTAL MOTOR SCALES AND ACTIVITY CARDS

M. Rhonda Folio and Rebecca R. Fewell

child

Purpose: Assesses the motor development of children during the first eight years of life. Identifies children whose gross or fine-motor skills are delayed or abnormal. Used to establish IEP's.

Description: Multiple item task performance test consisting of a comprehensive sequence of gross- and fine-motor skills from which the relative developmental skill level can be determined for children from birth to age 83 months. May be used to analyze a wide range of skills identified as questionable by prior screening or to diagnose specific characteristics of a motor problem. Norms are provided for each skill category at each level and for the total test. The instructional program components include a tab-indexed card file of 170 gross-motor and 112 fine-motor activities referenced to the items on the test. These activity cards provide an instructional curriculum to fill developmental gaps, strengthen emerging skills, and set objectives for skills not yet attained. Examiner required. May be administered individually or to groups of children using a station-testing procedure.

Untimed: 20-30 minutes

Range: Ages 0-83 months

Scoring: Examiner evaluated

Cost: Test kit (manual, 15 response scoring booklets, 282 activity cards in tab-indexed file box, and all materials for administering tests: cubes, pegboard, pegs, formboard and shapes, bottle, beads and laces, box, dowel and string, etc.) $135.00.

Publisher: DLM Teaching Resources

PIAGET TASK KIT

Willard Stibal

child

Purpose: Determines the Piagetian Level at which a child is functioning.

Description: Multiple item test in which the child is asked to perform a number of simple tasks involving the following test materials: clay, colored paper bars; wooden bars; glass containers, flat plastic containers; and the paper form of the patented Stibal's Modmath Kit. The Piaget Task Kit includes a complete set of materials, a description of materials and scoring, and one copy of the task interview procedure and recording sheet. Examiner required. Not suitable for group use.

Untimed: Varies

Range: Children

Scoring: Examiner evaluated

Cost: Piaget Task Kit $10.00.

Publisher: Bureau of Educational Measurements

PRESCHOOL AND EARLY PRIMARY SKILLS SURVEY (PEPSS)

child

Purpose: Measures developmental skills necessary for early school success. Identifies children in need of further evaluation.

Description: Four task performance subtests assessing four developmental skills related to learning ability. Subtests include: picture recognition (visual recognition), picture relationship (discrimination and association), picture sequences (cognition of picture story sequences), and form completion (perceptual motor skills). Norms provided for preschool, kindergarten, and first grade classes. Examiner required. Not suitable for group use.

Untimed: 15-20 minutes

Range: Ages 3-7 years

Scoring: Examiner evaluated

Cost: Test kit (10 test booklets, examiner's manual, technical manual, scoring keys) $28.00.

Publisher: Stoelting Co.

PRESCHOOL ATTAINMENT RECORD (RESEARCH EDITION)

Edgar A. Doll

child

Purpose: Measures the general development of preschool children.

Description: Multiple item inventory assessing the physical, social, and intellectual functions of preschool children. Examiner required. Not suitable for group use.

Untimed: Varies

Range: Ages 6 months-7 years

Scoring: Examiner evaluated

Cost: PAR specimen set $3.25.

Publisher: American Guidance Service

PRESCHOOL DEVELOPMENT INVENTORY

Refer to page 8.

PRESCHOOL LANGUAGE ASSESSMENT INSTRUMENT (PLAI)

Refer to page 170.

PRIDE: PRESCHOOL AND KINDERGARTEN INTEREST DESCRIPTOR

Refer to page 146.

PSYCHOEDUCATIONAL PROFILE (PEP)

devel. disabled child

Purpose: Measures learning abilities and characteristics of autistic and related developmentally disordered children. Used to establish individualized special education curricula or home programs for developmentally disabled children who were previously regarded as untestable.

Description: Multiple item task performance test assessing the learning abilities of autistic and developmentally disabled children. Test results comprise a learning profile reflecting the individual characteristics of the child. This profile is translated into an appropriately individualized special education curriculum or home program according to the teaching strategies described in Volume II of the manual. Test kit includes the following standard materials required for uniform and accurate administration of the test: bubbles, tactile blocks, kaleidoscope, call bell, clay, cat and dog puppets, three-piece geometric formboard, four-piece formboard, three-piece mitten formboard, four-piece kitten puzzle, six-piece cow puzzle, matching item, clapper, whistle, writing booklet and lotto letters, pouch and objects, felt board and nine felt pieces, scissors, blocks and box, number cards, beads and string, function cards, hand bell, category cards I and II, and language. Materials needed but not provided include: mirror, candy, large ball, styrofoam cups, and a wheeled walker. The manual *(Individualized Assessment for Autistic and Developmentally Disabled Children)* is published in two volumes by University Park Press. Volume I describes the psychoeducational profile, and Volume II discusses teaching strategies for parents and professionals. Examiner required. Not suitable for group use.

Untimed: Varies

Range: Autistic and developmentally disabled children

Scoring: Examiner evaluated

Cost: Test kit (including standard materials) $200.00; Volume I of manual $29.95; Volume II of manual $19.95.

Publisher: Orange Industries

THE PYRAMID SCALES

John D. Cone

all ages

Purpose: Assesses adaptive behavior in moderately-severely handicapped persons of all ages. Used to plan appropriate intervention programs, to monitor changes in adaptive functioning over long periods of time, and to establish relevant training priorities.

Description: 20 multiple item paper-pencil scales assessing a handicapped individual's adaptive functioning skills. The scales are completed by the examiner using one or all of three different modes: by interview with the handicapped individual, by interview with an informant, by direct observation. The 20 skills areas assessed are arranged in three categories. Sensory scales assess three skills: tactile, auditory, and visual responsiveness. Items in this category are appropriate for very young and/or low-functioning individuals (e.g., turns head toward sound source). Primary scales assess nine basic skills: gross motor, eating, fine motor, toileting, dressing, social interaction, washing and grooming, receptive and expressive language. Secondary scales assess eight skills appropriate for older, higher-functioning individuals: recreation and leisure, writing, domestic behavior, reading, vocational, time, numbers, and money. Items in the scale were selected from and curriculum-referenced to such sources as the Brigance Inventory, the Behavior Characteristics Progression (BCP), the Learning Accomplishment Profile (LAP), and the Uniform Performance Assessment System (UPAS). Tables are provided in the manual showing correlations between scores on this test and those of other measures of adaptive ability. Formerly known as The West Virginia Assessment and Tracking System. Examiner required. Not suitable for group use.

Untimed: Varies

Range: Ages birth-78 years

Scoring: Examiner evaluated

Cost: Complete kit (manual and 50 answer sheets in storage box) $28.00.

Publisher: Pro-Ed

SCALES OF INDEPENDENT BEHAVIOR

Robert H. Bruininks, Richard W. Woodcock, Richard F. Weatherman and Bradley K. Hill

all ages

Purpose: Evaluates adaptive behavior and social adjustment from infancy through adult levels. Used in school and institutional settings for determining eligibility for special services, program planning, and individual and program evaluation.

Description: Multiple item interview guide assessing adjustment in the social, behavioral, and adaptive areas. Information gained from parent, caregiver, or teacher is used to evaluate functional independence and adaptive behavior in motor skills, social and communication skills, personal living skills, and community living skills. A problem behavior scale focuses on more severe problems. This test is structurally and statistically related to the Woodcock-Johnson Psycho-Educational Battery. Common norms are provided for the two tests which make it possible to interpret an individual's adaptive behavior in relation to his cognitive ability. Obtained scores include: age scores, percentile ranks, standard scores, relative performance index (RPI) expected range of independence, and instructional range. Examiner required. Not suitable for group use.

Untimed: 45-50 minutes

Range: Infant-adult

Scoring: Examiner evaluated

Cost: Test kit (easel-style test book, interviewer's manual, 15 response booklets) $75.00.

Publisher: DLM Teaching Resources

VINELAND ADAPTIVE BEHAVIOR SCALES

Refer to page 8.

VERBAL LANGUAGE DEVELOPMENT SCALE (VLDS)

Refer to page 175.

Intelligence and Related

ARLIN TEST OF FORMAL REASONING (ATFR)

Patricia Kennedy Arlin

child, teen grades 6-12

Purpose: Assesses the ways children think and learn. Used to assess cognitive abilities, plan curriculum, modify teaching techniques, and identify gifted students.

Description: 36 item paper-pencil multiple-choice test assessing logical thinking based on the cognitive developmental theory of Jean Piaget. Test items are incomplete sentence stems with forced-choice responses. Includes nine subtests: classification, multiplicative compensations, probability, correlations, combinations, proportions, forms of conservation beyond direct verification, coordination of two or more systems of response, and mechanical equilibrium. Individual, class, group, grade level and school statistics are available for total test, subtest, and items. The interpretation of both the total test score and the nine subtest scores is based on Inhelder and Piaget's description of formal operational thought and the eight schemata associated with that thought. Two computer scoring packages are available. Package 1 provides alphabetical pupil list indicating subtest scores, total test scores, and cognitive level designation. Package 2 provides summary item statistics, coefficients of correlations, means, total test statistics, subtest statistics, total test report, number tested, grade, mean, standard deviation, highest and lowest scores, Hoyt, S.E., Gr. subtest 1-classification report, and total test histogram. Examiner required. Suitable for group use.

Untimed: One hour

Range: Grades 6-12

Scoring: Hand key; computer scoring available

Cost: Test kit (manual, test booklets, answer sheets, hand-scoring template) $38.00; scoring package 1, $1.00/pupil; scoring package 2, $.65/pupil.

Publisher: Slosson Educational Publications, Inc.

THE BRIGANCE® DIAGNOSTIC ASSESSMENT OF BASIC SKILLS—SPANISH EDITION

Refer to page 82.

CREATIVITY ASSESSMENT PACKET

Refer to page 146.

HENMON-NELSON TESTS OF MENTAL ABILITY

Joseph L. French, Tom A. Lamke and Martin J. Nelson

child, teen K-12

Purpose: Measures general mental abilities of elementary and high school students.

Description: Battery of multiple item paper-pencil tests assessing the cognitive abilities of students from kindergarten to grade 12. Available in four levels: grades K-2 (Primary Battery), grades 3-6, grades 6-9, and grades 9-12. The Primary Battery consists of three subtests: listening, picture vocabulary, and size and number. These subtests measure nine different abilities and require no reading on the part of the students. Tests for grades 3-12 are arranged in omnibus-cycle form and contain different types of items related to academic success: vocabulary, sentence completion, opposites, general information, verbal analogies, verbal classification, verbal inference, number series, arithmetic reasoning, and figure analogies.

Scores available include: raw score, DIQ (Deviation IQ—a standard score by age), age percentile rank and stanine, and grade percentile rank and stanine. Consumable test booklets are available for all levels. Reusable test booklets and MRC answer cards (for use with scoring service) are available for grades 3-12 only. The Primary Battery examiner's manual includes: directions for administering each test, information about the nature and purposes of the tests, and guidelines for interpreting and using the test results. The examiner's manual for grades 3-12 includes information for administering, understanding, and using the tests, technical information, and norms tables. The examination kit contains: consumable test booklets for each of the four levels, one reusable test booklet for grades 9-12, Primary Battery examiner's manual, grades 3-12 examiner's manual, MRC answer card, and class record sheet. Examiner required. Not suitable for group use.

Untimed: Grades K-2—25-30 minutes; grades 3-12—30 minutes

Range: Grades K-12

Scoring: Examiner evaluated; scoring service available for grades 3-12

Cost: 35 Primary Battery test booklets (includes examiner's manual and class record sheet) $25.41; consumable test booklets for grades 3-6, 6-9, or 9-12 (includes examiner's manual and class record sheet) $18.99; 35 reusable test booklets for grades 3-6, 6-9, or 9-12 $18.99; 100 MRC answer cards (includes all materials needed to obtain scoring service) $13.08; examiner's manual (grades K-2 or 3-12) $2.49; class record sheet $6.54; examination kit for grades K-12 $3.84.

Publisher: The Riverside Publishing Company

McGUIRE-BUMPUS DIAGNOSTIC COMPREHENSION TEST

Marion L. McGuire and Marguerite J. Bumpus

child grades 1-6

Purpose: Assesses the thinking and reasoning skills of grade school children. Used to develop remedial/corrective programs and IEP's.

Description: 12 item paper-pencil test measuring comprehension skills at four levels of reasoning: literal, interpretive, analytic, and critical. Test items range in difficulty from primary level to advanced. Criterion-referenced scoring procedure diagnoses deficiencies in any of the 12 skills assessed and identifies children with similar needs. Group record chart records test results for all 12 objectives. Available in three versions: early primary (grades 1-2), primary (grades 2-3), and intermediate (grades 4-6). Test kits for all versions include: spirit master book, directions for administration, individual progress charts and class record chart. Examiner required. Suitable for group use.

Untimed: Varies

Range: Grades 1-6

Scoring: Examiner evaluated

Cost: Test kit (early primary, primary, or intermediate) $79.95.

Publisher: CROFT, Inc.

MINNESOTA PRESCHOOL SCALE

Florence Goodenough, Katherine Maurer and M.J. Van Wagenen

child

Purpose: Measures the intelligence of preschool children. Used with normal, gifted, and retarded children.

Description: 109 item oral response and task performance test consisting of 26 short subtests measuring both verbal and non-verbal intelligence. The subtests include 12 practice items and 97 test items. Verbal subtests include: language comprehension, language facility, memory for digits, and incomplete picture and digits. Non-verbal subtests include: drawing, block building, discrimination recognition, tracing of forms, puzzle pictures, paper folding, recognition of omitted parts in picture and imitation position of clock hands. Verbal, non-verbal, and combined scores may be converted to percentile placement scores, IQ equivalents, or standard C scores. Examiner required. Not suitable for group use.

Untimed: Varies

Range: Ages 1 year 6 months-6 years

Scoring: Examiner evaluated

Cost: Complete set (test materials, manual, 25 individual record forms) $59.50; Specimen set (individual record form, manual, and sample test materials) $4.50.

Publisher: American Guidance Service

NON-LANGUAGE LEARNING TEST

Refer to page 12.

OTIS SELF-ADMINISTERING TEST OF MENTAL ABILITY

Refer to page 12.

PRIDE: PRESCHOOL AND KINDERGARTEN INTEREST DESCRIPTOR

Refer to page 146.

QUICK WORD TEST

Refer to page 170.

SILVER DRAWING TEST OF COGNITIVE AND CREATIVE SKILLS

Rawley A. Silver

all ages

Purpose: Identifies children with cognitive or creative strengths which may be overlooked by traditional tests of intelligence and achievement. Used by school psychologists, art therapists, speech and hearing specialists, resource teachers, teachers of art, rehabilitation counselors, and other professionals.

Description: Three multiple item paper-pencil subtests assessing the concepts of space, sequential order, and class-inclusion. The predictive drawing test assesses the ability to sequence and deal with hypothetical situations. Students are asked to add lines to outline drawings. Responses are scored for ability to show how the objects would appear if filled, tilted, or placed on a slope. The drawing from the observation test assesses concepts of space. Students are asked to draw an arrangement of cylinders. Responses are scored for ability to represent left-right, above-below, and front-back relationships. The drawing from imagination test assesses the ability to form associations on the basis of class or function. Students are asked to choose subjects from two arrays of drawings and to create a narrative drawing. Responses are scored for ability to select, to combine, and to represent. When appropriate, drawings are also scored for projection (emotional content) and language (titles). Drawing ability is not evaluated. Figures and tables are presented for interpretation of scores. Instructions for taking the test may be signed or pantomimed for used with handicapped populations in a variety of cultural settings. Examiner required. Suitable for use with small groups.

Untimed: 15 minutes

Range: Age 6 years-adult

Scoring: Examiner evaluated

Cost: Test kit (manual, 10 test booklets, stimulus photograph for drawing from observation test, classroom record sheet)$35.00; specimen set (manual and sample test book) $18.00.

Publisher: Special Child Publications

SOI PROCESS AND DIAGNOSTIC SCREENING TEST (FORM P)

SOI Institute staff

child grades K-3

Purpose: Assesses the learning abilities of young children. Screens for special education or gifted placement in Grades K-3. Used for early testing of bi-lingual and disadvantaged students to identify special needs or giftedness.

Description: 11 subtests evaluating the process abilities required for success in Grades K-3. Six subtests test processing abilities, the other five are diagnostic subtests. Designed for screening all students at Grades K-3 before an in-depth testing by a competency team for 94-142 or gifted placement. Includes auditory sequencing. Suitable for teacher administration to groups; some subtests are given individually to those students who cannot write. Spanish form available.

Untimed: Processing-30 minutes; Diagnostic-25 minutes

Range: Grades K-3

Scoring: Hand scored; computer scoring and analysis available

Cost: Form P $2.50 each; Spanish Form $2.50 each.

Publisher: SOI Institute

Reading

Elementary

ASSESSING READING DIFFICULTIES: A DIAGNOSTIC AND REMEDIAL APPROACH

Refer to page 158.

AUDITORY BLENDING TEST

Florence Rosewell and Jeanne Chall

child grades 2-6

Purpose: Evaluates a child's ability to blend sounds when the sounds are presented orally. Used for classroom and remedial work in elementary and secondary schools.

Description: Multiple item oral response test assessing a child's ability to blend sounds auditorily into whole words whether or not he has learned to associate the sounds with the corresponding letters. Indicates the ease or difficulty that students will experience in phonics instruction. Examiner required. Not suitable for group use.

Untimed: 5 minutes

Range: Grades 2-6

Scoring: Examiner evaluated

Cost: Get-acquainted set (manual and 2 copies of test) $4.00.

Publisher: Essay Press

BASIC SIGHT WORD TEST

E. W. Dolch

child

Purpose: Measures children's knowledge of basic sight words—the most commonly used words which cannot be learned from pictures and must be recognized instantly by sight before a child can read with interest and confidence. Identifies children in need of remedial work.

Description: 220 item paper-pencil multiple-choice test measuring children's knowledge of basic sight words (service words), such as commonly used pronouns, adjectives, adverbs, prepositions, conjunctions, and common verbs. Each test item consists of four words. The children are asked to circle the word read aloud by their teacher. The 100 sheets printed in primer type on both sides are enough to test 25 children on all the words. All the words should be known by the end of grade 2. Examiner required. Suitable for group use.

Untimed: Varies

Range: Children, beginning readers

Scoring: Examiner evaluated

Cost: 100 sheets $5.47.

Publisher: Garrard Publishing Company

BASIC VISUAL-MOTOR ASSOCIATION TEST

Refer to page 143.

BOTEL READING INVENTORY

Morten Botel

child

Purpose: Measures how well elementary school students can read. Used for academic placement and measuring student progress throughout the school year.

Description: Four paper-pencil and oral response tests assessing skills in three areas crucial to success in elementary reading and language arts: decoding, word recognition (oral reading ability), and word opposites (reading comprehension). The Decoding Test measures decoding competency at seven levels ranging from the awareness of sounds and letter correspondences to decoding multisyllabic nonsense words. The seven levels are covered by 12 subtests of 10 items each. All responses are scored according to the following code: correct word, mispronunciation, substitution, or no response. As on all of the tests, the student's highest instructional level is considered to be the first level at which he falls below 80% correct answers. The Spelling Test consists of five graded lists of 20 words each. The words are dictated and the students are asked to spell them.

The Word Recognition Test consists of eight 20-word samples, spanning eight graduated reading levels from preprimer through fourth grade. As the student reads the words, responses are graded as follows: correct word, mispronunciation, substitution, or no response. The Word Opposites Test is a group test consisting of ten scaled 10-word subtests that progress from first reader level through senior high school. For each test item, the student is asked to select from four words the one which means the opposite. The Word Opposites Test may be administered both as a reading test and as a listening test. As a reading test, it indicates the student's current reading performance; as a listening test, it indicates the student's reading potential. The reading placement tests yield three levels of reading competency: free reading level, instructional level, and frustration level. The Word Recognition and Word Opposites Tests are both available in forms A and B for pre- and posttesting. The administration manual includes information on administering, scoring, and interpreting the test, as well as technical data. Examiner required. Suitable for group use.

Untimed: Varies

Range: Elementary school children

Scoring: Examiner evaluated

Cost: Manual $8.00; Decoding Test, 35 Word Recognition Tests (Form A or B), or 35 Word Opposites Test (Form A or B) $6.58 each.

Publisher: Modern Curriculum Press

CLYMER-BARRETT READINESS TEST

Refer to page 118.

CONCISE WORD READING TESTS

Andrews

child

Purpose: Measures the word reading skills of primary and lower secondary school students. Used for class or school surveys and as a basis for grouping children for reading instruction.

Description: Four 20-item oral response tests measuring the word recognition and word attack skills of children ages 7-12 years. Each test is suitable for use with more than one age level. Age norms and standardized scores are provided for Australian students. Examiner required. Suitable for group use. AUSTRALIAN PUBLISHER

Untimed: Varies

Range: Ages 7-12 years

Scoring: Examiner evaluated

Cost: Basic kit (test materials for 4 forms, and 50 record forms with instructions and norms) $10.50.

Publisher: Teaching and Testing Resources

DIAGNOSTIC AND ACHIEVEMENT READING TESTS: DART PHONICS TESTING PROGRAM

child

Purpose: Measures student achievement of phonics skills. Diagnoses specific skills which have not been mastered. Used for instructional placement and planning.

Description: 10 multiple item paper-pencil multiple-choice test booklets measuring 66 phonics skills. Tests are arranged in three levels (A, B, and C) and assess the following phonics skills: test A-1 (readiness skills, initial and final consonants), test A-2 (alphabet letters, initial and final consonants), test A-3 (short and long vowels), test A-4 (consonant blends and digraphs), test B-1 (initial and final consonants, vowels, blends, digraphs), test B-2 (Y as a vowel, soft C and G, mumur diphthongs, plurals), test B-3 (prefixes, root words, irregular double vowels, diphthongs), test C-1 (monosyllabic and polysyllabic words with prefixes, roots, suffixes, long and short vowels, digraphs, diphthongs, and final e), test C-2 (synonyms, antonyms, homonyms, and contracted forms), and test C-3 (syllabication). Test pages look like familiar workbook pages. Tests may be administered in any order. All test booklets are supplied in spirit master form. Test sections are keyed to specific pages in the MCP Phonics Workbooks, but may be used with any reading program that employs the decoding approach to word recognition. Examiner required. Suitable for group use.

Untimed: Varies

Range: Elementary school students

Scoring: Examiner evaluated

Cost: Complete set (10 test booklets) $51.95.

Publisher: Modern Curriculum Press

DIAGNOSTIC READING TEST OF WORD ANALYSIS SKILLS (REVISED AND EXTENDED)

Florence Rosewell and Jeanne Chall

child grades K-4

Purpose: Assesses a child's ability to use fundamental phonic and word recognition skills. Used for diagnostic and prescriptive teaching purposes in classrooms, tutorial work, and reading clinics.

Description: Multiple item oral response test containing, among others, the following subtests: sight recognition of high frequency words, naming capital and lower case letters, consonant blends and digraphs, short vowels, long vowels with e, long vowel combinations, writing and spelling CVC words. Appropriate subtests are indicated for differing levels of reading ability. Results yield a comprehensive profile which indicates a grade level and classifies skills as: mastered, requiring review, or requiring systematic instruction. Available in Forms A and B for test-retest purposes. Suitable for use with older students who function at a grade 4 level or below on these skills. Examiner required. Not suitable for group use.

Untimed: 10-15 minutes

Range: Grades K-4

Scoring: Examiner evaluated

Cost: Get-acquainted set (manual, 2 copies Form A) $4.00.

Publisher: Essay Press

GILMORE ORAL READING TEST

John V. Gilmore and Eunice C. Gilmore

child grades 1-8

Purpose: Assesses the oral reading abilities of students grades 1-8. Used for program planning and academic placement.

Description: Oral reading test measuring three aspects of oral reading ability: accuracy, comprehension, and rate. The spiral-bound booklet of reading paragraphs and the manual of directions are needed to administer the test. A separate record blank is needed for each child tested. A five-level classification of accuracy, rate, and comprehension is provided, along with stanines and grade-equivalents for accuracy and comprehension scores. Available in two alternate and equivalent forms, C and D. Examiner required. Not suitable for group use.

Untimed: 15-20 minutes

Range: Grades 1-8

Scoring: Examiner evaluated

Cost: Examination kit (manual and record blank) $5.00; booklet of reading paragraphs $10.00; 25 record blanks Form C or D $16.00; manual $3.50.

Publisher: The Psychological Corporation

GROUP DIAGNOSTIC READING APTITUDE AND ACHIEVEMENT TESTS—INTERMEDIATE FORM

Marion Monroe and Eva Edity Sherman

child grades 3-9

Purpose: Measures reading aptitude and achievement for grades 3-9. Diagnoses specific skill deficits which may impair reading performance.

Description: 391 item paper-pencil battery consisting of eight achievement tests (paragraph meaning, speed of reading, vowels, consonants, reversals, additions and omissions, arithmetic, and spelling) and seven aptitude tests (visual letter memory, visual form memory, auditory letter memory, auditory orientation and discrimination, copying text, cross-out letters, and vocabulary). The paragraph reading test (28 items; 7 minutes) requires students to read a question, read a paragraph containing the answer to the question, and select the appropriate one-word or short-phrase answer from five given choices. The speed of reading test (45 items; 1½ minutes) requires students to read through a one-page text and indicate comprehension by performing simple game-like tasks (such as "put a dot in this circle" or "cross out the three"). The vowels, consonants, reversals, and additions and omissions tests (24 items each; 2 minutes each) measure word discrimination skills by presenting three sentences for each test item, one of which is correct with the other two containing errors appropriate to the test (vowel substitution, consonant substitution, reversals, or additions or omissions). Students underline the correct sentence.

The arithmetic computation test (30 items; 5 minutes) measures the ability to add, subtract, multiply, and divide with whole numbers, fractions, and decimals. The spelling test (40 minutes; untimed) provides a sentence with a blank provided for a missing word. The teacher reads the sentence with the missing word, and the students fill in the blank with the word pronounced by the teacher. In the visual letter memory test (18 items), the teacher shows the students a card on which a nonsense word is printed. Each card is flashed for five seconds, and students are asked to write as much of the nonsense word from each card as they can remember. In the visual form memory test (4 items) the teacher flashes cards with simple line-drawing designs for 10 seconds each, then asks the students to draw as much of each card as they can remember. The auditory letter memory test (16 items) is similar to the visual test, except the teacher spells aloud the letters of some nonsense words for the students to copy down. The auditory discrimination and orientation test (25 items) requires students to mark a grid of X's in response to aural stimuli dictated by the teacher. The copying text test (1 item; 1½ minutes) measures fine motor skills by requiring the students to copy a short story as quickly and plainly as they can.

In the crossing-out letters test (60 items; 1 minute) a text of nonsense words is provided in which every other word contains one letter "a." Students are directed to cross all the a's they can find. The vocabulary test (28 items; untimed) provides four pairs of words for each test item. Only one of the pairs of words makes sense (the other three pairs are abstract combinations or obvious malapropisms). The teacher reads each pair aloud, and students are directed to underline the pair that makes the best sense to them. The achievement tests are scored in terms of grade equivalents. The aptitude tests are scored in terms of percentiles by age. The front-sheet of the 14-page test booklet provides forms for developing educational and diagnostic profiles and deriving a mental age for each student tested. Examiner required. Suitable for group use.

Timed: 9 timed tests—24 minutes; 6 untimed tests—varies

Range: Grades 3-9

Scoring: Examiner evaluated

Cost: Test booklets each $.25; 22 visual test cards $2.50; set of norms $.75; directions to the examiner included free of charge.

Publisher: C.H. Nevins Printing Company

HARRISON-STROUD READING READINESS PROFILE

Refer to page 86.

INDIVIDUALIZED CRITERION REFERENCED TESTING (ICRT)

Refer to page 87.

INFORMAL READING COMPREHENSION PLACEMENT TEST

Eunice Insel and Ann Edson

child grades 1-6

Purpose: Measures reading comprehension. Determines instructional placement level for students grades 1-6.

Description: 68 item microcomputer administered test assessing word comprehension and passage comprehension. The 60 item word comprehension test measures students' knowledge of word meanings and thinking skills using a word analogy format. The passage comprehension test consists of a series of eight graded selections and questions ranging in difficulty from primer level through eighth grade. The level of difficulty for each of these selections was determined by using the Spache, Frye, and Dall Chall readability formulas. Students are placed in an instructional reading range of first through eighth grade in word comprehension and passage comprehension. The test is totally administered, scored, and managed by the microcomputer. Cassette or diskette available for Apple II + and IIe, TRS Models III and IV, and Commodore 64 microcomputers. All diskette programs include backups. Examiner required. Not suitable for group use.

Untimed: Varies

Range: Grades 1-6

Scoring: Microcomputer scored

Cost: 1 cassette (specify model) $44.95; 1 diskette (specify model) $49.95. All disk programs come with a backup.

Publisher: Educational Activities, Inc.

LANGUAGE DEVELOPMENT READING EVALUATION PROGRAM

Refer to page 166.

THE MACMILLAN DIAGNOSTIC READING PACK

Ted Ames

child, teen

Purpose: Diagnoses the reading problems of children ages seven years and older. Suggests appropriate remedial programs. Used for in-service teacher training programs.

Description: 16 multiple item paper-pencil and oral response test cards presenting tests on specific reading skills and sub-skills, such as letter-matching and consonant blending. Checklists, for recording student performance on the tests and providing a detailed picture of individual ability, are available for four stages in the development of reading skills: reading ages 5-6, 6-7, 7-8, and 8-9 years. The test cards and checklists together provide a means of observing and testing reading skills from beginning reading to fluency. A teacher's manual provides clear instructions for testing and diagnosis and prescribes source references for further remedial procedures. Examiner required. Suitable for group use.

BRITISH PUBLISHER

Untimed: Varies

Range: Reading ages 5-8 years

Scoring: Examiner evaluated

Cost: Test kit (manual, 16 test cards, and 10 copies of each of 4 checklists) £10.95.

Publisher: Macmillan Education

THE NELSON READING SKILLS TESTS: FORMS 3 AND 4

Gerald S. Hanna, Leo M. Schell and Robert L. Schreiner

child grades 3-9

Purpose: Assesses student achievement and progress in word attack skills, vocabulary, reading comprehension, and reading rate. Diagnoses individual students' reading strengths and weaknesses. Used with grades 3-9 to meet Chapter 1 (Title 1) requirements.

Description: Multiple item paper-pencil test consisting of two subtests: Word Meaning and Reading Comprehension. The Word Meaning test measures three kinds of vocabulary items: words in isolation, words in phrases, and words in sentences. The Reading Comprehension test measures literal, translational, and higher order tasks. A single test booklet presents three levels of each test: level A (grades 3-4), level B (grades 5-6), and level C (grades 7-9). The test booklet also includes the following two optional tests: the Word Parts test (for level A) diagnoses students' decoding skills, including sound/symbol correspondence, root words, and syllabication; and the Reading Rate test (for levels B and C) which also includes a short subtest measuring comprehension of the reading rate passage.

Test booklets are available in parallel forms 3 and 4. Scores provided for the Word Parts, Word Meanings, and Reading Comprehension tests include: raw scores, grade equivalent scores, national percentile ranks, national stanines, and normal curve equivalent scores. Verbal indicators of student performance on the Word Parts subtest are also provided. Words-per-minute and grade equivalent scores are provided for the Reading Rate test. Standardization and other studies are described in the technical manual. Administration and scoring procedures are described in the teacher's manual. Self-marking answer sheets are available for hand scoring; MRC answer sheets are available for machine scoring. The examination kit contains: Form 4 test booklet, teacher's manual, technical manual, student score report folder, class record sheet, level A self-marking answer sheet, and MRC answer sheet. Examiner required. Suitable for group use.

Timed: Word Parts—24 minutes; Word Meaning—8 minutes; Reading Comprehension—24 minutes; Reading Rate—3 minutes

Range: Grades 3-9

Scoring: Hand key; machine scoring available

Cost: 35 test booklets (form 3 or 4) $20.16; 35 MRC answer sheets (includes teacher's manual, 35 student score report folders, and materials for machine scoring) $14.13; 35 self-marking answer sheets (includes teacher's manual, 35 student score report folders, and 2 class record sheets) $18.69; set of 2 scoring masks $4.20; technical manual $2.97; examination kit $4.53.

Publisher: The Riverside Publishing Company

PRIMARY READING PROFILES

James B. Stroud, A.N. Hieronymus and Paul McKee

child grades 1-3

Purpose: Measures achievement of primary reading skills for students finishing first or second grade or entering second or third grade.

Description: Five multiple item paper-pencil tests assessing student progress in the following reading skills: aptitude for reading, auditory association, word recognition, word attack, and reading comprehension. A composite score for the word recognition, word attack, and reading comprehension tests indicates the student's grasp of the reading process. A comparison of this composite score with the student's score on the aptitude for reading test provides for a comparison between actual and expected reading performance. The scores on the auditory association, word attack, and word recognition tests will often indicate a reason for any divergence between actual and expected reading ability. Available in two levels: level 1 (late grade 1 or early grade 2) and level 2 (late grade 2 or early grade 3). Norms provided in the form of grade-equivalents and percentile ranks. Examiner required. Suitable for group use.

Untimed: 85 minutes

Range: Grades 1-3

Scoring: Hand key

Cost: 35 hand-scorable test booklets (includes manual, set of scoring masks, class record sheet, and 35 profile charts) level 1 or level 2 $21.15; examination kit $3.84.

Publisher: The Riverside Publishing Company

READING READINESS TESTS (FORM RR)

SOI Institute staff

child

Purpose: Assesses the reading readiness of young children.

Description: Multiple item oral response test assessing abilities that relate to reading readiness. Test includes instructions for administration. May be used as a prelude to the Reading Readiness Workbook (SOI). Examiner required. Suitable for group use (some sections must be individually administered).

Untimed: Varies

Range: Children

Scoring: Examiner evaluated

Cost: Form RR $2.15 each.

Publisher: SOI Institute

READING SKILLS CHECKLISTS

child, teen

Purpose: Measures individual students' growth in reading skills from kindergarten through junior high. Used for program planning, parent conferences, and as a part of a transferring student's permanent file.

Description: Multiple item paper-pencil checklist assessing student knowledge and mastery of important reading skills. Items on the list consist of descriptions of reading skills which the teacher must rate according to the following scale: the skill has not been taught, the skill has been taught but not mastered, the skill has been taught and mastered. Checklists are presented in the form of file-sized folders and are available in three levels: primary, intermediate, and junior high. Suitable for use with most basal reading programs (phonics or sight-word based). Examiner required. Not suitable for group use.

Untimed: Varies

Range: Primary-junior high students

Scoring: Examiner evaluated

Cost: Primary checklist (pkg. of 30) $10.60; intermediate checklist (pkg. of 30) $11.17; junior high checklist (pkg. of 30) $10.81.

Publisher: Modern Curriculum Press

ST. LUCIA GRADED WORD READING TEST

Andrews

child, teen

Purpose: Measures the word reading skills of primary and lower secondary school students. Diagnoses specific skill deficits.

Description: Multiple item oral response reading test measuring word recognition skills. Provides reading ages as well as diagnostic information on word attack skills and error patterns. Standardized in Australia. Examiner required. Not suitable for group use.
AUSTRALIAN PUBLISHER

Untimed: Varies

Range: Primary and lower secondary school children

Scoring: Examiner evaluated

Cost: Basic kit (manual test materials, and 50 record forms) $11.00.

Publisher: Teaching and Testing Resources

ST. LUCIA READING COMPREHENSION TEST

Elkins and Andrews

child grades 2-4

Purpose: Measures reading comprehension of children in the lower primary school.

Description: Multiple item paper-pencil cloze-type test measuring the reading ability of students grades 2-4. Available in alternate forms A and B. Australian norms allow scores to be expressed as reading ages, percentiles, or 15 point scale scores. Examiner required. Suitable for group use.
AUSTRALIAN PUBLISHER

Untimed: Varies

Range: Students grades 2-4

Scoring: Examiner evaluated

Cost: Basic kit (manual, 25 tests form A, and 25 tests form B) $11.50.

Publisher: Teaching and Testing Resources

High School and Above

BUFFALO READING TEST

Refer to page 212.

CALIFORNIA PHONICS SURVEY

Grace M. Brown and Alice B. Corrtell

teen, adult gr. 7 and up

Purpose: Measures the overall phonic adequacy of a group, class, or school system from grade 7 to college. Identifies individuals with some degree of phonic disability and determines the degree of impairment.

Description: 5 item oral response test assessing a student's phonic adequacy. Test items consist of exercises involving reading and listening which are constructed to reveal the most common reversals, confusions of blends and vowels, and other errors that reflect the inability to relate letter combinations to spoken sounds. The pattern of errors made by the student is interpreted in terms of eight diagnostic categories related to skills necessary for adequate reading, spelling, and language. Four general levels of phonic adequacy are defined by raw scores: adequate phonics, some phonic disability, serious phonic disability, and gross phonic disability. Available in two forms for pre- and posttesting. A single test booklet is used to administer either Form 1 or Form 2. Examiner required. Suitable for group use.

Untimed: 45 minutes

Range: Grade 7-college

Scoring: Examiner evaluated

Cost: Specimen set $10.00; manual $9.00; 25 test booklets $8.00; 50 answer sheets (profiles on back) $5.50; scoring stencils (diagnostic set; form 1) $8.50; scoring stencils (retest score; form 2) $1.50; cassette tape $10.00.

Publisher: Consulting Psychologists Press, Inc.

Multi-Level

INFORMAL READING ASSESSMENT

Paul C. Burns and Betty D. Roe

child, teen preK-12

Purpose: Measures the reading performance level of students from preschool to grade 12. Used by preservice as well as inservice teachers who have little or no experience with reading assessment.

Description: Multiple item inventory of oral reading ability consisting of graded word lists and graded reading passages. Two equivalent forms of the graded word lists and four equivalent forms of the graded passages are provided for each level. All forms are presented on reproducible pages. The equivalent forms provide a built-in provision for retesting to assure instructional flexibility. Test package includes detailed description of how to administer, score, and interpret the inventory, as well as a scoring aid and record-keeping sheets. Examiner required. Not suitable for group use. CANADIAN PUBLISHER

Untimed: Varies

Range: Preprimer-grade 12

Scoring: Examiner evaluated

Cost: Test kit $10.50.

Publisher: Nelson Canada

MICHIGAN PRESCRIPTIVE PROGRAM IN ENGLISH (GRAMMAR)

William E. Lockhart

teen, adult gr. 6 and up

Purpose: Measures student abilities in English grammar. Identifies skill deficits. Used to help students obtain a 10th grade equivalency and pass the GED test in English grammar.

Description: Multiple item paper-pencil test assessing the following high school level English grammar skills: capitalization, subjects, verbs, verb tense, moods, prepositions, case, possessive and indefinite pronouns, adjectives, adverbs, punctuation, synonyms, homonyms, plurals, and spelling. English study materials have allowed students .8 to 2-3 years gain in English achievement for 24 clock hours of study. Examiner required. Suitable for group use.

Untimed: Varies

Range: Middle school students-adult

Scoring: Examiner evaluated

Cost: Test book $1.50; 7 response and prescription sheet booklets $2.00; answer key $1.00; English study materials $5.00.

Publisher: Ann Arbor Publishers, Inc.

READING SPLIT FORM (FORM R)

Mary Meeker and Robert Meeker

teen grades 7 and up

Purpose: Assesses reading ability of elementary, intermediate, high school, and college students.

Description: Multiple item paper-pencil test measuring reading ability. Discipline-focused test items are selected from the SOI-LA Basic Test. Administration requires Basic Test manual. Examiner required. Suitable for group use.

Timed: 1 hour

Range: Intermediate, high school, and college students

Scoring: Hand key; computer scoring available

Cost: Examiner's manual $22.00; test forms $1.95 each.

Publisher: SOI Institute

SPADAFORE DIAGNOSTIC READING TEST (SDRT)

Gerald J. Spadafore

child, teen grades 1-12

Purpose: Assesses reading skills in students grades 1-12 and adults. Used for screening and diagnostic purposes for academic placement and career guidance counseling.

Description: Four subtests assess word recognition, oral reading and comprehension, silent reading comprehension, and listening comprehension. Criterion-referenced test items are graded for difficulty. Independent, Instructional, and Frustration reading and comprehension levels are designated for performance at each grade level. Test results may be used for screening to determine whether reading problems exist at a student's current grade placement. Administration for screening requires 30 minutes for all four subtests and determines whether reading problems exist at a student's current grade placement. Administration for diagnostic purposes requires 60 minutes for all four subtests and yields a comparison of decoding reading skills. Guidelines provided for interpreting performance in terms of vocational literacy. The test may be scored as it is administered. Provisions for conducting a detailed error analysis of oral reading are included. Examiner required. Not suitable for group use.

Untimed: 60 minutes

Range: Grades 1-12

Scoring: Examiner evaluated

Cost: Test kit (includes manual, test plates, 10 test booklets) $45.00; specimen set (includes manual and sample test booklet) $12.50.

Publisher: Academic Therapy Publications

Library Skills

DIAGNOSTIC TEST OF LIBRARY SKILLS

Barbara Feldstein and Janet Rawdon

child, teen grades 5-9

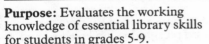

Purpose: Evaluates the working knowledge of essential library skills for students in grades 5-9.

Description: 50 item paper-pencil multiple-choice test measuring library skills in the following areas: definitions of library terms, use of the title page, use of the table of contents, use of an index, use of the card catalog, library arrangement, and use of reference materials. Results are recorded on an analytic sheet which indicates areas that require general class or small group attention. Further examination of individual answer sheets indicates specific needs. Available in equivalent forms A and B with interchangeable answer key. A bibliography of sources that provide instruction and learning experiences for concepts included in this test is provided in the teacher's guide. Examiner required. Suitable for group use.

Untimed: Varies

Range: Grades 5-9

Scoring: Hand key

Cost: Test kit (50 test booklets, 100 answer sheets, 1 scoring key, and teacher's guide) form A or B $24.95.

Publisher: Learnco, Inc.

LIBRARY SKILLS TEST

Illinois Association of College and Research Libraries

teen grades 7 and up

Purpose: Assesses students' skills in working with library materials.

Description: Multiple item paper-pencil test identifying students' strengths and weaknesses in working with library materials. Test items pertain to current terminology, the card catalog, classification systems, filing, parts of a book, indexes, reference tools, and bibliographic forms. Manual includes answer key, content outline, and norms for grades 7-12 and college freshmen. Scoring service provides three alphabetical lists and class summary data. Examiner required. Suitable for group use.

Timed: 45 minutes

Range: Grades 7-12 and college freshmen

Scoring: Computer scored

Cost: Test kit (manual and 20 test booklets) $17.60; scoring service $.80 per student; specimen set $6.00.

Publisher: Scholastic Testing Service, Inc.

TEST OF LIBRARY/STUDY SKILLS

Frances Hatfield and Irene Gullette

child, teen grades 2-12

Purpose: Measures knowledge of essential library/media skills for elementary and high school students.

Description: Multiple item paper-pencil multiple-choice test assessing library/media skills in the following areas: arrangement of books, parts of a book, card catalog, indexes, and reference books. Several types of media are used for examples. Available in three levels: level I (grades 2-5), level II (grades 4-9), and level III (grades 8-12). Answer key is common to all three levels. Complete test kits for all levels include 50 test booklets, 100 answer cards, and one answer key. Examiner required. Suitable for group use.

Timed: 50 minutes

Range: Grades 2-12

Scoring: Hand key

Cost: Complete kit (level I) $22.00; complete kit (level II or III) $25.00.

Publisher: Larlin Corporation

Sensory-Motor Skills

ADOLESCENT AND ADULT PSYCHOEDUCATIONAL PROFILE (AAPEP)

Refer to page 153.

ANN ARBOR LEARNING INVENTORY AND REMEDIATION PROGRAM

Barbara Meister Vitale and Waneta Bullock

child grades K-4

Purpose: Evaluates the central processing and perceptual skills necessary for reading, writing and spelling. Identifies learning difficulties and deficits and suggests appropriate remedial strategies. Used to establish IEP's.

Description: Multiple item task performance, oral response, and paper-pencil test measuring the following central processing skills: visual discrimination, visual memory, auditory discrimination, auditory memory, and modality strength (auditory or visual). Also identifies specific visual and auditory perceptual problems such as rotations, closure, omissions, directionality, and sequencing problems. Test items are presented in order of natural cognitive development, beginning with pictures, proceeding to objects and geometric forms, then to letters, words, and phrases. Tasks involve listening, manipulating, showing, matching, visualizing, telling, and writing. In addition to information on central processing skills and perceptual abilities, results also provide objective data on developmental levels for pre-reading readiness, pre-computational skills, kinesthetic and motor skills, and comprehension and critical thinking. Available for two levels: level A (grades K-1) and level B (grades 2-4). Manual provides remedial suggestions for immediate classroom use. Examiner required. Suitable for group use.

Untimed: Varies

Range: Grades K-4

Scoring: Examiner evaluated

Cost: Teacher's manual for level A or B $4.00; student booklet for level A or B $.50 each.

Publisher: Ann Arbor Publishers, Inc.

BASIC VISUAL-MOTOR ASSOCIATION TEST

James D. Battle

child grades 1-9

Purpose: Measures visual short-term memory. Predicts students' skills in reading, spelling, and arithmetic. Used by classroom teachers, resource teachers, school psychologists, and remedial therapists.

Description: 60 item paper-pencil symbol-copying test in two forms assessing the following visual-motor skills: recall of visual symbols, visual sequencing ability, visual association skills, visual-motor ability, visual integrative ability, and symbol-integration skills. Students are asked to copy 30 symbols (upper-case letters) on form A and 30 symbols (lower-case letters) on form B. Three minutes are allowed for each form. Conversion tables provide percentile ranks and t-scores derived from raw scores. Examiner required. Suitable for group use grades 2-9; individual use in grade one.

Timed: 6 minutes

Range: Grades 1-9

Scoring: Examiner evaluated

Cost: Test kit (manual, 25 forms A and B, scoring acetate) $19.50; specimen set (manual and sample test form) $12.50.

Publisher: Special Child Publications

EARLY LEARNING ASSESSMENT AND DEVELOPMENT

Refer to page 120.

EARLY SCREENING INVENTORY

Refer to page 121.

FROSTIG MOVEMENT SKILLS TEST BATTERY (EXPERIMENTAL EDITION)

Russel E. Orpet

child

Purpose: Evaluates the sensory-motor development of sensory-motor skills in children ages 6-12 years. Diagnoses areas of sensory-motor development requiring special attention.

Description: 12 item task performance test providing scaled scores on five factors: hand-eye coordination, strength, balance, visually guided movement, and flexibility. Norms by sex are provided for normally developing children from 6-12 years of age. Manual provides a rationale for the battery, statistical information, and instructions for administration and scoring. The needed equipment can be assembled or built from specifications provided in the manual or purchased in the standard equipment kit which includes the manual, 50 recording sheets, and all special items needed except for two 12-foot 2 x 4's and a stop watch (wooden blocks, block transfer kit, bean bags, floor targets, carpenter's rule, and brackets for walking board). Examiner required. Suitable for use with one to four children at a time.

Untimed: Approximately 20 minutes for a single child; about 45 minutes for a group of 3 or 4

Range: Ages 6-12 years

Scoring: Examiner evaluated

Cost: Standard equipment kit $85.00; manual $4.25; 50 recording sheets $5.00.

Publisher: Consulting Psychologists Press, Inc.

MOBILE VOCATIONAL EVALUATION (MVE)

Refer to page 213.

MOTOR SKILLS INVENTORY (MSI)

John Aulenta

child

Purpose: Evaluates the motor functioning of normal and handicapped preschool and primary-age children. Establishes motor functioning age levels and identifies children in need of further evaluation. Used by trained diagnostic personnel as part of a comprehensive psychological or developmental evaluation.

Description: 85 item paper-pencil observational inventory assessing skill development in two areas: fine motor (40 items) and gross motor (45 items). Test items represent individual motor abilities (such as "lifts cup with handle" or "turns single pages in book") which are scored "plus" or "minus" according to the child's success or failure at performing the task described in the item. Test items for the two areas are presented in order of normal development. Basal and ceiling levels are established using a guideline of five consecutive successes or failures. Examiners are encouraged to utilize information gained from parental report and results of other tests in completing the inventory. Intended for use with children ages six months to seven years, the inventory may also be used with older handicapped children functioning within that developmental age range. Results of the inventory can contribute significantly to the diagnosis of retardation, developmental language delays, learning disability, specific motor deficit, and general or specific developmental immaturities, as well as clarifying developmental discrepancies among cognitive, linguistic, social, and motor areas. The manual includes directions for administration and of the inventory and interpretation of results. Self-administered by examiner. Not suitable for group use.

Untimed: 5-15 minutes

Range: Developmental ages 6 months-7 years

Scoring: Examiner evaluated

Cost: Complete test kit (manual and 15 administration booklets) $9.00; manual $5.00; 15 administration booklets $5.00.

Publisher: Stoelting Company

RECEPTIVE-EXPRESSIVE OBSERVATION (REO)

Joan M. Smith

ages 6 and up

Purpose: Assesses simple memory and memory coding across sensory channels; visual-motor, visual-vocal, auditory-vocal, and auditory-motor. Identifies student deficiencies in the perceptual areas addressed.

Description: Multiple task test assessing performance in labeling, discrimination, sequencing, and short-term memory. Eighteen each of visual-vocal and visual-motor cards are provided. Auditory-vocal and auditory-motor responses are made to items read by the examiner. Items are progressively increased in length in each of the four cross-channel preceptual areas. Responses are observed and entered on the recording form. Conversion tables are provided for scores. Test manual includes suggestions for remediation. Examiner required. Not suitable for group use.

Untimed: 15 minutes

Range: Ages 6-12. May be used with adults.

Scoring: Examiner evaluated

Cost: Test kit (manual, two sets of visual-motor and visual-vocal cards, and a spirit response form) $45.00.

Publisher: Educational Research Consultants

Special Education

Gifted

CREATIVITY ASSESSMENT PACKET
Frank E. Williams

child, teen grades 3-12

Purpose: Measures cognitive and affective factors related to the creative process. Identifies gifted students in grades 3-12.

Description: Two multiple item paper-pencil tests assessing eight general areas of cognitive and affective behavior. The test of divergent thinking measures fluency, flexibility, elaboration, and originality. Test items require semantic transformation, thus combining right-left brain abilities. The divergent feelings test measures curiosity, imagination, complexity, and risk-taking (affective traits measured in a verbal analysis mode also requiring left-right brain synthesis). A parent-teacher inventory (the Williams scale) asks parents and teachers to rate each child on various manifestations of the eight subscores, providing a means of comparing observed behavior with measured potential. The manual includes: directions for administering and scoring the tests, scoring templates, and a list of teaching strategies related to the creative processes measured by the test. On the back of the test of divergent thinking is a pupil assessment matrix for profiling results of all three tests. Examiner required. Suitable for group use.

Untimed: Varies

Range: Grades 3-12

Scoring: Examiner evaluated

Cost: Complete kit (manual, 25 divergent thinking tests, 25 divergent feelings tests, and 25 Williams scale booklets) $19.95.

Publisher: D.O.K. Publishers, Inc.

EBY ELEMENTARY IDENTIFICATION INSTRUMENT (EEII)
Judy W. Eby

child, teen grades K-8

Purpose: Measures academic talent and gifted behavior. Used to select students for gifted programs.

Description: Three multiple item paper-pencil inventories assessing academic performance and classroom behavior as a means of identifying gifted students. Consists of the following three scales: general selection matrix, teacher recommendation form, and unit selection matrix. Together they provide a profile of the child's potential for academically challenging educational experiences. Examiner required. Suitable for screening groups of children.

Untimed: Varies

Range: Grades K-8

Scoring: Examiner evaluated

Cost: Test kit (manual, 50 general selection matrix, 50 teacher recommendation forms, 50 unit selection matrix) $20.00.

Publisher: Slosson Educational Publications, Inc.

MINNESOTA PRESCHOOL SCALE
Refer to page 130.

PRIDE: PRESCHOOL AND KINDERGARTEN INTEREST DESCRIPTOR
Sylvia B. Rimm

child

Purpose: Identifies creatively gifted preschool and kindergarten children.

Used for academic placement into gifted programs.

Description: 50 item paper-pencil inventory requiring parents to assess their child's attitudes and interests based on their personal observations. Each test item is a statement about attitudes and interests relevant to children ages 3-6 years. Parents rate each item on a five-point scale from "no" to "definitely" according to the extent to which the statement applies to their child. Scores are provided on four dimensions: many interests, independence-perseverance, imagination-playfulness, and originality. All scoring completed by Educational Assessment Service, Inc. Examiner required. Suitable for group use.

Untimed: 20-35 minutes

Range: Parents of children ages 3-6 years

Scoring: Computer scored

Cost: Specimen set $6.00.

Publisher: Educational Assessment Service, Inc.

SCALES FOR RATING THE BEHAVIORAL CHARACTERISTICS OF SUPERIOR STUDENTS (SRBCSS)

Joseph S. Renzulli, Linda H. Smith, Alan J. White, Carolyn M. Callahan and Robert K. Hartman

child, teen

Purpose: Assesses behavioral characteristics related to the objectives of gifted and talented elementary and junior high school programs. Used to supplement measures of intelligence, achievement and creativity in selecting students for gifted and talented programs.

Description: 95 item paper-pencil inventory consisting of ten subscales, each of which assesses a different dimension of behavioral characteristics related to gifted and talented educational objectives. The following ten dimensions are evaluated: learning, motivation, creativity, leadership, art, music, dramatics, planning, precise communication and expressive communication. Each scale consists of 4-15 statements describing behaviors attributed to gifted and talented students. The teacher is asked to rate each item on a four-point scale from "seldom" to "almost always," reflecting the degree to which the presence or absence of each characteristic has been observed. The ten subscales represent ten distinct sets of behavioral characteristics, therefore no total score is derived. Only those scales which are relevant to program objectives should be selected for use in a given program. Self-administered by teacher. Suitable for use with groups of children.

Untimed: Varies

Range: Elementary and junior high school students

Scoring: Examiner evaluated

Cost: Test kit $6.95.

Publisher: Creative Learning Press, Inc.

SOI PROCESS AND DIAGNOSTIC SCREENING TEST (FORM P)

Refer to page 131.

Learning Disabilities

AMERICAN SCHOOL ACHIEVEMENT TESTS

Refer to page 81.

ANN ARBOR LEARNING INVENTORY AND REMEDIATION PROGRAM

Refer to page 143.

THE BRIGANCE® DIAGNOSTIC ASSESSMENT OF BASIC SKILLS—SPANISH EDITION

Refer to page 82.

CAREER ASSESSMENT INVENTORIES: FOR THE LEARNING DISABLED

Carol Weller and Mary Buchanan

LD students

Purpose: Assesses the personality, ability, and interest of learning disabled students. Used to help learning disabled students make intelligent and realistic career choices.

Description: Multiple item paper-pencil test consisting of three inventories. The attributes inventory assesses the individual's dominant personality characteristics. The ability inventory provides a profile of strengths and weaknesses across the auditory, visual, and motor areas. The interest inventory determines whether the individual's career goals are realistic. The inventories are completed by the examiner after a period of observation. The interest inventory may be completed by the individual. Each inventory presents a list of descriptors that are evaluated using a numerical scale. The results are profiled and used to locate appropriate career options in the Job Finder section of the manual. The attributes and interests inventories are keyed to John I. Holland's theory of careers. Examiner required. Suitable for group use.

Untimed: 20-30 minutes

Range: Learning disabled students of all ages

Scoring: Examiner evaluated

Cost: Test kit (manual, 25 attributes/ability inventories, 25 interest inventories) $25.00; specimen set (manual and sample forms) $15.00.

Publisher: Academic Therapy Publications

DIAGNOSIS AND REMEDIATION OF HANDWRITING PROBLEMS (DRHP)

D.H. Stott, F.A. Moyes and S.E. Henderson

child, teen

Purpose: Evaluates children's handwriting skills. Identifies children with possible learning disabilities. Used in regular classroom, remedial clinics, and work with individual children.

Description: Multiple item paper-pencil test assessing handwriting problems. Objective analysis of handwriting faults identifies those faults which should yield to regular teaching procedures from those of a more serious nature requiring special treatment. Also measures fine motor problems due to unknown or suspected neurological dysfunction, or associated with stress. The manual includes programs of remediation which can be adapted to the type of fault and ages of the children involved. Examiner required. Suitable for clinical and group use and screening.

CANADIAN PUBLISHER

Untimed: 20 minutes

Range: 7½-16 years old

Scoring: Objective

Cost: Contact publisher.

Publisher: Brook Educational Publishing, Ltd.

DIAGNOSTIC ACHIEVEMENT BATTERY (DAB)

Refer to page 86.

EARLY LEARNING ASSESSMENT AND DEVELOPMENT

Refer to page 120.

EXPRESSIVE ONE-WORD PICTURE VOCABULARY TEST: UPPER EXTENSION

Refer to page 163.

HOWELL PREKINDERGARTEN SCREENING TEST

Refer to page 122.

INITIAL COMMUNICATION PROCESSES

Refer to page 5.

MARTINEZ ASSESSMENT OF THE BASIC SKILLS

Refer to page 88.

MOTOR SKILLS INVENTORY (MSI)

Refer to page 144.

THE POLLACK-BRANDEN BATTERY: FOR IDENTIFICATION OF LEARNING DISABILITIES, DYSLEXIA, AND CLASSROOM DYSFUNCTION

child, teen

Purpose: Diagnoses learning disabilities for students from six years of age through high school. Used by clinicians and special education teachers to establish treatment plans or educational programs (IEP's).

Description: Multiple item paper-pencil battery assessing receptive and expressive language skill areas, both in written and spoken form. Diagnoses and classifies learning disabilities, dyslexia, and other classroom dysfunctions. Consists of two sub-batteries: a clinical battery to inform clinicians on weaknesses and strengths in cognitive and emotional areas of development as a basis for a treatment plan; and a classroom battery to inform the educator as to an individualized educational program (IEP) and to identify individual problem areas. Both sub-batteries are based on the application of Luria's neuropsychological theories of functional learning systems in the brain. Criterion-reference scoring and interpretation offers a direct guide to effective remedial approaches. Examiner required. Classroom battery suitable for group use.

Untimed: Varies

Range: Age 6 years-high school

Scoring: Examiner evaluated

Cost: Contact publisher.

Publisher: Book-Lab

PSYCHOEDUCATIONAL PROFILE (PEP)

Refer to page 126.

READING FREE VOCATIONAL INTEREST INVENTORY–REVISED (RFVII Revised)

Refer to page 203.

THE REVERSALS FREQUENCY TEST

Richard A. Gardner

child, teen

Purpose: Assesses a child's letter and number reversals frequency. Identifies children in need of further evaluation for a neurologically based learning disability.

Description: Three multiple item paper-pencil tests of letter and number reversals frequency. The Reversals Execution Test requires the child to write a specific list of numbers and letters, after which the examiner records the number of items written in reversed orientation. The Reversals Recognition Test presents the child with an array of numbers and letters, some of which are correctly oriented and some of which are presented as mirror images. The child places a cross over the reversed items and the examiner records the number of errors. In the Reversals Matching test, each item consists of a model number or letter followed by four samples of the same letter or number. One of the four samples is correctly oriented like the model. The child places a circle around the one that matches the model and the examiner records the number of errors. Each test is scored separately. Means, standard deviations, and percentile ranks are provided for both normal children and those known to have neurologically based learning disabilities. The manual provides tabulated data, graphs, and theoretical material that enable the examiner to ascertain the significance of a child's score in learning disability assessment. Suitable for group use.

Untimed: Varies

Range: Ages 5-15½ years

Scoring: Examiner evaluated

Cost: Test $12.00.

Publisher: Creative Therapeutics

SEARCH: A SCANNING INSTRUMENT FOR THE IDENTIFICATION OF POTENTIAL LEARNING DISABILITY

Archie A. Silver and Rosa A. Hagin

child

Purpose: Detects learning difficulties in five- and six-year-old children. Identifies specific skill deficits in those children. Used to establish educational objectives for individual students and groups of students.

Description: Multiple item oral response and task performance test consisting of ten subtests: three tests of visual perception (matching, recall, and visual-motor), two auditory tests (discrimination and sequencing), two intermodal tests (articulation and initial consonants), and three body-image tests (directionality, finger schema, and pencil grip). The total score indicates the degree of each child's vulnerability to learning failure in the early grades. The subtest scores yield a profile of the child's perceptual skills (assets and deficits) which is used in guiding subsequent educational intervention (specific intervention procedures may be found in the test's companion program, TEACH). Test scores are interpreted by means of VABs (vulnerable ranges for each component) and stanines for completion of the student's profile. Two kinds of norms can be used: age norms and local norms.

The manual includes age norms ranging from 63-80 months for specific samples such as inner-city, small-town rural, suburban, and selected independent schools, as well as instructions for computing local norms. The test kit includes: the manual, which includes instructions for administering, scoring, and profiling the test results, as well as five removable test cards required for two of the subtests; 30 SEARCH record blanks (six-page forms used in the administration and scoring of each child's performance on each of the ten tests); and 12 miniature identification toys required for the auditory discrimination subtest (car, book, hat, pig, shoe, bat, bus, chair, bed, comb, clown, key). May be used independently or in conjunction with TEACH. Examiner required. Not suitable for group use.

Untimed: 20 minutes

Range: Ages 5-6 years

Scoring: Examiner evaluated

Cost: Complete kit $42.50.

Publisher: Walker Educational Book Corporation

SPELLMASTER DIAGNOSTIC SPELLING SYSTEM

Refer to page 66.

TEST LISTENING ACCURACY IN CHILDREN (TLAC)

Refer to page 159.

THE WORD TEST

Refer to page 175.

Mentally Handicapped

BALTHAZAR SCALES OF ADAPTIVE BEHAVIOR II: SCALES OF SOCIAL ADAPTATION

Refer to page 53.

BEHAVIOR ASSESSMENT BATTERY

Refer to page 14.

COGNITIVE DIAGNOSTIC BATTERY (CDB)

Stanley R. Kay

all ages

Purpose: Evaluates the nature and degree of intellectual disorders. May be used with intellectually limited, non-verbal, inattentive, overtly psychotic, or otherwise untestable patients for purposes of diagnostic evaluation and monitoring treatment progress.

Description: Multiple item non-verbal response and task performance tests assessing cognitive deficits due to impaired development versus later regression. Five tests utilize a Piagetian developmental framework to assess early conceptual maturation, higher order concept utilization, egocentric versus socialized thinking, perceputal motor development, attention span, arousal-related cognitive disturbance, and psychomotor rate. Normative data provided for schizophrenics, mentally retarded psychotics, normal adults, children, and the elderly. Results differentially diagnose mental retardation versus psychosis. Manual includes technical data. Examiner required. Not suitable for group use.

Untimed: 10-30 minutes

Range: Child, adult

Scoring: Examiner evaluated

Cost: Test kit (5 subtests, manual, and 50 of each scoring form) $42.95.

Publisher: Psychological Assessment Resources, Inc.

DEVELOPMENTAL ASSESSMENT FOR THE SEVERELY HANDICAPPED (DASH)

Refer to page 157.

DEVELOPMENTAL ASSESSMENT OF LIFE EXPERIENCES (DALE)

Gertrude A. Barber, John P. Mannino and Robert J. Will

all ages

Purpose: Assesses skill development in individuals who have been withdrawn from the mainstream of society for long durations of time at institutions for developmental and/or physical handicaps.

Description: Two 200 item paper-pencil observational inventories assessing two levels of skill development. Level I items describe tasks which reflect the functioning of individuals who are profoundly to severely mentally retarded and measure the following areas of self-help skills: sensory motor, language, self-help, cognition, and socialization. Level II items list behaviors which are of a higher functioning nature and assess the following community living skills: personal hygiene, personal management, communications, residence-home management, and community access. Test items describe skills in terms of the ways in which specific tasks are approached or completed and are expressed in positive terminology. Items within each skill area are listed in order of increasing difficulty. Two types of scores are utilized in rating every item on the inventory. A quantitative score indicates the frequency of the response: items are rated (1) responds less than 50%, (2) responds approximately 50%, (3) responds 90% or greater, (N/A) not applicable, (N/O) never observed, or (INCAP.) incapable of responding. Qualitative ratings identify responses for each behavioral item as: (a) inappropriate/incorrect, (b) fair approximation with reminders, or (c) excellent approximation with few reminders.

Initial evaluation identifies an individual's competencies which can then serve as a basis in determining what skills need to be expanded or developed. As specific strengths, related to a particular task or skill area, are observed and identified, they are recorded on pages opposite inventory items set aside for that purpose in the inventory booklets. Each strength-need page corresponds to the items in the inventory on the opposite page. A general strength-need list is also provided. A circular chart is used to provide a graphic illustration of an individual's progress.

Although the inventory is designed to be rated quarterly, items on which the individual has achieved competency are graphed immediately on the cumulative circle chart, showing on any given day all of the areas in which an individual has exhibited competency. The manual provides an instructional narrative which serves as a guide in the use of the system, as well as sample copies of pertinent data recording forms. Individual data forms are presented in separate booklets for levels I and II. A therapist's handbook is also available which discusses the assessment of strengths and needs of individuals being serviced and more effective programming for the therapist in planning goals. Examiner required. Not suitable for group use.

Untimed: Varies

Range: Child-adult

Scoring: Examiner evaluated

Cost: Manual $7.80; therapist's handbook $4.00; inventory list, profile fact sheet, and illustrative progress chart (level I or II) $3.50.

Publisher: Barber Center Press Publications

FLORIDA INTERNATIONAL DIAGNOSTIC-PRESCRIPTIVE VOCATIONAL COMPETENCY PROFILE

Refer to page 200.

MARTINEZ ASSESSMENT OF THE BASIC SKILLS

Refer to page 88.

MINNESOTA PRESCHOOL SCALE

Refer to page 130.

NISONGER QUESTIONNAIRE FOR PARENTS

Refer to page 155.

READING FREE VOCATIONAL INTEREST INVENTORY—REVISED (R-FVII Revised)

Refer to page 203.

SEQUENCED INVENTORY OF COMMUNICATION DEVELOPMENT

Refer to page 172.

SHELTERED EMPLOYMENT WORK EXPERIENCE PROGRAM (SEWEP)

Refer to page 204.

WASHER VISUAL ACUITY SCREENING TECHNIQUE (WVAST)

Refer to page 177.

Physically Handicapped

ADOLESCENT AND ADULT PSYCHOEDUCATIONAL PROFILE (AAPEP)

Mesibov, Schopler and Schaffer

handicapped teen, adult

Purpose: Measures learning abilities and characteristics for severely handicapped adolescents and adults. Used by service-providers, teachers, and parents in preparing and maintaining autistic and communications handicapped individuals in community-based programs. Used with individuals previously regarded as untestable.

Description: Multiple item task performance test assessing the learning abilities of autistic and communications handicapped individuals. The test results comprise a profile reflecting the individual characteristics of the person. The profile is translated into an appropriately individualized set of goals and objectives for each individual. Test kit includes the following standard materials required for uniform administration of the test: nerf ball and basket, checkers and board, pinball game, radio and battery, empty box, playing cards, tape of typical workshop sounds, five magic markers, work box, 100 pencils, erasers, target board with balls, magazine, catalog, pad of paper, pen wooden block, metal plate, nut and bolt, box sorting tray, green buttons, three wing nuts, five bolts, seven washers, five nuts, five sandwich bags, 10 dominoes, sewing block and lace, screwdriver, wrench, four-piece shape board, survival signs, comic book, paperback book, movie ticket, price signs, December calendar, #1, #2, and #3 cards, color jig, four color chips, written instruction cards, alphabet cards, five jig cards, schedule, five paper clips, clock, pill bottles, tops, 20 markers, and manual. The following materials are required but not included: nickels, dimes, quarters, $1 bill, $5 bill, pennies, package of nabs and soda, candy bar, stopwatch, typewriter, and tape recorder. Examiner required. Not suitable for group use.

Untimed: Varies

Range: Autistic, developmentally disabled, and communication handicapped adolescents and adults

Scoring: Examiner evaluated

Cost: Test kit (including standard materials and manual) $225.00.

Publisher: Orange Industries

THE BODY IMAGE OF BLIND CHILDREN

Bryant J. Cratty and Theresa A. Sams

blind child

Purpose: Evaluates the extent to which a blind child is able to identify his body parts and respond to requests for various types of movements.

Description: Multiple item oral response and task performance assessment procedure measuring the body image of blind children in the following areas: body parts, body planes, body movements, laterality, and directionality. Manual includes: norms for comparison among various subpopulations of blind children, suggested applications, interpretive guidelines, and a discussion of body-image training for blind children. Examiner required. Not suitable for group use.

Untimed: Varies

Range: Blind children ages 5-15 years

Scoring: Examiner evaluated

Cost: Manual $4.50.

Publisher: The American Foundation for the Blind

BEHAVIOR ASSESSMENT BATTERY

Refer to page 14.

CENTRAL INSTITUTE FOR THE DEAF PRESCHOOL PERFORMANCE SCALE (CID PRESCHOOL PERFORMANCE SCALE)

Ann E. Geers and Helen S. Lane

hear./lang. imp. child

Purpose: Measures intellectual potential using completely non-verbal testing procedures. Predicts school achievement in hearing-impaired and language-impaired preschoolers.

Description: Multiple item task performance test assessing the intellectual abilities of preschoolers without requiring a single spoken word from either the examiner or the child (optional verbal clues are provided for use with children who do hear). Six subtests assess intellectual abilities in the following areas, through the use of the tests indicated: manual planning (block building, Montessori cylinders and two-figure formboard), manual dexterity (buttons and Wallin pegs), form perception (Decroly pictures, Seguin formboard), perceptual/motor skills (Knox cube, drawing, and paper folding), preschool skills (color sorting and counting sticks), and part/whole relations (Manikin and Stutsman puzzles). Test materials were selected from existing mental tests for children between two and five years of age, to obtain a broad, clinical picture of the child's ability, as well as a numerical rating (Deviation IQ) that would correlate with a Stanford-Binet IQ. The test is an adaptation of the early Randall's Island Performance Series. Examiner required. Not suitable for group use.

Untimed: Varies

Range: Hearing-impaired and language-impaired preschoolers

Scoring: Examiner evaluated

Cost: Complete test kit (manual, record forms, and all manipulatives for subtests) $395.00; manual $4.50; 30 record forms $10.50.

Publisher: Stoelting Company

DEVELOPMENTAL ASSESSMENT FOR THE SEVERELY HANDICAPPED (DASH)

Refer to page 157.

MAXFIELD-BUCHHOLZ SOCIAL MATURITY SCALE FOR BLIND PRE-SCHOOL CHILDREN

Refer to page 6.

THE MOSSFORD ASSESSMENT CHART OF THE PHYSICALLY HANDICAPPED

Janet Whitehouse

handicapped teen

Purpose: Evaluates the daily living skills of handicapped children. Used in schools, hospitals, and residential and assessment centers for the physically handicapped, and by social workers making placement or employment decisions.

Description: Multiple item paper-pencil checklist of daily living skills relevant to children with mild to severe degrees of physical handicap. Items cover mobility, dressing, manipulative skills, personal hygiene, health, communicating, reading, writing, mathematics, financial and domestic skills, and leisure activities. Results are presented on a pie-chart, showing those skills which are being learned as well as those already mastered and identifying skills which may have been overlooked entirely. The chart enables annual comparisons of progress to be made and forms a visual record of the child's progress. Examiner required. Not suitable for group use.
BRITISH PUBLISHER

Untimed: Varies

Range: Ages 14-18 years

Scoring: Examiner evaluated

Cost: Manual £4.95; record forms (pkg. of 10) £3.95; transparency of chart £4.95.

Publisher: NFER-Nelson Publishing Co. Ltd.

NEALE ANALYSIS OF READING ABILITY—BRAILLE EDITION

N.B. Neale

blind child

Purpose: Assesses the braille reading ability of children ages 6-12 years. Used by teachers of the blind.

Description: Multiple item test consisting of six graded oral reading passages which have been standardized for different ages. The test booklet includes three parallel forms of the test (Forms A, B, and C) and three supplementary diagnostic tests. Results yield scores for reading rate, accuracy, and comprehension. The Individual Record Sheets contain scoring tables, comprehension questions, and charts to aid the assessment of reading characteristics and types of error. Not suitable for group use.
BRITISH PUBLISHER

Untimed: 10-15 minutes

Range: Ages 6-12 years

Scoring: Examiner evaluated

Cost: Braille test booklet £4.95; manual £2.95; record form A (pkg. of 10) £1.85; record form B (pkg. of 10) £1.85; record form C (pkg. of 10) £1.85.

Publisher: NFER-Nelson Publishing Company Ltd.

NISONGER QUESTIONNAIRE FOR PARENTS

W. Loadman, F.A. Benson and D. McElwain

handicapped child

Purpose: Gathers preliminary information on a handicapped child from the perspective of the parents.

Description: Multiple item paper-pencil questionnaire consisting of non-technical questions concerning the status of a handicapped child. Parents complete the form, which emphasizes current rather than historical information. A pocket is provided on the form for the child's picture. Self-administered. Suitable for group use.

Untimed: Varies

Range: Parents of handicapped children

Scoring: Examiner evaluated

Cost: 20 questionnaires $20.00; user's guide $.75; specimen set (includes user's guide and one questionnaire) $3.00.

Publisher: Nisonger Center, (The), Ohio State University

TEST FOR EXAMINING EXPRESSIVE MORPHOLOGY (TEEM)

Refer to page 173.

VINELAND ADAPTIVE BEHAVIOR SCALES

Refer to page 8.

Special Education

ADOLESCENT AND ADULT PSYCHOEDUCATIONAL PROFILE (AAPEP)

Refer to page 153.

THE AUTISM ATTITUDE SCALE FOR TEACHERS (AAST)

Refer to page 195.

BALTHAZAR SCALES OF ADAPTIVE BEHAVIOR I: SCALES OF FUNCTIONAL INDEPENDENCE

Earl E. Balthazar

handicapped—all ages

Purpose: Evaluates the self-help skills of profoundly or severely handicapped individuals. Used to plan and monitor goal-directed remedial programs.

Description: Multiple item paper-pencil observational inventory assessing the functional independence of profoundly and severely handicapped individuals. Data derived from direct observation of the individual is used to determine objective performance levels, which in turn identify appropriate remedial programs for developing self-help skills. Scoring form includes night-time supplements. Program effectiveness can be evaluated by readministering the scales. Personnel in residential treatment facilities can be trained within a week to become observers and raters. Also helpful in explaining the development of self-help skills to families. Examiner required. Not suitable for group use.

Untimed: Varies

Range: Profoundly and severely handicapped individuals of all ages

Scoring: Examiner evaluated

Cost: Manual set $10.00; 25 scoring forms $7.75; specimen set (2 vol. manual and scoring form) $10.50.

Publisher: Consulting Psychologists Press, Inc.

A BASIC SCREENING AND REFERRAL FORM FOR CHILDREN WITH SUSPECTED LEARNING AND BEHAVIORAL DISABILITIES

Robert E. Valett

child, teen grades 1-12

Purpose: Measures the development of learning and behavioral skills in students grades 1-12. Identifies students in need of further evaluation. Used by classroom and special education teachers.

Description: Multiple item paper-pencil observational inventory assessing classroom behavior and performance. Measures teacher ratings in eight areas: social-personal, conceptual-cognitive, language, perceptual-motor (visual-motor, visual, and auditory), sensory-motor, gross-motor, plus a pupil work sample. Self-administered by teacher. Not suitable for group use.

Untimed: Varies

Range: Grades 1-12

Scoring: Examiner evaluated

Cost: Package of 10 inventories $5.95.

Publisher: Pitman Learning, Inc.

BATTELLE DEVELOPMENTAL INVENTORY

Refer to page 115.

THE BEHAVIOR EVALUATION SCALE (BES)

Refer to page 177.

THE BRIGANCE® DIAGNOSTIC INVENTORY OF ESSENTIAL SKILLS

Refer to page 84.

CAREER ADAPTIVE BEHAVIOR INVENTORY (CAB)

Refer to page 197.

THE CHILD CENTER OPERATIONAL ASSESSMENT TOOL (OAT)

Refer to page 85.

DABERON SCREENING FOR SCHOOL READINESS

Refer to page 118.

DEVELOPMENTAL ASSESSMENT FOR THE SEVERELY HANDICAPPED (DASH)

Mary K. Dykes

child

Purpose: Assesses the development of severely handicapped individuals functioning between the developmental ages of birth to eight years. Used to establish IEP's.

Description: Five multiple item paper-pencil observational scales assessing development in the following domains: sensory-motor, language, preacademic, activities of daily living, and social-emotional. The five Pinpoint Scales are sensitive to small changes in skill performance. Skills assessed are identified as either present, emerging, task resistive, nonrelevant, or unknown. Examiner required. Not suitable for group use.

Untimed: Varies

Range: Developmental ages birth-8 years

Scoring: Examiner evaluated

Cost: Complete kit (manual, 5 each of 5 pinpoint scales, 25 daily plan sheets, 25 comprehensive program records, and 25 individualized education plans) $75.00.

Publisher: Pro-Ed

DEVELOPMENTAL ASSESSMENT OF LIFE EXPERIENCES (DALE)

Refer to page 151.

DEVELOPMENTAL INDICATORS FOR THE ASSESSMENT OF LEARNING—REVISED (DIAL-R)

Refer to page 119.

THE DYSINTEGRAL LEARNING CHECKLIST

Refer to page 16.

EXPLORE THE WORLD OF WORK (E-WOW)

Refer to page 199.

FLORIDA INTERNATIONAL DIAGNOSTIC-PRESCRIPTIVE VOCATIONAL COMPETENCY PROFILE

Refer to page 200.

PERFORMANCE ASSESSMENT OF SYNTAX: ELICITED AND SPONTANEOUS (PASSES)

Refer to page 169.

THE POLLACK-BRANDEN BATTERY: FOR IDENTIFICATION OF LEARNING DISABILITIES, DYSLEXIA, AND CLASSROOM DYSFUNCTION

Refer to page 149.

THE PYRAMID SCALES

Refer to page 127.

SCALES OF INDEPENDENT BEHAVIOR

Refer to page 128.

SCREENING TEST OF ADOLESCENT LANGUAGE (STAL)

Refer to page 171.

SOI PROCESS AND DIAGNOSTIC SCREENING TEST (FORM P)

Refer to page 131.

SPELLMASTER DIAGNOSTIC SPELLING SYSTEM

Refer to page 66.

TEST FOR EXAMINING EXPRESSIVE MORPHOLOGY (TEEM)

Refer to page 173.

Speech, Hearing and Visual

Auditory

ASSESSING READING DIFFICULTIES: A DIAGNOSTIC AND REMEDIAL APPROACH

Lynette Bradley

child

Purpose: Identifies children whose reading difficulties are the result of poor auditory organization. Indicates children who are likely to encounter future reading and spelling problems.

Description: Multiple item paper-pencil test with section for recording teacher observations assessing the problems of children who are making little or no progress towards learning to read. Test items are based on extensive longitudinal research which proved the close relationship between the inability to rhyme or identify rhyming words and reading failure. The manual provides full details for administering the schedule and interpreting the results. Guidelines for appropriate remedial action are also provided. Examiner required. Not suitable for group use.
BRITISH PUBLISHER

Untimed: Varies

Range: Children

Scoring: Examiner evaluated

Cost: Manual (36 pages) £2.50; 25 test sheets £1.95.

Publisher: Macmillan Education

EVALUATING COMMUNICATIVE COMPETENCE: A FUNCTIONAL PRAGMATIC PROCEDURE

Refer to page 163.

THE HEARING MEASUREMENT SCALE

William G. Noble

hearing impaired

Purpose: Measures degree of hearing impairment as reported by the hearing impaired individual.

Description: Multiple item paper-pencil self-report questionnaire assessing the degree to which an individual's hearing is impaired. Provides eight scores: speech hearing, hearing for nonspeech sounds, spatial localization, emotional response to hearing impairment, speech distortion, tinnitus, personal opinion of hearing, and total. Self-administered. Suitable for group use.
AUSTRALIAN PUBLISHER

Untimed: Varies

Range: Hearing impaired individuals

Scoring: Examiner evaluated

Cost: Test kit (60-page manual, 50 questionnaires, and transparent scoring matrix) $17.50.

Publisher: University of New England (Australia)

INVENTORY OF PERCEPTUAL SKILLS (IPS)

Refer to page 176.

SEQUENCED INVENTORY OF COMMUNICATION DEVELOPMENT

Refer to page 172.

TEST LISTENING ACCURACY IN CHILDREN (TLAC)

Merlin J. Mecham and J. Dean Jones

child grades K-5

Purpose: Measures the verbal listening abilities of elementary school children. Identifies children with listening and other language and learning disorders.

Description: Multiple item multiple-choice intelligibility type test measuring verbal listening skills. Available in two versions. The Individual Version is used with children ages 5-7 years and requires 20 minutes per child to administer. The Individual Version kit includes: administration manual, picture plates, cassette tape, and score sheets. The Group-Test Version is used with average classrooms of children grades 2-5 and requires 45 minutes to administer to the entire class. The Group-Test kit includes: administration manual, filmstrip, tape, acetate scoring key, and 35 scoring sheets. Both versions are percentile rated as well as having nominal descriptions. Examiner required. Suitable for group use as indicated above.

Untimed: 20-45 minutes

Range: Grades K-5

Scoring: Examiner evaluated; hand key

Cost: Individual Version test kit $25.00; Group-Test kit $25.00; Individual and Group Tests combined $45.00.

Publisher: Communication Research Associates, Inc.

TEST OF AUDITORY COMPREHENSION (TAC)

Los Angeles County Schools

hear. imp. child, teen

Purpose: Assesses comprehension in hearing impaired children. Used for academic placement and instructional planning.

Description: Ten subtests measuring auditory comprehension. Subtests begin with simple auditory discrimination tasks and conclude by assessing the child's understanding of complex stories given with a competing message background. The child responds to recorded messages by pointing to one of several pictures. Test results produce a profile of the child's performance on a continuum of auditory tasks, provide a basis for instruction, and allow comparison of results by age, degree of hearing loss, and type of placement. Administration requires the child's usual amplification, a quiet room, and a program-stop or cassette player. Norms provided for children ages 4-17 years with moderate through profound hearing losses. Directly correlated to a curriculum and training program. May also be used to assess auditory processing of learning disabled. Examiner required. Not suitable for group use.

Untimed: 30 minutes

Range: Hearing impaired-ages 4-17 years

Scoring: Examiner evaluated; hand key

Cost: Test of Auditory Comprehension (330 pages including manual) $75.00.

Publisher: Foreworks Publications

WRITTEN LANGUAGE SYNTAX TEST
Refer to page 68.

Speech and Language

AUDITORY BLENDING TEST
Refer to page 132.

BANKSON LANGUAGE SCREENING TEST (BLST)
Nicholas W. Bankson

child

Purpose: Assesses the language development of children ages 4-8 years. Identifies children in need of further evaluation. Used to plan language intervention programs.

Description: Multiple-item oral response test measuring the development of expressive language behavior and related auditory and visual perception skills. Picture stimuli are used to present test items based on a model that includes the morphological, syntactic, and semantic aspects of language necessary for linguistic performance. Results determine appropriate areas for follow-up diagnostic assessment and identify initial language areas in need of remediation. Examiner required. Not suitable for group use.

Untimed: Varies

Range: Ages 4-8 years

Scoring: Examiner evaluated

Cost: Test book (78 pages) $25.00; scoring sheets $13.00.

Publisher: Slosson Educational Publications, Inc.

BASIC INVENTORY OF NATURAL LANGUAGE (BINL)
CHECpoint Systems, Inc.

child, teen grades K-12

Purpose: Measures the language proficiency of students Grades K-12. Used in bilingual, ESL, language development, and speech and language remediation programs.

Description: 20 item oral response test in which each test item consists of a color photograph which is used to elicit language samples from the students. The language samples are transcribed and analyzed at three levels: word class (determiner, noun, verb, adjective, adverb, preposition, etc.), type of phrase employed (noun phrase, verb phrase, prepositional phrase, gerund phrase, etc.), and sentence type (simple sentence, compound sentence, compound/complex sentence, etc.). Four BINL kits are available: Forms A and B are elementary kits for use with grades K-6, Forms C and D are secondary kits for use with grades 7-12. The kits include: instructions manual, 20 full color photographs on heavy posterboard, 400 individual oral scoring sheets, individual and class profile sheets, sorting envelopes to prepare the tests for machine scoring, and materials for teaching the prescription activities included in the instructions manual.

Three BINL computer scoring programs are available. BINL I is available for IBM System 34 computers and Apple II microcomputers. The reports from this program include individual scores, class and grade level, graphs of student placement, and classification of students into four categories: Non, Limited, Functional, and Fluent. This program is available in English, Spanish, and 24 other languages. BINL II is available for Apple II microcomputers. BINL II provides a complete grammatical analysis of each student's sample as well as the reports provided by BINL I. Each student is reported separately and placed on a language continuum. Specific areas of strength and areas needing development are indicated. The Theme Correction and Analysis programs permits the correction of English written themes and scores each student's writing in an objective manner. Scores are correlated to an holistic scoring procedure used to evaluate themes for minimum competency testing. Examiner required. Not suitable for group use.

Untimed: Varies

Range: Grades K-12

Scoring: Computer scored

Cost: BINL kit A, B, C, or D $55.00 each.

Publisher: CHECpoint Systems, Inc.

CAMBRIDGE KINDERGARTEN SCREENING TEST

Ann M. Shahzade

kindergarten child

Purpose: Measures the speech and language abilities of kindergarten children. Identifies children in need of further evaluation or observation.

Description: Multiple item oral response and task performance test screening all major areas of speech and language. Various subtests are administered by means of realistic, full-color photographs of common objects, and with the use of ten wooden color cubes. May be administered by speech pathologist, classroom teacher, aide, or volunteer. Step-by-step directions for administering the test are provided in the spiral-bound testing book. The screener's manual contains instructions for administering, scoring, and record-keeping. Examiner required. Individually administered; suitable for screening groups of children.

Untimed: 10-20 minutes

Range: Kindergarten children

Scoring: Examiner evaluated

Cost: Test kit (testing book, manual, 10 wooden color cubes, vinyl carrying case) $35.00.

Publisher: DLM Teaching Resources

CENTRAL INSTITUTE FOR THE DEAF PRESCHOOL PERFORMANCE SCALE (CID PRESCHOOL PERFORMANCE SCALE)

Refer to page 154.

CHILD LANGUAGE ABILITY MEASURES (CLAM)

Albert Mehrabian and Christy Floynihan

child

Purpose: Measures the language production and language comprehension abilities of children ages 2-7 years. Identifies linguistic abilities and difficulties. Used by educators, speech-language pathologists, testers, and child psychologists to plan language development programs.

Description: Six multiple item oral response and non-verbal task performance tests measuring a child's expressive and receptive language abilities. Tests include: vocabulary comprehension, grammar comprehension, inflection production, grammar imitation, "grammar formedness" judgment, and grammar equivalence judgment. The tests assess a child's knowledge of syntactic, semantic, and phonological rules and do not confound measurement of language development with intellectual skills such as memory span, knowledge of real world facts, or ability to form abstract relationships. Administration procedures contain built-in safeguards against tester bias (such as encouraging one child more than another). The six tests may be administered separately or together, depending on the needs of the child in question (a selected pair of tests is usually sufficient to obtain a reliable and valid measure of a child's language skills). Norms are provided to calculate standardized scores for each test and for combinations of tests. In addition, norms are included to provide the age level corresponding to a child's language skills.

The manual (for all six tests) includes details regarding the construction of the tests, statistics on item selection and test reliabilities, appropriate age ranges for each test, and scoring procedures and norms. Two administration books are available: one for the vocabulary comprehension and grammar comprehension tests (238 pages; 111 photographs), and a second for the inflection production, grammar imitation, "grammar formedness" judgment, and grammar equivalence judgment (166 pages; 48 photographs). Detailed testing procedures and prompting procedures are provided for each test, followed by all practice items and test items for that test. Sample answer sheets are provided at the end of each test administration booklet and can be copied by the examiner for use in recording children's answers during testing. Examiner required. Not suitable for group use.

Untimed: 15 minutes per test

Range: Ages 2-7 years

Scoring: Examiner evaluated

Cost: Manual (100 pages) $12.00; test administration booklets each $20.00.

Publisher: Albert Mehrabian

THE COMMUNICATION SCREEN: A PRESCHOOL SPEECH-LANGUAGE SCREENING TOOL

Nancy Striffler and Sharon Willig

---

child

Purpose: Assesses the speech and language development of children ages 2-6 years. Identifies children in need of further evaluation. Used as a screening instrument by nursery school and Head Start teachers, health care personnel, and paraprofessionals who do not have specialized skills in the speech and language area.

Description: Multiple item oral response test measuring a child's development of the following language skill areas: speech, language comprehension, language expression, verbal imitation, and recall of digits (to tap short term auditory memory and sequencing and temporal ordering abilities). Skill areas appraised are based upon normal speech and language development, developmental norms, and criteria established by the author as to which skills would be most predictive of speech and language abilities. The laminated picture sheet is used to administer the test items. Responses are recorded on the test forms, three levels of which are available: 3-year screen (age 2.10-3.9), 4-year screen (age 3.10-4.9), and 5-year screen (age 4.10-5.9). The manual includes a description of the test, administration and scoring instructions, and interpretive information. Examiner required. Individually administered; suitable for screening groups of children.

Untimed: 5 minutes

Range: Language age 2.10-5.9 years

Scoring: Examiner evaluated

Cost: Test kit (manual, 25 each of 3-year, 4-year, and 5-year screen test forms, and laminated picture sheet) $12.95.

Publisher: CTB/McGraw-Hill

DIAGNOSTIC AND ACHIEVEMENT READING TESTS: DART PHONICS TESTING PROGRAM

Refer to page 134.

EXPRESSIVE ONE-WORD PICTURE VOCABULARY TEST: UPPER EXTENSION

Morrison F. Gardner

teen

Purpose: Assesses the expressive vocabulary of students ages 12 to 15 as a measure of verbal intelligence. Used to detect speech defects and learning disabilities.

Description: Multiple item oral-response test in which the student demonstrates his ability to understand and use words by naming pictures that range from simple objects to representations of abstract concepts. Each test item consists of one picture stimulus that requires a single word answer. Test results yield mental ages, percentiles, stanines, and deviation IQ scores which allow for comparing expressive language skills with other measures of receptive language, for detecting speech defects, identifying learning disorders related to hearing loss and imperceptions of the auditory modality, assessing auditory-visual association ability, and for evaluating a bilingual student's English/Spanish fluency. Examiner required. Suitable for use with small groups who respond in writing. Spanish Form available.

Untimed: 5-10 minutes

Range: Ages 12-15

Scoring: Examiner evaluated

Cost: Test kit (manual, test plates, 25 English Record forms, in vinyl folder) $33.50; 25 Spanish Record forms $6.00; specimen set (manual and sample forms) $10.00.

Publisher: Academic Therapy Publications

EVALUATING COMMUNICATIVE COMPETENCE: A FUNCTIONAL PRAGMATIC PROCEDURE

Charlann S. Simon

child, teen

Purpose: Appraises both listening and speaking communications skills of language-learning impaired children and adolescents ages 9-17 years.

Description: 21 informal communications tasks assessing a student's auditory and expressive language skills. Observations are made of the child's language behaviors in the following areas: abilities in language processing, skills in talking about language (metalinguistic skills), and functional uses of language for various communicative purposes. The student is involved in the tasks in both speaker and listener roles. Some of the tasks include: comprehension of directions, giving directions, creative storytelling, maintenance of tense in storytelling, stating similarities and differences, barrier games, expression, and justification of an opinion. The manual provides for each task: a description of the task (including materials needed), the rationale behind the task, directions for clinical administration of the task and analytical procedures for interpreting the student's language behaviors elicited by the task. All required stimulus materials are included in the test kit, along with recordkeeping forms and reproducible materials needed for test administration. Examiner required. Not suitable for group use.

Untimed: Varies

Range: Language age 9-17 years

Scoring: Examiner evaluated

Cost: Test kit (manual and the following materials: 6 blocks, 12 cards, and 3-ring binder) $49.95.

Publisher: Communication Skill Builders, Inc.

FISHER-LOGEMANN TEST OF ARTICULATION COMPETENCE

Hilda B. Fisher and Jerilyn A. Logemann

all ages   pre K and up

Purpose: Assesses students' ability to accurately articulate speech sounds. Used by speech therapists with individuals of all ages.

Description: 50 item oral response test assessing an individual's phonological functioning. Consists of two subtests: the picture test (35 items) and the sentence test (15 items). Both tests examine all the English phonemes in systematic occurrance according to syllabic function (prevocalic, intervocalic, and postvocalic) and include frequent reliability checks. The test portfolio of 36 cards converts into an easel setup for administration of test stimuli. The picture test materials include 109 large full-color illustrations on 35 cards that can be used with very young children as well as mentally retarded or easily distracted individuals. Materials for the sentence test consist of one card containing fifteen sentences (third grade reading level required). The record forms for each test are organized so that errors are grouped according to the nature of the deficiency. The therapist's manual provides complete instructions for administering and scoring the tests, guidelines for interpreting the responses, an outline of the linguistic processes involved, and suggestions for appropriate therapeutic intervention. Examiner required. Not suitable for group use.

Untimed: Varies

Range: Preschool-adult

Scoring: Examiner evaluated

Cost: Test portfolio (36 cards) $29.61; therapist's manual $5.52; 50 record forms (sentence test or picture test) $8.70.

Publisher: The Riverside Publishing Company

FLUHARTY PRESCHOOL SPEECH AND LANGUAGE SCREENING TEST

Nancy Buono Fluharty

child

Purpose: Evaluates the language performance of preschool children. Identifies children with delayed or abnormal language development.

Description: Multiple item oral response test assessing vocabulary, articulation, and receptive and expressive language performance. Picture stimuli ($8\frac{3}{8}$" x 5" cards) are used to elicit language samples. Cutoff scores provided for each age level of each area screened. Examiner required. Not suitable for group use.

Untimed: Varies

Range: Ages 2-6 years

Scoring: Examiner evaluated

Cost: Complete program (10 picture cards, 2 pads of 50 response forms, guide) $18.00.

Publisher: DLM Teaching Resources

FRENCHAY DYSARTHRIA ASSESSMENT

P. Enderby

teen, adult ☞ ✍

Purpose: Assesses dysarthria—speech impairment due to neuromuscular disorders—due to conditions such as cerebral palsy, Parkinson's disease, head injury and stroke. Used by speech therapists, doctors, psychiatrists and clinical psychologists to select and monitor appropriate treatment programs.

Description: 29 item task performance and behavioral observation test measuring speech impairment due to neuromuscular disorders. Test items cover the following areas: reflex, respiration, lips, jaw, palate, laryngeal, tongue, intelligibility, influencing factors (sight, teeth, language, mood, posture), rate, and sensation. Results are recorded graphically on multi-copy forms using a nine-point rating scale. Examiner required. Not suitable for group use.
BRITISH PUBLISHER

Untimed: Varies

Range: Ages 12 years and older

Scoring: Examiner evaluated

Cost: Manual and 100 record forms £19.95; activity cards £6.95.

Publisher: NFER-Nelson Publishing Company Ltd.

INTERPERSONAL LANGUAGE SKILLS ASSESSMENT—PRELIMINARY VERSION

Carolyn M. Blagden and Nancy L. McConnell

child, teen ☞ ✍

Purpose: Determines how effectively an 8-14 year old student uses language to participate in social situations. Identifies students with inadequate communication skills and pinpoints specific communication behavior problems.

Description: Multiple item paper-pencil observational inventory assessing a student's pragmatic use of the linguistic social skills necessary for successful interpersonal interactions. The student being tested is observed interacting in a group with two or three of his peers, and his interpersonal language skills are assessed according to percentage of utterances by age that are: negative; inadequate semantically, syntactically, morphologically or prosodically; statements of advice, deprecation, information, justification, requesting, support, commanding, accusation, and prompting. Results identify students with inadequate communication skills. Norms provided for students ages 8-14 years. Examiner required. One to four students may be evaluated at a time; suitable for group use.

Untimed: Varies

Range: Ages 8-14 years

Scoring: Examiner evaluated

Cost: Test kit (manual, 100 transcript forms, 20 test forms) $48.00.

Publisher: LinguiSystems, Inc.

THE JOLIET 3-MINUTE SPEECH AND LANGUAGE SCREEN (JMSLS)

Mary C. Kinzler and Constance Cowing Johnson

child grades K-5 ☞ ✍

Purpose: Measures speech and language development of school-age children. Identifies children with speech and language disorders. Used to screen large numbers of children.

Description: Multiple item oral response test assessing receptive vocabulary, expressive syntax, voice, fluency, and phonological competence. Line drawings are used to elicit receptive vocabulary. Sentences are used to identify expressive syntax, morphology, and phonological competence. Norms provided for grades K, 2, and 5. Examiner required. Individually administered; suitable for use with large groups of children.

Untimed: 3 minutes

Range: Grades K-5

Scoring: Examiner evaluated

Cost: Test kit (manual, 20 vocabulary plates, 2 scoring sheets) $19.95.

Publisher: Communication Skill Builders, Inc.

LANGUAGE DEVELOPMENT READING EVALUATION PROGRAM

Rosemary Courtney, Mimi Garry, Clayton Graves, Margaret Hughes and John McInnes

child grades 1-7

Purpose: Measures language development and reading abilities of students grades 1-7. Used for both diagnostic and achievement testing. Intended for use with the LANGUAGE DEVELOPMENT READING PROGRAM.

Description: 17 multiple item and oral response tests covering 22 levels of language and reading abilities. Assessment instruments include informal diagnostic tests, informal oral tests, and end-of-level written tests. Tests include: Evaluation Resource Books for grade 1 (levels 2-6), grade 2 (levels 7-10), and grade 3 (levels 11-14); Backpacks and Bumblebees (grades 3-4; level 15); Rowboats and Rollerskates (grade 4; level 16); Driftwood and Dandelions (grades 4-5; level 17); Hockey Cards and Hopscotch (grade 5; level 18); Northern Lights and Fireflies (grades 5-6; level 19); Kites and Cartwheels (grade 6; level 20); Sleeping Bags and Flying Machines (grades 6-7; level 21); and Toboggans and Turtlenecks (grade 7; level 22). Tests are presented in duplicating-master format and include follow-up strategies for teachers. Examiner required. Some tests suitable for group use.
CANADIAN PUBLISHER

Untimed: Varies

Range: Grades 1-7

Scoring: Examiner evaluated

Cost: Evaluation Resource Book (grade 1, 2, or 3) $27.35; all other tests (levels 15-22) each $15.85.

Publisher: Nelson Canada

LINGQUEST 1: LANGUAGE SAMPLE ANALYSIS

child

Purpose: Analyzes a child's use of English grammar. Used for comprehensive diagnostic purposes.

Description: Multiple item analysis of grammatical usage, including grammatical form, grammatical structure, lexical and verb tense analyses executed by microcomputer program. After eliciting a child's free-response utterance, contextual clues are used to produce an expanded (and grammatically correct) version of that utterance. A trained paraprofessional or secretary enters (types) both the actual and expanded utterances into the computer, which then executes the following form, structure, lexical and tense analyses: structure analysis (number of opportunities for occurrence, number of correct instances of use, percent of correct usage for three phrase structure types: noun, verb, and modifier), lexical analysis (lists expanded and actual vocabularies, number of times they are identical and different, and number of times expanded vocabulary items are omitted), Lexical Analysis Summary (total number of different words used over the total number of words present in the corpus is displayed, resulting in type/token ratio), form analysis summary (displays quantitative data depicting the child's grammatical form repertoire and usage; estimates developmental level), Mean Length of Utterance (MLU of both the actual and expanded versions are obtained for both words and morphemes), and verb tense analysis (number of opportunities for occurrence, total correct, total errors and percent correct for 12 verb tenses). Suitable for use with Apple II, Apple II Plus and Apple IIe with minimum 64K RAM, 2 disk drives, and an EPSON MX-80 printer with GRAFTRAX option. Currently being adapted for use on IBM PC and TRS-80 computers (contact publisher). Examiner required. Not suitable for group use.

Untimed: Varies

Range: Children

Scoring: Microcomputer scored

Cost: Complete set (analysis disk, backup analysis disk, 3 data disks, manual, 100 data collection sheets) $950.00.

Publisher: Slosson Educational Publications, Inc.

LINGQUEST 2: PHONOLOGICAL ANALYSIS

child

Purpose: Assesses a child's use of phonemes in spoken English. Used for comprehensive diagnostic purposes.

Description: Multiple item phonemic inventory analysis based on 23 consonants, 14 vowels and 5 diphthongs in English executed by micocomputer program. Picture stimuli (saw, pencil, house, spoon, skates, stars, zipper, scissors, keys) are used to elicit one word responses from the child.

Phonetic spellings of the child's responses are then entered into the computer, which compares the child's responses with the proper phonemic forms of the stimulus words and executes the following phonological analyses: speech sample (the orthographic spelling of each word along with the proper phonetic spelling of the word and the phonetic spelling of the child's responses are displayed for initial evaluation and easy reference), consonant error analysis (for 23 consonants: total opportunities for occurrence, total correct, percent correct and type of error—omission or substitution—are displayed for each initial, medial and final position consonant singleton and each initial position two and three element consonant cluster; also measures contrastivity, variability, and percent consonants correct for initial, medial and final position consonant singletons), consonant omission profile (number of omissions for initial, medial and final position consonant singletons and initial position two and three element clusters, as well as ratio of incorrect usage by manner of production and position in word), consonant substitution profile (identifies feature changes between the correct and the actual phonemes from which patterns of use become evident, and presents a ratio of incorrect usage), vowel error analysis (for 14 vowels and 5 dipthongs: total opportunities for occurance, total correct, percent correct and type of error—omission or substitution; also identifies feature changes between the correct and actual phonemes and presents ratio of correct usage), and phonological process summary (presents a summary of the conceptual rules upon which the child is operating and identifies 20 simplification processes).

Suitable for use with Apple II, Apple II Plus and Apple IIe microcomputers with minimum 64K RAM, 2 disk drives, and an EPSON MX-80 printer with GRAFTRAX option. Currently being adapted for use on IBM PC and TRS-80 computers (contact publisher). Examiner required. Not suitable for group use.

Untimed: Varies

Range: Children

Scoring: Microcomputer scored

Cost: Complete set (analysis disk, backup analysis disk, 3 data disks, manual, 25 data collection sheets) $950.00.

Publisher: Slosson Educational Publications, Inc.

MEEKER-CROMWELL BEHAVIOR DEVELOPMENTAL ASSESSMENT

all ages

Purpose: Measures the language development of severely impaired students from two years of age through adulthood. Used for instructional planning and placement.

Description: Multiple item behavioral observation inventory assessing the functional development of language skills in severely impaired individuals. The inventory consists of a list of language behaviors arranged in chronological developmental order. Someone who knows the student well rates him on a five-point scale for each behavioral item. There is a normal rating paralleled by a delayed or deficient scale; students are rated on both scales (one per student). The entry point for training is determined by the first score of "five" and will identify at what age the student is functioning. Examiner required. Not suitable for group use.

Untimed: Varies

Range: Age 2 years-adult

Scoring: Examiner evaluated

Cost: Test forms $1.25 each.

Publisher: SOI Institute

ORAL LANGUAGE EVALUATION (OLE)

Refer to page 72.

ORAL LANGUAGE SENTENCE IMITATION DIAGNOSTIC INVENTORY—FORMAT REVISED (OLSIDI-F)

Linda Zachman, Rosemary Huisingh, Carol Jorgensen and Mark Barrett

child

Purpose: Analyzes the syntactical, morphological, and grammatical errors of children ages 5-7 years. Used by clinicians to identify targets for intervention and to monitor changes in a child's language performance.

Description: 270 item sentence imitation test consisting of 27 subtests of 10 sentences each. Designed as a follow-up to the OLSIST-F, each subtest covers one of the 27 syntactical, morphological, and grammatic structures tested on the OLSIST-F. Only those subtests indicated by the results of the OLSIST-F are administered. Performances are scored in percentages. Revised format presents all 27 subtests and the diagnostic profile on one form. Examiner required. Not suitable for group use.

Untimed: Varies

Range: Ages 5-7 years

Scoring: Examiner evaluated

Cost: Test kit (20 test forms, 1 instruction manual, 1 statistical manual) $23.00.

Publisher: LinguiSystems, Inc.

ORAL LANGUAGE SENTENCE IMITATION SCREENING TEST—FORMAT REVISED (OLSIST-F)

Linda Zachman, Rosemary Huisingh, Carol Jorgensen and Mark Barrett

child

Purpose: Evaluates a child's use of language structures. Used by speech-language pathologists.

Description: 18-22 item sentence imitation test assessing syntax, morphology, and grammar at three stages of linguistic development. Stage III (for use with ages 3-4 years) assesses 18 linguistic structures with sentence length ranging from 4-9 morphemes. Stage IV (ages 4-5 years) assesses 22 linguistic structures with sentence length ranging from 5-11 morphemes. Stage V (ages 5-7 years) assesses 23 linguistic structures with sentence length ranging from 6-13 morphemes. One protocol for each stage combines the 20 sentence Test Form and Score Sheet. Examiner required. Not suitable for group use.

Untimed: 5 minutes

Range: Ages 3-7 years

Scoring: Examiner evaluated

Cost: Test kit (50 protocols each for stages III, IV, and V, 1 instruction manual, and 1 statistical manual) $30.00.

Publisher: LinguiSystems, Inc.

THE PATTERNED ELICITATION SYNTAX TEST (PEST)

Edna Carter Young and Joseph J. Perachio

child

Purpose: Determines whether a child's expressive grammatical skills are age appropriate. Identifies children in need of further evaluation.

Description: Multiple item oral response test using the delayed imitation technique to assess a child's use of 44 syntactic structures. The child listens to three consecutive modeled sentences with a common syntactic pattern but varying vocabulary while looking simultaneously at corresponding line illustrations. The child then repeats the sentences with the aid of the drawings. The first two sentences serve as carriers. The third sentence, which is most distant from the examiner's model, is used in scoring. The use of visual clues with delayed imitation allows the child's elicited responses to be closer to the student's spontaneous language. In addition to determining the child's language age, criterion-referenced interpretation of the child's responses provides an in-depth analysis of the child's use of grammatical structures. The manual includes: stimulus pictures, demonstration page, normative data, and instructions for administration and scoring. The response form is used to record the child's utterances, the assessment form includes the grammatical analysis, and the individual data form is used for recordkeeping. Examiner required. Not suitable for group use.

Untimed: 20 minutes

Range: Language age 3-7.5 years

Scoring: Examiner evaluated

Cost: Test kit (manual and response, assessment, and individual data forms) $19.95.

Publisher: CTB/McGraw-Hill

PERFORMANCE ASSESSMENT OF SYNTAX: ELICITED AND SPONTANEOUS (PASES)

Lila Coughran

child

Purpose: Assesses a child's ability to produce key syntactic structures.

May be used with young, severely impaired children, or children with short attention spans.

Description: Multiple item oral response test measuring the 11 most frequently exhibited errors in children's syntax: articles, personal pronouns, possessive pronouns, adjectives, verbs (is/are, present progressive), verbs (has/have), verbs (past tense, regular and irregular), plurality, negation, interrogation, and conjunctions. The child's spontaneous use of language is assessed when possible, but in the event of failure, stimulus items are provided for eliciting appropriate responses. The criterion-referenced nature of the test allows specific subtests rather than the entire battery to be administered. May be used with language impaired and normally developing children functioning within the 3-8 year age range. Examiner required. Not suitable for group use.

Untimed: Varies

Range: Ages 3-8 years

Scoring: Examiner evaluated

Cost: Complete kit (manual, stimulus items in an 8½″ x 11″ vinyl easel binder, and 10 response forms) $75.00.

Publisher: Pro-Ed

PRESCHOOL LANGUAGE ASSESSMENT INSTRUMENT (PLAI)

Marion Blank, Susan A. Rose and Laura J. Berlin

child

Purpose: Evaluates preschoolers' thinking and verbal reasoning skills. Used to make placement, remediation, and therapy decisions.

Description: Multiple item oral response test assessing how well a preschooler understands and uses classroom language to solve problems encountered in his academic world. Picture stimuli are used to present test items assessing four levels of thinking in developmental order. Level I assesses naming abilities, matching abilities, remembering relevant information, and imitating abilities. Level II assesses defining by function, describing a scene, recalling information, defining by attributes, attending to multiple attributes, and identifying differences. Level III assesses predicting, associating by function, assuming a role, following directions, identifying similarities, exclusion, defining words, and sequencing and event telling. Level IV assesses predicting, justifying decisions, determining causes, determining solutions, and explaining inferences. Test results provide means, percentile ranks, and standard deviations for ages 3-6 years. Examiner required. Not suitable for group use.

Untimed: Varies

Range: Ages 3-6 years

Scoring: Examiner evaluated

Cost: Test kit (hard-cover examiner's manual and therapy guide, picture stimuli book, 100 test forms) $74.00.

Publisher: LinguiSystems, Inc.

QUICK WORD TEST

Edgar F. Borgatta and Raymond J. Corsini

child-adult gr. 4 and up

Purpose: Measures verbal intelligence. Used for quick screening purposes in educational and clinical settings.

Description: 50 or 100 item paper-pencil multiple-choice vocabulary test measuring specific aspects of verbal mental ability. Test items present a word followed by four response choices. Individuals select from the four choices the word which has the same meaning as the first word. Available for three levels: elementary (50 items) for grades 4-6; level 1 (100 items) for grades 7-12 and average adult groups; and level 2 (100 items) for superior 11th and 12th grade students, college and professional groups. The vocabulary items for each level are printed one side of a single test sheet. IBM 1230 and combined IBM 805/Digitek test sheets are available in parallel forms Am and Bm. Hand-scoring and machine-scoring scoring stencils are available for all forms. The manual includes: directions for administering, scoring, and interpreting the test; comparative data and correlations with raw scores from other verbal intelligence tests; and developmental and normative data. Norms are provided in terms of percentile ranks and stanines for the following groups: grades 4, 5, and 6 (by grade) for the elementary level; grades 7-12 (by grade) for level 1; and college freshmen, adult education groups (by educational level), and various occupational groups for level 2. Examiner required. Suitable for group use.

Untimed: 15 minutes

Range: Grade 4-adult

Scoring: Hand key; machine scored; computer scored

Cost: Elementary test kit (35 test sheets, answer key, manual, and group record sheet) $3.00; level 1 or 2 test kit (45 test sheets, manual, and group record sheet) $6.00; scoring key for level 1 or 2 $1.00; specimen set (includes all three levels) $5.00.

Publisher: F.E. Peacock Publishers, Inc.

SCREENING KIT OF LANGUAGE DEVELOPMENT (SKOLD)

Lynn S. Bliss and Doris V. Allen

child

Purpose: Assesses the language development of young children. Used with children speaking both Black and Standard English to detect language impairments and disorders.

Description: 135 item oral response test measuring language development in both Black English and Standard English speaking children. Picture stimuli are used to assess vocabulary comprehension, story completion, individual and paired sentence repetition with pictures, individual sentence repetition without pictures, and comprehension of commands. Consists of six subtests, three for Black English and three for Standard English, in each of the following age ranges: 30-36 months, 37-42 months, and 43-48 months. Norms provided for speakers of Black and Standard English. Manual includes guidelines for administration and scoring and appendices covering normal language development, disordered language, and the linguistic characteristics of Black English. May be administered by trained paraprofessional. Examiner required. Not suitable for group use.

Untimed: Varies

Range: Ages 30-48 months (developmental age: 2½-4 years)

Scoring: Examiner evaluated

Cost: Test kit (manual, stimulus book, and 1 set of either Black or Standard English scoring forms) $50.00; 50 scoring forms—Black or Standard English $10.00.

Publisher: Slosson Educational Publications, Inc.

SCREENING TEST OF ADOLESCENT LANGUAGE (STAL)

Elizabeth M. Prather, Sheila Van Ausdal Breecher, Marimyn Lee Stafford and Elizabeth Matthews Wallace

teen grades 6 and up

Purpose: Assesses linguistic development and identifies junior and senior high school students in need of further testing. Used with large populations of students (public school settings) by speech-language pathologists, classroom teachers, school counselors and psychologists, and teachers of special education.

Description: 23 item oral response screening instrument consisting of four subtests assessing language skills often associated with learning/language disabilities. The Vocabulary subtest (12 items) assesses comprehension of word meaning, substitution of a synonym in a grammatically correct form, and word finding and retrieval competencies. The Auditory Memory Span subtest (3 items) requires repetition of a sentence in its original syntactical form and measures the aspect of memory span associated with related semantic and syntactic stimuli. The Language Processing subtest (5 items) requires the student to decode a message and to use language for reasoning and problem solving. The Proverb Explanation subtest (3 items) assesses paraphrasing and cognitive skills needed for verbal clarity. Standard instructions are given at the beginning of each subtest, and the student's oral responses are recorded and evaluated in accordance with the instructions included in the manual. Cut-off scores based on normative studies of sixth and ninth grade students identify students in need of further testing. Examiner required. Individually administered; suitable for use with large populations.

Untimed: 7 minutes

Range: Junior and senior high school students

Scoring: Examiner evaluated

Cost: Complete kit (two-part manual, 50 test forms, and pull-out laminated cards summarizing administration and scoring procedures) $30.00.

Publisher: University of Washington Press

SEQUENCED INVENTORY OF COMMUNICATION DEVELOPMENT

Dona Lea Hedrick, Elizabeth M. Prather and Annette R. Tobin

child

Purpose: Evaluates the communication abilities of normal and retarded children functioning between the ages of four months and four years. Used for remedial programming by speech-language pathologists, audiologists, psychologists, and teachers trained in speech and language assessment techniques.

Description: 210 item inventory assessing and diagnosing language disorders in young children. The receptive language section (92 items) includes behavioral items that test sound and speech discrimination and awareness, and understanding. The expressive language section (118 items) includes three types of expressive behaviors: imitating, initiating, and responding; and measures verbal output for length, grammatic and syntactic structure, and articulation. The resulting Communication Profile provides guidelines for developing remedial programs for young children with language disorders, mental retardation, specific language problems, and hearing or visual impairments. Some items have been adapted from the REP Scale, the Denver Development Scale, and the Illinois Test of Adaptive Abilities. Test kit includes over 100 objects used as stimuli for test items. Examiner required. Not suitable for group use.

Untimed: Varies

Range: Ages 4 months-4 years

Scoring: Examiner evaluated

Cost: Complete kit (manual, 50 receptive test booklets, 50 expressive test booklets, over 100 stimulus objects, all in a plastic carrying case)

$175.00.

Publisher: University of Washington Press

TEST FOR EXAMINING EXPRESSIVE MORPHOLOGY (TEEM)

Kenneth G. Shipley, Terry A. Stone and Marlene B. Sue

child, teen

Purpose: Assesses children's development and use of bound morphemes. Measures general language level and monitors student progress. Used in language remediation, hearing impaired, early childhood, special education, and speech therapy classes.

Description: 54 item oral response sentence-completion test assessing the allomorphic variations of six major morphemes: present progressives, plurals, possessives, past tenses, third-person singulars, and derived adjectives. Test items consist of a stimulus picture the child views while completing an orally administered stimulus phrase. Test items are familiar to children and can end in a variety of allomorphic variations. Test book allows examiner to present the stimulus pictures while reading the accompanying phrase. Results identify specific morphemes and allomorphic variations requiring stimulation or instruction. The manual includes administration and scoring instructions and technical data. Examiner required. Not suitable for group use.

Untimed: 7 minutes

Range: Language age 3-8 years; interest level 3-16 years

Scoring: Examiner evaluated

Cost: Test kit (manual, 25 scoring forms, test book) $20.00.

Publisher: Communication Skill Builders, Inc.

TEST LISTENING ACCURACY IN CHILDREN (TLAC)

Refer to page 159.

TEST OF ARTICULATION PERFORMANCE—DIAGNOSTIC (TAP-D)

Brian R. Bryant and Deborah L. Bryant

child

Purpose: Assesses a child's articulatory strengths and weaknesses. Used for educational planning and diagnostic evaluation.

Description: 82 item oral response test assessing the following components of a child's articulatory performance: isolated words (phonetic inventory, percent correct, error analysis of substitutions, omissions and distortions), distinctive features (place, manner, and voicing), selective deep test (adjacent sounds), continuous speech (key phonemes in sentences), stimulability (syllables, words, and sentences), and verbal communication scales (parent, teacher, and student). Picture stimuli are used to elicit the responses. The examiner selects those components which are needed to provide a comprehensive analysis of the child's articulatory performance. Test kit includes the Verbal Communication Scales as a measure of the child's practical use of language. Examiner required. Not suitable for group use.

Untimed: Varies

Range: Ages 3-8 years

Scoring: Examiner evaluated

Cost: Complete kit (manual, 82 picture cards, 25 profile forms, and complete VCS, all in a sturdy storage box) $66.00.

Publisher: Pro-Ed

TEST OF ARTICULATION PERFORMANCE—SCREEN (TAPS-S)

Brian R. Bryant and Deborah L. Bryant

child

Purpose: Identifies children with articulation problems in need of further evaluation. Used where large numbers of children must be screened in a short period of time.

Description: 31-item oral response test assessing articulation performance of children ages 3-8 years. Picture stimuli are used to elicit both spontaneous and imitative production. Quotients, percentiles, and age equivalents available for children 3 years 0 months to 8 years 11 months. Individually administered; suitable for use with large groups.

Untimed: 3-5 minutes

Range: Ages 3-8 years

Scoring: Examiner evaluated

Cost: Complete kit (manual, picture book, and 50 answer sheets, all in a sturdy box) $37.00.

Publisher: Pro-Ed

TEST OF PROBLEM SOLVING (TOPS)

Linda Zachman, Carol Jorgensen, Rosemary Huisingh and Mark Barrett

child

Purpose: Assesses the verbal reasoning and problem solving abilities of children ages 6-12 years.

Description: Multiple item oral response test assessing expressive language skills and problem solving abilities. Problems are presented with picture stimuli and test thinking skills such as: determining causes, answering negative why questions, determining solutions, avoiding problems, and explaining inferences. Results yield age equivalencies, percentile ranks, standard scores, and standard deviations. Examiner required. Not suitable for group use.

Untimed: Varies

Range: Ages 6-12 years

Scoring: Examiner evaluated

Cost: Test kit $58.00.

Publisher: LinguiSystems, Inc.

VERBAL COMMUNICATION SCALES (VCS)

Brian R. Bryant and Deborah L. Bryant

child

Purpose: Evaluates a child's use of language in the home and school. Used in conjunction with interviews in ecological assessments of spoken language skills.

Description: Three scales assess the attitudes of parents, teachers, and the student concerning his use of language. The Parent and Teacher scales consist of 25 items (each of which is a statement about the child's practical application of spoken language) to be rated on a numerical scale. The Student Scale consists of 20 questions asked by the examiner and requiring a simple yes or no response from the child. Norms for the Parent and Teacher scales are provided for children ages 3 years 0 months to 8 years 11 months. Student Scale norms are for children ages 5 years 0 months to 8 years 11 months. Not suitable for group use.

Untimed: Varies

Range: Ages 3-8 years

Scoring: Examiner evaluated

Cost: Complete kit (examiner's fact sheet, 25 teacher scales, 25 parent scales, and 25 student scales) $18.00.

Publisher: Pro-Ed

VERBAL LANGUAGE DEVELOPMENT SCALE (VLDS)

Merlin J. Mecham

child, teen

Purpose: Assesses the language development of children ages 1 month-16 years.

Description: Multiple item paper-pencil checklist assessing the language development of children. The checklist of developmental language behaviors is completed by the examiner during a structured interview with the child's parents or other adult informant with a thorough knowledge of the child's language behavior repertoire. Scale items are an extension of the communication section of the Vineland Social Maturity Scale. Examiner required. Not suitable for group use.

Untimed: Varies

Range: Ages 1 month-16 years

Cost: VLDS specimen set $2.00.

Publisher: American Guidance Service

THE WORD TEST

Carol Jorgensen, Mark Barrett, Rosemary Huisingh and Linda Zachman

child

Purpose: Assesses the expressive vocabulary and understanding of semantics of students age seven years and older. Used with language disabled, learning disabled, mentally disabled, and other exceptional children as a basis for planning therapy programs.

Description: Multiple item oral response subtests assessing vocabulary in six contexts: associations, synonyms, semantic absurdities, antonyms, definitions, and multiple definitions. All tasks are presented auditorially—no reading or pictures are involved. Vocabulary of test items is related to school curricula. Test results yield age equivalencies, percentile ranks, and standard scores for students ages 7-12 years. Ceilings and demonstration items provided. Examiner required. Not suitable for group use.

Untimed: 30 minutes

Range: Ages 7-12 years

Scoring: Examiner evaluated

Cost: Test kit (manual and 20 test forms) $36.00.

Publisher: LinguiSystems, Inc.

WRITTEN LANGUAGE SYNTAX TEST

Refer to page 68.

Visual

BIEGER TEST OF VISUAL DISCRIMINATION

Elaine Bieger

child-adult

Purpose: Measures visual discrimination abilities using letters and words.

Description: 112 item paper-pencil multiple-choice test consisting of seven subtests measuring levels of mastery in the following areas: larger and lesser contrasts in letters and words, orientation reversal in letters and words, and sequence reversals in words. This test may be administered independently or in conjunction with the Visual Discrimination of Words Training Program. Following the format of the test, the training program starts with contrasting words and systematically progresses to words with almost identical features. The whole word and parts of the word are presented to give systematic experiences relating parts of the word and the gestalt simultaneously. The individual is taught to scan works that are simultaneously positioned further and further apart. Examiner required. Suitable for group use.

Untimed: 5 minutes per subtest (35 minutes total)

Range: Child, adolescent, adult

Scoring: Examiner evaluated

Cost: Complete test kit (manual, test record forms, and workbook) $20.50; manual (for both test and training program) $5.50; 30 record forms (15 each tests A and B) $9.75; training program workbook $6.50.

Publisher: Stoelting Company

DEVELOPMENTAL VISION TEST

SOI Institute staff

child

Purpose: Assesses ten visual functions of young children. Used by teachers, nurses, and health service personnel to screen all students before vision problems cause academic problems.

Description: Nine subtests used as a screening instrument for detecting vision problems which may affect learning. Subtests are taken from the basic SOI Learning Abilities test, and the SOI-LA manual is used for administration. Scoring is keyed to the Developmental Vision Guide for complete interpretation. Includes Vision Checklist. Examiner required. Individually administered; suitable for screening large groups.

Untimed: Varies

Range: Children

Scoring: Examiner evaluated; computer scoring and analysis available

Cost: Test form $2.00.

Publisher: SOI Institute

INVENTORY OF PERCEPTUAL SKILLS (IPS)

Donald R. O'Dell

child

Purpose: Assesses visual and auditory perceptual skills and provides the structure for individual remedial programs. Aids in instructional planning for students at all age levels, and in the development of IEP's.

Description: 79 item oral response and task performance test assessing perceptual skills in the following areas: visual discrimination, visual memory, object recognition, visual-motor coordination, auditory discrimination, auditory memory, auditory sequencing, and auditory blending. Once scored and recorded on the student profile (included in the student record booklet), a graphic comparison can be made of all of the subtests. A score below the mean on any subtest would indicate a weakness in that area. May be administered by teachers, aides, or specialists without special training. The teacher's manual contains many educational activities in visual and auditory perception. Games, exercises, and activities provide the teacher with a variety of approaches and materials to use with the student. The student workbook includes 18 exercises to improve the areas in need of remediation. Examiner required. Not suitable for group use.

Untimed: Varies

Range: Children

Scoring: Examiner evaluated

Cost: Complete set (manual, student workbook, 10 student record booklets, and stimulus cards) $16.25; manual $3.25; student workbook $1.75; 10 student record booklets

$10.00; stimulus cards $2.25.

Publisher: Stoelting Company

WASHER VISUAL ACUITY SCREENING TECHNIQUE (WVAST)

Rhonda Wiczer Washer

mentally handicapped

Purpose: Measures the visual abilities of severely handicapped, low-functioning, and very young children. Used for screening groups of children to identify those with possible visual impairments.

Description: Multiple item vision test screening both near and far point acuity. The testing procedure omits as many perceptual, motor, and verbal skills as possible. A conditioning process is outlined for familiarizing the children with the symbols, matching skills, and eye occlusion used in the screening. May be administered by trained volunteers. Examiner required. Individually administered; suitable for screening groups of children.

Untimed: Varies

Range: 18 months or 2.6 years mental age to adult

Scoring: Examiner evaluated

Cost: Starter set (manual, symbol cards, stimulus cards, occluders, near point panel, 20 screening records) $49.00.

Publisher: Scholastic Testing Service, Inc.

Student Evaluation and Counseling

Behavior Problems and Counseling Tools

A BASIC SCREENING AND REFERRAL FORM FOR CHILDREN WITH SUSPECTED LEARNING AND BEHAVIORAL DISABILITIES

Refer to page 156.

THE BEHAVIOR EVALUATION SCALE (BES)

Stephen B. McCarney, James E. Leigh and Jane A. Cornbleet

child, teen grades 1-12

Purpose: Assesses the behavioral problems of students grades 1-12. Used by school personnel in making decisions about eligibility, placement, and programming for students with behavior problems.

Description: Multiple item paper-pencil observational inventory assessing the behavioral problems of students regardless of primary handicapping conditions. May be used with students who have learning disabilities, mental retardation, physical handicaps, or other handicapping conditions. Self-administered by examiner.

Untimed: Varies

Range: Grades 1-12

Scoring: Examiner evaluated

Cost: Complete kit (manual, 50 student record forms, one sample data collection form) $30.00.

Publisher: Pro-Ed

BEHAVIOUR PROBLEMS: A SYSTEM OF MANAGEMENT

Peter Galvin and Richard Singleton

child, teen

Purpose: Assesses and monitors the behavior of problem children. Used in the classroom by specialist and non-specialist teachers.

Description: Three paper-pencil record forms provide a framework for assessing and monitoring the classroom behavior of up to eight children over a six month period. The Behaviour Checklist enables the teacher to identify and describe inappropriate behaviors, note specific problems, and select two priority behaviors on which future work will concentrate. The Daily Record Sheet provides a record of observed classroom behavior, noting details concerning the priority behaviors (frequency, duration), positive behaviors, and other significant items. The Monthly Progress Chart records information about the child (age, IQ , reading age, etc.) along with a systematic account of the behavior management strategies adopted. The observations made help assess the success of the long-term program. The manual includes an explanation of the rationale behind the system, guidelines for its use, and references to books on appropriate remedial programs. Examiner required. Suitable for group use.
BRITISH PUBLISHER

Untimed: Varies

Range: Primary and secondary age children

Scoring: Examiner evaluated

Cost: Complete set (manual and set of 3 record forms) £8.45.

Publisher: NFER-Nelson Publishing Company Ltd.

CAREER PROBLEM CHECKLIST

Tony Crowley

teen

Purpose: Identifies problems secondary school and college students may be experiencing in making career plans. Used by careers teachers, officers and counselors in lessons, interviews and careers programs.

Description: 100 item four-page paper-pencil questionnaire identifying the problems individual students or groups of students may be experiencing in career planning. Students identify the kinds of problems they are experiencing from the 100 examples listed. Items cover information about school, home, getting information about jobs, starting work, applying for a job and decision making. Used to identify instructional needs of individuals and groups of students; to provide structure in guidance interviews; and to help form discussion groups in structured careers lessons and to plan and monitor the effects of careers programs. Examiner required. Suitable for group use.
BRITISH PUBLISHER

Untimed: Varies

Range: Ages 14-17 years

Scoring: Examiner evaluated

Cost: Manual £3.95; Checklists £7.95.

Publisher: NFER-Nelson Publishing Company Ltd.

CHILD BEHAVIOR CHECKLIST AND REVISED CHILD BEHAVIOR PROFILE

Refer to page 28.

CHILDREN'S ADAPTIVE BEHAVIOR SCALE

Refer to page 191.

CHILDREN'S VERSION/FAMILY ENVIRONMENT SCALE (CV/FES)

Refer to page 22.

DIFFERENTIAL PERSONALITY QUESTIONNAIRE

Refer to page 37.

EYBERG CHILD BEHAVIOR INVENTORY (ECBI)

Refer to page 38.

INDIVIDUAL PROBLEM INDEX (IPI)

Refer to page 41.

PERSONAL PROBLEM CHECKLIST

Refer to page 46.

PRE-MOD

Joseph Kaplan and Sandy Kent

child, teen & hand.

Purpose: Diagnoses behavior problems and prescribes appropriate interventions. Used by teachers or specialists working with mildly to moderately handicapped children; also applicable for teachers of normal and slow learners in the regular classroom. Used to establish IEP's in the affective domain and social skills areas.

Description: Multiple item computer-administered assessment instrument diagnosing the underlying causes of 14 of the most common behavior problems found in the classroom, including physical aggression, abusive-provocative language, noncompliance, and hyperactive-impulsive and withdrawn behavior. The program presents the teacher with a list of the 14 behaviors, from which the individual student's basic problems are identified. For each behavior identified, the program provides a socially appropriate behavior that is incompatible with the student's maladaptive behavior. The teacher is then presented with a list of prerequisite skills, knowledge, and attitudes necessary for the student to engage in the socially appropriate behavior. The teacher then identifies the prerequisites which the student lacks, and is provided with corresponding performance objectives and suggested interventions for each prerequisite the student lacks. Additional assessments are provided for determining the status of the prerequisites. The accompanying operator's manual is written in plain English. The program may be used independently or in conjunction with the textbook *Beyond Behavior Modification* (Kaplan, 1983) as an instructional aid in teaching behavior management strategies. Self-administered. Not suitable for group use.

Untimed: Varies

Range: Elementary and high school students; special education students of all ages

Scoring: Computer scored

Cost: Software package for Apple II + or IIe microcomputers (includes diskette, backup diskette, user's manual, and 10 test sheets) $169.95.

Publisher: ASIEP Education Company

PUPIL BEHAVIOR RATING SCALE

Nadine M. Lambert, Eli M. Bower and Carolyn S. Hartsough

child, teen grades K-7

Purpose: Assesses students' classroom behavior and interpersonal skills. Identifies students who are potentially educationally handicapped or gifted. Used to organize and manage appropriate instructional programs.

Description: Three multiple item paper-pencil and oral response rating scales measuring student effectiveness in nonintellectual or affective areas. The three scales include: one teacher-observation screening instrument, one peer-rating instrument and one self-rating instrument. The teacher-observation scale assesses three underlying dimensions of affective behavior: classroom adaptation, interpersonal skills, and intrapersonal behavior. These measures are obtained by using an interval scale of 11 observable attributes. The 11 scales are contained in the rating book; student scores are entered on the group record chart. Peer and self-rating are available for two levels: grades K-3 and grades 3-7.

The peer-rating instrument for grades K-3 is the Who Could This Be Game. The game consists of 20 scenes of school situations. The scenes portray both positive (or neutral) situations and situations that are potentially dysfunctional behavior. Students are asked individually to select a classmate for each situation. By tallying responses, a measure of how each student is perceived by the class is obtained. The self-rating instrument for grades K-3 is the picture game (separate forms for boys and girls). Seventy-two scenes depicting home, school and play situations are presented. Students circle a happy face next to the scenes they see as happy and a sad face next to the scenes they see as sad. A tally of sad and happy responses determines a child's self-rating. Results from the Who Could This Be Game and the Picture Game are entered on the group record chart for peer and self ratings. Peer and self ratings for grades 3-7 are both presented in the School Play test book. Part I of the play consists of 14 roles for which students choose classmates who they think could best play them. By tallying responses, a measure of how each student is perceived by the class is obtained. Part II elicits from the students responses concerning which roles they would or would not choose for themselves, and which roles they think they would or would not be chosen for by classmates and the teacher. Scores for both parts of the school play are entered on the group record chart for peer and self ratings.

The class screening summary chart combines scores of teacher, peer and self ratings. The pupil record folder provides space for recording scores of the teacher, peer and self ratings, data from other achievement tests, and other essential information related to the writing of IEP's. The manual includes information on administering and scoring the scales, interpreting results, and prescribing appropriate instructional intervention. Administered by classroom teacher. Teacher-observation scale is self-administered, the peer and self ratings for grades K-3 are individually administered, and the peer and self ratings for grades 3-7 are group administered.

Untimed: Varies

Range: Grades K-7

Scoring: Examiner evaluated

Cost: Manual $6.50; rating book $9.75; 20 group record charts $4.00; Who Could This Be Game (32 recording forms and 1 group record chart) $15.00; Picture Game (16 each boys and girls forms and 2 group record charts) $33.00; School Play (32 test books and 1 group record chart) $28.00; 20 class screening summary charts $5.50; and 32 pupil record folders $25.75.

Publisher: CTB/McGraw-Hill

THE REVISED BEHAVIOR PROBLEM CHECKLIST (RBPC)

Herbert C. Quay and Donald R. Peterson

child, teen

Purpose: Assesses the nature of problem behavior. Used in educational, mental health, pediatric, and correctional settings as well as for research purposes.

Description: 85 item paper-pencil observational inventory consisting of statements about problem behaviors commonly seen in children and adolescents. Each item on the inventory is rated by a knowledgeable observer (parent, teacher, child care worker, correctional staff member). Scores are provided for six subscales: conduct disorder, socialized aggression, attention problems-immaturity, anxiety-withdrawal, psychotic behavior, and motor excess. An *Interim Manual*, continuously updated, provides a description of the test's development, data on reliability and validity, and means and standard deviations from various normal and clinical samples. Examiner required. Not suitable for group use.

Untimed: 15 minutes

Range: Child, adolescent

Scoring: Hand key

Cost: Test kit (interim manual, 50 copies of the RPBC, and scoring stencil) $20.00.

Publisher: Herbert C. Quay

SCALE FOR THE IDENTIFICATION OF SCHOOL PHOBIA (SIS)

Jerome H. Want

child, teen

Purpose: Identifies school-phobic students from other chronically absent students.

Description: 24 item paper-pencil behavior rating scale consisting of two profiles: the School Phobia Profile and the School Truancy Profile. Each profile is completed and scored by the examiner in response to interviews with the student, parents, and other school personnel. Criterion-referenced evaluation of the two profiles identifies school-phobic behavior from school-truant behavior. Intervention strategies provided in manual. Examiner required. Not suitable for group use.

Untimed: Varies

Range: Students

Scoring: Examiner evaluated

Cost: Test kit (manual, 25 record forms, in vinyl folder) $18.50; specimen set (manual and sample forms) $12.50.

Publisher: Academic Therapy Publications

STOGDILL BEHAVIOR CARDS

child

Purpose: Assesses the attitudes of a delinquent child toward his past behavior and experiences. Used for initial screening of juvenile delinquents.

Description: Multiple item interview guide covering a wide range of delinquent behaviors and background information. Low-pressure questions deal with specific acts and observable behavior, not subjective feelings. The format provides a child with an opportunity to talk objectively about his problems and aids the examiner in understanding the child's attitudes toward his delinquencies. Examiner required. Not suitable for group use.

Untimed: 15-20 minutes

Range: Children

Scoring: Examiner evaluated

Cost: Test kit (150 cards, 100 record blanks, manual) $16.50.

Publisher: Stoelting Co.

STUDENT DEVELOPMENTAL PROFILE AND PLANNING RECORD

Refer to page 189.

STUDENT DEVELOPMENTAL TASK INVENTORY: REVISED SECOND EDITION (SDTI-2)

Refer to page 192.

TEST OF EARLY SOCIOEMOTIONAL DEVELOPMENT (TOESD)

Wayne P. Hresko and Linda Brown

child

Purpose: Evaluates the behavior of children ages 3-7 years. Identifies children with behavior problems and the setting in which those problems most often occur.

Description: Four multiple item paper-pencil components assessing problem behaviors in children. The 30-item student rating scale is completed by the student, the 34-item parent rating scale is completed by the parent(s), and the 36-item teacher rating scale is completed by the teacher or other professionals having contact with the child in a school setting. A sociogram provides information about peer perceptions of the child being evaluated. Results discriminate among normal, behavior disordered, learning disabled, and mentally retarded children. All four components yield percentile ranks and standard scores. This instrument is a downward extension of the Behavior Rating Profile (BRP), and resembles the BRP in both form and content. Examiner required. Suitable for group use.

Untimed: Varies

Range: Ages 3-0 to 7-11 years

Scoring: Examiner evaluated

Cost: Complete kit (manual, 50 student rating forms, 50 parent rating forms, and 50 teacher rating forms in a storage box) $44.00.

Publisher: Pro-Ed

LEARNING STYLE IDENTIFICATION SCALE (LSIS)

Paul Malcom, William C. Lutz, Mary A. Gerken and Gary M. Hoeltke

child

Purpose: Assesses the manner in which students prefer to learn. Used with low-functioning, average, and gifted students for academic planning.

Description: 24 item paper-pencil observational inventory assessing classroom behaviors related to students' preferred learning styles. Measures to what extent a student relies on internal sources of information (feelings, beliefs, and attitudes) and external sources of information (other people, events, and social institutions). Identifies five learning styles based on preferred manner in which a student reacts to situations and solves problems. The handbook contains directions for administering, scoring, and profiling the scale. Separate sections present teaching guidelines, techniques, and activities for each learning style, as well as data on development, reliability and validity, factor analyses, and rating differences by grade and sex. Examiner required. Suitable for evaluating groups of students.

Untimed: 15 minutes

Range: Children

Scoring: Examiner evaluated

Cost: Test kit (handbook, 30 rating, scoring, and profiling forms) $25.00.

Publisher: Slosson Educational Publications, Inc.

Student Attitudes

ADMINISTRATOR IMAGE QUESTIONNAIRE

Refer to page 194.

CANFIELD LEARNING STYLES INVENTORY (CLS)

Albert A. Canfield

teen, adult

Purpose: Identifies an individual's preferred learning methods. Identifies individuals with little or no interest in independent or unstructured learning situations. Used in conjunction with the Canfield Instructional Style Inventory to maximize teaching and learning efficiency.

Description: 30 item paper-pencil forced-rank inventory measuring individual learning needs (interacting with others, goal setting, competition, friendly relations with instructor, independence in study, classroom authority), preferred mediums (listening, reading, viewing pictures, graphs, slides, or direct experience), and areas of interest (numeric concepts, qualitative concepts, working with inanimate things and people). Also indicates student perceptions as to how they will perform in the learning situation. Identifies learning problems associated with either traditional or innovative teaching methods. Available in two forms: form S-A for use with most adults and form E for use with persons whose reading level is as low as the fifth grade. Test booklets are reusable. Answer sheets and profiles sheets are self-scoring. Separate norms for males and females. Self-administered. Suitable for group use.

Untimed: 30 minutes

Range: Adolescent, adult

Scoring: Self-scored

Cost: Starter set (25 test booklets, 50 answer sheets, profiles, and manual) $62.95; specimen set (includes manual) $19.95; manual $12.00.

Publisher: Humanics Media

CAREER PROBLEM CHECKLIST

Refer to page 178.

THE CLASSROOM ENVIRONMENT INDEX (CEI)

George Stern and associates

students grades 5 and up

Purpose: Measures the psychological environment of a classroom (grades 5-12 and certain college classes) in terms of the need-press paradigm of human behavior as conceptualized by Henry Murray. Used for research and teacher development purposes.

Description: 300 item paper-pencil true-false inventory assessing the environment of a classroom in terms of 30 press scales which reflect the 30 basic need scales established on the Stern Activities Index (AI). Test items refer to classroom environment, teacher personality, teaching style, creativity, and other facets of the teaching-learning process. Scores are provided for six first order dimensions (humanistic intellectual climate, group intellectual life, achievement standards, personal dignity, orderliness, and science) and two second order dimensions (development press and control press). The questionnaire is designed so that it is possible to divide it into two parts, requiring each student to answer only half of the 300 questions. Item content has been kept as similar as possible to that of the other Syracuse Indexes (especially the High School Characteristics Index), with a number of revisions to make the instrument applicable to individual classroom rather than to the institution as a whole. Analysis differentiates between classrooms, subjects, grades, and educational levels. Evidence for reliability and validity are presented in the technical manual. Self-administered. Suitable for group use.

Untimed: 40 minutes

Range: Grades 5-12 and college classes

Scoring: Examiner evaluated; computer scoring available

Cost: Test booklet $.50; answer sheet $.10; profile form $.10; technical manual $7.50; prices for computer scoring and analysis available on request.

Publisher: Evaluation Research Associates

THE COLLEGE CHARACTERISTICS INDEX (CCI)

George Stern and associates

college student

Purpose: Measures the perceived press found in college environments in terms of the need-press paradigm of human behavior as conceptualized by Henry Murray. Used for student survey and research purposes.

Description: 300 item (long form) or 92 item (short form) paper-pencil true-false inventory assessing the atmosphere of a college in terms of 30 press scales which reflect the 30 basic need scales established on the Stern Activities Index (AI). Test items refer to curriculum, teaching and classroom activities, rules, regulations, policies, student organizations, activities, interests, features of the campus, services and facilities, and to relationships among students and faculty. The long form provides scores on the 30 basic press scales (10 items per scale), 11 first order dimensions (aspiration level, intellectual climate, student dignity, academic climate, academic achievement, self-expression, group life, academic organization, social form, play-work, and vocational climate) and three second order dimensions (intellectual climate, non-intellectual climate, and impulse control). The short form provides scores on 11 first order dimensions and three second order dimensions. Evidence for reliability and validity are presented in the technical manual. Self-administered. Suitable for group use.

Untimed: Long form—40 minutes; short form—20 minutes

Range: College students

Scoring: Examiner evaluated; computer scoring available

Cost: Test booklet $.50; answer sheet $.10; profile form $.10; technical manual $7.50; prices for computer scoring and analysis available on request.

Publisher: Evaluation Research Associates

CULTURE-FREE SELF-ESTEEM INVENTORIES

James Battle

all ages gr. 3 and up

Purpose: Assesses the self-esteem of children and adults. Identifies individuals in need of psycholgical assistance.

Description: Multiple item paper-pencil test assesses five areas of self-esteem: general, school-related, peer-related, parent-related, and defensiveness. Raw scores for each subscale and a total score are obtained with acetate scoring template. Percentile ranks and standard scores provided for children Grades 3-9 and adults. Separate forms available for children and adults; parallel forms available for children for pre- and posttesting. May be administered orally or with cassette tape to low-level readers. Suitable for group use.

Untimed: 10-15 minutes

Range: Grade 3-adult

Scoring: Hand key. May be computer scored

Cost: Test kit (25 each of forms A and B for children, 25 of form AD for adults, manual quick-scoring acetates, 25 computer-scorable answer sheets, and oral administration on cassette tape) $45.50.

Publisher: Special Child Publications

CULTURE-FREE SELF-ESTEEM INVENTORIES FOR CHILDREN AND ADULTS

Refer to page 53.

THE HIGH SCHOOL CHARACTERISTICS INDEX (HSCI) AND THE ELEMENTARY AND SECONDARY SCHOOL INDEX (ESI)

George Stern and Associates

child, teen

Purpose: Measures the psychological characteristics of the academic environments of elementary and secondary schools in terms of the need-press paradigm of human behavior as conceptualized by Henry Murray. Used for student survey and research purposes.

Description: 300 item (HSCI) or 61 item (ESI) paper-pencil true-false inventory assessing the atmosphere of elementary and secondary schools along 30 basic press scales which reflect the 30 basic need scales established on the Stern Activities Index (AI). Both scales provide seven first order scores (intellectual climate, expressiveness, group social life, personal dignity/supportiveness, achievement standards, orderliness/control, and peer group dominance) and three second order dimensions (development press, orderliness/control, and peer group dominance). The 300 item HSCI contains 10 items for each of the press scales, which are identical in name and parallel in meaning to those used for the College Characteristics Index. Factor analysis was used to develop the ESI, which is essentially a short form of the HSCI. In addition to use for secondary schools, the ESI can be used at the elementary level down to grade four. The HSCI should not be used below the secondary school level. Evidence for reliability and validity are presented in the technical manual. Self-administered. Suitable for group use.

Untimed: HSCI—40 minutes; ESI—15 minutes

Range: Elementary and secondary school students

Scoring: Examiner evaluated; computer scoring available

Cost: Test booklet $.50; answer sheet $.10; profile form $.10; technical manual $7.50; prices for computer scoring and analysis available on request.

Publisher: Evaluation Research Associates

THE INTEREST-A-LYZER

Joseph A. Renzulli

child, teen

Purpose: Examines the present and potential interests of upper elementary and junior high school students. Used as a basis for group discussions and in-depth counseling.

Description: Multiple item paper-pencil instrument consisting of a series of open-ended questions that are structured to highlight general patterns of interest. Items cover the following interest areas: mathematical, historical, political, scientific, artistic and technical. Examiner required. Suitable for group use.

Untimed: Varies

Range: Elementary and junior high school students

Scoring: Examiner evaluated

Cost: 100 questionnaires $22.95.

Publisher: Creative Learning Press, Inc.

INTERPERSONAL STYLE INVENTORY—FORM E

Maurice Lorr and Richard P. Youniss

teen, adult

Purpose: Assesses the manner in which an individual interacts with other people and style of impulse control. Used for self-understanding, counseling and therapy, personnel guidance, and research.

Description: 300 item paper-pencil true-false inventory assessing an individual's style of interpersonal interactions along 15 bipolar scales: directive/non-directive, sociable/detached, help-seeking/self-sufficient, nurturant/withholding, conscientious/expedient, trusting/cynical, tolerant/hostile, sensitive to others/unaware of others, deliberate/impulsive, independent/conforming, rule-free/rule-bound, orderly/casual, persistent/lacks perseverance, stable/anxious, and approval seeking/admits frailties. Each test item is a statement that describes ways in which people relate and respond to each other. The individual reads each statement and decides whether it is mostly true or not true for himself. High school and college norms provided by sex. Self-administered. Suitable for group use.

Untimed: 40-50 minutes

Range: Adolescent, adult

Scoring: Examiner evaluated; computer scoring available

Cost: Contact publisher.

Publisher: Western Psychological Services

IRENOMETER

Refer to page 59.

JOB MATCH

Refer to page 222.

LEARNING STYLE IDENTIFICATION SCALE (LSIS)

Refer to page 182.

LEARNING STYLE INVENTORY (LSI)

Rita Dunn, Kenneth Dunn and Gary E. Price

child, teen grades 3-12

Purpose: Identifies the preferred learning environments of students grades 3-12. Used for designing instructional environments and counseling.

Description: 104 item paper-pencil true-false (grades 3-9) and Likert-scale (grades 6-12) test assessing the conditions under which students prefer to learn. Individual preferences are measured in the following areas: immediate environment (sound, heat, light and design), emotionality (motivation, responsibility, persistence and structure), sociological needs (self-oriented, peer-oriented, adult-oriented or combined ways), and physical needs (perceptual preferences, time of day, food intake and mobility). Test items consist of statements about how people like to learn. Students indicate whether they agree or disagree with each item. Results identify student preferences and indicate the degree to which a student's responses are consistent. Suggested strategies for instructional and environmental alternatives are provided to complement the student's revealed learning style. Computerized results are available in three forms: individual profile (raw scores for each of the 22 areas, standard scores, and a plot for each score in each area), group summary (identifies students with significantly high or low scores and groups individuals with similar preferences), and a sub-scale summary. Self-administered. Suitable for group use.

Untimed: 30 minutes

Range: Grades 3-12

Scoring: Computer scored

Cost: Specimen set (manual, research report, inventory booklet, and answer sheet) $12.00.

Publisher: Price Systems, Inc.

LEARNING STYLES INVENTORY (LSI)

Joseph S. Renzulli and Linda H. Smith

child grades 4-12

Purpose: Assesses the methods or ways through which students prefer to go about learning subject matter content. Used to assist teachers in individualizing the instructional process.

Description: 65 item paper-pencil inventory assessing student attitudes toward nine modes of instruction: projects, drill and recitation, peer teaching, discussion, teaching games, independent study, programmed instruction, lecture and stimulation. Various classrom learning experiences associated with these nine teaching/learning style approaches are described and students are asked to indicate their reaction to each activity along a five point scale ranging from very unpleasant to very pleasant. A teacher form of the LSI is included with each set of student materials. Teachers respond to items which parallel those of the student form in terms of how frequently each activity occurs in the clasroom. The resulting profile of instructional styles can be compared to individual student preferences and can serve to facilitate a closer match between how teachers instruct and the styles to which students respond most favorably. All forms are prepared on optical scanning sheets and are computer scored. Examiner required. Suitable for group use.

Untimed: Varies

Range: Grades 4-12

Scoring: Computer scored

Cost: Class set (30 student forms, 1 teacher form and computer scoring) $14.95 per 100; manual $6.95; specimen set (manual, 1 teacher form and 1 student form) $7.50.

Publisher: Creative Learning Press, Inc.

THE MAJOR-MINOR-FINDER

Arthur Cutler, Francis Ferry, Robert Kauk and Robert Robinett

teen, adult grades 10 and up

Purpose: Assesses an individual's aptitudes and interests and identifies appropriate college major choices. Used in college orientation courses at the upper high school and college level.

Description: Multiple item paper-pencil or computer administered college major exploration instrument matching student aptitudes and interests with 99 college majors. Includes information concerning: jobs related to 99 college majors, skills and interests required of the 99 majors, and college majors most compatible with educational goals and career interests. Reusable assessment booklets are used in conjunction with consumable insert answer folders for paper-pencil administration. Microcomputer programs available for TRS-80 Models I and III, Commodore PET/CBM, Commodore 64, Apple II + and IIe, IBM Personal Computer, and Franklin Ace 1000. Software packages include instructions, printed inventories, and additional information. Optional introductory filmstrip available. A supplement, the *College-Major Handbook*, is also available and includes: further data on each college major; a definition of the major; courses required; aptitudes most needed; job activities associated with the major; chances for employment in job associated with the major; related career opportunities; and where to write for further information. Paper-pencil version may be self-administered. Suitable for group use.

Untimed: Varies

Range: Grade 10-adult

Scoring: Self-scored; computer version available on diskettes

Cost: Reusable test booklet and one answer folder $1.40; additional answer folders $.22; manual $2.00; *College-Major Handbook* $4.00; diskettes $59.95; filmstrip $32.95.

Publisher: CFKR Career Materials, Inc.

MY BOOK OF THINGS AND STUFF: AN INTEREST QUESTIONNAIRE FOR YOUNG CHILDREN

Ann McGeevy

child ☞ ✍

Purpose: Assesses the interests of young children.

Description: Multiple item paper-pencil questionnaire including over 40 illustrated items focusing on the special interests and learning styles of students ages 6-11 years. The book also includes: a teacher's section, an interest profile sheet, sample pages from a Journal and bibliographies of interest centered books and magazines for children. All questionnaire pages are perforated and prepared on black line masters so that copies can be made for an entire class. Examiner required. Suitable for group use.

Untimed: Varies

Range: Ages 6-11 years

Scoring: Examiner evaluated

Cost: Questionnaire booklet $12.95.

Publisher: Creative Learning Press

QUALITY OF SCHOOL LIFE SCALE (QSL)

Joyce L. Epstein and James M. McPartland

child, teen grades 4-12 ☞ ✍

Purpose: Assesses emotions and feelings related to school life of students grades 4-12.

Description: Multiple item paper-pencil test measuring the affective domain in school settings. Three subscores relate to the individual student's satisfaction, commitment to classwork, and reactions to teachers. Also used to study and evaluate social, task, and authority structures of schools and classrooms. Technical manual summarizes research using the scale and provides reliability and validity data as well as item-to-scale and item-to-test correlations. Intended for use with local norms or in a criterion-referenced framework. Examiner required. Suitable for group use.

Untimed: 20 minutes

Range: Grades 4-12

Scoring: Hand key

Cost: Test kit (35 questionnaire folders, manual, and scoring key) $8.79; examination kit $2.07.

Publisher: The Riverside Publishing Company

SCHOOL INTEREST INVENTORY

William C. Cottle

teen grades 7-12 ☞ ✍

Purpose: Assesses school related attitudes and interests of junior and senior high school students. Identifies potential school dropouts. Used for counseling and program planning.

Description: 150 item paper-pencil inventory surveying student attitudes and interests. Weighted and unweighted scores may be obtained for males and females by using the appropriate scoring mask. Used in conjunction with other information such as teachers' evaluations and academic records to identify students with a high potential for dropping out of school. The manual contains information about the development of the test, validity studies used to develop the scale, scoring, interpretation, and use. Examiner required. Suitable for group use.

Untimed: 20 minutes

Range: Grades 7-12

Scoring: Hand key

Cost: 100 test booklets $34.50; manual $2.37; set of 2 scoring masks

$3.45.

Publisher: The Riverside Publishing Company

SELF-ESTEEM QUESTIONNAIRE (SEQ-3)

Refer to page 55.

STUDENT DEVELOPMENTAL PROFILE AND PLANNING RECORD

Roger B. Winston, Theodore K. Miller and Judith S. Prince

college students

Purpose: Identifies the immediate concerns of college students. Used for general guidance counseling with entering students during the orientation period or as a counseling or student development center intake form.

Description: Multiple item paper-pencil free response self-report assessment form collecting developmentally oriented biographical data and affording students the opportunity to respond to open-ended questions concerning their immediate concerns. The questionnaire is presented in form of a file folder. The inside provides a format for recording the student's past performance and continuing developmental goal accomplishment. The outside elicits data concerning previous development, current concerns, and special interests related to the college experience. May be administered in conjunction with the Student Developmental Task Inventory: Revised 2nd Edition. Information for both instruments is presented in a common manual. Self-administered. Suitable for group use.

Untimed: Varies

Range: College students ages 17-23 years

Scoring: Examiner evaluated

Cost: Individual folders $.35; 100 folders $30.00; manual $6.00; specimen set (includes SDTI-2 material and manual) $7.00.

Publisher: Student Development Associates

STUDENT DEVELOPMENTAL TASK INVENTORY: REVISED SECOND EDITION (SDTI-2)

Refer to page 192.

STUDENT OPINION INVENTORY

National Study of School Evaluation staff

child, teen

Purpose: Assesses students' opinions in reference to their school and its programs. Provides students with an opportunity to make direct recommendations. Used by school personnel as a part of a complete school evaluation program.

Description: 46 item paper-pencil opinion survey consisting of two parts. Part A contains 34 multiple-choice items assessing students' attitudes on various aspects of the school. Part B contains 12 open-ended questions constructed so that students can make direct recommendations for school improvement. The manual describes the development of the instrument, provides instructions for administering the inventory, and includes single copies of both parts A and B. May be administered independently as a measure of student attitudes and morale, or in conjunction with the Teacher Opinion Inventory and/or the Parent Opinion Inventory as a part of a complete school evaluation program. Self-administered. Suitable for group use.

Untimed: Varies

Range: Students

Scoring: Examiner evaluated

Cost: 50 copies of Part A $5.00; 50 copies of Part B $3.00; manual $2.00.

Publisher: National Study of School Evaluation

TLC-LEARNING PREFERENCE INVENTORY KIT

all students

Purpose: Assesses the manner in which students prefer to learn. Used for classroom planning and management.

Description: 144 item paper-pencil inventory assessing individual student preferences for perception and judgment and providing insights into students' attitudes toward things and ideas in their world. Test items and assessment procedures are based on Jung's Theory of Psychological Type. One adult Learning Style Inventory is included to allow teachers to compare their own preferred learning style with their preferred teaching style. Manual includes: guidelines for collecting student data and scoring, analyzing, and plotting student learning styles; guidelines for classroom planning and management based on test results; and sample lesson plans outlining how to use each of the four learning styles for maximum learning. Examiner required. Suitable for group use.

Untimed: Varies

Range: Elementary students-adult

Scoring: Examiner evaluated

Cost: Test kit (manual, 30 student inventories and scoring sheets, 30 student diagnostic folders, 1 student learning behavior checklist, 1 adult learning style inventory, and 1 teaching style inventory) $59.00.

Publisher: Mafex Associates, Inc.

TLC-LEARNING STYLE INVENTORY

adult

Purpose: Assesses the manner in which an individual prefers to learn. Used for adult self assessments.

Description: Multiple item paper-pencil test measuring individual preferences for how information is collected and judgments made about its significance. Test items and scoring procedures are based on Jung's Theory of Personality Type. The words/terms that individuals select to describe their learning styles correspond to the four distinct styles of learning. Self-administered. Suitable for group use.

Untimed: Varies

Range: Adult

Scoring: Self-scored

Cost: Six inventories $21.00.

Publisher: Mafex Associates, Inc.

WORLD GOVERNMENT SCALE

Panos D. Bardis

all ages

Purpose: Measures attitudes and beliefs concerning world government and the possible effects world government might have on society. Used for discussion and educational purposes.

Description: Six item paper-pencil inventory. Individuals rate six statements about world government and its effects on society on a five-point scale from 0 (strongly disagree) to 4 (strongly agree). All statements express positive attitudes toward world government. Score equals sum total of six numerical responses. Theoretical range is from 0 (complete rejection of the concept of world government) to 24 (complete acceptance). Self-administered. Suitable for group use.

Untimed: Varies

Range: Child-adult

Scoring: Self-scored

Cost: Free.

Publisher: Panos D. Bardis

Student Personality Factors

ADOLESCENT EMOTIONAL FACTORS INVENTORY

Refer to page 31.

CANFIELD LEARNING STYLES INVENTORY (CLS)

Refer to page 182.

CHILD & ADOLESCENT ADJUSTMENT PROFILE (CAAP)

Refer to page 28.

CHILDREN'S ADAPTIVE BEHAVIOR SCALE

Bert O. Richmond and Richard H. Kicklighter

child

Purpose: Assesses the adaptive behavior of children ages 5-11 years. Used to plan remediation programs.

Description: Multiple item paper-pencil observational inventory covering five areas of adaptive behavior: language development, independent functioning, family role performance, economic vocational activity, and socialization. Teacher or school psychologist completes the inventory based on direct observation of the child and evaluates the results according to guidelines presented in the manual. Self-administered. Suitable for use with groups of children.

Untimed: Varies

Range: Ages 5-11 years

Scoring: Examiner evaluated

Cost: Test kit (manual, picture book, and 5 record forms) $22.00.

Publisher: Stoelting Co.

CHILDREN'S VERSION/FAMILY ENVIRONMENT SCALE (CV/FES)

Refer to page 22.

PSYCHOEPISTEMOLOGICAL PROFILE (PEP)

J.R. Royce and L.P. Mos

teen, adult

Purpose: Evaluates an individual's epistemological hierarchy (approach to reality).

Description: 90 item paper-pencil test assessing the psychological processes and criterion for truth which determine an individual's particular world-view. Identifies and quantifies three basic epistemic styles: rationalism, empiricism, and metaphorism. An epistemic style is defined as a major personality integrator or higher order personality factor which determines an individual's basic approach to reality. Test items consist of value statements which the individual rates on a five-point scale from complete agreement to complete disagreement. There are 30 items pertaining to each of the three dimensions, yielding independent scores for each of the three epistemic styles. The highest of the three scores indicates the dominant epistemology for that person. Norms provided by sex for a junior college population. Self-administered. Suitable for group use. French version available (with separate norms). CANADIAN PUBLISHER

Untimed: 20-30 minutes

Range: High school students-adult

Scoring: Examiner evaluated; machine scoring available

Cost: Contact publisher.

Publisher: Center for Advanced Study in Theoretical Psychology/University of Alberta

QUALITY OF SCHOOL LIFE SCALE (QSL)

Refer to page 188.

ROGERS PERSONAL ADJUSTMENT INVENTORY—UK REVISION

Refer to page 30.

SCALES FOR RATING THE BEHAVIORAL CHARACTERISTICS OF SUPERIOR STUDENTS (SRBCSS)

Refer to page 147.

STUDENT DEVELOPMENTAL TASK INVENTORY: REVISED SECOND EDITION (SDTI-2)

Roger B. Winston, Theodore K. Miller and Judith S. Prince

college student

Purpose: Assesses the personal growth and development of college students according to constructs formulated by Arthur W. Chickering as reported in *Education and Identity.* Used for general guidance counseling with college students.

Description: 140 item paper-pencil true-false test assessing behaviors and feelings which reflect the personal growth and development of college students. Identifies the accomplishment of three developmental tasks (each of which is defined by three subtasks): developing autonomy (emotional, instrumental, and interdependence), developing purpose in life (appropriate educational plans, mature career plans, and mature lifestyles), and developing mature interpersonal relationships (intimate relationships with the opposite sex, relationships with peers, and tolerance). The inventory contains 16 items for eight of the subtasks and 12 items for the ninth subtask. Each item is a statement describing behavior or reports of feelings representative of a level of development within the specified subtask. Students indicate whether the statement is an accurate (true) or inaccurate (false) self-description. Scoring guidelines emphasize self-understanding, planning, and goal setting, and the scoring procedure (using the SDTI-2 Data Sheet) is designed to stimulate the students to plan for and assume responsibility for their own intentional development. May be used in conjunction with the Student Developmental Profile and Planning Record (SDPPR). Information for both instruments is presented in a common manual. Self-administered. Suitable for group use.

Untimed: Varies

Range: College students ages 17-23 years

Scoring: Self-scored

Cost: Test booklet $.75; answer sheets $.35; 100 data sheets $5.00; manual $6.00; specimen set (includes SDPPR material and manual) $7.00.

Publisher: Student Development Associates

PRODUCTIVITY ENVIRONMENTAL PREFERENCE SURVEY (PEPS)

Refer to page 239.

Study Skills Attitudes

No new tests available. Please refer to the First Edition of ***TESTS*** *for a complete listing and description of tests currently available in this area.*

Teacher Evaluation

Student Opinion of Teachers

CLASS ACTIVITIES QUESTIONNAIRE (CAQ)

Refer to page 196.

McCORMICK AFFECTIVE ASSESSMENT TECHNIQUE (MAAT)

Ronald R. McCormick

college student, adult

Purpose: Measures student *commitment* to instructor determined topical objectives. Used in professional skills training programs typically offered by the College of Business as well as other college-level classroom settings. May be used to assess the learning needs of business professionals and others. This assessment technique operationalizes the *Affective Domain Handbook* for use in higher education

Description: Multiple item paper-pencil questionnaire assessing taxonomic affective reactions to instructor determined topical goals and objectives in higher education classroom instruction. The affective domain instructional objective is to move the students towards *commitment* to the instructor determined cognitive goals and objectives. The three levels of affective domain categories surveyed are: I, receiving; II, responding; and III, valuing; with simple awareness (1) the lowest and commitment (9) the highest of the nine affective domain sub-categories measured. The instructor designs the questionnaire by constructing three subtopic stimulus word items for each instructional topic. Students respond to these subtopic items in a sentence completion format by selecting affective domain word stems which best describe their relationship to the instructor-determined sub-topic item. Any number of subtopic items may be used, but 15 sub-topic items surveying 5 course topics is optimum. Scoring keys are provided for tabulation and grouping of questionnaire scores into three affective domain categories and nine sub-categories. Interpretive guidelines are provided. Three forms of the questionnaire are included in the manual that may be reproduced for classroom use. Examiner required. For group use. May also be self-administered for survey use.

Untimed: 20 minutes for a 15 item questionnaire

Range: Undergraduate and Graduate college students, and business professionals

Scoring: Examiner evaluated

Cost: Manual and three reproducible questionnaire forms $25.00.

Publisher: Dr. R.R. McCormick & Associates

STUDENT OPINION INVENTORY

Refer to page 189.

TEACHER IMAGE QUESTIONNAIRE

teen grades 7-12

Purpose: Evaluates student perceptions of their classroom teacher. Used for faculty appraisal and self-improvement.

Description: 16 item paper-pencil inventory assessing how students feel about and perceive important characteristics of their teacher. Students rate their teacher on a five-point scale from poor to excellent for test items in the following areas: knowledge of subject, fairness, control, attitude toward students, variety in teaching procedures, encouragement of student participation, and sense of humor. Completed questionnaires are returned to the Educator Feedback Center for analysis. A teacher image profile is developed and sent to the teacher on whom the student feedback was gathered. The teacher also receives an interpretive discussion of factors which might be causing problems indicated by the profile and suggestions for possible behavioral changes designed to improve teacher effectiveness. Student responses are confidential, as is the feedback sent to the teacher, which is sent directly and only to the person on whom it was obtained. It is also possible to gather feedback for comparisons of images across time as well as comparisons for different reference groups. Such comparisons are represented by superimposing designated image profiles. Typical comparisons are: self-ideal-real, two different classes, and time (1)-time (2). Test kit includes: instructions to examiner (temporary substitute teacher), class ID form, teacher ID form, one-page questionnaire (with space on the back for responses concerning the teacher's strengths and weaknesses), and interpretive guidelines for the teacher. Examiner required. Suitable for group use.

Untimed: 15-20 minutes

Range: Grades 7-12

Scoring: Evaluated by Educator Feedback Center

Cost: Materials for assessing one class $10.00.

Publisher: Educator Feedback Center

Teacher Attitudes

ADMINISTRATOR IMAGE QUESTIONNAIRE

teen, adult

Purpose: Evaluates the image of an administrator held by groups such as teachers, parents, students, service personnel, or board members. Used for administrator appraisal and self-improvement.

Description: 25 item paper-pencil survey measuring reactions of relevant groups of people concerning the effectiveness of an administrator. These groups are usually teachers, but may be other administrators or non-certified personnel. Items 1-23 are statements about the administrator's abilities which must be rated on a five-point scale from poor to excellent. Items 24 and 25 are free response questions concerning the administrator's strengths and weaknesses. Completed questionnaires are returned to the Educator Feedback Center for analysis. A leader image profile is developed and sent to the administrator on whom the feedback was gathered. The administrator also receives an interpretive discussion of factors which might be causing problems indicated by the profile and suggestions for possible behavioral changes designed to improve administrator effectiveness. Group responses are confidential, as is the feedback sent to the administrator, which is sent directly and only to the person on whom it was obtained. It is also possible to gather feedback for comparisons of images across time as well as comparisons for different reference groups. Such comparisons are represented by superimposing designated image profiles. Typical comparisons are: self-ideal-real, two different groups, and time (1)-time (2). Test kit includes: instructions for using the questionnaire, group ID form, administrator ID form, one-page questionnaire (both sides), and interpretive guidelines for the administrator. Examiner required. Suitable for group use.

Untimed: Varies

Range: High school student-adult

Scoring: Evaluated by Educator Feedback Center

Cost: Materials for assessing one group $15.00.

Publisher: Educator Feedback Center

THE AUTISM ATTITUDE SCALE FOR TEACHERS (AAST)

J. Gregory Olley, Robert F. Devellis, Brenda McEvoy Devellis, A. Jack Wall and Carolyn E. Long

adult

Purpose: Assesses teachers' attitudes toward the inclusion of autistic children in public schools. Used to measure attitudes of teachers whose schools are about to receive autistic children for the first time and to evaluate the effect of inservice training for those teachers.

Description: 14 item paper-pencil questionnaire assessing attitudes and beliefs concerning the inclusion of autistic children in public schools. May be administered as two alternate forms A and B for pre- and post-testing. Each item is a statement about beliefs concerning autistic children and their behavioral problems, educational needs, and potential impact on a public school classroom. Teachers rate each item on a five-point scale from one (strongly disagree) to five (strongly agree) according to their personal beliefs. A total score is derived by summing the scores on the individual items. Teacher information questionnaire assesses background and experience with autistic children of teachers completing the scale. Examiner required. Suitable for group use.

Untimed: Varies

Range: Public school teachers

Scoring: Examiner evaluated

Cost: Contact publisher (order number ED204922).

Publisher: Distributed by ERIC Document Reproduction Service

CANFIELD INSTRUCTIONAL STYLES INVENTORY (CIS)

Albert A. Canfield and Judith S. Canfield

adult

Purpose: Identifies a teacher's preferred instructional methods. Used in conjunction with the Learning Styles Inventory to maximize teaching and learning efficiency.

Description: 25 item paper-pencil forced-rank inventory assessing a teacher's preferences concerning learning environments, instructional modalities, and topical interests. Also measures how much responsibility the instructor will assume for student learning (instead of measuring performance expectancy). Identifies areas where instructional training would be most beneficial and provides information to help instructors interpret classroom problems and student reactions. Measures the same dimensions as the Canfield Learning Styles Inventory to allow for one-to-one comparison between the two inventories. Test booklets are reusable. Answer sheets and profiles are self-scoring. Separate norms provided for male and female instructors. Self-administered. Suitable for group use.

Untimed: 25-40 minutes

Range: Adult

Scoring: Self-scored

Cost: Starter set (15 test booklets, 25 answer sheets, 25 profile sheets, and guide) $32.95; specimen set (includes manual) $12.95.

Publisher: Humanics Media

CHANGE AGENT QUESTIONNAIRE (CAQ)

Refer to page 225.

CLASS ACTIVITIES QUESTIONNAIRE (CAQ)

Joe M. Steele

teen, adult

Purpose: Assesses the instructional climate of upper elementary and high school classrooms. Enables teachers to see if goals and expectations are clearly defined in the classroom. Assesses affective factors such as openness, independence, divergence and emphasis on grades.

Description: 30 item paper-pencil questionnaire assessing five dimensions of instructional climate in the classroom: lower thought processes, higher thought processes, classroom focus, classroom climate, and student opinions. Items 1-27 assess cognitive emphasis and classroom conditions by asking students to rate statements about classroom experiences on a four point scale from strongly agree to strongly disagree according to the degree to which the statement applies to their classroom. Items 28-30 allow the students to describe in their own words what they perceive to be the strengths and weaknesses of their class. Teachers complete the questionnaire twice, once to indicate what they intend to emphasize in the classroom and a second time to indicate what they predict the students as a group will say. Computer scoring compares the teacher's responses to those provided by the students. Examiner required. Suitable for group use.

Untimed: 20-30 minutes

Range: Elementary and high school teachers and students

Scoring: Computer scored

Cost: Test kit (30 student forms, two teacher forms, manual, and computer analysis) $16.95.

Publisher: Creative Learning Press, Inc.

PERFORMANCE LEVELS OF A SCHOOL PROGRAM SURVEY (PLSPS)

Frank E. Williams

adult

Purpose: Evaluates teacher and administrator perceptions of the value of a classroom, a building, or a district program. Used to insure compliance with federal, state, and local guidelines concerning the quality and content of academic programs.

Description: Multiple item paper-pencil inventory evaluating the following eight areas of multiple abilities that are specifically defined in federal, state, and local guidelines: general intellectual, specific academics, leadership, creative productive thinking, psychomotor, visual performing arts, affective, and vocational career. Pinpoints those areas receiving insufficient emphasis. Self-administered. Suitable for group use.

Untimed: Varies

Range: Teachers and administrators

Scoring: Self-scored

Cost: Test kit (survey materials for 30 participants) $13.95.

Publisher: D.O.K. Publishers, Inc.

TEACHER OPINION INVENTORY

National Study of School Evaluation Staff

adult

Purpose: Assesses teachers' opinions in reference to their school and its programs. Provides an opportunity for direct faculty recommendations. Used by school personnel in decision-making relative to program development, policy formulation, administrative organization, faculty development, and community relations.

Description: 72 item paper-pencil opinion survey consisting of two parts. Part A contains 64 multiple-choice items assessing teacher opinion on various aspects of the school. Part B contains eight open-ended questions constructed so that teachers can make recommendations for school improvement. The manual describes the development of the instrument, provides instructions for administering the inventory, and contains a single copy of both parts A and B. May be administered independently or in conjunction with the Parent Opinion Inventory and/or the Student Opinion Inventory or as part of a complete school evaluation program. Self-administered. Suitable for group use. Available in Spanish.

Untimed: Varies

Range: Classroom teachers

Scoring: Examiner evaluated

Cost: 25 copies of Part A $3.00; 25 copies of Part B $2.00; manual $2.00.

Publisher: National Study of School Evaluation

TROUBLE-SHOOTING CHECKLIST (TSC) FOR HIGHER EDUCATIONAL SETTINGS

Refer to page 207.

TROUBLE-SHOOTING CHECKLIST (TSC) FOR SCHOOL-BASED SETTINGS

Refer to page 207.

Vocational

ARMED SERVICES—CIVILIAN INTEREST SURVEY (ACSVIS)

Refer to page 221.

BALL APTITUDE BATTERY

Refer to page 211.

CAREER ADAPTIVE BEHAVIOR INVENTORY (CAB)

Thomas P. Lombardi

developmentally delayed students

Purpose: Assesses the behavior of developmentally disabled students in relation to career planning. Determines readiness for placement in prevocational or vocational education courses. Used to monitor student progress in vocational education courses.

Description: 120 item paper-pencil observational inventory assessing 12 specific behaviors in each of 10 areas: academics, communication, interest, leisure time, motor, responsibility, self-concept, self-help, socialization, and task performance. Parent, teacher, or clinician rates the student's level of ability on a five-point scale for each behavior. Results are charted on a graphic profile of strengths and weaknesses. The CAB Activity Book provides 360 teaching ideas keyed to the behaviors assessed. Examiner required. Not suitable for group use.

Untimed: Varies

Range: Developmentally delayed students; ages 3-15 years

Scoring: Examiner evaluated

Cost: Test kit (activity book, manual, 25 rating forms) $26.75.

Publisher: Stoelting Co.

CAREER AND VOCATIONAL FORM OF THE SOI-LA BASIC TEST

teen, adult

Purpose: Measures 24 cognitive abilities patterned to predict career and vocational options.

Description: Multiple item paper-pencil test consisting of subtests of the SOI-LA Basic Test. Instructions included with each form for self-administration. The MSI subtest has been replaced with a test of MMI. The scoring keys and instructions in the Basic Test manual apply. Career and vocational choices are listed on an accompanying sheet for selection. Augmented by the Career and Vocation Choice Guide. Materials available for training any low abilities required for a desired occupation. Self-administered. Suitable for group use.

Timed: 24 tests at 3-5 minutes each

Range: All ages

Scoring: Hand scored; computer scoring and analysis available

Cost: Examiner's manual $22.00; test form $2.25 each.

Publisher: SOI Institute

CAREER DECISION SCALE (2nd EDITION)

Refer to page 221.

CAREER EXPLORATION SERIES (CES)

Arthur Cutler, Francis Ferry, Robert Kauk and Robert Robinett

teen, adult

Purpose: Assesses an individual's job-related interests and identifies appropriate vocational choices. Used in vocational education programs.

Description: Six multiple item paper-pencil or computer administered inventories matching job interests with job characteristics in the following fields: AG-O (agriculture, conservation, forestry), BIZ-O (business, sales, management, clerical), CER-O (consumer/home econ-related fields), DAC-O (design, performing arts, communication), IND-O (industrial, mechanics, construction), and SCI-O (scientific, mathematical, health). Each of the inventories includes the following features: reusable booklets for self-assessment and self-scoring of job matches; answer insert folders that give job information for exploration and decision making; matching of job interests with the job characteristics of selected jobs in each field; listings of 300-500 related job titles in each field; and job duties, pay range, and outlook of job titles within each occupational field. Microcomputer programs available for TRS-80 Models I and III, Commodore PET/CBM, Commodore 64, Apple II + and IIe, IBM Personal Computer, and Franklin Ace 1000. Software packages include instructions, printed inventories, and additional information. An introductory filmstrip is also available. Paper-pencil version may be self-administered. Suitable for group use.

Untimed: Varies

Range: High school students-adult

Scoring: Self-scored; computer version available on diskette

Cost: Class set (materials for 35 students) $45.00; additional answer folders to use with reusable booklets $.22; specimen set (one copy of each inventory with user's guide) $7.75; diskettes (complete series) $249.95; filmstrip $32.95.

Publisher: CFKR Career Materials, Inc.

THE DECISION MAKING INVENTORY

Refer to page 225.

DOLE VOCATIONAL SENTENCE COMPLETION BLANK

Arthur A. Dole

teen grades 7-12

Purpose: Evaluates an individual's career-related interests and abilities. Used with high school students for educational and vocational counseling, rehabilitation, diagnosis or therapy.

Description: 21 item paper-pencil projective inventory assessing a student's concerns, emphases, and preferences concerning future vocational choices. Test items consist of sentence stems to be completed in the student's own words. Results yield 29 scores, including: problems, achievement, independence, satisfaction, material possessions, vocation, effectiveness, recognition from others, relaxation, intellectual qualities, activity, relationships with other people, recreation, outdoor activities, mechanical interest, computational interest, scientific interest, persuasive influence, artistic interest, literary interest, musical activities, social service, clerical interests, domestic interests, academic interests, armed forces, and homemaking interests (household arts). Scores also available for nine optional categories: peace of mind, security, value, obligation, health, religion, social studies, negative academic, and unclassifiable. This test supplements and amplifies, in the student's own words, the results of standardized inventories such as the Kuder or Strong. Examiner required. Suitable for group use.

Untimed: 20 minutes

Range: Grades 7-12

Scoring: Examiner evaluated

Cost: Test kit (manual, 30 record forms, 30 individual score profiles) $15.00.

Publisher: Stoelting Co.

EXPLORE THE WORLD OF WORK (E-WOW)

Arthur Cutler, Francis Ferry, Robert Kauk and Robert Robinett

child grades 4-6

Purpose: Measures vocational interests for students grades 4-6, special education students at any level, and those who read at the third to fifth grade level. Used for early introduction to vocational education.

Description: 36 item paper-pencil rating inventory assessing students' interests in 36 job activities in the following job clusters: Business-office-sales, industry-mechanics-transportation-construction, art-communication-design, health-education-social service, forestry-agriculture-natural resources, and scientific-technical-health. Thirty-six pictures with brief captions identify the job activities. Students use colored pencils or crayons to color the drawings green (like), yellow (not sure), or red (don't like). Six activities are listed for each of the six job clusters. After indicating preferred job activities within the clusters, students then select preferred job titles and explore one job in depth by following an exploration process outlined in the folder (including a visit to workers on the job). Two copies of the JOB-O Dictionary are included with each class set for further job research. E-WOW is also tied in with Exploring Careers, a junior edition of the *Occupational Outlook Handbook.* Computer version available July 1, 1984 (contact publisher for further information). Self-administered. Suitable for group use.

Untimed: Varies

Range: Grades 4-6, special education

Scoring: Hand scored

Cost: Class set (35 folders, 2 JOB-O Dictionaries, and user's guide) $16.00; individual folders $.40; Exploring Careers $12.00; diskettes $79.95.

Publisher: CFKR Career Materials, Inc.

FLORIDA INTERNATIONAL DIAGNOSTIC-PRESCRIPTIVE VOCATIONAL COMPETENCY PROFILE

Howard Rosenberg and Dennis G. Tesolowski

teen, adult

Purpose: Evaluates vocational behaviors related to work adjustment, job readiness and employability. Used with mentally retarded, specific learning disabled, seriously emotionally disturbed, and economically disadvantaged adolescents and adults

Description: 70 item paper-pencil rating scale assessing an individual's development in terms of job readiness and employability. Includes the following subscales: vocational self-help skills, social-emotional adjustment, work attitudes-responsibility, cognitive-learning ability, perceptual-motor skills, and general work habits. Performance on each of the test items is assessed on a five-point rating scale representing five developmental levels of vocational competency. The profile assists in the selection of training programs and determines an individual's present vocational functional level. Used in special education classes, work-study programs and vocational education classes as well as sheltered workshops, work activities centers, rehabilitation facilities, adult education classes and vocational schools. Self-administered by examiner. Not suitable for group use.

Untimed: Varies

Range: Adolescent; adult

Scoring: Examiner evaluated

Cost: Test kit (manual, 10 five-page record forms, and 10 individualized vocational prescription forms) $25.50.

Publisher: Stoelting Co.

HIGH SCHOOL CAREER-COURSE PLANNER

Arthur Cutler, Francis Ferry, Robert Kauk and Robert Robinett

teen

Purpose: Evaluates career interests of high school students. Used to develop a high school course plan that is consistent with self-assessed career goals. Especially useful with eighth grade, ninth grade, and transfer students.

Description: 6 item paper-pencil test measuring interests in the following six occupational areas: working with tools, working with people, creating new things, solving problems, and doing physical work. Students rate each area on a three-point scale from one (high interest) to three (low interest). A profile of these six ratings is then compared with similar profiles from the following 16 occupational clusters: industrial production, clerical, computer, banking-insurance-administrative, service (food, personal, protectice), education, sales, construction, transportation, scientific-technical, mechanics-repairers, health, social scientists-social service, performing arts-communications-design, agriculture-forestry-conservation, and mining petroleum. Related job titles, suggested high school course work, and job entry requirements are provided for each of the 16 occupational clusters, providing a basis for making a high school career-course plan. Each class set includes two copies of the JOB-O Dictionary for further job research. Computer version available July 1, 1984 (contact publisher for further information). Self-administered. Suitable for group use.

Untimed: Varies

Range: High school students

Scoring: Hand key

Cost: Class set (35 folders, 2 JOB-O Dictionaries, and user's guide) $16.00; individual folders $.40; diskettes $79.95.

Publisher: CFKR Career Materials, Inc.

INTEREST DETERMINATION, EXPLORATION AND ASSESSMENT SYSTEM (IDEAS)

Charles B. Johansson

teen grades 6-12

Purpose: Assesses career related interests of junior high and high school students. Used in career planning and occupational exploration at the junior high and high school level.

Description: 112 item paper-pencil multiple-choice inventory assessing a range of career interests. Test items present five response choices and require a sixth-grade reading ability. Scales include: mechanical/fixing, electronics, nature/outdoors, science/numbers, writing, arts/crafts, social service, child care, medical service, business, sales, office practices and food service. Norms provided for grades 6-8 and grades 9-12. Available in two forms: self-scoring form which allows students to plot their own scores on a profile chart, and Psychometer diskette which provides a plotted report identical to that provided by the self-scoring form. Examiner required. Suitable for group use.

Untimed: 30-40 minutes

Range: Grades 6-12

Scoring: Self-scored; microcomputer scoring available

Cost: Specimen set (manual and inventory booklet) $3.50; 25 inventory booklets $19.00; Psychometer diskette (20 administrations) $45.00.

Publisher: NCS/Professional Assessment Services

INTEREST INVENTORY (II)

Refer to page 222.

JOB-O

Arthur Cutler, Francis Ferry, Robert Kauk and Robert Robinett

teen, adult grades 7 and up

Purpose: Assesses an individual's aspirations and interests and identifies appropriate career and occupational choices. Used in career counseling and vocational guidance.

Description: Multiple item paper-pencil or computer administered career exploration instrument assessing nine variables related to educational aspirations, occupational interests, and interpersonal and physical characteristics of occupations. The *Dictionary of Occupational Titles*, the *Occupational Outlook Handbook*, and Dr. William B. Schutz's FIRO-B provide the theoretical basis relating test responses to current labor statistics, trends, and predictions for 120 job titles. The reusable assessment booklet contains complete directions and guides the student in recording responses in the consumable answer folder. The folder displays information on the number of people employed, job outlook, training requirements, and job clusters for the 120 job titles. The JOB-O Dictionary contains precise definitions of all job titles, related job titles, and unusual jobs, and indicates which characteristics are related to each job. The manual includes information on development and rationale and instructions for administration and use. Computer programs available for TRS-80 Models I and III, Commodore PET/CBM, Commodore 64, Apple II + and IIe, IBM Personal Computer, and Franklin Ace 1000. Optional introductory filmstrip also available. Paper-pencil version may be self-administered. Suitable for group use.

Untimed: Varies

Range: Grade 7-adult

Scoring: Hand key; computer version available on diskette

Cost: Reusable test booklet and one answer folder $1.40; additional answer folders $.22; manual $2.00; JOB-O dictionary $1.75; filmstrip $32.95; diskettes $59.95.

Publisher: CFKR Career Materials, Inc.

MY VOCATIONAL SITUATION

Refer to page 231.

OCCUPATIONAL APTITUDE-INTEREST MEASUREMENT (AIM)

Refer to page 223.

OCCUPATIONAL PERSONALITY QUESTIONNAIRES (OPQ)

Refer to page 232.

PHOENIX ABILITY SURVEY SYSTEM (PASS)

Refer to page 213.

PRG INTEREST INVENTORY

visually handicapped

Purpose: Measures vocational/occupational interests of visually handicapped individuals.

Description: 150 item paper-pencil questionnaire assessing interests in the following ten areas: mechanical, computational, scientific, persuasive, artistic, literary, musical, social service, clerical, and outdoor. Questionnaires and answer sheets presented in large print format. Examiner required. Suitable for group use.

Untimed: Varies

Range: Visually handicapped individuals

Scoring: Examiner evaluated

Cost: Test kit (test booklet, 10 answer sheets, and instructions for administration and scoring) $10.00.

Publisher: Associated Services for the Blind

PROGRAM FOR ASSESSING YOUTH EMPLOYMENT SKILLS (PAYES)

Educational Testing Service

teen

Purpose: Measures attitudes, knowledge, and interests of students preparing for entry level employment. Used by program directors, counselors, and teachers working with dropouts, potential dropouts, and disadvantaged youth in government training programs, skill centers, vocational high schools, ABE centers, and correctional institutions.

Description: Three orally administered paper-pencil tests assessing attitudes, knowledge, and interests related to entry level employment. Test booklet I measures attitudes in: job-holding skills (supervisor's requests, appropriate dress, punctuality), attitudes toward supervision by authority figures (judge, supervisor, teacher, police officer and parent), and self-confidence in social and employment situations. Measurements are done by assessing responses to multiple choice questions based on statements, real-life situations and scenes. Test booklet II provides cognitive measures including: job knowledge (understanding of education required, salary, task performed, location of work, working hours and tools), job seeking skills (interpretation of newspaper want ads and job application forms), and practical job-related reasoning in situations which require following directions. Test booklet III measures seven vocational interest clusters (aesthetic, business, clerical, outdoor, service, science, technical). The respondents indicate their degree of interest in specific job tasks that are described verbally and pictured. All three tests are administered orally to small groups in an informal manner. Students mark answers directly in test booklets. Examiner required. Suitable for group use.

Untimed: Varies

Range: Adolescents

Scoring: Examiner evaluated

Cost: Complete set (10 each of the following: test booklets I, II, and III, and score sheets) $40.00; user's guide $2.00; administrators's manual $3.60; technical manual $4.40.

Publisher: Cambridge

READING FREE VOCATIONAL INTEREST INVENTORY—REVISED (R-FVII REVISED)

Ralph Leonard Becker

teen, adult

Purpose: Measures vocational preferences of mentally retarded, learning disabled, and disadvantaged persons in job areas that are realistically within their capabilities. Used in vocational guidance counseling and for selection of prospective job trainees.

Description: 165 item paper-pencil multiple-choice test measuring the vocational preferences of the educable mentally retarded (EMR), the learning disabled (LD), and the adult trainable mentally retarded (TMR). Test items consist of 55 sets of three drawings each, depicting job tasks from the unskilled, semiskilled, and skilled levels. Each artist-drawn picture is typical of the kind and type of job in which EMR, LD, and TMR individuals are known to be proficient and productive. Individuals select the one picture or job task they most prefer of the three alternatives in each set. Choices are indicated by marking the picture directly in the booklet. Scores are obtained for 11 vocational interest clusters: automotive, building trades, clerical, animal care, food service, patient care, horticulture, housekeeping, personal service, laundry service, and materials handling.

A single test booklet is used for both males and females in compliance with federal Title IX requirements. Test booklets include a detachable scoring sheet and individual profile sheet. The manual includes: sections on administration and scoring, statistical data, analysis of scores, cluster descriptions, and percentile ranks, T-scores, and stanines for ten different norm groups by type of handicap, age, and sex for EMR, LD, and TMR individuals. For each interest cluster a list of appropriate job titles is suggested for individuals who score high in each occupational category. The revised edition includes updated norms and drawings which have been modified to avoid persons appearing in stereotypic occupational roles. Examiner required. Suitable for group use.

Untimed: 20 minutes or less

Range: Age 13 years-adult

Scoring: Examiner evaluated

Cost: Contact publisher.

Publisher: Elbern Publications

SHELTERED EMPLOYMENT WORK EXPERIENCE PROGRAM (SEWEP)

Gertrude A. Barber, Ceal Barber, Audree M. Blodgett, John Dobrosky and Alfred P. Riccomini

MR teen, adult

Purpose: Assesses the development of vocational capabilities of mentally retarded teenagers and adults. Provides both individual skill assessment and program development for mentally retarded individuals enrolled in vocational training programs.

Description: 546 item paper-pencil observational checklist assessing personal/social development (21 items), general vocational development (21 items), and 504 specific skills related to 50 skill areas arranged in the following ten vocational competency areas: factory work training, carpentry, print shop, laundry, building maintenance, general and outdoor maintenance, transportation aide, library aide, food service, and housekeeping. Each of the 504 specific skills is rated by someone familiar with the individual as either mastered, approaching mastery, inadequate approximation, not responding, not yet exposed, or not applicable. Circular program charts are used for each of the ten vocational competency areas to assess an individual's strengths and weaknesses. As the individual is enrolled into an appropriate work setting, the vocational counselor utilizes the personal/social development scale (assessing personal and social aspects of the work world), the general vocational development scale (assessing work habits which are important for success in any work setting), and the appropriate vocational competency scale to evaluate the individual's progress.

Quarterly re-evaluation indicates the percentage of specific vocational skills and personal/social and general vocational skills achieved and retained during each quarter. Suitable for use with traditional programs, such as Sheltered Employment and Personal and Work Adjustment Training, as well as innovative training techniques, such as Projects with Industry, Service Contracts, and Work Centers. Examiner required. Not suitable for group use.

Untimed: Varies

Range: Mentally retarded teenagers and adults

Scoring: Examiner evaluated

Cost: Manual $6.00; 1 set of program sheets $3.50.

Publisher: The Barber Center Press

SPACE RELATIONS (PAPER PUZZLES)

Refer to page 215.

WORK ASPECT PREFERENCE SCALE

Refer to page 245.

WORK VALUES INVENTORY

Donald E. Super

teen, adult gr. 7 and up

Purpose: Measures values which are of particular importance in determining an individual's vocational satisfaction and success. Used for career counseling and vocational guidance.

Description: 45 item paper-pencil inventory measuring 15 values related to vocational satisfaction and success: intellectual stimulation, job achievement, way of life, economic returns, altruism, creativity, relationships with associates, job security, prestige, management of others, variety aesthetics, independence, supervisory relations, and physical surroundings. Students are asked to rate 45 statements having to do with work values and it is from these weighted ratings that the strength of each value is determined. Norms are provided for junior and senior high school grades by sex. Examiner required. Suitable for group use. (In Canada, materials and scoring are available from the Thomas Nelson Company).

Untimed: 15 minutes

Range: Grades 7-12, college, adult

Scoring: Hand key; machine scoring available

Cost: Test kit (100 MRC machine-scorable test booklets, manual, and materials needed to obtain scoring services) $49.50.

Publisher: The Riverside Publishing Company

Miscellaneous

MASTERY TEST IN CONSUMER ECONOMICS

Les Dlabay

teen grades 8-12

Purpose: Measures knowledge of major consumer economics topics as set forth in various state education agencies and professional organization curriculum guides.

Description: Multiple item paper-pencil test measuring achievement in the field of consumer economics. Topics covered include: the individual consumer in the market place; the consumer in the economy; personal money management; consumer credit; wise use of credit; food buying; housing; transportation; furniture, appliances, and clothing; personal and health services; banking services; saving and investments; insurance; taxes and government; and the consumer in society. Each test item is keyed to one of these fifteen topics. Results identify concepts that have been mastered and those on which students perform poorly. Manual includes scoring key. Scoring service provides three alphabetical lists, class analysis data, and one set of pressure-sensitive labels. Examiner required. Suitable for group use.

Timed: 40 minutes

Range: Grades 8-12

Scoring: Hand scored; computer scoring available

Cost: Starter set (manual, 20 test booklets, 20 answer sheets) $24.00; scoring service $1.00 per pupil; specimen set $5.00.

Publisher: Scholastic Testing Service, Inc.

NUTRITION ACHIEVEMENT TESTS: K-6

child grades K-6

Purpose: Evaluates the nutrition education needs and achievements of elementary school children.

Description: Multiple item paper-pencil test measuring knowledge of basic nutrition facts which are generally included in primary school nutrition education programs. Separate tests are included for grades K-2, 3-4, and 5-6. The effectiveness of nutrition education programs is determined by measuring gains from pretest to posttest. Manual includes: directions for administration, guidelines for interpretation of test scores, mean scores achieved by nationwide sample, difficulty level, and reliability statistics. Test forms are provided in the form of reproducible masters. Examiner required. Suitable for group use.

Untimed: Varies

Range: Grades K-6

Scoring: Examiner evaluated

Cost: Test kit (42-page manual and reproducible test forms) $5.00.

Publisher: The National Dairy Council

PARENT OPINION INVENTORY

National Study of School Evaluation Staff

adult

Purpose: Evaluates parents' opinions in reference to their children's school and its programs. Provides an opportunity for parents to make direct recommendations. Used by school personnel in the decision-making process relative to program development, policy formulation, administrative organization, faculty development, and community relations.

Description: 58 item paper-pencil opinion survey consisting of two parts. Part A contains 53 multiple-choice items assessing parent opinion on various aspects of the school. Part B contains five open-ended items constructed so parents can make recommendations for school improvement. The manual describes the development of the instrument, provides instructions for administering the inventory, and contains a single copy of both parts A and B. May be administered independently or in conjunction with the Student Opinion Survey and/or the Teacher Opinion Survey or as part of a complete school evaluation program. Self-administered. Suitable for group use. Available in Spanish.

Untimed: Varies

Range: Parents of school age children

Scoring: Examiner evaluated

Cost: 25 copies of Part A $3.00; 25 copies of Part B $2.00; manual $2.00.

Publisher: National Study of School Evaluation

SCHOOL PRINCIPAL JOB FUNCTIONS INVENTORY (SP-JFI)

Melany E. Baehr, Frances M. Burns, R. Bruce McPherson and Columbus Salley

adult

Purpose: Assesses the work elements involved in a particular school principal position. Used to clarify a school principal's job description, to diagnose training needs, and to select personnel for school principalships.

Description: Multiple item paper-pencil inventory assessing the relative importance of 17 basic functions for overall successful performance in a given principalship. Functions include: personal handling of student adjustment problems, organizations and extracurricular activities, individual student development, utilization of specialized staff, evaluation of teacher performance, collegial contacts, racial and ethnic group problems, trouble shooting and problem solving, community involvement and support, dealing with gangs, curriculum development, instructional materials, staffing, working with unions, working with central office, safety regulations, and fiscal control. Items are rated by incumbent principal. May also be used to have incumbents rate their relative ability to perform these functions. Separate forms available for rating the importance of various job elements and for self-rating of incumbent's abilities. Examiner required. Suitable for group use.

Untimed: 40-60 minutes

Range: Adult

Scoring: Computer or hand-scored

Cost: $35.00/pkg. of 25 (includes

users' manual and scoring sheets) $10 per specimen set.

Publisher: London House Press

SCHOOL SUPERINTENDENT JOB FUNCTIONS INVENTORY (SS-JFI)
Columbus Salley and Melany E. Baehr

adult

Purpose: Assesses the work elements involved in a particular school superintendency. Used to clarify job descriptions and to resolve possible differences between the superintendent's view of job priorities and the expectations of such groups as school boards, principals, and community or political leaders.

Description: Multiple item paper-pencil inventory assessing the relative importance of 17 basic functions for overall success in a given superintendency. Items are rated by incumbent superintendent. May also be used to have incumbents assess their relative ability to perform the functions. Separate forms available for rating the importance of various job elements and for self-rating of incumbent's abilities. Examiner required. Suitable for group use.

Untimed: 45-60 minutes

Range: Adult

Scoring: Computer or hand-scored

Cost: $34/pkg. of 25 (includes users manual and scoring sheets) $10 per specimen set.

Publisher: London House Press

TROUBLE-SHOOTING CHECKLIST (TSC) FOR HIGHER EDUCATIONAL SETTINGS
B.A. Manning

adult

Purpose: Measures organizational variables which predict an educational institution's potential for successfully adopting innovations. Identifies areas of acceptance and resistance. Used by personnel involved in implementing innovations in higher educational settings.

Description: 100 item paper-pencil questionnaire assessing an institution's potential for adopting innovations along the following five scales: organizational climate, organizational staff, communications, innovative experience, and students. Scores for the five scales provide a profile of an institution's particular strengths and weaknesses with respect to the adoption process. Self-administered. Suitable for group use.

Untimed: Varies

Range: Adult

Scoring: Examiner evaluated

Cost: Instrument and manual (42 pages) $2.50.

Publisher: Distributed by ERIC Document Reproduction Service

TROUBLE-SHOOTING CHECKLIST (TSC) FOR SCHOOL-BASED SETTINGS
B.A. Manning

adult

Purpose: Measures organizational variables which predict a school's potential for successfully adopting and implementing educational innovations. Identifies areas of acceptance and resistance. Used by school personnel involved in implementing educational innovations.

Description: Multiple item paper-pencil checklist assessing a school's potential for adopting innovations along the following seven scales: communication patterns, innovative experience, school-based staff, central administration, relations with the community, organizational climate, and students. Scores on the seven scales provide a profile of a school's particular strengths and weaknesses with respect to the adoption process. Self-administered. Suitable for group use.

Untimed: Varies

Range: Adult

Scoring: Examiner evaluated

Cost: Instrument and manual (47 pages) $2.50.

Publisher: ERIC Document Reproduction Service

WHAT I USUALLY EAT

Iowa State University

child grades 3-6 ☞ ✍

Purpose: Assesses the eating habits of elementary school children. Used in conjunction with nutrition education programs and to assess student diets across large numbers of classrooms, schools, or school districts.

Description: Multiple item computer-administered survey assessing children's eating habits. The program asks students (grades 3-6) what they usually have for breakfast, lunch, supper, and snacks. As students answer, the computer generates color graphics of the food identified to assure the accuracy of the responses and to maintain student interest. The program then analyzes the meals and snacks selected in terms of the basic food groups and provides students, teachers, and administrators with the results. Group and classroom profiles of food choice behaviors are also provided. May be used with students in higher grades who are reviewing food groups and daily eating patterns. May be administered before nutrition units to motivate student interest, to identify individual and class needs, and to give baseline date for evaluating students' progress. May also be administered during the nutrition unit to reinforce lessons on food choices, meal patterns, and food groups, and after nutrition units to provide students with feedback and review, to measure learning, and to pinpoint concepts in need of additional reinforcement. Educational researchers can use the program to obtain hard-to-get food behavior data from students grade 3 and above. The software is programmed in color, with sound cues, for use with: either Apple II + (48K) or Apple IIe (64K); single disk drive (second disk drive optional); any television monitor compatible with the computer; and printer (optional). Examiner required. Individually administered on the computer; suitable for use with groups of children.

Untimed: Varies

Range: Grades 3-6

Scoring: Computer scored

Cost: Software package includes: two floppy disks, master copies of two student handouts for duplication, and a manual describing the administration and use of the program. Contact publisher for information concerning cost and availability.

Publisher: National Dairy Council

Driving and Safety Education

*No new tests available. Please refer to the First Edition of **TESTS** for a complete listing and description of tests currently available in this area.*

Business and Industry

Tests presented and described in the Business and Industry Section have been selected on the basis of their appropriate usage in the business world. In general, tests found in this section are those which might be used by personnel professionals or human resource specialists to aid in the assessment, selection, development, and promotion of personnel.

Tests in this section have been arranged into twelve subsections on the basis of "typical usage or function." The twelve subsections listed in the Business and Industry Section Index are identical to those listed in the First Edition of **TESTS**, *and the same guidelines for classification have been applied to the tests listed in both volumes.*

Some subsections contain no new test entries in this supplement. In such cases, the title of the subsection will be listed and readers will find the following instructions: "No new tests available. Please refer to the First Edition of **TESTS** *for a complete listing and description of tests currently available in this area."*

The classification of tests on the basis of "typical usage or function" is, of course, an arbitrary one, and the reader is encouraged to review the Psychology Section and the Education Section for additional assessment techniques. Readers are also encouraged to refer to the First Edition of **TESTS** *in addition to this supplement for a more complete knowledge of the range of tests available within each of the twelve subsections.*

Business and Industry Section Index

Business and Industry Section

Aptitude and Skills Screening

BALL APTITUDE BATTERY

Yong H. Sung and Rene V. Davis

teen, adult

Purpose: Measures aptitude for a wide variety of occupational and industrial jobs. Used for employee selection, classification, and placement, as well as individual career planning.

Description: Standardized battery of 15 multiple item paper-pencil and task performance tests evaluating aptitude based on an individual's performance based on selected work samples. Tests include: Clerical Test (240 items; 5 minutes) in which the task is to identify as quickly as possible all pairs of identical numbers from two columns of numbers; Idea Fluency Test (4 items; 8 minutes) in which the task is to generate as many alternative uses as possible that can be made of a given object; Inductive Reasoning Test (30 items; 8 minutes) in which the task is to identify three pictures in each series of six pictures that have a common theme among them; Word Association Test (100 items; 8 minutes) in which the task is to give a word associated with the given stimulus word; Writing Speed Test (15 lines; 1 minute) in which the task is to write the sentence given as fast and as many times as possible during the alloted time; Paper Folding Test (24 items; 10 minutes) in which the task is to identify from among five choices what would result when a sheet of paper is folded in the manner shown and one or two holes are punched through the paper; Vocabulary Test (80 items; 22 minutes) in which the task is to select from five choices the word most equivalent in meaning to the test word; Ideaphoria Test (1 item; 10 minutes) in which the task is to generate and write down as many ideas as possible about or in response to a novel situation; Numerical Computation Test (40 items; 13 minutes) in which the task is to perform simple arithmetic computations as quickly as possible; Numerical Reasoning (40 items; 20 minutes) in which the task is to identify the pattern in a series of numbers and give the next number that extends the series according to the pattern; Finger Dexterity Test (2 trials each hand; 6 minutes) in which each task is to place three small pins into holes on a board as rapidly as possible; Grip Test (3 trials each hand; 6 minutes) in which the task is to squeeze the dynamometer as hard as possible; Analytical Reasoning Test (18 items; 5-13 minutes) in which the task is to arrange five, six, or seven words (printed on chips) on a diagram-board in the most logical order; and the Shape Assembly Test (6 items; 15-35 minutes) in which the task is to assemble a disassembled wooden geometric shape. For all tests, except Ideaphoria, Finger Dexterity, and Grip, items are arranged in ascending order of difficulty.

Time of administration for each test was chosen at the point where 95% of the individuals taking the test were able to complete all of the items. The order of administration for the tests in the battery is designed to minimize test anxiety and maximize test motivation.

A short break is called after the first hour of testing. All tests are suitable for group use with the exception of

Grip, Analytical Reasoning, and Shape Assembly. For operational reasons, the group tests are administered first and the individual tests after. Reliability, validity, and normative data provided in the Technical and Administrator's Manuals. Examiner required. Suitable for group use (with the exceptions described above).

Timed: 3-3½ hours

Range: High school juniors-adult

Scoring: Hand key; examiner evaluated

Cost: Contact publisher.

Publisher: The Ball Foundation

BUFFALO READING TEST

Herman J.P. Schubert

teen, adult

Purpose: Measures reading abilities. Used for selection purposes with high school and college students and adults.

Description: Multiple item paper-pencil test measuring reading speed and reading comprehension. Provides a total score. Used for selecting personnel who read rapidly and/or understandingly and for identifying persons in need of remedial training. Examiner required. Suitable for group use.

Untimed: Varies

Range: High school student-adult

Scoring: Examiner evaluated

Cost: 25 tests $8.75; specimen set (with manual) $3.00.

Publisher: Herman J.P. Schubert

CLERICAL SELECTION BATTERY

Refer to page 217.

DAILEY VOCATIONAL TESTS

Refer to page 114.

DENTAL ASSISTANT TEST

Mary Meeker and Robert Meeker

adult

Purpose: Measures aptitude for work as a dental assistant. Used for selection of dental assistants.

Description: Multiple item paper-pencil screening instrument assessing the abilities and aptitudes of prospective dental assistants. Criterion-referenced test items developed in conjunction with practicing dental groups. Scoring keys and criteria graph for selection available separately. Examiner required. Suitable for group use.

Untimed: Varies

Range: Adult

Scoring: Hand key

Cost: Test form $2.00 each; scoring key $12.00.

Publisher: SOI Institute

INVENTORY OF INSURANCE SELLING POTENTIAL

Refer to page 259.

MANAGEMENT INVENTORY ON LEADERSHIP AND MOTIVATION (MILM)

Donald L. Kirkpatrick

adult

Purpose: Measures knowledge of the theories and recommendations of five major behavioral scientists: Maslow, Herzberg, McGregor, McClelland, and Likert. Used in conjunction with training or reading programs in the behavioral sciences.

Description: 75 item paper-pencil two-choice test assessing an individual's knowledge of the philosophy and approaches of five major behavioral scientists. Test items cover theories on motivation, leadership, productivity, and effectiveness. The individual reads statements about the philosophies of Abraham Maslow (8 items), Frederick Herzberg (30 items), Douglas McGregor (21 items), David McClelland (9 items), and Rensis Likert (7 items) and indicates whether each statement applies or does not apply to the actual philosophies proposed by the behavioral scientist for which it is listed. The answer booklet includes explanations of all correct answers. The manual also includes a list of suggested reading and guidelines for establishing a training program related to the inventory. Self-administered and self-scored. Suitable for group use.

Untimed: 20 minutes

Range: Adult

Scoring: Self-scored

Cost: 20 tests and answer booklets $20.00; manual $1.00; review set (test, answer booklet, and manual) $2.00.

Publisher: Donald L. Kirkpatrick

MEEKER BEHAVIOR CORRELATES FOR MANAGEMENT MATCHING OF TEAMS

Refer to page 230.

MOBILE VOCATIONAL EVALUATION (MVE)

Edward J. Hester

teen, adult

Purpose: Measures vocationally related abilities as a basis for identifying specific jobs which fit an individual's abilities and special needs. Used for home applications and as a service of several small workshops or multi-campus school systems.

Description: Multiple test battery assessing the following factors of an individual's ability: finger dexterity, wrist finger speed, arm hand steadiness, manual dexterity, two arm coordination, two hand coordination, perceptual accuracy, special perception, aiming, reaction time, abstract reasoning, verbal reasoning, numerical reasoning, reading arithmetic, leadership-structure, and following directions. Yields 19 ability factor scores as well as the 17 personal characteristics. Ability factors and personal characteristics are computer analyzed to identify appropriate jobs. The data base contains computer analysis of over 700 jobs taken from the current dictionary of occupational titles (DOT) published by the United States Department of Labor. The computer printout provides scaled scores along with a listing of up to 100 jobs which are realistic opportunities for the individual, arranged in order from those which are most feasible to those which are less feasible. All components are contained in a single carrying case weighing less than 30 pounds. All electronic components are battery powered. Tests may be administered by non-professional personnel such as clerks and assistants. Examiner required. Eighty-five percent of the testing may be accomplished in a group setting.

Untimed: 4-5 hours

Range: Adolescent, adult

Scoring: Computer scored

Cost: Contact publisher.

Publisher: Lafayette Instrument Company, Inc.

PHOENIX ABILITY SURVEY SYSTEM (PASS)

Edward J. Hester

teen, adult

Purpose: Measures vocationally related abilities as a basis for identifying specific jobs which fit an individual's abilities and special needs. Used for on-sight applications.

Description: Multiple test battery measuring 30 ability factors and 21 personal characteristics related to a person's vocational aptitudes and interests. Specific ability factors measured include: three measures of unilateral motor functions, six measures of bilateral motor functions, four measures of perceptual factors, four factors of perceptual motor coordination, five factors of intelligence, two factors of achievement, two factors of strength, and four factors of people/relationships abilities. The data base used in the computer analysis consists of over 2,000 jobs taken from the current dictionary of occupational titles (DOT) published by the United States Department of Labor. The jobs in the data base range from physician to laborer, representing virtually every industrial and occupational group in America. A typical computer printout is up to six pages long and includes physical limitations, working conditions, people relationships and individual test scores, ability scores profile sheet, and several job title listings which are realistic for the individual, arranged in order from those which are most feasible to those which are less feasible. May be used to augment job sample testing systems such as Valpar, Singer, JEVS or VIEWS. Examiner required. Eighty-five percent of the testing may be accomplished in a group setting.

Untimed: Varies

Range: Adult, adolescent

Scoring: Computer scored

Cost: Contact publisher.

Publisher: Lafayette Instrument Company, Inc.

PROGRAM FOR ASSESSING YOUTH EMPLOYMENT SKILLS (PAYES)

Refer to page 202.

SMELL IDENTIFICATION TEST™

Richard L. Doty

all ages

Purpose: Provides an accurate straight-forward quantitative measure of an individual's ability to smell without the use of chemicals or complex odorant presentation equipment. Designed for use in industrial, academic or medical settings—applications include screening of industrial smell and taste panels; evaluation of industrial exposure to airborne chemicals; medical examinations; longitudinal tracking of smell loss or return; and legal determinations of smell function.

Description: Consists of four booklets containing 10 odorants apiece, an odorant per page. The stimuli are embedded in "scratch 'n sniff" crystals located on brown strips positioned at the bottom of each page. The individual is required to complete a multiple-choice question for each of the 40 odorant items. The test can be self-administered, can detect most malingerers, and is sensitive to numerous subject variables, including smoking habits, age, gender and a number of medical conditions. Total test score is the sum of the number of items correct out of the 40 total. Norms provide percentile values for men and women in 5-year age categories from 5 years of age to 100 years of age, and specific function classifications (i.e., normosmia, microsmia or hyposmia, anosmia, probable malingering). Norms are based upon over 2000 subjects. Scores also correlate with levels of specific neurotransmitter metabolites in cerebral spinal fluid.

Also available is *The Pocket Smell Test™*, designed to be used by a medical practitioner, consisting of items selected from the *Smell Identification Test* arranged in a pocket-sized folded card with instructions. It allows gross olfactory screening.

Olfactory abnormalities discovered by this test should be fully characterized using the 40-item *Smell Identification Test.* Scoring is by Pass/Fail.

Currently both tests are available only for English-speaking persons. Japanese, French and German versions under development. Self-administerable only by reasonably literate persons in 10 to 70 year age range. Should be administered by a test administrator to persons below 10 years of age or over 70 years of age, as per administration manual.

Untimed: 10-15 minutes

Range: Child-adult

Scoring: Examiner evaluated

Cost: $19.95/test (minimum order of 5 tests—includes manual); *Pocket Smell Test,* $1.25 each plus shipping—minimum order of 100 tests.

Publisher: Sensonics, Inc.

SOI-LA: DENTAL RECEPTIONIST TEST

Mary Meeker and Robert Meeker

adult

Purpose: Measures aptitude for work as a dental receptionist. Used for selection of dental receptionists.

Description: Multiple item paper-pencil screening instrument assessing the abilities and aptitudes of prospective dental receptionists. Criterion-referenced test items developed in conjunction with practicing dental groups. Scoring keys and criteria graph for selection available separately. Self interpreted. Examiner required. Suitable for group use.

Untimed: 1 hour

Range: Adult

Scoring: Hand key; machine scoring available

Cost: Test form $2.00 each; scoring key $12.00. Computer analysis available.

Publisher: SOI Institute

SPACE RELATIONS (PAPER PUZZLES)

L.L. Thurstone and T.E. Jeffrey

adult

Purpose: Measures the ability to visualize a rigid configuration (a stable figure, drawing, or diagram) when it is moved into different positions.

Description: Multiple item paper-pencil test of mechanical interest and ability. Useful in vocational counseling or selection, identifying individuals with high mechanical interest and ability. Examiner required. For individual or group use.

Timed: 9 minutes

Range: Adult

Scoring: Hand key; computer scoring available

Cost: 25 test booklets (includes interpretation, Research Manual and scoring key) $16.25; specimen set $8.00.

Publisher: London House Press

SUPERVISORY INVENTORY ON SAFETY (SIS)

Refer to page 254.

SYSTEM FOR TESTING & EVALUATION OF POTENTIAL (STEP)

Melany E. Baehr

adult

Purpose: Estimates potential for successful performance (PSP) in present and future positions. Useful for hiring, training, and promotion decisions at all levels of skill from first-line supervisors, to vice-president officer level.

Description: STEP Battery consists of two interlocking measurement procedures; the Managerial and Professional Job Functions Inventory (MP-JFI) and the Managerial and Professional Test Battery. Both are paper-pencil batteries. The MP-JFI is a standardized and quantified job analysis procedure which provides a common grid for the description of higher-level positions with respect to 16 factorially-determined dimensions or generic job functions. Composite job profiles and norms have been developed for the 12 Key Positions based upon a national sample of incumbents. The *MP Test Battery* is a systematic and quantified procedure which provides measures of abilities, skills, and attributes of individuals over a wide range of behavior. The test battery has been specifically developed and validated for managers and other high-level personnel. Composite profiles and normative data have been developed for each of the 12 Key Positions based upon a national sample.

These key positions include: *Line Personnel*—First line supervisors, middle managers, general managers, vice presidents; *Professionals*—First-level professionals (engineers, R&D, etc.), managers of one type of professional, managers of different types of professionals, vice presidents; *Sales Personnel*—Sales representatives, district managers, regional and general managers, vice presidents; *Technical Specialists*—First-level specialists (analysts, accountants, programmers), managers of one type of specialist, managers of different types of specialists, vice presidents. Used together, and anchored to the 12 Key Positions as reference points, these instruments provide information about: the position (the relative importance of the functions to be performed) and the individual (the level of job skill (or competency) in the important job functions—the areas of strengths and weaknesses as revealed by the MP Test Battery,—and estimates of potential for successful performance (PSP) in present and possible future positions). Examiner required. Suitable for group or individual use.

Timed: 3-4 hours for entire battery

Range: Adult

Scoring: Mail scoring or ITAC (Immediate Telephone Analysis by Computer)

Cost: Contact publisher. $150-$250 per test, depending on volume.

Publisher: London House Press

TEST OF ENGLISH FOR INTERNATIONAL COMMUNICATION (TOEIC)

LPI 1.0-LPI 4.0

Purpose: Measures English language skills required in the work environment of business, commerce, and industry. Used as a basis for employee selection and placement decisions as well as decisions concerning assignment, placement, and achievement in company sponsored English language programs. Used with non-native speakers of English.

Description: 200 item paper-pencil multiple-choice test of English language skills consisting of two parts: Part I contains 100 listening comprehension items administered via audio tape; Part II contains 100 reading items. Total test scores range from 10-990; subscores for Parts I and II range from 5-495. Scores are correlated to direct measures of reading, writing, and speaking ability as well as to indirect measures. Used by multi-national corporations, language schools, government agencies, public and private organizations for hiring, assignment to overseas posts requiring communication skills in English, assignment to or promotion within departments where English is needed or desirable, identification of employees who know English well enough to benefit from training programs abroad, and determination of the effectiveness of English language training programs. Currently offered in Japan, Korea, and Taiwan on a regular basis. (ETS is in the process of establishing similar programs in Hong Kong and Indonesia as well as an off-the-shelf international corporate program.) Application to take the test is made through offices in those respective countries. Examiner required. Suitable for group use.

Timed: 2½ hours

Range: Non-native speakers of English, LPI 1.0-LPI 4.0

Scoring: Hand key; computer scoring available

Cost: Contact publisher for information concerning prices and availability.

Publisher: TOEIC Program—Educational Testing Service

Clerical

CLERICAL SELECTION BATTERY

adult

Purpose: Identifies applicants with good potential for long-term success as clerical employees.

Description: The battery includes three types of paper and pencil testing instruments to provide a complete picture of the applicant's background, abilities and aptitudes. Biographical Data is a specially-constructed, 75-item version of the Personal Background Inventory measuring work history, educational experiences, drive, leadership, financial responsibility, and health. Self-Assessment assesses applicant's ability in a wide variety of areas in comparison with others of similar age, education, and work experience in a specially-constructed, 55-item version of the Skills and Attributes Inventory. Cognitive Ability measures applicant's cognitive abilities in four short tests. These four tests measure mathematical ability in the areas of simple computation and error recognition; name and number comparison (an ability necessary for many clerical tasks such as proofreading and credit card verification); number sequence and verbal comprehension and verbal reasoning. Examiner required. Suitable for group use.

Timed/Untimed: 50 minutes for total battery

Range: Adult

Scoring: ITAC (Immediate Test Analysis by Computer) and mail scoring

Cost: $8-15, depending on volume.

Publisher: London House Press

Computer

FOGEL WP OPERATOR TEST

Max Fogel

adult

Purpose: Measures aptitudes and personality dimensions which predict success as a word processor operator. Used for employee selection and placement.

Description: Multiple item paper-pencil test assessing an applicant's potential for success as a word processor operator. Sections include:

problem solving (the ability to assess information and to make decisions based upon the information and general analytical skills), vocabulary, proofreading, figural transformations, mechanical-spatial relationships, and personality (including attitudes toward machinery and equipment). Examiner required. Suitable for group use.

Untimed: 45 minutes

Range: Adult

Scoring: Examiner evaluated; scoring service available

Cost: Corporate kit (50 test booklets, complete answer key, and interpretive manual) $2,000.00; 10 test booklets (includes partial key) $425.00; scoring service per test $20.00.

Publisher: Association of Information Systems Professionals

I.P.I. JOB TEST FIELD SERIES: COMPUTER PROGRAMMER

Industrial Psychology, Inc.

adult

Purpose: Assesses skills and aptitudes of applicants for entry level computer programmer positions. Used for employee selection and placement.

Description: Multiple item paper-pencil battery of five aptitude tests measuring skills which predict success as an entry level computer programmer. Tests include: Office Terms (54 item test measuring the ability to understand special terms used in business and industry), Numbers (54 item test measuring aptitude for working quickly and accurately with numbers), Judgment (54 item test of aptitude for logical thinking, planning, and dealing with abstract relations), Parts (48 item test measuring aptitude for visualizing size, shape, and spatial relations of objects in two or three dimensions), and Perception (54 item test of ability to rapidly scan and locate details and errors in words and numbers, and to recognize likenesses and differences). Examiner required. Suitable for group use. All tests available in French.

Timed: 30 minutes (6 minutes per test)

Range: Adult

Scoring: Hand key

Cost: Contact publisher.

Publisher: Industrial Psychology, Inc.

Engineering

*No new tests available. Please refer to the First Edition of **TESTS** for a complete listing and description of tests currently available in this area.*

Intelligence and Related

DAP QUALITY SCALE (DRAW-A-PERSON)

Herman J.P. Schubert

adult

Purpose: Measures intelligence and motivation. Used for selection purposes.

Description: 1 item paper-pencil free response test assessing non-verbal intelligence. Individuals are asked to draw a picture of a person which is then scored according to objective guidelines. The overall quality score contributes to the prediction of available intelligence and motivation. Examiner required. Suitable for group use.

Untimed: Varies

Range: Adult

Scoring: Examiner evaluated

Cost: Test kit $3.00.

Publisher: Herman J.P. Schubert

GENERAL ABILITY BATTERY

Herman J.P. Schubert

adult

Purpose: Measures general mental abilities. Used for personnel-selection purposes with executives, supervisors, salesmen, foremen, and clerks.

Description: Multiple item paper-pencil battery of tests assessing general mental abilities as a measure of occupational aptitude and ability. Provides scores for: verbal skills, precise thinking, arithmetic reasoning, and logical analysis. Examiner required. Suitable for group use.

Timed: Varies

Range: Adult

Scoring: Examiner evaluated

Cost: 25 complete tests $12.50; specimen set (with manual) $3.00.

Publisher: Herman J.P. Schubert

HUMAN INFORMATION PROCESSING SURVEY: HIP SURVEY

E. Paul Torrance, William Taggart and Barbara Taggart

adult

Purpose: Assesses the manner in which an individual processes information. Used as a training tool in human resource development programs and for research purposes.

Description: Multiple item paper-pencil inventory assessing an individual's processing preference: left hemisphere, right hemisphere, integrated, or mixed. Results provide a description of a person's overall approach as well as specific tactics in problem solving and decision making. The manual outlines applications of the survey and its use in a one-day workshop. Research edition available. Examiner required. Suitable for group use.

Untimed: Varies

Range: Adult

Scoring: Examiner evaluated

Cost: Professional edition starter set (manual, 10 survey forms, 10 profile forms) $25.00; specimen set $8.00.

Publisher: Scholastic Testing Service, Inc.

MULTIDIMENSIONAL APTITUDE BATTERY

Refer to page 11.

OTIS SELF-ADMINISTERING TEST OF MENTAL ABILITY

Refer to page 12.

PERFORMANCE EFFICIENCY TEST (PET)

Thomas Rex Long

adult

Purpose: Measures the ability to use intellectual potential for satisfactory performance in any job situation. Used for employee screening and placement.

Description: Multiple item oral response test assessing intellectual ability. Applicants are asked to read color names or identify colors from three stimulus cards (A, B, and C). Card A contains four color names, printed in black, in random order. Card B contains four colors, printed in quarter-inch squares. Card C contains color names, printed in colors different from what the word reads. The number of incorrect answers identifies those applicants least likely to compete successfully. The format suggests nothing regarding what psychological variables are being measured, and consequently, is nonthreatening to the subjects. "Faking" presents no problem, as subjects are unaware of what constitutes an acceptable time score. Examiner required. Not suitable for group use.

Untimed: 5-6 minutes

Range: Adult

Scoring: Examiner evaluated

Cost: Complete set (manual and set of three stimulus cards) $6.50.

Publisher: Stoelting Co.

PSYCHOSOCIAL HISTORY REPORT

Refer to page 47.

SCOTT MENTAL ALERTNESS TEST

adult

Purpose: Measures general mental alertness. Used for employee selection and vocational guidance counseling.

Description: Multiple item paper-pencil test assessing arithmetic reasoning, quickness and accuracy of judgment, clearness of perception, degree of comprehension, and ability to follow instructions. The time limits are so short that the most alert person cannot make a perfect score, yet the test is easy enough to permit the less mentally alert make an appreciable score. Test items are as free as possible from the influence of formal schooling and no difficult words are used. Examiner required. Suitable for group use.

Timed: 20 minutes

Range: Adult

Scoring: Examiner evaluated

Cost: Test kit (50 test booklets and manual) $18.50.

Publisher: Stoelting Co.

TIME PERCEPTION INVENTORY (TPI)

adult

Purpose: Measures the difference between physical and mental presence. Helps employees understand how much of their time is wasted due to mental preoccupations. Identifies an individual's particular preoccupations and evaluates their causes and debilitating nature.

Description: Multiple item paper-pencil inventory measuring an individual's tendencies to focus attention on the past, future, or present. Also provides percentile comparison on perceived time effectiveness (typically related to an individual's motivation to improve). All scales provide opportunities to consider positive and negative aspects of thinking in a particular time reference. Test booklets are self-scoring and self-profiling. Group patterns can be identified through a simple show of hands. Test booklet provides interpretations of scales and implications of scores on scales. Recommendations for additional reading are included. Normative data available. Self-administered. Suitable for group use.

Untimed: 10 minutes

Range: Adult

Scoring: Self-scored

Cost: Demonstration kit (30 inventories and manual) $45.95; specimen set (includes manual) $9.95.

Publisher: Humanics Media

Publisher: CFKR Career Materials, Inc.

Interests

ARMED SERVICES-CIVILIAN INTEREST SURVEY (ASCVIS)

Robert Kauk

teen, adult

Purpose: Assesses an individual's interests in high-tech occupational fields and identifies armed forces and related civilian jobs that match those interests. Used by armed forces recruiters and career counselors with clients who want technical training which might be offered by the armed services.

Description: Six-page multiple item paper-pencil or computer-administered inventory assessing levels of interest within high-tech occupational clusters. Identifies appropriate occupational choices and shows how the armed services can be a source of immediate employment and basic and advanced technical training that can be utilized in either a military or civilian career. A career profile is developed for making tentative career decisions, including selection of an educational plan—either civilian or military—to reach career goals (a two-path plan is explained, step by step). The individual is free to take the completed career profile to a recruiter or civilian counselor to make the training connection. Self-administered. Suitable for group use.

Untimed: Varies

Range: High school students-adult

Scoring: Self-scored; computer version available

Cost: Class set (materials for 35 students and user's guide) $15.00; diskette $79.95.

Publisher: CFKR Career Materials, Inc.

CAREER DECISION SCALE (2nd EDITION)

Samuel H. Osipow, Clarke G. Carney, Jane Winer, Barbara Yanico, and Maryanne Koschir

teen grades 9-college

Purpose: Identifies barriers preventing an individual from making career decisions. Used as a basis for career counseling, to monitor the effectiveness of career counseling programs, for research on career indecisiveness.

Description: 18 item paper-pencil inventory assessing a limited number of circumstances which cause problems in reaching and implementing educational and career decisions. Each item describes a separate reason for career indecisiveness. Individuals rate each item on a four-point scale from one ("not like me") to four ("like me") to indicate the extent to which each item describes their personal situation. The manual includes data regarding validity and reliability and norms for various age and grade levels. Examiner required. Suitable for group use.

Untimed: 10-15 minutes

Range: High school and college students

Scoring: Examiner evaluated

Cost: 25 scale booklets $6.00; manual $5.95.

Publisher: Marathon Consulting and Press

CAREER EXPLORATION SERIES (CES)

Refer to page 198.

DIFFERENTIAL PERSONALITY QUESTIONNAIRE

Refer to page 37.

INTEREST INVENTORY (II)

United States Employment Service

teen, adult

Purpose: Measures an individual's vocational preference. Used in vocational guidance and career counseling.

Description: 162 item paper-pencil inventory measuring an individual's interest in each of the 12 vocational categories identified in the GOE *(Guide to Occupational Exploration).* Test items consist of descriptions of various vocational duties and settings. Individuals respond by indicating "like," "don't know," or "dislike" for each item. All testing materials are contained in a single booklet that can be scored manually or by machine. Computer scoring provides a one-page report which includes: a narrative description of the inventory, standard scores and percentiles for all 12 interest scales, and an interpretive graphic display of scores. Scores are cross-referenced to relevant Work Group pages in the GOE and to relevant occupational aptitude patterns (OAP's) for the General Aptitude Test Battery (GATB). The manual explains how to administer the inventory, provides intepretive guidelines and norms for hand-scoring, and explains how the inventory was developed. Examiner required. Suitable for group use.

Untimed: 15-20 minutes

Range: Adolescent, adult

Scoring: Examiner evaluated; computer scoring available

Cost: 100 inventory booklets $9.00; manual $4.50; computer scoring service $.70-$.95 per individual.

Publisher: Intran Corporation

JOBMATCH

Industrial Training Unit (ITRU) in association with the Manpower Services Commission

teen, adult

Purpose: Identifies jobs or job areas which non-academic secondary and college students would find most compatible with their personal job-related likes and dislikes. Used by LEA careers advisors, in training and personnel departments of large companies, and for use in schemes organized under the (British) Government's New Training Initiative.

Description: 49 item paper-pencil or computer-administered questionnaire assessing personal preferences related to four basic aspects of employment: physical environment, social environment, work content, and work method. In the paper-pencil version, students respond to items presented in the six-page questionnaire on self-profiling answer sheets. These profiles are then compared to the forty profile stencils provided in the *Jobmatch Profiles Book* to identify jobs or job areas which should be of interest to the students. Profiles in the *Jobmatch Profiles Book* are based on workers responses to a Job Disposition Questionnaire assessing the likes and dislikes of individuals actually working in the forty jobs covered by the system. Each of these jobs is discussed in further detail in the *Job Facts Book,* which provides: illustrated descriptions of each job (including basic information, qualifications required, and a list of the likes and dislikes of persons who work in it), a list of appropriate books and pamphlets, useful addresses, and a glossary of employment terms.

The teacher's guide provides notes on administration and scoring procedures and research background, as well as guidelines for extending the range of the questionnaire by relating jobs not directly covered by the system to those which are. Two computer versions are available. The Interactive Computer Version computer-administers the questions and scores the answers, leaving students to follow up on the results with the *Job Facts Book*. The Scoring and Matching Computer Version is designed for group use where individual computer time is not available. Students answer questions using an answer sheet, and the computer matches the profiles of their responses with the profiles of the forty jobs. Both programs are suitable for use with the Commodore PET (32K), RML 380Z, and the BBC Micro. The paper-pencil version is self-administered and self-scored. The paper-pencil version and the Scoring and Matching Computer Version are both suitable for group use. BRITISH PUBLISHER

Untimed: Varies

Range: Adolescent, adult

Scoring: Self-scored; computer software scoring available

Cost: Complete pack (5 questionnaires, 20 answer sheets, the *Jobmatch Profiles Book*, the *Job Facts Book*, and teacher's guide) £17.95; contact publisher concerning cost and availability of software.

Publisher: Macmillan Education

JOB-O

Refer to page 201.

LIMRA CAREER PROFILE SYSTEM

Refer to page 259.

THE MAJOR-MINOR-FINDER

Refer to page 187.

MY VOCATIONAL SITUATION

Refer to page 231.

OCCUPATIONAL APTITUDE-INTEREST MEASUREMENT (AIM)

teen, adult

Purpose: Measures occupational aptitudes and interests simultaneously. Used for vocational guidance and career counseling.

Description: Multiple item paper-pencil inventory combining forms B, C, and D of the General Aptitude Test Battery (GATB) with an Interest Inventory (II). Computer scoring yields a multipage narrative report which provides: a discussion of the 12 interest areas identified in the GOE *(Guide to Occupational Exploration)*, standard scores and percentiles for the 12 interest areas, and aptitude levels for each of the 66 OAP's (occupational aptitude patterns) based on the GATB results. This report links interests and OAP's to work groups in the GOE, integrating aptitudes and interests to provide a comprehensive picture of an individual's best vocational opportunities. A one-page counselor's profile report combining interest inventory scores and OAP's is also available. The manual provides norms and OAP's and a discussion of test results. Examiner required. Suitable for group use.

Untimed: Varies

Range: Adolescent, adult

Scoring: Examiner evaluated; computer scoring required

Cost: 100 inventory booklets (with combined GATB BCD answer sheet and interest inventory) $19.00; narrative reports $1.80-$2.60 per individual; counselor profile reports each $1.40-$2.00.

Publisher: Intran Corporation

PAPI SYSTEM

Refer to page 233.

PAPI SYSTEM: RATING OF JOB REQUIREMENTS—FORM D REVISED

Refer to page 237.

PERSONAL RESOURCES QUESTIONNAIRE: FORM E-2

Refer to page 238.

Interpersonal Skills and Attitudes

ADULT PERSONALITY INVENTORY

Refer to page 32.

ALIENATION INDEX SURVEY (AI SURVEY)

adult

Purpose: Assesses work-related attitudes of job applicants. Identifies individuals with alienated attitudes that reduce performance and cause poor morale. Used for applicant screening and employee selection.

Description: Multiple item paper-pencil pre-employment survey assessing the attitudes of job applicants toward: employers, supervisors, co-workers, work, pay, and benefits. Identifies applicants with alienated attitudes in these areas who have a high potential for becoming problem employees. Administered, scored, and interpreted in-house for immediate use by personnel/human relations/security specialists by license to Psychological Systems Corporation. Also available as part of the PASS Booklet (which includes the Trustworthiness Attitude Survey and the Emotional Stability Survey) or PASS-II Booklet (along with Trustworthiness Attitude Survey) for more complete applicant assessment. Examiner required. Suitable for group use.

Untimed: 8-12 minutes

Range: Adult

Scoring: Examiner evaluated

Cost: Contact publisher.

Publisher: Psychological Systems Corporation

BANK PERSONNEL SELECTION INVENTORY (BPSI)

adult

Purpose: Identifies banking job applicants who might engage in counter-productive behavior in the workplace.

Description: 108 item paper-pencil test examining behavior that could result in theft, violence or drug-abuse on the job. A distortion scale is included. Basic literacy is required. Self-administered. Suitable for group use.

Untimed: 30-40 minutes

Range: Adult

Scoring: Computer scored by phone

Cost: \$8.50-\$14.50 depending on volume.

Publisher: London House Press

THE BIPOLAR PSYCHOLOGICAL INVENTORY (BPI)

Refer to page 34.

CANFIELD LEARNING STYLES INVENTORY (CLS)

Refer to page 182.

CAREER DECISION SCALE (2nd EDITION)

Refer to page 221.

CHANGE AGENT QUESTIONNAIRE (CAQ)

Jay Hall and Martha S. Williams

adult

Purpose: Evaluates attitudes toward change. Used in programs on the dynamics of change with teachers, trainers, managers, members of the clergy, politicians, probation officers, counselors, and social workers—individuals whose role is to bring about positive changes in organizations, institutions, or individuals.

Description: Multiple item paper-pencil self-report inventory assessing an individual's philosophies, strategies, and approaches concerning the concept of change. Measures basic assumptions regarding the process and duration of change, particularly change which is brought about through the efforts of change agents (individuals who effect change by actively influencing the thoughts and behaviors of others). Yields five scores which are profiled according to a grid format based on the work of Herbert Kelman concerning change agents. Self-administered. Suitable for group use.

Untimed: Varies

Range: Adult

Scoring: Self-scored

Cost: Individual instrument $4.50.

Publisher: Teleometrics International

CLAYBURY ASSESSMENT BATTERY

Refer to page 35.

CONFLICT MANAGEMENT SURVEY (CMS)

Jay Hall

adult

Purpose: Assesses the manner in which group members interpret the meaning of conflict and, consequently, the manner in which they handle it. Used in labor-management sessions, community relations laboratories, and programs on the dynamics of conflict to identify constructive outcomes to conflict.

Description: Multiple item paper-pencil self-report inventory assessing an individual's reaction to—and consequent handling of—interpersonal, group, and inter-group conflict. Analysis employs a grid format measuring two dimensions: concern for personal goals and concern for relationships. Identifies five styles of conflict management: win-lose, yield-lose, lose-leave, compromise, and synergistic. Normative data and conversion tables are provided for transforming raw scores on the five styles into a fivefold conflict management profile. These profiles provide a basis for establishing constructive conflict-handling behavior. Examiner required. Suitable for group use.

Untimed: Varies

Range: Adult

Scoring: Examiner evaluated

Cost: Individual instrument $4.50.

Publisher: Teleometrics International

CUSTOMER REACTION SURVEY (CRS)

Refer to page 258.

THE DECISION MAKING INVENTORY

Richard Johnson, William Coscarelli and JaDean Johnson

teen, adult

Purpose: Identifies an individual's preferred decision making style. Used in career counseling, marriage therapy, task groups, and instructional programs.

Description: 20 item paper-pencil one-page instrument assessing an individual's preferred style of making decisions. Individuals rate a series of statements concerning steps in the decision making process on a six-point scale from "never" to "always" to indicate the degree to which each item is true for themselves. Scoring and interpretation is based on Johnson's theory which suggests that information can be gathered in a systematic or spontaneous manner and this information is analyzed either externally or internally. The manual describes the theory in detail, as well as the development of the scale, scoring procedures, and examples of its use in counseling and task groups. Examiner required. Suitable for group use.

Untimed: Varies

Range: Adolescent, adult

Scoring: Examiner evaluated

Cost: 30 inventories $6.00; manual $10.00; scoring grid (set of 2) $1.00.

Publisher: Marathon Consulting and Press

DEROGATIS STRESS PROFILE (DSP)

Refer to page 36.

EMOTIONAL STABILITY SURVEY (ES SURVEY)

adult

Purpose: Measures the emotional stability of applicants for sensitive positions. Used for applicant screening and employee selection.

Description: Multiple item paper-pencil pre-employment survey measuring emotional stability and control. Highly job related for police and security positions. The self-report questionnaire format requires no interpretive analysis. In addition to the standard scoring template, a critical factor score template is also provided to identify false positive scores indicating attempts to bias answers. Developed according to guidelines established by the EEOC and reviewed by FEPC and EEOC examiners. May be administered, scored, and interpreted in-house by personnel/human resource/security specialists by license to Psychological Systems Corporation. Also available as part of the PASS Booklet (which includes the Trustworthiness Attitude Survey and the Alienation Index Survey) for more complete applicant assessment. Examiner required. Suitable for group use.

Untimed: 5-10 minutes

Range: Adult

Scoring: Hand key

Cost: Contact publisher.

Publisher: Psychological Systems Corporation

GIANNETTI ON-LINE PSYCHOSOCIAL HISTORY (GOLPH)

Refer to page 39.

GROUP ENCOUNTER SURVEY (GES)

Jay Hall and Martha S. Williams

adult

Purpose: Assesses attitudes which affect an individual's ability to participate in group decision making processes. Used in training programs aimed at improving group decision-making dynamics.

Description: Multiple item paper-pencil self-report inventory assessing previously formed assumptions about the group decision-making process which determine an individual's effectiveness in such situations. Measures concerns about the quality of the group decision and about the other members' commitment to the decision. A decision-making grid is used to identify for the individual a personal style of group interaction. Dominant group styles are portrayed, as well as leadership preference, conflict resolution, intergroup relations, and feelings about groups per se. Normative data provided. Examiner required. Suitable for group use.

Untimed: Varies

Range: Adult

Scoring: Examiner evaluated

Cost: Individual instrument $4.50.

Publisher: Teleometrics International

HOGAN PERSONALITY INVENTORY

Robert Hogan

college student-adult

Purpose: Assesses normal personality characteristics. Used for counseling, employment decisions, research, and self-development.

Description: 300 item paper-pencil true-false inventory assessing six primary traits (intellectance, adjustment, prudence, ambition, sociability, likeability), one validity scale, and six occupational scales (service orientation, clerical performance, sales performance, management performance, stress tolerance, and reliability). Test items presented at eighth-grade reading level. Hand-scoring materials allow for the scoring and profiling of six primary traits and validity scale. Two-page computerized profile report presents raw and percentile scores for six primary traits, one validity scale, and six occupational scales along with a listing of 45 homogeneous item composites. Examiner required. Suitable for group use.

Untimed: 30-40 minutes

Range: College students-adults

Scoring: Examiner evaluated; computer scoring available

Cost: Specimen set (manual, reusable test booklet, profile score form, and a sample report) $12.00.

Publisher: NCS/Professional Assessment Services

HOGAN SELECTION SERIES

Robert Hogan

college student-adult

Purpose: Assesses aspects of personality related to job performance. Used for employee selection and placement.

Description: Four paper-pencil batteries, each consisting of 20-90 true-false items presented at an eighth-grade reading level. The Primary Performance Battery indicates conscientiousness, honesty, dependability, even-tempered disposition, and tendency toward insubordination, theft, alcohol and substance abuse as well as proneness toward illness and worker compensation claims. The Clerical Performancy Battery predicts success in occupations requiring close attention to details, following instructions, and the ability to communicate effectively. The Sales Performance Battery predicts success in occupations requiring initiative, persistence, and the ability to influence others. The Managerial Performance Battery predicts success in occupations requiring leadership, planning and the ability to motivate others. Scores are provided on four scales for each of the four batteries: validity, service orientation, reliability, and stress tolerance. The clerical, sales, and managerial batteries each include one additional scale designed to predict success in the relevant class of occupations. Norms provided for college students and adults. Examiner required. Suitable for group use.

Untimed: 5-20 minutes

Range: College students-adults

Scoring: Hand scored

Cost: Specimen set (1 test booklet, 1 rediscore answer sheet for each battery, and user's guide) $20.00.

Publisher: NCS/Professional Assessment Services

HUMAN FACTORS PERSONNEL SELECTION INVENTORY (HFPSI)

adult

Purpose: Identifies job applicants who might engage in counterproductive or unsafe behavior in the workplace.

Description: Multiple item paper-pencil test examining behavior that could result in theft, violence, drug-abuse or accidents on the job. A distortion scale is included. Basic literacy is required. Self-administered. Suitable for group or individual use. Available in Spanish.

Untimed: 30-40 minutes

Range: Adult

Scoring: Computer scored by phone or by microprocessor on-site

Cost: Complete $8.50-$13.50 depending on volume.

Publisher: London House Press—offered through St. Paul Companies

INDUSTRIAL SENTENCE COMPLETION FORM

Martin M. Bruce

teen, adult

Purpose: An aid in assessing personal adjustment and attitudes. Used for personnel evaluation and employee selection in business and industry as well as clinical assessment.

Description: 50 item paper-pencil projective test of personal adjustment and attitudes. Fifty sentence stems are provided for the individual to complete. No separate manual or key. Self-administered. Suitable for group and individual use.

Untimed: Varies

Range: Adolescent, adult

Scoring: Examiner evaluated

Cost: 20 tests $18.15.

Publisher: Martin M. Bruce, Ph.D., Publishers

INTERPERSONAL STYLE INVENTORY—FORM E

Refer to page 185.

I.P.I. JOB TEST FIELD SERIES: COMPUTER PROGRAMMER

Refer to page 218.

THE LAKE ST. CLAIR INCIDENT

Albert A. Canfield

adult

Purpose: Examines individual and group decision-making processes. Used to improve decision-making, communication skills, and teamwork.

Description: Multiple item paper-pencil test requiring a team of three to seven individuals to work together to solve a hypothetical problem situation involving cold weather and cold water survival. Participants are provided with considerable information on the subject, maps, charts, drawings, and a list of 15 items available for them to use in their struggle for survival. The team must reach a decision on what action to take and the relative importance of the 15 items. Three different decision-making processes are required: independent, consultive, and participative/consensual. Scoring procedure uses Coast Guard officer decisions and rankings as "expert" opinions. Scores provided for three types of decision making processes: autocratic, consultive, and consensual. Data is produced on which to evaluate the decision-making process, individual and team behaviors, and on which to compare the performance of different teams. Two-color test booklet includes table for recording the results of up to 12 teams. The manual includes: situation analysis, Coast Guard opinions and rationales, information on hypothermia, and averages of scores from other teams. Self-administered and self-scored (teams must cooperate to get team performance scores). Intended for group use.

Untimed: 1½-2 hours

Range: Adult

Scoring: Self-scored

Cost: Demonstration kit (30 test booklets and manual) $45.95; specimen set (includes manual) $9.95.

Publisher: Humanics Media

LEADERSHIP APPRAISAL SURVEY (LAS)

Jay Hall

adult

Purpose: Evaluates a leader's behavior from the associates' point of view. Used for assessment and development purposes with non-management supervisory personnel, campus and community groups, volunteer organizations and administrative personnel.

Description: Multiple item paper-pencil inventory assessing a leader's impact on and stimulus value for the group from the associates' point of view. Identifies blindspots, pinpoints strengths and weaknesses, and confirms the way leadership practices come across to associates. Yields analyses of overall leadership style including four components of leadership: philosophy, planning, implementation, and evaluation. May be administered in conjunction with Styles of Leadership Survey (SLS) to provide a comparison of the associates' ratings with the leaders self-ratings on the SLS. Normative data provided. Examiner required. Suitable for group use.

Untimed: Varies

Range: Adult

Scoring: Examiner evaluated

Cost: Individual instrument $4.50.

Publisher: Teleometrics International

MANAGEMENT APPRAISAL SURVEY (MAS)

Refer to page 247.

MANAGEMENT BURNOUT SCALE

John W. Jones and Donald M. Moretti

adult

Purpose: Assesses burnout or work stress among managerial-level employees

Description: Multiple item paper-pencil test, self-administered to individuals or groups. Assesses burnout or work stress through four types of factors: Cognitive Reactions, Affective Reactions, Behavioral Reactions, Psychophysiological Reactions.

Untimed: 10 minutes

Range: Adult

Scoring: Computer or hand-scored

Cost: $10/package of 25 (includes interpretation manual and validation studies); $5 specimen set.

Publisher: London House Press

MANAGEMENT OF MOTIVES INDEX (MMI)

Refer to page 249.

MANAGEMENT RELATIONS SURVEY (MRS)

Refer to page 248.

MANAGEMENT TRANSACTIONS AUDIT (MTA)

Refer to page 249.

MEEKER BEHAVIOR CORRELATES FOR MANAGEMENT MATCHING OF TEAMS

adult

Purpose: Assesses the abilities and attitudes of current and prospective employees. Used for employee selection and placement.

Description: Multiple item self-report paper-pencil rating scale consisting of a three-way evaluation survey to be completed by supervisors, personnel directors, and prospective employees. Assesses major dimensions of intellectual abilities found to be correlates of personality characteristics. Identifies team patterns. Self-administered. Suitable for group use.

Untimed: 20 minutes

Range: Adult

Scoring: Examiner evaluated

Cost: 10 survey forms $20.00.

Publisher: SOI Institute

MEETING EFFECTIVENESS INVENTORY

Refer to page 250.

THE MINER SENTENCE COMPLETION SCALE: FORM H

John B. Miner

adult

Purpose: Measures an individual's hierarchic (bureaucratic) motivation. Used for employee counseling and development and organizational assessment.

Description: Multiple item paper-pencil free-response or multiple-choice sentence completion test measuring an individual's motivation in terms of motivational patterns which fit the hierarchic (bureaucratic) organizational form. Both forms (free-response version or multiple choice version offering six alternatives for each stem) measure the following subscales: authority figures, competitive games, competitive situations, assertive role, imposing wishes, standing out from the group, and routine administrative functions. The basic scoring guide (for use with the free response version) discusses: categorizing the responses, the subscales, supervisory jobs, total scores, and sample scoring sheet. A supplementary scoring guide is available describing the scoring of the multiple-choice version and variations in scoring the free response version. Examiner required. Suitable for group use.

Untimed: Varies

Range: Adult

Scoring: Examiner evaluated

Cost: 50 scales (specify free response or multiple-choice version) $15.00; basic scoring guide (64 pages) $5.00; supplementary scoring guide (15 pages) $2.50.

Publisher: Organizational Measurement Systems Press

THE MINER SENTENCE COMPLETION SCALE: FORM P

John B. Miner

adult

Purpose: Measures an individual's professional (specialized) motivation. Use for employee counseling and development and organizational assessment.

Description: Multiple item paper-pencil free-response sentence completion test measuring an individual's motivation in terms of motivational patterns which fit the professional (specialized) organizational form. Measures the following subscales: acquiring knowledge, independent action, accepting status, providing help, and professional commitment. Each test item consists of a sentence stem which the individuals complete in their own words. The scoring guide discusses: categorizing the responses, the subscales, actual scoring, reliability, normative data, use of form P, and bibliographic notes. Examiner required. Suitable for group use.

Untimed: Varies

Range: Adult

Scoring: Examiner evaluated

Cost: 50 scales $15.00; scoring guide (49 pages) $5.00.

Publisher: Organizational Measurement Systems Press

MY VOCATIONAL SITUATION

John L. Holland, Denise Daiger and Paul G. Power

adult

Purpose: Assesses the problems which may be troubling an individual seeking help with career decisions. Used in career counseling and guidance.

Description: Two-page multiple item paper-pencil questionnaire determining which of three possible difficulties may be troubling an individual in need of career counseling: lack of vocational identity, lack of information or training, and/or environmental or personal barriers. The questionnaire is completed by the individual just prior to the counseling interview, and may be tabulated by the counselor at a glance. Responses may offer clues for the interview itself and treatments relevant to each individual's need. The manual discusses development of the diagnostic scheme and reports statistical properties of the three variables. Examiner required. Suitable for group use.

Untimed: 5-10 minutes

Range: Adult

Scoring: Examiner evaluated

Cost: 25 questionnaires $4.85; specimen kit (includes manual and sample questionnaire) $1.25.

Publisher: Consulting Psychologists Press, Inc.

OBSERVATIONAL ASSESSMENTS OF TEMPERAMENT

Melany E. Baehr

adult

Purpose: Measures an individual's insight into own behavior and representation to others. Used for career counseling and guidance. Predictive of performance in higher-level specialized and managerial positions.

Description: Paper-pencil test to assess three behavior factors which have been shown to be the most effective in predicting significant aspects of performance in higher-level positions. Behavioral factors measured are reserved/cautious vs. extroversive/impulsive, emotionally controlled vs. emotionally responsive, dependent/group oriented vs. self-reliant/individually oriented. Self-administered.

Timed/Untimed: 10 minutes

Range: Adult

Scoring: Computer or hand-scoring

Cost: $13.75/package of 25.

Publisher: London House Press

OCCUPATIONAL ENVIRONMENT SCALES: FORM E-2

Samuel H. Osipow and Arnold R. Spokane

adult

Purpose: Measures different kinds of stresses people experience in their work, regardless of occupational field or level of employment. Used to redesign jobs to reduce stress and to plan counseling programs aimed at reducing on-the-job stress.

Description: 60 item paper-pencil inventory assessing six aspects of work environment related to role-related stress that workers often encounter in their work environments: responsibility for others, role ambiguity, role insufficiency, role overload, boundary roles, and stresses induced by physical environment. Test items consist of statements about work-related stress. Individuals rate each statement on a five-point scale from one (rarely or never) to five (most of the time) to indicate the degree to which each statement applies to their own work environment.

Scores are yielded for each of the six scales (10 items per scale). The manual includes: the theoretical basis for the scales, information on reliability and validity, normative data procedures for scoring and interpretation, and potential applications. May be administered in conjunction with the Personal Strain Questionnaire and the Personal Resources Questionnaire for a more complete assessment of work environment and stress (all three tests share a common manual and profile form). Self-administered. Suitable for group use.

Untimed: Varies

Range: Adult

Scoring: Examiner evaluated

Cost: 10 inventories $4.00; manual $10.00; 10 profiles $3.00; 10 interpretive flyers $2.00.

Publisher: Marathon Consulting and Press

OCCUPATIONAL PERSONALITY QUESTIONNAIRES (OPQ)

Saville & Holdsworth Ltd.

adult

Purpose: Measures personality and motivational factors which are critical to a person's job success. Used with managerial, graduate, and professional groups for purposes of selection, career development, counseling, and placement.

Description: 50-400 item paper-pencil or computer-administered questionnaire assessing personality characteristics important to future job success. Available in several forms: short forms measuring five factors, nine and seventeen factors, and long forms measuring 30 factors. Personality factors measured on all forms are arranged in the following three domains: relating to people (influence, affiliation, empathy), ideas and thinking (fields of use, styles of thinking, methods of evaluation), and feelings (anxieties, emotional control, energies). Paper-pencil versions may be scored with a hand-key and interpreted immediately by trained personnel. Two training courses for examiners are offered: one for individuals inexperienced in the use of personality questionnaires and a second for experienced individuals. Examiner required. Suitable for group use.
BRITISH PUBLISHER

Timed: Varies

Range: Adult

Scoring: Examiner evaluated; computer scoring available

Cost: Contact publisher for information concerning sponsorship, training courses, and availability and cost of materials.

Publisher: Saville & Holdsworth Ltd.

THE ORGANIZATIONAL CLIMATE INDEX (OCI)

George Stern and associates

adult

Purpose: Measures the psychological climate of institutionalized work settings in terms of the need-press paradigm of human behavior as conceptualized by Henry Murray. Used in schools and colleges, industrial settings, and in conjunction with Peace Corps training programs for employee survey and research purposes.

Description: 300 item (long form) or 80 item (short form) paper-pencil true-false inventory assessing institutional work environments along 30 basic press scales which reflect the 30 basic need scales established on the Stern Activities Index (AI). Both forms provide scores for six first order dimensions and two second order dimensions. Slightly different factor structures have been developed for school and college work environments. Analysis of school work environments yields first order scores for intellectual climate, achievement standards, personal dignity, organizational effectiveness, orderliness, and impulse control; and second order scores for development and task effectiveness. Analysis of college work environments yields first order scores for achievement standards, intellectual climate, practicalness, supportiveness, orderliness, and impulse control; and second order scores for development and control. Factor structures, reliabilities, and norms have also been established for industrial, school district, and Peace Corps settings. Evidence for reliability and validity are presented in the technical manual. Self-administered. Suitable for group use.

Untimed: Long form—40 minutes; short form—20 minutes

Range: Employees in institutionalized work settings

Scoring: Examiner evaluated; computer scoring available

Cost: Test booklet $.50; answer sheet $.10; profile form $.10; technical manual $7.50; prices for computer scoring and analysis are available on request.

Publisher: Evaluation Research Associates

PAPI SYSTEM

M.M. Kostick

adult

Purpose: Measures employees' work preferences, assesses behavioral job requirements as seen from several perspectives, and evaluates workers' self-images. Explores areas which managers need to know about in order to motivate, develop, and manage others more effectively. Used to establish in-service training objectives.

Description: Seven multiple item paper-pencil inventories assisting in the development and management of staff. Inventories include: PA Preference Inventory (90 items measuring work preferences), three questionnaires rating behavioral job requirements from three perspectives (incumbent's view, supervisor's view, and subordinate's view), an ideal job requirements questionnaire, and two personal image questionnaires ("how I see you," and "how I see myself"). Employees complete one or more of the questionnaires depending upon the objectives to be reached. Responses may be scored manually without being sent away for specialist interpretation. Computerized scoring for norm bulding is also available. Individuals can be trained to interpret the PAPI System questionnaires during a short intensive training program. Personnel staff and selected managers are trained in the use of the system by experienced consultants. Those companies without the facilities or personnel to use the system for themselves can be serviced by PA Management Consultant Staff or its distributors. Other consultants can be trained and licensed to use the system with their own clients. Licensing with PA Consulting, Inc. or its distributors is required for purchase of all instruments in the system. Examiner required. Suitable for group use. Available in Arabic, Danish, Dutch, French, German, Italian, Norwegian, Portugese, Spanish, and Swedish.

Untimed: 5-15 minutes per questionnaire

Range: Adult

Scoring: Examiner evaluated; computer scoring available

Cost: PA license for organizations $4,000.00; PA license for consultants $2,000.00; see individual listings for prices of components.

Publisher: PA Consulting Services, Inc.

PAPI SYSTEM: HOW I SEE MYSELF

M.M. Kostick

adult

Purpose: Measures an employee's self-image in terms of work-related needs and roles. Used to establish in-service training objectives.

Description: 20 item paper-pencil rating scale assessing an individual's work-related self-image along with the following subscales: work direction, work style, activity, leadership, followership, social nature, and temperament. Test items consist of statements about needs (motivations) and roles (behavior). Individuals indicate the strength of the needs and the ease of playing the roles by rating each item on a ten-point scale from 0 (exceptionally low) to nine (exceptionally high). Subscales correlate directly with those of the PA Preference Inventory and the other components of the PAPI System. May be administered separately or in conjunction with other PAPI System components. Available only to organizations and consultants licensed with PA Consulting Services, Inc. or its distributors. Examiner required. Suitable for group use. Available in Arabic, Danish, Dutch, French, German, Italian, Norwegian, Portugese, Spanish, and Swedish.

Untimed: 5 minutes

Range: Adult

Scoring: Examiner evaluated

Cost: 100 one-page questionnaires $120.00.

Publisher: PA Consulting Services, Inc.

PAPI SYSTEM: HOW I SEE YOU

M.M. Kostick

adult

Purpose: Measures an individual's perception of a fellow employee in terms of work-related needs and roles. Used to establish in-service training objectives.

Description: 20 item paper-pencil rating scale assessing an individual's perception of a co-worker along the following subscales: work direction, work style, activity, leadership, followership, social nature, and temperament. Test items consist of statements about needs (motivations) and roles (behavior). Individuals evaluate their co-workers (peer, subordinate, or supervisor) by rating each item on a ten-point scale from 0 (exceptionally low) to nine (exceptionally high) to indicate the strength of the needs and the ease of playing the roles. Subscales correlate directly with those of the PA Preference Inventory and the other components of the PAPI System. May be administered independently or in conjunction with other PAPI System components. Available only to organizations and consultants licensed with PA Consulting Services, Inc. or its distributors. Examiner required. Suitable for group use. Available in Arabic, Danish, Dutch, French, German, Italian, Norwegian, Portugese, Spanish, and Swedish.

Untimed: 5 minutes

Range: Adult

Scoring: Examiner evaluated

Cost: 100 one-page questionnaires $120.00.

Publisher: PA Consulting Services, Inc.

PAPI SYSTEM: PA PREFERENCE INVENTORY

M.M. Kostick

adult

Purpose: Assesses an individual's work preferences in terms of needs and behavioral roles. Used to establish in-service training objectives.

Description: 90 item paper-pencil two-choice test measuring an individual's needs and preferred roles along the following subscales: work direction, work style, activity, leadership, followership, social nature, and temperament. Each item consists of a pair of simple descriptive statements. The individual selects the one statement from each pair which most accurately describes himself. Responses are tallied according to subscales and plotted on a circular profile chart. Subscales correlate directly to those of the other PAPI System components. May be administered independently or in conjunction with other components of the PAPI System. Available only to organizations and consultants licensed with PA Consulting Services, Inc. or its distributors. Examiner required. Suitable for group use. Available in Arabic, Danish, Dutch, French, German, Italian, Norwegian, Portugese, Spanish, and Swedish.

Untimed: 15 minutes

Range: Adult

Scoring: Examiner evaluated

Cost: Reusable test booklet $50.00; non-reusable test booklet $12.00; 100 answer sheets $192.00; 100 profile sheets $60.00.

Publisher: PA Consulting Services, Inc.

PAPI SYSTEM: RATING OF JOB REQUIREMENTS—FORM A REVISED

M.M. Kostick

adult

Purpose: Evaluates the requirements of a particular job from the incumbent job holder's point of view. Used to establish in-service training objectives.

Description: 20 item paper-pencil multiple-choice questionnaire assessing the manner in which an incumbent job holder would describe the requirements of his job in terms of work-related needs (motivations) and behavioral roles. Measures the following subscales: work direction, work style, activity, leadership, followership, social nature, and temperament. Each item consists of nine statements describing possible job requirements (the statements for each item represent a continuum between two bipolar extremes, such as adaptable/routine-oriented and leadership/subordinate). Incumbents circle the number of the statement which best describes the requirements of their job and cross out the numbers of any statements which are definitely uncharacteristic. Subscales correlate directly with those of other PAPI System components. May be administered independently or in conjunction with other PAPI System components. Available only to organizations and consultants licensed by PA Consulting Services, Inc. or its distributors. Examiner required. Suitable for group use. Available in Arabic, Danish, Dutch, French, German, Italian, Norwegian, Portugese, Spanish, and Swedish.

Untimed: 15 minutes

Range: Adult

Scoring: Examiner evaluated

Cost: 100 questionnaires $132.00.

Publisher: PA Consulting Services, Inc.

PAPI SYSTEM: RATING OF JOB REQUIREMENTS—FORM B REVISED

M.M. Kostick

adult

Purpose: Evaluates the requirements for a subordinate's job from the supervisor's point of view. Used to establish in-service training objectives.

Description: 20 item paper-pencil multiple-choice questionnaire assessing the manner in which a supervisor would describe the job requirements of a subordinate in terms of work-related needs (motivations) and behavioral roles. Measures the following subscales: work direction, work style, activity, leadership, followership, social nature, and temperament. Each item consists of nine statements describing possible job requirements (the statements for each item represents a continuum between two bipolar extremes, such as adaptable/routine-oriented and leadership/subordinate). The supervisor circles the number of the statement which best describes the requirements of the subordinate's job and crosses out the numbers of any statements which are definitely uncharacteristic. Subscales correlate directly with those of the other PAPI System components. May be administered independently or in conjunction with other components of the PAPI System. Available only to organizations and consultants licensed with PA Consulting Services, Inc. or its distributors. Examiner required. Suitable for group use. Available in Arabic, Danish, Dutch, French, German, Italian, Norwegian, Portugese, Spanish, and Swedish.

Untimed: 15 minutes

Range: Adult

Scoring: Examiner evaluated

Cost: 100 questionnaires $132.00.

Publisher: PA Consulting Services, Inc.

PAPI SYSTEM: RATING OF JOB REQUIREMENTS—FORM C REVISED

M.M. Kostick

adult

Purpose: Evaluates the requirements for a boss' job from the subordinate's point of view. Used to establish in-service training objectives.

Description: 20 item paper-pencil multiple-choice questionnaire assessing the manner in which a subordinate would describe the job requirements of supervisor in terms of work-related needs (motivations) and behavioral roles. Measures the following subscales: work direction, work style, activity, leadership, followership, social nature, and temperament. Each item consists of nine statements describing possible job requirements (the statements for each item represent a continuum between two bipolar extremes, such as adaptable/routine-oriented and leadership/subordinate). The subordinate circles the number of the statement which best describes the requirements of the supervisor's job and crosses out the numbers of any statements which are definitely not characteristic. Subscales correlate directly with those of the other PAPI System components. May be administered separately or in conjunction with other components of the PAPI System. Available only to organizations and consultants licensed with PA Consulting Services, Inc. or its distributors. Examiner required. Suitable for group use. Available in Arabic, Danish, Dutch, French, German, Italian, Norwegian, Portugese, Spanish, and Swedish.

Untimed: 15 minutes

Range: Adult

Scoring: Examiner evaluated

Cost: 100 questionnaires $132.00.

Publisher: PA Consulting Services, Inc.

PAPI SYSTEM: RATING OF JOB REQUIREMENTS—FORM D REVISED

M.M. Kostick

adult

Purpose: Evaluates the job requirements an individual would select to describe the ideal job. Used to establish in-service training objectives.

Description: 20 item paper-pencil multiple-choice questionnaire assessing the manner in which an individual would describe the requirements for an ideal job in terms of work-related needs (motivations) and behavioral roles. Measures the following subscales: work direction, work style, activity, leadership, followership, social nature, and temperament. Each item consists of nine statements describing possible job requirements (the statements for each item represent a continuum between two bipolar extremes, such as adaptable/routine-oriented and leadership/subordinate). The individual circles the number of the statement which best describes the requirements of an ideal job and crosses out the numbers of any statements which are definitely undesirable or uncharacteristic. Subscales correlate directly with those of the other PAPI System components. May be administered independently or in conjunction with other components of the PAPI System. Available only to organizations and consultants licensed with PA Consulting Services, Inc. or its distributors. Examiner required. Suitable for group use. Available in Arabic, Danish, Dutch, French, German, Italian, Norwegian, Portugese, Spanish, and Swedish.

Untimed: 15 minutes

Range: Adult

Scoring: Examiner evaluated

Cost: 100 questionnaires $132.00.

Publisher: PA Consulting Services, Inc.

PERSONAL BACKGROUND INVENTORY

Refer to page 258.

PERSONAL PROBLEM CHECKLIST

Refer to page 46.

PERSONAL REACTION INDEX (PRI)

Jay Hall

adult

Purpose: Measures the degree to which employees feel they are encouraged to participate in the decision-making process. Used in programs evaluating job satisfaction at all occupational levels and in management training and development programs.

Description: Multiple item paper-pencil inventory assessing the attitudes of subordinates toward the decision structure which governs their work. Measures the amount of influence subordinates feel they have in making work-related decisions and their consequent satisfaction with and commitment to those decisions. The resulting information provides information concerning the manager's use or lack of use of the participative ethic with subordinates. Normative data provided. Examiner required. Suitable for group use.

Untimed: Varies

Range: Adult

Scoring: Examiner evaluated

Cost: Individual survey $2.00.

Publisher: Teleometrics International

PERSONAL RELATIONS SURVEY (PRS)

Refer to page 252.

PERSONAL RESOURCES QUESTIONNAIRE: FORM E-2

Samuel H. Osipow and Arnold R. Spokane

adult

Purpose: Measures the extent to which resources are available to people to counteract the effects of occupational stress. Used in conjunction with counseling programs aimed at reducing occupational stress.

Description: 40 item paper-pencil inventory assessing the potential individuals have for dealing effectively with work stress. Measures the following four dimensions: recreation, self-care, rational/coping behaviors, and social support system. Scores are yielded for each of the four scales (10 items per scale). Test items describe activities or feelings which help to relieve stress. Individuals rate each statement on a scale from one ("rarely or never") to five ("most of the time") to indicate the degree to which each item describes their own activities or feelings. Scores are yielded for each of the four scales (10 items per scale). The manual includes: the theoretical basis for the scales, information on reliability and validity, normative data procedures for administration and scoring, and potential applications. May be administered in conjunction with the Occupational Environment Scales and the Personal Strain Questionnaire for a more complete assessment of work environment and stress (all three tests share a common manual and profile form). Self-administered. Suitable for group use.

Untimed: Varies

Range: Adult

Scoring: Examiner evaluated

Cost: 10 inventories $4.00; manual $10.00; 10 profiles $3.00; 10 interpretive flyers $2.00.

Publisher: Marathon Consulting and Press

PERSONAL STRAIN QUESTIONNAIRE: FORM E-2

Samuel H. Osipow and Arnold R. Spokane

adult

Purpose: Measures different kinds of strains people experience in their lives which may be the result of occupational stress. Used in conjunction with counseling programs aimed at reducing occupational stress.

Description: 40 item paper-pencil inventory assessing four dimensions of occupational stress: vocational (productivity and work attitudes), psychological (adjustment and/or mood disruptions), interpersonal (disruption in interpersonal relations), and physical (self-care habits and health). Test items describe behaviors and attitudes which may be symptomatic of personal stress. Individuals rate each statement on a five-point scale from one ("rarely or never") to five ("most of the time") to indicate the degree to which each item describes their own behaviors or attitudes. Scores are yielded for each of the four scales (10 items per scale). The manual includes: the theoretical basis for the scales, information on reliability and validity, normative data procedures for scoring and interpretation, and potential applications. May be administered in conjunction with the Personal Resources Questionnaire and the Occupational Environment Scales for a more complete assessment of work environment and stress (all three tests share a common manual and profile form). Self-administered. Suitable for group use.

Untimed: Varies

Range: Adult

Scoring: Examiner evaluated

Cost: 10 inventories $4.00; manual $10.00; 10 profiles $3.00; 10 interpretive flyers $2.00.

Publisher: Marathon Consulting and Press

POWER MANAGEMENT PROFILE (PMP)

Refer to page 253.

PROCESS DIAGNOSTIC (PD)

Jay Hall

adult

Purpose: Assesses interpersonal group dynamics. Used in training programs aimed at raising a group's awareness of its own internal processes.

Description: Multiple item paper-pencil inventory assessing the internal processes of a group. A matrix format and scoring wheel are used to identify behavioral cluster scores for individual group members. Group members receive individual assessments of the dynamics underlying their behavior and of their impact on the group. Diagnostic information is also provided concerning the group's climate resulting from the problem solving, "flight," or "fight" behaviors of its members. Requires several hours to initiate in-depth, free-wheeling interchange. Trained process specialists or outside consultants are not required. Examiner required. Suitable for group use.

Untimed: Several hours

Range: Adult

Scoring: Examiner evaluated

Cost: Individual instrument $4.50.

Publisher: Teleometrics International

PRODUCTIVITY ENVIRONMENTAL PREFERENCE SURVEY (PEPS)

Rita Dunn, Kenneth Dunn and Gary E. Price

adult

Purpose: Assesses the manner in which adults prefer to function, learn, concentrate, and perform in their occupational or educational activities. Used for employee placement and counseling and office design and lay-out.

Description: 100 item paper-pencil Likert scale inventory measuring the following environmental factors related to educational or occupational activities: immediate environment (sound, temperature, light and design), emotionality (motivation, responsibility, persistence and structure), sociological needs (self-oriented, peer-oriented, authority-oriented and combined ways), and physical needs (perceptual preferences, time of day, intake and mobility). Test items consist of statements about ways people like to work or study. Respondents are asked to indicate whether they agree or disagree with each statement. Computerized results are available in three forms: individual profile (raw scores for each of the 20 areas, standard scores, and a plot for each score in each area), group summary (identifies individuals with signifcantly high or low scores and groups individuals with similar preferences), and subscale summary. Results provide a basis for supervisor- or instructor-individual interaction in the ways that permit each person to concentrate best and allow instructors or supervisors to group individuals or design work settings based on similarity among productivity elements. May be self-administered. Suitable for group use.

Untimed: 20-30 minutes

Range: Adult

Scoring: Computer scored

Cost: Specimen set (manual and answer sheet) $11.00.

Publisher: Price Systems, Inc.

PROGRAM FOR ASSESSING YOUTH EMPLOYMENT SKILLS (PAYES)

Refer to page 202.

RAHIM ORGANIZATIONAL CONFLICT INVENTORIES: EXPERIMENTAL EDITION (ROCI)

Afzalur Rahim

adult

Purpose: Measures conflict experienced within an organization and assesses varying styles of handling conflict.

Description: 105 item paper-pencil self-report inventory assessing types of conflict (part I) and varying styles of handling conflict (part II) found within an organization. Part I contains 21 items and assesses three dimensions or types of organizational conflict: intrapersonal, intergroup, and intragroup. Part II consists of three 28-item forms assessing conflict with one's boss (form A), with one's subordinates (form B), and with one's peers (form C) and identifies five styles of handling interpersonal conflict: integrating, obliging, dominating, avoiding, and compromising. Both parts use a five-point Likert scale. Limited norms provided for college students and managerial groups categorized by organizational level, functional area, and educational level. Examiner required. Suitable for group use.

Untimed: 45 minutes

Range: Adult

Scoring: Examiner evaluated

Cost: 25 ROCI-I inventories $18.00; 50 ROCI-I answer sheets $20.50; 25 ROCI-II inventories (includes 25 each of forms A, B, and C) $10.00; 50 ROCI-II answer sheets $20.50; manual $9.50; specimen set $10.50.

Publisher: Consulting Psychologists Press, Inc.

SALES RELATIONS SURVEY (SRS)

Refer to page 260.

SALES TRANSACTION AUDIT (STA)

Refer to page 260.

STAFF BURNOUT SCALE FOR HEALTH PROFESSIONALS

John W. Jones

adult

Purpose: Assesses burnout or work stress among health care professionals.

Description: Multiple item paper-pencil test self-administered to individuals or groups. Assesses burnout or work stress through four types of factors: Cognitive Reactions, Affective Reactions, Behavioral Reactions, Psychophysiological Reactions.

Untimed: 10 minutes

Range: Adult

Scoring: Computer or hand-scored

Cost: $10/package of 25 (includes intepretation manual and validation studies); $5 specimen set.

Publisher: London House Press

STAFF BURNOUT SCALE FOR POLICE AND SECURITY PERSONNEL

John W. Jones

adult

Purpose: Assesses burnout or work stress among police and security personnel.

Description: Multiple-item paper-pencil test self-administered to individuals or groups. Assesses burnout or work stress through four types of factors: Cognitive Reactions, Affective Reactions, Behavioral Reactions, Psychophysiological Reactions.

Untimed: 10 minutes

Range: Adult

Scoring: Computer or hand-scored

Cost: $10/package of 25 (includes interpretation manual and validation studies); $5 specimen set.

Publisher: London House Press

STRESS EVALUATION INVENTORY (SEI)

Raymond W. Kulhavy and Samuel E. Krug

adult

Purpose: Evaluates the stress that individuals are experiencing in their lives, identifies probable sources of stress, and suggests methods of controlling or preventing stress. Used in conjunction with stress management programs in business, health care, education, government, and private counseling settings.

Description: 30 item paper-pencil multiple-choice inventory administered in conjunction with either form A or form B of the 16 Personality Factor Questionnaire as a part of the Individualized Stress Management Program. The SEI provides indices of perceived stress in three areas of an individual's life (job, family, and personal), while diagnostic data from the 16 PF yields personality and lifestyle information which is used to identify sources of the individual's stress. Each individual receives a book-length, computer-based report which includes: indices of job, family, and personal stress, as well as overall "distress" level; a discussion of stress and its symptoms; and a variety of work sheets, exercises, and educational materials which address the types of stress reported by each individual. The first three chapters of this report are the same for all individuals; chapters 4-10 vary according to individual needs.

A four-page computer-based professional summary includes: scores on each of the 16 primary factors, seven broad influence patterns, and two validity scales of the 16 PF; a profile of the stresses reported by the individual; and a brief explanation of the factors that determined which chapters and exercises would be included in the individual's report. A group profile summary is also provided for groups of seven or more. Materials for the Individualized Stress Management Program (including the SEI) are available only to qualified program coordinators. Attendance at one of IPAT's training seminars is the preferred method of qualification. These seminars are offered free of charge;

participants must pay for their own training materials. Supplementary materials available to program coordinators include: training manual, prepared presentations (slides, overhead transparencies, and audio tapes), demonstration workbook, and brochures. Examiner required. Suitable for group use.

Untimed: Varies

Range: Adult

Scoring: Computer scored

Cost: Assessment materials, computer scoring, and preparation of the individual's report $30.00 per person; professional summary $4.00 per person; for further cost information contact the publisher's Individualized Stress Management Program Coordinator.

Publisher: Institute for Personality and Ability Testing, Inc.

STYLES OF LEADERSHIP SURVEY (SLS)

Jay Hall and Martha S. Williams

adult

Purpose: Assesses leadership styles in terms of "concern for people" and "concern for purpose." Used with non-management supervisory personnel, campus and community groups, volunteer organizations and administrative personnel.

Description: Multiple item paper-pencil self-report inventory assessing leadership behavior in terms of the Blake-Mouton model of management behavior. The Blake-Mouton managerial grid is an extension of Likert's production-morale theory and measures two dimensions of leadership behavior: concerns for people and concerns for purpose. Yields analyses of overall leadership style including four components of leadership: philosophy, planning, implementation and evaluation. Normative data provided. May be administered in conjunction with the Leadership Appraisal Survey for a more complete assessment of leadership styles and effectiveness. Self-administered. Suitable for group use.

Untimed: Varies

Range: Adult

Scoring: Self-scored

Cost: Individual instrument $4.50.

Publisher: Teleometrics International

SUPERVISORY INVENTORY ON COMMUNICATION (SIC)

Donald L. Kirkpatrick

adult

Purpose: Measures knowledge of proper supervisory use of communication procedures within an organization. Used in conjunction with training programs aimed at improving the communication effectiveness of supervisors.

Description: 80 item paper-pencil two-choice test assessing knowledge and understanding of communication philosophy, principles, and methods for supervisors. Each test item describes an action or belief concerned with on-the-job communication. Individuals indicate whether they agree or disagree with each statement. Test results identify topics which should be emphasized in training programs, serve as a tool for conference discussions, measure the effectiveness of training programs, provide information for on-the-job coaching, and assist in the selection of supervisory personnel. The manual includes: a discussion of the inventory's development, normative data, research data, and interpretive guidelines. The answer booklet includes the rationale behind all correct answers. Self-administered and self-scored. Suitable for group use.

Untimed: 20 minutes

Range: Adult

Scoring: Self-scored

Cost: 20 tests and answer booklets $20.00; instructor's manual $1.00; review set (test, answer booklet, manual, and leader's guide) $3.00.

Publisher: Donald L. Kirkpatrick

SUPERVISORY INVENTORY ON HUMAN RELATIONS (SIHR)

Donald L. Kirkpatrick

adult

Purpose: Measures knowledge of basic human relations principles involved in effective supervisory job performance. Used in conjunction with management training programs aimed at increasing knowledge and improving attitudes in dealing with people.

Description: 80 item paper-pencil two-choice test measuring the extent to which supevisors understand and accept the principles, facts, and techniques of human relations in management. Test items cover human relations issues in the following areas: the supervisor's role in management, understanding and motivating employees, developing positive employee attitudes, problem solving techniques, and principles of learning and training. Individuals indicate whether they agree or disagree with the statement about beliefs or behaviors presented in each test item. Answer booklet provides rationale for each correct answer. Test results identify topics which should be emphasized in training programs, serve as a tool for conference discussions, measure the effectiveness of training programs, provide information for on-the-job coaching, and assist in the selection of supervisory personnel. The manual includes norms for foremen and plant supervisors, office supervisors, and middle and top management; a discussion of validity and reliability, interpretive guidelines, and an answer key providing the rationale behind all correct answers. Self-administered and self-scored. Suitable for group use.

Untimed: 15 minutes

Range: Adult

Scoring: Self-scored

Cost: 20 tests and answer booklets $20.00; instructor's manual $1.00; review set (test, answer booklet, and manual) $2.00.

Publisher: Donald L. Kirkpatrick

SUPERVISORY PRACTICES INVENTORY (SPI)

Refer to page 254.

SURVEY OF ORGANIZATIONS (SOO)

Rensis Likert Associates, Inc.

adult

Purpose: Measures perceptions of organizational behavior and evaluates employee attitudes and morale. Used for human resource assessments, survey-guided organizational development, and organizational research.

Description: 125 item paper-pencil questionnaire measuring certain critical dimensions of organizational climate, supervisory leadership, peer relationships, group functioning, job characteristics, and satisfaction. Subscales include: guidance system, job design, shape, coordination moderators, supervisory leadership, perceived causes of supervisory leadership, peer relationships, and end results. Scores are provided for subscales, 3-5 factors contained within each subscale, and individual items. Completed questionnaires are strictly confidential. Responses are summarized in statistical form by group.

Scoring service available at two levels: A and B. Level A includes machine-scorable questionnaires, advice on survey coding and administration, scanning of questionnaires, and the following analytical printouts: grand means printout providing an overall tabulation for the entire survey population and workgroup printouts (a work group includes all those who report to the same supervisor).

Optional printouts available with Level A service include: pyramid printouts for manager's with subordinates who are supervisors themselves (summarizes the results from all respondents directly below that manager), hierarchical level printouts summarizing the results of all respondents at the same level in the organization, and confidential feedback packages providing the supervisor of each work group with a sealed confidential package containing that group's printout and a supervisor's handbook for interpretation. Level B provides everything noted in level A, including all options, as well as a written narrative report which splits the organization's results into hierarchical levels. This organization-wide diagnosis identifies strengths and weaknesses at each level, evaluates similarities and differences between levels, and traces possible causes through the organization. Normative data is available by hierarchical level as a basis for comparison with other users. Internal norms may be created for comparison of groups within the organization. The format provides for the option of including up to 75 supplemental questions at no extra charge. Consulting services are available to assist organizations in the use of this instrument. The Small Business Assessment (SBA) is available for use with organizations of less than 100 employees. Examiner required. Intended for group use.

Untimed: Varies

Range: Adult

Scoring: Computer scored

Cost: 100 questionnaires with level A scoring service $1,500.00; 100 questionnaires with level B scoring service $1,500.00; contact publisher concerning quantity discounts.

Publisher: University Associates, Inc.

TEAM EFFECTIVENESS SURVEY (TES)

Jay Hall

adult

Purpose: Assesses team functioning and identifies individuals who are primarily responsible for the team's style of functioning. Used for employee training and development and discussion purposes.

Description: Multiple item paper-pencil inventory assessing team functioning on the exposure and feedback dimensions inherent in the Johari Window model of interpersonal relations. Each team member rates self and others on items related to both dimensions. The resulting individual and team profiles serve as immediate feedback to confirm or deny self-ratings and furnish an overview of team functioning. Defensive versus supportive climate scores are also obtained. Examiner required. Suitable for group use.

Untimed: Varies

Range: Adult

Scoring: Examiner evaluated

Cost: Individual instrument $4.50.

Publisher: Teleometrics International

TEMPERAMENT INVENTORY TESTS

Refer to page 27.

TIME PROBLEMS INVENTORY (TPRI)

Albert A. Canfield

adult

Purpose: Evaluates an individual's time use problems. Identifies personal and internal causes of time use problems. Used for group discussions and to assess organizational time use problems.

Description: Multiple item paper-pencil inventory measuring the comparative level of an individual's time use problems in four areas: priority setting, planning, task clarification, and self-discipline. Questions are largely work-related, representing time problems encountered in any organization, but scores may be related to time use problems in all aspects of daily living. Test booklets are self-scoring and self-profiling. Interpretation focuses on internal causes of time use problems and may be used to identify time use problems common to members of any organization. Scoring provides information for the discussion of internal and external factors that are related to ineffective time use. Self-administered. Suitable for group use.

Untimed: 30 minutes

Range: Adult

Scoring: Self-scored

Cost: Demonstration kit (30 test booklets and manual) $45.95; specimen set (includes manual) $9.95.

Publisher: Humanics Media

TIME USE ANALYSIS (TUA)

adult

Purpose: Evaluates a person's time use habits. Provides a basis for discussions of time quality versus time quantity.

Description: Multiple item paper-pencil test assessing how individuals feel about how their time is being spent in eight aspects of life: at work, asleep, on personal hygiene, taking care of personal/family business, in community and church activities, with family or home members, in education and development, and on recreational and hobby activities. Test booklets are self-scoring and self-profiling and contain a discussion of the implications of the results and the general findings. Produces an awareness of common areas in which most people express some level of dissatisfaction with their time use. Helps individuals differentiate between time efficiency and time effectiveness and stimulates concerns for improvement in both areas. Norms provided for comparing levels of dissatisfaction among groups of supervisors and managers. Self-administered. Suitable for group use.

Untimed: 20 minutes

Range: Adult

Scoring: Self-scored

Cost: Demonstration kit (30 test booklets and manual) $45.95; specimen set (includes manual) $9.95.

Publisher: Humanics Media

TLC—LEARNING STYLE INVENTORY

Refer to page 190.

TWELVE O'CLOCK HIGH

Refer to page 255.

WORK ASPECT PREFERENCE SCALE

R. Pryor

teen, adult gr. 10 and up

Purpose: Measures the qualities of work that individuals consider important to them. Used in career counseling, vocational rehabilitation, the study of personal and work values, and research on career development and worker satisfaction.

Description: 52 item paper-pencil inventory assessing an individual's work values along 13 scales: altruism, co-workers, creativity, detachment, independence, life style, management, money, physical activity, prestige, security, self development, and surroundings. Answer sheets are scorable by hand or machine. Examiner required. Suitable for group use. AUSTRALIAN PUBLISHER

Untimed: 10-20 minutes

Range: Grade 10-adult

Scoring: Hand key; machine scoring available

Cost: Contact publisher.

Publisher: The Australian Council for Educational Research Ltd.

WORK ATTITUDES QUESTIONNAIRE

M.S. Doty and N.E. Betz

adult

Purpose: Measures an individual's commitment to work and the degree to which such commitment is psychologically healthy or unhealthy. Used for research purposes and to identify "workaholics."

Description: 45 item paper-pencil questionnaire consisting of two scales: one assessing high versus low commitments to work (23 items) and the second assessing the degree to which work attitudes are psychologically healthy or unhealthy (22 items). Test items consist of statements regarding work or career orientation or the role which work plays in the larger scheme of life. Individuals rate each item on a five-point scale from one ("strongly disagree") to five ("strongly agree") to indicate the degree to which the statement expresses their personal beliefs. Results differentiate the "workaholic" or the Type A personality from the highly committed worker who, while strongly committed to and involved in his work, manages at the same time to lead a balanced psychologically healthy life. The manual includes: procedures for administration and scoring, interpretive guidelines, information on the development of the scales, data on reliability and validity, and normative data. Examiner required. Suitable for group use.

Untimed: Varies

Range: Adult

Scoring: Examiner evaluated

Cost: 25 questionnaires $5.00; manual $3.95.

Publisher: Marathon Consulting and Press

WORK MOTIVATION INVENTORY (WMI)

Jay Hall and Martha S. Williams

adult

Purpose: Assesses the work-related needs and motivations of both managers and subordinates. Used for employee training and development and as a basis for discussion.

Description: Multiple item paper-pencil self-report inventory assessing work-related needs actually experienced by an individual. Yields five scores which provide a personal motivational profile according to the five need systems established in Maslow's need-hierarchy concept. May be administered in conjunction with the Management of Motives Index (MMI) in two ways. When used as a subordinate instrument and compared to the manager's MMI profile, discrepancies are identified between what an employee feels is important and what the manager offers in the way of motivational support. When completed by the manager and the results compared with scores on the MMI, areas are indicated in which the manager's own needs may be influencing motivational methods used to meet the needs of others. Normative data provided. Examiner required. Suitable for group use.

Untimed: Varies

Range: Adult

Scoring: Examiner evaluated

Cost: Individual instrument $4.50.

Publisher: Teleometrics International

WORK VALUES INVENTORY

Refer to page 204.

Management and Supervision

INCENTIVES MANAGEMENT INDEX (IMI)

Refer to page 259.

THE LAKE ST. CLAIR INCIDENT

Refer to page 228.

MANAGEMENT APPRAISAL SURVEY (MAS)

Jay Hall, Jerry Harvey and Martha S. Williams

adult

Purpose: Assesses an individual's style of management from the subordinates' point of view. Used for management training and development and as a basis for discussion.

Description: Multiple item paper-pencil inventory assessing subordinates' perceptions of their manager's practices. Analysis is based on the Blake-Mouton managerial grid—a model of management behavior which is an extension of Likert's production-morale theory relating production concerns with people concerns. Provides a total score for each of the five management styles described by the model as well as scores for each style on four components: philosophy, planning, implementation, and evaluation. May be administered in conjunction with the Styles of Management Inventory to provide a comparison between subordinate ratings and manager self-ratings on the SMI. Normative data provided. Examiner required. Suitable for group use.

Untimed: Varies

Range: Adult

Scoring: Examiner evaluated

Cost: Individual instrument $4.50.

Publisher: Teleometrics International

MANAGEMENT INVENTORY ON LEADERSHIP AND MOTIVATION (MILM)

Refer to page 212.

MANAGEMENT INVENTORY ON MANAGING CHANGE (MIMC)

Donald L. Kirkpatrick

adult

Purpose: Measures the attitudes and knowledge of a manager in regard to managing change within an organization. Used in conjunction with training programs aimed at teaching managers how to deal with change. Used with all levels of management from first level supervisors and foremen to top executives.

Description: 65 item paper-pencil inventory measuring attitudes, knowledge, and opinions regarding principles and approaches for managing change. Items 1-50 are statements of beliefs or attitudes concerning organizational change and various ways of implementing such change. Individuals indicate for each of these items whether they agree or disagree with the statement. Items 51-60 are free-response questions asking for a list of reasons why people might accept or resist change. Items 61-65 are multiple-choice items asking for an assessment of a situation involving change within an organization. Objective scoring key allows for the fact that more than one answer may be "correct" for some of the questions. Answer booklet provides rationale for answers. Results of the test identify topics which should be emphasized in management training courses, serve as a tool for conference discussions, measure the effectiveness of training programs, provide information for on-the-job coaching, and assist in the selection and promotion of managers. Item content is intended to help managers understand their role in managing change, reasons why people resist change, reasons why people accept change, principles for effective management of change, and specific approaches for managing change in their department. Self-administered and self-scored. Suitable for group use.

Untimed: 20 minutes

Range: Adult

Scoring: Self-scored

Cost: 20 tests and answer booklets $20.00; instructor's manual $1.00; review set (test, answer book, and manual) $2.00.

Publisher: Donald L. Kirkpatrick

MANAGEMENT INVENTORY ON TIME MANAGEMENT (MITM)

Donald L. Kirkpatrick

adult

Purpose: Measures a manager's knowledge and attitudes regarding the effective management of time. Used in conjunction with training programs on time management.

Description: 60 item paper-pencil two-choice test assessing managers' knowledge of principles and practices concerning the effective management of time. Test items are statements about time use within an organization. Individuals indicate for each item whether they agree or disagree with the statement. Answer booklet includes rationale for all correct answers. Test results identify topics which should be emphasized in training programs, serve as a tool for conference discussions, measure the effectiveness of training programs, and provides information for on-the-job coaching. A list of books and films for use in time management training programs is also included. Self-administered and self-scoring. Suitable for group use.

Untimed: 15 minutes

Range: Adult

Scoring: Self-scoring

Cost: 20 tests and answer booklets $20.00; instructor's manual $1.00; review set (test, answer booklet, and manual) $2.00.

Publisher: Donald L. Kirkpatrick

MANAGEMENT RELATIONS SURVEY (MRS)

Jay Hall

adult

Purpose: Measures a manager's communications/employee relations skills from the subordinates' point of view. Used for employee training and development.

Description: Multiple item paper-pencil inventory assessing management/employee relations from the subordinates' point of view. Provides a manager with feedback from associates and subordinates and allows subordinates to examine their own practices with the manager. May be administered in conjunction with the Personnel Relations Survey for self-other comparisons of management communication skills and effectiveness. Normative data provided. Examiner required. Suitable for group use.

Untimed: Varies

Range: Adult

Scoring: Examiner evaluated

Cost: Individual instrument $4.50.

Publisher: Teleometrics International

MANAGEMENT OF MOTIVES INDEX (MMI)

Jay Hall

adult

Purpose: Assesses a manager's approach to employee motivation in terms of Maslow's need-hierarchy concept. Used for management training and development and as a basis for discussion.

Description: Multiple item paper-pencil self-report inventory assessing a manager's theories of what stimulates subordinates, assumptions about why people work, and the approaches to motivation which result from those assumptions. Yields five scores which indicate the relative emphasis that managers place on each of Maslow's five need systems to manage others. Normative profiles provide a basis for comparing what managers emphasize with what subordinates say they need. May be administered in conjunction with the Work Motivation Inventory of subordinates for a more complete assessment of managerial motivational techniques. Self-administered. Suitable for group use.

Untimed: Varies

Range: Managerial personnel

Scoring: Self-scored

Cost: Individual instrument $4.50.

Publisher: Telometrics International

MANAGEMENT TRANSACTIONS AUDIT (MTA)

Jay Hall and C. Leo Griffith

adult

Purpose: Assesses management communications skills in terms of Eric Berne's model of transactional analysis. Used for employee training and development and as a basis for discussion.

Description: Multiple item paper-pencil self-report inventory measuring the size of the parent, adult, and child (the three positions from which individuals can communicate according to the model of transactional analysis) in a manager's transactions with subordinates, colleagues, and superiors. Also provides scores for transaction contamination, crossed and complementary transactions, and constructive and disruptive tension. Normative data provided. Examiner required. Suitable for group use.

Untimed: Varies

Range: Managerial personnel

Scoring: Examiner evaluated

Cost: Individual instrument $4.50.

Publisher: Teleometrics International

MANAGERIAL AND PROFESSIONAL JOB FUNCTIONS INVENTORY (MP-JFI)

Melany E. Baehr, Wallace G. Lonergan and Bruce A. Hunt

adult

Purpose: Assesses the work elements involved in the performance of higher-level managerial and professional positions. Used to clarify job positions and organizational structure, to diagnose individual and group training needs, and to classify higher-level positions.

Description: Multiple item paper-pencil inventory assessing the relative importance of various job functions in the following 16 categories: setting organizational objectives, financial planning and review, improving work procedures and practices, inter-departmental coordination, developing technical ideas, judgment and decision-making, developing teamwork, coping with difficulties and emergencies, promoting safety attitudes and practices, communications, developing employee potential, supervisory practices, self-development and improvement, personnel practices, promoting community-organization relations, and handling outside contacts. Items are related by incumbent employees for each particular position. May also be used to have incumbents rate their own relative abilities to perform the various job functions. Separate forms available for rating the importance of the job elements and for self-rating of incumbent's abilities. Examiner required. Suitable for group use.

Untimed: 45-60 minutes

Range: Managerial and professional personnel

Scoring: Hand key; machine scoring available

Cost: 25 test booklets (importance or ability) $13.75; interpretation and research manual $5.00; scoring sheets (25) $2.50; specimen set $10.00.

Publisher: London House Press

MANAGERIAL PHILOSOPHIES SCALE (MPS)

Jacob Jacoby and James Terborg

adult

Purpose: Evaluates managers in terms of Douglas McGregor's theory X and theory Y types of managers. Differentiates between high, average, and low achieving managers.

Description: Multiple item paper-pencil self-report inventory measuring the degree to which managers adhere to either of two theories concerning the philosophical motivation behind management practice: theory X and theory Y. Theory X managers are authoritarian and intent on others' compliance with their commands. Theory Y managers see the potential of satisfaction and self-fulfillment for all who work. Yields scores for both X and Y dimensions. Normative data and interpretive guidelines are provided for purposes of comparison, reflection, and evaluation. May be used for pre- and posttesting to measure the impact of training intervention programs. Examiner required. Suitable for group use.

Untimed: Varies

Range: Managerial personnel

Scoring: Examiner evaluated

Cost: Individual instrument $4.50.

Publisher: Teleometrics International

MEETING EFFECTIVENESS INVENTORY

R. Dean Harrington, Walter E. Natemeyer, Selina L. Harrington and Paul Hersey

adult

Purpose: Measures the effectiveness of people who conduct meetings. Used in training programs concerned with situational leadership.

Description: Multiple item paper-pencil inventory assessing three factors related to an individual's effectiveness in leading meetings: preplanning, conduct of the meeting, and follow-up. Available in two forms: self-report and other-report. Examiner required. Suitable for group use.

Untimed: Varies

Range: Adult

Scoring: Examiner evaluated

Cost: 10 inventories (self-report or other-report form) $2.65; individual inventories to colleges and universities for research purposes $.95 each.

Publisher: University Associates, Inc.

OCCUPATIONAL PERSONALITY QUESTIONNAIRES (OPQ)

Refer to page 232.

THE OLIVER ORGANIZATION DESCRIPTION QUESTIONNAIRE (OODQ)

John E. Oliver

adult

Purpose: Evaluates the organizational form of a particular organization or its components.

Description: Multiple item paper-pencil questionnaire measuring the extent to which four organizational forms exist within a particular organization. The forms are: hierarchic (bureaucratic), professional (specialized), task (entrepeneurial), and group (socio-technical). The scoring guide discusses: the form of the instrument, the four domains, scoring, potential uses of the scores, development of the instrument, interpretation of individual scores, and interpretation of organization scores. Examiner required. Suitable for group use.

Untimed: Varies

Range: Adult

Scoring: Examiner evaluated

Cost: 50 questionnaires $15.00; scoring guide (13 pages) $2.50.

Publisher: Organizational Measurement Systems Press

PAPI SYSTEM: RATING OF JOB REQUIREMENTS—FORM A REVISED

Refer to page 235.

PAPI SYSTEM: RATING OF JOB REQUIREMENTS—FORM B REVISED

Refer to page 236.

PAPI SYSTEM: RATING OF JOB REQUIREMENTS—FORM C REVISED

Refer to page 236.

PERFORMANCE MANAGEMENT SIMULATION: AN INDIVIDUAL/GROUP DECISION-MAKING EXERCISE

Paul Hersey and Walter E. Natemeyer

adult

Purpose: Assesses the ability of managers to evaluate their professional staff and to work as a group to reach decisions by consensus. Used for management training and development programs.

Description: Multiple item paper-pencil exercise measuring the ability of a group of managers to work independently and as a group in response to a situation which requires them to rate the relative importance and potential for leadership of the members of their "staff" of professional personnel. Individuals participating in the exercise are designated as department heads within a hypothetical company involved in the development of highly innovative computer software programs. Each of the participants is asked to rate their staff of eight employees on the basis of merit to be used as a major factor in assigning salary increases. Detailed descriptions of the eight staff members are provided as a basis for the assessments. In addition, each of the participants is told that he is being promoted and must rank the employees from the "most qualified" to the "least qualified" candidate for promotion. After the participants make their individual assessments, the group meets together to work toward consensus decisions regarding the same two rankings (merit ranking and promotion ranking) for the same eight employees. The individual and group rankings are then scored according to the rankings provided by personnel experts. This exercise also provides insight into the participants' personal preferences, tendencies, and assumptions about others. The manual reviews the major criteria used to evaluate the exercise and the legal aspects of performance management. It also includes the case answers and rationale underlying the expert's rankings. Detailed options for using the simulation and for designing training activities are also included. Examiner required. Intended for group use.

Untimed: Varies

Range: Management personnel

Scoring: Examiner evaluated

Cost: 10 instruments $26.50; manual $9.95.

Publisher: Center for Leadership Studies

PERSONAL RELATIONS SURVEY (PRS)

Jay Hall and Martha S. Williams

adult

Purpose: Assesses the communications skills of managers. Used for employee training and development.

Description: Multiple item paper-pencil self-report inventory assessing the communications tendencies of managers in three areas: with employees, with colleagues, and with superiors. Normative data provides a basis for comparison with the "average" manager on both the exposure and feedback dimensions. May be administered in conjunction with the Management Relations Survey for a more complete assessment of managers' communications skills. Self-administered. Suitable for group use.

Untimed: Varies

Range: Managerial personnel

Scoring: Self-scored

Cost: Individual instruments $4.50.

Publisher: Teleometrics International

PERSONNEL PERFORMANCE PROBLEMS INVENTORY (PPPI)

Albert A. Canfield

adult

Purpose: Assesses the use of delegation skills at all levels of management. Identifies specific elements in the delegation process which are creating problems. Used for manager/supervisor training and development.

Description: 30 item paper-pencil test assessing the effectiveness of a supervisor's delegation relationships in the following areas: mutual understanding of job responsibilities, authority, accountability, results expected and employment conditions. Each test item describes a common performance problem of subordinates. The supervisor or manager must indicate the extent to which each is a problem with a present employee or group of employees. Test booklets are self-scoring and self-profiling and contain complete descriptions of areas for improvement. Norms provided for supervisors/managers to identify key areas for improvement. Bibliography for additional reading also included.

Self-administered. Suitable for group use.

Untimed: 30 minutes

Range: Adult

Scoring: Self-scored

Cost: Demonstration kit (30 test booklets and manual) $45.95; specimen set (includes manual) $9.95.

Publisher: Humanics Media

POWER MANAGEMENT INVENTORY (PMI)

Jay Hall and James Hawker

adult

Purpose: Evaluates a manager's use of power. Used for management training and development and as a basis for discussion.

Description: Multiple item paper-pencil self-report inventory assessing the motivations for power and power styles of managers. The first part of the inventory examines personal motivations for power, including needs for impact, strength, and influence that guide their behavior. The second part of the inventory analyzes how the individual uses power and assesses two bipolar dimensions of power style: autocratic-democratic and permissive-authoritarian. The analysis of individual power dynamics includes assessments of both motive and style, focusing on the interaction between the two. Normative data provided. May be administered in conjunction with the Power Management Profile to provide a comparison of the managers' self-ratings with the ratings of their subordinates. Self-administered. Suitable for group use.

Untimed: Varies

Range: Managerial personnel

Scoring: Self-scored

Cost: Individual instrument $4.50.

Publisher: Teleometrics International

POWER MANAGEMENT PROFILE (PMP)

Jay Hall and James Hawker

adult

Purpose: Evaluates a manager's use of power from the viewpoint of subordinates or associates. Used for management training and development and as a basis for discussion.

Description: Multiple item paper-pencil inventory assessing a manager's power style and related behaviors as seen by the manager's subordinates or co-workers. Elicits feedback for managers concerning how their approaches to power are viewed by those on the receiving end of their behavior. Analysis of responses provides a structure for after-the-fact discussions with their subordinates and develops a statement of the general morale that exists in the workplace as a function of the manager's use of power. Normative data provided. May be administered in conjunction with the Power Management Inventory to provide a comparison of managers' self-ratings with those of his subordinates. Examiner required. Suitable for group use.

Untimed: Varies

Range: Adult

Scoring: Examiner evaluated

Cost: Individual instrument $4.50.

Publisher: Teleometrics International

SCHOOL PRINCIPAL JOB FUNCTIONS INVENTORY (SP-JFI)

Refer to page 206.

SCHOOL SUPERINTENDENT JOB FUNCTIONS INVENTORY (SS-JFI)

Refer to page 207.

STYLES OF MANAGEMENT INVENTORY (SMI)

Jay Hall, Jerry B. Harvey and Martha S. Williams

adult

Purpose: Evaluates an individual's style of management in terms of the assumptions made about the relationship between production concerns and people concerns. Used for management training and development and as a basis for discussion.

Description: Multiple item paper-pencil self-report inventory assessing styles of management based on the Blake-Mouton managerial grid (a model of management behavior based on Likert's morale-production theory). Yields a total score for each of the five styles described by the Blake-Mouton model, as well as subscores for each style on four components of management: philosophy, planning, implementation, and evaluation. Provides managers with a way of relating their behavior with their on-the-job practices and discovering areas in need of change. Normative data and conversion tables afford personal comparison with both the "average" manager and a theoretical ideal. May be administered in conjunction with the Management Appraisal Survey for a more complete assessment of management styles. Examiner required. Suitable for group use.

Untimed: Varies

Range: Managerial personnel

Scoring: Examiner evaluated

Cost: Individual instrument $4.50.

Publisher: Teleometrics International

SUPERVISORY INVENTORY ON COMMUNICATION (SIC)

Refer to page 242.

SUPERVISORY INVENTORY ON HUMAN RELATIONS (SIHR)

Refer to page 243.

SUPERVISORY INVENTORY ON SAFETY (SIS)

Donald L. Kirkpatrick

adult

Purpose: Measures supervisors' knowledge of basic facts and principles concerning on-the-job safety and accident prevention. Used in training courses aimed at increasing job safety and reducing accidents.

Description: 80 item paper-pencil two-choice test assessing knowledge of the principles, facts, and techniques related to safety and accident prevention. Items are related to the job of foreman, supervisor, and manager in industry, business, and government. Test results identify topics which should be emphasized in training programs, serve as tools for conference discussions, measure the effectiveness of training programs, provide information for on-the-job coaching, and assist in the selection of supervisory personnel. Revised in 1980 to include new items based on the Occupational Safety & Health Act as well as recommendations from safety engineers. Norms provided for first level supervisors and foremen, middle and top-level supervisors, and safety and personnel professionals. Answer booklet provides rationale for all correct answers. Self-administered and self-scoring. Suitable for group use.

Untimed: 20 minutes

Range: Adult

Scoring: Self-scoring

Cost: 20 tests and answer booklets $20.00; instructor's manual $1.00; review set (test, answer booklet, and manual) $2.00.

Publisher: Donald L. Kirkpatrick

SUPERVISORY PRACTICES INVENTORY (SPI)

Judith S. Canfield and Albert A. Canfield

adult

Purpose: Evaluates how an individual prefers to be supervised, how the individual's supervisor actually functions, and the difference between preferred and actual supervisory behaviors. Identifies areas in which to reduce "stress points" in supervisor/subordinate working relationships.

Description: 20 item paper-pencil inventory assessing a subordinate's view of 10 areas of supervisory behavior in 10 areas: setting objectives, planning, organization, delegation, problem identification, decision making, performance evaluation, subordinate development, team building, and conflict resolution. Test items consist of a list of supervisory behaviors which the subordinate must rank once in order of personal preference and a second time to indicate how his supervisor actually functions. Questions measure supervisory behavior rather than trait or personality characteristics. Dissonance scores are developed from the difference between preferred and actual rankings. Test booklets are self-scoring and self-profiling and include explanations of the scales and possible interpretations. Norms available for supervisors/managers from diverse organizations. Self-administered. Suitable for group use.

Untimed: 20-40 minutes

Range: Adult

Scoring: Self-scored

Cost: Demonstration kit (30 test booklets and manual) $45.95; specimen set (includes manual) $9.95.

Publisher: Humanics Media

TWELVE O'CLOCK HIGH

Paul Hersey and Kenneth H. Blanchard

adult

Purpose: Assesses leadership style and leader effectiveness. Used in training programs concerned with situational leadership.

Description: Multiple item paper-pencil test measuring leader effectiveness and leadership style according to the 3-D leader effectiveness model. Group member needs are assessed using Maslow's hierarchy of needs model. The case analysis is based on the characters in the 918th Bomber Group in the film "Twelve O'Clock High." Examiner required. Suitable for group use.

Untimed: Varies

Range: Adult

Scoring: Examiner evaluated

Cost: 10 tests $8.00; individual tests to colleges and universities for research purposes $.95 each.

Publisher: University Associates, Inc.

WORK MOTIVATION INVENTORY (WMI)

Refer to page 246.

Mechanical Abilities and Manual Dexterity

CARD SORTING BOX

adult

Purpose: Measures progress in motor learning where it is necessary to make rapid recognition of materials and to quickly coordinate visual discrimination with hand movements.

Description: Multiple item task performance test consisting of a 15-hole sorting box and 10 sets of 15 cards each. Individuals are provided with the sorting box, a set of cards, and instructions as to how they are to be sorted. The task is to place each card in the proper pigeon-hole. Problems of inhibition and facilitation can be studied by changing the pattern for appropriate pigeon-holes for given cards. Once the cards have been sorted, the backless sorting apparatus may be lifted and the cards readily picked up in packs for counting. An extra supply of numbers is provided which may be attached to the back of the three wood strips forming the first scoring key to form a second key. Examiner required. Not suitable for group use.

Timed: Varies

Range: Adult

Scoring: Examiner evaluated

Cost: Test kit (sorting box, 150 cards, and one random scoring key) $75.00.

Publisher: Lafayette Instrument Company, Inc.

DAILEY VOCATIONAL TESTS

Refer to page 114.

MOBILE VOCATIONAL EVALUATION (MVE)

Refer to page 213.

PHOENIX ABILITY SURVEY SYSTEM (PASS)

Refer to page 213.

PURDUE HAND PRECISION TEST

adult

Purpose: Measures upper level perceptual-motor skills. Used in selection of hosiery mill operators and other positions requiring precision perceptual-motor skills.

Description: Multiple item task performance test assessing an individual's ability to make contact between a hand-held stylus and a rapidly rotating shutter. The testing apparatus consists of a rotating shutter, variable speed control, and hand stylus. The speed control provides a continuously variable shutter speed from 30 to 60 rpm. Three measures may be recorded with this instrument: total number of correct responses, total number of attempts can be recorded with the use of an impulse counter, and actual shutter contacts (recorded with the use of a stop clock). Examiner required. Not suitable for group use.

Timed: Varies

Range: Adult

Scoring: Examiner evaluated

Cost: Testing apparatus (110 volt) $315.00; testing apparatus (220 volt) $350.00.

Publisher: Lafayette Instrument Company, Inc.

PYRAMID PUZZLE

adult

Purpose: Measures motor learning and problem solving abilities.

Description: Multiple item task performance test assessing problem solving, insight learning, and concept formation. The task involves placing a series of graduated blocks on one of three posts such that a larger block is never placed over a smaller block. Average solution time is about 20 minutes for the first trial. Repeated trials with the same individual will produce successively shorter solution time. Examiner required. Suitable for group use.

Timed: Varies

Range: Adult

Scoring: Examiner evaluated

Cost: Test kit (test board with three

posts and set of graduated blocks) $24.00.

Publisher: Lafayette Instrument Company, Inc.

STEADINESS TESTER–GROOVE TYPE

adult

Purpose: Measures the steadiness aspect of psychomotor control.

Description: Multiple item task performance test assessing the degree of steadiness with which an individual can move a stylus in a straight line on a frictionless surface. The testing unit consists of adjustable stainless steel plates which form the sides of a progressively narrowing slit. The sides are indexed in centimeters to accurately measure an individual's performance. The bottom surface of the unit is mirror finished glass to assure no friction artifact. The unit may be connected to a tone response unit for immediate feedback studies, or to any number of data collection devices. Replacement stylus available. Examiner required. Not suitable for group use.

Untimed: Varies

Range: Adult

Scoring: Examiner evaluated

Cost: Testing apparatus $45.00.

Publisher: Lafayette Instrument Company, Inc.

STEADINESS TESTER—HOLE TYPE

adult

Purpose: Measures one aspect of the psychomotor phenomena of steadiness.

Description: Multiple item task performance test assessing the steadiness with which an individual can place a stylus in circular holes of varying sizes. The testing instrument provides nine holes of diminishing size. Analysis can be made of the subject's total score or for each hole separately. Considerable differences in performance may be determined for different individuals. The apparatus may be used with a counter or stop clock to record scores. The unit may also be connected to a tone reponse unit to provide immediate feedback. Replacement stylus available. Examiner required. Not suitable for group use.

Timed: Varies

Range: Adult

Scoring: Examiner required

Cost: Testing apparatus $25.00; single impulse counter $70.00.

Publisher: Lafayette Instrument Company, Inc.

TAPPING BOARD

adult

Purpose: Measures elementary psychomotor skills.

Description: Multiple item task performance test assessing an individual's ability to tap with a stylus, as rapidly as possible, the two stainless steel plates located at each end of an 18 inch fiberesin board (stainless steel plates measure 3½″ square). May be used to evaluate a number of basic psychomotor skills. Replacement stylus available. Examiner required. Not suitable for group use.

Timed: Varies

Range: Adult

Scoring: Examiner evaluated

Cost: Testing apparatus $25.00; single impulse counter $70.00.

Publisher: Lafayette Instrument Company, Inc.

TWO ARM COORDINATION TEST

adult

Purpose: Measures perceptual motor abilities involving the use of both arms together.

Description: One item task performance test assessing an individual's ability to use both arms together in the performance of a fine motor task. The testing unit consists of a stylus mounted on an apparatus with two handles. The individual grasps both handles simultaneously and moves the stylus around a six-point star pattern. The testing unit may be connected to an impulse counter to record the number of errors and/or a stop clock to record the amount of time outside the path. A stop clock may be used to time the total test time. Examiner required. Not suitable for group use.

Timed: Varies

Range: Adult

Scoring: Examiner evaluated

Cost: Testing apparatus $115.00; single impulse counter $70.00.

Publisher: Lafayette Instrument Company, Inc.

Municipal Services

THE BIPOLAR PSYCHOLOGICAL INVENTORY (BPI)

Refer to page 34.

CHANGE AGENT QUESTIONNAIRE (CAQ)

Refer to page 225.

EMOTIONAL STABILITY SURVEY (ES SURVEY)

Refer to page 226.

PERSONAL BACKGROUND INVENTORY

Melany E. Baehr and Frances M. Burns

adult

Purpose: Evaluates an individual's personal background history. Determines level of motivation. Predicts performance of transit operators, police officers, and entry-level positions which carry some responsibility. Also useful for structuring and quantifying background interviews.

Description: Multiple item paper-pencil inventory assessing 10 motivational areas of an individual's personal background history. The 10 motivational areas are arranged in the following five categories: success orientation (group participation and school achievements, drive, mobility), responsibility (financial responsibility, early family responsibility), stability (job and personal stability, education-vocational consistency), background (parental family adjustment, successful parental background), and general health. Examiner required. Suitable for group use.

Untimed: 20 minutes

Range: Adult

Scoring: Hand key; computer scoring available

Cost: 25 test booklets $25.00 (includes interpretation and research manual, scoring sheet); specimen set $10.00.

Publisher: London House Press

Sales

CUSTOMER REACTION SURVEY (CRS)

Jay Hall and C. Leo Griffith

adult

Purpose: Assesses customer reaction to a salesperson's interpersonal style and customer preferences regarding salesperson behavior. Used for employee training and development and as a basis for discussion.

Description: Multiple item paper-pencil inventory assessing an individual's success as a salesperson from the customer's point of view. Consists of two parts. The customer first rates the salesperson's use of exposure and feedback, then states preferred salesperson behavior. The resulting profiles may be combined with self-ratings from the Sales Relations Survey to make sales training relevant to the realities of the field. Normative data provided. Examiner required. Suitable for group use.

Untimed: Varies

Range: Adult

Scoring: Examiner evaluated

Cost: Individual instrument $4.50.

Publisher: Teleometrics International

INCENTIVES MANAGEMENT INDEX (IMI)

Jay Hall and Norman J. Seim

adult

Purpose: Assesses the incentives used by a sales manager to motivate the sales force. Used for training and development of sales managers and as a basis for discussion.

Description: Multiple item paper-pencil self-report inventory identifying which incentives a sales manager emphasizes and assessing the sales manager's personal theories about what motivates the sales force. Yields a managerial profile which may be used as feedback for the sales force. May be administered in conjunction with the Sales Motivation Survey (SMS) in two ways: to indicate areas in which the sales manager's own needs influence the incentives which are emphasized with the sales force, and to assess the sales manager's own motivational theory in light of the needs of the sales force. Normative data provided. Examiner required. Suitable for group use.

Untimed: Varies

Range: Adult

Scoring: Examiner evaluated

Cost: Individual instrument $4.50.

Publisher: Teleometrics International

INVENTORY OF INSURANCE SELLING POTENTIAL

adult

Purpose: Measures an individual's potential as an insurance salesperson. Used for employee screening and selection.

Description: 190 item paper-pencil test measuring aptitudes and abilities related to success as an insurance salesperson. Results indicate the probability of success of an individual considering an insurance sales career. The higher the rating, the higher the probability of success. May be used with experienced and inexperienced applicants. Available to insurance company home offices only. Examiner required. Suitable for group use. Available in French (may be administered in Canada).

Untimed: Varies

Range: Adult

Scoring: Computer scored

Cost: Test booklet $5.00; answer sheet (including scoring) $8.50.

Publisher: Life Insurance Marketing and Research Association, Inc.

LIMRA CAREER PROFILE SYSTEM

adult

Purpose: Evaluates career experience and expectations of individuals considering an insurance sales career. Used for employee screening and selection.

Description: 183 or 158 item paper-pencil questionnaire assessing career information related to future success as an insurance salesperson. The 183-item Initial Career Profile questionnaire is for use with applicants who have no prior insurance sales experience. The 158-item Advanced Career Profile questionnaire is for use with experienced applicants. Both forms may be administered in Canada and are available in French. Available to insurance company home offices only. Examiner required. Suitable for group use.

Untimed: Varies

Range: Adult

Scoring: Computer scored

Cost: Test booklet (Initial or Advanced)$5.00; answer sheet (Initial) $10.00; answer sheet (Advanced) $12.00; cost includes scoring.

Publisher: Life Insurance Marketing and Research Association, Inc.

SALES MOTIVATION SURVEY (SMS)

Jay Hall and Norman J. Seim

adult

Purpose: Assesses the needs and motivations of salespersons. Used for employee training and development and as a basis for discussion.

Description: Multiple item paper-pencil self-report inventory measuring the personal needs and goals of salespersons. Provides a profile of personal motivations. Results may serve as a basis for reordering personal priorities and better understanding of personal performance. Normative data provided. May be administered in conjunction with the Incentive Management Index for assessment of sales managers. Self-administered. Suitable for group use.

Untimed: Varies

Range: Salespersons

Scoring: Self-scored

Cost: Individual instrument $4.50.

Publisher: Teleometrics International

SALES RELATIONS SURVEY (SRS)

Jay Hall

adult

Purpose: Assesses an individual's interpersonal sales style. Used for employee training and development and as a basis for discussion.

Description: Multiple item paper-pencil self-report inventory assessing the quality of a salesperson's relationships with customers along exposure and feedback dimensions. Used to introduce and assess concepts such as blindspots, facades, and hidden potentials. Scores may be used to plot Johari Window profiles for an entire sales force. Normative data provided. May be administered in conjunction with the Customer Reaction Survey for a more complete assessment of an individual's interpersonal sales style. Examiner required. Suitable for group use.

Untimed: Varies

Range: Salespersons

Scoring: Examiner evaluated

Cost: Individual instrument $4.50.

Publisher: Teleometrics International

SALES TRANSACTION AUDIT (STA)

Jay Hall and C. Leo Griffith

adult

Purpose: Assesses the interpersonal transactions of salespeople with their customers in terms of Eric Berne's model of transactional analysis. Used for employee training and development and as a basis for discussion.

Description: Multiple item paper-pencil self-report inventory measuring the size of the parent, adult, and child (the three positions from which individuals can communicate according to the model of transactional analysis) in a salesperson's transactions with customers. Also provides scores for transaction contamination, crossed and complementary transactions, and constructive and disruptive tension in the sales relationship. Normative data provided. Examiner required. Suitable for group use.

Untimed: Varies

Range: Salespersons

Scoring: Examiner evaluated

Cost: Individual instrument $4.50.

Publisher: Teleometric International

Teachers

No new tests available. Please refer to the First Edition of ***TESTS*** *for a complete listing and description of tests currently available for this area.*

Appendix: Selected Test Ilustrations

The test elements illustrated in this section have been published or revised since 1980. The selection offered here was determined cooperatively between the editors and the test publishers, and choices were made on the basis of providing the reader with useful samples while avoiding the breach of test security. The editors gratefully acknowledge the participation of these tests publishers.

Test Illustrations

ADULT GROWTH EXAMINATION (AGE)

Refer to page S14.

ADULT GROWTH EXAMINATION
Score Sheet

Name ______________________ Date of Birth ____________
Identifying Number ______________________________
Address ______________________________
Telephone ____________________ Sex ____________
Occupation ____________________ Education ____________
Marital Status ____________________ Referred by ____________
Medical Problems ______________________________

I know the purpose of this test and consent to take it of my own free will. I understand the results will be handled in a professional and ethical manner.

____
Signature and Date

The Examiner: ______________________

==

Time test begun ________

Measurements

Body Temperature ____________

SBP-1 Systolic blood pressure ______ mm/hg
HL Hearing loss at 1000 cps: Right ear ____ db Left ear ____ db
HL Hearing loss at 6000 cps: Right ear ____ db Left ear ____ db
HL Hearing loss at 6000 cps Better ear ____ db*
SBP-2 Systolic blood pressure ______ mm/hg
NPV Near point of vision ______ inches*
SBP-3 Systolic blood pressure ______ mm/hg
SBP Average of three readings ______ mm/hg*

Time test concluded ______ Total testing time ______ minutes

==

Results

*HL raw score _____ HL age score _____ BODY AGE ____________
*NPV raw score _____ NPV age score _____ BIRTH AGE ____________
*SBP raw score _____ SBP age score _____ Difference ____________

==

ADULT PERSONALITY INVENTORY

Refer to page S32.

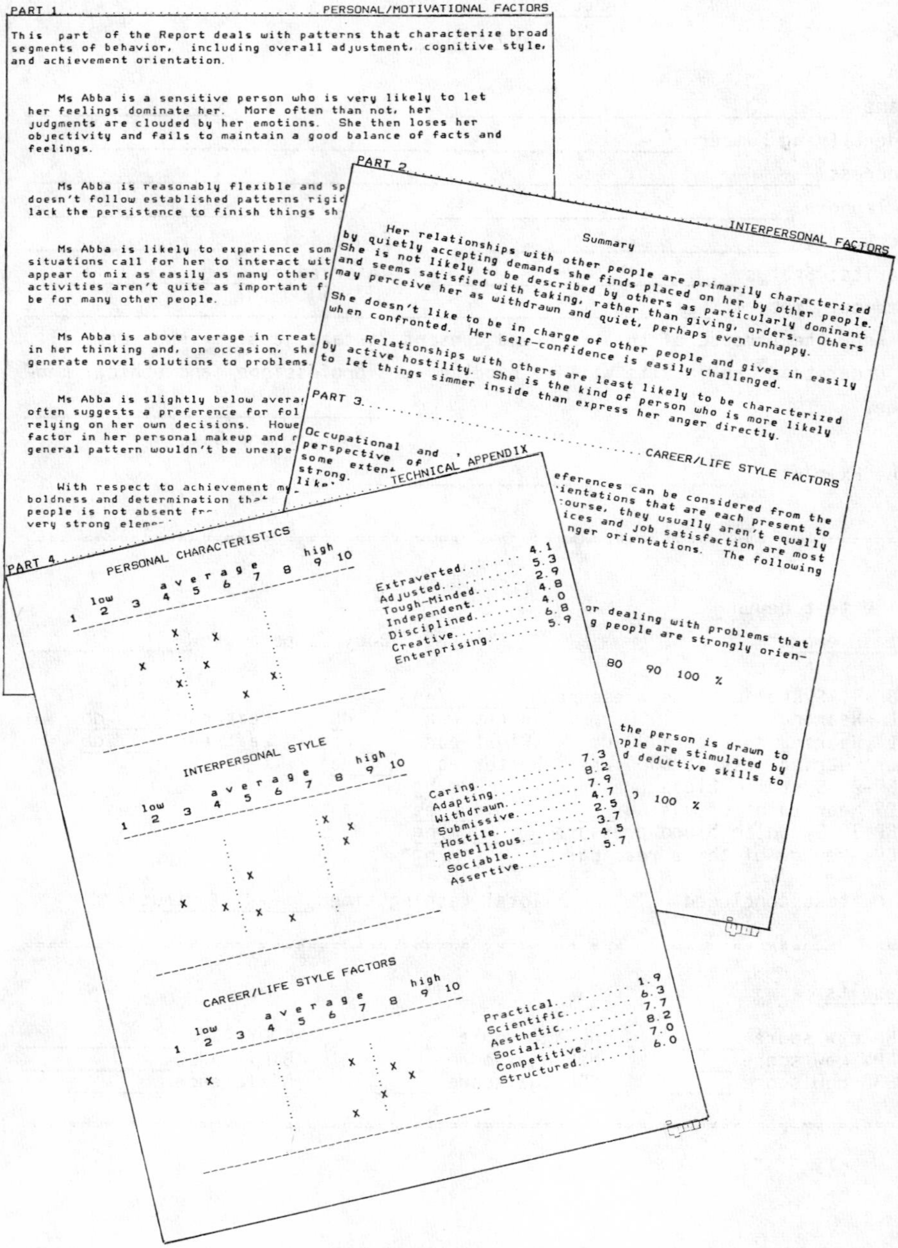

ALIENATION INDEX SURVEY (A.I. SURVEY)

Refer to page S224.

personnel security preview®
A. I. Survey®

INSTRUCTIONS:

A. ANSWER **ALL** QUESTIONS GIVING YOUR OPINION AS TO THE ACCURACY OF THE FOLLOWING STATEMENTS.
B. PUT AN **X** IN THE APPROPRIATE BOX.
C. USE THE QUESTION MARK **(?) ONLY** IF YOU ABSOLUTELY CANNOT ANSWER THE QUESTIONS WITH A YES OR NO.
D. DO NOT LEAVE ANY QUESTIONS UNANSWERED OR WITH MORE THAN ONE ANSWER.

	YES	?	NO
1. Few jobs are 100% satisfying.	☐	☐	☐
2. Quality work is the primary responsibility of every worker.	☐	☐	☐
3. People would work harder if they shared in the profits.	☐	☐	☐
4. American working hours should be reduced.	☐	☐	☐
5. Business managers are responsible for most economic problems.	☐	☐	☐
6. Most companies pay their employees according to the value of their work.	☐	☐	☐
7. Most employers try to underpay their workers if they can.	☐	☐	☐
8. Most employers will increase pay when the employee deserves it.	☐	☐	☐
9. There is a limited amount an employer can pay for any job.	☐	☐	☐
10. Most companies make too much profit.	☐	☐	☐
11. Companies should be limited as to how much they make.	☐	☐	☐
12. Most jobs are boring an unch lenging.	☐	☐	☐
13. Most people really like w they work at.	☐	☐	☐
14. The interesting jobs are given to those people with lots of schooling.	☐	☐	☐
15. Most bosses are fair to their employees.	☐	☐	☐
16. Most bosses know what's going on at work.	☐	☐	
17. Most supervisors really don't lead; they drive their people.	☐		
18. Most supervisors got where they are by hard work and merit.			
19. Most supervisors are honest w their people.			
20. One of the best parts about c work is the people.			
21. Most workers stick togr			
22. It's a nice thing to sr low workers.			
23. Most workers w look bad in ord selves.			
24. Most wor the com			
25. Most imp th			
26.			

	YES	?	NO
27. Most employers demand too much for too little pay.	☐	☐	☐
28. Worker's rights usually come last as far as most companies are concerned.	☐	☐	
29. Most people get ahead because of being in the right place at the right time.	☐		
30. Most companies try to help th people advance.			
31. Favoritism is the most comm son that workers are rewa			
32. Most jobs are really de			
33. There isn't really m unless you know t			
34. Loyalty, honest off now as m past.			
35. d			
36.			
37. M			
38			

SPECIMEN COPY

BALL APTITUDE BATTERY

Refer to page S211.

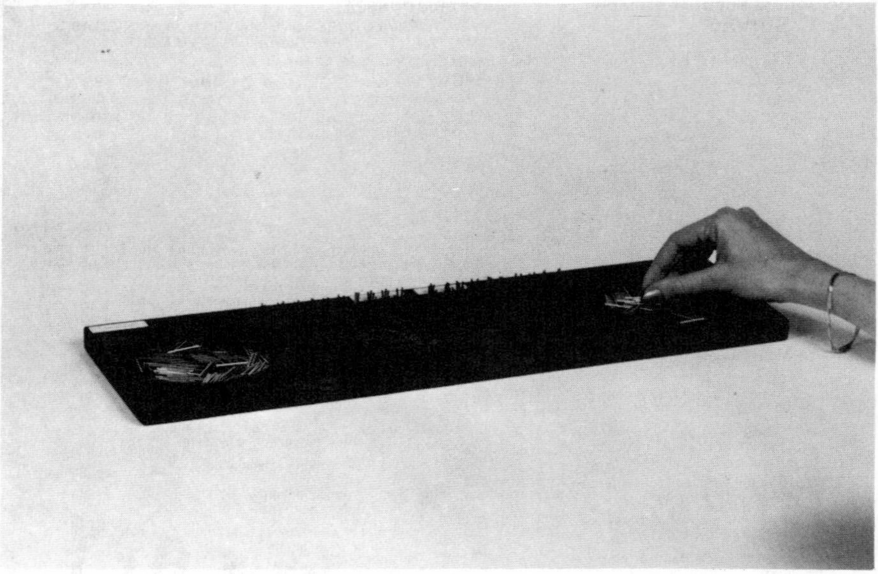

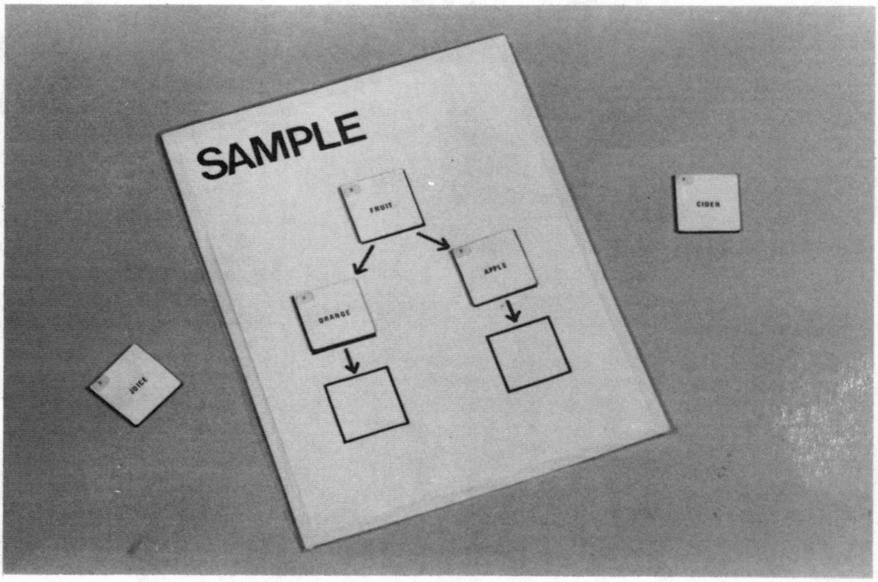

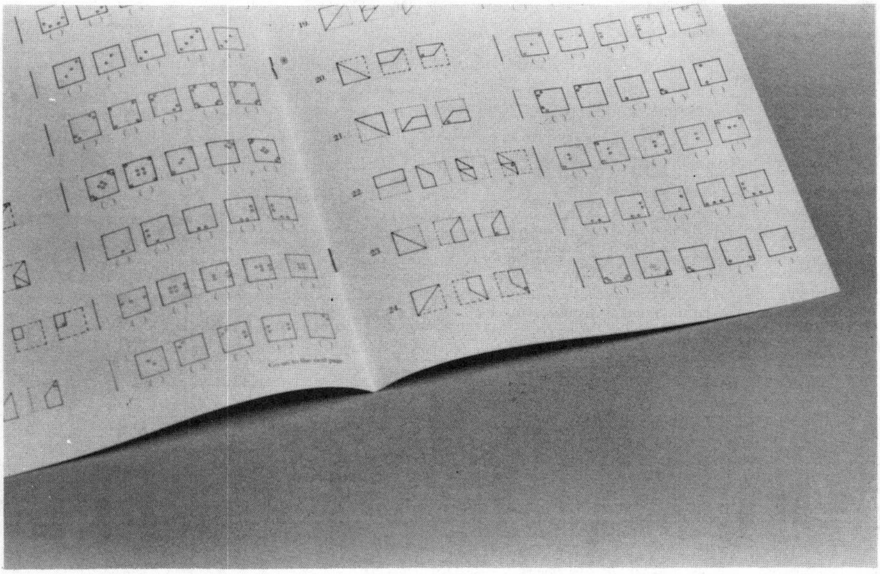

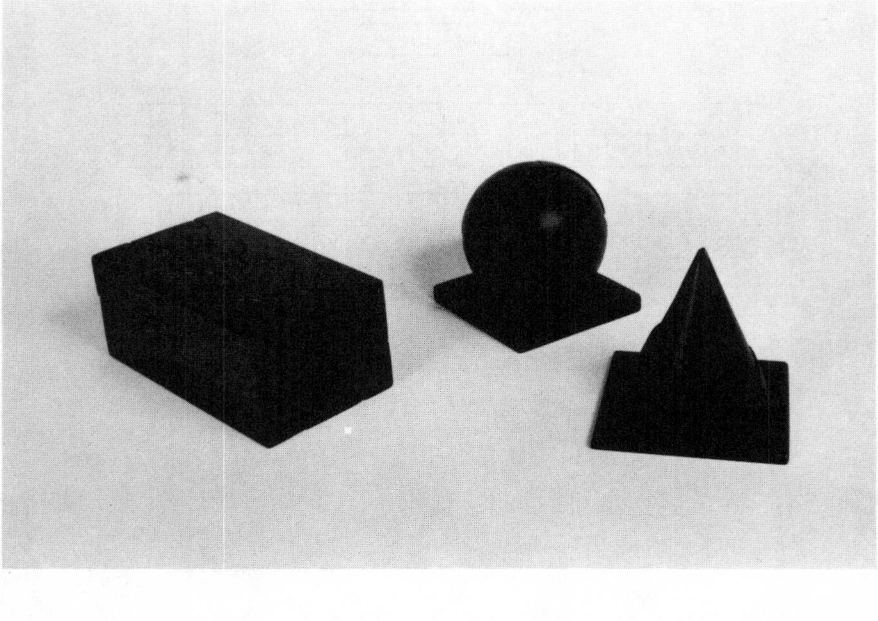

BASIC VISUAL-MOTOR ASSOCIATION TEST (BVMAT)

Refer to page S143.

BVMAT–FORM A

Name: . . . . Today's Date: . . . . Sex: . . . .

School: . . . . Date of Birth: . . . . Grade: . . . .

Examiner: . . . . Chronological Age: . . . . Teacher: . . . .

Key

A	B	C	D	E	F	G	H	I	J
0	+	V	−	>	Λ	<	C	⊥	Ɔ

Sample

B	D	H	J	B
+				

I	A	D	F	E	B	A	I	H	D	E	I	B	A	J	F	G	B	C	I
⊥	0	−	Λ	>	+	0	⊥	C	−	>	⊥	+	0	Ɔ	Λ	<	+	V	⊥

A	J	B	C	F	G	H	J	D	E	I	B	E	C	J	G	C	H	F	C
0	Ɔ	+	V	Λ	<	C	Ɔ	−	>	⊥	+	>	V	Ɔ	<	V	C	Λ	V

B	D	I	E	G	C	H	J	D	H	G	F	H	A	G	F	J	E	A	D
+	−	⊥	>	<	V	C	Ɔ	−	C	<	Λ	C	0	<	Λ	Ɔ	>	0	−

BVMAT–FORM B

Key

a	b	c	d	e	f	g	h	i	j
0	+	V	−	>	Λ	<	C	⊥	Ɔ

Sample

b	d	h	j	b
+				

i	a	d	f	e	b	a	i	h	d	e	i	b	a	j	f	g	b	c	i
⊥	0	−	Λ	>	+	0	⊥	C	−	>	⊥	+	0	Ɔ	Λ	<	+	V	⊥

a	j	b	c	f	g	h	j	d	e	i	b	e	c	j	g	c	h	f	c
0	Ɔ	+	V	Λ	<	C	Ɔ	−	>	⊥	+	>	V	Ɔ	<	V	C	Λ	V

b	d	i	e	g	c	h	j	d	h	g	f	h	a	g	f	j	e	a	d
+	−	⊥	>	<	V	C	Ɔ	−	C	<	Λ	C	0	<	Λ	Ɔ	>	0	−

	RS		%		*t*	
Category	Form A	Form B	Form A	Form B	Form A	Form B
A						
B						
C						
D						

BESSEMER SCREENING TEST

Refer to page T567.

Cat. No. 33150S Scoring Sheet
BESSEMER SCREENING TEST

Name of Student: ______________________ **Age:** ______ **Grade:** ______
School: ______________________ **Date of Test:** ______
Raw Score: ______ **Percentile Rank:** ______ **Emotional Indicator:** ______
Recommendations: ______________________

NAME WRITING (check if present).. **Score:** ______
all letters of first name in correct order ______
all letters of last name in correct order ______
contains no letter reversals ______
capitalization is correct ______
no more than 2 letters above or below line ______

HUMAN FIGURE DRAWING (check if present).. **Score:** ______
head ______
eyes ______
nose ______
mouth ______
feet ______
body ______
legs ______
arms ______
hair ______
neck ______
arms pointing downward ______
arms two-dimensional ______
legs two-dimensional ______
arms attached to shoulder ______

....

EMOTIONAL INDICATORS (check if present).. **Total:** ______
eyes omitted ______
nose omitted ______
body omitted ______
mouth omitted ______
arms omitted ______
legs omitted ______
feet omitted ______
(score only for girls age 7 up; boys age 9 up)
neck omitted ______
(score only for girls age 9 up; boys age 10 up)
hand and fingers both omitted ______
figure over 9″ ______
teeth present ______
monster or grotesque figure ______
extremities not attached ______
gross asymmetry of extremities ______
face or cheeks shaded ______
figure slants by 30° or more ______
transparent clothing ______
head very small ______
arms very short ______
arms very long ______
hands very large ______
no space between legs ______
no space between arms & body ______
three or more figures drawn ______
eyes appear crossed ______
clouds appear in drawing ______
genitals drawn ______
figure under 2″ ______

TOTAL EMOTIONAL INDICATORS: ______

BIEGER TEST OF VISUAL DISCRIMINATION

Refer to page S175.

Bieger Test of Visual Discrimination and Visual Discrimination of Word Training Program

Name: ______________________ **School:** ____________ **Class:** ________ **Date:** ________

TEST 1A—Visual Discrimination of Letters with Larger Contrasts

Circle the letter that is the same as the first letter.

1. t	s	y	o	t	14. n	o	x	n	z
2. v	s	o	v	t	15. m	z	o	m	i
3. l	c	l	z	o	16. f	o	f	w	q

TEST 3A—Visual Discrimination of Letters that are Almost Identical

Circle the letter that is the same as the first letter.

1. b	p	d	b	g
2. d	p	b	d	g
3. q	g	p	d	q

TEST 5A—Visual Discrimination of Words with Lesser Contrasts

Circle the word that is the same as the first word.

1. if	it	of	if
2. me	me	he	we
3. fat	tat	tax	fat

TEST 7A—Visual Discrimination of Almost Identical Words—Sequencing

Circle the word that is the same as the first word.

1. to	to	ot	ot	ot
2. be	eb	eb	be	eb
3. shy	yhs	hsy	shy	hys

BILINGUAL TWO LANGUAGE BATTERY OF TESTS

Refer to page S71.

Student Score Profiles Card
Bilingual Two Language Battery of Tests

Profile 1: Composite Scores

	Sessions:		(1) Pre		(2) Post			(3) Pre		(4) Post			(5) Pre		(6) Post			
	Date:																	
	Sittings:		NL	Eng	NL	Eng		NL	Eng	NL	Eng		NL	Eng	NL	Eng	Max	Pts
	Sections:																	
I	1st letter	A					A					A					24	
	2 letters	B					B					B					10	
	Spelling	C					C					C					16	50
II	Opposites	D					D					D					10	
	Similarities	E					E					E					10	
	Comparisons	F					F					F					20	
	Reading	G					G					G					10	
	Listening	H					H					H					10	60
III	Items	I					I					I					30	
	Actions	J					J					J					30	
	Relationships	K					K					K					30	90
Composite Score																		200
	Sitting/Session		(1)	(1)	(2)	(2)		(3)	(3)	(4)	(4)		(5)	(5)	(6)	(6)		

Profile 2: Proficiency Levels, Language Dominance, Point of Bilinguality

Session			1 Pre	2 Post	3 Pre	4 Post	5 Pre	6 Post		**Session**	
P	Full	200							200	Full	P
R	___	180							180	___	R
O	___	160							160	___	O
F	Medium	140							140	Medium	F
I	___	120							120	___	I
C	___	100							100	___	C
I	Low	80							80	Low	I
E	___	60							60	___	E
N	___	40							40	___	N
C	None	20							20	None	C
Y	___	0							0	___	Y

Using the Composite Scores from Profile 1, left to right (Pre to Post), write the number of each language Sitting/Session (NL and English) across from the point column. Circle the number of the Sitting/Session, and draw:

SOLID or RED lines for Native Language
BROKEN or BLUE lines for English

Note: LAU Category "C" – Bilingual, may be established where the two lines cross, or closely parallel each other by not more than 20 points between each. Bilinguality can be measured in terms of proficiency from "None" (lowest level) to "Full" (highest).

THE BRIGANCE K&1 SCREEN

Refer to page S117.

(Oriented for the student facing the assessor)

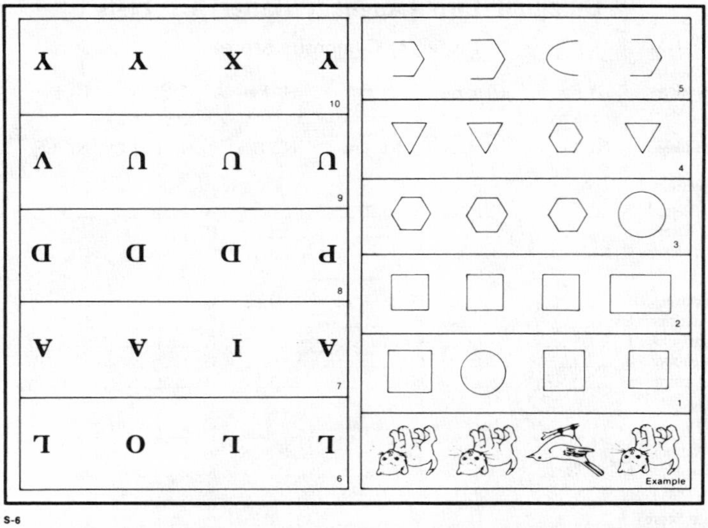

VISUAL DISCRIMINATION—A

(1) **SKILL:** Visually discriminates which one of four printed symbols is different.

Geometric Designs
1. ○ 2. □ 3. ○ 4. ⬡ 5. ⊃

Upper Case Letters
6. O 7. I 8. P 9. V 10. X

(2) **PUPIL DATA SHEET:** Kindergarten.

(3) **ASSESSMENT METHOD:** Student performance.

(4) **MATERIAL:** S-6.

(5) **DISCONTINUE:** After two consecutive errors.

(6) **TIME:** Your discretion. Ten seconds for each item is recommended.

(7) **ACCURACY:** Give credit for each correct response.

(8) **POINT VALUE:** 1 point each.

STUDENT PAGE FORMAT AND ANSWERS FOR S-6

(9)

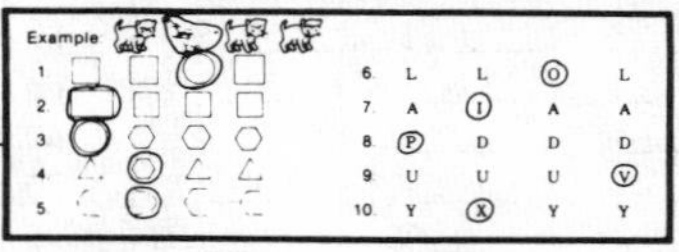

(10) **NOTES:**

1. **Possible Observations:** As the student responds to the items on S-6, you may wish to observe for the following:
   a. *Comprehends the Concept of Different:* Are the student's responses incorrect because he or she does not comprehend the concept of *different*? If you feel that the student is performing poorly because of a language deficit, you may wish to use the phrase *not the same* for *different*.
   b. *Focusing Difficulties:* Does the student appear to experience difficulty focusing on one item because of being distracted by other items on the page? Does the student lose his or her place on the page? See **NOTE #3**.
   c. *Type of Response:* Does the student prefer to respond by pointing, or does he or she respond verbally by naming the design or letter that is different? The latter response would suggest a more capable student.
2. **Supplemental Assessment:** The items on S-6 may be used to informally assess the student's ability to recognize and name the geometric designs and upper case letters used. This may be accomplished by asking questions such as the following:
   a. Can you show me a (*name of design or letter*)?
   b. Pointing to the design or letter, ask, "What do we call this?"
3. **Screen If Needed:** If it appears that the student is having difficulty focusing on one item at a time because of the visual stimuli of the entire page, you should cover the other items on the page by using blank sheets of paper.

(11) **DIRECTIONS:** This assessment is made by asking the student to identify the symbol in each box on page S-6 that is different.

Place your finger on the outer edge of the Example box as shown below and

Say: **One of the pictures in this box is different. Put your finger on the picture that is different.**

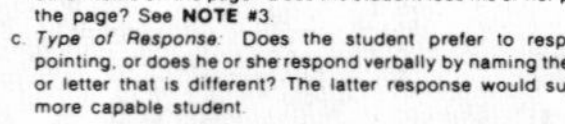

If the student does not appear to comprehend or does not respond correctly, point to the cats and

Say: **These are cats.**

Point to the bird and

Say: **This is a bird. It is different.**

Do not give any additional help. Continue with the other items. Point to each box and

Ask: **Which one is different?**

6 ○ **Visual Discrimination 4A**

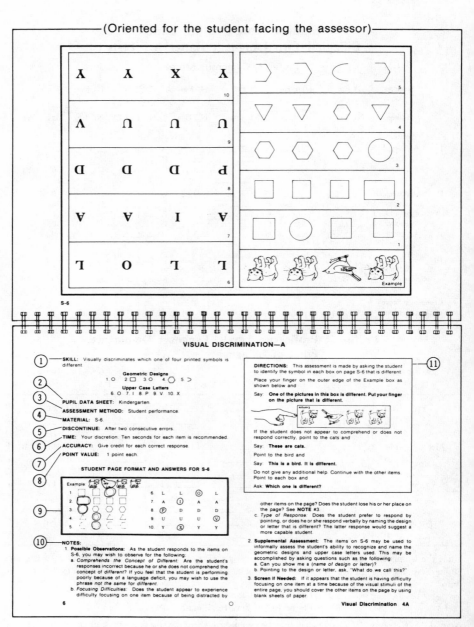

ASSESSOR'S PAGE

KINDERGARTEN Pupil Data Sheet for the *BRIGANCE® K & 1 SCREEN*

K

A. Student's Name ______ Date of Screening (Year / Month / Day) ______ ______ ______ School/Program ______

Parents/ Guardian ______ Birthdate ______ ______ ______ Teacher ______

Address ______ Age ______ ______ ______ Assessor ______

B. BASIC SCREENING ASSESSMENTS / **C. SCORING**

Page	Assessment Number	Skill (*Circle the skill for each correct response and make notes as appropriate.*)	Number of Correct Responses	Point Value	Student's Score
2	1	**Personal Data Response:** Verbally gives: 1. first name 2. full name 3. age 4. address (street or mail) 5. birthdate (month and day)	×	2 points each	/10
3	2	**Color Recognition:** Identifies and names the colors: 1. red 2. blue 3. green 4. yellow 5. orange 6. purple 7. brown 8. black 9. pink 10. gray	×	1 point each	/10
5	3	**Picture Vocabulary:** Recognizes and names picture of: 1. dog 2. cat 3. key 4. girl 5. boy 6. airplane 7. apple 8. leaf 9. cup 10. car	×	1 point each	/10
6	4A	**Visual Discrimination:** Visually discriminates which one of four symbols is different: 1. ○ 2. □ 3. O 4. ⬭ 5. Ↄ 6. O 7. I 8. P 9. V 10. X	×	1 point each	/10
8	5	**Visual-Motor Skills:** Copies: 1. ○ 2. – 3. + 4. □ 5. △	×	2 pts. ea.	/10
9	6	**Gross Motor Skills:** 1. Hops 2 hops on one foot. 2. Hops 2 hops on either foot. 3. Stands on one foot momentarily. 4. Stands on either foot momentarily. 5. Stands on one foot for 5 seconds. 6. Stands on either foot for 5 secs. 7. Walks forward heel and toe 4 steps. 8. Walks backward toe and heel 4 steps. 9. Stands on one foot momentarily with eyes closed. 10. Stands on either foot momentarily with eyes closed.	×	1 point each	/10
12	8	**Rote Counting:** Counts by rote to: (*Circle all numerals prior to the first error.*) 1 2 3 4 5 6 7 8 9 10	×	.5 point each	/5
13	9	**Identification of Body Parts:** Identifies by pointing or touching: 1. chin 2. fingernails 3. heel 4. elbow 5. ankle 6. shoulder 7. jaw 8. hips 9. wrist 10. waist	×	.5 point each	/5
15	11	**Follows Verbal Directions:** Listens to, remembers, and follows: 1. one verbal direction 2. two verbal directions	×	2.5 points each	/5
17	12	**Numeral Comprehension:** Matches quantity with numerals: 2 1 4 3 5	×	2 pts. ea.	/10
21	15	**Prints Personal Data:** Prints first name. Reversals: Yes____ No____	×	5 points	/5
22	16	**Syntax and Fluency:** 1. Speech is understandable. 2. Speaks in complete sentences.	×	5 pts. ea.	/10
				Total Score	/100

D. OBSERVATIONS:
1. Handedness: Right____ Left____ Uncertain____
2. Pencil grasp: Correct____ Incorrect____
3. Maintained paper in the proper position when writing: Yes____ No____
4. Record other observations below or on the back.

______

______

______

E. SUMMARY: (*Compared to other students included in this screening*)
1. this student scored: .... Lower____ Average____ Higher____
2. this student's age is: .... Younger____ Average____ Older____
3. the teacher rates this student: .... Lower____ Average____ Higher____
4. the assessor rates this student: .... Lower____ Average____ Higher____

F. RECOMMENDATIONS:
Place in: Preschool____ Low Kindergarten____ Average Kindergarten____ High Kindergarten____

Other (*Indicate.*) ______

Refer for: (*Indicate if needed.*) ______

COPY I

FIRST GRADE Pupil Data Sheet for the *BRIGANCE® K & 1 SCREEN*

1

A. Student's Name ______ Date of Screening (Year / Month / Day) ______ ______ ______ School/Program ______

Parents/ Guardian ______ Birthdate ______ ______ ______ Teacher ______

Address ______ Age ______ ______ ______ Assessor ______

B. BASIC SCREENING ASSESSMENTS / **C. SCORING**

Page	Assessment Number	Skill (*Circle the skill for each correct response and make notes as appropriate.*)	Number of Correct Responses	Point Value	Student's Score
2	1	**Personal Data Response:** Verbally gives: 1. first name 2. full name 3. age 4. address (street or mail) 5. birthdate (month and day)	×	1 point each	/5
3	2	**Color Recognition:** Identifies and names the colors: 1. red 2. blue 3. green 4. yellow 5. orange 6. purple 7. brown 8. black 9. pink 10. gray	×	.5 point each	/5
5	3	**Picture Vocabulary:** Recognizes and names picture of: 1. dog 2. cat 3. key 4. girl 5. boy 6. airplane 7. apple 8. leaf 9. cup 10. car	×	.5 point each	/5
7	4B	**Visual Discrimination:** Visually discriminates which one of four symbols is different: 1. o 2. c 3. c 4. b 5. n 6. on 7. be 8. can 9. they 10. was	×	1 point each	/10
8	5	**Visual-Motor Skills:** Copies: 1. ○ 2. – 3. + 4. □ 5. △	×	1 point ea.	/5
11	7	**Draw a Person (Body Image):** Draws picture of person that includes the body parts: 1. head 2. legs 3. eyes 4. nose 5. mouth 6. arms 7. trunk 8. hands 9. ears 10. neck	×	1 point each	/10
12	8	**Rote Counting:** Counts by rote to: (*Circle all numerals prior to the first error.*) 1 2 3 4 5 6 7 8 9 10 11 12 13 14 15 16 17 18 19 20	×	1 pt./4 in seq.	/5
14	10	**Recites Alphabet:** Recites alphabet to: (*Circle all letters prior to the first error.*) a b c d e f g h i j k l m n o p q r s t u v w x y z	×	1 pt./5 in seq.	/5
17	12	**Numeral Comprehension:** Matches quantity with numerals: 2 1 4 3 5 7 9 6 8 10	×	1 point ea.	/10
18	13	**Recognition of Lower Case Letters:** Recognizes and names lower case letters: o a d g q b p c e l t i f j n m r h u v w y x z k s	×	.5 point each	/13
20	14	**Auditory Discrimination:** (*Circle the number or letter if both responses are correct.*) 1. m— met-met; sum-sun 2. b— tab-tab; bit-mit 3. h— hide-wide; hat-mat 4. j— jet-wet; just-just 5. g— gate-late; sag-sat 6. r— rid-bid; raid-raid 7. s— set-wed; bus-bud 8. d— hid-hid; dab-dab 9. n— next-next; nut-mutt 10. f— fix-mix; fan-fan	×	1 point each letter	/10
21	15	**Prints Personal Data:** Prints: 1. first name 2. last name Reversals: Yes____ No____	×	5 pts. ea.	/10
23	17	**Numerals in Sequence:** Writes numerals to: 1 2 3 4 5 6 7 Reversals: Yes____ No____	×	1 pt. ea.	/7
				Total Score	/100

D. OBSERVATIONS:
1. Handedness: Right____ Left____ Uncertain____
2. Pencil grasp: Correct____ Incorrect____
3. Maintained paper in the proper position when writing: Yes____ No____
4. Record other observations below or on the back.

______

______

______

E. SUMMARY: (*Compared to other students included in this screening*)
1. this student scored: .... Lower____ Average____ Higher____
2. this student's age is: .... Younger____ Average____ Older____
3. the teacher rates this student: .... Lower____ Average____ Higher____
4. the assessor rates this student: .... Lower____ Average____ Higher____

F. RECOMMENDATIONS:
Place in: First Grade____ Low First Grade____ Average First Grade____ High First Grade____

Other (*Indicate.*) ______

Refer for: (*Indicate if needed.*) ______

COPY I

CAREER ADAPTIVE BEHAVIOR INVENTORY (CAB)

Refer to page S197.

Academics

		Behavior Level 0	1	2	3	4	5	Rating Method 1	2	3	
1.	Sorts objects according to shape, size, and color.						x			x	used 5 trials
2.	Counts 10 objects in proper sequence.						x			x	used blocks
3.	Counts 30 objects in proper sequence.	x								x	can count to 15
4.	Prints and/or writes own name.						x			x	Prints; not always
5.	Prints and/or writes simple sentences when given verbally.	x								x	legible.
6.	Reads common signs (Stop, Go, Danger, Men's, Women's).		x							x	once in a while; guess?
7.	Reads and understands simple directions (cooking, building a model).	x								x	we'll work on these
8.	Identifies coins and paper currency (up to $10.00).	x								x	no interest
9.	Makes proper change up to $1.00.	x								x	no interest
10.	Tells time.	x								x	understands concept
11.	Measures by inches and feet; by centimeters and meters.	x								x	somewhat
12.	Names days of the week in succession.	x								x	yes; not in sequence

Academics Score 16 36 *Rating Score*

Communication

		0	1	2	3	4	5	1	2	3	
1.	Establishes and maintains eye contact.		x							x	only w/ hands on shoulders
2.	Speaks so that needs are understood.				x					x	speech is slurred
3.	Responds to and makes verbal greetings and farewells.					x				x	usually quite, courteous
4.	Listens to, and follows one simple verbal command.				x					x	depends on command
5.	Responds to two or more verbal commands.		x							x	depends on command
6.	Makes general introductions.					x				x	
7.	Uses appropriate volume when speaking.				x					x	sometimes very soft spoken
8.	Maintains appropriate social distance when speaking to another.					x				x	
9.	Initiates or pursues appropriate conversation topics.				x					x	doesn't talk to all students
10.	Accepts criticism and attempts to implement suggestions.	x								x	gets upset no matter what
11.	Uses telephone with assistance (dialing, holding receiver).			x						x	will talk and hold
12.	Uses telephone unassisted.	x								x	

Communication Score 28 36 *Rating Score*

Interest

		0	1	2	3	4	5	1	2	3	
1.	Enjoys working alone.						x			x	prefers it
2.	Enjoys working as a group member.		x							x	a struggle
3.	Enjoys physical work.	x								x	
4.	Enjoys working outdoors.	x								x	claims too hot or cold
5.	Likes to work with hands.		x							x	
6.	Enjoys stacking and/or sorting items.			x						x	
7.	Likes to help or care for others.						x			x	if request is simple
8.	Likes to work with tools and machinery.	x								x	
9.	Enjoys working in kitchen and preparing food.					x				x	stirring food, pouring
10.	Enjoys household duties (making beds, ironing, doing laundry).	x								x	milk
11.	Enjoys general cleaning duties (mopping, polishing, dusting).	x								x	
12.	Likes to make repairs.	x								x	

Interest Score 18 36 *Rating Score*

Leisure Time

		0	1	2	3	4	5	1	2	3	
1.	Initiates spare-time activities.		x							x	sometimes plays a record
2.	Willing to engage in new activities.		x							x	must be encouraged

Socialization

		0	1	2	3	4	5	1	2	3	
1.	Cooperates with peers.					x				x	
2.	Respects the work results of others.					x				x	
3.	Sits beside others and interacts.			x						x	
4.	Gives assistance when requested.		x							x	if something she wants
5.	Offers assistance without being requested.		x							x	if something she wants
6.	Requests help when needed.						x			x	raises hand to do
7.	Shares materials/supplies with others.		x							x	with reminders
8.	Displays social manners ("Thank you," "Excuse me," etc.).					x				x	
9.	Gives reinforcement to others ("I like your drawing," etc.).					x				x	
10.	Listens/attends to others who are talking.			x						x	
11.	Accepts authority figures.		x						x		not if an unknown
12.	Is sensitive to the feelings of others.		x							x	person

Socialization Score 30 35 *Rating Score*

Task Performance

		0	1	2	3	4	5	1	2	3	
1.	Completes simple manual routines (folding laundry, storing materials).	x								x	
2.	Washes various items (dishes, table tops, windows).	x								x	
3.	Uses a dishwasher properly.	x								x	We have in Lab.
4.	Uses a vacuum cleaner properly.	x								x	We have in Lab.
5.	Uses a stove properly.	x								x	We have in Lab.
6.	Prepares and serves a simple meal.	x								x	
7.	Sets a table in correct manner (silverware, napkins in proper place).	x								x	
8.	Makes a bed properly.	x								x	We have in Lab.
9.	Uses a washing machine properly.	x								x	We have in Lab.
10.	Uses a dryer properly.	x								x	We have in Lab.
11.	Can sew and mend by hand.	x								x	
12.	Can use a sewing machine to make simple items (apron, dishtowels).	x								x	We have in Lab.

Task Performance Score 0 36 *Rating Score*

CAREER ASSESSMENT INVENTORY (PROFILE)

Refer to page T656.

CAI DATE SCORED

I. ADMINISTRATIVE INDICES

RESPONSE PERCENTAGES

	L%	l%	I%	d%	D%
ACTIVITIES	17	12	15	21	36
	28		15		57
SCHOOL SUBJECTS	33	7	16	5	40
	40		16		44
OCCUPATIONS	10	11	17	20	42
	21		17		62

TOTAL RESPONSES	FINE ARTS-MECHANICAL	OCCUP EXTROV-INTROV	EDUC ORIENT	VARIAB OF INTERESTS
305	39	52	46	35

II. GENERAL THEMES

	SCALE	STD SCR.	VERY LOW	LOW 35	AVERAGE 43 57	HIGH 65	VERY HIGH
R	REALISTIC	27					
I	INVESTIGATIVE	39					
A	ARTISTIC	61					
S	SOCIAL	41					
E	ENTERPRISING	59					
C	CONVENTIONAL	48					

III. BASIC INTEREST AREAS

	SCALE	STD SCR.	VERY LOW	LOW 35	AVERAGE 43 57	HIGH 65	VERY HIGH
R	MECHANICAL/FIXING	31					
	ELECTRONICS	34					
	CARPENTRY	29					
	MANUAL/SKILL. TRADES	37					
	AGRICULTURE	35					
	NATURE/OUTDOORS	34					
	ANIMAL SERVICE	34					
I	SCIENCE	41					
	NUMBERS	39					
A	WRITING	70					
	PERFORMING/ENTERTAINING	59					
	ARTS/CRAFTS	43					
S	SOCIAL SERVICE	47					
	TEACHING	40					
	CHILD CARE	36					
	MEDICAL SERVICE	34					
	RELIGIOUS ACTIVITIES	41					
E	BUSINESS	54					
	SALES	44					
C	OFFICE PRACTICES	61					
	CLERICAL/CLERKING	49					
	FOOD SERVICE	42		35	57	65	

IV. OCCUPATIONAL SCALES

THEME CODE	OCCUPATION	STD SCORE	VERY DISS. 15	DISSIMILAR 25	MID-RANGE 44	SIMILAR 54	VERY SIMILAR	
RI	AIRCRAFT MECHANIC	3						R
R	AUTO MECHANIC	4						
R	BUS DRIVER	4						
RI	CAMERA REPAIR TECH.	11						
R	CARPENTER	5						
RI	CONSERVATION OFFICER	1						
RI	DENTAL LAB. TECHNICIAN	17						
RI	DRAFTER	12						
R	ELECTRICIAN	6						
RS	EMERGENCY MEDICAL TECH.	7						
R	FARMER/RANCHER	21						
R	FIREFIGHTER	1						
RI	FOREST RANGER	1						
RC	HARDWARE STORE MGR.	2						
R	JANITOR/JANITRESS	12						
R	MACHINIST	1						
RC	MAIL CARRIER	4						
RIA	MUSICAL INST. REPAIR	12						
RI	NAVY ENLISTED	9						
RI	ORTHOTIST/PROSTHETIST	2						
R	PAINTER	7						
RI	PARK RANGER	1						
R	PIPEFITTER/PLUMBER	2						
RS	POLICE OFFICER	21						
R	PRINTER	9						
RI	RADIO/TV REPAIR	11						
RC	SECURITY GUARD	21						
R	SHEET METAL WORKER	1						
RI	TELEPHONE REPAIR	9						
RI	TOOL/DIE MAKER	1						
R	TRUCK DRIVER	4						
RI	VETERINARY TECHNICIAN	1						
IS	CHIROPRACTOR	13						I
I	COMPUTER PROGRAMMER	31						
ISA	DENTAL HYGIENIST	1						
IR	ELECTRONIC TECHNICIAN	14						
I	MATH-SCIENCE TEACHER	12						
IR	MEDICAL LAB. TECHNICIAN	3						
IRS	RADIOLOGICAL TECHNICIAN	13						
IRS	RESPIRATORY THER. TECH.	6						
IR	SURVEYOR	14						
A	ADVER. ARTIST/WRITER	46						A
AE	ADVERTISING EXECUTIVE	55						
A	AUTHOR/WRITER	59						
ASE	COUNSELOR-CHEM. DEPEND.	51						
A	INTERIOR DESIGNER	28						
AE	LEGAL ASSISTANT	57						
AI	LIBRARIAN	57						
A	MUSICIAN	38						
AE	NEWSPAPER REPORTER	63						
A	PHOTOGRAPHER	40						
ARI	PIANO TECHNICIAN	18						
SR	ATHLETIC TRAINER	1						S
SA	CHILD CARE ASSISTANT	17						
SA	COSMETOLOGIST	19						
SA	ELEMENTARY SCHOOL TCH.	38						
SC	LICENSED PRACTICAL NURSE	16						
SC	NURSE AIDE	1						
SR	OCCUPATIONAL THER. ASST.	1						
SIR	OPERATING ROOM TECH.	14						
S	PHYSICAL THER. ASSISTANT	1						
SI	REGISTERED NURSE	4						
ER	BARBER/HAIRSTYLIST	7						E
EAS	BUYER/MERCHANDISER	52						
E	CARD/GIFT SHOP MANAGER	52						
ES	CATERER	30						
E	FLORIST	34						
ECS	FOOD SERVICE MANAGER	23						
ECS	HOTEL/MOTEL MANAGER	41						
ESC	INSURANCE AGENT	37						
E	MANUFACTURING REP.	26						
EAS	PERSONNEL MANAGER	54						
EA	PRIVATE INVESTIGATOR	52						
EC	PURCHASING AGENT	20						
E	REAL ESTATE AGENT	40						
ESA	RESERVATION AGENT	35						
ECS	RESTAURANT MANAGER	31						
EC	TRAVEL AGENT	49						
CE	ACCOUNTANT	40						C
CE	BANK TELLER	34						
C	BOOKKEEPER	39						
C	CAFETERIA WORKER	8						
CE	COURT REPORTER	58						
CE	DATA ENTRY OPERATOR	42						
CS	DENTAL ASSISTANT	19						
CSE	EXECUTIVE HOUSEKEEPER	27						
CS	MEDICAL ASSISTANT	29						
CS	PHARMACY TECHNICIAN	29						
C	SECRETARY	42						
CS	TEACHER AIDE	35						
CSE	WAITER/WAITRESS	23	15		44	54		

CAREER ASSESSMENT INVENTORIES (CAI)

Refer to page S148.

ATTRIBUTES INVENTORY

Instructions. For each item, circle the number that best describes the characteristic of the individual you are rating. Degrees of likeness to a characteristic are represented by numbers 1 through 6. Number 1 should be circled if the individual is *least like* the characteristic; number 6, if the individual is *most like* the characteristic.

REALISTIC						
Asocial (Shy)	1	2	3	4	5	6
Conforming	1	2	3	4	5	6
Frank	1	2	3	4	5	6
Genuine	1	2	3	4	5	6
Materialistic	1	2	3	4	5	6

INVESTIGATIVE						
Analytical	1	2	3	4	5	6
Cautious	1	2	3	4	5	6
Curious	1	2	3	4	5	6
Independent	1	2	3	4	5	6
Intellectual	1	2	3	4	5	6

ARTISTIC						
Complicated	1	2	3	4	5	6
Disorderly	1	2	3	4	5	6
Emotional	1	2	3	4	5	6
Idealistic	1	2	3	4	5	6
Imaginative	1	2	3	4	5	6

SOCIAL						
Cooperative	1	2	3	4	5	6
Friendly	1	2	3	4	5	6
Sensitive	1	2	3	4	5	6
Generous	1	2	3	4	5	6
Helpful	1	2	3	4	5	6

ABILITY INVENTORY

Instructions. For each item, circle the number that best describes the individual you are rating. Use the following criteria to rate the individual in comparison to other individuals who are making career decisions. (Note: Do not compare the individual with *only* other learning disabled individuals. Make all comparisons to the population at large.)

1. *Very Poor:* Skill is practically non-existent.
2. *Poor:* Skill is present, but basically non-useful.
3. *Low Average:* Skill is considered low for any individual.
4. *Average:* Skill is considered average for any individual.
5. *Above Average:* Skill is considered an asset to any individual.
6. *Excellent:* Skill far exceeds the expectation for most persons.

VERBAL UNDERSTANDING						
Listening at a Distance	1	2	3	4	5	6
Culling Main Ideas	1	2	3	4	5	6
Interpretation of Information	1	2	3	4	5	6
Following Directions	1	2	3	4	5	6
Verbal to Manual Sequencing	1	2	3	4	5	6
Verbal to Verbal Sequencing	1	2	3	4	5	6
Auditory Memory	1	2	3	4	5	6
Figure Ground in Noisy Places	1	2	3	4	5	6
Humor	1	2	3	4	5	6
Idioms/Slang	1	2	3	4	5	6

Score________

CONVERSATION						
Persuasion	1	2	3	4	5	6
Articulation	1	2	3	4	5	6
Response Time	1	2	3	4	5	6
Functional Usage	1	2	3	4	5	6
Questioning Strategies	1	2	3	4	5	6
Word Usage	1	2	3	4	5	6
Coherency	1	2	3	4	5	6
Speaking to the Point	1	2	3	4	5	6
Initiation of Conversation	1	2	3	4	5	6
Fluency	1	2	3	4	5	6

Score________

CENTRAL INSTITUTE FOR THE DEAF PRESCHOOL PERFORMANCE SCALE (CID PERSONAL PERFORMANCE SCALE)

Refer to page S154.

Cat. No. 37020R
Summary Sheet
Central Institute for the Deaf
Preschool Performance Scale

Name ______________________ Date Tested ______________

School ______________________ Date of Birth ______________

Examiner ______________________ Chronologic Age __________ IQ __________

Subtest	Point Score	Scaled Score
Manual Planning	______	______
Manual Dexterity	______	______
Form Perception	______	______
Perceptual Motor Skills	______	______
Preschool Skills	______	______
Part-Whole Relations	______	______
SUM OF SCALED SCORES		______

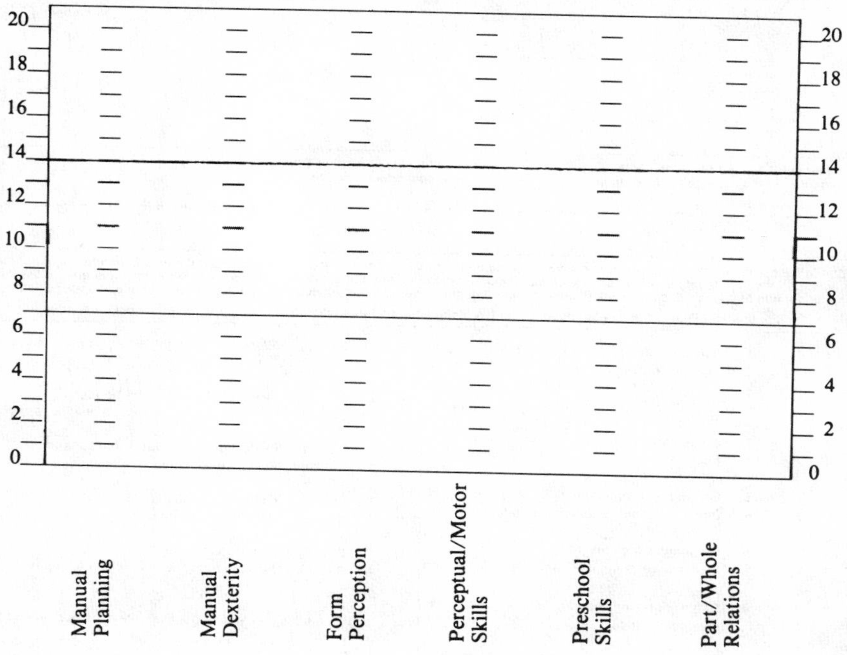

CHILD BEHAVIOR CHECKLIST AND REVISED CHILD BEHAVIOR PROFILE

Refer to page S28.

CHILD BEHAVIOR CHECKLIST FOR AGES 4-16

For office use only
ID #

CHILD'S NAME

SEX ☐ Boy ☐ Girl | AGE | RACE

TODAY'S DATE Mo. ______ Day ______ Yr. ______

CHILD'S BIRTHDATE Mo. ______ Day ______ Yr. ______

GRADE IN SCHOOL

PARENT'S TYPE OF WORK *(Please be specific—for example: auto mechanic, high school teacher, homemaker, laborer, lathe operator, shoe salesman, army sergeant, even if parent does not live with child.)*

FATHER'S TYPE OF WORK: ______________________

MOTHER'S TYPE OF WORK: ______________________

THIS FORM FILLED OUT BY:

☐ Mother

☐ Father

☐ Other *(Specify)*:

I. Please list the sports your child most likes to take part in. For example: swimming, baseball, skating, skate boarding, bike riding, fishing, etc.

☐ None

	Compared to other children of the same age, about how much time does he/she spend in each?				Compared to other children of the same age, how well does he/she do each one?			
	Don't Know	Less Than Average	Average	More Than Average	Don't Know	Below Average	Average	Above Average
a. ______	☐	☐	☐	☐	☐	☐	☐	☐
b. ______	☐	☐	☐	☐	☐	☐	☐	☐
c. ______	☐	☐	☐	☐	☐	☐	☐	☐

II. Please list your child's favorite hobbies, activities, and games, other than sports. For example: stamps, dolls, books, piano, crafts, singing, etc. (Do not include T.V.)

☐ None

	Compared to other children of the same age, about how much time does he/she spend in each?				Compared to other children of the same age, how well does he/she do each one?			
	Don't Know	Less Than Average	Average	More Than Average	Don't Know	Below Average	Average	Above Average
a. ______	☐	☐	☐	☐	☐	☐	☐	☐
b. ______	☐	☐	☐	☐	☐	☐	☐	☐
c. ______	☐	☐	☐	☐	☐	☐	☐	☐

III. Please list any organizations, clubs, teams, or groups your child belongs to.

☐ None

Compared to other children of the same age, how active is he/she in each?

VIII. Below is a list of items that describe children. For each item that describes your child **now or within the past 6 months,** please circle the **2** if the item is **very true** or **often true** of your child. Circle the **1** if the item is **somewhat** or **sometimes true** of your child. If the item is **not true** of your child, circle the **0.** Please answer all items as well as you can, even if some do not seem to apply to your child.

0 = Not True (as far as you know) **1 = Somewhat or Sometimes True** **2 = Very True or Often True**

0 1 2 1. Acts too young for his/her age 16
0 1 2 2. Allergy (describe): ______________________
0 1 2 3. Argues a lot
0 1 2 4. Asthma
0 1 2 5. Behaves like opposite sex 20
0 1 2 6. Bowel movements outside toilet
0 1 2 7. Bragging, boasting
0 1 2 8. Can't concentrate, can't pay attention for long
0 1 2 9. Can't get his/her mind off certain thoughts; obsessions (describe): ______________________
0 1 2 10. Can't sit still, restless, or hyperactive 25

0 1 2 31. Fears he/she might think or do something bad
0 1 2 32. Feels he/she has to be perfect
0 1 2 33. Feels or complains that no one loves him/her
0 1 2 34. Feels others are out to get him/her
0 1 2 35. Feels worthless or inferior 50
0 1 2 36. Gets hurt a lot, accident-prone
0 1 2 37. Gets in many fights
0 1 2 38. Gets teased a lot
0 1 2 39. Hangs around with children who get in trouble
0 1 2 40. Hears things that aren't there (describe): ______________________ 55

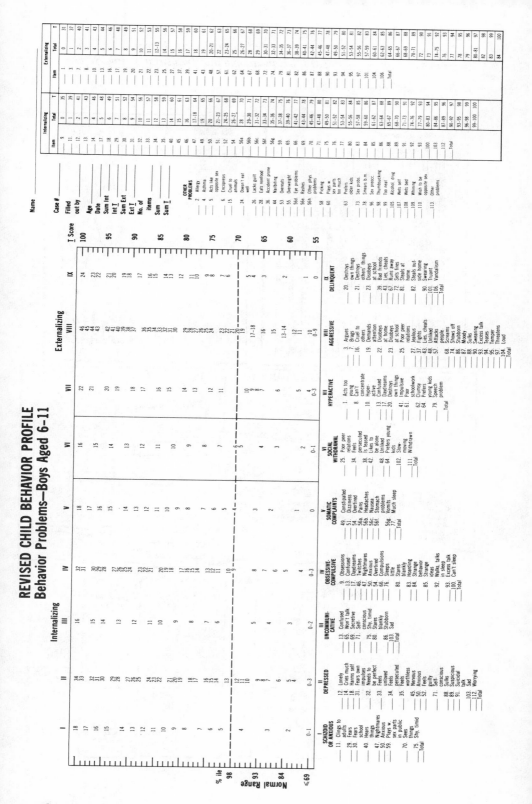

REVISED CHILD BEHAVIOR PROFILE
Behavior Problems—Boys Aged 6–11

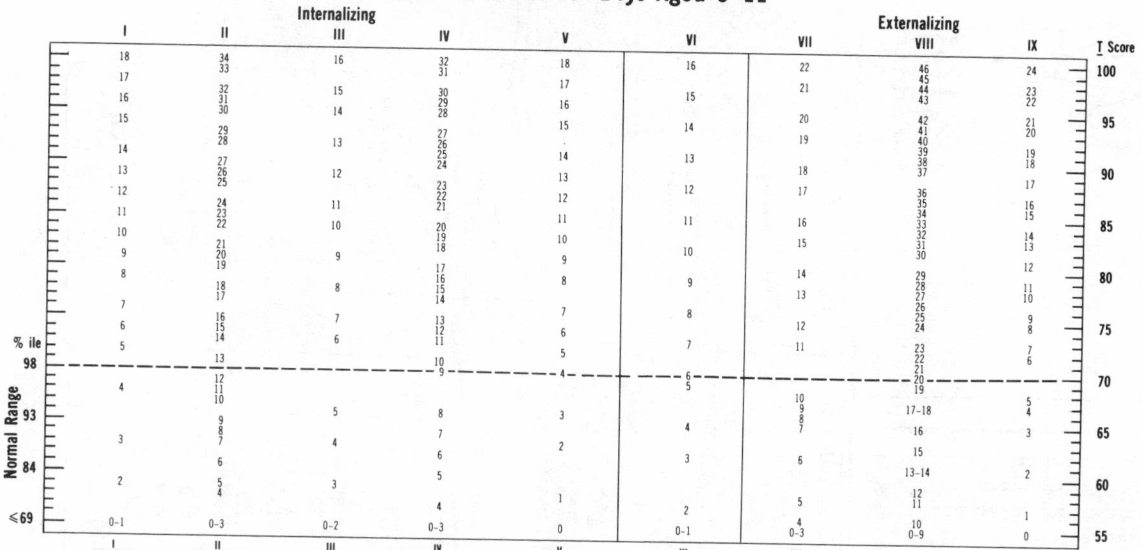

I SCHIZOID OR ANXIOUS
___ 11. Clings to adults
___ 29. Fears
___ 30. Fears school
___ 40. Hears things
___ 47. Nightmares
___ 50. Anxious
___ 59. Plays w. sex parts in public
___ 70. Sees things
___ 75. Shy, timid
___ Total

II DEPRESSED
___ 12. Lonely
___ 14. Cries much
___ 18. Harms self
___ 31. Fears own impulses
___ 32. Needs to be perfect
___ 33. Feels unloved
___ 34. Feels persecuted
___ 35. Feels worthless
___ 45. Nervous
___ 50. Anxious
___ 52. Feels guilty
___ 71. Self-conscious
___ 88. Sulks
___ 89. Suspicious
___ 91. Suicidal talk
___ 103. Sad
___ 112. Worrying
___ Total

III UNCOMMUNICATIVE
___ 13. Confused
___ 65. Won't talk
___ 69. Secretive
___ 71. Self-conscious
___ 75. Shy, timid
___ 80. Stares blankly
___ 86. Stubborn
___ 103. Sad
___ Total

IV OBSESSIVE-COMPULSIVE
___ 9. Obsessions
___ 13. Confused
___ 17. Daydreams
___ 46. Twitches
___ 47. Nightmares
___ 50. Anxious
___ 54. Overtired
___ 66. Compulsions
___ 76. Sleeps little
___ 80. Stares blankly
___ 83. Hoarding
___ 84. Strange behavior
___ 85. Strange ideas
___ 92. Walks, talks in sleep
___ 93. Excess talk
___ 100. Can't sleep
___ Total

V SOMATIC COMPLAINTS
___ 49. Constipated
___ 51. Dizziness
___ 54. Overtired
___ 56a. Pains
___ 56b. Headaches
___ 56c. Nausea
___ 56f. Stomach problems
___ 56g. Vomits
___ 77. Much sleep
___ Total

VI SOCIAL WITHDRAWAL
___ 25. Poor peer relations
___ 34. Feels persecuted
___ 38. Is teased
___ 42. Likes to be alone
___ 48. Unliked
___ 64. Prefers young kids
___ 102. Slow-moving
___ 111. Withdrawn
___ Total

VII HYPERACTIVE
___ 1. Acts too young
___ 8. Can't concentrate
___ 10. Hyper-active
___ 13. Confused
___ 17. Daydreams
___ 20. Destroys own things
___ 41. Impulsive
___ 61. Poor schoolwork
___ 62. Clumsy
___ 64. Prefers young kids
___ 79. Speech problem
___ Total

VIII AGGRESSIVE
___ 3. Argues
___ 7. Brags
___ 16. Cruel to others
___ 19. Demands attention
___ 22. Disobeys at home
___ 23. Disobeys at school
___ 25. Poor peer relations
___ 27. Jealous
___ 37. Fights
___ 43. Lies, cheats
___ 48. Unliked
___ 57. Attacks people
___ 68. Screams
___ 74. Shows off
___ 86. Stubborn
___ 87. Moody
___ 88. Sulks
___ 90. Swearing
___ 93. Excess talk
___ 94. Teases
___ 95. Temper
___ 97. Threatens
___ 104. Loud
___ Total

IX DELINQUENT
___ 20. Destroys own things
___ 21. Destroys others' things
___ 23. Disobeys at school
___ 39. Bad friends
___ 43. Lies, cheats
___ 67. Runs away
___ 72. Sets fires
___ 81. Steals at home
___ 82. Steals outside home
___ 90. Swearing
___ 101. Truant
___ 106. Vandalism
___ Total

Name ______________________

Case # __________
Filled out by __________
Age __________
Date __________
Sum Int __________
Int T __________
Sum Ext __________
Ext T __________
No. of items __________
Sum __________
Sum T __________

OTHER PROBLEMS
___ 2. Allergy
___ 4. Asthma
___ 5. Acts like opposite sex
___ 6. Encopresis
___ 15. Cruel to animals
___ 24. Doesn't eat well
___ 26. Lacks guilt
___ 28. Eats nonfood
___ 36. Accident prone
___ 44. Nailbiting
___ 53. Overeats
___ 55. Overweight
___ 56d. Eye problems
___ 56e. Rashes
___ 56h. Other phys. problems
___ 58. Picking
___ 60. Plays w. sex parts too much
___ 63. Prefers older kids
___ 73. Sex probs.
___ 78. Smears b.m.
___ 96. Sex preocc.
___ 98. Thumbsucking
___ 99. Too neat
___ 105. Alcohol, drug
___ 107. Wets self
___ 108. Wets bed
___ 109. Whining
___ 110. Wish to be opposite sex
___ 113. Other problems

Internalizing			Externalizing		
Item	Total	T	Item	Total	T
___ 9	0	35	___ 1	0	31
___ 11	1	39	___ 3	1	37
___ 12	2	41	___ 7	2	40
___ 13	3	43	___ 8	3	41
___ 14	4	46	___ 10	4	43
___ 17	5	48	___ 13	5	44
___ 18	6	49	___ 16	6	46
___ 29	7	51	___ 17	7	48
___ 30	8	52	___ 19	8	49
___ 31	9	54	___ 20	9	51
___ 32	10	56	___ 21	10	52
___ 33	11	57	___ 22	11	53
___ 34	12	58	___ 23	12-13	55
___ 35	13	59	___ 25	14	56
___ 40	14	60	___ 27	15	57
___ 45	15	61	___ 37	16	58
___ 46	16	63	___ 39	17	59
___ 47	17-18	64	___ 41	18	60
___ 49	19	65	___ 43	19	61
___ 50	20	66	___ 48	20-21	62
___ 51	21-23	67	___ 57	22	63
___ 52	24-25	68	___ 61	23-24	65
___ 54	26-27	69	___ 62	25	66
___ 56a	28	70	___ 64	26-27	67
___ 56b	29-30	71	___ 67	28	68
___ 56c	31-32	72	___ 68	29	69
___ 56f	33-34	73	___ 72	30-31	70
___ 56g	35-36	74	___ 74	32-33	71
___ 59	37-38	75	___ 79	34-35	72
___ 65	39-40	76	___ 81	36-37	73
___ 66	41-42	77	___ 82	38-39	74
___ 69	43-44	78	___ 86	40-41	75
___ 70	45-46	79	___ 87	42-44	76
___ 71	47-48	80	___ 88	45-46	77
___ 75	49-50	81	___ 90	47-48	78
___ 76	51-52	82	___ 93	49-50	79
___ 77	53-54	83	___ 94	51-52	80
___ 80	55-56	84	___ 95	53-54	81
___ 83	57-58	85	___ 97	55-56	82
___ 84	59-60	86	___ 101	57-59	83
___ 85	61-62	87	___ 104	60-61	84
___ 86	63-64	88	___ 106	62-63	85
___ 88	65-67	89	___ Total	64-65	86
___ 89	68-70	90		66-67	87
___ 91	71-73	91		68-69	88
___ 92	74-76	92		70-71	89
___ 93	77-79	93		72	90
___ 100	80-83	94		73	91
___ 103	84-86	95		74-75	92
___ 112	87-89	96		76	93
___ Total	90-92	97		77	94
	93-95	98		78	95
	96-98	99		79	96
	99-100	100		80-81	97
				82	98
				83	99
				84	100

COPYSYSTEM

Refer to pages T660-62.

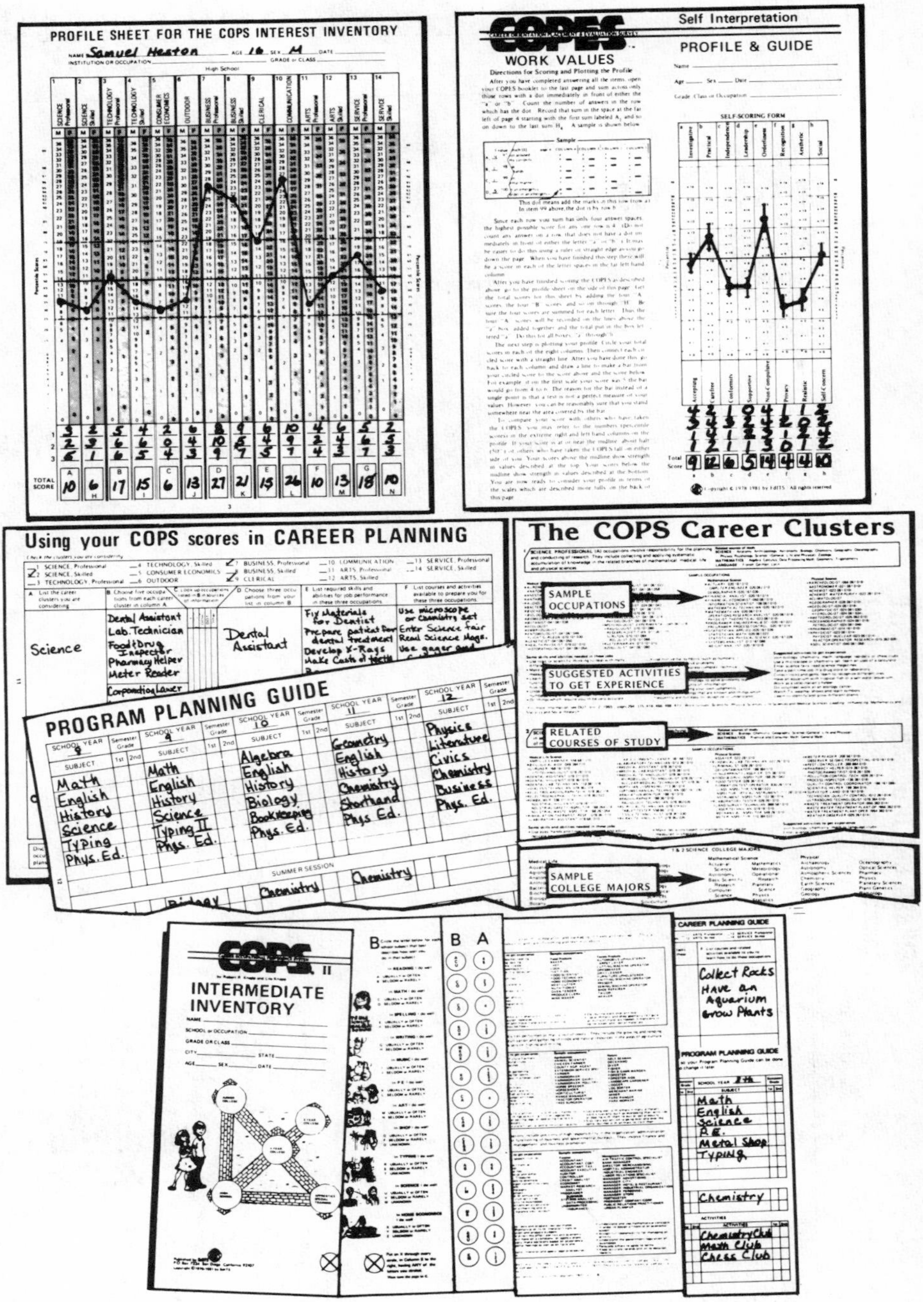

CULTURE-FREE SELF-ESTEEM INVENTORIES, FORM A

Refer to page S184.

CULTURE-FREE SEI, FORM A

Name____________________________Age_____Date of Birth____________

School___________________________Today's Date______________

Examiner___________________________Total___G___S___A___P___L___

Directions

Please mark each statement in the following way: If the statement describes how you usually feel, make a check mark (✓) in the "yes" column. If the statement does not describe how you usually feel, make a check mark (✓) in the "no" column. Please check only one column (either "yes" or "no") for each of the 60 statements. This is *not* a test, and there are no "right" or "wrong" answers.

		Yes	***No***
1.	I spend a lot of time daydreaming.	☐	☐
2.	Boys and girls like to play with me	☐	☐
3.	I like to spend most of my time alone	☐	☐
4.	I am satisfied with my school work	☐	☐
5.	I have lots of fun with my mother	☐	☐
6.	My parents never get angry at me.	☐	☐
7.	I wish I were younger	☐	☐
8.	I have only a few friends	☐	☐
9.	I usually quit when my school work is too hard	☐	☐
10.	I have lots of fun with my father	☐	☐
11.	I am happy most of the time	☐	☐

46.	Other boys and girls are mean to me.	☐	☐
47.	I know myself very well	☐	☐
48.	I am doing the best school work that I can	☐	☐
49.	People can depend on me to keep my promises	☐	☐
50.	My parents think I am a failure.	☐	☐
51.	I always tell the truth	☐	☐
52.	I need more friends	☐	☐
53.	I always know what to say to people	☐	☐
54.	My teacher feels that I am not good enough.	☐	☐
55.	My parents love me	☐	☐
56.	I never do anything wrong	☐	☐
57.	Most boys and girls are stronger than I am	☐	☐
58.	I am proud of my school work.	☐	☐
59.	I often get upset at home	☐	☐
60.	I am never unhappy	☐	☐

DENVER HANDWRITING ANALYSIS (DHA)

Refer to page S65.

DENVER HANDWRITING ANALYSIS

SCORING PROFILE

Peggy L. Anderson, PhD

Name ______________________________ **Date** ______________

SUBSKILL ANALYSIS	**Part I: Near-Point Copying (119)**	**Part II-A: Writing Capitals (26)**	**Part II-B: Writing Lower Case (26)**	**Part III: Far-Point Copying (155)**
Mastery Levels	/ = %	/ = %	/ = %	/ = %
Closure				
Looping				
Rounding				
Connection				
Transition				
Reversal				
Poor Formation				
Substitution				
Omission				
Insertion				

Note: Values in parentheses indicate total number possible.

PERFORMANCE ANALYSIS	**Part I**	**Part II-A**	**Part II-B**	**Part III**
Spatial Organization				
Speed				
Slant				
Appearance				

Total: Parts I-III (326)	**Part IV: Manuscript-Cursive Transition**	**Part V: Dictation**
______ = % Mastery Level	______ / 26 = % Mastery Level	______ / 10 = % Mastery Level

DEVELOPMENTAL INDICATORS FOR THE ASSESSMENT OF LEARNING—REVISED (DIAL-R)

Refer to page S119.

DIAL-R™ SCORESHEET

Child's Name ______ (LAST / FIRST / NICKNAME)
Address ______ (NUMBER / STREET / CITY/STATE/ZIP)
Phone Number (____) ______ (AREA CODE)
Parents' Names ______ (MOTHER / FATHER)
1 2 3

1	2	3
Potential Problem	OK	Potential Gifted

School ______ Class ______
Hearing + − Vision + −
Today's Date ___ ___ ___ (YEAR / MONTH / DAY)
Birth Date ___ ___ ___
C.A. ___ ___
Boy ___ Girl ___

MOTOR (red)

	Scaled Score 0	1	2	3	4
1. Catching	0	—	1	2	3
2. Jumping, Hopping, and Skipping jumps: 0 1 + hops: (right) 0 1 2 3 4 5 6 (left) 0 1 2 3 4 5 6 + skip: 0-any 1-slide 2-step/hop 3-skip	0	1-2	3-8	9-12	13-16
3. Building	0	1	2	3	4
4. Touching Fingers	0	1	2	3	4
5. Cutting	0-1	2	3	4	
6. Matching I ○ + □ △ ◊ E N D S ⧣ ⧣	0	1-7	8-9	10-11	12
7. Copying I 0 1 2 E 0 1 2 ○ 0 1 2 N 0 1 2 + 0 1 2 D 0 1 2 □ 0 1 2 S 0 1 2 △ 0 1 2 ⧣ 0 1 2 ◊ 0 1 2 ⧣ 0 1 2	0	1-7	8-11	12-18	19-24
8. Writing Name	0	—	—	1	2
TOTAL (Max.= 31)	OBSERVATIONS 1 2 3 4 5 6 7 8				

CONCEPTS (green)

	Scaled Score 0	1	2	3	4
1. Naming Colors R O W G BL Y B BR P	0	1-7	8-15	16-18	
2. Identifying Body Parts nose neck chin ankle hair stomach shoulder hip ear knee chest waist teeth thumb heel tongue elbow wrist	0	1-9	10-12	13-15	16-18
3. Counting (Rote)	0-2	3-4	5-8	9-10	11
4. Counting (Meaningful) 1 3 5 7 9	0	1	3	5-7	9
5. Positioning on under corner between middle	0	1-2	3	4	5
6. Identifying Concepts biggest big hot empty night longest long most more fastest fast littlest little cold full day shortest short least less slowest slow	0	1-14	15-20	21-26	27-28
7. Naming Letters O B P E R W Y G	0	—	—	1-10	11-16
8. Sorting Chips by color: R B Y by size: big little by shape: ○ □ △	0	—	—	1-4	5-8
TOTAL (Max.= 31)	OBSERVATIONS 1 2 3 4 5 6 7 8				

LANGUAGE (purple)

	Scaled Score 0	1	2	3	4
1. Articulating pin rabbit truck bed chair dress cup knife sandwich towel leg thumb hand fish mouth/teeth	0	1-14	15-26	27-29	
2. Giving Personal Data first name sex phone # last name street age city/state	0	1-3	4	5	6-7
3. Remembering clapping 1 2 3 numbers 1 2 3 sentences 1 2 3	0	1-3	4-5	6-7	8-9
4. Naming Nouns cat phone comb plane TV pencil car clock ambulance	0	1-15	16	17	18
5. Naming Verbs sleep call comb fly watch write drive time go to hospital	0	1-9	10-14	15-16	17-18
6. Classifying Foods Tally ______	0	1-2	3-4	5-6	7-8
7. Problem Solving hungry 0 1 2 dark room 0 1 2 rain 0 1 2 broken 0 1 2	0	1	2-3	4-5	6-8
8. Sentence Length ______ ______ ______	0	1-2	3	4	5-8
TOTAL (Max.= 31)	OBSERVATIONS 1 2 3 4 5 6 7 8				

Cut-off Points

Age (Yrs. – Mos.)

Age	1	3	Age	1	3	Age	1	3	Age	1	3	Age	1	3
2-0 to 2-2	0	30	3-0 to 3-2	15	50	4-0 to 4-2	34	67	5-0 to 5-2	51	77	6-0 to 6-2	58	82
2-3 to 2-5	2	40	3-3 to 3-5	18	57	4-3 to 4-5	37	70	5-3 to 5-5	53	78	6-3 to 6-5	59	83
2-6 to 2-8	4	44	3-6 to 3-8	26	62	4-6 to 4-8	41	73	5-6 to 5-8	55	80	6-6 to 6-8	60	84
2-9 to 2-11	10	47	3-9 to 3-11	32	65	4-9 to 4-11	47	75	5-9 to 5-11	57	81	6-9 to 6-11	61	85

Motor score ______
Concepts score ______
Language score ______
TOTAL ______

CHILDCRAFT EDUCATION CORP

THE DEVEREUX ELEMENTARY SCHOOL BEHAVIOR RATING SCALE (DESB-II)

Refer to page T617.

RATING GUIDE

1. Base rating on student's recent and current behavior.	Consider only the behavior of the student over the past month.
2. Compare the student with normal children his age.	The standard for comparison should be the average youngster in the normal classroom situation.
3. Base rating on your own experience with the student.	Consider only your own impression. As much as possible, ignore what others have said about the student and their impressions.
4. Consider each question independently.	Make no effort to describe a consistent behavioral picture or personality. It is known that children may show seemingly contradictory behavior.
5. Avoid interpretations of "unconscious" motives and feelings.	As much as possible, base ratings on outward behavior you actually observe. Do not try to interpret what might be going on in the student's mind.
6. Use extreme ratings whenever warranted.	Avoid tending to rate near the middle of all scales. Make use of the full range offered by the scales.
7. Rate each item quickly.	If you are unable to reach a decision, go on to the next item and come back later to those you skipped.
8. Rate every question.	Attempt to rate each item. If you are unable to rate a particular item because it is not appropriate to the child in question, or because of lack of information, circle the item number.
9. He or him are used as generic pronouns for ease of reading. The scale is standardized for both girls and boys.	See the manual for norms for girls and boys.

YOU ARE GOING TO RATE THE OVERT BEHAVIOR OF A STUDENT. FOR ITEMS 1 - 30 USE THE RATING SCALE BELOW. MARK YOUR RATING (NUMBER) FOR EACH ITEM ON THE MARKING SHEET NEXT TO THE ITEM NUMBER.

Very frequently	Often	Occasionally	Rarely	Never
5	4	3	2	1

COMPARED WITH THE AVERAGE CHILD IN THE NORMAL CLASSROOM SITUATION, **HOW OFTEN** DOES THE CHILD...........

Rating	Item
☐	1. Hand in work without checking it first?
☐	2. Give an answer that has nothing to do with a question being asked?
☐	3. Show worry or get anxious about knowing the "right" answers?
☐	4. Say that the teacher doesn't help him enough (i.e., won't show him how to do things, or answer his questions)?
☐	5. Forget the directions that are given?
☐	6. Rush through work just to get the job done?
☐	16. Introduce into class discussion personal experiences or things he has heard which relate to what is going on in class?
☐	17. Start working on something before getting the directions straight?
☐	18. Say he doesn't like the work assigned?
☐	19. Make irrelevant remarks during a classroom discussion?
☐	20. Seek out the teacher before or after class to talk about school or personal matters?
☐	21. Just sit and not participate (e.g., not raise

DESB II PROFILE *

Marshall Swift, Ph.D.

Student's Name ______________ **Teacher's Name** ______________

Student's Sex ________ **Age** ________ **Academic Subject** ______________

Grade ______ **School** ______________ **Date of Rating** ______________

Behavior Factor	Factor Item Raw Scores	Tot. Raw Sc.
1. Work Organization	Complete 10 ___ 39 ___ Independ. Organize 36 ___ 45 ___ To work	
2. Creative Initiative/ Involvement	Initiate 12 ___ 29 ___ Listen Talk exper 16 ___ Bring in 24 ___ 30 ___ Act. Imag.	
3. Positive Toward Teacher	Seek out 20 ___ 35 ___ Close Praise 31 ___ 49 ___ Respons.	
4. Need for Direction in Work	Unab. corr. 42 ___ Direct. 43 ___ 48 ___ Reliant	
5. Socially Withdrawn	Avoid 11 ___ 40 ___ Withdrawn Not Part. 21 ___ 46 ___ Obliv.	
6. Failure Anxiety	Worry 3 ___ 25 ___ Upset Test 7 ___ 50 ___ Sensitive	
7. Impatience	Not check 1 ___ 17 ___ Start Rush 6 ___ 44 ___ Go back	
8. Irrelevant Thinking/ Talk	Answers 2 ___ 19 ___ Irrelev. Jump 9 ___ 22 ___ Unrelated	
9. Blaming	No help 4 ___ 18 ___ Not like No call 13 ___ 41 ___ Blame	
10. Negative/ Aggressive	Tease 14 ___ 27 ___ Belittle Destroy 26 ___ 28 ___ Rules	
Behavior Clusters	**Cluster Item Raw Scores**	
11. Perseverance	Complete 23 ___ 33 ___ Persist	
12. Peer Cooperation	Work well 32 ___ 38 ___ Share	
13. Confusion	Forget 5 ___ 43 ___ Directions Confused 34 ___	
14. Inattention	No attn. 8 ___ 37 ___ Not reach Lose attn. 15 ___ 47 ___ Distract	
Achievement	**Achievement Item Raw Scores**	
15. Compared to	Average 51 ___	
16. Compared to own	Ability 52 ___	

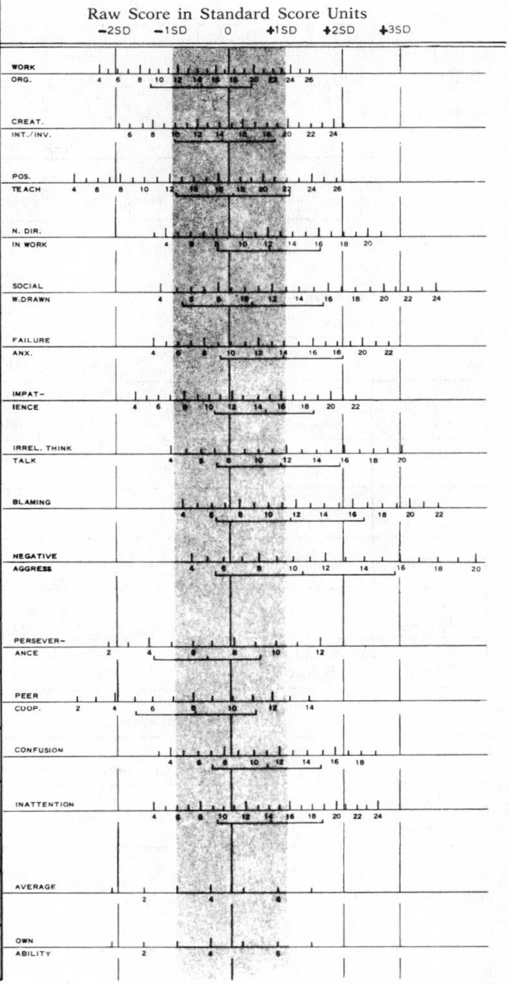

DIAGNOSTIC SPELLING POTENTIAL TEST (DSPT)

Refer to page S68.

DSPT Form A-1

Name ______________________ Date _____yr _____mo _____day

School ______________________ Date of Birth _____yr _____mo _____day

Teacher ______________________ Age _____yr _____mo _____day

Examiner ______________________ Grade _____yr _____mo Sex_____

Score Box

TYPE OF SCORE	Spelling	WORD RECOGNITION: Sight	WORD RECOGNITION: Phonetic	SPELLING RECOGNITION: Visual	SPELLING RECOGNITION: Aud-Vis
Raw Score	____	____	____	____	____
Standard Score	____	____	____	____	____
Percentile Rank	____	____	____	____	____
Grade Rating	____	____	____	____	____

Profile Chart

Verbal Description	Standard Score	Spelling	WORD RECOGNITION: Sight	WORD RECOGNITION: Phonetic	SPELLING RECOGNITION: Visual	SPELLING RECOGNITION: Aud-Vis	Percentile Rank
Superior	130 and above						98 and above
Above Average	115-129						84-97
Average	85-114						16-83
Below Average	70-84						2-15
Low	69 and below						2 and below

Spelling Error Analysis Chart

	Reversal or Transposition	Phonetic	Other
Number	____	____	____
Percent	____	____	____

Word Recognition

DSPT Form A-1

S P I		S P I		S P I	
1. ____ ____ ____	look	31. ____ ____ ____	damage	61. ____ ____ ____	honorable
2. ____ ____ ____	she	32. ____ ____ ____	blizzard	62. ____ ____ ____	engagement
3. ____ ____ ____	had	33. ____ ____ ____	confine	63. ____ ____ ____	criticism
4. ____ ____ ____	but	34. ____ ____ ____	sword	64. ____ ____ ____	pronunciation
5. ____ ____ ____	can	35. ____ ____ ____	jewel	65. ____ ____ ____	forfeit

Sight Raw Score (column S) ________

Phonetic Raw Score (column S + column P) ________

DIAGNOSTIC TEST OF LIBRARY SKILLS

Refer to page S142.

FORM B

DIAGNOSTIC TEST OF LIBRARY SKILLS

DIRECTIONS: Read each question carefully and indicate your choice for the correct answer by marking in the box under the letter on the answer sheet. Do not make any mark on the test itself.

1. The person who writes the book is the
   a. illustrator
   b. publisher
   c. distributor
   d. author
2. The publisher
   a. prints the book
   b. writes the book
   c. draws the pictures
   d. is the subject of a biography
3. The person who draws the pictures is the
   a. illustrator
   b. publisher
   c. distributor
   d. author

Look at this sample title page then answer questions 4, 5, 6 and 7.

Mrs. Frisby and the
Rats of NIMH
by
Robert C. O'Brien
illustrated by

8. The copyright date tells
   a. when the book was first published
   b. when the author was born
   c. when the publishing company was founded
   d. when the illustrator was born
9. The copyright date is usually found
   a. on the spine
   b. in the Index
   c. in the Table of Contents
   d. on the back of the title page
10. In the library a story that never happened called **Tuck Everlasting** by Natalie Babbitt could be located in the
    a. non-fiction section
    b. biography section
    c. fiction section
    d. reference section
11. Of the following fiction books, which one will come last on the shelves?
    a. **Beat the Turtle Drum** by Constance Greene
    b. **The Wind in the Willows** by Ken
    Grahame
    c. **At the Mouth of th**
    Arnold Gr
    d. **Sc**

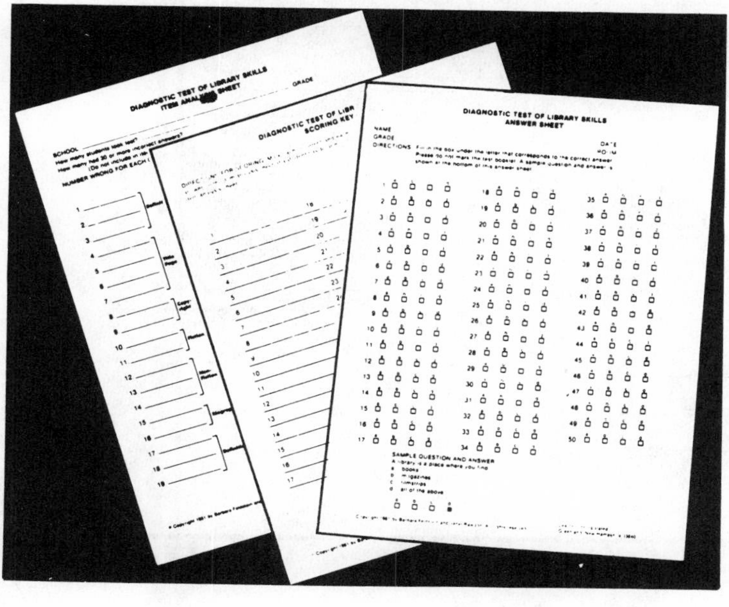

THE ENRIGHT™ DIAGNOSTIC INVENTORY OF BASIC ARITHMETIC SKILLS

Refer to page S74.

C-6 MULTIPLICATION OF WHOLE NUMBERS
3-Digit Number by a 1-Digit Number, Regrouping Ones

Diagnostic Inventory of Basic Arithmetic Skills
©1983 Curriculum Associates, Inc.

NAME:

a.	b.	c.	d.	e.
328 × 3	419 × 2	227 × 3	118 × 4	216 × 2

216 × 4	346 × 2	127 × 3	427 × 2	219 × 3

C. *Multiplication of Whole Numbers* — *3-Digit Number by a 1-Digit Number, Regrouping Ones*

SKILL: Multiplies a 3-digit number by a 1-digit number, regrouping ones.

GRADE LEVEL TAUGHT: 3.6

ARITHMETIC RECORD BOOK: Page 4

MATERIALS: Copy of S-96 and a pencil.

ASSESSMENT METHODS: Individual or group written response.

DISCONTINUE: When student has completed the five test items at the top of S-96.

ACCURACY: At least 4/5 (80%) on the test items is required. When the review items are used for post testing, 4/5 (80%) is also required.

NEXT: If the student's accuracy is 4/5 (80%) on this skill test, proceed to the next higher test.

If the student has responded incorrectly to two or more test items, do not proceed to the next higher skill test. Instead, begin remediation based on the error analysis shown here.

NOTES:
- * Check to see if student works left to right instead of right to left. Working left to right also results in answers shown here.
- † These answers show that student regroups, if necessary, when adding.

REVIEW ITEMS

a.	b.	c.	d.	e.
216 × 4 = 864	346 × 2 = 692	127 × 3 = 381	427 × 2 = 854	219 × 3 = 657

(C-6)
OBJECTIVE: By ________ (date), when given five test items for multiplying a 3-digit number by a 1-digit number, regrouping ones, ________ (student's name) will correctly compute at least four of the five test items (80%).

DIRECTIONS: Give each student a copy of **S-96** and a pencil. Tell the students to do the five items at the top of **S-96**. Tell the students to work carefully and take as much time as needed.

a.	b.	c.	d.	e.
328 × 3 = 984	419 × 2 = 838	227 × 3 = 681	118 × 4 = 472	216 × 2 = 432

ERROR ANALYSIS

a.	b.	c.	d.	e.	Error	Example
9624	8218	6621	4432	4212	***Regrouping 13:*** *Writes entire product of each column without regrouping.**	328 × 3 = 9624
912	811	672	463	441	***Regrouping 14:*** *Writes tens value of each subproduct, and regroups ones value into next column.*	328 × 3 = 912
964	828	661	442	422	***Regrouping 15:*** *Writes ones value of each subproduct, but doesn't regroup tens value into next column.*	328 × 3 = 964
971	831	670	452	428	***Process Substitution 29:*** *Adds ones column, and multiplies other column(s).†*	328 × 3 = 971
661	641	560	562	438	***Process Substitution 30:*** *Adds using multiplication process.†*	328 × 3 = 661
1224	848	921	862	442	***Process Substitution 32:*** *Regroups, but adds regrouped value to next column before multiplying.*	328 × 3 = 1224
325	417	224	114	214	***Attention to Sign 193:*** *Subtracts.*	328 − 3 = 325

Examiner's Notes:

C-6 MULTIPLICATION OF WHOLE NUMBERS:
3-Digit Number by a 1-Digit Number, Regrouping Ones

96

EXPRESSIVE ONE-WORD PICTURE VOCABULARY TEST: UPPER EXTENSION

Refer to page S163.

INDIVIDUAL TEST FORM

Name: ____
Last First Middle

School: ____

Grade: ____

Sex: __________ Examiner: ______________________________

Date of Test: ____
Year Month Day

Date of Birth: _______________________________________
Year Month Day

Chronological Age: ____________________________________
Year Month Day*

*If the number of days exceeds 15, consider as a full month and increase the months by one.

Test Results:

Raw Score .... ________

Mental Age .... ________

Deviation IQ .... ________

Percentile .... ________

Stanine .... ________

Basal: **Established by (8) consecutive correct verbal responses.**

Ceiling: **Established by six (6) consecutive errors.**

Begin with plate 10 for individuals 12 through 13 years old and plate 15 for individuals 14 years old and above. If basal is not established, work backwards until eight (8) consecutive correct responses are made.

Record in writing in space after word all responses whether right or wrong. This will avoid having the child make his own analysis of his or her successes or failures.

1 lobster ____________________

crayfish ____________________

2 microscope ____________________

22 fire extinguishers ____________________

23 Eiffel Tower ____________________

24 hammock ____________________

Obtaining a Raw Score:

Ceiling item .... ____________

Minus errors .... ____________

Raw score .... ____________

*Any response that contains the root of the stimulus word is correct.

Note to Examiner:

After completing the administration of the test, draw a slanted line through the numbers of the items that are incorrect. This will reduce the number of scoring errors. Underline any of the responses that indicate a speech distortion.

EMOTIONAL STABILITY SURVEY (E.S. SURVEY)
© *Copyright Robert W. Cormack & Alan L. Strand.*
Reprinted by permission of Psychological Systems Corporation.

Refer to page S226.

personnel security preview©
E. S. Survey®

REMINDER: You are being examined by a psychological technique that identifies biasing of answers. It is therefore important that your answers are truthful since any falsification will be gradeable when the test is scored.

	Yes	(?)	No
1. Do you usually feel cheerful?	☐	☐	☐
2. Do you frequently do things on sudden impulse?	☐	☐	☐
3. Do you flare up in anger if you cannot have the things you want right away?	☐	☐	☐
4. Did you ever become intoxicated?	☐	☐	☐
5. Do you tremble or feel weak when someone shouts at you?	☐	☐	☐
6. Is it difficult for you to make up your mind?	☐	☐	☐
7. Do you have to be on your guard with friends?	☐	☐	☐
8. Does it bother you to eat anywhere except in your home?	☐	☐	☐
9. Have you ever intentionally damaged someone's property?	☐	☐	☐
10. Did you ever hurt anyone in anger?	☐	☐	☐
11. Are you often awakened out of your sleep by frightening dreams?	☐	☐	☐
12. Are you often bothered by thumping or a pain of the heart?			
13. Do you have the feeling that people are watching you or talking about you on the street?			
14. Do you get spells of exhaustion or fatigue?	☐	☐	☐
15. Do cold hands or feet trouble you even in hot weather?	☐	☐	
16. Did you ever go out of your way to get even with someone?	☐		
17. Do people usually pick on you?			
18. Do you become scared at sudden movements or noises at night?			
19. Does it make you angry to have one tell you what to do?			
20. Have you usually been tr			
21. Do you feel you are people?			
22. Are you extrem			
23. Do you cry			
24. Is your			
25. Are at			
26.			
2			

	Yes	(?)	No
28. Do you often have fits of temper?	☐	☐	
29. Have you at times had a twitching of the face, head, or shoulders?	☐	☐	
30. Do you sometimes get emotional to the point of tears?			
31. Are you considered a nervous person?			
32. Do you have any unusual fea			
33. Do you often have difficu ing asleep or staying as			
34. Does your thinking fused when you h quickly?			
35. Do you sometir out reason?			
36. Did you anger?			
37. Do yo in kr			

SPECIMEN COPY

ESCALA DE INTELIGENCIA WECHSLER PARA NIÑOS-REVISADA (EIWN-R)—Spanish Edition of WISC-R.

Refer to page T36.

EIWN-R

ESCALA DE INTELIGENCIA WECHSLER PARA NIÑOS—REVISADA

EDICIÓN DE INVESTIGACIÓN

HOJA DE CALIFICACIÓN

NOMBRE ____________ EDAD ____ SEXO ____

DIRECCIÓN ____________

PADRE O MADRE ____________

ESCUELA ____________ GRADO ____

LUGAR DEL EXAMEN ____________

EXAMINADOR ____________

PERFIL EN LA EIWN-R

El examinador que desee lograr un perfil debe primero transferir las *calificaciones en escala* del niño a la fila de recuadros abajo. Después debe marcar una X en el punto que corresponda a la calificación en escala para cada prueba, y dibujar una línea conectando las X.

	PRUEBAS VERBALES							PRUEBAS DE EJECUCIÓN						
Calificación en Escala	Información	Semejanzas	Aritmética	Vocabulario	Comprensión	Retención de Dígitos	Calificación en Escala	Figuras Incompletas	Arreglo de Dibujos	Diseños con Bloques	Composición de Objetos	Claves	Laberintos	Calificación en Escala
	☐	☐	☐	☐	☐	☐		☐	☐	☐	☐	☐	☐	
19	•	•	•	•	•	•	19	•	•	•	•	•	•	19
18	•	•	•	•	•	•	18	•	•	•	•	•	•	18
17	•	•	•	•	•	•	17	•	•	•	•	•	•	17
16	•	•	•	•	•	•	16	•	•	•	•	•	•	16
15	•	•	•	•	•	•	15	•	•	•	•	•	•	15
14	•	•	•	•	•	•	14	•	•	•	•	•	•	14
13	•	•	•	•	•	•	13	•	•	•	•	•	•	13
12	•	•	•	•	•	•	12	•	•	•	•	•	•	12
11	•	•	•	•	•	•	11	•	•	•	•	•	•	11
10	•	•	•	•	•	•	10	•	•	•	•	•	•	10
9	•	•	•	•	•	•	9	•	•	•	•	•	•	9
8	•	•	•	•	•	•	8	•	•	•	•	•	•	8
7	•	•	•	•	•	•	7	•	•	•	•	•	•	7
6	•	•	•	•	•	•	6	•	•	•	•	•	•	6
5	•	•	•	•	•	•	5	•	•	•	•	•	•	5
4	•	•	•	•	•	•	4	•	•	•	•	•	•	4
3	•	•	•	•	•	•	3	•	•	•	•	•	•	3
2	•	•	•	•	•	•	2	•	•	•	•	•	•	2
1	•	•	•	•	•	•	1	•	•	•	•	•	•	1

NOTAS

	Año	Mes	Día
Fecha de la Prueba	____	____	____
Fecha de Nacimiento	____	____	____
Edad	____	____	____

	Calificación en Bruto	Calificación en Escala*
PRUEBAS VERBALES		
Información	____	____
Semejanzas	____	____
Aritmética	____	____
Vocabulario	____	____
Comprensión	____	____
(Retención de Dígitos)	(____)	(____)
Calificación Verbal		____
PRUEBAS DE EJECUCIÓN		
Figuras Incompletas	____	____
Arreglo de Dibujos	____	____
Diseños con Bloques	____	____
Claves	____	____
(Laberintos)	(____)	(____)
Calificación de Ejecución		____

	Calificación en Escala*	IQ*
Calificación Verbal	____†	____
Calificación de Ejecución	____†	____
Calificación Completa	____	____

*Las calificaciones en escala y los IQ se deben formular en base a normas para un grupo apropiado de individuos de habla hispana.
†Prorrateado de 4 pruebas, si es necesario.

THE FIVE P'S: PARENT PROFESSIONAL PRESCHOOL PERFORMANCE PROFILE

Refer to page S122.

the five P's

ID.—Routines and Self Help/ Mealtime Behaviors

Age Norms		Fall School	Fall Home	Spring School	Spring Home
48-60	1. Eats in socially acceptable manner	N			
	2. Uses knife for spreading	N			
	3. Cleans up spills, getting own cloth	S			
	4. Independently prepares simple meals (e.g. bowl of cereal; sandwich)	N			
	5. Helps set table	N			
	Interfering Behaviors				
	16 Cannot be part of group at mealtime because of distractions by others	X			
	17 Does not sit at high chair/table	X			
	18 Runs around at mealtime	X			
	19 Needs to be reminded/encouraged to eat	O			

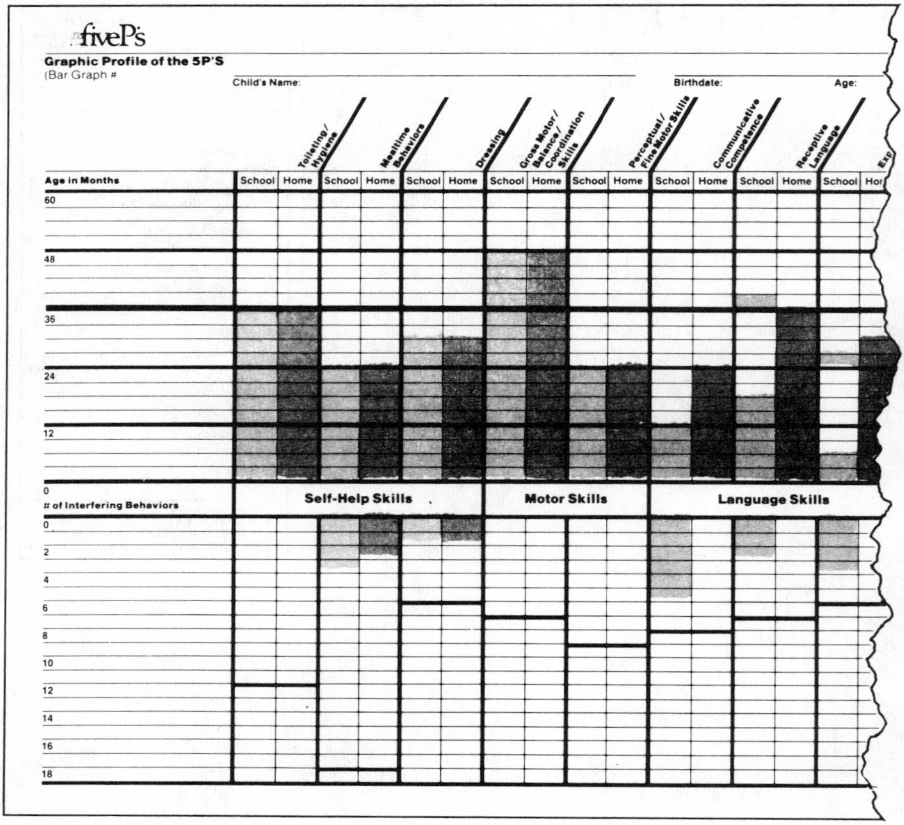

FLORIDA INTERNATIONAL DIAGNOSTIC-PRESCRIPTIVE VOCATIONAL COMPETENCY PROFILE

Refer to page S200.

DIRECTIONS

Each item in this Profile should be evaluated by indicating a numerical level of vocational competency. Indicate only ONE level for each item. The following key includes all 5 levels of vocational competency. Refer to the manual of directions for a comprehensive behavioral description of individual items. This scale is to be used for interpretive purposes only.

RATING SCALE

LEVEL

5 = Excellent	=	**Ready for placement in competitive employment**
4 = Good	=	**Above Average performance in training program**
3 = Average	=	**Average performance in training program**
2 = Fair	=	**Below Average performance in training program**
1 = Poor	=	**Essentially unable to perform task**

I. VOCATIONAL SELF-HELP SKILLS (14)

____ 1. Attendance
____ 2. Punctuality
____ 3. Grooming
____ 4. Personal Hygiene
____ 8. Ability to use Classified Ads
____ 9. Ability to use Employment Agencies
____10. Ability to fill out a Job Application Form
____11. Ability to Cash a Paycheck

II. SOCIAL-EMOTIONAL ADJUSTMENT (14)

____ 1. Frustration Tolerance (Reaction to vocational pressure)
____ 2. Relationship to Peers
____ 3. Relationship to Supervisors
____ 4. Self-Confidence as a Worker
____ 8. Social Judgement (Level of maturity)
____ 9. Cooperativeness with Peers (Reaction to group tasks)
____10. Leadership Ability
____11. Reaction to Criticism

V. PERCEPTUAL-MOTOR SKILLS (12)

____ 1. Gross Motor Coordination
____ 2. Finger Dexterity
____ 3. Eye-Hand Coordination
____ 4. Operating Powered Tools and Machines
____ 5. Bi-Manual Coordination (Using right and left hands simultaneously)
____ 6. Manual Dexterity
____ 7. Eye-Hand-Foot Coordination
____ 8. Color Discrimination
____ 9. Form Discrimination
____10. Texture Discrimination
____11. Spatial Discrimination
____12. Size Discrimination

TOTAL POINTS ________
Comments: ____

____

____

____

GOODMAN LOCK BOX

Refer to page T451.

LOCK BOX CODE SHEET

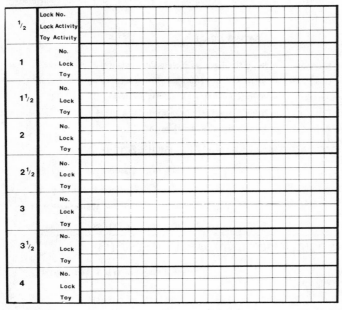

Time in minutes		
1/2	Lock No.	
	Lock Activity	
	Toy Activity	
1	No.	
	Lock	
	Toy	
1 1/2	No.	
	Lock	
	Toy	
2	No.	
	Lock	
	Toy	
2 1/2	No.	
	Lock	
	Toy	
3	No.	
	Lock	
	Toy	
3 1/2	No.	
	Lock	
	Toy	
4	No.	
	Lock	
	Toy	

4 1/2	No.	
	Lock	
	Toy	
5	No.	
	Lock	
	Toy	
5 1/2	No.	
	Lock	
	Toy	
6	No.	
	Lock	
	Toy	
6 1/2	No.	
	Lock	
	Toy	

CODING KEY

LOCK ACTIVITY

I	Inhibition
\	Unsuccessful attempt to unlock
X	Unlocks
o	Opens without unlatching
c	Closes without attempting to relock
|	Unsuccessful attempt to relock
✓	Relocks
L	Leaves
S	Scans
P	Primitive Lock approach

TOY ACTIVITY

Ar	Attempts to remove toy
r	Removes Toy
AR	Attempts to return toy
R	Returns toy
T	Tactile/Visual exploration
A	Adaptive play
M	Combination play
P	Primitive play
W	Shares toy

GROUP INVENTORY FOR FINDING CREATIVE TALENT (GIFT)—ELEMENTARY LEVEL-GRADES 3-4

Refer to page T542.

DATE ______________________________ GRADE ________

NAME ____

SCHOOL ____

Read each sentence below. Fill in the circle in the YES column next to each sentence if you agree with it and in the NO column if you don't agree. If you're not sure if you agree or not or think you sometimes agree, fill in the answer which is closest to the way you feel. There are no right or wrong answers. We only want to know how you think and how you feel about things, and what you like to do.

	Yes	No
1. I like to make up my own songs.	O	O
2. I like to take walks alone.	O	O
3. My mom or dad like to play with me.	O	O
4. I ask a lot of questions.	O	O
5. Making up stories is a waste of time.	O	O
6. I like to have only one or two friends.	O	O

GROUP INVENTORY FOR FINDING INTERESTS (GIFFI)—LEVEL 2-GRADES 9-12

Refer to page T542.

Name ________________________________ Grade __________ SEX M — F
LAST FIRST MIDDLE

School ________________________________ Date of Test __________

City ________________________________ State __________

INSTRUCTIONS TO STUDENTS:

Read each sentence and mark how much you agree with it. Use a pencil and fill in the appropriate circle completely. There are no right or wrong answers. We only want to know how you think and how you feel about things.

Sample Questions:

	NO	TO A SMALL EXTENT	AVERAGE	MORE THAN AVERAGE	DEFINITELY
1. I like to eat ice cream.	○	○	○	○	●
2. I like to play golf.	○	●	○	○	○

	NO	TO A SMALL EXTENT	AVERAGE	MORE THAN AVERAGE	DEFINITELY
1. I have a very good sense of humor.	○	○	○	○	○
2. I have always been active in drawing or painting.	○	○	○	○	○
3. I would like to get a pilot's license.	○	○	○	○	○
4. I would like to explore new cities alone, even if I get lost.	○	○	○	○	○
5. I enjoy thinking of new and better ways of doing things.	○	○	○	○	○
45. Sometimes I get so interested in a new idea that I neglect what I should be doing.	○	○	○	○	○
46. I have taken things apart just to find out how they work.	○	○	○	○	○
47. I read over 20 books a year.	○	○	○	○	○
48. When I was a child, I remember creating games, stories, poems, or art work more than other children did.	○	○	○	○	○
49. I have invented new gadgets for my own personal use.	○	○	○	○	○
50. My parents have encouraged my creative efforts by hanging my pictures, helping with my projects, or offering me out-of-school instruction.	○	○	○	○	○

HARDING STRESS-FAIR COMPATIBILITY TEST

Refer to page S58.

HARDING STRESS-FAIR COMPATIBILITY TEST

We present over the page a short test which we believe makes a fair statement about the human frame of reference relationship. It is not a personality test and we are not concerned with how closely you conform to some particular pattern of response other than producing another persons response that matches yours. That is our job, and from the enormous numbers we receive, we select the one that best matches your 'profile'. Your job is to answer as truthfully as possible in order to make this possible.

If you choose to distort your response to the questions you will only make the problem of finding the best matching person to you all the harder, if not impossible. There is no lie scale in our test, so it is really up to you to help us be of assistance to you. There is another person who also needs to meet you. Being fair to them is being fair to the person who **deserves** your kindness most ! and it cuts both ways.

....

(25) I find that there are only limited numbers of people I can talk to. (A) YES. (B) NO (C) I FIND THE QUESTION IRRELEVANT.

(26) I associate numbers with colours. (A) TRUE (B) FALSE.

(27) I need stimulation. (A) YES (B) ONLY RARELY (C) NEVER.

(28) I find people in general to be mentally dead. (A) TRUE (B) FALSE.

(29) I consider that people are most compatible when they (A) HAVE THE SAME EDUCATION LEVEL (B) HAVE THE SAME COMMON INTERESTS (C) HAVE THE SAME MECHANISM OR PATTERNS OF THOUGHT.

(30) If I cannot solve a problem immediately, I (A) PUT IT ASIDE UNTIL LATER (B) FORGET IT UNLESS NEW EVIDENCE COMES TO LIGHT (C) CEASE TO BE INTERESTED IN THE QUESTION.

(31) I would rate my bodily energy as (A) HIGH (B) LOW (C) ABOVE AVERAGE (D) AT THE COMMON LEVEL.

COMPATIBILITY OF PAIRED MATCHES :

LEVEL	X^2 RANGE	%ILE RANGE (approx.)	DESCRIPTION
12	759- 1,047	99.92 ± 0.02	Optimum Compatibility
11	1,048- 1,445	99.84 ± 0.05	Beginnings of Identity Fusion
10	1,446- 1,995	99.66 ± 0.13	Complete Mutual Reciprocation
9	1,996- 2,754	99.2 ± 0.3	Equivalent Evaluations
8	2,755- 3,801	98 ± 0.8	"Best Friend" Status
7	3,802- 5,248	95 ± 2	Deep Friendship Possible
6	5,249- 7,244	88 ± 5	Reciprocation with reservations in certain areas
5	7,245-10,000	73 ± 9	Awareness of others viewpoint
4	10,001-13,803	50 ± 13	Indifferent Relationship
3	13,804-19,054	24 ± 12	Mild Antagonism
2	19,055-26,302	6.5 ± 5	Antagonism
1	26,303-36,307	0.8 ± 0.7	Complete Alienation

For determination of X^2 range vide scoring sheet.

HOME OBSERVATION FOR MEASUREMENT OF THE ENVIRONMENT (HOME)

Refer to page S58.

HOME Inventory (Preschool)

Place a plus (+) or minus (-) in the box alongside each item if the behavior is observed during the visit or if the parent reports that the conditions or events are characteristic of the home environment. Enter the subtotals and the total on the front side of the Record Sheet.

I. LEARNING STIMULATION

1. Child has toys which teach color, size, shape.	
2. Child has three or more puzzles.	
3. Child has record player and at least five children's records.	
4. Child has toys permitting free expression.	
5. Child has toys or games requiring refined movements.	
6. Child has toys or games which help teach numbers.	
7. Child has at least 10 children's books.	
8. At least 10 books are visible in the apartment.	
9. Family buys and reads a daily newspaper.	
10. Family subscribes to at least one magazine.	
11. Child is encouraged to learn shapes.	
Subtotal	

II. LANGUAGE STIMULATION

12. Child has toys that help teach the names of animals.	
13. Child is encouraged to learn the alphabet.	
14. Parent teaches child simple verbal manners (please, thank you).	
15. Mother uses correct grammar and pronunciation.	
16. Parent encourages child to talk and takes time to listen.	
17. Parent's voice conveys positive feeling to child.	
18. Child is permitted choice in breakfast or lunch menu.	
Subtotal	

III. PHYSICAL ENVIRONMENT

19. Building appears safe.	
20. Outside play environment appears safe.	
21. Interior of apartment not dark or perceptually monotonous.	
22. Neighborhood is esthetically pleasing.	
23. House has 100 square feet of living space per person.	
24. Rooms are not overcrowded with furniture.	
25. House is reasonably clean and minimally cluttered.	
Subtotal	

IV. WARMTH AND ACCEPTANCE

26. Parent holds child close 10-15 minutes per day.	
27. Parent converses with child at least twice during visit.	
28. Parent answers child's questions or requests verbally.	
29. Parent usually responds verbally to child's speech.	
30. Parent praises child's qualities twice during visit.	
31. Parent caresses, kisses, or cuddles child during visit.	
32. Parent helps child demonstrate some achievement during visit.	
Subtotal	

V. ACADEMIC STIMULATION

33. Child is encouraged to learn colors.	
34. Child is encouraged to learn patterned speech (songs, etc.).	
35. Child is encouraged to learn spatial relationships.	
36. Child is encouraged to learn numbers.	
37. Child is encouraged to learn to read a few words.	
Subtotal	

VI. MODELING

38. Some delay of food gratification is expected.	
39. TV is used judiciously.	
40. Parent introduces visitor to child.	
41. Child can express negative feelings without reprisal.	
42. Child can hit parent without harsh reprisal.	
Subtotal	

HOWELL PREKINDERGARTEN SCREENING TEST

Refer to page S122.

Page 8 — Rhyming and Letter Writing

Rhyming

We are going to be listening for words that rhyme or sound the same. FAT and CAT rhyme. HAIR and CHAIR rhyme. BOY and TOY rhyme. *(Do example on board now.)*

TEACHER: Draw  on board. This example will be used after the oral examples of rhyming.

Now that you know what to do, put your marker under the row with the DISH.

1. Put your finger on the DISH. Look at the pictures in the row as I say them: GATE, DUCK, FISH. Mark the picture that rhymes with DISH. *(Repeat the words in capital letters in each item.)*
   Move your marker down.
2. Put your finger on the EYE. Look at the other pictures in the row as I say them: PAN, PIE, PEAR. Mark the one that rhymes with EYE.
   Move your marker down.
3. Put your finger on the MOP. Look at the other pictures in the row as I say them: TOP, MAN, TIE. Mark the one that rhymes with MOP.
   Move your marker down.
4. Put your finger on the MOON. Look at the other pictures in the row as I say them: SPOOL, SPOON, STOOL. Mark the one that rhymes with MOON.

****

Letter Writing

Find the box with the SPOON. In this box, make the letter S.

Find the box with the SCISSORS. In this box, make the letter P.

Find the box with the SAD FACE. In this box, make the letter K.

END OF PART I - SECOND SITTING

rhyming letter write

INDEX OF SOMATIC PROBLEMS

Refer to page S41.

222-22-2222 Jonathan Doe 32 yr old white male 16-Feb-84

ISP	INDEX OF SOMATIC PROBLEMS

The respondent reports no problems with sex organs, muscle pains and nausea. However the respondent reports specific problems as follows:

abdominal pains	-sudden onset -lasting longer than 30 minutes -located in lower middle area
abdominal swelling	-located in upper middle area -located in upper part -located in upper left area -located in upper right area
chest pains	-sudden onset -causes sweating -several attacks -constricting
headaches	-steady, long-lasting -caused by tension
thyroid	-recent operation
seizures	
coughing	
nervous complaints	-tremor -fainting -light-headed dizziness -room-spinning dizziness

FAMILY HISTORY

....

He reports that his mother and father would physically attack each other and would frequently lose their tempers. His mother is viewed as having been domineering and cruel. His father is seen as having been brutal and unfaithful. He complains of generally impaired relationships with them manifested by exclusion from conversation, frequent disagreements, running away from home and severe restrictions.

CHILDHOOD AND ADOLESCENCE

He admits to childhood difficulties with overt aggression (temper tantrums and quick to anger), hyperactivity (always on the go) and emotional lability (frequent crying). He reports engaging in lying, thievery and fire-setting at an early age. In school he was slow in learning to read. He received failing grades and was not promoted normally. He admits to having trouble with school authorities. As an adolescent he states that he was generally happy. He had friends but did not date...........

INTEREST DETERMINATION, EXPLORATION AND ASSESSMENT SYSTEM (IDEAS)

Refer to page S201.

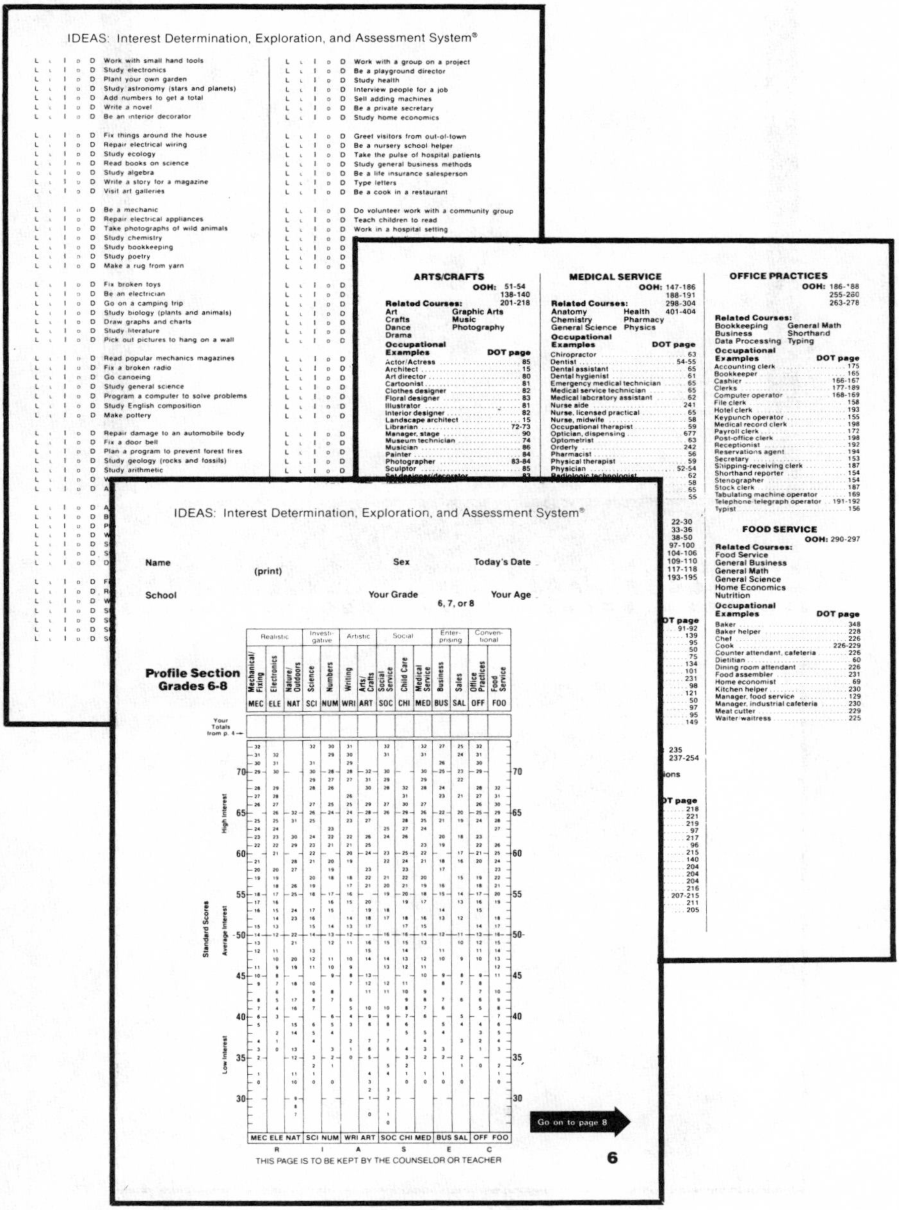
IDEAS: Interest Determination, Exploration, and Assessment System®

L L I D D Work with small hand tools
L L I D D Study electronics
L L I D D Plant your own garden
L L I D D Study astronomy (stars and planets)
L L I D D Add numbers to get a total
L L I D D Write a novel
L L I D D Be an interior decorator

L L I D D Fix things around the house
L L I D D Repair electrical wiring
L L I D D Study ecology
L L I D D Read books on science
L L I D D Study algebra
L L I D D Write a story for a magazine
L L I D D Visit art galleries

L L I D D Be a mechanic
L L I D D Repair electrical appliances
L L I D D Take photographs of wild animals
L L I D D Study chemistry
L L I D D Study bookkeeping
L L I D D Study poetry
L L I D D Make a rug from yarn

L L I D D Fix broken toys
L L I D D Be an electrician
L L I D D Go on a camping trip
L L I D D Study biology (plants and animals)
L L I D D Draw graphs and charts
L L I D D Study literature
L L I D D Pick out pictures to hang on a wall

L L I D D Read popular mechanics magazines
L L I D D Fix a broken radio
L L I D D Go canoeing
L L I D D Study general science
L L I D D Program a computer to solve problems
L L I D D Study English composition
L L I D D Make pottery

L L I D D Repair damage to an automobile body
L L I D D Fix a door bell
L L I D D Plan a program to prevent forest fires
L L I D D Study geology (rocks and fossils)
L L I D D Study arithmetic

L L I D D Work with a group on a project
L L I D D Be a playground director
L L I D D Study health
L L I D D Interview people for a job
L L I D D Sell adding machines
L L I D D Be a private secretary
L L I D D Study home economics

L L I D D Greet visitors from out-of-town
L L I D D Be a nursery school helper
L L I D D Take the pulse of hospital patients
L L I D D Study general business methods
L L I D D Be a life insurance salesperson
L L I D D Type letters
L L I D D Be a cook in a restaurant

L L I D D Do volunteer work with a community group
L L I D D Teach children to read
L L I D D Work in a hospital setting

ARTS/CRAFTS
OOH: 51-54, 138-140, 201-218
Related Courses: Art, Crafts, Dance, Drama, Graphic Arts, Music, Photography

Occupational Examples	DOT page
Actor/Actress	85
Architect	15
Art director	80
Cartoonist	81
Clothes designer	82
Floral designer	83
Illustrator	81
Interior designer	82
Landscape architect	15
Librarian	72-73
Manager, stage	90
Museum technician	74
Musician	86
Painter	84
Photographer	83-84
Sculptor	85

MEDICAL SERVICE
OOH: 147-186, 188-191, 298-304, 401-404
Related Courses: Anatomy, Chemistry, General Science, Health, Pharmacy, Physics

Occupational Examples	DOT page
Chiropractor	63
Dentist	54-55
Dental assistant	65
Dental hygienist	61
Emergency medical technician	65
Medical service technician	65
Medical laboratory assistant	62
Nurse aide	241
Nurse, licensed practical	65
Nurse, midwife	58
Occupational therapist	59
Optician, dispensing	677
Optometrist	63
Orderly	242
Pharmacist	56
Physical therapist	59
Physician	52-54

OFFICE PRACTICES
OOH: 186-188, 255-260, 263-278
Related Courses: Bookkeeping, Business, Data Processing, General Math, Shorthand, Typing

Occupational Examples	DOT page
Accounting clerk	175
Bookkeeper	165
Cashier	166-167
Clerks	177-189
Computer operator	168-169
File clerk	158
Hotel clerk	193
Keypunch operator	155
Medical record clerk	198
Payroll clerk	172
Post-office clerk	198
Receptionist	192
Reservations agent	194
Secretary	153
Shipping-receiving clerk	187
Shorthand reporter	154
Stenographer	154
Stock clerk	187
Tabulating machine operator	169
Telephone-telegraph operator	191-192
Typist	156

FOOD SERVICE
OOH: 290-297
Related Courses: Food Service, General Business, General Math, General Science, Home Economics, Nutrition

Occupational Examples	DOT page
Baker	348
Baker helper	228
Chef	226
Cook	226-229
Counter attendant, cafeteria	226
Dietitian	60
Dining room attendant	226
Food assembler	231
Home economist	69
Kitchen helper	230
Manager, food service	129
Manager, industrial cafeteria	230
Meat cutter	229
Waiter/waitress	225

IDEAS: Interest Determination, Exploration, and Assessment System®

Name (print) Sex Today's Date
School Your Grade 6, 7, or 8 Your Age

Profile Section Grades 6-8

Realistic: Mechanical/Fixing (MEC), Electronics (ELE), Nature/Outdoors (NAT)
Investigative: Science (SCI), Numbers (NUM)
Artistic: Writing (WRI), Arts/Crafts (ART)
Social: Social Service (SOC), Child Care (CHI), Medical Service (MED)
Enterprising: Business (BUS), Sales (SAL)
Conventional: Office Practices (OFF), Food Service (FOO)

Your Totals from p. 4

Standard Scores: 30–70 (High Interest, Average Interest, Low Interest)

MEC ELE NAT | SCI NUM | WRI ART | SOC CHI MED | BUS SAL | OFF FOO
R I A S E C

Go on to page 8

THIS PAGE IS TO BE KEPT BY THE COUNSELOR OR TEACHER

6

KAUFMAN ASSESSMENT BATTERY FOR CHILDREN (K-ABC)

Refer to page T558.

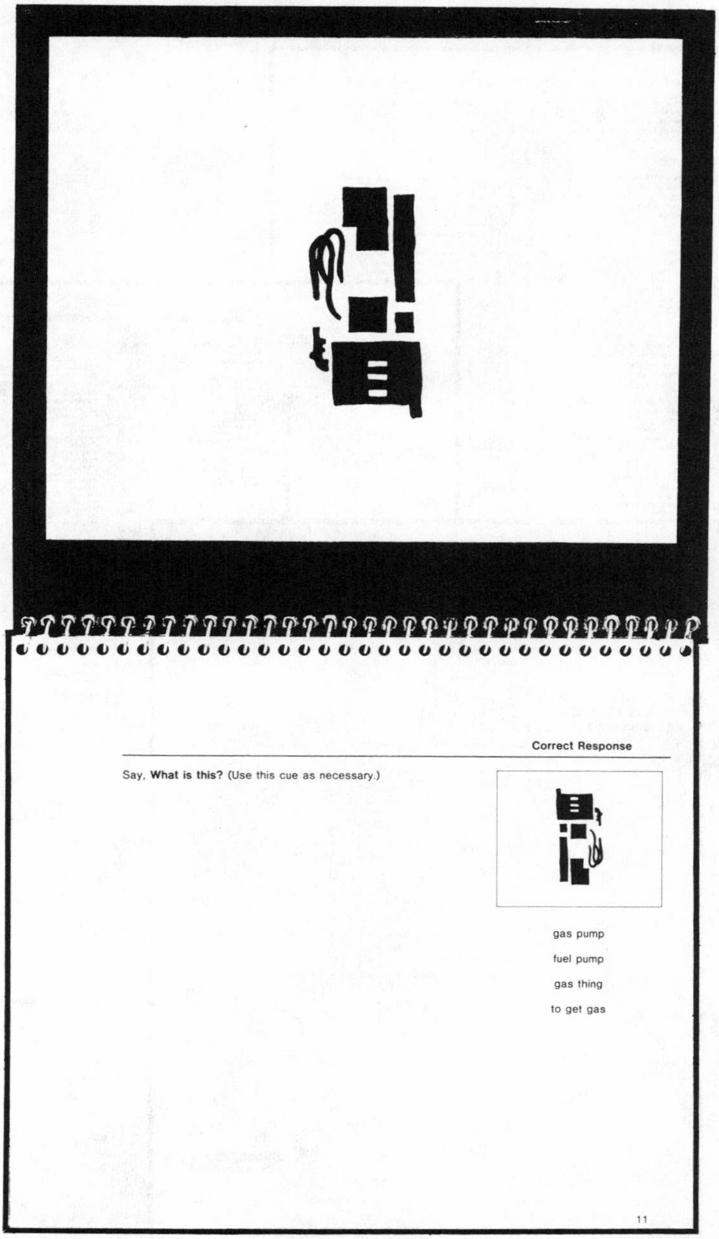

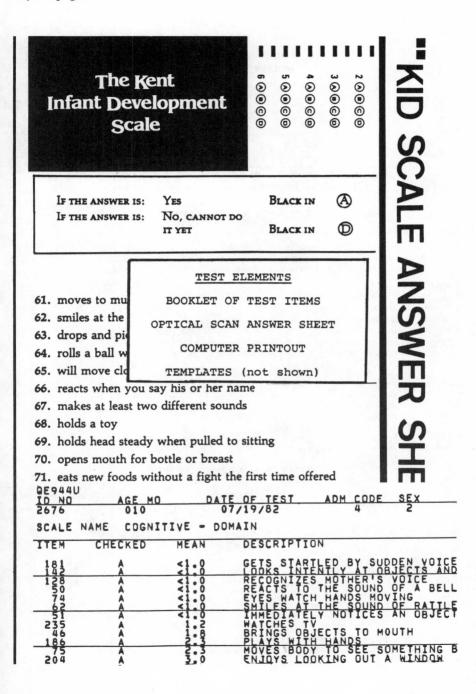

THE KENT INFANT DEVELOPMENT SCALE (KID SCALE)

Refer to page S5.

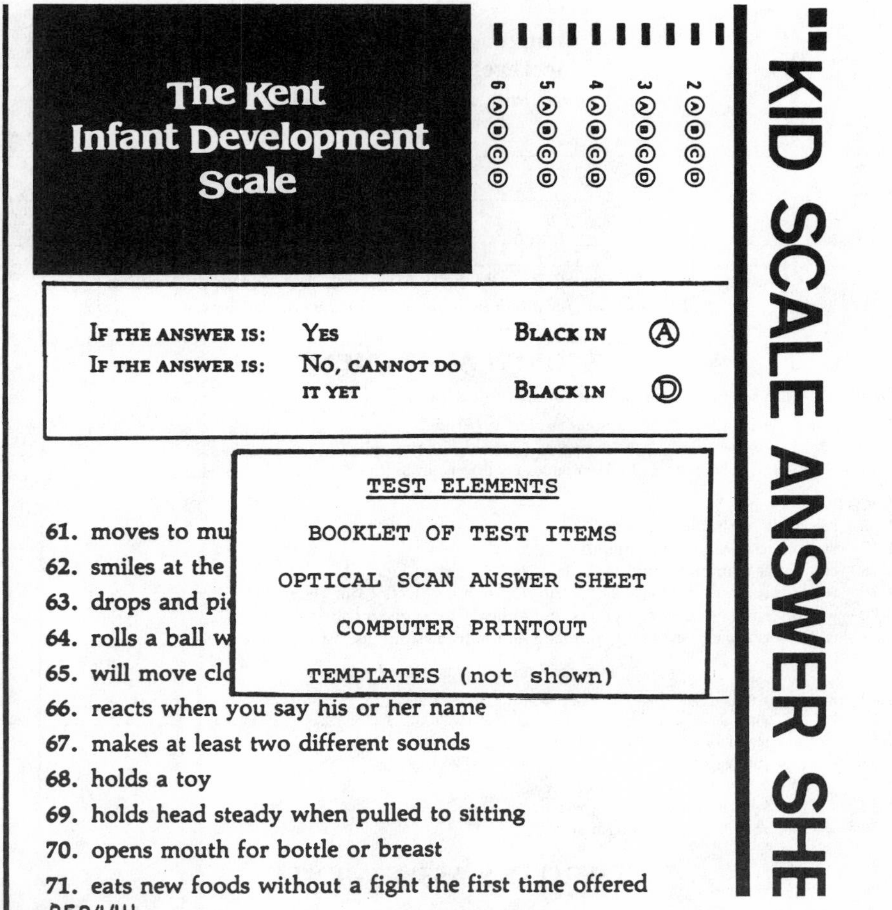
The Kent Infant Development Scale
"KID SCALE ANSWER SHE
2 Ⓐ Ⓑ Ⓒ Ⓓ
3 Ⓐ Ⓑ Ⓒ Ⓓ
4 Ⓐ Ⓑ Ⓒ Ⓓ
5 Ⓐ Ⓑ Ⓒ Ⓓ
6 Ⓐ Ⓑ Ⓒ Ⓓ
IF THE ANSWER IS: YES BLACK IN Ⓐ
IF THE ANSWER IS: NO, CANNOT DO IT YET BLACK IN Ⓓ
TEST ELEMENTS
BOOKLET OF TEST ITEMS
OPTICAL SCAN ANSWER SHEET
COMPUTER PRINTOUT
TEMPLATES (not shown)
61. moves to mu
62. smiles at the
63. drops and pi
64. rolls a ball w
65. will move clo
66. reacts when you say his or her name
67. makes at least two different sounds
68. holds a toy
69. holds head steady when pulled to sitting
70. opens mouth for bottle or breast
71. eats new foods without a fight the first time offered
QE944U

ID NO	AGE MO	DATE OF TEST	ADM CODE	SEX
2676	010	07/19/82	4	2

SCALE NAME COGNITIVE - DOMAIN

ITEM	CHECKED	MEAN	DESCRIPTION
181	A	<1.0	GETS STARTLED BY SUDDEN VOICE
142	A	<1.0	LOOKS INTENTLY AT OBJECTS AND
128	A	<1.0	RECOGNIZES MOTHER'S VOICE
50	A	<1.0	REACTS TO THE SOUND OF A BELL
74	A	<1.0	EYES WATCH HANDS MOVING
62	A	<1.0	SMILES AT THE SOUND OF RATTLE
51	A	<1.0	IMMEDIATELY NOTICES AN OBJECT
235	A	1.2	WATCHES TV
46	A	1.8	BRINGS OBJECTS TO MOUTH
186	A	2.3	PLAYS WITH HANDS
75	A	2.3	MOVES BODY TO SEE SOMETHING B
204	A	3.0	ENJOYS LOOKING OUT A WINDOW

LANGUAGE INVENTORY FOR TEACHERS (LIT)

Refer to page T222.

LIT
Language Inventory for Teachers Checklist

Arlene Cooper, PhD and Beverly A. School, PhD

Name ______________________________________ Date__________

School ____________________________ Grade______ Teacher________________

Birthdate____________ Age________ Examiner __________________________

Coding: M = Mastered; P = Partially Mastered; N = Needs Instruction
Full instructions for administration are explained in the manual

SPOKEN ASSESSMENT

Goal #1 Will correctly name and use nouns (objects) expressively.

1.1 - 1.5 uses simple N-V sentences (The boy runs) ______ ______ ______ ______ ______
1.6 - 1.12 use simple N-V-N sentences (Harold hits the ball) ______ ______ ______ ______ ______
1.13 - 1.15 uses N-V (to be)-N sentences (A dog is an animal) ______ ______ ______

Concepts

1.16 - responds to simple question ______
1.17 - can name at least four animals ______
1.18 - can name inanimate objects (at least 6) ______
1.19 - will discriminate between living and non-living objects from given list of items ______
1.20 - will discriminate between plants and animals from given list of items ______
1.21 - will discriminate between man-made and natural from given list of items ______

Can extend animal classification by naming:

1.22 farm mammals ______ 1.25 wildlife mammals ______ 1.28 wildlife insects ______

5.50 describes cause and effect ______
5.51 makes prediction ______
5.52 generalizes prediction ______
5.53 relates to personal experience ______
5.54 makes a value judgment ______

WRITTEN ASSESSMENT

Have lined paper and pencil available for student use. Please note that some items under the following Goals are repeated because they are assessing more than one concept.

Goal #6 Will produce the following legible written forms:

Student will make:

6.1 printed upper case letters ______
6.2 printed lower case letters ______
6.3 all capital forms in cursive ______
6.4 all letter forms in cursive ______
6.5 connected cursive letters (words) ______

NOTE: Letters and words spaced and contained between three lines ______
Letters and words spaced and contained between two lines ______

LEARNING STYLE INVENTORY/PRODUCTIVITY ENVIRONMENTAL PREFERENCE SURVEY

Refer to pages S186 and S239.

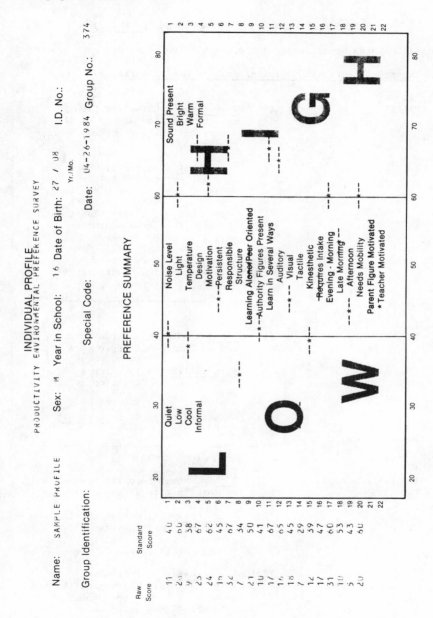

INDIVIDUAL PROFILE
PRODUCTIVITY ENVIRONMENTAL PREFERENCE SURVEY

Name: SAMPLE PROFILE Sex: M Year in School: 16 Date of Birth: 27 / 08 (Yr./Mo.) I.D. No.:

Group Identification: Special Code: Date: 04-26-1984 Group No.: 374

PREFERENCE SUMMARY

	Raw Score	Standard Score
1	11	40
2	25	60
3	9	38
4	25	67
5	24	62
6	15	45
7	32	67
8	7	34
9	21	50
10	10	41
11	17	67
12	16	65
13	18	45
14	7	29
15	12	39
16	17	47
17	31	60
18	10	53
19	5	43
20	20	60
21		
22		

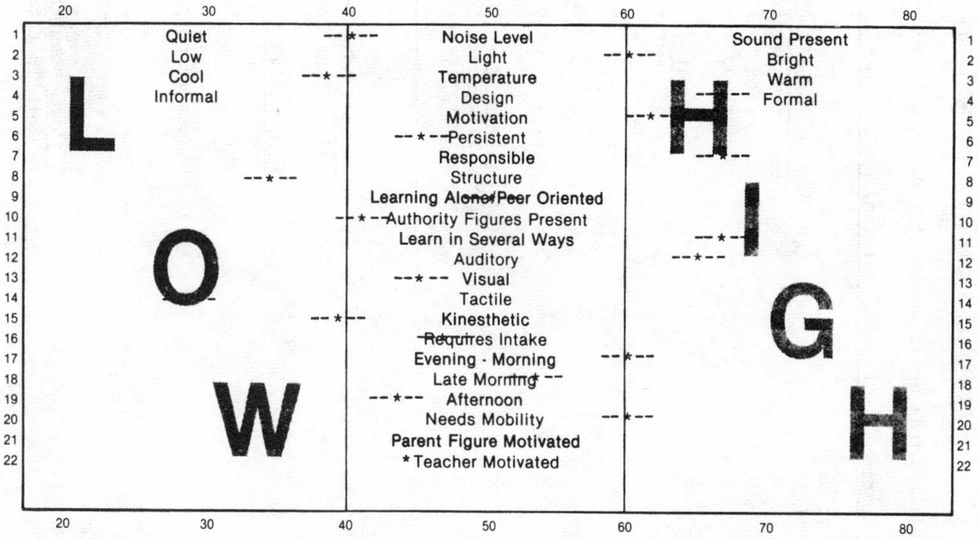

McCORMICK AFFECTIVE ASSESSMENT TECHNIQUE (MAAT)

Refer to page S193.

McCORMICK AFFECTIVE ASSESSMENT TECHNIQUE (MAAT)

Topical Learning Needs Survey -- Representative Learning Needs Statements

Question 3 - Problem Solving/Decision Making Skills

(LEVELS OF TRAINING NEEDS: I-III)

III VALUING

(9) I am convinced that problem solving/decision making skills are essential if a program is to succeed

(8) I seek out opportunities to increase my problem solving/decision making skills and to apply these skills within the organization. I seek also to increase the level of these skills among my managers

(7) I believe that my problem solving/decision making skills are highly developed

---

II RESPONDING

(6) I enjoy both in joint efforts and in individual approaches

(5) I am willing to learn more problem solving/decision making skills

(4) No usable response to I comply with

I AWARENESS (RECEIVING)

(3) I think about becoming more capable in this area

(2) I do not avoid problem solving or decision making because the nature of the organization demands decisiveness

(1) I am conscious of problem solving/decision making skills among very few of the members with whom I have come in contact

MILLER ASSESSMENT FOR PRESCHOOLERS (MAP)
© Copyright The Foundation for Knowledge in Development. Reprinted by permission of KID Technology, Inc.

Refer to page S6.

Continued on page S312.

SUPPLEMENTAL OBSERVATIONS SHEET

MILLER ASSESSMENT FOR PRESCHOOLERS

☐ Preferred Hand

VISION

- ☐ Obvious crossed eyes
- ☐ Red or watery eyes
- ☐ Crusty eye lids
- ☐ Rubs eyes excessively
- ☐ Abnormal head posture/movement
- ☐ Squints or frowns when looking at objects
- ☐ Gets very close to work
- ☐ Abnormal eye movements i.e., restrictions, nystagmus

TOUCH

- ☐ Rubs, scratches area touched
- ☐ Negative verbal reaction to touch
- ☐ Uses fingertips rather than palms to manipulate objects
- ☐ Hands tend to be fisted
- ☐ Tendency to walk on toes when shoes are off

MOVEMENT

Extension/Flexion

- ☐ Resting postures and position changes often incorporate excessive neck hyperextension
- ☐ Anterior pelvic tilt
- ☐ Uses only some muscle groups actively when flexing—may "fix"

Weight Shifting/Rotation

- ☐ Compensates by "fixing" when shifts weight
- ☐ Does not use diagonal movements
- ☐ Uses lateral flexion rather than rotation
- ☐ Loses balance during rotation activities

Appearance

- ☐ Hypotonic muscle tone
- ☐ Hypertonic muscle tone
- ☐ Poor mouth closure
- ☐ Trunk or facial asymmetry

Stability

- ☐ Excessive internal or external rotation at shoulders and/or hips
- ☐ Arms tend to go into high guard position
- ☐ Bears weight medially or laterally on feet
- ☐ Hyperextends knee when walking
- ☐ Tends to "W" sit

Postural/Movement Patterns

- ☐ Overflow or associated movements
- ☐ Falls frequently, clumsy or awkward movements
- ☐ Movement always initiated to same direction
- ☐ Frequent postural readjustments in chair
- ☐ Holds body rigidly; seems unwilling to move quickly
- ☐ Primitive grasp
- ☐ Does not automatically assist with alternate hand

DRAW-A-PERSON

- ☐ Body parts not attached (1)
- ☐ Sides strikingly dissimilar (2)
- ☐ Draws monster, dinosaur, etc. (3)
- ☐ Much scribbling (4)
- ☐ Not identifiable as human figure (5)
- ☐ Shape of parts grossly inappropriate (6)
- ☐ Part usually drawn at older age present (*i.e.* toes, fingers, eyebrows) but elementary part missing (*i.e.* trunk, head, arms) (7)
- ☐ Much detail to one part at expense of total picture (8)
- ☐ Bizarre, disturbing quality (9)
- ☐ Unenclosed (*i.e.* facial features with no head) (10)
- ☐ Vague overall shape but individual parts hard to distinguish (11)
- ☐ Body parts definitely out of proportion (12)

SPEECH AND LANGUAGE

Expression

- ☐ Uses inappropriate vocabulary
- ☐ Does not use grammatical sentence structure
- ☐ Difficulty "finding" words
- ☐ Uses many vague or indefinite words or circumlocutions
- ☐ Tends to respond in simple sentences and short phrases
- ☐ Voice quality inappropriate for age or sex, *i.e.* harsh, hoarse, pitch too high or low, volume too soft or loud
- ☐ Dysfluent, *e.g.* stutters, repeats words or sounds, prolongs sounds, tension in body when speaks
- ☐ Echoes or shadows directions vocally or subvocally
- ☐ Excessive nonverbal response, *e.g.* nods, smiles, etc.
- ☐ Sounds reversed within words
- ☐ Words reversed within sentences

Auditory Ability

- ☐ Needs directions repeated
- ☐ Needs volume of directions increased
- ☐ Watches lips excessively
- ☐ Wears hearing aid
- ☐ Difficulty localizing sound, *i.e.* turning in direction of voice or sounds
- ☐ Seems to have difficulty discriminating similar sounds, *e.g.*, penny, pencil; gum, come; wait, wade

Intelligibility

- ☐ Difficult to understand
- ☐ Words run together
- ☐ Talks too fast/too slow
- ☐ Many articulation errors

Comprehension

- ☐ Responses usually delayed
- ☐ Need directions reworded
- ☐ Difficulty understanding task expected

BEHAVIOR DURING TESTING

ATTENTION	ACTIVITY LEVEL					...e
	CONCENTRATION					...ask ...xed
	ABILITY TO STRUCTURE TIME/ COMPLETE TASKS	...complete tasks Needs total management	...organize time and activities	Needs minimal aid	Needs a push	...s; ...te even if prompted
	NEED FOR REWARD/ ABILITY TO DELAY GRATIFICATION	Needs instant, constant gratification Cannot delay reward until task is done	Needs reward quickly to proceed to next task	Wants gratification as expected for age Can delay	Somewhat indifferent to reward	Not aware of end product or interested in reward
SOCIAL INTERACTION	REACTION TO SEPARATION FROM CARETAKER	Clings; refuses to go along with examiner Avoids contact with unfamiliar adult	Very resistant to leaving Must be coaxed or promised reward	May have a little difficulty but goes with examiner as expected for age	Goes immediately with examiner Little concern about leaving caretaker	Seems unaware of caretaker. No verbal communication with caretaker
	INTERACTION WITH EXAMINER	Requires attention Either hostile and non-compliant or clingy and dependent	Demanding, manipulative Seeks constant physical or verbal attention	May be open or shy but interacts without difficulty Accepts limits	Cautious, may look at adult but not initiate contact Submissive Imitates adult exactly	Avoids contact Isolated Withdrawn
	VERBAL INTERACTION	Inappropriate speech or sounds Extremely rapid or incoherent speech	Very talkative Does not listen to others or interact	Facility with words Uses to make needs known and communicate with others	Slow to respond Seldom verbalizes Acts out needs by pointing, pulling, crying, etc.	No verbalization
SENSORY REACTIVITY	REACTION TO MOVEMENT	Extremely sensitive to movement, e.g. tends to get nauseated, pale, sweaty particularly with rotation Extremely fearful of moving	Does not like movement Tends to avoid whenever possible	Enjoys moving Likes to play, run	Seeks fast movement No dizziness or somatic response Heedless, i.e. lacks caution in movement activities	Does not seem to prepare when falling Moves in same pattern over and over without tiring, e.g. wishes to spin endlessly
	REACTION TO TOUCH	Startles or withdraws from touch; experiences touch as painful	Becomes uneasy when touched Avoids touch whenever possible	Interested in feeling different textures Likes to be hugged	Slow to respond when touched Doesn't explore toys by handling them	Oblivious to touch or pain Doesn't notice when bumps into things or falls down
		Compulsion to touch people and objects; can't stop even when directed to	Overexploratory; often annoys people by touching too much			

MILLION ADOLESCENT PERSONALITY INVENTORY (MAPI)

Refer to page T118.

NAME: 0123456789 ID: UNIT G DATE: 23-FEB-84 · PAGE: 6

135. I MAKE NASTY REMARKS TO PEOPLE IF THEY DESERVE IT. (T)

EMOTIONAL DIFFICULTIES:

16. I BECOME VERY EXCITED OR UPSET ONCE A WEEK OR MORE. (T)
55. I DO NOT SEEM TO KNOW WHAT I WANT OUT OF LIFE. (T)
89. OTHERS MY AGE SEEM TO HAVE THINGS TOGETHER BETTER THAN I DO. (T)
91. I OFTEN FEEL SO ANGRY I WANT TO THROW AND BREAK THINGS. (T)
113. I AM JEALOUS OF THE SPECIAL ATTENTION THAT THE OTHER CHILDREN IN THE FAMILY GET. (T)
133. SO LITTLE OF WHAT I HAVE DONE HAS BEEN APPRECIATED BY OTHERS. (T)
148. IT IS VERY DIFFICULT FOR ME TO STOP FEELINGS FROM COMING OUT. (T)
150. I CAN CONTROL MY FEELINGS EASILY. (F)

THERAPEUTIC IMPLICATIONS

THE FOLLOWING CONSIDERATIONS ARE LIKELY TO BE OF GREATER UTILITY AND ACCURACY DURING EARLY TREATMENT PLANNING THAN IN LATER MANAGEMENT PHASES.

IT IS PROBABLE THAT THIS YOUNGSTER WILL ACTIVELY SOLICIT AND DEMAND MORE
ATTENTION AND NURTURANCE THAN MAY BE CALLED FOR. SHOULD THESE MANIPULATIONS
FAIL TO GAIN SPECIAL CONSIDERATIONS, THE PATIENT MAY
MOODINESS AND VOICED DISAPPOINTMENT IN THE CARE SHOWN
CLINICIAN. THE FRAGILE TRUST THAT THIS YOUNGSTER FEE
SHAKEN, LEADING TO DEMANDS, FEELING SORRY FOR ONESELF
STANDING PATTERN IS LIKELY TO BE DISPLAYED NUMEROUS
LONG HISTORY OF PRIOR THERAPEUTIC EXPERIENCES, ALL OF
TO SPEAK, TO PROVIDE THE ATTENTIONS SOUGHT. PROBLEMS
TO ARISE WITH THIS YOUNGSTER. ALTHOUGH COOPERATIVE
LITTLE SUSTAINING POWER. THERE IS A HIGH PROBABILIT
BE ERRATIC IN ADHERING TO ANY RECOMMENDED BEHAVIORAL
FAILURE TO PERSEVERE OVER THE LONG HAUL OR SLIPPING
FREQUENT CONTACT IS STRONGLY RECOMMENDED SINCE IT CA
PROGRESS WILL BE MAINTAINED WITHOUT CLOSE SUPERVISIO
RESPOND TO ANGRY OUTBURSTS, PASSIVE-RESISTANT BEHAV
OF REASSURANCE WITHOUT EXASPERATION OR THE APPLYING
CHANGE. SYMPATHETIC EXPRESSIONS OF CONCERN, CONVEY
INTEREST AND COMPETENCE, ARE LIKELY TO COUNTERACT A
ACTIONS. ALSO, A FIRM AND AUTHORITATIVE MANNER WIL
THE ERRATIC AND NEGATIVE PATTERN. A GOOD POLICY TO
OF RULES, FOLLOWED WITH FREQUENT CONTACTS THAT ARE

CONFIDENTIAL INFORMATION FOR PROFESSIONAL USE ONLY

REPORT FOR: 0123456789 SEX: MALE AGE: 13

ID NUMBER: UNIT G QUESTIONABLE RELIABILITY DATE: 23-FEB-84

CODE:

8 2 **- * - + 3 6 " 1 4 5 7 //A H B E G **D C F * - + - " - //WWSSUUTT**- * //

SCALES		RAW	BR	PROFILE OF BR SCORES (35 60 75 85 100)	DIMENSIONS
	1	9	15	XXX	INTROVERSIVE
	2	28	109	XXXXXXXXXXXXXXXXXXXXXXXXXXXXXXXXXXXXXXXXXX	INHIBITED
	3	18	50	XXXXXXXXX	COOPERATIVE
PERSNLTY	4	10	13	XXX	SOCIABLE
STYLES	5	9	3	X	CONFIDENT
	6	13	35	XXXXXX	FORCEFUL
	7	6	1	X	RESPECTFUL
	8	33	111	XXXXXXXXXXXXXXXXXXXXXXXXXXXXXXXXXXXXXXXXXX	SENSITIVE
	A	30	112	XXXXXXXXXXXXXXXXXXXXXXXXXXXXXXXXXXXXXXXXXX	SELF-CONCEPT
	B	27	99	XXXXXXXXXXXXXXXXXXXXXXXXXXXXXXXXXXXXXXXXX	PERSONAL ESTEEM
	C	14	75	XXXXXXXXXXXXXXXXXXXXX	BODY COMFORT
EXPRESSD	D	16	76	XXXXXXXXXXXXXXXXXXXXXX	SEXUAL ACCEPTNCE
CONCERNS	E	17	97	XXXXXXXXXXXXXXXXXXXXXXXXXXXXXXXXXXXXXXXX	PEER SECURITY
	F	12	75	XXXXXXXXXXXXXXXXXXXXX	SOCIAL TOLERANCE
	G	16	95	XXXXXXXXXXXXXXXXXXXXXXXXXXXXXXXXXXXXXX	FAMILY RAPPORT
	H	21	101	XXXXXXXXXXXXXXXXXXXXXXXXXXXXXXXXXXXXXXXXXX	ACADEMIC CONFDNCE
	SS	23	99	XXXXXXXXXXXXXXXXXXXXXXXXXXXXXXXXXXXXXXXXX	IMPULSE CONTROL
BEHAVIOR	TT	23	85	XXXXXXXXXXXXXXXXXXXXXXXXXXXXXXXX	SOCIAL CONFORMITY
CORRE-	UU	28	98	XXXXXXXXXXXXXXXXXXXXXXXXXXXXXXXXXXXXXXXX	SCHOLAST ACHVMNT
LATES	WW	28	101	XXXXXXXXXXXXXXXXXXXXXXXXXXXXXXXXXXXXXXXXXX	ATTNDNCE CNSTNCY

NAME: 0123456789 ID: UNIT G DATE:

THE BEHAVIOR OF THIS YOUNGSTER IS TYPIFIED BY HIS EM
SHAKY SELF-CONCEPT, FEELINGS OF HOPELESSNESS AND THE PRES
SO-CALLED NEUROTIC SYMPTOMS. THERE IS A HIGH DEGREE OF L
OF IMPULSIVE ACTING-OUT, DEPRESSIVE COMPLAINTS, EXCESSIVE
BEHAVIORS. NOTABLE IS HIS HYPERSENSITIVITY TO CRITICISM,
TOLERANCE, RESTLESSNESS, PERIODIC SELF-ACCUSATIONS AND GU
EMOTIONS SURGE READILY TO THE SURFACE, CHARACTERIZING HIS
TRACTIBLE AND ERRATIC.

THE MOODS OF THIS YOUNGSTER TEND TO BE VARIABLE, WIT
EXCITEMENT ALTERNATING WITH LETHARGY, FATIGUE, OVERSLEEPI
OVERUSE OF DRUGS OR ALCOHOL. HIS FEELINGS MAY SWING FROM
EXCITED DESPERATION, AND TEND TO BE EXPRESSED MORE INTENS
BY THE SITUATION. IN A SELF-FULFILLING PROPHECY, HE OFTE
WITH FAMILY MEMBERS AND WILL ACT IN A MANNER THAT PROMOTE
IF CUT OFF FROM NEEDED SUPPORT AND NURTURANCE, HE WILL BE
AND CONTENTIOUS OR DEJECTED AND FORLORN.

THIS YOUNG MAN FEELS MISUNDERSTOOD AND IS DISAPPOINT
AND WITH HIS MATURATION AND LOOKS. HE IS OFTEN CRITICAL
GOOD FORTUNES OF OTHERS, GRUDGES THEIR GOOD LUCK, AND REA
ANY SLIGHT THAT OTHERS COMMUNICATE. HE MAY EXHIBIT UNUSU
WITH BODILY FUNCTIONS AND HEALTH, OVERREACT TO ILLNESS, A
COMPLAINTS ABOUT THE INJUSTICES IN HIS LIFE. COMPLAINTS
MAY BE DISPLAYED PROMINENTLY SO AS TO GAIN THE ATTENTION
HE CANNOT OTHERWISE ELICIT. PARTICULARLY PAINFUL ARE THE
WITHIN HIS FAMILY RELATIONSHIPS AND THE LACK OF ACCEPTANC
PEERS.

EXPRESSED CONCERNS

THE SCALES COMPRISING THIS SECTION PERTAIN TO THE PERSONAL PERCEPTIONS OF THIS YOUNGSTER CONCERNING SEVERAL ISSUES OF PSYCHOLOGICAL DEVELOPMENT, ACTUALIZATION AND CONCERN. BECAUSE EXPERIENCES DURING THIS AGE PERIOD ARE NOTABLY SUBJECTIVE, IT IS IMPORTANT TO RECORD HOW THIS TEENAGER SEES EVENTS AND REPORTS FEELINGS, AND NOT ONLY HOW OTHERS MAY OBJECTIVELY REPORT THEM TO BE. FOR COMPARATIVE PURPOSES, THESE SELF-ATTITUDES REGARDING A WIDE RANGE OF PERSONAL, SOCIAL, FAMILIAL AND SCHOLASTIC MATTERS ARE CONTRASTED WITH THOSE EXPRESSED BY A BROAD CROSS-SECTION OF TEENAGERS OF THE SAME SEX AND AGE.

THIS YOUNGSTER EXPRESSES CONSIDERABLE CONCERN OVER FEELING CONFUSED IF NOT LOST IN LIFE. HE DOES NOT HAVE A CLEAR SENSE OF HIS IDENTITY AND SEEMS NOTABLY UNFOCUSED AS TO HIS FUTURE GOALS AND VALUES. HE IS TROUBLED BY HIS INABILITY TO WORK TOWARD A CLEARER SENSE OF SELF AND A MEANS OF FINDING A DIRECTION FOR HIS FUTURE.

THIS TROUBLED YOUNGSTER REPORTS EXPERIENCING GLOBAL DISSATISFACTION. HE FEELS NOT ONLY CONSIDERABLE DISTRESS WHEN VIEWING HIMSELF, BUT FINDS MINIMAL ACCEPTANCE FROM OTHERS AS WELL. FALLING FAR SHORT OF WHAT HE ASPIRES TO BE, HIS LOW PERSONAL ESTEEM AND LACK OF FULFILLMENT INTRUDES PAINFULLY INTO ALL ASPECTS OF FUNCTIONING.

MINNESOTA PRESCHOOL INVENTORY (MPI)

Refer to page T456.

Instructions

First, print your child's name in the boxes at the top of the answer sheet. Print last name first, skip one box, then print as much of the first name as space will allow. Next, indicate your child's sex by filling in the correct circle. Then, fill in your child's birthdate and the date you complete the Minnesota Preschool Inventory. Finally, complete the Family Information section at the bottom of the answer sheet.

This booklet contains statements describing behaviors of children. These statements describe the things that children do as a part of growing up. Read each statement carefully. If the statement describes your child's present behavior, answer YES. If the statement does not describe your child's present behavior, answer NO. Answer YES or NO by what you have seen your child do, not by what you think he may be able to do. Answer YES by filling in the circle marked Y on the answer sheet; answer NO by filling in the circle marked N.

Please do not make any marks in this booklet.

1. Crosses the street alone.
2. Washes face without help.
3. Pours a drink.
4. Dresses and undresses without help.
5. Puts shoes on the correct feet.
6. Goes to a playmate's house alone.
7. Uses table knife for spreading.
8. Goes about neighborhood unattended.
9. Uses table knife for cutting.
10. Gets ready for bed without help.
11. Puts on boots without help.
12. Takes a bath without help.
13. Uses money to buy things.
14. Goes to the toilet without help.

31. Draws or copies a cross.
32. Cuts across paper with scissors from one side to the other.
33. Draws or copies a square.
34. Prints a few simple words from a copy.
35. Draws a picture of a man or woman that has at least three parts, such as head, body, arms, legs, eyes, nose, mouth.
36. Asks questions beginning with "why."
37. Tells what he (she) dreams about.
38. Recites at least one nursery rhyme, such as "Little Bo Peep" or "Little Miss Muffet."
39. Talks clearly; is easily understandable.
40. Makes conditional statements, such as "If I do . . ., then I can . . .," or "When I . . ., then . . ."

---

104. Overtalkative; "chatters," is seldom silent.
105. Overly excitable.
106. Impulsive; acts without thinking.
107. Easily frustrated; often gets upset or angry.
108. Does not take turns or follow the rules in group activities.
109. Careless or irresponsible; gets into trouble unless constantly looked after.
110. Disobedient; doesn't mind well.
111. Often takes advantage of others.
112. Feels abused; tries to get even and punish others.
113. Quarrelsome, defiant, a "troublemaker."
114. Boistrous, loud, noisy.

136. Clumsy, awkward; runs poorly, stumbles or falls, etc.
137. Avoids participation in physical games such as tag, hopscotch, catch, jumprope.
138. Clumsy in doing things with hands.
139. Draws and colors poorly.
140. Talks only in short phrases (less than 5 words long).
141. Stutters or stammers.
142. Has trouble expressing ideas — frequently gets things "all mixed up."
143. Speech is difficult to understand.
144. Often uses "baby talk."
145. Complains of being tired, appears sluggish,

MINNESOTA PRESCHOOL INVENTORY PROFILE

Harold R. Ireton and Edward J. Thwing

Name ______________________ Date Completed ______________ Age ______

\# ______________________ Birthdate ______________ Sex ______

Mother's Education ______________________ Mother's Occupation ______________________

Child's Problems or Handicaps ____

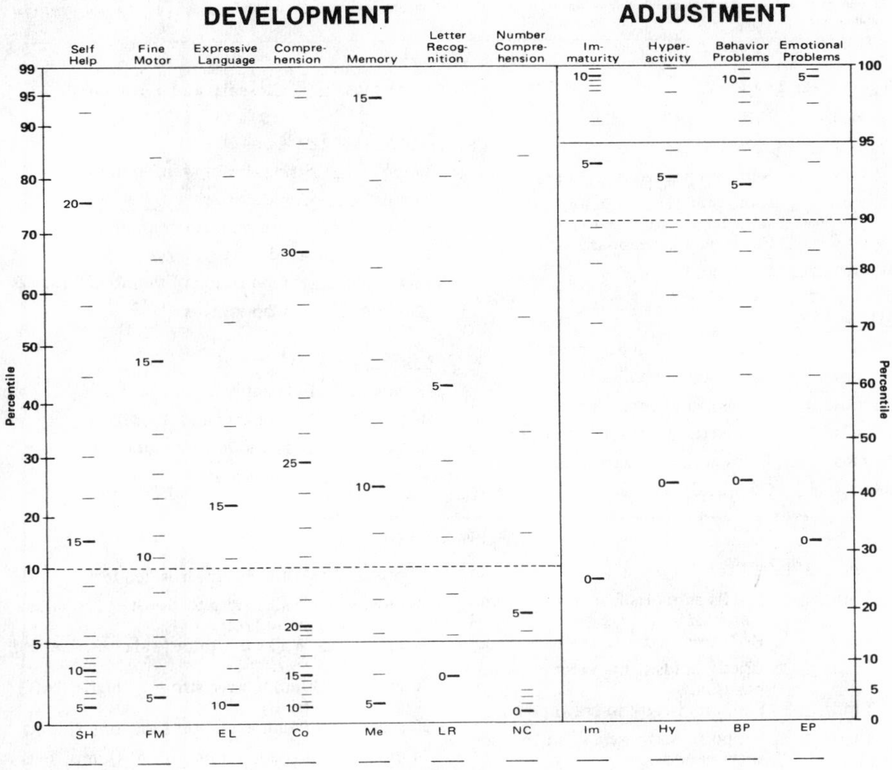

SYMPTOMS

Percent	Motor	Language	Somatic	Sensory
0–5	136 Clumsy, awkward 137 Avoids physical games 138 Clumsy with hands	140 Talks only in short phrases 141 Stutters, stammers	145 Tired, sluggish, low energy 146 Sleeps poorly	149 Vision?
5–10		142 Trouble expressing ideas 143 Speech difficult to understand 144 "Baby Talk"		150 Hearing?
10	139 Draws, colors poorly		147 Eating problems 148 Aches and pains	

MOTOR SKILLS INVENTORY (MSI)

Refer to page S144.

Cat. No. 33485R Record Form

MOTOR SKILLS INVENTORY

by: John Aulenta, M.A.

ADMINISTRATION

Review the manual and administer items as described in Appendix A. Seek to establish basal and ceiling levels using a guideline of five consecutive successes and failures. To reduce administration time, estimate approximate motor functioning level and start testing at a level slightly below this. Indicate successes with a check or plus mark. Indicate failed items with a zero or minus sign. Utilize parental report and items scoreable from other tests whenever possible. Consult the manual when determining age estimates and functional ability levels.

FINE MOTOR

0 to 1 Year Level

6 mos. ____ Lifts cup with handle.
6 mos. ____ Palmar grasp.
7 mos. ____ Removes peg from pegboard.
8 mos. ____ Hand preference (reaches with same hand, 5 of 6 trials).
9 mos. ____ Pokes hole in pegboard with finger.
10 mos. ____ Pincer grasp.

1 to 2 Year Level

14 mos. ____ Places one peg in pegboard.
14 mos. ____ Opens round box.
16 mos. ____ Closes round box.
16 mos. ____ Completes pegboard when urged.
18 mos. ____ Turns group of pages in book.
18 mos. ____ Completes pegboard without urging.

30-35 mos. ____ Close fist and move thumb.

3 to 4 Year Level

36 mos. ____ Strings beads (4 in 2 minutes).
36 mos. ____ Copies circle.
36 mos. ____ Draws cross (in imitation).
42 mos. ____ Winds up toy.
42-47 mos. ____ Opposition of thumb and fingers.
42-47 mos. ____ Copies cross.

4 to 5 Year Level

48 mos. ____ Puts paper clip on paper.
48 mos. ____ Folds paper and creases.
50 mos. ____ Draws square (in imitation).
54 mos. ____ Copies square.

GROSS MOTOR

0 to 1 Year Level

6 mos. ____ Briefly supports fraction of weight standing.
6 mos. ____ Rolls over.
7 mos. ____ Briefly holds trunk erect in sitting position.
7 mos. ____ Supports weight in crawl position.
8 mos. ____ Supports body weight on feet for short periods.
9 mos. ____ Creeping position.
10 mos. ____ Pulls self to knees, standing position.
10 mos. ____ Stands with support/stands briefly unsupported.

2 to 3 Year Level

24 mos. ____ Jumps off floor, both feet.
24 mos. ____ Walks straight line.
25 mos. ____ Walks upstairs alone, both feet on each step.
25 mos. ____ Jumps from bottom step of stairs.
26 mos. ____ Walks downstairs, both feet on each step.
27 mos. ____ Walks backwards, ten feet.
30 mos. ____ Walks up and down stairs, alternating feet.
30 mos. ____ Walks on tiptoe/walks on line, ten feet.
30 mos. ____ Jumps over string 2″ high (1 of 3 trials).
30 mos. ____ Balance on one foot, one second.
34 mos. ____ Broad jump, 8½″ (jump over paper, 8½ x 11″).

5 to 6 Year Level

60-72 mos. ____ Balances on toes for several seconds.
60-72 mos. ____ Walks easily on tiptoe.
72 mos. ____ Stands on each foot alternately, eyes closed.

6 to 7 Year Level

72-84 mos. ____ Stands heel to toe, ten seconds.
72-84 mos. ____ Hops skillfully.
72-84 mos. ____ Throws ball well with adult-like stance/catches well.

Refer to page S11.

MULTIDIMENSIONAL APTITUDE BATTERY

PICTURE ARRANGEMENT

Here are some sets of pictures for you to arrange. In each case, they are mixed up and you are to put them in the right order so that they make the most sensible story.

Look at these pictures. Put them in the right order so they will tell a story.

Choose the correct one of the following possible orders:

1. 

2. 

A. 1 2 4 3
B. 2 3 1 4
C. 1 4 3 2
D. 4 1 3 2
E. 4 3 2 1

3. 

4. 

The correct order is **(C), 1 4 3 2.** In the **1** frame, the mother puts her son's pants in his boots. Second, in **4,** the boy begins to take his pants out of his boots. In the third scene, frame **3,** two girls from school admire his bell-bottoms, and in the final scene, frame **2,** as he arrives home, his mother is upset because of his wet and dirty pants.

For each question, mark the correct choice on your answer sheet. Do not begin until the examiner gives the signal. You will have **seven minutes.** Continue until time is called.

WAIT FOR THE SIGNAL.

Continued on page S318.

PRACTICE PROBLEMS

Picture Completion — Choose the letter that begins the word describing the missing part of the picture.

A. L
B. E
C. B
D. W
E. F

The answer is **Light,** so **A** should be marked.

Spatial — Choose one figure to the right of the vertical line which is the same as the figure on the left. One figure can be turned to look like the figure on the left; the others would have to be flipped over.

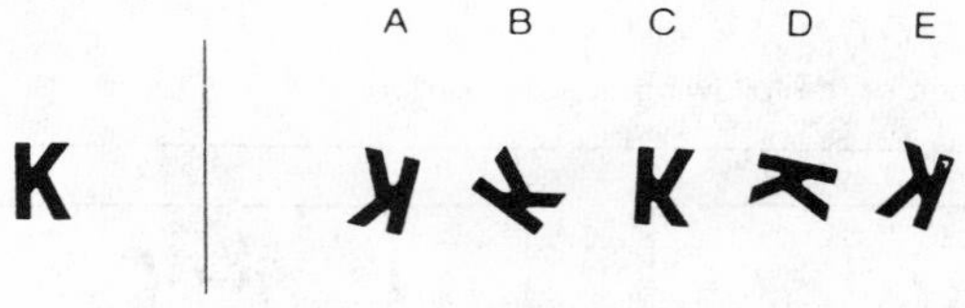

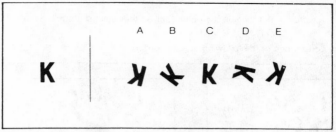

The correct answer is **A,** so **A** should be marked. The others **BCDE** would have to be flipped over.

Object Assembly — Choose the order, from left to right, in which these parts should be placed to form the object.

A.	3	2	1
B.	2	1	3
C.	1	3	2
D.	2	3	1
E.	3	1	2

The correct answer is **C-132** so **C** should be marked. Only this order would create the object **teacup.**

When the examiner gives the signal, turn the page to Test 1—Digit Symbol.

Arithmetic — Solve the following problem.

1. If it costs $8 for two students to go to the theatre, how much will it cost for three students?

A. $10 B. $16 C. $12 D. $4 E. $6

The answer is **C,** $12, therefore one should mark **C.**

THE OHIO VOCATIONAL ACHIEVEMENT TESTS IN DISTRIBUTIVE EDUCATION—APPAREL AND ACCESSORIES

Refer to page T421.

Note: Use the following "Receiving Record" to answer questions 69 through 71.

RECEIVING RECORD

Received from Aiken Dress Company — NO. 16181

Address 1400 Broadway — City New York, N.Y. 10018 — Date Received 9/5/8-

Department	Order No.	Transportation Charges: Total Paid	Charge Shipper	Buyers Approval or Remarks		Received Via		
42	M184925	48.00		Jane Dean 9/16		IOU Service		
Invoice Date	**Terms**	**Invoice Passed**	**Discount Date / Amount**	**Amt. of Inv.**	**Retail Value**	**Pkg.'s**	**Pieces**	**Cartons**
9/5/8-	8/10 EOM	9/12/8-	10/10 / 189.89	2373.60	4816.00		86 (Hangers)	

ATTACH INVOICE HERE

Received from ______ NO. 16181

Vendor No.	Unit Cost	Color	Description	Size 8	Size 10	Size 12	Size 14	Quantity Amt.	Quantity Unit	Class	Unit Price
482	27.60	Blk	Style 253, 2 pc	6	9	9	6	30	ea	123	56.00
483	27.60	Red	Style 253, 2 pc	6	8	8	4	26	ea	123	56.00
484	27.60	Gold	Style 253, 2 pc	3	4	4	4	13	ea	123	56.00
485	27.60	Blue	Style 253, 2 pc	3	4	4	4	15	ea	123	56.00

Order Checked	Date	Mdse. Checked	Date	Price Tickets	Date	Mdse Marked	Date	Cost Extension	Retail Extension	Merchandise Rec'd Date: Stock Room	Department
HLC	9/6	FBJ	9/6	ATL	9/6	MNJ	9/9	2373.60	4816.00	a.22 9/10	

69. There was an error made on the receiving report above when the quantity of items was recorded. This error is the quantity received for vendor number:
    1. 482
    2. 483
    3. 484
    4. 485

70. Referring to the report above, who attached the tickets to the merchandise?
    1. A.T.L.
    2. F.B.J.
    3. M.N.J.
    4. H.L.C.

71. Referring to the report above, the retail price that should appear on the sales ticket is:
    1. $27.60
    2. $54.20
    3. $56.00
    4. $112.00

SECTION 8 - SUPPORT FUNCTIONS

72. An example of an accident caused by poor housekeeping is:
    1. cutting fingers with knife while opening boxes.
    2. electrical shock while repairing a light switch.
    3. being hit with a swinging door.
    4. puncturing foot with discarded pin-ticket.

73. A customer has just fallen in a wet aisle. As a salesperson, you sould immediately:
    1. dry the floor.
    2. assist the customer.
    3. notify the security department.
    4. call an ambulance.

74. The most likely cause of a fire would be:
    1. a missing fire extinguisher.
    2. an overloaded elevator.
    3. a frayed electrical cord.
    4. a cluttered aisle.

7

THE OHIO VOCATIONAL ACHIEVEMENT TESTS IN BUSINESS AND OFFICE EDUCATION—DATA PROCESSING

Refer to page T418.

SECTION 3 - PROGRAMMING LANGUAGES

58. A type of report in which the data from each input record is examined and a line is printed for each record is known as:
    1. a detail report.
    2. a summary report.
    3. an exception report.
    4. an audit report.

59. The multiple-card layout form is used to:
    1. compare the data with the source document.
    2. help the operator in keying data.
    3. verify the data punched in all cards.
    4. aid in the design of several related cards.

64. A programming language which is machine-dependent is:
    1. PL/1.
    2. COBOL.
    3. FORTRAN.
    4. BAL.

65. High-level languages like FORTRAN, COBOL, and BASIC are used for:
    1. applications programming.
    2. software programming.
    3. system utility programming.
    4. control language programming.

66. Consider the following:

    10 LET A = 500

THE OHIO VOCATIONAL ACHIEVEMENT TESTS IN ELECTRONICS—INDUSTRIAL ELECTRONICS

Refer to page T423.

Use the following illustration to answer questions 29 through 31.

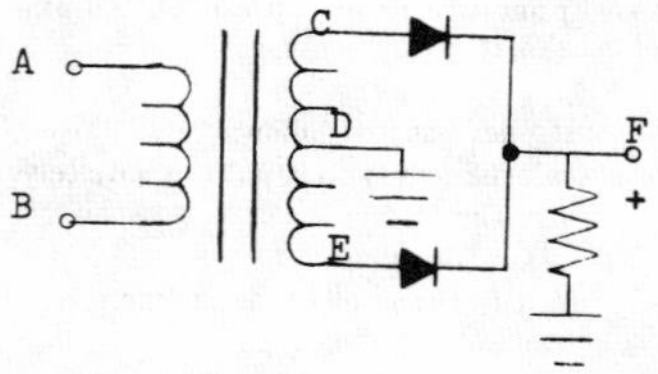

29. The voltage read between Points C and E in the illustration above would best be described as:
    1. AC.
    2. DC.
    3. ripple DC.
    4. pulsating DC.

30. The circuit described in the illustration above is a:
    1. bridge rectifier.
    2. voltage doubler.
    3. full wave rectifier.
    4. half wave rectifier.

31. In the illustration above, the voltage read between Points D and F would best be described as:
    1. AC.
    2. DC.
    3. sinusodial.
    4. pulsating DC.

THE OHIO VOCATIONAL ACHIEVEMENT TESTS IN HEALTH OCCUPATIONS EDUCATION—MEDICAL ASSISTING

Refer to page T425.

86. Field corn is classified as:
    1. sweet corn.
    2. popcorn
    3. flower corn.
    4. dent corn.

87. The most critical time for weed control for corn is when weeds emerge:
    1. before crop emergence.
    2. with crop emergence.
    3. when the crop starts to tassel.
    4. when the crop is nearing maturity.

88. A possible disadvantage of full tillage would

93. An ideal goal for field corn yield per acre is:
    1. 1 metric ton.
    2. 2 tons.
    3. 150 bushels.
    4. 200 pounds.

94. The nutrient needed in the largest amount for corn production is:
    1. potassium.
    2. zinc.
    3. phosphorus.
    4. nitrogen.

THE OHIO VOCATIONAL ACHIEVEMENT TESTS IN AGRICULTURAL EDUCATION—PRODUCTION AGRICULTURE

Refer to page T416.

105. The surgical operation performed on males in which the foreskin is removed from the penis is called a:
    1. vasectomy.
    2. castration.
    3. circumcision.
    4. orchidectomy.

106. When preparing a patient for a pelvic examination in the doctor's office, it is important for the medical assistant to:
    1. administer a douche.
    2. administer a low enema.
    3. scrub the perineal area with soap.
    4. have the patient empty bladder.

107. A tonometer is used to:
    1. measure a refraction.
    2. check prescription lenses.
    3. measure intraocular tension.
    4. examine the interior of the eye.

108. When administering the Snellen vision test, how far away from the standard chart should the patient stand?
    1. 10 feet
    2. 20 feet
    3. 10 meters
    4. 20 yards

109. The surgical procedure called D & C involves:
    1. drainage and cutting of the ovary.
    2. removal of cervical tissue samples.
    3. x-ray examination of the reproductive tract.
    4. dilation of the cervix and scraping of the uterus.

110. While taking a blood pressure, the mercury should be lowered at the rate of:
    1. 1-2 mm. per heartbeat.
    2. 2-4 mm. per heartbeat.
    3. 4-6 mm. per heartbeat.
    4. 6-8 mm. per heartbeat.

OHIO VOCATIONAL INTEREST SURVEY: SECOND EDITION (OVIS II)

Refer to page T810.

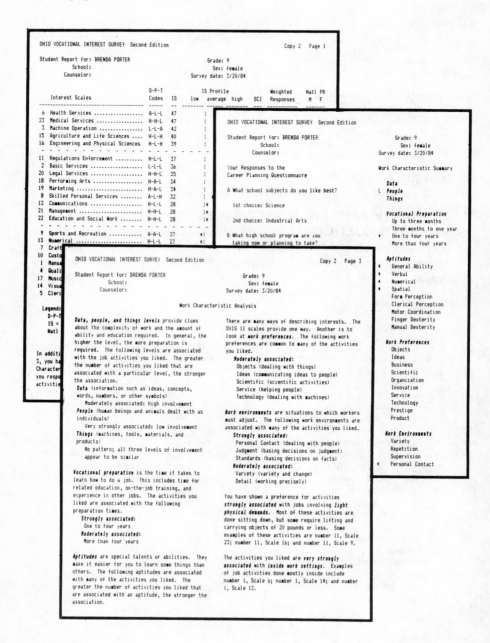

OHIO VOCATIONAL INTEREST SURVEY Second Edition — Copy 2 Page 1

Student Report for: BRENDA PORTER — Grade: 9
School: — Sex: female
Counselor: — Survey date: 3/20/84

	Interest Scales	D-P-T Codes	IS	IS Profile low average high	SCI	Weighted Responses	Natl PR M F
6	Health Services	A-L-L	47	:			
23	Medical Services	H-H-L	47	:			
3	Machine Operation	L-L-A	42	:			
15	Agriculture and Life Sciences	H-L-H	40	:			
16	Engineering and Physical Sciences	H-L-H	39	:			
11	Regulations Enforcement	H-L-L	37	:			
2	Basic Services	L-L-L	36	:			
20	Legal Services	H-H-L	35	:			
18	Performing Arts	H-A-L	34	:			
19	Marketing	H-A-L	34	:			
8	Skilled Personal Services	A-L-H	32	:			
12	Communications	H-L-L	28	:*			
21	Management	H-H-L	28	:*			
22	Education and Social Work	H-H-L	28	:*			
9	Sports and Recreation	A-A-L	27	*:			
13	Numerical	H-L-L	27	*:			
7	Craft…						
10	Custo…						
1	Manua…						
4	Quali…						
17	Music…						
14	Visua…						
5	Cleri…						

Legend:
D-P-T…
IS = …
Natl …

In additi… 3, you ha… Character… you respo… activitie…

OHIO VOCATIONAL INTEREST SURVEY Second Edition

Student Report for: BRENDA PORTER — Grade: 9
School: — Sex: female
Counselor: — Survey date: 3/20/84

Your Responses to the Career Planning Questionnaire

A What school subjects do you like best?

1st choice: Science

2nd choice: Industrial Arts

B What high school program are you taking now or planning to take?

Work Characteristic Summary

Data
L ***People***
Things

Vocational Preparation
Up to three months
Three months to one year
* One to four years
More than four years

Aptitudes
* General Ability
* Verbal
* Numerical
* Spatial
Form Perception
Clerical Perception
Motor Coordination
Finger Dexterity
Manual Dexterity

Work Preferences
Objects
Ideas
Business
Scientific
Organization
Innovation
Service
Technology
Prestige
Product

Work Environments
Variety
Repetition
Supervision
* Personal Contact

OHIO VOCATIONAL INTEREST SURVEY Second Edition — Copy 2 Page 3

Student Report for: BRENDA PORTER — Grade: 9
School: — Sex: female
Counselor: — Survey date: 3/20/84

Work Characteristic Analysis

Data, people, and things levels provide clues about the complexity of work and the amount of ability and education required. In general, the higher the level, the more preparation is required. The following levels are associated with the job activities you liked. The greater the number of activities you liked that are associated with a particular level, the stronger the association.

Data (information such as ideas, concepts, words, numbers, or other symbols)
Moderately associated: high involvement
People (human beings and animals dealt with as individuals)
Very strongly associated: low involvement
Things (machines, tools, materials, and products)
No pattern; all three levels of involvement appear to be similar

Vocational preparation is the time it takes to learn how to do a job. This includes time for related education, on-the-job training, and experience in other jobs. The activities you liked are associated with the following preparation times.
Strongly associated:
One to four years
Moderately associated:
More than four years

Aptitudes are special talents or abilities. They make it easier for you to learn some things than others. The following aptitudes are associated with many of the activities you liked. The greater the number of activities you liked that are associated with an aptitude, the stronger the association.

There are many ways of describing interests. The OVIS II scales provide one way. Another is to look at ***work preferences***. The following work preferences are common to many of the activities you liked.
Moderately associated:
Objects (dealing with things)
Ideas (communicating ideas to people)
Scientific (scientific activities)
Service (helping people)
Technology (dealing with machines)

Work environments are situations to which workers must adjust. The following work environments are associated with many of the activities you liked.
Strongly associated:
Personal Contact (dealing with people)
Judgment (basing decisions on judgment)
Standards (basing decisions on facts)
Moderately associated:
Variety (variety and change)
Detail (working precisely)

You have shown a preference for activities ***strongly associated*** with jobs involving ***light physical demands.*** Most of these activities are done sitting down, but some require lifting and carrying objects of 20 pounds or less. Some examples of these activities are number 11, Scale 23; number 11, Scale 16; and number 11, Scale 9.

The activities you liked are ***very strongly associated*** with ***inside work settings.*** Examples of job activities done mostly inside include number 1, Scale 6; number 1, Scale 14; and number 1, Scale 12.

PERSONAL CAREER DEVELOPMENT PROFILE (from Sixteen Personality Factor Questionnaire)

Refer to page T138.

SAMPLE PCDP REPORT

MARK SAMPLE -3- 8/17/1981

RELATED OCCUPATIONS OF INTEREST

MR SAMPLE'S STRONGEST INTEREST THEMES ARE SIMILAR TO THOSE OF PEOPLE EMPLOYED IN SOME OF THE FOLLOWING OCCUPATIONS. IN REVIEWING THIS LIST, HE MAY FIND SUPPORT FOR PAST OR PRESENT CAREER CHOICES. ALTERNATIVELY, HE MAY FIND IT HELPFUL TO REVIEW HIS INTERESTS, SKILLS, AND EXPERIENCE WITH RESPECT TO OCCUPATIONS HE MAY NOT HAVE CONSIDERED. THERE ARE INDICATIONS HE MAY FIND IT RELATIVELY EASY TO IDENTIFY WITH AND RELATE TO PEOPLE WHO ARE SUCCESSFULLY PURSUING CAREERS IN SOME OF THESE OCCUPATIONS: BANK TELLER, CASHIER, CLERK/STENOGRAPHER, CREDIT REFERENCE CLERK, HOSPITAL WARD ATTENDANT, RESERVATION AGENT, SECRETARY. ADDITIONAL OCCUPATIONS MR SAMPLE MAY WISH TO CONSIDER INCLUDE: BOOKKEEPER, CLAIMS EXAMINER, INSURANCE UNDERWRITER, PERSONNEL SECRETARY, RECEPTIONIST, RETAIL COUNTER CLERK, SALES CORRESPONDENT, AND ACCOUNTING CLERK, BILLING CLERK, COMPUTER SYSTEMS ANALYST, ESTIMATOR, MEDICAL LABORATORY ASSISTANT, OFFICE WORKER, PRODUCTION PLANNER, TECHNICAL SECRETARY.

THE OCCUPATIONAL INFORMATION REPORTED HERE IS BASED ON CAREER PREFERENCES SUGGESTED BY MR SAMPLE'S GENERAL PERSONALITY ORIENTATION. THE OCCUPATIONAL LISTINGS SHOULD NOT BE TREATED AS SPECIFIC JOB SUGGESTIONS. SOME MAY NOT APPEAL TO HIM. OTHERS MAY NOT RELATE WELL TO HIS TRAINING AND EXPERIENCE. HOWEVER, EACH REPRESENTS AN OPTION OPEN TO MR SAMPLE IN HIS PERSONAL GROWTH AND CAREER PLANNING AT THIS POINT IN TIME. A CAREFUL REVIEW MAY BRING TO MIND OTHER ALTERNATIVES THAT REPRESENT EVEN MORE APPEALING CAREER PATHS.

PERSONAL-CAREER DEVELOPMENT CONSIDERATIONS

AT THE PRESENT TIME, MR SAMPLE APPEARS TO PREFER PERSONAL AND WORK-RELATED SITUATIONS WHEREBY HE IS ABLE TO WORK OUT THINGS BY HIMSELF, RATHER THAN TO WORK THEM OUT WITH OTHERS. MR SAMPLE IS NORMALLY MOST PRODUCTIVE AND FEELS MOST SECURE WHEN HE IS DOING WHAT HE KNOWS BEST, SINCE HE TENDS TO BE HESITANT ABOUT EXPERIMENTING WITH NEW APPROACHES TO WHAT HE DOES. MR SAMPLE IS APT TO FEEL MOST COMFORTABLE AND EXPERIENCE MOST PERSONAL GRATIFICATION IF HE IS ASSIGNED WORK-RELATED RESPONSIBILITIES IN A CONTROLLED AND STRUCTURED ENVIRONMENT. CONSEQUENTLY, HIS CONFIDENCE IN HIMSELF IS GENERALLY ENHANCED WHEN HE IS PROVIDED A GRADED SERIES OF EXPERIENCES WHICH ENABLE HIM TO FEEL SUCCESSFUL. SIMILARLY, A CLOSE, SUPPORTIVE WORKING RELATIONSHIP WITH SUPERIORS WHOM HE CAN RESPECT WOULD BE OF ASSISTANCE TO MR SAMPLE IN HIS EFFORTS TO PERFORM WITH OVERALL EFFECTIVENESS. AT THIS TIME, MR SAMPLE SHOWS RATHER LIMITED INTEREST FOR THE KINDS OF DISCIPLINED ACTIVITIES REQUIRED BY FORMAL ACADEMIC TRAINING SITUATIONS.

IN TERMS OF MR SAMPLE'S NEEDS FOR SELF-GROWTH AND PERFORMANCE IMPROVEMENT, HE COULD BE ENCOURAGED TO GUARD AGAINST: (*) HIS TENDENCY TO BE SO SELF-CONCERNED AND SELF-CONSCIOUS AT TIMES THAT

PRIDE©: PRESCHOOL AND KINDERGARTEN INTEREST DESCRIPTOR

Refer to page S146.

Name of Child ______________________________ Age ________

Name of Parent ________________ Name of Teacher ________________

School ______________________________ Date ________

City ______________________________ State ________

INSTRUCTIONS TO THE PARENT: Consider your child's interests and activities and your own relationship to your child in responding to these statements. In determining your responses, it will be helpful to compare your child's interests with other similar aged children that you know. Be sure to answer all the questions.

	NO	TO A SMALL EXTENT	AVERAGE	MORE THAN AVERAGE	DEFINITELY
19. I enjoy make-believe play with my child.	O	O	O	O	O
20. My child has many interests.	O	O	O	O	O
21. My child enjoys painting at home.	O	O	O	O	O
22. My child is quite reflective, rather than impulsive.	O	O	O	O	O
23. I laugh with my child a lot.	O	O	O	O	O
24. I have many interests.	O	O	O	O	O
25. My child has unusual ideas.	O	O	O	O	O
26. My child usually does whatever other children do.	O	O	O	O	O
27. My child often does two things at the same time that aren't usually done					

PSYCHO-EPISTEMOLOGICAL PROFILE (PEP)

Refer to page S191.

<u>Directions</u>

For each of the following statements, you are to indicate your personal agreement or disagreement on the scale provided on the answer sheet. 'CD' means complete disagreement with the statement, 'MD' means moderate disagreement, 'N' means neutral, 'MA' means moderate agreement, and 'CA' means complete agreement.

Here is a sample question:

The Roman Empire fell because of moral degeneration of its rulers.

CD	MD	N	MA	CA
===	===	===	■■■	===

In this example, the person agrees with the statement, but not entirely, so they have blacked out the space under 'MA' -- moderate agreement.

Your personal preference alone is required. There are no right or wrong responses. <u>It is necessary</u>, however, <u>that you answer all of the questions</u>. Be sure to clearly mark the appropriate space for each question. Use a pencil and erase any extra marks. <u>Trust your first impression</u>. There is no time limit.

....

67. I prefer to associate with people who stay in close contact with the facts of life.
68. Many T.V. programs are based on inadequate background research.
69. Higher education should place greater emphasis on natural science.
70. I like to think of myself as logical.
71. When people are arguing a question from two different points of view, I would say that each should endeavor to assess honestly his own attitude and bias before arguing further.
72. When reading an historical novel, I am most interested in the factual accuracy found in the novel.
73. The greatest evil inherent in a totalitarian regime is distortion of the facts.
74. A good driver is considerate.
75. Our understanding of the meaning of life has been furthered most by biology.

READING FREE VOCATIONAL INTEREST INVENTORY—REVISED (R-FVII REVISED)

Refer to page S203.

MALE AND FEMALE

READING-FREE VOCATIONAL INTEREST INVENTORY: M F

Devised by Ralph L. Becker

Last Name ______ First Name ______ Date ______

Birthdate ______ Age: ___ Yrs. ___ Mos. ___ Grade (circle one) 9 10 11 12 Other

School or Institute ______ City ______ State ______

HOW TO USE THIS BOOKLET: This is not a test. There are no wrong or right answers. Your answers will tell about the kind of work you like best.

On each page of this booklet there are groups of three pictures in a straight row, just like the three pictures at the bottom of this page. Look at the example, below. If you liked best the picture of raking leaves, you would make a big **circle** on this picture, as shown. You can only choose **one** picture of the three, so choose the one you like best.

If you like all three pictures, you must decide on only one, so make a circle on the picture you like best. If you do not like any of the three pictures, choose the one you would do for only a very short time.

There are 55 rows of pictures of people working at different jobs just like the pictures below. Be sure you **circle one** picture in each group of the 55 rows of pictures.

Turn the page and begin.

EXAMPLE

INDIVIDUAL PROFILE SHEET

Last Name Wilson, First Tom Date 8-29-81

Grade 9 Age: 15 yrs. 2 mos. Date of Birth

School C. C. S. City Columbus State OHIO

Male Norm Used EMR, 13 To 15 Female Norm Used

Key Letter	Raw Score	T Score	Percentile	Stanine	Interest Area	Symbol	Interest High	Interest Low
A	1	31	3	1	Automotive	Auto		✓
B	4	31	3	1	Building Trades	B Tr		✓
C	11	66	95	8	Clerical	Cl	✓	
D	1	34	5	2	Animal Care	An Cr		✓
E	2	40	15	3	Food Service	F S		✓
F	10	66	95	8	Patient Care	P Cr	✓	
G	3	40	15	3	Horticulture	Hort		✓
H	7	43	25	4	Housekeeping	Hsk		
I	16	71	98	9	Personal Service	P Sv	✓	
J	5	55	70	6	Laundry Service	Ly		
K	5	49	45	5	Materials Handling	M Hg		

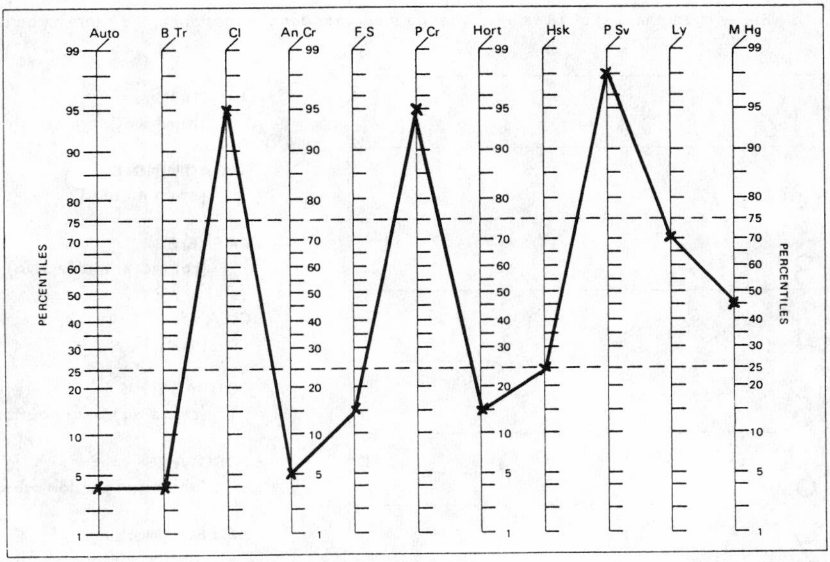

ROKEACH VALUE SURVEY: FORM G

Refer to page S54.

1		**A COMFORTABLE LIFE** (a prosperous life)
2		**AN EXCITING LIFE** (a stimulating, active life)
3		**A SENSE OF ACCOMPLISHMENT** (lasting contribution)
4		**A WORLD AT PEACE** (free of war and conflict)
5		**A WORLD OF BEAUTY** (beauty of nature and the arts)
6		**EQUALITY** (brotherhood, equal opportunity for all)

Below is another list of 18 values. Arrange them in order of importance, the same as before.

1		**AMBITIOUS** (hard-working, aspiring)
2		**BROADMINDED** (open-minded)
3		**CAPABLE** (competent, effective)
4		**CLEAN** (neat, tidy)
5		**COURAGEOUS** (standing up for your beliefs)
6		**FORGIVING** (willing to pardon others)
7		**HELPFUL** (working for the welfare of others)
8		**HONEST** (sincere, truthful)
9		**IMAGINATIVE** (daring, creative)

SCALE FOR THE IDENTIFICATION OF SCHOOL PHOBIA (SIS)

Refer to page S181.

Instructions: Use this rating scale to assess the frequency of occurrence of each behavior or characteristic listed. Refer to the following rating scheme and write the appropriate number in the space provided next to each item.

Almost never	Not very often	Sometimes	Often	Very frequently
0	1	2	3	4

The source of information should also be noted in the space provided next to each item. More than one source may be listed. Use the following codes to identify sources: "P" for parent, "ST" for student, "SC" for school, and "O" for other.

20. **REQUIRES PARENT TO DRIVE HIM/HER TO SCHOOL.** Rating ______
Reluctance to ride bus to school; requires parent to drive him/her to and from school; requires parent to drive him/her to other places that could normally be reached by walking or riding bicycle. Source ______
Comments: ______

21. **SLEEP DISORDERS.** Rating ______
Reports of recurring nightmares; night terrors; insomnia; hypersomnia (excessive sleep at night or during the day); sleeping at odd times. Source ______
Comments: ______

22. **ASSERTING INDEPENDENCE FROM FAMILY LIFE.** Rating ______
Infrequently involved in family activities (trips, vacations, meals, church, Sunday outings, etc.); fails to comply with wishes/directions of parents (e.g., curfews, family chores, etc.); seems to set own lifestyle outside family. Source ______
Comments: ______

23. **NOT MOTIVATED FOR ACADEMIC ACHIEVEMENT.** Rating ______
Infrequently completes homework or school assignments; history of poor academic achievement in school, below average grades or grades not reflective of student's potential. Source ______
Comments: ______

24. **PANIC REACTIONS AT SCHOOL OR HOME.** Rating ______
Crying; screaming; demands to return home; runs from class, office, or building; withdrawal; quivering; hand-wringing; atypical seating; physical resistance or crying when required to leave home, ride to school, or to enter school building. Source ______
Comments: ______

School Phobia Profile

Item No.	Behavior	Item Rating	×	Weight	=	Item Score	Source: Parent	Student	School	Other
1	Remain at Home	____	×	1	=	____				
3	Depend. on Parent	____	×	2	=	____				
4	Intol. Separation	____	×	3	=	____				
8	Parental Illness	____	×	1	=	____				
9	Missing Parent	____	×	2	=	____				
12	Complaints of Illness	____	×	1	=	____				
14	Homebound Instr.	____	×	1	=	____				
15	Anxiety	____	×	1	=	____				
16	Depression	____	×	1	=	____				
20	Driven to School	____	×	1	=	____				
21	Sleep Disorders	____	×	1	=	____				
24	Panic Reaction	____	×	1	=	____				

Total Score ____ ÷ 16 = ☐ **School Phobia Profile Score**

SCHEDULE OF RECENT EXPERIENCE (SRE)

Refer to page S55.

SCHEDULE OF RECENT EXPERIENCE (SRE)

CARD NO. 1 (1) DATE ____ ____ (4) ____ (5)
GROUP NO. ____ (2) ____ (3) ID NO. ____ (6) ____ (7) ____ (8) ____ (9) ____ (10)

NAME________________ ADDRESS________________

AGE____ (11, 12) SEX: (13) Male____ Female____

MARITAL STATUS: (14) Married ____ Divorced ____ Separated ____ Widowed ____ Never married ____
EDUCATION: (15) Grade school____ High school ____ Trade school ____ College ____ Advanced degree ____

INSTRUCTIONS:

For each life event item listed below please do the following:

Think back on the event and decide if it happened during the last 12 months. If the event did happen, indicate the *number of times* it happened by placing a number in the column labeled 0–12 months ago.

	0–12 months ago
1. A lot more or a lot less trouble with the boss.	____ 16
2. A major change in sleeping habits (sleeping a lot more or a lot less, or change in part of day when asleep).	____ 17
3. A major change in eating habits (a lot more or a lot less food intake, or very different meal hours or surroundings).	____ 18
4. A revision of personal habits (dress, manners, associations, etc.).	____ 19
5. A major change in your usual type and/or amount of recreation.	____ 20
6. A major change in your social activities (e.g., clubs, dancing, movies, visiting, etc.).	____ 21
7. A major change in church activities (e.g., a lot more or a lot less than usual).	____ 22
8. A major change in number of family-get-togethers (e.g., a lot more or a lot less than usual).	____ 23
9. A major change in financial state (e.g., a lot worse off or a lot better off than usual).	____ 24
10. In-law troubles.	____ 25
33. Wife beginning or ceasing work outside the home.	____ 48
34. Taking out a mortgage or loan for a major purchase (e.g., purchasing a home, business, etc.).	____ 49
35. Taking out a mortgage or loan for a lesser purchase (e.g., purchasing a car, TV, freezer, etc.).	____ 50
36. Foreclosure on a mortgage or loan.	____ 51
37. Vacation.	____ 52
38. Changing to a new school.	____ 53
39. Changing to a different line of work.	____ 54
40. Beginning or ceasing formal schooling.	____ 55
41. Marital reconciliation with mate.	____ 56
42. Pregnancy.	____ 57

SCREENING TEST OF ADOLESCENT LANGUAGE (STAL)

Refer to page S171.

Name________________ Birthdate__________ School__________ Grade_____

Date______________ Examiner______________

	Raw Score	Pass for ____ grade	INTERPRETATION
Total Test Score	______	______	
Vocabulary	______	______	
Aud. Memory	______	______	
Lang. Probe	______	______	
Prov. Expl.	______	______	

Recommendation: ☐ Pass - No further testing
☐ Fail - Further assessment:

MINIMUM PASSING SCORES FOR THE SCREENING TEST OF ADOLESCENT LANGUAGE

	GRADES 6-8	GRADES 9-12
TOTAL TEST SCORE	11 pass responses	13 pass responses
Vocabulary	5 pass responses	6 pass responses
Auditory Memory Span	1 pass response	1 pass response
Language Processing	2 pass responses	2 pass responses
Proverb Explanation	1 pass response	1 pass response

I. *VOCABULARY*

______ 1. Gigantic — The room is gigantic.______________

______ 2. Kettle — The kettle is copper.______________

______ 3. Unmarried — My teacher is unmarried.______________

II. *AUDITORY MEMORY SPAN*

______ 1. The fire drill that we had last week/turned out to be the real thing.

______ 2. The school on the west side of town/has more new students than our own school.

______ 3. Last night I went to a movie with my friend/at the theater that takes coupons.

III. *LANGUAGE PROCESSING*

	what	why	
______	☐	☐	1. The sun was shining so brightly last week on Tuesday that I had to wear my sunglasses in the movie theater.
______	☐	☐	2. I went with my sister to the shoe store to buy a pair of combat boots to wear to the Junior Prom.
______	☐	☐	3. After climbing up ten flights of stairs two steps at a time yesterday morning, the man finally reached the basement.
______	☐	☐	4. The most recent set of identical twins born at the hospital was a girl and a boy.

IV. *PROVERB EXPLANATION*

______ 1. Practice makes perfect.

______ 2. Actions speak louder than words.

______ 3. Better late than never.

TOTAL IV______

TOTAL TEST SCORE__________

SILVER DRAWING TEST OF COGNITIVE AND CREATIVE SKILLS

Refer to page S131.

PREDICTIVE DRAWING

Suppose you took a few sips of an ice cream soda, then a few more, and more, until your glass was empty. Draw lines in the glasses to show how the soda would look if you gradually drank all of it.

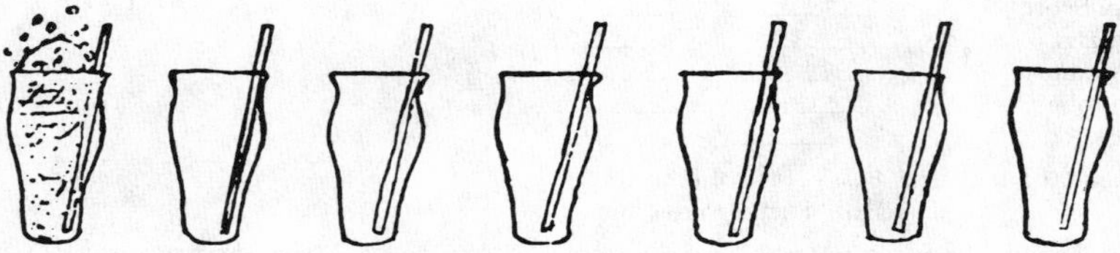

Suppose you tilted a bottle half filled with water. Draw lines in the bottles to show how the water would look.

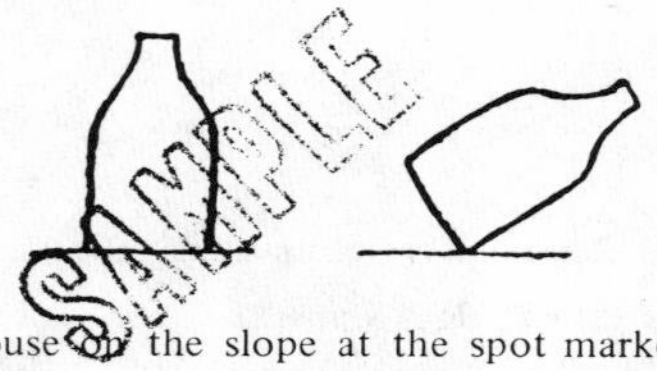

Suppose you put the house on the slope at the spot marked X. Draw the way it would look.

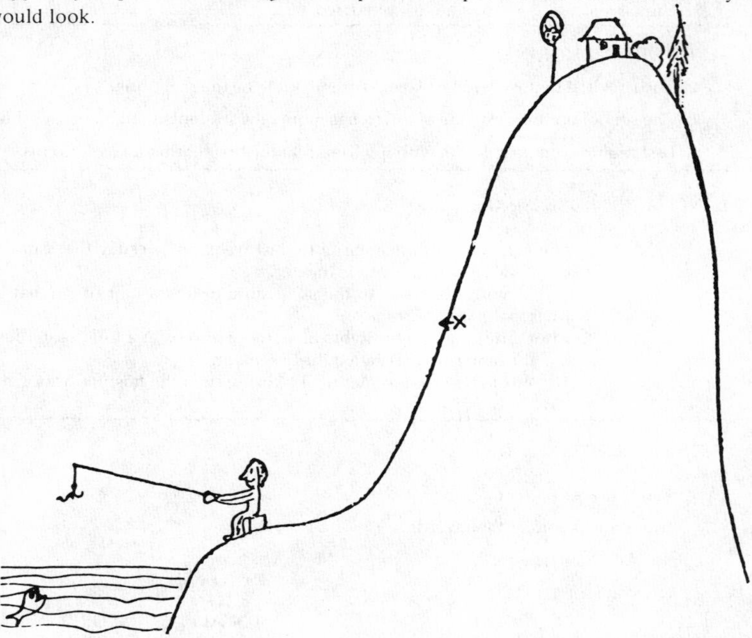

THE SMELL IDENTIFICATION TEST™

Refer to page S214.

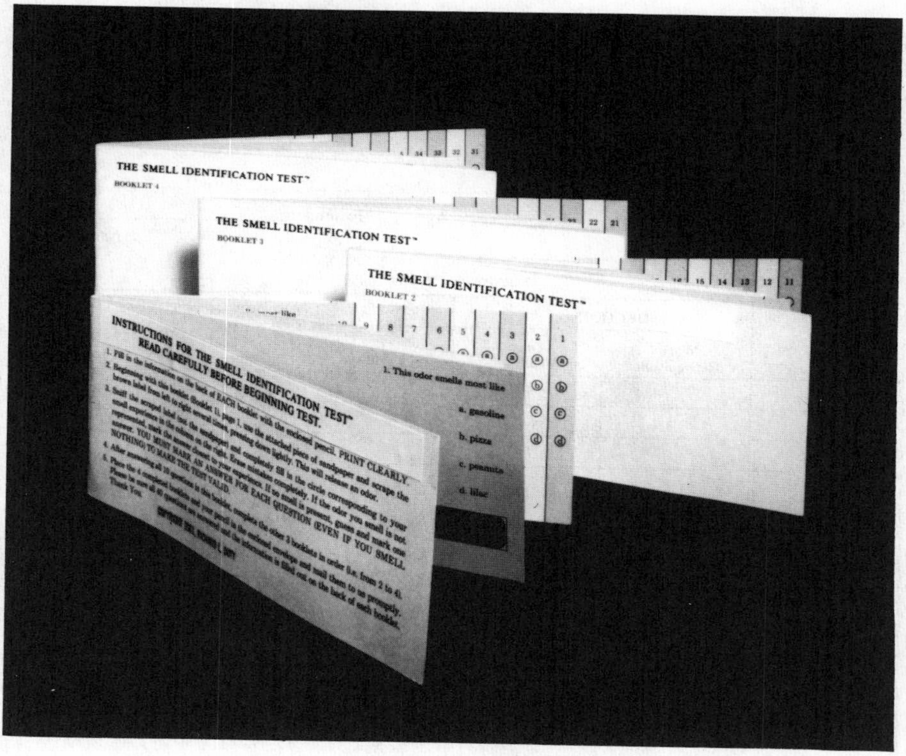

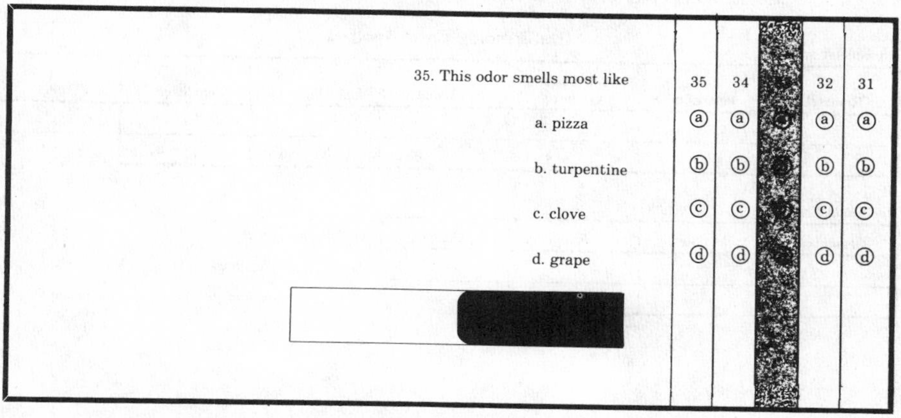

SPADAFORE DIAGNOSTIC READING TEST (SDRT)

Refer to page S141.

SDRT

SPADAFORE DIAGNOSTIC READING TEST

Gerald J. Spadafore, EdD

Name____________________ Date__________ Grade__________

School ____________________ Age_____ Examiner__________

Scoring Profile

GRADE LEVEL	DECODING		COMPREHENSION		
	Word Recognition	Oral Reading	Oral Reading	Silent Reading	Listening
Primer					
1st					
2nd					
3rd					
4th					
5th					
6th					
7th					
8th					
9th					
10th					
11th					
12th					

Note: Use the following abbreviations when completing this profile: Ind. – Independent level, Ins. – Instructional level, Frus. – Frustration level.

Oral Reading Error Analysis

Pronunciation Errors

Reversal	Insertion	Mispronunciation	Omission	Substitution	Repetition	TOTAL
%	%	%	%	%	%	

Positional Errors

Beginning	Middle	End	TOTAL
%	%	%	

Literacy Level

____Professional

____Vocational

____Technical

____Functional

Grade: Primer	Grade: 2	Grade: 4	Grade: 6
1. _____ dog	1. _____ breakfast	1. _____ whether	1. _____ disaster
2. _____ we	2. _____ dinner	2. _____ strange	2. _____ encounter
3. _____ one	3. _____ name	3. _____ public	3. _____ disarm
4. _____ look	4. _____ sent	4. _____ squirrel	4. _____ gusher
5. _____ big	5. _____ time	5. _____ target	5. _____ transport
6. _____ something	6. _____ church	6. _____ hurricane	6. _____ wrench
7. _____ jump	7. _____ donkey	7. _____ courage	7. _____ wealth
8. _____ boy	8. _____ people	8. _____ museum	8. _____ subscribe
9. _____ up	9. _____ morning	9. _____ knowledge	9. _____ twilight
10. _____ at	10. _____ teacher	10. _____ stretch	10. _____ distant
11. _____ of	11. _____ care	11. _____ claimed	11. _____ interrupted
12. _____ no	12. _____ believe	12. _____ camera	12. _____ trousers
13. _____ my	13. _____ town	13. _____ design	13. _____ bought
14. _____ all	14. _____ please	14. _____ lame	14. _____ defeated
15. _____ the	15. _____ lunch	15. _____ future	15. _____ acquire
16. _____ she	16. _____ farmer	16. _____ brought	16. _____ structure
17. _____ did	17. _____ every	17. _____ membership	17. _____ devoted
18. _____ red	18. _____ friend	18. _____ phony	18. _____ organize
19. _____ book	19. _____ children	19. _____ engine	19. _____ transportation
20. _____ road	20. _____ knew	20. _____ marriage	20. _____ caterpillar
_____Ind. (0-1 errors)	**_____Ind. (0-1 errors)**	**_____Ind. (0-1 errors)**	**_____Ind. (0-1 errors)**
_____Ins. (2-3 errors)	**_____Ins. (2-3 errors)**	**_____Ins. (2-3 errors)**	**_____Ins. (2-3 errors)**
_____Frus. (4 or more errors)	**_____Frus. (4 or more errors)**	**_____Frus. (4 or more errors)**	**_____Frus. (4 or more errors)**

ORAL READING AND COMPREHENSION

Grade: 6

People and the Ocean

For ages people have discovered new lands by sail-/ ing on the ocean. But now a great deal of money and/ time is spent investigating the ocean. A great deal is/ already known about this last frontier, as it has been/ called. But there is still a great deal of new information/ we need to learn. It is known that the ocean is rich in/ minerals which are needed by the world. Also, it con-/ tains enough food to provide protein for all the people/ in the world. If there were a way to remove salt from/ ocean water, there would be enough irrigation water to/ turn the deserts into productive farm land./

Better equipment needs to be developed so we can/ safely explore the oceans. The ocean is of great value to/ people because it is rich in food and minerals. Perhaps/ in the distant future we will have colonies of people/ living under the ocean.

	Questions	**Answers**
1.	____ What are people spending a great deal of time and money investigating?	the ocean
2.	____ What are two things needed by people which the ocean contains?	minerals and food
3.	____ What must we do to ocean water before it can be used for irrigation?	remove the salt
4.	____ What must we develop in order for man to safely explore the oceans?	better equipment
5.	____ In the distant future how might we use the ocean?	we will have colonies of people living under the ocean

Decoding Errors: ____Ind. (2 or less) ____Ins. (3-8) ____Frus. (9 or more)

TOTAL______

Comprehension Errors: ____Ind. (0) ____Ins. (1) ____Frus. (2 or more)

Pronunciation Errors

RV	IS	MP	OM	SB	RP

Positional Errors

Beg.	Mid.	End

SUPERVISORY INVENTORY ON COMMUNICATION (SIC)

Refer to page S242.

On the following pages are 80 items concerned with the job of supervisor. Some of them deal with principles, while others are concerned with everyday supervisory practices.

You are to read each statement and indicate whether you "agree" or "disagree" as follows:

If you "agree," mark an X in the "A" box	[X A] [DA]
If you "disagree," mark an X in the "DA" box	[A] [X DA]

46. Most employes would like to know more about company products and customers. [A] [DA]

47. The use of effective visual-aids by a speaker usually provides a significant increase in the understanding of the audience. [A] [DA]

48. The use of a large vocabulary helps greatly in a person's communication effectiveness. [A] [DA]

---

46. A Most employes, whether they be management or hourly, would like to know more about company products and customers. It makes them feel important and that they "belong" to the organization.

47. A Most of what we learn, we see rather than just hear. Therefore, a speaker who uses effective visual aids is usually more effective in getting across the message so that the audience understands it.

48. DA This question is aimed at the sender. The use of a large vocabulary by the sender frequently results in lack of understanding on the part of the receiver who does not understand the words that are being used. Sometimes it results in antagonism because the receiver feels the sender is trying to impress rather than communicate. The sender must be sure that the vocabulary is understood by the receiver, and a small vocabulary usually accomplishes this. (From a receiver's standpoint, a large vocabulary is very important to understand whatever words the sender may use.)

SUPERVISORY INVENTORY ON SAFETY (SIS)

Refer to page S254.

If you "agree," mark an X in the "A" box	[X A] [DA]
If you "disagree," mark an X in the "DA" box	[A] [X DA]

You may not be as sure about some statements as you are about others. However, if you "agree" more than you "disagree," mark the "A" box. Or, if you "disagree" more than you "agree," mark the "DA" box. BE SURE TO MARK AN ANSWER FOR EACH STATEMENT.

54. The best way to develop positive safety attitudes is to show pictures of some horrible accidents. [A] [DA]
55. Safety posters are the most effective way of building positive employe safety attitudes. [A] [DA]
56. If safety is stressed when an employe starts a new job, the supervisor can depend on the employe to follow through with safe methods of working. [A] [DA]
57. In training an employe, the first thing the supervisor should do is to point out the job hazards. [A] [DA]

DA 54. This is similar to item 50. It may have a positive effect by scaring some people into being safe. However, items 53 and 60 describe better ways.

DA 55. Safety posters can *only* be effective if they are used by the supervisor as a discussion point and if they relate to concerns felt by the employe. They are reminders about brief, single concept topics — not safety programs. Items 53 and 60 are better ways.

DA 56. Safety is something that must be constantly stressed. Experienced workers, for example, may become careless because they feel that they won't have an accident. Also, they may be so experienced and skillful that they will do the work "mechanically" while thinking about something else. This lack of concentration may result in an accident. It is important to add that new workers are more apt to have accidents and must be thoroughly oriented on safety.

THE TEST OF MOTOR IMPAIRMENT (Henderson Revision)

Refer to page T540.

AGE BAND 1

TASK	ENTER CHILD'S PERFORMANCE BELOW		AGE FIVE PASS	AGE FIVE BORDERLINE	AGE FIVE FAIL	AGE FIVE Enter Score		AGE SIX PASS	AGE SIX BORDERLINE	AGE SIX FAIL	AGE SIX Enter Score
MANUAL DEXTERITY 1 **POST COINS**	*Time taken (secs)* RIGHT HAND Trial 1 .... 2		0	1/2	1			0	1/2	1	
		Pr.	21–	22-23	24+		Pr.	18–	19-21	22+	
	LEFT HAND Trial 1 .... 2		0	1/2	1			0	1/2	1	
		Oth.	22–	23-25	26+		Oth.	20–	21-22	23+	
MANUAL DEXTERITY 2 **THREAD BEADS**	*Time taken (secs)* Trial 1 .... 2		**0**	**1**	**2**			**0**	**1**	**2**	
			58–	59-65	66+			55–	56-65	66+	
MANUAL DEXTERITY 3 **FLOWER TRAIL**	*Number of deviations* HAND USED [ ] 1 Trial		**0**	**1**	**2**			**0**	**1**	**2**	
			12–	13-18	19+			5–	6-9	10+	
BALL SKILLS 1 **CATCH BEAN BAG**	*Number of catches* 10 Trials		**0**	**1**	**2**			**0**	**1**	**2**	
			6+	4-5	3–			9+	7-8	6–	
BALL SKILLS 2 **ROLL BALL INTO GOAL**	*Number of goals* HAND USED [ ] 10 Trials		**0**	**1**	**2**			**0**	**1**	**2**	
			5+	3-4	2–			7+	5-6	4–	
STATIC BALANCE **ONE LEG BALANCE**	*Time balanced (secs)* RIGHT LEG Trial 1 .... 2		0	1/2	1			0	1/2	1	
		R:	9+	6-8	5–		R:	15+	8-14	7–	
	LEFT LEG Trial 1 .... 2		0	1/2	1			0	1/2	1	
		L:	9+	6-8	5–		L:	15+	8-14	7–	
DYNAMIC BALANCE 1 **JUMP OVER CORD**	*One correct jump* (1st / 2nd / 3rd) KNEE HEIGHT 3 Trials; LOWER HEIGHT 3 Trials		**0**	**1**	**2**			**0**	**1**	**2**	
			Pass at Knee Height	Pass at Lower Height	Fail			Pass at Knee Height	Pass at Lower Height		
DYNAMIC BALANCE 2 **WALK HEELS RAISED**	*Number of steps* Trial 1 .... 2 .... 3		**0**	**1**	**2**			**0**	**1**	**2**	
			13+	7–12	6–			15+	11-14	10–	
			AGE FIVE TOTAL **Range 0—16**			—		**AGE SIX TOTAL** **Range 0—16**			—

In the scoring blocks 'Pr' means 'Preferred hand' as ascertained by the hand used in writing or drawing; 'Oth' means 'Other hand'.

A number followed by a minus sign signifies that number or less; by a plus sign, that number or more.

TRUSTWORTHINESS ATTITUDE SURVEY (T.A. SURVEY)

Refer to page T832.

personnel security preview©
T. A. Survey©

Reminder: You are being examined by a psychological technique that identifies biasing of answers. It is therefore important that your answers are truthful since any falsification will be gradeable when the test is scored.

Yes (?) No

1. People who steal really are mental cases.
2. Our society seems to be going down hill morally.
3. The courts are too easy on law breakers.
4. Employers should do a better job of investigating the background of people before they are hired if they are trying to prevent theft.
5. Most people just cannot be trusted.
6. There should be a tougher penalty for employee theft.
7. A lot of employees steal because they are not satisfied in their job.
8. Most people will lie if they can gain by it.
9. Most employers try to take advantage of their workers and pay as little as the law permits.
10. If someone does you a wrong, do you feel you should pay him back if you can, just for the principle of the thing?
11. If the facts were known, most bosses take more from the company than their workers but are better able to get away with it.
12. The manager who gets caught stealing usually gets to "resign" where the little guy goes to jail.
13. When you get bored, do you like to stir up some excitement?
14. The reason why a lot of people ste... because the compa... is ... les...
15. Have you be... n...n to ... almo... an... thing ... da...?
16. Most c...ani... expe... certain amount of emplo... th...ft and think it's o.k. because th... an deduct it from their taxes and come out ahead.
17. Do you always tell the truth?
18. Employee theft is chicken feed compared to income tax evasion by company executives.
19. Government employees are generally more honest than business employees.
20. It's always a good thing to know people in the right places in order to get traffic tickets and such things taken care of.
21. There are some legitimate reasons for a person to take merchandise or money without permission.
22. Are you stricter about right and wrong than most people?
23. Too many people think in terms of right and wrong and do not consider the circumstances.
24. The closer an employee is watched on his job the more he will try to "beat the system."
25. It is all right to get around the law if you don't actually break it.
26. Kids from strict homes are just as likely to do things as kids from lenient homes.

Yes (?) No

28. Disinterested parents are the reason kids go bad.
29. A person with a mental problem should be excused for his actions.
30. A person should adapt his ideas and behavior to the group that he happens to be with at the time.
31. Heavy drinking usually leads to other kinds of delinquency.
32. Stealing is a part of growing pains in youth.
33. Using marijuana is worse than drinking liquor.
34. Most parents disapprove of their children's friends.
35. Most people would take the money out of a lost wallet or purse that had identification in it and leave the empty for someone else to return.
36. Most people are honest mainly because of the fear of being caught.
37. It is really dishonest for a food store employee to take food off the shelf to eat while at work.
38. Most people fin... themselves in trouble with the ... a... s...me time.
39. M...os... rul... ...re m...de for the little guy not th... p...vil...ed.
40. It ... th... system that makes people dis-...onest more than their upbringing.
41. Do you keep out of trouble at all costs?
42. Most people do not "settle down" until they are in their thirties.
43. Have you ever purposely told a lie?
44. Low wages are the main reason person becoming dishonest.
45. Turning in a fellow employee see something probably gets the in as much hot water as the t
46. Anyone who provides tempta ing valuable property lying much to blame for its the who steals it.
47. People generally make they will probably be
48. Law breakers are a and punished.
49. Loyalty to fellow important than
50. Most people
51. An employ workers at of mercha
52. Do you the ru suppo
53. It's
54. P
55

VINELAND ADAPTIVE BEHAVIOR SCALES

Refer to page S8.

ITEM SCORES
2 Yes, usually
1 Sometimes or partially
0 No, never
N No opportunity
DK Don't know

EXPRESSIVE
WRITTEN

	Item				COMMENTS
	34. Uses phrases or sentences containing "but" and "or."				
	35. Articulates clearly, without sound substitutions.				
	36. Tells popular story, fairy tale, lengthy joke, or television show plot.				
5	37. Recites all letters of the alphabet from memory.			2	
	38. Reads at least three common signs.			2	
	39. States month and day of birthday when asked.		2		
	40. Uses irregular plurals.		2		
6	41. Prints or writes own first and last name.			2	
	42. States telephone number when asked. N MAY BE SCORED.		2		
	43. States complete home address, including city and state, when asked.		2		
	44. Reads at least 10 words silently or aloud.			0	
	45. Prints or writes at least 10 words from memory.			0	
	46. Expresses ideas in more than one way, without assistance.		0		
	47. Reads simple stories aloud.			0	
7,8	48. Prints or writes simple sentences of three or four words.			0	
	49. Attends to school or public lecture more than 15 minutes.	1			
	50. Reads on own initiative.			0	
	51. Reads books of at least second-grade level.			0	
	52. Arranges items or words alphabetically by first letter.			0	
	53. Prints or writes short notes or messages.			0	
9	54. Gives complex directions to others.		1		
	55. Writes beginning letters. DO NOT SCORE 1.			0	
	56. Reads books of at least fourth-grade level.			0	
	57. Writes in cursive most of the time. DO NOT SCORE 1.			0	
10 to 18+	58. Uses a dictionary.			0	
	59. Uses the table of contents in reading materials.			0	
	60. Writes reports or compositions. DO NOT SCORE 1.			0	
	61. Addresses envelopes completely.			0	
	62. Uses the index in reading materials.				
	63. Reads adult newspaper stories. N MAY BE SCORED.				
	64. Has realistic long-range goals and describes in detail plans to achieve them.				
	65. Writes advanced letters.				
	66. Reads adult newspaper or magazine stories each week. N MAY BE SCORED.				
	67. Writes business letters. DO NOT SCORE 1.				

Count items before basal as 2, items after ceiling as 0.

1.	1	9	6	Sum of 2s, 1s, 0s page 3
2.	24	42	–	Sum of 2s, 1s, 0s page 2
3.				Number of Ns pages 2 and 3
4.				Number of DKs pages 2 and 3
	25	51	6	SUBDOMAIN RAW SCORE (Add rows 1 – 4 above)

COMMENTS ______________________

EXPRESSIVE

WRITTEN

VISUAL FUNCTIONING ASSESSMENT TOOL (VFAT)

Refer to page T611.

XII. C. VISUAL PERCEPTION: FORM CONSTANCY: SIZE____________________

Range: NV, V: P, E, S,

Preceding Skills: Receptive language of shapes or hand use, concept of same/different, knowledge of shapes in 3-D flat forms and as forms and outlines in 2-D.

Materials/Environment:

Three-dimensional teacher-made flat shapes:

small, medium and large sizes of ● ■

small and medium sizes of ▬ ⬬ ▲ ◆

Frostig Developmental Test of Visual Perception, Test III; Barraga Visual Efficiency Scale, Form Constancy, Size Items; Worksheets, pages 85-105 in this Testing Manual.

Techniques for Assessing:

Present all the above shapes in the following manner.

	Receptive Language/Hand Use	Expressive Language
3-D Flat Shapes	1. Present the different sizes of one shape at the same time, being careful that they are all in the same position (e.g., ■ ■ ■). "Point to or put a penny on all the squares, etc." 2. Present differing sizes of different shapes at the same time, again being careful that they are all in the same position (e.g., ■ ▲ ■ ▲ ● ● . "Point to or put a penny on all squares, etc."	1. Present shapes as directed under Receptive Language/Hand Use. 2. Teacher points to each shape. "What is this?"

Refer to page T759.

PERSONNEL TEST

FORM I

NAME .... Date ....
(Please Print)

READ THIS PAGE CAREFULLY. DO EXACTLY AS YOU ARE TOLD.
DO NOT TURN OVER THIS PAGE UNTIL YOU ARE
INSTRUCTED TO DO SO.

PROBLEMS MUST BE WORKED WITHOUT THE AID OF A CALCULATOR OR OTHER PROBLEM-SOLVING DEVICE.

This is a test of problem solving ability. It contains various types of questions. Below is a sample question correctly filled in:

REAP is the opposite of

1 obtain, 2 cheer, 3 continue, 4 exist, 5 sow .... [5]

The correct answer is "sow." (It is helpful to underline the correct word.) The correct word is numbered 5. Then write the figure 5 in the brackets at the end of the line.

Answer the next sample question yourself.

Paper sells for 23 cents per pad. What will 4 pads cost? .... [___]

The correct answer is 92¢. There is nothing to underline so just place "92¢" in the brackets.

Here is another example:

MINER MINOR — Do these words have

1 similar meaning, 2 contradictory, 3 mean neither same nor opposite? .... [___]

The correct answer is "mean neither same nor opposite" which is number 3 so all you have to do is place a figure "3" in the brackets at the end of the line.

When the answer to a question is a letter or a number, put the letter or number in the brackets.
All letters should be printed.

This test contains 50 questions. It is unlikely that you will finish all of them, but do your best. After the examiner tells you to begin, you will be given exactly 12 minutes to work as many as you can. Do not go so fast that you make mistakes since you must try to get as many right as possible. The questions become increasingly difficult, so do not skip about. Do not spend too much time on any one problem. The examiner will not answer any questions after the test begins.

Now, lay down your pencil and wait for the examiner to tell you to begin!

Do not turn the page until you are told to do so.

INTERPRETING GUIDE FOR THE WONDERLIC PERSONNEL TEST **Table 2**

SCORE	PERSONNEL TEST SCORES 0 TO 50	JOB POTENTIAL	EDUCATION POTENTIAL	TRAINING POTENTIAL
35 34 33 32 31 30	28 OVER	Upper level management; only upper 17% of population score within this range.	College graduate mean IQ 120; WPT 29. Central tendency for graduate students is WPT 30.	Able to gather and synthesize information easily; can infer information and conclusions from on-the-job situations.
29 28 27 26	26 TO 30	Managerial potential and upper level clerical positions; 24% of the population score within this range; gathers information; analyzes and makes decisions from a limited number of choices.	May enter college; mean score for college freshmen—IQ 115; WPT 24	Above average individuals; can be trained with typical college format; able to learn much on their own; e.g. independent study or reading assignments.
25 24 23 22	20 TO 26	General clerical and first line supervisors; able to train others for routine positions; gathers information; may require help with making decisions. 29% of the population score within this range.	Mean for High School grads. is IQ 110; WPT 21; Central tendency for College Freshmen WPT 24—have a better than average chance of completing High School curriculum. 50 50 chance of graduating from college.	Able to learn routines quickly; train with combination of written materials with actual on the job experience.
21 20 19 18 17 16	16 TO 22	Routine office worker can run routinized equipment; 27% of the population scores in this range. Given enough time can learn and perform jobs with lengthy routinized steps; perform simple operations with lists of names and numbers.	May enter High School; will probably select classes which are less academic track; Central tendency for High School Junior, WPT 16.	Successful in elementary settings and would benefit from programmed or mastery learning approaches; important to allow enough time and "hands on" (on the job) experience previous to work.
15 14 13 12	10 TO 17	Operate simple process equipment; 21% of the population score within this range. Given ample time can learn limited number of steps for routinized jobs; if deviations occur on the job will have difficulty establishing or using contingencies.	Slightly better than average chance of reaching the 9th grade or entering high school. Central tendency for High School Sophomore WPT 15, High School Freshmen WPT 13, 8th grade WPT 11.	Need to be "explicitly taught" most of what they must learn; successful approach is to use apprenticeship program; may not benefit from "book learning" training.
11 10 9 8 7	12 OR LESS	Use very simple tools and equipment; repair furniture; assist electrician; simple carpentry; domestic work. 13% of the population score within this range.	Armed forces IQ cut off score between 75–80. Central tendency for 7th grade WPT 9.	Unlikely to benefit from formalized training setting; successful using simple tools under consistent supervision.

WORLD GOVERNMENT SCALE

Refer to page S190.

WORLD GOVERNMENT SCALE

Panos D. Bardis, Ph.D.

The University of Toledo, Ohio 43606, USA

Below is a list of issues concerning world government. Please read ALL statements very CAREFULLY and respond to ALL of them on the bases of YOUR OWN TRUE beliefs, WITHOUT consulting any other persons. Do this by reading each statement and then writing, in the space provided at its left, ONLY ONE of the following numbers: 0, 1, 2, 3, 4. The meaning of each of these figures is:

0 = Strongly disagree.
1 = Disagree.
2 = Undecided.
3 = Agree.
4 = Strongly agree.

(For research purposes, you must consider ALL statements AS THEY ARE, without modifying any of them in any way.)

_____1. Our planet needs world government.
_____2. World government is possible.
_____3. World government will promote cooperation among the people of our planet.
_____4. World government will promote understanding among the people of our planet.
_____5. World government will promote general prosperity.
_____6. World government will promote universal peace.

(Score equals sum total of 6 numerical responses. Theoretical range: 0, complete rejection of world government, to 24, complete acceptance.)

(Source: "Student Attitudes Toward World Government, Universal Peace, and International Law," in Pacific Cultural Foundation, In Search of a New World Order: The Need for New Initiatives, Taipei, Taiwan: 1980, pp. 127-145.)

Cumulative Indexes

Publishers Index

S = TESTS: Supplement
T = TESTS: First Edition

Academic Therapy Publications, 20 Commercial Boulevard, Novato, California 94947; (415)883-3314—S65, S68, S141, S148, S163, S181[T49, T208, T219, T222, T230, T250, T333, T338, T363, T458, T469, T478, T484, T527, T532, T534, T536, T540, T547, T550, T551, T554, T556, T573, T575, T577, T579, T610, T693]

Administrative Research Associates, Inc., Irvine Town Center, Box 4211, Irvine, California 92644: no business phone—[T651, T653]

Allington Corporation, (The), P.O. Box 125, Remington, Virginia 22734; (703)825-5722—[T587]

American Association of Bible Colleges, P.O. Box 1523, Fayetteville, Arkansas 72701; (501)521-8164—[T256]

American Association of Teachers of German, Inc. (AATG), 523 Building, Suite 201, Cherry Hill, New Jersey 08034; (609)663-5264—S69

American Automobile Association (AAA), Traffic Safety Department, 8111 Gatehouse Road, Falls Church, Virginia 22047; (703)AAA-6621—[T695]

American College Testing Program, (The), 2201 North Dodge Street, P.O. Box 168, Iowa City, Iowa 52243; (319)337-1000—[T293, T294, T295, T296, T297, T298, T299, T300, T301, T302, T303, T304, T305, T306, T307, T308, T309, T310, T311, T312, T313, T659, T683]

American Dental Association, 211 East Chicago Avenue, Chicago, Illinois 60611; (312)440-2500—[T364]

American Foundation for the Blind, 15 West 16th Street, New York, New York 10011; (212)620-2000—S6, S154[T92, T147]

American Guidance Service, Publisher's Building, Circle Pines, Minnesota 55014; (800)328-2560, in Minnesota (612)786-4343—S8, S67, S126, S130, S176[T16, T244, T388, T448, T492, T528, T532, T535, T558, T572, T574, T586, T668, T856, T859]

American Optical (AO), Scientific Instruments Division, Warner-Lambert Technologies, Inc., P.O. Box 123, Buffalo, New York 14240; (716)891-3000—[T602]

American Orthopsychiatric Association, Inc., (The), 1775 Broadway, New York, New York 10019; (212)586-5690—[T37]

American Printing House for the Blind, 1839 Frankfort Avenue, P.O. Box 6085, Louisville, Kentucky 40206-0085; (502)895-2405—[T467, T608]

Andrews University Press, Berrien Springs, Michigan 49104; (616)471-3392—S27, S61

Ann Arbor Publishers, Inc., P.O. Box 7249, Naples, Florida 33940; (813)775-3528—S76, S141, S143

ASIEP Education Company, 3216 N.E. 27th, Portland, Oregon 97212; (503)281-4115—S52, S88, S118, S179

Associated Services for the Blind (ASB), 919 Walnut Street, Philadelphia, Pennsylvania 19107; (215)627-0600—S12, S31, S53, S202

Associates for Research in Behavior, Inc. (ARBOR), The Science Center, 34th & Market Streets, Philadelphia, Pennsylvania 19104; (215)387-5300—[T685]

Association of American Medical Colleges, 1 Dupont Circle NW, Suite 200, Washington, D.C. 20036; (202)828-0400—[T375]

Association of Information Systems Professionals (ASIP), 1015 N. York Road, Willow Grove, Pennsylvania 19090; (215)657-6300—S218

Aurora Publishing, 1709 Bragaw Street, Suite B, Anchorage, Alaska 99504; (907)279-5251—[T139]

Australian Council for Educational Research Limited (ACER), Radford House, Frederick Street, Hawthorn, Victoria 3122, Australia; (03)818-1271—S245[T4, T17, T18, T19, T25, T28, T45, T125, T150, T153, T162, T252, T257, T284, T332, T393, T403, T438, T439, T453, T472, T487, T493, T494, T516, T574, T593, T599, T628, T680, T681, T685, T760, T761, T783, T851]

Ball Foundation, Room 314, Building B, 800 Roosevelt Road, Glen Ellyn, Illinois 63017; (312)469-6270—S211

Barber Center Press, (The), 136 East Avenue, Erie, Pennsylvania 16507; no business phone—S151, S204

Bardis, (Panos D.), Ph.D., The University of Toledo, 2801 W. Bancroft Street, Toledo, Ohio 43606; (419)537-4242—S59, S190[T56, T57, T60, T63, T64, T65, T66, T67, T68, T73, T74, T78, T80, T124, T144, T279]

Behar, (Lenore), Division of Mental Health, Albemarle Building, 325 N. Salisbury Street, Raleigh, North Carolina 27611; (919)733-4660—[T87]

Behavior Arts Center, 77 Lyons Place, Westwood, New Jersey 07675; (201)664-3237—S45

Behavior Science Press, P.O. Box BV, University, Alabama 35486; (205)759-2089—[T109, T151, T159, T160, T709]

Behavior Science Systems, Inc., Box 1108, Minneapolis, Minnesota 55440; no business phone—S8[T11, T456]

Belwin-Mills Publishing Company, 25 Deshon Drive, Melville, New York 11747; (516)293-3400—[T226, T227]

Bilingual Media Productions, Inc., P.O. Box 9337, North Berkeley Station, Berkeley, California 94709; (415)548-3777—S70

Bingham Button Test, 46211 North 125th Street East, Lancaster, California 93534; (805)943-3241—[T4]

Biometrics Research, Research Assessment and Training Unit, New York State Psychiatric Institute, 722 West 168th Street, Room 341, New York, New York 10032; (212)960-5534—[T174, T177, T178, T186, T187, T188]

BJK Associates, 2104 South 135th Avenue, Omaha, Nebraska 68144; (402)330-3726—[T842]

Bobbs-Merrill Educational Publishing, 4300 West 62nd Street, P.O. Box 7080, Indianapolis, Indiana 46206; (317)298-5479—[T364]

Bond Publishing Company, 787 Willett Avenue, Riverside, Rhode Island 02915-9990; (401)437-0421—[T226]

Book-Lab, 500 74th Street, North Bergen, New Jersey 07047; (201)861-6763 or (201)868-1305—S122, S149[T390, T525, T526]

Brador Publications Inc., Education Division, 36 Main Street, Livonia, New York 14487; (716)346-3191—[T476, T503]

Branden Press, Inc., 21 Station Street, P.O. Box 843, Brookline Village, Massachusetts 02147; (617)734-2045—S71

Brandywine Associates, P.O. Box 1, Concordville, Pennsylvania 19331; (215)358-3957—[T43]

Brook Educational Publishing Limited, Box 1171, Guelph, Ontario N1H 6N3, Canada; (519)836-2920—S148[T540]

Brown, (William C.), Company Publishers, 2460 Kemper Boulevard, Dubuque, Iowa 52001; (319)588-1451—[T510, T517]

Bruce, (Martin M.), Ph.D., Publishers, 50 Larchwood Road, Larchmont, New York 10538; (914)834-1555—S228[T92, T128, T148, T228, T630, T696, T762, T795, T814, T832, T849, T868, T870]

Bureau of Business and Economic Research, College of Business Administration, University of Iowa, Iowa City, Iowa 52242; (319)353-2121—[T280]

Bureau of Educational Measurements, Emporia State University, 1200 Commercial, Emporia, Kansas 66801; (316)343-1200—S125[T199, T203, T205, T206, T207, T211, T214, T216, T217, T231, T232, T235, T242, T254, T257, T259, T260, T270, T276, T278, T280, T281, T283, T410, T411, T493, T494, T530, T657, T658]

Callier Center for Communication Disorders, The University of Texas at Dallas, 1966 Inwood Road, Dallas, Texas 75235; (214)783-3000—S3

Cambridge, The Adult Education Company, 888 Seventh Avenue, New York, New York 10106; West of the Mississippi or Louisiana, Alabama, Mississippi, and the Florida panhandle (800)221-4764, east of the Mississippi (except New York) (800)221-4600, in New York (212)957-2563—S89, S112, S202

Camelot Behavioral Systems, P.O. Box 3447, Lawrence, Kansas 66044; (913)843-9159—[T556]

Carlson, (Bernadine P.), c/o Western Michigan University, 720 Sprau Tower, Kalamazoo, Michigan 49008; (616)383-0788—[T407, T759]

Carroll Publications, 704 South University, Mount Pleasant, Michigan 48858; (517)772-3956—[T509]

Center for Advanced Study in Theoretical Psychology, University of Alberta, 6-102 Education North, Edmonton, Alberta, Canada; (403)432-5271—S191

Center for Child Development and Education, College of Education, University of Arkansas at Little Rock, 33rd and University, Little Rock, Arkansas 72204; (501)569-3422—S58

Center for Epidemiologic Studies, Department of Health and Human Services, 5600 Fishers Lane, Rockville, Maryland 20857; (301)443-4513—[T95]

Center for Improvement of Undergraduate Education, (The), 115 Rand Hall, Cornell University, Ithaca, New York 14850; (607)256-1000—[T646]

Center for Leadership Studies (available from Learning Resources Corp.), 8517 Production Avenue, P.O. Box 26240, San Diego, California 92126; (714)578-5900—S251[T62, T64, T826, T838, T839, T841, T843, T844]

Center for Psychological Service, (The), 1511 K Street NW, Suite 430, Washington, D.C. 20005; (202)347-4069—S112

CFKR Career Materials, Inc., P.O. Box 437, Meadow Vista, California 95722; (800)553-3313, in California (916)878-0118—S187, S198, S199, S200, S201, S221

Chambers, (Jay L.), College of William and Mary, Williamsburg, Virginia 23185; (703)253-4000—[T128]

Chapman, Brook & Kent, 1215 De La Vina, Suite F, Santa Barbara, California 93101; (805)962-0055—S118

CHECpoint Systems, Inc., 1520 N. Waterman Avenue, San Bernadino, California 92404; (714)888-3296—S160

CHILD Center, (The), Childhood Help in Learning and Development, P.O. Box 144, Kentfield, California 94914; (415)456-0440—S86

Child Development Centers of the Bluegrass, Inc., 465 Springhill Drive, Lexington, Kentucky 40503; (606)278-0549—S124

Childcraft Education Corporation, 20 Kilmer Road, Edison, New Jersey 08818; (800)631-5652, in New Jersey (201)572-6100—S119[T447]

Chronicle Guidance Publications, Inc., Moravia, New York 13118; (315)497-0330—[T664]

Clinical Psychology Publishing Company, Inc., 4 Conant Square, Brandon, Vermont 05733; (802)247-6871—S44[T46, T446, T469, T600]

Clinical Psychometric Research, 1228 Wine Spring Lane, Towson, Maryland 21204; (301)321-6165—S26, S32, S34, S36, S40, S47, S49, S50

Coddington, (R. Dean), School of Medicine in New Orleans, Louisiana State University Medical Center, 1542 Tulane Avenue, New Orleans, Louisiana 70112; (504)568-4006—[T115]

Coffin Associates, 21 Darling Street, Marblehead, Massachusetts 01945; (617)631-9491—[T276, T280]

College Board Publications, (The), Box 2815, Princeton, New Jersey 08541; (609)771-7600—[T13, T285, T286, T287, T288, T289, T290, T291, T292, T293, T317, T318, T319, T320, T321, T322, T323, T324, T325, T326, T327, T328, T329, T330, T339, T340, T341, T342, T343, T344, T345, T346, T347, T348, T349, T350, T351, T352, T353, T354, T355, T356, T357]

Collins Educational/A Division of Collins Publisher, Box 9, 29 Frogmore, St. Albans, Hertfordshire, AL2 2NF, England; no business phone—[T506]

The Committee on Diagnostic Reading Tests, Inc., Mountain Home, North Carolina 28758; (704)693-5223—[T518, T519, T520, T521, T522, T523]

Communication Research Associates, Inc., P.O. Box 11012, Salt Lake City, Utah 84147; (801)292-3880—S159[T466, T587, T595, T600]

Communication Skill Builders, Inc., 3130 N. Dodge Blvd., P.O. Box 42050, Tucson, Arizona 85733; (602)323-7500—S163, S165, S173

Consulting Psychologists Press, Inc., 577 College Avenue, P.O. Box 60070, Palo Alto, California 94306; (415)857-1444—S27, S28, S30, S31, S45, S46, S53, S57, S140, S144, S156, S231, S240[T58, T62, T81, T90, T91, T93, T94, T95, T98, T99, T105, T106, T113, T122, T140, T143, T148, T151, T153, T159, T169, T171, T173, T176, T178, T181, T182, T190, T191, T192, T449, T458, T464, T556, T562, T580, T585, T591, T592, T633, T644, T645, T648, T656, T678, T694, T811, T812, T832, T833]

Counseling and Self-Improvement Programs, 710 Watson Drive, Natchitoches, Louisiana 71457; (318)352-5313—[T69, T75, T79, T111, T817]

C.P.S. Inc., Box 83, Larchmont, New York 10538; no business phone—[T82, T83, T136]

CRAC Publications, Hobsons Press (Cambridge) Ltd., Bateman Street, Cambridge CB2 1LZ, England; (0223)354551—[T665, T677]

Crane Publishing Company, Division of MLP, 1301 Hamilton Avenue, P.O. Box 3713, Trenton, New Jersey 08629; (609)393-1111—[T583]

Creative Learning Press, Inc., P.O. Box 320, Mansfield Center, Connecticut 06250; (203)423-8120—S147, S185, S186, S188, S196

Creative Learning Systems, Inc., 936 C Street, San Diego, California 92101; (619)231-3599—[T553, T557, T568]

Creative Therapeutics, P.O. Box R, Cresskill, New Jersey 07626; (201)567-8989—S149

Croft, Inc., Suite 200, 7215 York Road, Baltimore, Maryland 21212; (800)638-5082, in Maryland (301)254-5082—S130[T361, T489]

CTB/McGraw-Hill, Publishers Test Service, Del Monte Research Park, 2500 Garden Road, Monterey, California 93940; (800)538-9547, in California (800)682-9222, or (408)649-8400—S5, S19, S162, S169, S179[T210, T217, T218, T223, T224, T234, T235, T237, T240, T255, T334, T336, T359, T360, T361, T367, T368, T392, T393, T394, T395, T402, T403, T444, T448, T467, T491, T501, T515, T555, T560, T561, T621, T677, T679]

Curriculum Associates, Inc., 5 Esquire Road, North Billerica, Massachusetts 01862-2589; (800)225-0248, in Massachusetts (617)667-8000—S74, S82, S83, S84, S116, S117

Datascan, 1134 Bobbie Lane, Garland, Texas 75042; (214)276-3978—[T74, T670]

Delaware County Intermediate Unit, State Building, Sixth and Olive Streets, Media, Pennsylvania 19063; (215)565-4880—[T489, T490, T491]

Developmental Reading Distributors, 1944 Sheridan Avenue, Laramie, Wyoming 82070; (307)745-9027—[T513]

Devereaux Foundation Press, (The), 19 South Waterloo Road, Box 400, Devon, Pennsylvania 19333; (215)964-3000—[T533, T558, T616, T617]

Diagnostic Specialists, Inc., 1170 North 660 West, Orem, Utah 84057; (801)224-8492—S34

DLM Teaching Resources, P.O. Box 4000, One DLM Park, Allen, Texas 75002; (800)527-4747, in Texas (800)442-4711—S75, S115, S125, S128, S161, S164

D.O.K. Publishers, Inc., 71 Radcliffe Road, Buffalo, New York 14214; (716)837-3391—S146, S196

Economy Company, (The), P.O. Box 25308, 1901 North Walnut Street, Oklahoma City, Oklahoma 73125; (405)528-8444—[T507]

Educational Activities, Inc., P.O. Box 392, Freeport, New York 11520; (800)645-3739, in Alaska, Hawaii, and New York (516)223-4666—S136[T470, T500, T569, T598, T695]

Educational and Industrial Testing Service (EdITS), P.O. Box 7234, San Diego, California 92107; (619)222-1666—[T65, T74, T89, T98, T100, T103, T104, T107, T117, T121, T125, T126, T129, T180, T401, T443, T614, T621, T643, T655, T658, T660, T661, T662]

Educational and Industrial Test Services Ltd. (EITS), 83, High Street, Hemel Hempstead, Herts, HP1 3AH, England; (0442)56773—[T678, T741, T750, T763, T764, T796, T798, T799, T801, T806, T808, T814, T852, T855, T858]

Educational Assessment Service, Inc., Route One, Box 139-A, Watertown, Wisconsin 53094; (414)261-1118—S146

Educational Development Corporation, P.O. Box 45663, Tulsa, Oklahoma 74145; (800)331-4418, in Oklahoma (800)722-9113—S87

Educational Guidance, Inc., P.O. Box 511, Main Post Office, Dearborn, Michigan 48121; (313)274-0682—[T657, T664]

Educational Records Bureau Inc., Bardwell Hall, 37 Cameron Street, Wellesley, Massachusetts 02181; (617)235-8920—[T359]

Educational Research Consultants, 4436 Engle Road, Sacramento, California 95821; (916)483-6417—S145

Educational Research Council of America, Rockefeller Building, 614 West Superior Avenue, Cleveland, Ohio 44113; (216)696-8222—[T624]

Educational Resources, 19 Peacedale Grove, Nunawading, Victoria 3131, Australia; no business phone—[T502]

Educational Studies and Development, 1357 Forest Park Road, Muskegon, Michigan 49441; (616)780-2053/755-1041—[T439]

Educational Testing Service (ETS), Rosedale Road, Princeton, New Jersey 08541; (609)921-9000—S112, S216[T232, T234, T236, T370, T629, T648, T649, T687, T693, T694, T757]

Educator Feedback Center, College of Education, Western Michigan University, Kalamazoo, Michigan 49008; (616)383-1690—S193, S194

Educators Publishing Service, Inc. (EPS), 75 Moulton Street, Cambridge, Massachusetts 02238-9101; (800)225-5750, in Massachusetts (800)792-5166—[T6, T335, T457, T463, T495, T505, T523, T525, T547, T549, T552, T566, T574, T596]

Edwards, (Carl N.), Four Oaks Institute, 61 Winthrop Street, West Newton, Massachusetts 02165; (617)332-1246—S50

Effective Study Materials, P.O. Box 603, San Marcos, Texas 78666; (512)442-7979—[T641, T642, T644]

Elbern Publications, P.O. Box 09497, Columbus, Ohio 43209; (614)235-2643—S203[T679]

El Paso Rehabilitation Center, 2630 Richmond, El Paso, Texas 79930; (915)566-2956—[T7, T15]

EMC Publishing, 300 York Avenue, St. Paul, Minnesota 55101; (612)771-1555—S72

Employers' Tests and Services Association (ETSA), 120 Detzel Place—Dept. G-180, Cincinnati, Ohio 45219; (513)281-5389—[T87, T646, T709, T710; T711, T712]

Endeavor Information Systems, Inc., 1317 Livingston Street, Evanston, Illinois 60201; no business phone—[T647]

ERIC Document Reproduction Service, P.O. Box 190, Arlington, Virginia 22210; (703)841-1212—S195, S207

Essay Press, P.O. Box 2323, La Jolla, California 92037; (619)565-6603—S132, S134

Evaluation Research Associates, P.O. Box 6503, Teall Station, Syracuse, New York 13217; (315)422-0064—S56, S183, S184, S185, S233

Examinations Committee, American Chemical Society (ACS), University of South Florida, Chemistry, Room 112, Tampa, Florida 33620; (813)974-2730—S79, S80[T258, T259, T260, T261, T262, T263, T265, T266, T267, T406]

Eyberg, (Sheila), Ph.D., Associate Professor of Medical Psychology, The Oregon Health Sciences University, School of Medicine, Department of Medical Psychology—OP336, 3181 S.W. Sam Jackson Park Road, Portland, Oregon 97201—S26, S38

Facilitation House, Box 611-E, Ottawa, Illinois 61350; (815)434-2353—[T161, T219, T241, T512, T546, T552, T567, T642]

Family Life Publications, Inc., Box 427, Saluda, North Carolina 28773; (704)749-4971—[T61, T67, T68, T69, T70, T71, T72, T73, T75, T76, T77, T78]

Fast, (Charles C.), Northeast Missouri State University, Kirksville, Missouri 63501; (816)785-4000—[T270]

Federation of Societies for Coatings Technology, 1315 Walnut Street, Philadelphia, Pennsylvania 19107; (215)545-1506—[T704]

Fetler, (Daniel), & Associates, P.O. Box 3473, Arlington Station, Poughkeepsie, New York 12603; (914)471-9340—[T141]

Foreworks, Box 9747, North Hollywood, California 91609; (213)982-0467—S159

Foundation for Knowledge in Development, (The), KID Technology, 11715 East 51st Avenue, Denver, Colorado 80239; (303)373-1916—S6

Frost, (Brian), University of Calgary, 2500 University Drive N.W., Calgary, Alberta, Canada T2N 1N4; (403)284-5651—[T85]

Gallaudet College Press, Distribution Office, 800 Florida Avenue NE, Washington, D.C. 20002; (202)651-5591 (voice), or (202)651-5355 (TDD)—S68

Garrard Publishing Company, 1607 North Market Street, Post Office Box A, Champaign, Illinois 61820; (217)352-7685—S132

Gibson, (Robert), Publisher, 17, Fitzroy Place, Glasgow, Scotland G3 7BR; (041)248-5674—[T481]

Girona, (Ricardo), 428 Columbus Avenue, Sandusky, Ohio 44870; no business phone—[T91]

Gleser, (Goldine C.), 7710 Medical Sciences Building, 231 Bethesda Avenue, Cincinnati, Ohio 45267; no business phone—[T175]

Gough, (Harrison G.)/Institute of Personality and Research, University of California, Berkeley, California 94720; (415)642-6000—[T617]

Goyer, (Robert S.), Centre for Communication Studies, Ohio University, Athens, Ohio 45701; (602)965-5095—[T369]

Grassi, (Joseph R.), Inc., Mailman Center for Child Development, P.O. Box 016820, University of Miami, Miami, Florida 33101; (305)547-6631—[T42]

Grune & Stratton, Inc., 111 Fifth Avenue, New York, New York 10003; (212)741-6800—S38[T55, T85, T88, T165, T223, T508, T537, T548, T593]

Guidance Center, Faculty of Education, University of Toronto, 252 Bloor Street West, Toronto, Ontario, Canada M5S 2Y3; (416)978-3206/3210—[T8, T250, T282, T517]

H & H Enterprises, now published by Pro-Ed, 5341 Industrial Oaks Boulevard, Austin, Texas 78735; (512)892-3142—[T561]

Halgren Tests, 873 Persimmon Avenue, Sunnyvale, California 94807; (408)738-1342—S54[T164]

Harding, (Christopher), Harding Tests, Box 5271, Rockhampton Mail Centre, Q. 4701, Australia; no business phone—S58[T221, T222, T479]

Harrap Ltd., 19-23 Ludgate Hill, London, England EC4M 7PD; (01)248-6444; USA: Pendragon House, Inc., 2898 Joseph Avenue, Campbell, California 95008; (408)371-2737—[T22, T250, T263, T264, T497, T514]

Harvard Personnel Testing, Box 319, Oradell, New Jersey 07649; (201)265-5393—[T766, T791, T800]

Harvard University Press, 79 Garden Street, Cambridge, Massachusetts 02138; (617)495-2600—[T143]

Haverly Systems, Inc., 78 Broadway, P.O. Box 919, Denville, New Jersey 07834; (201)627-1424—[T787]

Hayes Educational Tests, 7040 North Portsmouth Avenue, Portland, Oregon 97203; (503)285-3745—[T246, T247]

Heath, (S. Roy), Ph.D., 1193 South East Street, Amherst, Massachusetts 01002; (413)253-7756—[T49, T161]

Hill, (William Fawcett), California State Polytechnic University, Pomona, 3801 West Temple Avenue, Pomona, California 91768; (714)626-0128—[T150, T155, T156]

Hiskey-Nebraska Test, (The), 5640 Baldwin, Lincoln, Nebraska 68507; (402)466-6145—[T565]

Hodder & Stoughton Educational, A Division of Hodder & Stoughton Ltd., P.O. Box 702, Mill Road, Dunton Green, Sevenoaks, Kent TN13 2YD, England; (0732) 50111—S65, S121[T11, T99, T125, T152, T157, T221, T225, T238, T243, T245, T247, T251, T331, T370, T378, T451, T488, T496, T503, T504, T506, T508, T512, T533, T551, T614, T671]

Humanics Media, 5457 Pine Cone Road, La Crescenta, California 91214; (818)957-4332—S182, S195, S220, S228, S244, S245, S252, S254

Human Sciences Research Council, Private Bag X41, 0001 Pretoria, South Africa; (012)28-3944—[T24, T26, T31, T32, T110, T111, T113, T167, T198, T207, T225, T231, T233, T236, T241, T245, T273, T283, T284, T330, T331, T369, T371, T373, T374, T379, T388, T392, T393, T438, T465, T478, T479, T480, T482, T577, T597, T620, T635, T653, T668, T670, T674, T679, T682, T685, T696]

Illinois Thinking Project, Education Building, University of Illinois, Urbana, Illinois 61801; (217)333-1000—[T214, T362, T363]

Industrial Psychology Incorporated (IPI), 515 Madison Avenue, New York, New York 10022; (212)355-5330—S218[T719, T720, T721, T722, T723, T724, T725, T726, T727, T728, T729, T730, T731, T732, T733]

Institute for Personality and Ability Testing, Inc. (IPAT), P.O. Box 188, 1602 Coronado Drive, Champaign, Illinois 61820; (217)352-4739—S32, S241[T21, T81, T83, T84, T96, T102, T108, T111, T112, T122, T132, T138, T179, T704, T822, T836, T866]

Institute for Psycho-Imagination Therapy, c/o Joseph Shorr, Ph.D., 111 North La Cienega Boulevard #108, Beverly Hills, California 90211; (213)652-2922—[T107, T137]

Institute for Psychosomatic & Psychiatric Research & Training/Daniel Offer, Michael Reese Hospital and Medical Center, 29th Street and Ellis Avenue, Chicago, Illinois 60616; (312)791-3826—[T123]

Institute for the Development of Human Resources, 1201 Second Street, Corpus Christi, Texas 78404; (512)883-6442—[T824]

Institute of Psychological Research, Inc., 34, Fleury Street West, Montreal, Quebec, Canada H3L 1S9; (514)382-3000—[T28, T51, T140, T164, T180, T191, T358, T456, T484, T565, T572, T593, T595, T640, T740, T831, T850]

Instructional Materials & Equipment Distributors (IMED), 1520 Cotner Avenue, Los Angeles, California 90025; (213)879-0377—[T528, T529, T530, T548]

Instructional Materials Laboratory, The Ohio State University, 1885 Neil Avenue, Columbus, Ohio 43210; (614)422-2345—[T413, T414, T415, T416, T417, T418, T419, T420, T421, T422, T423, T424, T425, T426, T427, T428, T429, T430]

Integrated Professional Services, Inc. (IPS), 5211 Mahoning Ave., Suite 135, Youngstown, Ohio 44515; (216)799-3282—S42

Interstate Printers and Publishers, Inc., (The), (IPP), P.O. Box 594, Jackson at Van Buren, Danville, Illinois 61832; (217)446-0500—[T564, T580, T581, T591, T601, T654]

Intran Corporation, 4555 West 77th Street, Minneapolis, Minnesota 55435; (612)835-5422—S222, S223[T335]

IOX Assessment Associates, 11411 West Jefferson Boulevard, Culver City, California 90230; (213)391-6295—[T204, T212, T238, T253, T488, T511]

JAIM Research, Inc., 1808 Collingwood Road, Alexandria, Virginia 22308; (703)765-5903—[T808]

Jamestown Publishers, P.O. Box 6743, 544 Douglas Avenue, Providence, Rhode Island 02940; (401)351-1915—[T496, T497, T500, T516, T517]

Jansky, (Jeannette J.), 120 East 89th Street, New York, New York 10028; (212)876-8894—[T498]

Jastak Associates, Inc., 1526 Gilpin, Wilmington, Delaware 19806; (302)652-4990—[T170, T408, T511, T686]

Joint Council on Economic Education, 1212 Avenue of the Americas, New York, New York 10036; (212)582-5150—[T275, T279, T280, T282]

Kahn, (Marvin W.), Department of Psychology, The University of Arizona, Tucson, Arizona 85721; (602)626-2921—[T174]

Karger, (S.), AG, Basel, P.O. Box, Postfach, CH-4009 Basel, Switzerland; no business phone—[T151]

Katz, (Martin M.), 6305 Walhonding Road, Bethesda, Maryland 20816; (301)229-1511—[T113]

Keeler Instruments Inc., 456 Parkway, Lawrence Park Industrial District, Broomall, Pennsylvania; (800)523-5620, in Pennsylvania (215)353-4350—[T603]

Kent Developmental Metrics, 126 W. College Avenue, P.O. Box 3178, Kent, Ohio 44240-3178; (216)678-3589—S5

Kew, (Clifton E.), 245 East 19th Street, New York, New York 10003; (212)473-3082—[T106]

Keystone View, Division of Mast Development Company, 2212 East 12th Street, Davenport, Iowa 52803; (319)326-0141—[T607, T612]

Kiesler, (Donald J.), Ph.D., Virginia Commonwealth University, Department of Psychology College of Humanities and Sciences, 810 West Franklin Street, Richmond, Virginia 23284-0001; (804)257-1179—S40

Kirkpatrick, (Donald L.), Ph.D., 1080 Lower Ridgeway, Elm Grove, Wisconsin 53122; (414)224-1891—S212, S242, S243, S247, S248, S254

Knobloch, (Hilda), 230 E. Oglethorpe Avenue, Savannah, Georgia 31401; no business phone—[T13]

Krantz, (David S.), Department of Medical Psychology, Uniformed Services University of the Health Sciences, 4301 Jones Bridge Road, Bethesda, Maryland 20014; (301)295-3030—S59

Kreiger, (Robert E.), Publishing Company, Inc., P.O. Box 9542, Melbourne, Florida 32901; (305)724-9542—[T147]

Kundu, (Ramanath), Department of Psychology, University of Calcutta, 92, Acharya Prafulla Chandra Road, Calcutta 700 009 India; (35)9666/7089—[T114]

L & T Educational Materials, P.O. Box 403, Yorktown Heights, New York 10598; no business phone—S66

Ladoca Publishing Foundation, Laradon Hall Training and Residential Center, East 51st Avenue & Lincoln Street, Denver, Colorado 80216; (303)629-6379—[T7, T61, T459, T570, T584, T603]

Lafayette Instrument Company, P.O. Box 5729, Lafayette, Indiana 47903; (317)423-1505—S18, S213, S255, S256, S257, S258[T25, T41, T42, T45, T54, T536, T537, T538, T539, T603, T607, T719, T856, T858, T861]

LaForge, (Rolfe), 83 Homestead Blvd., Mill Valley, California 94941; (415)388-8121—[T110]

Larlin Corporation, P.O. Box 1523, 119 Cobb Parkway, South Marietta, Georgia 30062; (404)424-6210—S142[T531]

Lawrence, (Trudys), 5916 Del Loma Avenue, San Gabriel, California 91775; (213)286-2027—[T635]

Leach, (Glenn C.), Wagner College, 631 Howard Avenue, Staten Island, New York 10301; (212)390-3100—[T271, T272, T273]

Learnco, Inc., 128 High Street, Greenland, New Hampshire 03840; (603)778-0813—S66, S142

Learning Publications, Inc., P.O. Box 1326, Dept. C-1, Holmes Beach, Florida 33509; (616)372-1045—[T544]

Leonard, (Hal), Publishing Corporation, 960 E. Mark Street, Winona, Minnesota 55987; (507)454-2920—[T227, T229]

Lewis, (H.K.), & Co. Ltd., 136 Gower Street, London, England WC1E 6BS; (01)387-4282—[T19, T21, T28, T33]

Life Insurance Marketing and Research Association, Inc. (LIMRA), P.O. Box 208, Hartford, Connecticut 06141; (203)677-0033—S259[T868]

Life Office Management Association, Inc. (LOMA), 100 Colony Square, Atlanta, Georgia 30361; (404)892-7272—[T734, T735, T736, T737, T738]

LinguiSystems, Inc., Suite 806, 1630 Fifth Avenue, Moline, Illinois 61265; (800)ALL-TIME, in Illinois (309)762-5112—S165, S168, S169, S174, S175

London House Press, 1550 N. Northwest Highway, Park Ridge, Illinois 60068; (800)323-5923, in Illinois (312)298-7311—S206, S207, S215, S217, S224, S228, S229, S231, S240, S241, S249, S259[T681, T751, T758, T760, T771, T792, T796, T801, T804, T813, T816, T818, T822, T824, T825, T835, T836, T838, T844, T849, T855, T856, T865, T868]

M.A.A. Committee on High School Contests, Department of Mathematics and Statistics, University of Nebraska, Lincoln, Nebraska 68588-0322; (402)472-7211—S78[T252]

Macmillan Education, Houndmills, Basingstoke, Hampshire RG21 2XS, England; (0256)29242—S73, S77, S85, S120, S123, S137, S158, S222[T500]

Mafex Associates, Inc., 90 Cherry Street, Box 519, Johnstown, Pennsylvania 15907; (814)458-0151, in Pennsylvania (800)535-3597—S190[T240, T440, T451, T460, T672]

Manasayan, 32 Netaji Subhash Marg, Delhi 110006, India; no business phone—[T213, T365, T393, T660]

Marathon Consulting and Press, P.O. Box 09189, 575 Enfield Road, Columbus, Ohio 43209-0189; (614)237-5267—[T221, T225, T232, T246]

Marriage Council of Philadelphia, Inc., 4025 Chestnut Street, Suite 210, Philadelphia, Pennsylvania 19104; (215)222-7574—[T64, T67, T71, T77]

Martinus Nijhoff, Postbuss 566, 2501 CN, Lange Voorhout, 9-11, The Hague, Netherlands; (070)469 460—[T153]

McCann Associates, 2755 Philmont Avenue, Huntington Valley, Pennsylvania 19006; (215)947-5775—[T863, T864, T865, T866, T867]

McCartney, (William A.), P.O. Box 507, Kaneohe, Hawaii 96744; (808)239-8071—[T216]

McCormick, (Dr. R.R.) & Associates, P.O. Box 2010, Boca Raton, Florida 33432; no business phone—S193

Medical Research Council, Department of Psychological Medicine, Royal Free Hospital, Pond Street, London, England NW3 2QG; (01)794-0500—[T48]

Meeting Street School, The Easter Seal Society of Rhode Island, Inc., 667 Waterman Avenue, East Providence, Rhode Island 02914; (401)438-9500—[T12, T454]

Mehrabian, (Albert), Ph.D., 9305 Beverlycrest Drive, Beverly Hills, California 90210; (213)829-2524—S23, S24, S43, S44, S161

Merrell-National Laboratories, Division of Richardson-Merrell, Inc., 2110 East Galbraith Road, Cincinnati, Ohio 45215; (513)948-9111—[T136]

Merrill, (Charles E.), Publishing Company, 1300 Alum Creek Drive, Box 508, Columbus, Ohio 43216; (614)258-8441—[T249, T338, T363, T373, T374, T378, T379, T442, T461, T468, T483, T488, T538, T557, T582, T583, T588, T589, T592, T599, T613, T619]

Miami University Alumni Association, Murstein Alumni Center, Oxford, Ohio 45056; (513)529-5211—[T510]

Midwest Music Tests, c/o Newell H. Long, 1304 East University Street, Bloomington, Indiana 47401; (812)332-0211—[T227]

Ministry Inventories, P.O. Box 8265, Dallas, Texas 75205; (214)276-3978—[T682]

Ministry of Education, The Ontario Institute for Studies in Education, 252 Bloor Street West, Toronto, Ontario, M5S 1V6, Canada; (416)965-6789—[T232, T386]

Minnesota Moral Research Projects (MMRP), 206 Burton Hall, 178 Pillsbury Drive SE, University of Minnesota, Minneapolis, Minnesota 55455; (612)373-5539, or (612)373-5213—S57

Mississippi State University Rehabilitation Research Training Center, P.O. Drawer 5365, Mississppi State, Mississippi 39762; (601)325-2001—[T853, T854, T857, T861]

MKM, 809 Kansas City Street, Rapid City, South Dakota 57701; (605)342-7223—[T535, T606, T607]

Modern Curriculum Press, Inc., 13900 Prospect Road, Cleveland, Ohio 44136; (216)238-2222—S16, S120, S132, S134, S139

Monitor, P.O. Box 2337, Hollywood, California 90028; no business phone—[T63, T101, T144, T146, T159, T202, T255, T264, T265, T409, T544, T624, T674, T675, T676]

Moore, (Joseph E.), and Associates, Perry Drive, R.F.D. 12, Box 309, Gainesville, Georgia 30501; no business phone—[T536]

Morgan (Robert), Ph.D., Dean for Academic and Professional Affairs, California School of Professional Psychology, 1350 M Street, Fresno, California 93721; (209)486-8420—S14

Morrison, (James H.), 9804 Hadley, Overland Park, Kansas 66212; (913)642-2258—[T179, T192]

Morstain, (Barry R.), Department of Urban Affairs, University of Delaware, Newark, Delaware 19711; (302)738-2394—[T629]

Munsell Color, Macbeth, A Division of Kollmorgen Corporation, 2411 N. Calvert Street, Baltimore, Maryland 21218; (301)243-2171—[T189, T712]

National Business Education Association, 1914 Association Drive, Reston, Virginia 22091; (703)860-8300—[T199, T200, T201, T202, T204]

National Dairy Council, 6300 North River Road, Rosemont, Illinois 60018-4233; (312)696-1020—S205, S208

National Educational Laboratory Publishers, Inc., 813 Airport Boulevard, Austin, Texas 78702; (512)385-7084—[T475, T506, T578, T584, T634]

National Institute for Personnel Research, P.O. Box 32410, Braamfontein, 2017 South Africa; (011)39-4451—[T129, T139, T703, T709, T716, T740, T742, T753, T757, T762, T796, T797, T798, T801, T802, T825, T827]

National League for Nursing, Inc. (NLN), Ten Columbus Circle, New York, New York 10019; (212)582-1022—S89, S90, S91, S92, S93, S94, S95, S96, S97, S98, S99, S100, S101, S102, S103, S104, S105, S106, S107, S108, S109, S110, S111

National Occupational Competency Testing Institute, 45 Colvin Avenue, Albany, New York 12206; (518)482-8864—[T430, T431, T432, S433, T434, T435, T436, T437, T872, T873, T874, T875, T876, T877, T878, T879, T880, T881, T882, T883, T884, T885, T886, T887, T888, T889, T890]

National Study of School Evaluation, 5201 Leesburg Pike, Falls Church, Virginia 22041; (703)820-2727—S189, S197, S206

NCS Professional Assessment Services, P.O. Box 1416, Minneapolis, Minnesota 55440; (800)328-6759, in Minnesota (612)933-2800—S21, S33, S37, S39, S41, S42, S201, S227[T118, T119, T120, T409, T656, T669, T810, T831]

Nelson Canada, 1120 Birchmount Road, Scarborough, Ontario M1K 5G4, Canada; (416)752-9100—S66, S140, S166[T336, T337, T524, T680, T806]

Nevins, (C.H.), Printing Company, 311 Bryn Mawr Island, Bayshore Gardens, Bradenton, Florida 33507; (813)755-5330—S135[T499, T500]

Newbury House Publishers, Inc., 54 Warehouse Lane, Rowley, Massachusetts 01969; (617)948-2840—[T217, T220, T233, T587]

New Zealand Council for Educational Research (NZCER), P.O. Box 3237, Wellington, New Zealand; no business phone—[T208, T389, T405, T643]

NFER-Nelson Publishing Company Ltd., Darville House, 2 Oxford Road East, Windsor, Berkshire SL4 1DF, England; (07535)58961—S10, S11, S14, S15, S17, S30, S35, S39, S50, S75, S154, S155, S165, S177, S178[T13, T15, T39, T59, T60, T68, T84, T92, T101, T105, T114, T123, T124, T127, T146, T170, T205, T220, T229, T237, T239, T243, T245, T247, T248, T252, T255, T272, T335, T366, T391, T402, T403, T404, T405, T406, T411, T412, T430, T441, T445, T447, T452, T454, T470, T472, T473, T474, T476, T483, T487, T498, T502, T503, T504, T507, T509, T510, T511, T527, T555, T559, T576, T596, T609, T614, T664, T770, T810]

Nisonger Center, (The), The Ohio State University, 434 McCampbell Hall, 1580 Cannon Drive, Columbus, Ohio 43210-1205; (614)422-0825—S155[T439, T563]

Northwestern University Press, Dept. SLD-82, 1735 Benson Avenue, Evanston, Illinois 60201; (312)492-5313—[T590]

Nursing Research Associates, 3752 Cummings Street, Eau Claire, Wisconsin 54701; (715)836-4731—[T636, T637, T649]

Oliver and Boyd, Robert Stevenson House, 1-3 Baxter's Place, Leith Walk, Edinburgh EH1 3AF, Scotland. U.S. Representative: Longman Inc., 19 West 44th Street, New York, New York 10036; (212)764-3950—[T476, T491, T504]

Orange Industries, 229 West Tyron Street, Hillsborough, North Carolina 27278; (919)732-8124—S126, S153

Organizational Measurement Systems Press, P.O. Box 81, Atlanta, Georgia 30301; (404)355-9472—S230, S251

Organizational Tests (Canada) Ltd., Box 324, Fredericton, New Brunswick, Canada E3B 4Y9; (506)455-8366—[T815, T828, T830, T834, T835, T841, T842, T843, T846, T847, T848, T849, T850, T870]

Oxford University Press, 200 Madison Avenue, New York, New York 10016; (212)679-7300—[T53, T532, T540]

PA Consulting Services, Inc., 708 Alexander Road, Princeton, New Jersey 08540; (609)452-1734—S233, S234, S235, S236, S237

Peace Research Laboratory, 6251 San Bonita, St. Louis, Missouri 63105; (314)721-8219—[T279, T625, T652]

Peacock, (F.E.), Publishers, Inc., Test Division, 115 N. Prospect Road, Itasca, Illinois 60143; (312)773-1590—S170

Perceptual Learning Systems, P.O. Box 864, Dearborn, Michigan 48121; (313)277-6480—[T569, T571, T576]

The Perfection Form Company, 8350 Hickman Road, Suite 15, Des Moines, Iowa 50322; (800)831-4190, in Iowa (800)432-5831—[T209, T211, T213, T215, T216, T274, T275, T277, T282, T283, T531]

Person-O-Metrics, Inc., Evaluation & Development Services, 20504 Williamsburg Road, Dearborn Heights, Michigan 48127; no business phone—[T626, T628, T639, T640]

Personnel Research Institute, Psychological Research Services, Case Western Reserve University, 11220 Bellflower Road, Cleveland, Ohio 44106; (216)368-3546—[T772, T773, T774, T802]

Phi Delta Kappa, Eighth and Union, P.O. Box 789, Bloomington, Indiana 47402; (812)339-1156—[T689, T690, T691, T692]

Phoenix Institute of California, (The), 248 Blossom Hill Road, Los Gatos, California 95030; (408)354-6122—[T79]

Phonovisual Products, Inc., 12216 Parklawn Drive, P.O. Box 2007, Rockville, Maryland 20852; (301)881-4888—[T207]

Pikunas, (Justin), 335 Briggs Building, University of Detroit, Detroit, Michigan 48221; (313)927-1000—[T89, T91]

Pitman Learning, Inc., 19 Davis Drive, Belmont, California 94002; (415)592-7810—S123, S156[T39, T162, T390, T446, T537]

Price Systems, Inc., P.O. Box 3067, Lawrence, Kansas 66044; (913)843-7892—S186, S239

Priority Innovations, Inc., P.O. Box 792, Skokie, Illinois 60076; (312)729-1434—[T457, T460, T465]

Pro-Ed, 5341 Industrial Oaks Boulevard, Austin, Texas 78735; (512)892-3142—S73, S77, S78, S81, S86, S119, S127, S157, S169, S173, S174, S177, S182[T34, T209, T225, T333, T334, T507, T524, T527, T568, T597, T598, T599, T613, T626, T627, T654, T676, T677]

Professional Examinations Division/The Psychological Corporation, 7500 Old Oak Boulevard, Cleveland, Ohio 44130; (216)234-5300—[T284, T313, T314, T315, T316, T317, T739]

Programs for Education, Inc., Dept. W-16, 82 Park Avenue, Flemington, New Jersey 08822; (212)689-3911—[T449, T450, T464]

Psychodiagnostic Test Company, Box 859, East Lansing, Michigan 48823; no business phone—[T47]

Psychodynamic Instruments, c/o Gerald Blum, Dept. of Psychology, University of California, Santa Barbara, California 93106; no business phone—[T149]

Psychological Assessment and Services, Inc., P.O. Box 1031, Iowa City, Iowa 52240; no business phone—[T86]

Psychological Assessment Resources, Inc., P.O. Box 98, Odessa, Florida 33556; (813)977-3395—S19, S21, S23, S35, S37, S38, S44, S46, S48, S49, S151[T38, T46, T47, T55, T115, T494]

Psychological Corporation, (The), (PsyCor), A Subsidiary of Harcourt Brace Jovanovich, Inc., 7500 Old Oak Boulevard, Cleveland, Ohio 44130; (216)234-5300—S9, S12, S15, S54, S81, S135[T3, T5, T10, T19, T20, T21, T28, T29, T33, T35, T36, T37, T38, T41, T54, T56, T84, T101, T106, T121, T124, T132, T156, T180, T228, T230, T234, T254, T365, T375, T376, T377, T387, T388, T396, T397, T398, T399, T411, T441, T447, T455, T485, T492, T499, T513, T546, T585, T603, T604, T631, T644, T665, T678, T682, T688, T699, T719, T747, T749, T759, T766, T770, T782, T785, T795, T810, T813, T837, T851, T852, T853, T860, T862]

Psychological Development Publications, P.O. Box 3198, Aspen, Colorado 81612; (303)925-4432—[T446]

Psychological Documents, American Psychological Association, 1200 17th Street NW, Washington, D.C. 20036; (202)955-7600—S22

Psychological Publications, Inc., 5300 Hollywood Boulevard, Los Angeles, California 90027; (213)4163—[T59, T142]

Psychological Service Center of Philadelphia, Suite 904, 1422 Chestnut Street, Philadelphia, Pennsylvania 19102; (215)568-2555—T666

Psychological Services, Inc., 3450 Wilshire Boulevard, Suite 1200, Los Angeles, California 90010; (213)738-1132—[T705, T706, T707, T708, T752, T775, T776, T777, T778, T779, T780, T781, T804, T840]

Psychological Systems Corporation, Oak Brook Executive Plaza, 1301 West 22ndStreet—Suite 714, Oak Brook, Illinois 60521; (312)325-8000—S224, S226[T832]

Psychological Test Specialists, Box 9229, Missoula, Montana 59805; no business phone—[T23, T26, T29, T30, T44, T45, T154, T157, T683, T816]

Psychologistics, Inc., P.O. Box 3896, Indialantic, Florida 32903; (305)727-7900—S4, S47

Psychologists and Educators, Inc., 211 West State Street, Jacksonville, Illinois 62650; (217)243-2135—[T53, T73, T89, T93, T109, T116, T134, T137, T166, T459, T501, T541, T615, T622, T624, T636, T638, T641, T650, T669, T672, T871]

Psychometric Affiliates, 1620 East Main Street, Murfreesboro, Tennessee 37130; no business phone—[T14, T29, T30, T56, T58, T109, T127, T131, T135, T144, T271, T272, T380, T381, T382, T383, T384, T385, T412, T542, T619, T743, T762, T765, T771, T792, T806, T807, T814, T815, T816, T833, T852, T855, T869]

PSYCH Systems, 600 Reisterstown Road, Baltimore, Maryland 21208; (301)486-2206—S32, S33, S37, S41, S51

Pumroy, (Donald K.), College of Education, University of Maryland, College Park, Maryland 20742; (301)454-2027—[T62]

Purdue University Bookstore, P.O. Box 3028, Station 11, 360 State Street, West Lafayette, Indiana 47906; (317)743-9618—[T627, T647, T650, T651, T748, T749, T763, T782, T793, T802, T825, T826, T845, T846, T860]

Quay, (Herbert C.), Ph.D., Box 248074, University of Miami, Coral Gables, Florida 33124; (305)284-5208—S180

Reid Psychological Systems, 233 North Michigan Avenue, Chicago, Illinois 60601; (312)938-9200—[T827]

Reitan Neuropsychology Laboratory, 1338 East Edison Street, Tucson, Arizona 85719; (602)795-3717—S17, S20[T49]

Research and Development Center for Teacher Education, The University of Texas at Austin, Education Annex 3.203, Austin, Texas 78712-1288; (512)471-1343—[T97, T645, T646, T652, T687]

Research Concepts, A Division of Test Maker, Inc., 1368 East Airport Road, Muskegon, Michigan 49444; (616)739-7401—[T155, T448, T463, T688]

Research Press, Box 317760, Champaign, Illinois 61820; (217)352-3273—[T59, T66, T75]

Research Psychologists Press, Inc., 1110 Military Street, P.O. Box 984, Port Huron, Michigan 48061-0984; (800)265-1285, in Michigan (313)982-4556—S11[T95, T112, T130, T138, T163, T543, T670]

Revrac Publications, Inc., 207 West 116th Street, Kansas City, Missouri 64114; no business phone—[T515]

Rimland, (Bernard), Ph.D., Director, Institute for Child Behavior Research, 4758 Edgeware Road, San Diego, California 92116; (619)281-7165—S29

Riverside Publishing Company, (The), 8420 Bryn Mawr Avenue, Chicago, Illinois 60631; (800)323-9540, in Alaska, Hawaii, or Illinois call collect (312)693-0040—S67, S69, S71, S86, S88, S113, S114, S115, S129, S137, S138, S164, S188, S204[T33, T338, T372, T401, T406, T514, T524, T630]

Rocky Mountain Behavioral Science Institute, Inc. (RMBSI), P.O. Box 1066, Fort Collins, Colorado 80522; no business phone—[T117, T120, T190, T640, T641]

Rosenzweig, (Saul), 8029 Washington Avenue, St. Louis, Missouri 63114; no business phone—[T165]

Rucker-Gable Associates, P.O. Box 927, Storrs, Connecticut 06268; (203)423-7880—[T651]

Saleh, (S.D.), University of Waterloo, Faculty of Engineering, Department of Management Sciences, Waterloo, Ontario, Canada N2L 3G1; (519)885-1211—[T818]

Sauls, (Charles), Department of Curriculum and Instruction, Louisiana State University, Baton Rouge, Louisiana 70803; (504)388-3202—[T239, T240, T248, T251]

Saville & Holdsworth Ltd. (SHL), Windsor House, Esher Green, Esher, Surrey KT10 9SA, England; (0372)66476/67766/68634—S232[T699, T700, T701, T702, T705, T715, T743, T744, T745, T746, T747, T748, T753, T754, T755, T756, T757, T805, T807]

Schmidt, (Paul F.), 1209 West Main Street, Shelbyville, Kentucky 40065; (502)456-1990—[T96]
Scholastic Testing Service, Inc. (STS), 480 Meyer Road, P.O. Box 1056, Bensenville, Illinois 60106; (312)766-7150—S25, S116, S142, S177, S205, S219[T204, T332, T365, T367, T373, T400, T443, T457, T462, T464, T468, T531, T544, T545, T554, T556, T615, T618, T623, T656, T667, T669]
Schubert, (Herman J.P.), M.E., Ph.D., Schubert-Wagner Aptitude and Psychological Tests, 500 Klein Road, Buffalo, New York 14221; no business phone—S212
Science Research Associates, Inc. (SRA), 155 North Wacker Drive, Chicago, Illinois 60606; (800)621-0664, in Illinois (312)984-2000—[T142, T372, T386, T395, T461, T672, T673, T713, T714, T738, T750, T752, T771, T783, T784, T786, T787, T795, T803, T804, T823, T830, T831, T841, T860, T862, T869]
Scott, Foresman and Company, Test Division, 1900 East Lake Avenue, Glenview, Illinois 60025; (312)729-3000—[T6, T358, T377, T477, T625]
Search Institute, 122 West Franklin, Suite 215, Minneapolis, Minnesota 55404-2466; (612)870-3664—[T256]
Sensonics, Inc., 408 S. 47th Street, Philadelphia, Pennsylvania 19143; (215)471-4117—S214
Sheridan Psychological Services. Inc., P.O. Box 6101, Orange, California 92667; (714)639-2595—[T25, T27, T107, T171, T172, T173, T175, T176, T177, T179, T181, T182, T183, T184, T185, T189, T190, T191, T192, T444, T619, T631, T663, T666, T716, T717, T718, T803, T815, T837, T863]
Skillcorp Software, Inc., 1711 McGraw Avenue, Irvine, California 92714; (714)549-3246—[T249, T463, T505]
Slosson Educational Publications, Inc., P.O. Box 280, East Aurora, New York 14052; (800)828-4800, in New York (716)652-0930—S12, S22, S128, S146, S160, S166, S167, S171, S182[T31, T51]
SOARES Associates, 111 Teeter Rock Road, Trumbull, Connecticut 06611; (203)375-5353—[T622, T632]
SOI Institute, 343 Richmond Street, El Segundo, California 90245; (213)322-5532—S16, S79, S131, S138, S141, S168, S176, S198, S212, S215, S218, S219, S220, S230
South, (John C.), Duquesne University, Pittsburgh, Pennsylvania 15282; (412)434-6000—[T792]
Southern Illinois University Press, P.O. Box 3697, Carbondale, Illinois 62901; (618)453-2281—[T649]
Special Child Publications(SCP), P.O. Box 33548, Seattle, Washington 98133; (206)771-5711—S131, S143, S184
Speech and Hearing Clinic, 110 Moore Building, University Park, Pennsylvania 16802; (814)865-5414—[T577]
Springer Publishing Company, 200 Park Avenue South, New York, New York 10003; (212)475-2494—[T89, T129, T140]
Stanford University Press, Stanford, California 94305; (415)497-9434—[T811]
Stanton Corporation, (The), 417 South Dearborn Street, Chicago, Illinois 60605; (800)621-4152, in Illinois (312)922-0970—[T829]
Stanwix House, Inc., 3020 Chartiers Avenue, Pittsburgh, Pennsylvania 15204; (412)771-4233—[T579, T583, T584, T590, T594]
Statistical Publishing Society, Indian Statistical Institute, 203 Barrackpore Trunk Road, Calcutta, India 700 035; no business phone—[T482]
Steck-Vaughn Company, P.O. Box 2028, Austin, Texas 78768; (800)531-5015, in Texas (800)252-9317—[T369, T399]
Stein, (Morris), Graduate School of Arts and Science, Research Center for Human Relations, NewYork University, 6 Washington Place, 7th Floor, New York, New York 10003; (212)598-1212—[T793, T794, T823, T846]
Stevens, Thurow and Associates, 100 West Monroe Street, Chicago, Illinois 60603; (312)332-6277—[T764, T765, T800, T859]
Stoelting Company, 1350 S. Kostner Avenue, Chicago, Illinois 60623; (312)522-4500—S10, S33, S42, S53, S124, S126, S144, S154, S175, S176, S181, S191, S197, S199, S200, S219[T3, T8, T9, T10, T20, T24, T27, T40, T43, T50, T79, T94, T102, T110, T115, T148, T149, T166, T228, T451, T452, T453, T458, T480, T481, T534, T541, T542, T543, T549, T559, T567, T588, T604, T611, T817, T857, T858]
Stratton-Christian Press, Inc., Box 1055, University Place Station, Des Moines, Iowa 50311; no business phone—[T214, T215]
Student Development Associates, 110 Crestwood Drive, Athens, Georgia 30605; (404)549-4122—S189, S192
SWETS Test Services, Heereweg 347b, 2161 CA Lisse, The Netherlands; 02521-19113—[T32]
Tabin, (Johanna Krout), 162 Park Avenue, Glencoe, Illinois 60022; (312)835-0162—[T126, T166]
TAV Selection System, 12807 Arminta Street, North Hollywood, California 91605; no business phone—[T830]

Teachers College Press, Teachers College, Columbia University, 1234 Amsterdam Avenue, New York, New York 10027; (212)678-3929—S121[T413, T442, T495, T648]

Teaching and Testing Resources, P.O. Box 984, Woden, A.C.T. 2606, Australia; (062)88 5777—S76, S77, S133, S139

Teaching Resources Corporation, now DLM Teaching Resources, P.O. Box 4000, One DLM Park, Allen, Texas 75002; (800)527-4747, in Texas (800)442-4711—[T209, T244, T390, T408, T409, T445, T471, T573, T575, T576, T578, T581, T582, T585, T601, T602, T620]

T.E.D. Associates, 42 Lowell Road, Brookline, Massachusetts 02146; (617)734-5868—[T622]

Telometrics International, 1755 Woodstead Court, The Woodlands, Texas 77380; (713)367-0060—S225, S226, S229, S239, S242, S244, S246, S247, S248, S249, S250, S252, S253, S254, S258, S259, S260

Test Agency, (The), Cournswood House, North Dean, High Wycombe, Bucks, HP14 4NW, England; (024)3384—S51, S76[T22, T23, T115, T154, T206, T250, T497, T750, T809]

Test Analysis and Development Corporation, 2400 Park Lane Drive, Boulder, Colorado 80301; (303)666-8651—S24, S57

Titmus Optical Company, Petersburg, Virginia 23803; (800)446-1802, in Virginia (800)552-1869—[T601, T605, T606, T608, T609, T610, T612, T758]

Trademark Design Products, Inc., now Dr. R.R. McCormick & Associates, P.O. Box 2010, Boca Raton, Florida 33432; no business phone—[T820]

Touliatos, (John), Ed.D., Department of Home Economics, Texas Christian University, Fort Worth, Texas 76129; (817)921-7309—S25

Twitchell-Allen, (Doris), Bangor Mental Health Institute, Maine Department of Mental Health and Mental Retardation, Box 926, Bangor, Maine 04401; (207)947-6981—[T168]

Union College, Character Research Project, 207 State Street, Schenectady, New York 12305; (518)370-6012—[T3, T162, T634]

United States Department of Defense, Testing Directorate, Headquarters, Military Enlistment Processing Command, Attn: MEPCT, Fort Sheridan, Illinois 60037; (312)926-4111—[T655]

United States Department of Labor, Division of Testing, Employment and Training Administration, Washington, D.C. 20213; (202)376-6270—[T703, T715, T742, T751, T762, T807, T812]

University Associates, Inc., Learning Resources Corporation, 8517 Production Avenue, P.O. Box 26240, San Diego, California 92121; (619)578-5900—S243, S250, S255[T133, T134, T819, T828, T835, T839]

University of Illinois Press, 54 E. Gregory Drive, Box 5081, Station A, Champaign, Illinois 61820; institutions (800)233-4175, individuals (800)638-3030, or (217)333-0950—S3[T564, T586]

University of Minnesota Press, 2037 University Avenue S.E., Minneapolis, Minnesota 55414; (612)373-3266. Tests are distributed by NCS Professional Assessment Services, P.O. Box 1416, Minneapolis, Minnesota 55440; (800)328-6759, in Minnesota (612)933-2800—[T119, T120, T513, T589]

University of New England, Publications Office, Armidale, N.S.W. 2351, Australia; no business phone—S158

University of Vermont, College of Medicine, Department of Psychiatry, Section of Child, Adolescent, and Family Psychiatry, 1 South Prospect Street, Burlington, Vermont 05401; (802)656-4563—S28

University of Washington Press, P.O. Box 85569, 4045 Brooklyn Avenue N.E., Seattle, Washington 98105; (206)543-4050, business department (206)543-8870—S55, S171, S172[T14]

University Park Press, Inc., 300 North Charles Street, Baltimore, Maryland 21201; (800)638-7511, in Maryland (301)547-0700—[T5]

University Press of America, University of Detroit, 4001 W. McNichols Road, Detroit, Michigan 48221; (313)927-1000—[T163]

Variety Pre-Schooler's Workshop, 47 Humphrey Drive, Syosset, New York 11791; (516)921-7171—S122

Vocational Psychology Research, University of Minnesota, Elliott Hall, 75 East River Road, Minneapolis, Minnesota 55455; (612)376-7377—[T809, T821]

Vocational Research Institute, 1700 Sansom, Suite 900, Philadelphia, Pennsylvania 19103-5281; (215)893-5911—[T563, T654, T671, T683]

Walker Educational Book Corporation, 720 Fifth Avenue, New York, New York 10019; (212)265-3632—S150

Warner/Chilcott, 201 Tabor Road, Morris Plains, New Jersey 07950; (201)540-2000—[T135]

Weider, (Arthur), 300 Central Park West, New York, New York 10024; (212)873-2322—S36[T99]

Western Psychological Services, A Division of Manson Western Corporation, 12031 Wilshire Boulevard, Los Angeles, California 90025; (213)478-2061—S61, S185[T15, T31, T34, T38, T40, T44, T48, T50, T51, T52, T63, T65, T70, T80, T81, T86, T88, T92, T100, T103, T104, T108, T116, T130, T131, T132, T141, T145, T152, T155, T157, T158, T160, T163, T164, T167, T169, T184, T391, T440, T453, T462, T466, T471, T483, T486, T509, T526, T539, T550, T553, T562, T569, T570, T579, T580, T592, T594, T595, T605, T608, T611, T615, T616, T617, T618, T620, T623, T632, T633, T643, T655, T665, T673, T684, T805, T820, T840]

Westwood Press, Inc., 770 Broadway, 3rd Floor, New York, New York 10003; (212)420-8008—[T514]
The Wilmington Collection, 13315 Wilmington Drive, Dallas, Texas 75234; (214)620-8431—[T47, T76, T87, T131, T659]
Williams, (Robert L.), & Associates, Inc., 6372 Delmar Boulevard, St. Louis, Missouri 63130; (314)862-0055—[T94, T146, T168]
Winch, (B.L.), & Associates, 45 Hitching Post Drive, Bldg. 21B, Rolling Hills Estates, California 90274; (213)539-6430—[T333]
Wolfe Computer Personnel Testing, Inc., P.O. Box 319, Oradell, New Jersey 07649; (201)265-5393—[T786, T787, T788, T789, T790, T791]
Wonderlic, (E.F.), & Associates, Inc., P.O. Box 7, Northfield, Illinois 60093; (312)446-8900—[T759, T767, T768, T785]
Woolner, (Rosestelle B.), 3551 Aurora Circle, Memphis, Tennessee 38111; (901)454-2365—[T638]
Work Making Productions, P.O. Box 15038, Salt Lake City, Utah 84115-0038; (801)484-3092—[T591]
World of Work, Inc., 2923 N. 67th Place, Scottsdale, Arizona 85251; (602)946-1884—[T813]
Wright Group, (The), 7620 Miramar Road, Suite 4100, San Diego, California 92126; (614)464-7811—[T652]
Yuker, (H.E.), Hofstra University, Hempstead, New York 11550; (516)560-5635—[T628]
Zalk, (Susan Rosenberg), Hunter College, 695 Park Avenue, New York, New York 10021; (212)570-5118—[T627]
Zung, (William W.K.), M.D., Veterans Administration Medical Center, 508 Fulton Street, Durham, North Carolina 27705; (919)286-0411—S60[T136]

Test Title Index

S = TESTS: Supplement
T = TESTS: First Edition

Author Index

S = TESTS: Supplement
T = TESTS: First Edition

Scoring Service Index

Academic Therapy Publications *software* 20 Commercial Blvd., Novato, California 94947; (415) 883-3314.

American College Testing Program, (The) *computer scoring service* 2201 North Dodge Street, P.O. Box 168, Iowa City, Iowa 52243; (319) 337-1000.

American Dental Association *computer scoring service* 211 East Chicago Avenue, Chicago, Illinois 60611; (312) 440-2500.

American Guidance Service *computer scoring service* Publishers' Building, Circle Pines, Minnesota 55014; (800) 328-2560, in Minnesota (612) 786-4343.

Associates for Research in Behavior, Inc. (ARBOR) *computer scoring service* The Science Center, 34th & Market Streets, Philadelphia, Pennsylvania 19104; (215) 387-5300.

Association of Information Systems Professionals (ASIP) *scoring service* 1015 N. York Road, Willow Grove, Pennsylvania 19090; (215) 657-6300.

Australian Council for Educational Research Limited (ACER) *machine scoring service* Radford House, Frederick Street, Hawthorn, Victoria 3122, Australia; (03)818-1271.

Behaviordyne *computer scoring service* 599 College Avenue, Suite One, Palo Alto, California 94306; (415) 857-0111.

Biometrics Research *software* Research Assessment and Training Unit, New York State Psychiatric Institute, 722 West 168th Street, Room 341, New York, New York 10032; (212) 960-5534.

BJK Associates *computer scoring service* 2104 South 135th Avenue, Omaha, Nebraska 68144; (402) 330-3726.

Bureau of Educational Measurements *machine scoring service* Emporia State University, Emporia, Kansas 66801; (316) 343-1200.

Caldwell Report *computer scoring service* 3122 Santa Monica Boulevard, Santa Monica, California 90404; (213) 829-3644.

Carlson, (Bernadine P.) *computer scoring service* c/o Western Michigan University, 720 Sprau Tower, Kalamazoo, Michigan 49008; (616) 383-0788.

Center for Applied Psychology *software* 2245 Manhattan Boulevard, Harvey, Louisiana 70058; (504) 361-3330.

Center for Improvement of Undergraduate Education *computer scoring service* 115 Rand Hall, Cornell University, Ithaca, New York 14850; (607) 256-1000.

CFKR Career Materials, Inc. *software* P.O. Box 437, Meadow Vista, California 95722; (800) 553-3313, in California (916) 878-0118.

Chambers, (Jay L.) *computer scoring service* College of William and Mary, Williamsburg, Virginia 23185; (703) 253-4000.

CHECpoint Systems, Inc. *computer scoring service and software* 1520 North Waterman Avenue, San Bernadino, California 92404; (714) 888-3296.

Clinical Psychometric Research *computer scoring service and software* 1228 Wine Spring Lane, Towson, Maryland 21204; (301) 321-6165.

College Board Publications, (The) *computer scoring service* Box 2815, Princeton, New Jersey 08541; (609) 771-7600.

Creative Learning Press, Inc. *computer scoring service* P.O. Box 320, Mansfield Center, Connecticut 06250; (203) 423-8120.

CTB/McGraw-Hill *computer scoring service* Del Monte Research Park, Monterey, California 93940; (408) 649-8400, (800) 538-9547, in California (800) 682-9222.

Datascan *computer scoring service* 1134 Bobbie Lane, Garland, Texas 75042; (214) 276-3978.

Delphic Systems, Ltd. *computer scoring service* P.O. Box 1019, Coconut Grove, Florida 33133; no business phone.

Diagnostic Specialists, Inc. *computer scoring service and software* 1170 North 660 West, Orem, Utah 84057; (801) 224-8492.

Educational and Industrial Test Services Ltd. (EITS) *computer scoring service* 83, High Street, Hemel Hempstead, Herts. HPI 3AH England; (0442) 56773.

Educational and Industrial Testing Service (EdITS) *computer scoring service* P.O. Box 7234, San Diego, California 92107; (619) 222-1666.

Educational Assessment Service, Inc. *scoring service* Route One, Box 139-A, Watertown, Wisconsin 53094; (414) 261-1118.

Educational Development Corporation *computer scoring service and software* P.O. Box 45663, Tulsa, Oklahoma 74154; (800) 331-4418, in Oklahoma (800) 722-9113.

Educational Records Bureau Inc. *computer scoring service* Bardwell Hall, 37 Cameron Street, Wellesley, Massachusetts 02181; (617) 235-8920.

Educational Testing Service (ETS) *computer scoring service* Rosedale Road, Princeton, New Jersey 08541; (609) 921-9000.

Educator Feedback Center *scoring service* College of Education, Western Michigan University, Kalamazoo, Michigan 49008; (616) 383-1992.

Employers' Tests and Services Associates (ETSA) *computer scoring service* 120 Detzel Place—Dept. G—180, Cincinnati, Ohio 45219; (513) 281-5389.

Endeavor Information Systems, Inc. *computer scoring service* 1317 Livingston Street, Evanston, Illinois 60201; no business phone.

Evaluation Research Associates *computer scoring service* P.O. Box 6503, Teall Station, Syracuse, New York 13217; (315) 422-0064.

Grassi, (Joseph R.), Inc. *scoring service* Mailman Center for Child Development, P.O. Box 016820, University of Miami, Miami, Florida 33101; (305) 547-6631.

Grune & Stratton, Inc. *scoring service* 111 Fifth Avenue, New York, New York 10003; (212) 741-6800.

Harding, (Christopher), Harding Tests *scoring service* Box 5271, Rockhampton Mail Centre, Q.4701, Australia; no business phone.

Hartley Software *software* 1776 Thornapple River Drive, Grand Rapids, Michigan 49506; (616) 676-9176.

Harvard Personnel Testing *computer scoring service* Box 319, Oradell, New Jersey 07649; (201) 265-5393.

Haverly Systems, Inc. *computer scoring service* 78 Broadway, P.O. Box 919, Denville, New Jersey 07834; (201) 627-1424.

Hill, (William Fawcett) *computer scoring service* California State Polytechnic University, Pomona, 3801 West Temple Avenue, Pomona, California 91768; (714) 626-0128.

Illinois Thinking Project *scoring service* Education Building, University of Illinois, Urbana, Illinois 61801; (217) 333-1000.

Institute for Personality and Ability Testing, Inc. (IPAT) *computer scoring service* P.O. Box 188, 1602 Coronado Drive, Champaign, Illinois 61820; (217) 352-4739.

Institute for Psychosomatic & Psychiatric Research & Training/Daniel Offer *scoring service* Michael Reese Hospital and Medical Center, 29th Street and Ellis Avenue, Chicago, Illinois 60616; (312) 791-3826.

Institute for the Development of Human Resources *computer scoring service* 1201 Second Street, Corpus Christi, Texas 78404; (512) 883-6442.

Institute of Psycholgical Research, Inc. *computer scoring service* 34, Fleury Street West, Montreal, Quebec H3L 9Z9; (514) 382-3000.

Instructional Materials Laboratory *computer scoring service* The Ohio State University, 1885 Neil Avenue, Columbus, Ohio 43210; (614) 422-2345.

Integrated Professional Systems *computer scoring service, hardware and software* 5211 Mahoning Avenue, Suite 135, Youngstown, Ohio 44515; (216) 799-3282.

Intran Corporation *computer scoring service* 4555 West 77th Street, Minneapolis, Minnesota 55435; (612) 835-5422.

JAIM Research, Inc. *computer scoring service* 1808 Collingwood Road, Alexandria, Virginia 22308; (703) 765-5903.

Jansky, (Jeannette J.) *computer scoring service* 120 East 89th Street, New York, New York 10028; (212) 876-8894.

Kent Developmental Metrics *computer scoring service* 126 West College Avenue, P.O. Box 3178, Kent, Ohio 44240-3178; (216) 678-3589.

Learning Publications, Inc. *computer scoring service* P.O. Box 1326, Dept. C-1, Holmes Beach, Florida 33509; (616) 372-1045.

Life Insurance Marketing and Research Association, Inc. (LIMRA) *computer scoring service* P.O. Box 208, Hartford, Connecticut 06141; (203) 677-0033.

London House Press *computer scoring service* 1550 Northwest Highway, Park Ridge, Illinois 60068; (312) 298-7311 in Illinois; (800) 323-5923.

M.A.A. Committee on High School Contests, Department of Mathematics and Statistics *computer scoring service* 917 Oldfather Hall, University of Nebraska, Lincoln, Nebraska 68588; (402) 472-7211.

Macmillan Education *software* Houndmills, Basingstoke, Hampshire RG21 2XS, England; (0256)29242.

McCann Associates *computer scoring service* 2755 Philmont Avenue, Huntingdon Valley, Pennsylvania 19006; (215) 947-5775.

Medical Research Council, Department of Psychological Medicine, Royal Free Hospital *scoring service* Pond Street, London NW3 2QG, England; (01) 794-0500.

Merrill, Charles E., Publishing Company *computer scoring service* 1300 Alum Creek Drive, Box 508, Columbus, Ohio 43216; (614) 258-8441.

Ministry Inventories *computer scoring service* P.O. Box 8265, Dallas, Texas 75205; (214) 276-3978.

Monitor *scoring service* P.O. Box 2337, Hollywood, California 90028; no business phone.

Morstain (Barry R.) *computer scoring service* Department of Urban Affairs, University of Delaware, Newark, Delaware 19711; (302) 738-2394.

National Dairy Council *software* 6300 N. River Road, Rosemont, Illinois 60018-4233; (312) 696-1020.

National League for Nursing (NLN) *computer scoring service* Ten Columbus Circle, New York, New York 10019; (212) 582-1022.

National Occupational Competency Testing Institute *scoring service* 45 Colvin Avenue, Albany, New York 12206; (518) 482-8864.

NCS Professional Assessment Services *computer scoring service* P.O. Box 1416, Minneapolis, Minnesota 55440; (800) 328-6759 or, in Minnesota (612) 933-2800.

Nelson Canada *computer scoring service* 1120 Birchmount Road, Scarborough, Ontario, Canada M1K 5G4; (416) 752-9100.

NFER-Nelson Publishing Company Ltd. *computer scoring service* Darville House, 2 Oxford Road East, Windsor, Berkshire SL4 1DF, England; (07535) 58961.

Nisonger Center (The), Ohio State University *scoring service* 1580 Cannon Drive, Columbus, Ohio 43210; (614) 422-0825.

Nursing Research Associates *scoring service* 3752 Cummings Street, Eau Claire, Wisconsin 54701; (715) 836-4731.

Person-O-Metrics, Inc., Evaluation & Development Services *scoring service* 20504 Williamsburg Road, Dearborn Heights, Michigan 48127; no business phone.

Phoenix Institute of California (The) *computer scoring service* 248 Blossom Hill Road, Los Gatos, California 95030; (408) 354-6122.

Precision People, Inc. *software* 3452 North Ride Circle S., Jacksonville, Florida 32217; (904) 262-1096.

Professional Examinations Division/The Psychological Corporation *computer scoring service* 7500 Old Oak Boulevard, Cleveland, Ohio 44130; (216) 234-5300.

Psych Systems *hardware and software* 600 Reisterstown Road, Baltimore, Maryland 21208; (301) 486-2206.

Psychological Assessment Resources, Inc. *computer scoring service and software* P.O. Box 98, Odessa, Florida 33556; (813) 977-3395.

Psychological Corporation Scoring Center (The) *MRC Answer Documents scoring service* Highway 1 and Interstate 80, Iowa City, Iowa 52240; (212) 888-3602 or

The Psychological Corporation Scoring Service (for Arizona, California, Idaho, Nevada, Oregon, Utah and Washington) 770 Lucerne Way, Sunnyvale, California 94086; (212) 888-3602.

Psychological Corporation Scoring Service (The) *OpScan scoring service* 7500 Old Oak Boulevard, Cleveland, Ohio 44130.

Psychological Corporation (The) *software* 7500 Old Oak Boulevard, Cleveland, Ohio 44130.

Psychological Software Specialists *software* 1776 Fowler, Richland, Washington 99352; (509) 735-3427.

Psychologistics, Inc. *software* P.O. Box 3896, Indialantic, Florida 32903; (305) 727-7900.

Purdue University Bookstore *computer scoring service* P.O. Box 3028, Station 11, 360 State Street, West Lafayette, Indiana 47906; (317) 743-9618.

Reid Psychological Systems *computer scoring service* 233 North Michigan Avenue, Chicago, Illinois 60601; (312) 938-9200.

Research Concepts, A Division of Test Maker, Inc. *computer scoring service* 1368 East Airport Road, Muskegon, Michigan 49444; (616) 739-7401.

Research Psychologists Press Inc. *computer scoring service* P.O. Box 984, Port Huron, Michigan 48060; (313) 982-4556; (800) 265-1285.

Riverside Publishing Company (The) *computer scoring service* 8420 Bryn Mawr Avenue, Chicago, Illinois 60631; (800) 323-9540, in Alaska, Hawaii or Illinois call collect (312) 693-0040.

Rucker-Gable Associates *computer scoring service* P.O. Box 927, Storrs, Connecticut 06268; (203) 423-7880.

Saville & Holdsworth Ltd. (SHL) *scoring service* Windsor House, Esher Green, KT10 9SA, England; (0372) 66476.

Scholastic Testing Service, Inc. *computer scoring service* 480 Meyer Road, P.O. Box 1056, Bensenville, Illinois 60106; (312) 766-7150.

Science Research Associates, Inc. (SRA) *computer scoring service* 155 North Wacker Drive, Chicago, Illinois 60606; (800) 621-0664, in Illinois (312) 984-2000.

Scientific Software Associates, Ltd. *software* Box 208, Wausau, Wisconsin 54401; (715) 845-2066.

Scott, Foresman and Company, Test Division *computer scoring service* 1900 East Lake Avenue, Glenview, Illinois 60025; (312) 729-3000.

Search Institute *computer scoring service* 122 West Franklin, Suite 215, Minneapolis, Minnesota 55404-2466; (612) 870-3664.

Skillcorp Software, Inc. *software* 1711 McGraw Avenue, Irvine, California 92714; (714) 549-3246.

Slosson Educational Publications, Inc. *software* P.O. Box 280, E. Aurora, New York 14052; (800) 828-4800, in New York (716) 652-0930.

SOI Institute *computer scoring service* 343 Richmond Street, El Segundo, California 90245; (213) 322-5532.

South (John C.) *scoring service* Duquesne University, Pittsburgh, Pennsylvania 15282; (412) 434-6000.

Southern Illinois University Press *computer scoring service* P.O. Box 3697, Carbondale, Illinois 62901; (618) 453-2281.

Special Child Publications (SCP) *scoring service* J.B. Preston, Editor & Publisher, P.O. Box 33548, Seattle, Washington 98133; (206) 771-5711.

Stanford University Press *computer scoring service* Stanford, California 94305; (415) 497-9434.

Stanton Corporation (The) *computer scoring service* 417 South Dearborn Street, Chicago, Illinois 60605; (800) 621-4152, in Illinois (312) 922-0970.

Stoelting Company *computer scoring service* 1350 S. Kostner Avenue, Chicago, Illinois 60623; (312) 522-4500.

Sysdata International Inc. *computer scoring service* 7671 Old Central Avenue NE, Minneapolis, Minnesota 55432; (612) 780-1750.

Test Analysis and Development Corporation *computer scoring service* 2400 Park Lake Drive, Boulder, Colorado 80301; (303) 666-8651.

United States Department of Defense, Testing Directorate *computer scoring service* Headquarters, Military Enlistment Processing Command, Attn: MEPCT, Fort Sheridan, Illinois 60037; (312) 926-4111.

United States Department of Labor, Division of Testing *computer scoring service* Employment and Training Administration, Washington, D.C. 20213; (202) 376-6270.

University Associates, Inc. *scoring service* Learning Resource Corporation, 8517 Production Avenue, P.O. Box 26240, San Diego, California 92121; (619) 578-5900.

University of Vermont *software* College of Medicine, Department of Psychiatry, Section of Child, Adolescent and Family Psychiatry, 1 South Prospect Street, Burlington, Vermont 05401; (802) 656-4563.

Vocational Psychology Research *scoring service* University of Minnesota, Elliott Hall, 75 East River Road, Minneapolis, Minnesota 55455; (612) 376-7377.

Vocational Research Institute *software* 1700 Sansom, Suite 900, Philadelphia, Pennsylvania 19103-5281; (215) 893-5911.

Western Psychological Services *computer scoring service* 12031 Wilshire Boulevard, Los Angeles, California 90025; (213) 478-2061.

Wolfe Computer Personnel Testing Inc. *scoring service* P.O. Box 319, Oradell, New Jersey 07649; (201) 265-5393.

Visually Impaired Index—Revised

S = TESTS: Supplement
T = TESTS: First Edition

ABOUT THE EDITORS

RICHARD C. SWEETLAND, Ph.D. A graduate of Baylor University (1953), the University of Texas (1959) and Utah State University (1968). Dr. Sweetland completed post-doctoral training in psychoanalytically oriented clinical psychology at the Topeka State Hospital in conjunction with the training program of the Menninger Foundation in 1969. Following appointments in Child Psychology at the University of Kansas Medical Center and in Neuropsychology at the Kansas City Veterans Administration Hospital, he entered the practice of psychotherapy in the Kansas City area. In addition to his clinical work in neuropsychology and psychoanalytic psychotherapy, Dr. Sweetland has been extensively involved in the development of computerized psychological testing. He is currently president of the Test Corporation of America.

DANIEL J. KEYSER, Ph.D. A graduate of the University of Kansas (1974), the University of Missouri (1965) and the University of Wisconsin (1959). Dr. Keyser specializes in biofeedback and behavioral psychology, currently a medical psychologist at the Veterans Administration Hospital in Kansas City in the Ambulatory Care Unit. He specializes in the medical applications of psychology—pain control, stress management, psychological testing, individual and group therapy. Dr. Keyser also has a private practice in Raytown, Missouri. He has made significant contributions to computerized psychological testing. Dr. Keyser is currently Chairman of the Board of Test Corporation of America.